W9-CDC-874

THE GREEK
AND
ROMAN WORLDS

Brian G. Walton
and
William R. Higgins

University Press
of America

Wingate College Library

Copyright © 1980 by

University Press of America, Inc.™

4720 Boston Way, Lanham, MD 20801

All rights reserved
Printed in the United States of America

ISBN: 0-8191-1254-2
Library of Congress Number: 80-5791

MY 24 '82

086518

THE GREEK AND ROMAN WORLDS

TABLE OF CONTENTS

vi

ILLUSTRATIONS (MAPS)

vii

INTRODUCTION

The purposes of this work are to provide an outline of the civilizations of ancient Greece and Rome and to discuss some of the important and distinguishing elements of those civilizations. The first task is to explain in the broadest sense what this involves.

A civilization is an advanced or complicated society. What is meant by advanced or complicated will vary with the standards of the day and the views of the observer. In general, though certainly not necessarily, the "requirements" for calling a society civilized tend to increase with time, as societies are able to do more complicated things. An example is the mastery of writing, something now taken for granted but which is used as an indication of civilization in judging ancient societies.

The word culture describes the habits or style of any group of people or society, so that all humans belong to a culture. The more advanced cultures can be called civilizations. Unfortunately, we also use the word culture to indicate fine or educated tastes, so that a cultured person, or a person of culture, stands out from the mass. In a sense, and most confusingly, we make this use of the word culture mean much the same as when we call a man civilized.

The U.S.A. is civilized, both by today's standards and by all previous standards. It can do many complicated things. This does not mean, though, that all Americans are civilized. How many we would include would depend on the strictness of the standards to be applied. Appalachia, for example, has a culture of its own — usually we do not say that it has a civilization of its own, since at the present, as at all times in the past, the things we think of as Appalachian are not complicated or difficult enough by customary standards. Similarly, when Elvis Presley died, Jimmy Carter correctly spoke about Presley's big contribution to American culture. Rock and Roll is too simple to be described as civilized, although it exists in a civilized society.

It is very important to note that civilization generally

1

refers only to how complicated things are; it does not involve any question of whether a culture becomes <u>better</u> as it becomes civilized. Civilized people can do more than (can "outsmart") uncivilized ones, but we can only debate whether they are better in any moral sense. At the same time, however, and again confusingly, we do use civilized in the sense of "good" habits (of cleanliness, decency, etc.).

A <u>civilization</u> includes the areas which share and exchange roughly the same knowledge. In the world today there is more and more only one civilization, the <u>Western</u>, which for the most part originated in Europe, in fact in Greece, and has spread with Europeans across the world. Britain, France, the U.S.A., Canada — these are all part of the same civilization. Less obviously, so in some degree are places such as Japan and India. In fact Japan, an Asian country, is one of the most successful examples of this Western civilization. This is true even of Russia and China, since Marxist communism is a western system of thought. In that sense, when China went communist, it went western. In the Arab countries, as well as in many other places, we can see people protesting the impact of this civilization, trying to stop what is happening.

Because this is a new state of affairs in the world, it is one whose implications are difficult to grasp. Always, until this century, there have been several <u>independent</u> civilizations. Independent civilizations are ones which know relatively little of each other and exist largely separately from each other. They often do a lot of things in similar ways, for many of the problems people face are the same everywhere, but generally they do not do so simply by copying from each other, although there may be extensive contact among them. It is the difference between, say, Japan and the U.S.A. developing automobiles separately and their sharing, as in fact they do, a common store of knowledge. Of course, there can be many different degrees of independence. 300 years ago there were two outstanding independent civilizations, the Western and the Chinese, which had very little to do with one another, and a further two major independent civilizations, the Indian and the

2

Arab/Moslem.

The ancient Greeks and Romans made up independent
civilizations in their day. It is because we are the heirs
of these Greek and Roman civilizations that they look so
much more "modern" to us than do the other ancient civilizations, such as those in Egypt or Mesopotamia, or China
or India. The Greeks and Romans are also much better known
to us than any other ancient civilizations. They are, in
fact, the earliest civilizations we can describe in any great
detail. This is not just a matter of luck. One of the values
we obtain from the ancient Greeks and Romans, a value not
present in the same degree elsewhere in the ancient world,
is a great interest in ourselves as human beings, a value
which made it natural for them to take note of and record
what they were doing or saying or thinking.

Greece and Rome are numbered among the ancient civilizations. Rather than just meaning old, ancient in this
sense refers specifically to the whole period of development,
in Egypt and Mesopotamia as well as in Greece and Rome,
before the collapse of the Roman Empire, an event which is
seen as ending the ancient world and bringing the beginning
of the medieval (the Middle Ages). In line with this
reasoning, this work finishes with the success of Christianity toward the end of the Roman Empire around 300 A.D.

The period covered runs from around 2000 B.C. to 300
A.D. The term Classical applies only to Greece and Rome
and only to a portion of this period, that which begins
around 500 B.C. with the climax of the Greek achievement
and runs through the Roman Empire. In the case of Rome,
then, to say Ancient Rome and Classical Rome is to say more
or less the same thing. The terms Ancient Greece and Classical Greece are also used a lot to indicate the same thing,
but in a more specific use the long earlier Greek period,
that before 500 B.C., is ancient but not classical (pre-
classical). More narrowly still, it is common to limit the
term Classical Greece to the period from 500 to the 300's
B.C.

Our dating system, with B.C. and A.D., is a Christian
one which was introduced at the end of the Roman Empire

3

several hundred years after the birth of Christ. The birth of Christ is used in this dating system as the fixed point of reference. With the year of Christ's birth as 1 A.D., we can count forward indefinitely. A.D. indicates ANNO DOMINI, which is Latin (the language of the Romans) for In the Year of the Lord, the Lord being Christ. From the year immediately before 1 A.D., which is 1 B.C., we can count backwards indefinitely in ascending numbers. In this system, we have

1. no year 0
2. no "missing" 33 years for Christ's life, since A.D. is not After Death

The difficulties occur in the B.C. period, where you must count down in order to count forward. January 396 B.C. is followed by February 396 B.C.; December 396 B.C. is followed by January 395 B.C. In addition, terms such as "first" or "second" centuries, etc., whether B.C. or A.D., need to be used carefully:

1st century A.D. = 1-99 A.D.
1st century B.C. = 99-1 B.C.
2nd century A.D. = 100-199 A.D.
2nd century B.C. = 199-100 B.C.
5th century A.D. = 400-499 A.D.
5th century B.C. = 499-400 B.C.

In this work, initials B.C. are always included when reference is made to a year before the birth of Christ. A.D. is omitted and the number alone used for other years unless there is a risk of confusion.

Since this dating system is Christian, it is not the one used by either the Greeks or the Romans. The structure of the year, however, which is a solar year of 365 days with an extra day every four years, and the arrangement and names of the months, are Roman, being largely the work of Julius Caesar some 50 years before the birth of Christ. Oddly, the date of Christ's birth was fixed wrongly when our dating system came into use, so that on its reckoning the actual birth is usually placed several years before 1 A.D. (at 8-4 B.C.)

In examining ancient Greek and Roman civilization, we will look at all aspects of those societies, a task which in the most general sense can be called history, which is

the study of the past. We will direct our attention to
those things which are the best-known or the most readily
available or the most enlightening. In the case of the
Greeks and Romans this means particularly their <u>literature</u>,
their <u>art</u>, their <u>philosophy</u> and <u>religion</u> and their <u>politics</u>.
Other elements receive less attention. Some parts of
Classical Civilization we hardly know at all. This is most
true of <u>music</u>; we do not know a great deal more about
Greek and Roman <u>technology</u> or <u>economic</u> and <u>social</u> <u>structure</u>.

THE MEDITERRANEAN

The geographical unit we are dealing with is the <u>Mediterranean</u>. It is a large area. From <u>Gibraltar</u> to modern-day <u>Israel</u> it is 2500 miles in a direct line, a distance equal to the breadth of the continental U.S.A. (New York-San Francisco). Nonetheless, the Mediterranean area is a distinct natural unit. Despite many variations, the lands around the Mediterranean Sea have:

1. <u>a common climate</u>: hot, dry summers; cool winters with rain. The climate in the Classical period seems to have been similar to what it is now. The closest approach in the U.S.A. to this Mediterranean climate is found in Southern California. The following figures give an indication of the climate. Atlanta, Georgia is inserted for example's sake:

Average Daily Temperature by Month

	J	F	M	A	M	J	J	A	S	O	N	D	average annual rainfall
Athens													
high	54	55	60	67	77	85	90	90	83	74	64	57	14 inches
low	42	43	46	52	60	67	72	72	66	60	52	46	
Cairo													
high	65	69	75	83	91	95	96	95	90	86	78	68	1 inch
low	47	48	52	57	63	68	70	71	68	65	58	50	
Rome													
high	54	56	62	68	74	82	88	88	83	73	63	56	33 inches
low	39	39	42	46	55	60	64	64	61	53	46	41	
Los Angeles													
high	65	66	69	71	74	77	83	84	82	77	73	67	15 inches
low	45	47	49	52	55	58	62	62	60	56	51	48	
Atlanta													
high	53	56	63	73	81	88	89	89	84	74	62	54	48 inches
low	36	37	42	51	59	67	70	69	64	53	42	37	

2. <u>a common vegetation</u>: sparse evergreens, usually bushes, in the hotter and drier lowlands; richer growths of oak and beech forests, etc., in the uplands.

6

3. a common isolation from the interior away from the Mediterranean. The sea ties the coastal areas together
while mountains (in Europe and Asia Minor) and deserts
(in North Africa and the Near East) limit access to the
interior.
4. a common easy access via water. While it is stormy in
winter, so that in ancient times trade and travel was
halted for the storm season, the Mediterranean is easy
to travel in summer, when there are good winds. There
are no strong tides or currents. On the other hand,
because of the insecurity of the rainfall and the mountainous interior, there are few reliable rivers to provide easy movement inland.

Cereal crops can be produced reliably with care. Generally they must be sown in early spring and harvested before
the summer drought sets in. Fruits are victime of the lack
of rainfall in most sections, but the olive (to provide oil
and take the place of our butter), the fig, and the vine
(for wine and grapes) can do well. Pasture farming requires
seasonal movement between the wetter uplands in summer and
the lowlands in winter. In the Mediterranean area, bread
and wine were the staples of the diet in the Classical
Period, along with olives and occasional meat.

GREECE

The Greek mainland south of Mt. Olympus contains only
about 30,000 square miles, appreciably less than 2/3rds the
size of New York or North Carolina. It is very mountainous,
to heights of about 8,000 feet, and very rugged and broken-
up. Except on the west coast, rainfall is a considerable
problem. As a result, there are few extensive sections of
good farmland. In many places in the Classical Period a
cereal crop could be sown only one year in two, and in some
places, including Athens, only barley could be raised, not
the preferred wheat. Even in the highlands good pasturage
was in short supply, so that animals were few. Goats were
preferred; they supplied such milk as the Greeks had.
Greece also lacked substantial deposits of most of the basic
minerals of the Classical Period -- little copper or iron,
no tin and little gold or silver until 500 B.C.

7

While it was difficult to get around Greece on land, the problem of the mountains being compounded by the usual absence of good rivers, access to the sea was available everywhere. The coastline of the Greek mainland is very irregular, particularly the remarkable Gulf of Corinth, and with the mountains reaching to the sea there are many good harbors.

Having easy access to the sea, and finding difficulty in feeding themselves, the Greeks naturally looked outwards. They traded olives and finished products for cereals and metals; at the same time they tried to find places to settle their surplus population. By necessity, perhaps, they early became a seafaring, outgoing, trading people. They established themselves all across the Aegean area, which is a natural geographical sub-unit of the Mediterranean, and then beyond in every direction.

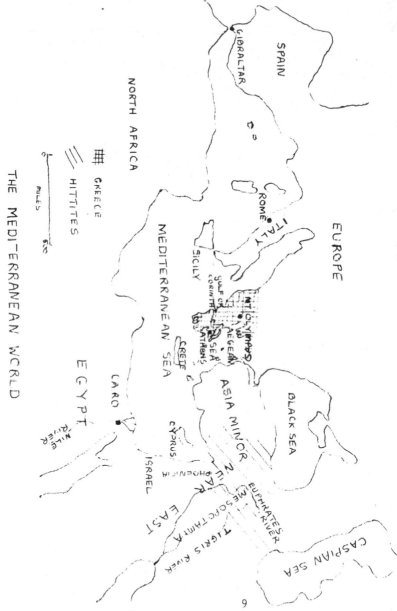

THE MEDITERRANEAN WORLD

⊞ GREECE
/// HITTITES

MILES
0 ——— 600

NORTH AFRICA

SPAIN
GIBRALTAR
ROME
ITALY
EUROPE
MEDITERRANEAN SEA
SICILY
GULF OF CORINTH
IONIAN SEA
ATHENS
MT. OLYMPUS
AEGEAN
CRETE
ASIA MINOR
BLACK SEA
EGYPT
CAIRO
NILE RIVER
CYPRUS
ISRAEL
PHOENICIA
MESOPOTAMIA
MIDDLE EAST
TIGRIS RIVER
EUPHRATES RIVER
CASPIAN SEA

6

BACKGROUND: TO 2000 B.C.

We do not know much about what happened in Greece before the 500's B.C. Classical Greece bursts out suddenly
from a dim background. It is not likely that we will be
able to change this state of affairs, although it would be
very useful to know more about earlier Greece. Such knowledge might do a lot to alter the way we see the Greeks.

Before 2000 B.C.
Very little at all can be said about the Greek world
before 2000 B.C. The area was backward (uncivilized by the
standards of its day) and unimportant until well after 2000
B.C. Pottery can be dated on the Greek mainland to before
6000 B.C., but there is nothing that is exceptional or worth
special notice. It is widely believed that the entire
Aegean area was then inhabited by one people (not Greek)
with a more or less common culture.

Around 3000 B.C. the Neolithic Age (New Stone Age) was
succeeded by the Bronze Age. Tin and copper were combined
to produce the harder bronze, which was better for weapons
than the copper of the late Neolithic period. At about the
same time (3000 B.C.) there developed in EGYPT and
MESOPOTAMIA what are usually called the first civilizations.
These areas were the first to achieve developed writing
systems and the efficient administration of large territorial units. The Nile River and Delta area in ancient
Egypt, for example, was not much smaller than a state such
as New York or North Carolina.

Around 2000 B.C.
There seems to have been an upheaval of some kind on
the Greek mainland around 2000 B.C. What happened is not
known. Many people believe that over a period perhaps of
several centuries new groups came into the area from the
north and displaced or absorbed the existing population.
These newcomers are often supposed to have been Greeks,
here making their first appearance.

The Greeks are Indo-Europeans, a term which applies
correctly to language, not to race. The term Indo-European
describes a group of related languages spoken in the

10

beginning by people from the plains north of the <u>Black</u> and
<u>Caspian Seas</u>. The peoples speaking these languages (and
who are also called Indo-Europeans) probably were at first
similar in race, looking something like Europeans now.

The impact of these newcomers is far from clear (some
refuse to believe that there were such arrivals) and it
varied a great deal across the Greek world. These people
do not seem to have moved into <u>Crete</u> or the <u>Cyclades</u> at
this time. There is no way to say with confidence how any
newcomers interacted with the earlier population. Since
any newcomers, however, are likely to have been more backward than the people already living in Greece, the effect
probably was to slow development. The population of the
mainland in the 1000's B.C., which we call <u>Mycenaean</u>, was
the result of whatever process of change took place.

MINOAN CIVILIZATION, 2000 B.C. - 1400 B.C.

The first part of the Aegean area to develop enough to
be called a civilization was the island of CRETE. Its
civilization is known as MINOAN. This civilization arose
soon after 2000 B.C. Its reputation dates from the discoveries of the British archaeologist <u>Sir Arthur Evans</u> around
the beginning of this century.

The term MINOAN comes from a figure of Greek legend,
King MINOS of Crete, most probably of CNOSSOS. In legend,
Minos had <u>Athens</u> under his control. He kept the <u>Minotaur</u>,
a monster half-man and half-bull, the offspring of his
wife, in a great <u>labyrinth</u> or maze-like building on Crete.
He fed the monster with young men and women supplied by
Athens, until the hero <u>Theseus</u>, disguising himself as one
of intended victims, went to Crete and killed it.

The origins of this civilization are little known.
The population of the island of Crete is believed <u>not</u> to
have been Greek, so that this is <u>not</u> the first Greek civilization, just the first civilization in the Greek world.
The Minoan people are thought to have belonged to that
earlier people which had existed across the Aegean area
and which was being affected on the mainland around 2000
B.C. by the newcomers called Greeks.

11

Crete, lying 400 miles from the Nile Delta, can be thought of as undergoing a natural development, particularly as a profitable trading center, under the influence of the great old civilizations. Crete had an abundant supply of lumber, which was always in great demand in Egypt, and good stretches of cereal-producing land, especially on its south coast. In the same way, we can imagine Crete in its turn having a civilizing influence on the Greek mainland, which was less than 100 miles to the north. The story of Minos is an example of this.

The Minoan Style

A number of palaces have been excavated, beginning with the one found at CNOSSOS by Evans. These palaces are much the most important source of our knowledge concerning the Minoan civilization. The first palaces, dated from soon after 2000 B.C., seem to have been destroyed around 1700 B.C. The destruction probably came from natural causes--earthquakes, for example, occur commonly in the area. The palaces were quickly rebuilt on a much bigger scale and the next period, from 1650 to 1450 B.C., marks the high-point of Minoan civilization and prosperity.

While we have no idea of the island's political structure, it is often supposed that the kings or rulers at Cnossos had some sort of influence over the rulers of the other palaces and cities. The Classical Greeks saw things that way, with Minos as the great figure on Crete. The legend of Theseus and the Minotaur is an example. Both Herodotus and Thucydides, the great historians of Classical Greece, believed that Minos had controlled much of the Aegean. The palace on Cnossos is much larger than any of the others: the main buildings cover about 3 acres.

The layout of the palaces was pleasantly informal. They were rambling collections of rooms (think of the labyrinth of the Minotaur) with no real focus except for the open central courtyard. The courtyard at Cnossos is 170 feet long and 80 feet wide. The Cnossos palace had two floors, with the important rooms on the upper floor. The foundations and lower courses were of stone, the rest of the walls of unbaked brick, with wooden beams for support. The roofs were flat. Cnossos and the other palaces, furthermore, were not fortified, something which suggests that

there was ordinarily a considerable sense of security on
the island. There is in general little evidence of an interest in military things in Minoan civilization.

The informality and the sense of security of the palaces support the very clear general impression we have of
Minoan civilization. We see a wealthy, carefree, luxury-
loving people, with a style of life attuned to the natural
world, to the sea particularly, one in which women played a
very important role.

Minoan art was graceful and natural. Minoan pottery,
which was of very great quality, developed from semi-
abstract beginnings to a highly naturalistic style. The
favorite subjects for vases were nature scenes, with
flowers, plants, fish, dolphins, octopuses. The few
pieces of sculpture which have survived and the great
quantity of wall paintings in the palaces (called frescoes
because they are painted on fresh plaster) indicate the
same kind of friendly attitude toward nature and a generally pleasant outlook on life. Animals and birds were
frequently represented, along with a variety of young people, gift-bearers and elegant ladies. These last, with
their ornate hair styles, their topless dresses with tight
bodices and flounced skirts and puffed sleeves, express the
luxury and grace of the civilization's wealthy class very
clearly. Scenes shown included dancing and bull-leaping,
the latter with young men somersaulting over the backs of
bulls. Military subjects were avoided.

Minoan religion also had more happiness than fear
about it. Of course, it was a polytheism (system with more
than one god). No temples have been found, and religion
seems to have centered on nature, perhaps with open air
services in the large palace courtyards and elsewhere.
Female figures dominate in religious art, especially earth-
mother types. The snake-goddesses from the palace at
Cnossos are very famous. There are no lavish burial sites;
their absence suggests that the Minoans did not have the
common fear of the afterlife.

Our impression of Minoan civilization, as consistently lively and charming, and with a solid emphasis on
enjoying life, encourages some people to believe that many

13

Wingate College Library

of the roots of Greek civilization lie here; that the civilization on Crete had already freed itself from the otherworldly worries of the East (Egypt and Mesopotamia) to concentrate on man and his life on earth.

MYCENAEAN CIVILIZATION, 1700 B.C. - 1200 B.C.

Mycenaean is the name given to the civilization on the
Greek mainland which overlaps in time the Minoan civilization on Crete. The word Mycenaean comes from Mycenae which
is in the fertile Argive plain (plain of Argos) in the
northern Peloponnesus. Mycenae is the best-known and, it is
thought, the most important center of this Mycanaean civilization. The importance of Mycenaean civilization lies in
its role as the first Greek civilization. It is usually
seen as the work of the Indo-Europeans (Greeks) who are
thought to have entered Greece around 2000 B.C. This identification assumes that such newcomers became the dominant,
ruling group in Greece. It further rests upon
1.   the acceptance by later Greeks of the Mycenaeans as
     their ancestors;
2.   the numerous links between the Mycenaeans and later
     Greeks;
3.   the identification of the Mycenaean writing system as
     Greek.

Very little can be said for certain about Mycenaean
civilization. Once again, however, as with the Minoans,
the general image we have of Mycenaean civilization is a
very clear one. It seems to have been a much more warlike
and masculine society than the Minoan. It is often suggested that this difference reflects the harsh conditions
to the north of Greece from which the Mycenaeans had only
recently come and the rougher, less settled way of life on
the mainland compared to that on Crete.

Minoan civilization had a great deal of influence on
the Greek mainland and on many of the islands of the
Aegean. A strong connection between the Minoan and the
later Mycenaean civilizations is taken for granted in later
Greek legends, as we have seen already in the story of
Theseus and the Minotaur. Hesiod, writing around 700 B.C.,
believed that Zeus, who was by then the chief among the
Greek gods, had been born in Crete. Certainly, the Minoan
influence on early Mycenaean art styles is obvious and substantial. Evans even believed that the Minoans conquered
some parts of the mainland, but this idea is no longer accepted. Instead, we see the Mycenaeans developing under

15

Minoan encouragement and influence, being heavily dependent
in the beginning upon Minoan styles, themes, and craftsmen,
but gradually asserting their own distinctive preferences.

Mycenae, the first and major site, was opened up by
the German archaeologist Heinrich Schliemann from 1876
(before Cnossos was excavated). At Mycenae Schliemann
found both a palace and a town. Other important sites
since discovered are at Pylos and Thebes. Pylos gives us
our most vivid impression of a Mycenaean palace, since it
was abandoned after being destroyed around 1200 B.C.;
Thebes, where the ruins lie below the present city, was
remembered by later Greeks as having been a town of great
wealth in Mycenaean times, and it is well known to us as
the location of the famous story of Oedipus. Athens does
not seem to have been very important in the Mycenaean period, although there are traces of a Mycenaean palace on the
rock known as the ACROPOLIS in the center of the city.

Mycenae seems to have been well-developed and flourishing (civilized) by the 1600's B.C., but the "Golden Age" of
Mycenaean Greece ran from about 1400 to about 1250 B.C. By
that time, the Mycenaeans dominated the Aegean and traded
with Egypt and throughout the Mediterranean. They may be
the people referred to as the AHHIYAWA (= Achaeans?, a word
Homer uses for the Mycenaeans) in clay tablet records which
have survived from the great HITTITE Empire of Asia Minor.
In these records, which are dated to some point between the
late 1400's B.C. and the 1200's B.C., the Ahhiyawa are seen
as a great power; their king is termed "brother" by the
Hittite emperor. Much of this Mycenaean success in the
Aegean had come at the expense of the Minoans. Around 1400
B.C., in fact, Minoan civilization, which had played a
great role in early Mycenaean development, seems to have
been largely destroyed.

The End of Minoan Civilization
     The circumstances surrounding the collapse of the de-
lightful world on Crete are much in dispute. The palaces
seem to have been destroyed by fire, with the fire coming
perhaps from some natural disaster or from attacks. This
destruction is usually dated around 1450 B.C. The palace
at Cnossos, however, while it was damaged at this time,
seems to have survived until 1400 B.C. or a little later
before being destroyed.

    At some point in this period, an enormous volcanic explosion took place on the island of THERA 80 miles to the north of Crete. It blew the middle out of the island and, with the tidal wave and earthquake which must have followed, may have caused great damage on Crete. Some people have suggested that this explosion is linked to the destruction of the palaces on Crete. Two points can be noted in this connection:
1. the explosion is dated fairly securely to about 1500 B.C., some 50 years before the palaces were destroyed;
2. Cnossos survived the destruction while other palaces did not.

    At the time it was destroyed, it is believed around 1400 B.C., Cnossos was using a writing system called LINEAR B (linear means that it was written horizontally rather than vertically). It has been widely accepted that this Linear B is a Greek language rather than a Minoan one, a point which encourages the belief that Linear B had been brought to Crete from the Greek mainland and that Cnossos was in Greek (Mycenaean) hands when it was destroyed around 1400 B.C. It is not likely that a Greek Linear B from the mainland was simply copied by the non-Greek Minoans on Crete.

    The earliest Minoan writing was picture-writing and has not been deciphered. A little after 2000 B.C. this picture-writing developed into an abstract script which Evans called Linear A. Linear A has not been deciphered either. Evans gave the name Linear B to the later writing he found in the Cnossos ruins dated around 1400 B.C. He assumed that Linear B was simply a Minoan outgrowth of the earlier Linear A. Scratched with wedge-shaped instruments (the name cuneiform for such writing comes from wedge) on wet clay and allowed to dry, the writing survived because the tablets were baked when the palace was destroyed.

    Like Linear A, Linear B was a syllabary; almost all the signs stood for a combination of consonant and following vowel, although there were some signs for single vowels standing alone. This is inconvenient since it requires a large number of signs and it cannot represent a consonant without a following vowel or two consonants in succession. Final consonants at the end of a word, for example, are left out in Linear B.

17

The Linear B writing found on Crete has also been found on the Greek mainland, most notably at Mycenaean Pylos. It was deciphered in the early 1950's by a young Englishman, Michael Ventris, as an early form of Greek rather than a Minoan language. We can note that the translations of Linear B, both on Crete and on the mainland, are only administrative and commercial lists about palace business, so that the writing is of no further use in explaining what happened, or in telling us much in any way about Minoan or Mycenaean civilization. The limited nature of these Linear B sources also raises a question about how extensively writing was used in the Mycenaean period. Was it limited only to a very few, in the service of the kings? It is tempting to assume this, since such a belief would help to explain how literacy came to disappear later.

How to account for the presence of a Greek language and of Greeks (Mycenaeans) at Cnossos? The most common explanation is that the warlike Mycenaeans were raiding widely in Crete in the 1400's B.C., adding to and taking advantage of the weaknesses caused by natural disasters such as the explosion on Thera. There is evidence of disturbance and destruction on the Greek mainland in this same period. The Mycenaeans may have devastated much of Crete while operating out of Cnossos as their headquarters. Then, after a couple of generations, Cnossos itself was burned and the Mycenaeans withdrew. They left a Crete which was much damaged and was only a shadow of its old self, a Crete which recovered little over the next 200 years (1400-1200 B.C.) while Mycenaean power and civilization were at their peak on the mainland and across the Aegean area.

If this is what happened, it is odd to find the Mycenaeans more or less abandoning Crete in such a way. Some people have argued that the Mycenaeans stayed in Crete, or at least at Cnossos, for some 200 years until the collapse of their own civilization around 1200 B.C. Encouragement for this view comes from the fact that the Linear B writing found on the mainland at Pylos and dated to about 1200 B.C. is very similar to the Linear B writing at Cnossos which is dated to about 1400 B.C. Such a lack of change in a young language over so long a period is surprising. Putting the final destruction of Cnossos at 1200 B.C. would make the Linear B writings there and at Pylos

contemporary, thereby removing this problem. It would
also accommodate the Greek legends about Theseus which
later placed that hero, the killer of the Minotaur, in the
1200's B.C. Unfortunately, while radiocarbon or carbon 14
dating can give only an approximate indication of time, it
does not seem reasonable to argue for an error of 200
years. The archaeological evidence, including the dating
of the Linear B tablets, puts the destruction of Cnossos at
around 1400 B.C., not 1200 B.C., and all the signs are that
after 1400 B.C. Crete was a much reduced society.

The Mycenaean Style
     Despite the early and heavy Minoan influence, the
Mycenaeans had their own distinguishing styles from the
start, styles which were harsher and blunter than the
Minoan. Their palaces, as at Mycenae and Pylos, are relatively small and simple compared to the Minoan even though
they date from the 1300's B.C., well along in Mycenaean
development. They are centered upon a royal hall, apparently the administrative center and throne room of the palace complex. The hall itself was large, with a balcony
around it, an open hearth in the center of the floor, and
benches along the frescoed walls. These palaces are much
darker, less open to the sun, than their Minoan counterparts. They are also fortified, being surrounded by thick
walls and located on dominating hilltops. The Mycenaean
palaces, however, do follow the same principles of construction as those on Crete, being of brick built up on
stone and having flat roofs.

     Mycenaean frescoes, the best of which are from Pylos,
frequently depict, in addition to processions and nature or
religious scenes in the Minoan manner, hunting episodes,
soldiers, and battle scenes. The same can be said of their
pottery, the best-known example of which, the so-called
Warrior Vase from Mycenae, shows armed men marching off to
fight. Often the figures shown are more angular, stiff,
heavier, and less pleasant than those on Crete. Even so,
there is always plenty to remind us of the Minoan connection. An example is provided by the famous pair of golden
cups from Vappheio in the Peloponnesus. Dating from
around 1400 B.C., when Crete perhaps had already fallen to
the Mycenaeans, the cups have scenes of wild bulls being
caught, a distinctly Minoan theme. The brilliant

workmanship of these cups is very likely to have been the
achievement of an artist from Crete.

The Mycenaean style is also seen in the boastfulness
of the rich objects left in Mycenaean tombs. Inside the
walls of the city of Mycenae, Schliemann dug out a grave
circle of six vertical shafts at the bottom of which lay
corpses in splendid life-size gold masks. The most famous
of these pieces is the one called the Mask of Agamemnon.
The bodies were surrounded by thousands of pieces of gold
jewelry, cups, etc., and a great abundance of weapons, including gold daggers and long, bronze swords in an enormous
variety of styles. These graves and their contents are
dated to the 1500's B.C. There is a good possibility that
at such an early date in Mycenaean development much of this
work would be done by men from Crete. These shaft tombs
were covered with small mounds of dirt and usually they had
stones bearing designs as markers. It is generally believed that they contained the bodies of members of the
royal family of Mycenae. Most were used more than once,
one of them as many as five times. These graves were
treated carefully by the Mycenaeans, being surrounded by a
circular wall and preserved. Another circle of 14 shaft
graves was neither so rich in its contents nor so well preserved. It is usually believed that those buried in this
second circle belonged to leading families, the aristocrats, of Mycenae.

Shaft tombs are not found elsewhere, and they were
soon replaced even at Mycenae by the mound or tholos tombs.
These mound tombs were even more spectacular. They were
round and domed and well constructed with massive blocks of
limestone. Built into a hillside, a mound tomb was approached by a long, walled entry way that led to a single
large entrance. When the tomb was completed and the body
(presumably that of a member of the local royal family) put
in, the entire structure was covered with earth, hiding it
from view. While these mound tombs are found most commonly
in Messenia in the southwestern Peloponnesus, the best
known of them is the one called the Treasury of Atreus at
Mycenae, which is dated around 1300 B.C. Its dome is 50
feet in diameter and 43 feet high; the entrance passage is
115 feet long and 19 feet wide; the block over the entrance
doorway weighs more than 100 tons. The treasury, however,

is missing, for graverobbers, here and elsewhere, have long since taken the gold contents. In one sense, these mound tombs are misleading. Generally, and in this they were like the Minoans, the Mycenaeans did not develop a tradition of monumental (large-scale) sculpture. The best-known exception is the Lion Gate Sculpture, a large work over a gateway at Mycenae which is dated to about 1250 B.C.

We do not know much about Mycenaean religion. There were some similarities to Minoan religion, with an apparent absence of temples and a heavy reliance upon goddesses. At the same time, it is generally believed that the Mycenaeans developed, or brought with them into Greece, most of the great gods of the much later Classical period. There is doubt about some of the great names among the gods of later Greece, particularly Apollo and Dionysius, but in general they are thought to have existed already in Mycenaean times. These gods are known to us, however, mostly through Homer, as quarrelsome, warlike, and very undependable. To the Mycenaeans, however, the chief god seems to have been Poseidon, the Earth-Shaker, who by Homer's day (700's B.C.) had lost out to his brother Zeus and had taken up a lesser role as ruler of the oceans. Similarly, some of the great sacred places of Classical Greece, such as Delphi and Olympia, were probably already religious centers at this time.

We know even less about Mycenaean political structure. As with Cnossos in Crete, it is often claimed that Mycenae exercised some kind of authority over the kings of at least some of the other centers. This is how Homer saw Agamemnon of Mycenae, as "the most kingly," centuries later. It is possible that the Hittite tablet references to the king of the Ahhiyawa provide some support for this idea of the importance of Mycenae. Pylos is associated with King Nestor, another of the participants in the war against Troy which is described by Homer in the Iliad.

The End of Mycenaean Civilization
It is possible that new groups continued to move into Greece through the Mycenaean period. There are signs of occasional trouble and devastation. Such changes as that from the shaft graves of the 1500's B.C. to the mound graves of 1300 B.C. may be linked to disruptions of this

21

nature. So, too, may what seems to have happened to Crete around 1400 B.C. At present, we cannot be more definite than this.

Then, toward 1200 B.C., a great wave of destruction swept across Mycenaean Greece. Walls were built around several of the palaces, enclosing large areas and presumably offering shelter for the local populations. An attempt seems to have been made to build a protective wall across the isthmus at Corinth against newcomers from the north. None of this worked. The palace at Pylos, along with many others, was destroyed around 1200 B.C. or a little earlier. Some places survived at that time, and others were reconstructed. Mycenae appears to have been overwhelmed in stages, with a first devastation before 1200 B.C., a second at about 1200 B.C., and a third some 50 years later. Finally, the destruction reached almost everywhere.

It is often argued that a haphazard series of raids took place over several generations, weakening the Mycenaeans and leading eventually, perhaps not until toward the end of the 11th century (toward 1000 B.C.), to permanent conquest and occupation by the incoming groups. By that time, certainly, poverty and backwardness were apparent in Greece. Large-scale buildings and such splendors as the mound tombs, as well as writing, had disappeared.

In this period there occurred (about 1200 B.C.) the Trojan War, which thanks to the description of it in Homer's Iliad is the most famous episode in Mycenaean history. The attack on Troy, a place inhabited by Indo-Europeans closely related to the Mycenaeans, is often seen as a last effort at aggression by the Mycenaeans as they themselves fell on hard times. Later Greek legend, for example, placed the destruction of Mycenaean Thebes in the 1200's B.C., before the war against Troy, and, as we have seen, the archaeological evidence also provides support for placing the early destruction before 1200 B.C. Schliemann in 1870 dug out a site in Asia Minor which is widely accepted as Troy. This was Schliemann's first big discovery; he went from this site to Mycenae. The location fits what we are told by Homer, but there is no archaeological evidence of a Mycenaean destruction of the town around 1200 B.C. Some believe that the whole episode is an invention.

The difficulties in the Mycenaean world coincided with trouble across much of the eastern Mediterranean, with great movements of peoples. Heavy raids from the sea were noted in Egyptian records. Egypt survived, but the Hittite Empire, which had been a great power since about 2000 B.C., broke up at this time. All this occurred as the Iron Age slowly replaced the Bronze Age. This technological change used to be a favorite device for explaining what happened. It was claimed that the newcomers, such as those who wrecked Mycenaean civilization, owed some part of their success to the use of the new iron. Iron, however, did not replace bronze extensively for centuries, and we know far too little about what was going on to make such statements. The Mycenaeans, an outgoing and aggressive people, may have been participating in as well as suffering from these raids and disturbances--the story of the expedition against Troy suggests as much. In any event, the Mycenaeans had their best days behind them by 1200 B.C. and over the next several generations they experienced very considerable further decline.

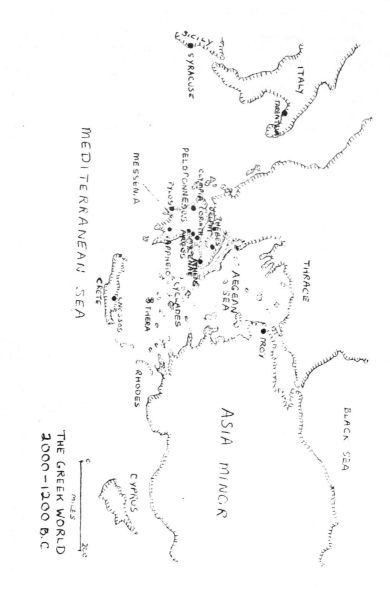

MEDITERRANEAN SEA

ITALY

SICILY
SYRACUSE

TARENTUM

MESSENIA

PELOPONNESUS
OLYMPIA
CORINTH
DELPHI
THEBES
PYLOS
MYCENAE
SAPPHEIC
ARGOS
ATHENS
CYCLADES

CRETE
KNOSSOS
THERA

RHODES

THRACE

AEGEAN
SEA

TROY

ASIA MINOR

BLACK SEA

CYPRUS

THE GREEK WORLD
2000–1200 B.C

0   MILES   200

24

THE GREEK DARK AGES, 1200 B.C. - 800 B.C.

Our knowledge of the period after the fall of the Mycenaeans is very limited. The evidence is all drawn from weak archaeological sources, from Homer, and from what we know of later Greeks. Writing disappeared for centuries. For the later Classical Greeks this was their Dark Age. It is clear that they knew little more about it than we do.

What can we say about the identity of those who conquered Mycenaean Greece? It is agreed that the newcomers were Greeks. Such barbarian Greeks, with no written language (illiterate), are likely to have come from the northern edges of the Mycenaean Greek world. They were the primitive relatives of the men who built the shaft and mound tombs. The newcomers seem to have shared the gods of the Mycenaeans. They promoted Zeus to the father-god role and gave the gods a home on Mt. Olympus. This location, well to the north and beyond the limit of the Mycenaean world, may be an indication of the newcomers' northern origins.

Later Greeks definitely saw the newcomers as Greeks. For them, this Dark Age marked the coming into Greece of the DORIAN Greeks from around Epirus. In legend the Dorians came to help the Heracleidae, the three sons of Hercules, who had gone to the north to look for such aid in order to challenge the grandson of Agamemnon for the throne of Mycenae from which they had been expelled. The involvement of the family of Hercules, the strong man, may suggest the primitive, warlike nature of the newcomers. The legend has two attacks from the north upon Mycenaean Greece 100 years apart, which supports the idea of a series of raids from that direction followed by settlement. The first attack came 10 years before the Mycenaeans sailed for Troy--another indication that the expedition occurred after the trouble had started. The attackers on that occasion failed to break into the Peloponnesus by land and were told by an oracle (a medium through which the gods communicate with people) that they would have to wait 100 years. When they returned at the end of that period they came by sea, resting at sacred Delphi before crossing the Gulf of Corinth. Since the Mycenaeans seem to have built a wall across the isthmus at Corinth, the newcomers may

indeed have come by sea. This second time the Heracleidae
succeeded. The three brothers founded the Dorian kingdoms
of <u>Argos</u>, <u>Sparta</u>, and <u>Messenia</u>.

Although, apart from legend, almost nothing is known
of their coming into Greece or of their experiences in
Greece for several centuries, the <u>Dorians</u> have a very strong
position in later Greek thought and tradition, and the term
Dorian is used almost automatically by scholars. Frequently, though, the Dorians are seen now as only the final
stage in the overwhelming of Mycenaean Greece, a process
which had been going on since before 1200 B.C. It is often
suggested that these particular newcomers appeared in
Greece only in the 1000's B.C., and that they then took
the place of or merged with earlier attackers.

A variety of relationships between Dorians and the
earlier population is assumed, based on what Greeks wrote
and believed in the much later Classical Period about what
had happened; specifically, about religious, tribal, and
social-political differences between Dorians and non-
Dorians, and, most importantly, about the distribution of
Greek dialects (branches of the language) in their day and
what lay behind them.

In the Classical Period, after 500 B.C., Greeks refer-
red to a <u>Doric</u> (Dorian) <u>Greek</u>, a dialect which they believed had originated with the Dorian invaders. Doric Greek is
now regarded as belonging to <u>West Greek</u>, a category which
includes also <u>North-West Greek</u>, another dialect of newcomers
in the Dark Ages. Classical Greeks also distinguished
<u>Ionic</u> and <u>Aeolic Greek</u> dialects, together termed <u>East Greek</u>,
which they saw as the Greek of the older Mycenaean inhab-
itants. We now distinguish also in the later Classical
Period an <u>Arcado-Cyprian</u> dialect of Greek, found in distant
<u>Cyprus</u> and in <u>Arcadia</u>, a rugged and backward mountainous
section of the Peloponnesus. This Arcado-Cyprian dialect
is seen as the closest thing to the old Mycenaean <u>Linear B</u>,
surviving in distant or undeveloped parts of the Greek
world. Thus we have:

North-West Greek ⎫		language of the newcomers
Doric Greek ⎬ West Greek =		in the Classical Period
Aeolic Greek ⎫ East Greek =		language of most pre-
Ionic Greek ⎬		Dorians, Mycenaeans, in
		the Classical Period
Arcado-Cyprian Greek	=	closest surviving link in
		the Classical Period to
		Linear B

Greeks speaking different dialects could understand one
another reasonably well in the Classical Period, but Doric
Greek was less developed than the East Greek dialects,
containing elements which seem to have been out of style
even in the Mycenaean Greek of Linear B. This suggests
that the Doric dialect belonged to a people who had not
shared much in the various advances of the Mycenaean day,
which is what we would expect of a group from the backward
northern fringes of the Mycenaean world.

Later in the Classical Period, Dorians and non-
Dorians had some separate cults and festivals and had to
stay out of one another's holy places. They also did not
mix in the colonies which were set up outside Greece. The
groups recognized as Dorian always were divided into three
tribes, always with the same names--and often with a
fourth (perhaps the earlier Greeks). There was, though, no
connection between the tribes of the same name from one
part of Greece to another. There was less order in uniformity of tribal names among the non-Dorians, but the four
tribal names at Athens crop up often, with others, among
other East Greeks.

The relationships between the Dorians or newcomers and
the earlier population can be placed into three general
groups:
1. Where the newcomers lasted as a ruling or "master"
group, controlling a distinct, subject, and presumably
older, population. Generally, in such cases, the newcomers
seem to have been heavily outnumbered by the older population, a situation which we also meet in what are in some
ways similar circumstances when large parts of the Roman
Empire fell to barbarian tribes.
The best example of this situation is SPARTA, whose
entire nature and development as a military and slave state
are often explained in these terms. All who lived in

Sparta spoke <u>Doric</u> Greek in the Classical Period, the slaves having picked up the language of their conquerors. <u>Corinth</u>, the wealthiest city in the Peloponnesus in the Classical Period, is another example. <u>Thessaly</u>, in the north, which like Sparta was ruled by a small class in the Classical Period, belongs in the same group, although there the newcomers and the population they had conquered spoke a common <u>mixed</u> dialect, a mixture of the newcomers' <u>North-West</u> Greek and the older population's <u>Aeolic</u> Greek. These ruling classes had legends which told how they were descended from conquerors who had arrived from the north in the Dark Ages. In Thessaly, for example, legend had it that the newcomers arrived two generations after the fall of Troy (that is, in the 1100's B.C.), drove out to the south many of the earlier <u>Boeotian</u> people, and held the rest in serfdom (part-slave, part-free).

2. Where the newcomers and the earlier population merged more or less indistinguishably. Such places might use an East or a West Greek dialect, or some mixture of the two. Usually, if with some confusion, these places considered themselves Dorian, identifying with the conquerors. An example is BOEOTIA, just to the north of <u>Athens</u>. The <u>Boeotians</u> believed they were newcomers during the Dark Ages, but they are found among the Mycenaeans in Homer's <u>Iliad</u> and, as we have seen, they were identified in Thessaly as an earlier people who had been driven out of that region by newcomers. Like the men of Thessaly, the Boeotians spoke a mixture of <u>North-West</u> and <u>Aeolic</u> Greek.

3. Places which seem to have remained "unconquered" by the newcomers. By far the most important of these is Ionic-speaking <u>Athens</u>. This "survival" of a "civilized" Athens in a collapsing Greek world, with the Athenians seeing themselves as being descended from the Mycenaeans rather than from the more primitive newcomers, is a favorite theme for Greeks of the Classical Period. It does much to explain how Athenians later understood themselves and how they contrasted themselves to others such as the Spartans. Athens was seen as the great link with the past, as the banner-bearer of civilization, superior to the Dorian Greek areas.

Archaeological evidence seems to support the likelihood that Athens largely escaped direct Dorian occupation, although there was some damage. If the Dorians did enter the Peloponnesus by sea across the Gulf of Corinth, as

legend has it, then they may have bypassed Athens. In
legend, the Heracleidae did attack Athens. An oracle
promised them victory if they spared the life of the king
of Athens, Codrus. Codrus saved Athens by managing to get
himself killed.

It is in fact in the Dark Ages, and perhaps for this
reason, that Athens becomes very important for the first
time. Athens was dominant in Dark Age pottery, the best-
known and the most impressive art form produced by the
Greek world in the period. It makes sense that such a
leadership role would fall to a place which had escaped
the worst of the devastation. Dark Age pottery developed
gradually, without any apparent sharp break, out of the
natural style of Mycenaean vase painting. Gradually, a
geometric style of decoration was developed, with circles,
lozenges (◊), swastikas (✕), stripes, etc. By 800 B.C.,
as the Dark Ages ended, animals and men reappeared, but
they were drawn in a stick-like style in which the body
was reduced to geometric shapes. The black and white
colors, and the abstract nature of the designs, give an
austere look to this work. Reflecting its style and its
gradual development, this pottery work is called in turn--
  - PROTOGEOMETRIC, meaning before or leading to geo-
    metric, from about 1050 to about 850 B.C.
  - GEOMETRIC, from about 850 B.C. to about 700 B.C.

The high quality of Dark Age pottery marks it as the
first flourishing of Athenian civilization. Even so,
Athens, like the rest of Greece, seems to have been illiterate in this period. This is difficult to understand if
Athens escaped destruction, unless we assume again that
literacy had been rare in the Mycenaean world and that it
had been limited largely to administrative detail. Athens
itself, in general terms, even if it did escape conquest,
was much reduced from the levels of Mycenaean civilization,
so that it was not carrying the banner of Greek civilization very high.

The Dark Ages witnessed a great movement of Greeks
out of mainland Greece to the islands of the Aegean Sea
and to the coast of Asia Minor. These areas had been
dominated already by Mycenaeans, but they now received a
rush of population from the mainland as refugees fled the
disorder. Generally, the line of flight was more or less
directly eastwards across the Aegean. Aeolians went out
from such places as Thessaly to the northern part of Asia

Minor; the _Ionians,_ many of them perhaps using "unconquered" Athens as a channel for emigration, settled most of the islands and the central coast of Asia Minor.

While we know very little of the details of these movements, and must suppose that there was a good deal of confusion and mixing-up in the process, it seems that these emigrants retained some bonds of feeling for the areas they left and had some common practices. The _Ionians,_ for example, held as their common sacred island _Delos,_ which had already been a holy place in Mycenaean times. They also developed a special common attachment to _Apollo,_ who was probably originally a non-Greek god from _Asia Minor,_ although it is possible that Apollo is identified already in Mycenaean sources. Delos was supposed to be a birthplace of Apollo (a god often had many birthplaces, as ancient local beliefs were gathered up into great regional or all-Greek practices). The Ionians also shared a major shrine and oracle of Apollo at _Didyma_ on the coast of Asia Minor, which was another of his birthplaces. Didyma was a little south of _Miletus,_ the chief Ionian city on the Asian mainland. Another Ionian favorite was _Poseidon,_ who, as we have seen, had been preferred by the Mycenaeans to _Zeus,_ the favorite of the Dorian newcomers. The worship of Poseidon centered on the shrine of the _Panionion_ at _Mycale_ beside _Samos,_ which was believed to be the site of the first landings on the mainland.

Like Athens, and perhaps for the same reasons, these settlements in and across the Aegean provide relative bright spots in the Dark Ages, and they were to play a great part in leading Greece out of the Dark Ages in the 700's B.C. At this time, however, and again like Athens, these settlements seem to have been illiterate, raising the old question about writing in the Mycenaean period.

The Dorians themselves must have raided widely in the Aegean. They actually settled some of the southern islands, including _Crete_ and _Rhodes,_ as well as the southwestern tip of Asia Minor. Further afield, in _Cyprus,_ earlier Greek inhabitants may have escaped the troubles, leading to the maintenance of the primitive Arcado-Cyprian dialect here and in the remote mountains of the central Peloponnesus.

THE ARCHAIC PERIOD, 800-500 B.C.

The Archaic (Old) Period covers the years from the end
of the Dark Ages to the beginning of the Classical Age. It
was a period of very rapid development and its general outline is reasonably well known to us. Despite the reappear-
ance of writing, however, our evidence for these centuries
still comes primarily from archaeology, legend, and later
Greek accounts, so that little detail is available for much
of what happened. This is especially true for the early
part of the Archaic Period.

700's B.C.: END OF THE DARK AGES

The Dark Ages end with the 700's B.C., although Greek
society in many ways remained primitive and poor. The
writings of Homer and Hesiod provide us with our first
good look at the Greeks as they saw themselves. The way
out of the Dark Ages was led by the Ionian settlements,
then perhaps the wealthiest and most advanced parts of the
Greek world, by Athens (also Ionian), and by the great
Dorian trading city of Corinth. Among the things we can
observe in the 700's B.C. are:

1. The Greeks saw themselves as one people. Whatever
their backgrounds or dialects, the Dorians and the various
other and earlier groups had become one people. The name
they used for themselves was Hellenes (and for Greece
Hellas). The name was in use by 700 B.C. but it may then
have been fairly new. It is used by Hesiod (around 700
B.C.), whereas the writings of Homer, which are usually
dated a little earlier, use the word to identify just one
group of Greeks in Thessaly. We do not know how this word
Hellenes came to be adopted to identify the Greeks, but
in any case this question is less important than the knowledge that the sense of oneness existed. This sense is
in fact very clear in Homer, even though the word Hellenes
was not yet being used. It is not known when, or even
if, a specific individual named Homer lived, or when the
writings associated with him were composed or written down.
He is usually supposed to have been a real person who
lived in the 700's B.C., perhaps in the developed Ionia
on the island of Chios.

2. The sense of oneness may be seen in the development of the great games which were for all Hellenes. The oldest and most famous of these games, the OLYMPIAN (Olympic) GAMES, were held at Olympia in the Peloponnesus every 4th year. Later tradition claimed that they had begun in 776 B.C. This may be approximately correct, although we know very little about the Games for a long time. These games were religious as well as sporting events. Olympia, for example, was a great holy place of Zeus and the Olympian Games were held in his honor. This was in a Dorian area; Zeus was the Dorian favorite. The Games at first were aristocratic (the expensive chariot-racing was the early favorite). Gradually, they became professional.

3. The Greeks had a common set of gods. These were called the Olympian gods because the chief among them lived on Mt. Olympus in the north under the supervision of Zeus. These gods had been obtained from various sources at various times, but, as we have seen, most of them seem to have existed in Mycenaean Greece before the Dark Ages. Despite many local variations, all Greeks by the 700's B.C. shared a common religious framework.

The way the Greeks thought of these gods is best seen in Homer (below) and in the poem Theogony by Hesiod of Boeotia which we have in form dating from around 700 B.C. The Theogony describes relationships among the early gods, concentrating upon the emergence of Zeus as the chief among the gods.

4. Literacy returned. The Greeks had a new written language. This writing probably came into use around 750 B.C. It was copied from the writing of the Phoenicians, a great commercial people based north of Israel who were building up trade and settlements all across the Mediterranean at this time, including the West. The Phoenicians crop up frequently in Homer's writings, particularly in the Odyssey.

The symbols of Phoenician writing were nearly all for consonants, although some had a limited vowel sound. The Greeks used some of these symbols for vowels, producing by 700 B.C. a written language which developed gradually into Classical Greek and which was based on the same principles as ours. This written language was the most efficient means of expression the world had produced to this time.

The ancient Greeks, however, never fully standardized
their writing. No city used all of the 27 letters (22 of
which are thought to have come from the Phoenicians). At
first, writing went from right to left, then from right
to left and left to right on alternating lines. Finally,
around 500 B.C., the format of left to right was settled
on.

The sense of oneness encouraged by this common written
language is seen in the term barbarian which the Greeks
applied to those who did not speak or write Greek.

5. The Greeks were rapidly increasing their contact with
the more advanced eastern civilizations, particularly
through Asia Minor. The new writing was one result of
this. Hesiod's Theogony from around 700 B.C. shows heavy
eastern influence in its structure and contents. So do
the Fables associated with AESOP which we have from around
600 B.C. The ORIENTALIZING Style which dominated Greek
arts between 700 and 600 B.C. is an indication of the
eastern influence. In pottery, for example, the Geometric
Style of the late Dark Ages gave way to a freer style.
The stick figures became more realistic and varied and
patterns were replaced by scenes of myth and everyday life
(the latter are called genre).

6. The Greeks, even while they were continuing to occupy
the Aegean, were already moving further out in all directions. The Greek world which resulted stretched eventually from the northern and eastern parts of the Black Sea
across the northern coasts of the Mediterranean world to
Spain, with a few settlements along the coast of Africa.
Nowhere did the Greeks show any great interest in moving
into the interior; their attention remained centered on
the sea. This movement may have developed naturally from
the migrations of the Dark Ages. It also perhaps came
from the general advances the Greeks were making, a
return to the busy trading activity of the Mycenaeans
before the Dark Ages. In addition, the idea of more
colonization seems to have been encouraged by a population
problem which was already severe in some parts of the Greek
world. Such a problem was a constant worry in an area of
such poor soil. As Greece recovered from the damages of
the Dark Ages, the problem returned. Thucydides wrote
later that the population problem had been the main factor

in the movement out from Greece. The movement swelled in
the 700's B.C., and it may in fact have been not much older
than this century. It is portrayed in the Odyssey of Homer
of the 700's B.C. That work, which recounts the adventures
of Odysseus around the Mediterranean after the Trojan War,
presents its hero as more the tough sea-dog captain than
one of the great aristocratic heroes of the Iliad—though
Odysseus is very insistent that he is not a merchant.

The most important directions of movement were into
the Black Sea area in the northeast and to South Italy and
Sicily in the West. The Ionian islands people dominated
the movement into the Black Sea; the larger trading cities
on the mainland, especially Corinth, dominated the movement
west. Syracuse in Sicily, which became by 400 B.C. the
largest and wealthiest of all Greek cities anywhere, was
founded by Corinth before 700 B.C. Founded about the same
time, Tarentum in South Italy was the only colony sent out
by Sparta. That great Greek state had little need of
further land. Athens, which had played a big role in the
migrations of the Dark Ages, was now slow to put out
colonies. Being a large state by Greek standards, it may
have had enough land for its growing population. Corinth,
the islands, and other small city-states, were not so
fortunate.

Most colonies were set up as planned projects by individual Greek states. From the beginning, though, there
were a few joint projects, and many colonies set up by one
state allowed Greeks from other states to go along. Generally, while a sort of dependent status was not uncommon,
colonies were independent rather than remaining as part of,
or extensions of, their founding states. Even so, they
shared the official religious practices of the founding
cities and tended to work together in foreign policy, etc.

7. The city-state (POLIS, from which we take all our words
about politics) was already the normal Greek type of
"country." Usually a polis was a piece of territory center-
ing upon an urban area. The best-known example is the city
of Athens as the central point of the "country" called
Attica. We call the country or city-state Athens rather
than Attica: the Greeks used the term "the Athenians"
instead of both. The development of the polis, the bringing together of villages and groups which were at first
independent into these larger units, is generally a process

of the Dark Ages about which we know very little. Most of
the city-states were very small.

Athens, at about 1000 square miles, was large. Sparta
was enormous. The development of the polis as the basic
unit was more than just a product of the mountainous, cut-
up nature of the Greek mainland or the sense of separateness natural to the islands. Small, independent city-
states often existed alongside one another with no natural
barriers intervening. The polis, though, was not universal
among the Greeks. Thessaly, on the largest fertile plain
in the region, did not become split up into a federation of
city-states until the 400's B.C. And even then, like the
large Boeotia, it was a federation rather than a single
polis. Nor was the polis unique to Greeks. The Phoenicians used it, and we will find it in Italy too.
    The Greeks gave their most basic loyalty to the polis.
The Greeks' high option of the importance of the state,
their generous attitude in thinking about what the state
was entitled to, is one of the most significant things to
be borne in mind when thinking about Greek values, particularly their "individualism." Faithfulness to the polis
meant that the Greeks, even though they saw themselves as
one people, were hopelessly divided politically. These
divisions encouraged competitiveness, and many rivalries
and wars grew out of the Greeks' aggressive and eager
localism. War was necessarily a big part of life for the
Greeks, even though many of them seem to have had no
special liking for war in general. The Greeks would
continue to believe, as Hesiod put it around 700 B.C., that
"strife is wholesome to man." The difficulty they had in
working together was no help to the Greeks in their deal-
ings with others. It explains why no Greek "empire" was
possible and why there was so little movement toward bigger
political units.

8. Long before the 700's B.C. generally, the kings who
seem to have ruled in earlier days and who are described
in legend and by Homer had given way to control by
ARISTOCRACIES. We know almost nothing about how this
happened.
    The kings do not seem to have been theocrats (claim-
ing to rule by right drawn from the gods, divine-right)
such as were common in the East. Thucydides and Aristotle

both said later that royal power had always been limited. We do not know if there were such kings everywhere in the Greek world earlier. The clearest examples of kings come mostly from places conquered by Dorian invaders, such as Sparta. In some large areas, Thessaly, Boeotia, perhaps even Athens, there may never have been kings in our sense of the word. The many little villages in an area such as Attica (Athens) may have had "kings" of a sort and have given them up as they came together in the larger unit of the polis. "Kings" continued to exist in the Greek world long after the 700's B.C., but they were usually only religious officials.

The aristocracies which were in control by the 700's B.C. gave power to a few men who owed their position to birth and/or wealth. The word aristocracy itself means rule by the best. The aristocracies probably began with the relatives, or the right-hand men, of the kings they pushed out. Many remained very restrictive and included only small numbers born into certain families. They drew strength from the blood relationships which were still important in Greek life, the identification of the ordinary citizen with his extended family (clan) and his tribe and with the leaders of these groups. Some aristocracies, though, were more open, involving a larger number of families and/or letting rich people get into the aristocracy.

All the inhabitants of a state were divided into tribes; whatever their early role or nature, these tribes had become just territorial units by 700 B.C. Early Greek armies usually were based on the tribes, on a kinship or local basis, but this too disappeared. By 600 B.C., in the writings of the Spartan poet Tyrtaeus, the Spartan army had become regionally based, probably recently--the old tribal basis had been given up. There were also kinship clans, probably just for the aristocracy--certainly this was the case later, by 500 B.C.--these supplied the priests for some cults, including some big state services. There were brotherhoods, too. These are usually seen as very old kinship groups. We can only guess at what they were-- perhaps at first the local following of a big clan. Homer treats them very casually, although Nestor in the Iliad says they were military subdivisions of the tribes. Like the clans, they had probably become unimportant long before

36

500 B.C. They did survive, though, as social and religious units. In general, it is apparent that Greek society was moving away from a __tribal__ or __kinship__ basis (which we know little about).

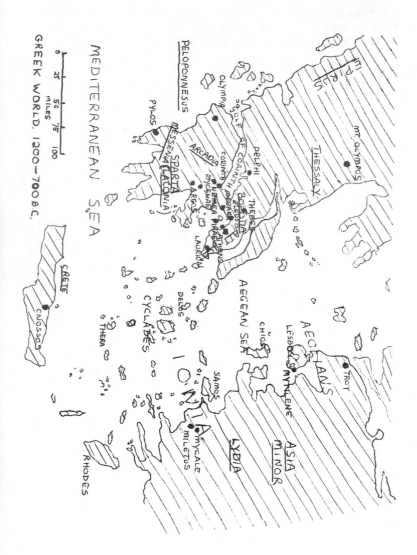

MEDITERRANEAN SEA

PELOPONNESUS

GREEK WORLD, 1200–700 B.C.

0 25 50 75 100
MILES

PYLOS

MESSENIA

SPARTA (LACONIA)

ARCADIA

OLYMPIA

GULF OF CORINTH

CORINTH

DELPHI

BOEOTIA

THEBES

MYCENAE

ARGOS

NEMEA

LAURION

EPIRUS

THESSALY

MT. OLYMPUS

DELOS

CYCLADES

THERA

AEGEAN SEA

CHIOS

AEOLIANS

LESBOS

MYTILENE

TROY

ASIA MINOR

LYDIA

SAMOS

MYCALE

MILETUS

IONIA

CRETE

CNOSSOS

RHODES

38

GREEK CIVILIZATION IN THE ARCHAIC PERIOD, 700-500 B.C.

Only toward the end of the Archaic Period, in the 500's B.C., did the Greek world become developed enough to leave us with much to talk about in terms of its art, literature, and thought. This is not surprising--as late as 700 B.C. the Greeks were still barely literate and probably poor. Remember that we have Homer only as he is given to us in the 500's B.C. By the 500's B.C., though, the Greeks were developing at a very rapid speed-- something they were very much aware of and which shaped the way they saw themselves and their world.

ART IN THE ARCHAIC PERIOD

Pottery.
Pottery is the only art we can follow from the earlier Dark Ages. The Orientalizing Style was still dominant in the 600's B.C. In the 500's B.C. it gave way to a new pottery style, the Black Figure style. This kind of pottery was difficult and costly to achieve, and it provides perhaps the best example of the technological advances which had been made already by the Greeks at this time (500's B.C.). An extremely fine clay material was needed to produce the black areas. This was obtained by stirring clay with water and an alkali and then letting it stand. Only the very fine clay particles would remain suspended. Then the liquid was drawn off, and what remained was allowed to evaporate. This fine clay mate- rial (the clay slip) was arranged in the desired pattern on the natural surface of smooth red or orange clay of the piece. The firing system which followed was very elabo- rate. The piece was fired to a little less than 1000°C. Then the kiln openings were closed. This blackened the entire surface. The temperature was then reduced to a little below 800°C and the kiln was opened to the air again. The fine clay sliped stayed black, while the rest of the surface gradually turned a clear red.

Black Figure pottery was of high technical quality, very elegant and expensive-looking. With its sharp out- lines and constant contrast between dark and light areas, it gives a very pleasing clear and simple impression.

The best Black Figure work came from <u>Athens</u> in the late
500's B.C., in the last stages of the style. It was appropriate that it should be in pottery that Athens first
recaptured leadership in the arts at this time (the age
of the tyrant Peisistratus). The Athenian Black Figure
work was more controlled and linear (in lines) than the
swirling, more flamboyant style of <u>Corinth,</u> the early
leader in Black Figure pottery.

Pottery was actually nearing the end of its career
as a major art form. As society developed, and technical
abilities developed with it, attention turned away from
pottery toward grander and artistically more rewarding
forms. Pottery lost prestige, remaining a matter for
technicians, almost for tradesmen, rather than for
artists—one result is that we have very little information,
or even names, for the men who did the best work of their
day in pottery.

Attempts were made in pottery to meet this problem.
The Black Figure style had only a limited appeal for
artists. With its flat style, they could not easily show
volume or put in such effects as hair or thin clothing.
Lines to show detail had to be scratched on through the
black slip rather than painted on. These limitations led
to the development of the <u>Red Figure</u> style in the late
500's B.C. This change came out of Athens—its introduction was one of the achievements of the tyrant Peisistratus.
Red Figure pottery became the dominant style through the
400's B.C. It reversed the arrangement of the Black
Figure style: now the background was black, with the
design or figures left as the red of the clay pot. This
made it much easier to develop details. The Red Figure
pottery was a great achievement—the finest work produced
anywhere to that time—but it could not prevent the shifting of attention away from pottery.

By the 500's B.C. the subject-matter of the pottery,
the Athenian especially, was generally humans or myths
rather than the abstract or geometrical designs which had
been favored earlier. Women appeared on early vases much
less frequently than men (women alone, or women with men,
appear on only 500 of 2000 vases between 570 and 480 B.C.,
compared to 2000 of 3000 between 480 and 400 B.C.). The

tone of the pottery in the 500's B.C. is aristocratic and male-centered, with a heavy emphasis on athletic activities, particularly involving horses (which in the Greek framework indicates the upper class). Men are frequently naked; so, sometimes, are women, although in such cases they seem to have been "ladies of the night." The figures are shown in the same stiff, Archaic style of the sculpture of the period, with the same gradual loosening, freeing toward 500 B.C.

Sculpture.

As late as the 700's B.C., with Greece still a poor place, there was no large-scale sculpture or architecture. Larger works came in as the society continued to develop—the spreading use of iron tools, in particular, made it easier and quicker for the man with skill to show his talent in larger works. There was also the example of the large-scale works which were to be seen in the East, above all in Egypt—the larger Greek sculpture as it developed was for a long time under very obvious Egyptian influence.

The small bronze statuettes, cast solid, which are the predominant form of sculpture around 700 B.C. and for some time after, were patterned after Eastern counterparts—stiff, angular, with wig-like hair, forearms pushed forward. Bigger works appeared in the 600's B.C. as workmen used the idea of hammering bronze plates over a wooden core. By 600 B.C., though, and perhaps for a generation or so before that, the Greeks were making life-size or larger (colossal) statues of humans—of marble and limestone, chiefly the latter, but with some still of bronze.

This is the beginning of a period of sculpture called simply the Archaic, lasting from 600 B.C. to about 480 B.C. The basic form is the life-size young man (kouros, singular; kouroi, plural) or young woman (kore, singular; korai, plural). Some were grave markers; others were gods and goddesses; others represented athletes who had won in the games; others were simply monuments, representing noone. Most of the korai (young women) come from a landfill on the sacred Acropolis, or rock, at Athens, which was discovered in the late 1800's. Probably they had been knocked over and broken by the Persians who took Athens

41

in 480 B.C. (see below); later, the Athenians carefully buried them. Representative examples of this Archaic style in sculpture are the marble <u>Kouros of Sounion</u> from about 600 B.C. and the <u>Kore from Samos</u>, dated a little later.

The statues are rigid and formal. The faces are abstracted and expressionless, save for the famous Archaic <u>smile</u>. They cannot be attempts to reproduce the appearance of the subject. The <u>kouroi</u> are <u>naked</u>. Their poses are Egyptian—left foot advanced, weight equally on both feet, hands clenched and attached to the sides, basically at attention. The wide shoulders and long arms produce a rectangular impression—a hint of the old geometric style which is also seen in the abstracted lines used to indicate the divisions of the trunk. The <u>korai</u> are always fully clothed—a clear indication of a social distinction. They range from the severe, linear appearance of the Kore of Samos to a considerable fussiness in the complicated drapery which was the fashion of the day. As the decades passed, the Archaic style became increasingly free, showing movement and expressing some feeling—the women, in particular, were sometimes quite lavishly and fancily presented.

It can be argued that the Archaic sculpture is in <u>spirit</u> very definitely Greek, despite the eastern influences on the style. The emphasis is on <u>humans</u>—we are looking at people who are people. In the case of the <u>kouroi</u> especially, the emphasis is squarely on the beauty and dignity of the body—expressed in the nakedness of the figures, a most un-Egyptian thing. Even the female figures give something of the same impression. The Greek emphasis was on humans—on the glory that was the body and the greater glory that was the mind.

The Greek emphasis on human beings dictated the attitude toward the rest of nature. The world was a place to be dominated, reduced to order, turned to profit. This was why they turned their gods, which often began as natural forces, into representations of themselves. Few people can have been as indifferent to nature and to animals as the Greeks were: the Egyptians were obsessed with cats, the Greeks used the term "like a dog" as a strong insult. The benefits of nature--olives and olive groves, for example, were appreciated, but toward nature itself, the wild, they were at best indifferent, sometimes hostile. The Greeks for this reason avoided confusing man and animals--as Easterners, with their hawk--headed men, etc., were very prone to do; Greeks also avoided confusion in nature, a favorite theme in the East, with winged serpents, hoofed lions, etc. Thus it is perhaps very significant that in Archaic sculpture the subject already is man.

Since the most remarkable thing about this remarkable human race was the power to reason, it followed that the Greeks would emphasize that element. From the beginning, so far as we can see, Greeks sought a rational understanding of the world and themselves. So we see about the Greeks a relentless search for generalizations, looking for common bases. This led them to analyze things into their parts; it also led them to represent specific things as types, to abstract in the light of the generality. One result in art is that the range of subject-matter, in sculpture or pottery or painting, and the range of building types, in architecture, is limited--they are after what they have decided is the appropriate type. We see this already in the sculpture of the Archaic Period--the abstraction, the desire for order, the search for a type.

The price of this pursuit was that the exuberance and freedom of nature had to be brought under control--not for the Greeks the outright enjoyment of the pleasures of nature and the senses such as characterized the Minoans on Crete. The individual had to bring himself under control in order to bring the world under control--the senses had to be watched very carefully, since they were the part of man "closest to nature." Individualism did not mean freedom; it meant the opportunity to accept discipline, to work with others. By our standards, the Greeks were group-oriented (as in the polis), accepting all kinds of restrictions which would seem unreasonable to many of us. It was not by accident that the great shrine to Apollo at Delphi carried the slogans "Know Yourself" and "Nothing to Excess"--the aim was a sensible discipline. The style of fighting developed in this period, the hoplite phalanx, emphasized the same qualities, requiring men to fight together in close formation--bravery was steadiness and discipline, not a crazed individualism. In the Archaic sculpture, we can see the lack of individuality (the type) and the refusal to show strong emotion, right alongside the delight in what a fine thing a human is. In this reading, the famous Archaic smile is a symbol that the figures know that the right mixture is hard to find--and that they have achieved it.

Architecture.
        We have little Greek architecture from before 600 B.C. We have the foundations of a number of buildings so that we can, in a poor way, trace the development of architecture from the 900's B.C. Even as late as the 700's B.C. Greek public buildings were primitive wooden things. Our oldest temple (late 700's B.C.) is to Zeus and Hera at Olympia--of sun-baked bricks on lower courses of stone, with wooden Doric (see below) columns. It was replaced with a stone temple on the same ground plan about 600 B.C. Stone buildings came in the 600's B.C. with both the Doric and the more ornate Ionic (see below) styles. We have an Ionic Temple of Artemis at Ephesus from about 650 B.C., for example. Still, there is very little any-where until the late 500's B.C. Then we have a group of Doric temples at Athens, Delphi, Corinth, and Olympia. Even these, though, are little more than ruins--Greek architecture has not survived well at all. The only good Archaic temple sculptures from before 500 B.C. are from the Temple of Artemis on Corfu (early 500's B.C.). From the Treasury at Delphi, about 525 B.C., we have an example of late Archaic style, in a scene of Hector fighting Menelaus, with plenty of movement.

PHILOSOPHY/SCIENCE/RELIGION IN THE ARCHAIC PERIOD

Philosophy, which is the search for understanding about the nature of the universe and of man, was to become one of the greatest glories of the Greek world—and it certainly was one very revealing of the Greeks' values. What we can call the beginnings of Greek philosophy came late, around 600 B.C.—late because it is a very sophisticated undertaking and one which requires a distinctive attitude toward the world. It means that, even by 600 B.C., Greeks were rejecting the haphazard, take-it-as-you-find-it world of Homer and his gods; they were trying to impose order, to explain, to make sense, of what was around them. The fatalism of the old attitude, expressed in the remark credited to Solon that he "counted no man lucky till he had seen how he ended," would be made to give way to order. Even after 600 B.C., it was a long time before philosophy separated itself from religion (theology = the study of god or the gods) and science; in many ways, for the Greeks, it never did so.

The Milesians.
          The earliest figures associated with the story all came from Miletus, the greatest Ionian city, on the coast of Asia Minor. That was probably still in 600 B.C. the wealthiest and the most developed part of the Greek world. We have three early names:
1. Thales, 600 B.C. and a little after
2. Anaximander, about 600-550 B.C.
3. Anaximenes, about 590-520 B.C.
These men may get more credit from us than they are due, but whatever developments lay behind their work are not known to us. Thales seems to have written nothing. The other two wrote prose works, but they are lost. What we know about all of them depends on tradition, for which Aristotle, who lived 200 years later, is our first major source. However, some things about the three men seem fairly clear:
1. They were what we would call scientists (of a sort), discussing the physical origins (cosmogony) and the physical make-up (cosmology) of the world: why things are as they are and how they came to be that way—the nature of the physical matter which is the basis of the world. Kosmos (the world) = order.

2. They looked for <u>rational</u> answers to these problems.
While these three (the <u>Milesians</u>, or men from <u>Miletus</u>) are
not anti-religious, they are detached from religion and
religious explanations. This is the same loose attitude
to the gods we find in Homer, who was from the same part
of the Greek world.
3. Many of the skills they used came from the East--the
characteristic borrowing from the East in this period. In
the East, astronomy and mathematics had long been associated with magic/religion. The Milesians' interest in
these skills, though, was distinctively Greek--it is not
usually believed that they picked up on a Mesopotamian or
Egyptian "philosophical tradition"--what they were doing
was new. The Milesians were practical astronomers, land-
surveyors, geographers:
--THALES, the earliest, the "Father of Science," was said
later to have been part non-Greek, with <u>Phoenician</u> or
<u>Carian</u> blood. He is said to have predicted the <u>eclipse</u>
<u>of the sun</u> of May 28, 585 B.C., but such precise knowledge
was impossible at the time, and the historian <u>Herodotus</u>
in the 400's B.C. said that Thales only predicted the
eclipse within a year. Thales worked in geometry and is
associated with the <u>isosceles</u> triangle. He used tri-
angulation to measure distances at sea from land; to help
navigate by the stars. There is a story that he fell
down a well while studying the stars--on the opposite side,
there is a story that he made a fortune in olives by
predicting the weather.
--ANAXIMANDER, a little later, is said to have invented
the <u>sundial</u>, to have made the first <u>map of the world</u>, and
to have reached several important astronomical discoveries.

Practically all we know about the <u>philosophy</u> of these
men involves their cosmogony and their cosmology. They all
have a common approach. They all are looking for the
<u>permanent</u>. The reality is a <u>single living</u> stuff--from
this the world and all things developed spontaneously
(that is, without the activity of a god or gods). We still
have this idea in the form of the principle of the
conservation of matter or of energy. These men offered the
first "scientific" rather than religious or supernatural
explanation of what had happened. They call the one
substance or stuff divine, but they mean that it is alive
and lasts for ever. What is permanent can be known by man,

they claim. However, they have no explanation of what gives rise to the single, first stuff, to the essence. For us, they miss the first stage.

For Thales, the single stuff was "the moist," which is usually translated as water. He guessed that the earth floated on water, as well as having been formed from water. He came to this by common sense, observation, and intuition--the underlying importance of water was also a common idea in the East. This is a very clear materialism (a stuff that you can touch is the essence).

For Anaximander, the one original stuff was the "indefinite"--something without special qualities. Clearly, this is a big step forward from Thales. He used the idea of a rotating movement, like that of a vortex in a liquid, to explain the variations in his indefinite basic substance and so to account for the origins of our world. He contributed to evolution theory, claiming that animals came originally from a moist environment and that man evolved from a fish. He thought that the earth was a disc, its diameter three times its depth; this disc needed no support but was suspended freely, moving for ever--a cold disc for an earth, surrounded by hot, round atmospheres produced from the "indefinite." He may have believed that worlds such as ours succeeded one another without number through time.

For ANAXIMENES, the first stuff was air or breath. The world is like a man--kept going by breath, which is always in motion. He watched rain coming from clouds, earth which seemed to condense from water, water evaporating into air--so he thought that the density of air decided how it became fire, water, stone, wind, etc.

Out of this first stuff, the universe developed in ways they thought of in terms of the weather--which they were interested in, and which they could measure. They seem to have thought automatically in terms of pairs, or opposites, a style of thought very common in early Greek philosophy, and one which has had tremendous impact on the way we see things. The stuff split apart and came back together in opposites--hot/cold, wet/dry. This was all regulated by a rhythm which they called Justice.

47

Anaximander said that the elements which came out of the
one stuff "give justice and do right by one another,
according to how things are arranged in time." Justice
punished one element for being in excess by pushing forward its opposite: too much heat, say, is punished by
cold. The sense of a natural balance, operating through
opposites, is a long way from a simple materialism. So
they are at least aware, even if they don't know much
or ask how matter comes into existence, that a theory
of physics must start with some sort of belief about
matter. With black holes into which matter disappears,
and white holes from which matter appears, we are not in
better shape.

What these men say is like the old Greek stories of
the origins of the gods and the world (say in Hesiod's
Theogony). The one stuff replaces Chaos or Night;
Justice is like old Fate, the ruler, stronger than the
stuff or the gods; the Opposites are like the pairings
among the gods, which produce the succeeding generations.
Above all, as in the old stories, the world was born,
not made--the gods are a part of the universe, not beyond
it, and are subject to the rules (Justice or Fate). It
was perhaps easier for Greeks, given their religious
structure, to proceed to the kind of thing the Milesians
were doing, than it was for other peoples.

Even the willingness to put forward a grand account
of the origins of the universe, something which can
hardly be defended by much in the way of a reasoned
argument, with only a few more or less haphazard observations to uphold it, is a lot more like a myth than it is
a science. Logic was tending to push out observation very
early here--the observation was limited in extent and it
centered on what was easily observed (astronomy). This
was a trap into which Greeks fell all too easily and all
too frequently. Aware of the newness of what they were
doing, trying to reduce the world to order and understanding, they tended to rush on to answers, trying to run
before they could walk well. They were, to their credit,
well aware of this problem--they agreed that arrogance
(hubris) brought punishment, another example of the balance of opposites. "Nothing to excess" was something
the Greeks believed in, but had trouble practicing.

Pythagoras (580–500 B.C.) and the Pythagoreons.

In the late 500's B.C. Ionia fell to the Persians.
The city of Miletus was destroyed in 494 B.C. Greek
intellectual life shifted westwards; many Ionians actually
fled in that direction. Athens benefitted greatly from
this development as it moved toward cultural leadership.
At first, though, the greatest benefit was felt by the
Greek cities in south Italy, which by their wealth and
their distance from the Persians were attractive to many
Ionians. PYTHAGORAS of Samos (580–500 B.C.) left Ionia
for south Italy around 530 B.C., settling at Croton. As
the greatest Greek intellectual figure of his day, he gave
enormous prestige to south Italy. Pythagoras stands next
in time after the Milesians, with whose work he must
have been familiar in Ionia, but what he had to say was
very different. The greatest difference was that
Pythagoras was not willing to just leave aside religion--
he intended to preserve the traditional identification
of religion, science, and philosophy.

It is likely that all Greeks, as they developed so
rapidly, felt some unease with their old religious
explanations (or, rather perhaps, non-explanations) of
things. Their gods seemed absurd, even embarrassing,
even bad--both contrary to good sense and emotionally
unsatisfying. Some Greeks were not concerned; like the
Milesians, they could ignore the gods and go ahead. It
is not likely, though, that this was possible for many--
and even the Milesians had an idea of balance, of judgment, although it was physical. Greeks generally could
not turn their backs on the gods so quickly or so completely, no matter how proud they were of their development.
That would be hubris, pride, an unreasonable act of self-
assertion that would call the gods' attention to a man.
The word we translate as sin meant to the Greeks going
too far, overshooting the mark. For such people the
task was to make religion more fulfilling and/or to
reconcile it with intellectual developments.

In the 500's B.C. new religious forms flourished,
forms which offered things beyond what the old Homeric
gods knew: emotion, a personal contact with the supernatural, even life after death. While we know very little
about any of them (one of their emotional tricks was

49

secrecy), we can identify the most prominent of the new
religious forms, all Panhellenic:
1. a new, wild form of the worship of <u>Dionysius</u>, with
crazed dancing at night, religious ecstasies, fits. This
had a big popular appeal for centuries, picking up along
the way an association with sex and drink orgies.
2. the <u>Eleusinian Mysteries</u>--Panhellenic but also a state
religion of Athens at <u>Eleusis</u>. This was associated with
the earth-mother <u>Demeter</u> and with the underworld, picking
up eventually through this last connection a line to
Dionysius. The Mysteries were secret, so there is not much
to say about them; there seems to have been no great system
of doctrine, but the religion did offer <u>immortality</u>, the
greatest of all secrets, to those who passed all the tests
and became initiated.
3. <u>Orphism</u>--the most important, which only seems to
appear in the 500's B.C. It was named for a legendary
singer, Orpheus. We hear of purification-rituals, small
brotherhoods of believers, an ascetic life (self-denial,
doing without). It had no single set of beliefs. There
were fantastic cosmogonies, including a <u>World-Egg</u>, and
sometimes a story that man was a mix of the earth and the
divine, born from the ashes of the <u>Titans</u>. The idea of
<u>two separate worlds</u> was basic to the Orhic way. There
was a divine element in man, the soul, an immortal god
which was imprisioned in and hurt by the body. The believer wanted to purify and release his sould so that it could
return to the company of all the other gods. Until
that happened, the soul had to go round the wheel of
<u>reincarnation</u>, being punished or rewarded after death
according to what had happened to it in its most recent
existence, and then reborn at a fitting place on the
scale of existence. At fixed times, it seems, there were
total reincarnations of all souls at once (similar to an
idea that <u>Anaximander</u> may have had). Purifying and
releasing the souls came through ritual services, magic
formulas, and asceticism (such as not eating animal meat--
since all living things were kin, souls being imprisoned
in a variety of forms). This Orphism should look much
closer to the kind of things Christians took for granted
for a long time than anything we have run across so far--
especially the other-worldliness, the contempt for the
body, the preference for the unseen over the physical
world. It was also to have enormous effect on the Greek

world for centuries. It is the system of opposites which we saw among the Milesians carried to an extreme—two opposing worlds.

For many, we can suppose, these new religious experiences were enough of an answer in themselves. For others, it was necessary to combine such religious ideas with learning. Pythagoras and the group (Brotherhood—although it included women) he formed in south Italy are the most important attempt to do this that we know of. A good deal of "magic" was involved, as well as crazy diet rules (including a fanatic insistence on not eating beans). We do not know much about what Pythagoras himself thought, as opposed to his associates and later followers, but we can make out a basic outline of his sytem. Accepting the Orphic idea of the imprisoned soul, he wanted to explain what the soul was.

Pythagoras decided that what made the soul divine was intellect, the power to know the truth which never changes and which lasts forever. What is the truth, then? It is the element of form, order, proportion, harmony, limit in the universe. This, the one reality for Pythagoras, can be expressed in numbers (as we do in modern physics). Thus "Things are numbers"—numbers are the essence. Mathematics, primarily geometry, had a very obvious natural appeal to any Greek trying to explain his world and himself—clear, precise, always valid, a model to which all thought should try to relate—and one which required no observation, or "experimenting." Pythagoras was a mathematician—we all have heard of the Pythagoras theorem involving right-angled triangles. He also discovered the laws of musical harmony, that the chief musical intervals (the fixed proportions of the scale) can be expressed in simple numerical ratios. This kind of knowledge fascinated him—he decided that numbers, which express proportion, order, etc., were of the essence. So we get things like "the music of the spheres," the Pythagorean idea that the heavens moved in similar harmony. Justice, similarly, could be expressed mathematically, as returning equal for equal. This is the kind of jump from a few observations to a grand theory that we found among the Milesians.

The difference between Pythagoras and the Milesians was that he had decided that the essence was <u>not</u> material and could <u>not</u> be known to the senses (and indeed, with the Orphics, that material things were bad). He also proceeded to talk of good and evil instead of just neutral matter. For Anaximander, cold and hot were opposites, but not moral opposites--neither one was good or bad. For Pythagoras, everything was either good or bad, in neat pairs of opposites:

good = unchanging form, order, the soul, shape, light, rest (all male);
bad = matter, the body, disorder, the indefinite, darkness, motion (all female).

Somehow, he had decided, if you contemplated all this in the correct way, your soul would be purified, released at your death from the prison that was your body to return to the godlike state (a state of rest).

Like the Milesians, Pythagoras seems to have had no explanation of what lay behind this, of why it was all happening--there is no "Creator" trying to test men or their souls. Nor, given their two-worlds system, could Pythagoreans find much of an explanation of how the material world came into existence at all. In their cosmology, it seems, some sort of dark, indefinite (bad) vapor was drawn continually (by???) into the universe through a process like breathing, and order and shape (good) were imposed. Later Pythagoreans argued that there was a fire at the center of the universe, with the earth and the sun revolving around it; the earth was shaped like a sphere (the Orphic World-Egg?); the sun and the moon had independent movements of their own. This at least gave up <u>geocentricity</u> (putting the earth at the center of things). 200 years later, though, Aristotle carried the day for geocentricity--it became a required belief.

The Pythagoreans were active politically in south Italy. Reasonably, since they worshipped order and discipline, they were oligarchs (anti-democrats). This is an early example of two characteristics of Greek philosophy: thinkers were expected to be politically active--no ivory-tower for the Greeks; and thinkers were just about always anti-democrats. When you emphasize the power to reason, it's hard not to notice that some people don't have as much

of that power as do others. Actually, failure in politics
soon nearly wiped out the Pythagorean circle--but they
experienced many revivals later and their influence on
all later thought was very, very great. Greek thought at
this point, in 500 B.C., had come a long way since Thales--
but it was in a strange direction.

A voice raised in protest against Pythagoras even in
his day was that of Xenophanes of Colophon, 550-500 B.C.,
a sort of wandering religious teacher whom we know only
in scraps. He settled in Elea in south Italy, in
Pythagorean territory. He, too, attacked the traditional
gods, of Homer, etc., and their values, but he also attacked as ridiculous the newer religions and the new systems
of thought (that of Pythagoras included) which were based
on them. All he had to preach, though, was a variation of
the Milesians' Justice--a force which was one, whole, not
to be moved, which governed all--a total world soul, one
which was, it seems, still material, not spiritual.

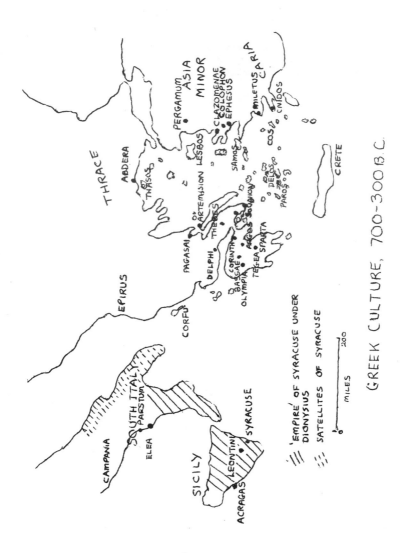

GREEK CULTURE, 700-300 B.C.

THRACE

ABDERA

THASOS

PERGAMUM
ASIA
MINOR

ARTEMISION LESBOS

CLAZOMENAE
COLOPHON
EPHESUS

SAMOS

MILETUS CARIA

CNIDOS

COS

DELOS

PAROS

CRETE

PAGASAI

DELPHI

THEBES

CORINTH

BASSAE

OLYMPIA

ARGOS SALAMIS

TEGEA SPARTA

EPIRUS

CORFU

CAMPANIA

SOUTH ITALY

PAESTUM

ELEA

SICILY

LEONTINI

ACRAGAS

SYRACUSE

///// 'EMPIRE' OF SYRACUSE UNDER
DIONYSIUS

≡≡≡ SATELLITES OF SYRACUSE

0   200
MILES

INTRODUCTION TO HOMER

Homer's works, the _Iliad_ and the _Odyssey_, are very important to the study of the western mind. In the ancient world, many civilizations were mor militarily and economically important than the Greek, including the Babylonian and Egyptian. Furthermore, these other civilizations had a recorded and surviving literature. But for us, Homer's awareness that he was dealing with something special, the Greek view of things, makes his poems of great value.

However, before we can read Homer, we have to establish what we are reading, and about this there is great dispute and uncertainty. The "Trojan War" took place around 1200 B.C. Was homer alive then or soon after? Did he compose his poems and pass them on to other poets word for word? Did he write them down? Did a series of stories about Trojan War heroes pass down from generation to generation, to be composed on the spot from a general store of related stories? Did a poet we call "Homer" merely compile a group of these stories in 600 B.C.? We know that Peisistratus, a tyrant of Athens, put the epic poems into about the form we know now in about 540 B.C., but we do not know whether he collected written or memorized material, or whether he collected from one source (one poet) or many. Remember, a span of six centuries separates the Trojan War and Peisistratus' "rescension."

One view holds that poets devoted their lives to learning by heart the Homeric works, which were composed soon after the Trojan War and passed down from poet to poet with very few alterations until the poems were written down. We know that in Albania in modern times illiterate reciters, whose memories are much better than those of people who rely on writing, can commit poems of this length to memory with great accuracy (on the other hand, recent research has shown that they often make mistakes without realizing it). The Greek of the poems is also very rigidly "poetic" in a way not possible to convey in English and thus easier to remember. The view that the poems were composed early and passed down accurately received support from the archeological work of Heinrich Schleimann, who took Homer most literally and was rewarded with wonderful results.

Another view holds that many poets made up songs as they went along about heroes associated with the Trojan War, and that Peisistratus, on purpose or by accident, happened to collect only those about Achilles (Iliad), and Odysseus (Odyssey). If the collection was this random, we can explain some of the historical inconsistencies in the poems. The methods of warfare, especially the use of chariots and horses, seem to reflect a much latter period than 1200 (the Greeks of this period seem to have travelled in small, shallow boats that would hardly have carried horses, much less the food required to keep them). The poems refer to bronze and steel weapons in a confused way, regarding them as equals in effectiveness. The people in the poem always burn their bodies after death(cremate them), while we have many elaborate tombs from the time of the War which reflect burial as the common way of disposing of the dead. Most importantly, we know that the Greeks of this time could write ("Linear A and Linear B"), but the people in the poem seem to know nothing of writing (the Greeks of the Dark Ages apparently could not). Each of these difficulties offer fascinating areas of study.

However, since all these questions are unsettled, perhaps we should, for our purposes, look at Homer as a kind of text book from which the Greeks learned proper Greek behavior. In the Iliad, homer is clearly trying to get his point across by two contrasts, on between two types of men and the other between men and the gods. By using these contrasts, Homer reases some important questions about the world that men live in and makes us think about how men should behave.

First, Homer takes advantage of a contrast which we find throughout Greek mythology, a contrast between people whose names end with --os and those whose names end with --eus. This contrast may reflect the difference between the settled people, the --os people, and the invaders, the --eus people, because old Greek place names tend to end in --os (Corinthos, Lesbos, Melos, Delos). In this pattern, the --os people in mythology tend to stay at home, to live in cities, to have stronger ties to parents than to mates, and to be losers. The -eus people tend to be away from home, to live more nomadic lives, to take varriage very seriously, and to be winners. Thus Zeus takes over from his father

Chronos and kills him. Theseus of Athens kills the bull of Minos in Crete. Odysseau kills Polyphemos among the Cyclops. In the Iliad, Menelaus fights for Helen against Alexandros (Paris) and Menelaus wins. Priamos is the king of Troy, while the Greeks are led by Odysseus. The pattern does not hold at all times, since Nestoros and Patroclos are important Greeks.

The main contrast by which Homer makes his point is the contrast between Achilleus and Hectoros. Achilleus is very strong, very loyal to his friend Patroclos and his girlfriend Briseis, he is move more by emotions than by thinking—he almost kills Agamemnon in anger, and he eventually kills Hectoros because he is angry about the death of his friend, not because he wants to help the Greeks. Obviously, such a warrior fights well, but like all -eus Greeks, he does not fit well into military organizations. Achilleus never thinks—but he does play the harp well and sing well.

Hectoros, on the other hand, fights because he sees the necessity of defending his city and would be ashamed to appear to be a coward (Achilleus does not worry at all about what people think of him). Although Hector is very fond of his wife Andromache, his father has many wives. When Hector drives the Greeks back toward their ships, he thinks a great deal about whether to camp outside the city overnight or to return to the safety of the city. When he finally decides to stay out overnight, he makes sure that the army is well supplied with food and wine.

However, when the thoughtful, dedicated Hector fights the violent, irrational Achilleus, Achilleus is the winner, and the city of Troy is destroyed by the nomadic Greeks. The theme, or point, of Homer seems to be that the two men represent human alternatives of behavior. As the Greeks settled down, they were conscious that city life, settled life, offered many advantages, but that the disciplined life was less fun than the life of pure individualism. This understanding is what makes the Greeks so important. They realized, when no other people did, that man chose among different ways of living, and that he could thereby control at least a part of his fate.

The second contrast which homer uses to get his point across is between men and gods. All of the men in the Iliad except Agamemnon try very hard to be decent to their wives or mistresses. They also have an elaborate code of conduct--they give back prisoners when a ransom is paid, they live up to their obligations as hosts and guests, and they are kind to those weaker than themselves, especially women and children. Hector foresees the day when he will be killed and his wife made to work as a slave. He does not, however, fear that she will be raped or physically abused. Achilleus can become angry enough to drag Hector's body behind his chariot, but he cannot hurt a defenseless old man like Priam.

The gods, however, have no concept of good or bad behavior at all. They use all the power they have to do whatever they want, and continually scheme to get more power. In contrast to the men in the Iliad, Zeus rapes women quite often (the Earth is littered with his illegitimate children-- Helen of Troy is one). Hera, unlike the dutiful and loving human women, nags her husband Aeus without mercy. Indeed, the marriage of Hera and Zeus look like the worst of human marriages. Zeus threatens Hera with violence many times, and Hera's son Hephaistos remembers Zeus having hung Hera up by her ankles at one time. Hera, more treacherous than human wives, tempts Zeus into sexual over-indulgence so that she can go against his orders while he is asleep.

Since the gods are more immoral than the human beings in Homer, we are obviously dealing with a complicated religion which is very different from the one we know, and very different from other religions of the world. Gods normally do two differnt things for the people who believe in the--they give reason for moral (or good) behavior and they have reasons for making things happen to humans. The Greek gods do neither. In contrast to Confusianism, Buddhism, Hinduism and Hebraism, all of which grew up in the same era as Homer deals with, the Greeks have no sense of a creator of the universe, no holy writings, no theology, no sense of an eternal god (Greek gods are all doomed to die). There is no "earth-mother"godesses, and no sense of a "point" to human existence. For the Greeks to say, "Zeus did it" is about the

same as saying, "It just happened.' It is not the same at
all as our saying, " We must accept this as God's will"
is very different, for our God, whether he is the God of
Christianity, Hebraism or of Islam, has a plan and does
things for the greater good of all. Zeus just does things.

Furthermore, the Greek gods are not pagan in the same way
as the gods of Egypt or of Mesopotamia. While Apollo is
identified with the sun, and while some personalities are
identified with rivers, the Greeks did not worship the
moon, the sun or river gods. Their gods instead represent
abstract human qualities. Athena represents wisdom, Aphrodite sexual pleasure, Artemis chastity, Ares war, Apollo
civilize cleverness, Hephaistos manufacturing, Dionysios
the dark and irrational side of the mind (hence wine), and
Hera the home and marriage. According to Greek religion,
each human was especially dear to one god (had the gifts
that a special god gives), and therefore tended to solve
his problems by cleverness or by strength, by reason or by
intuition, according to which god helps him. Perhaps when
we hear a person in the Iliad say, "Athena held me back,"
we should no think of a goddess actually holding him by
the hair, but should think of him as merely saying, as we
would, "Suddenly it occured to me that I should think more
about it." Frequently, the gods and goddesses appear to
people in the form of a human, so when a Greek says,
"Athena appeared to me in the form of my mother," he may
only mean "my mother gave me some smart advice." True, the
Greeks built temples to these gods and worshipped them in
elaborate rituals, but then how "Christian" does one have
to be in order to get drunk at a "Christmas" party at the
country club?

This leads us to the most important thing we must learn
from the Iliad, the Homeric Greek way of seeing the world.
The Homeric Greeks have no sense of an after-life (at
death, all go "with Hades," who is a person, not a place),
and live forever as "shadows." Homer gives us a picture of
these shadows, and they are miserable. The Homeric Greeks
have no concept of the soul. Achilles says Zeus scatters
blessings and curses without even looking where he is
throwing them, so some people seem to get all of one or the

other, while most men get a little of each before disappearing into nothingness. Nothing makes any sense at all. Human beings often have their personalities taken over by forces (gods) beyond their control.

However, the effect of this bleak view of the world had the opposite effect of what we might at first think. Instead of depressing the, this view inspired them to live intensely. The enthusiasm for life we have seen in Minoan and Mycenaean art is also apparent in Homer. We see the same joy in two Homeric characteristics of these epics, the epithets and the similes. Most of the major characters have several little tags which Homer attaches to their names, which are called epithets. Zeus is, according to his mood, a 'storm-cloud gatherer" or "earth-shaker"; Achilleus is "swift-footed" or "shining" (our word brilliant); Hera is "white-armed" or "large-eyed" (actually "cow-headed" but the term refers to the large, liquid, long-lashed eyes cows have); the lovliest epithet belongs to Thetis, who is called "silver-footed," refering to the lovely motion of graceful girls when they walk.

Likewise, the longer comparisons of two things, called similes, show an enthusiasm for the beauty of the natural world. Thes long comparisons may go on for several hundred words, and for us seem to slow down the story. Instead, we must try to see them as important things in themselves (like the 'background' of movies, beautiful scenery, nice settings, and so forth). Homer never says, "the sun came up." He says "The lovely lady of dawn, Eo, got up from her soft bed and touched the eastern sky with her rosey fingers, and walked just on the other side of the eastern hills in a dress of red and yellow, giving the sky its lovely colors of sunrise." Paris is compared to a horse, but not just any horse--he is a horse which has been cooped up for a long time and who gets away and enjoys running because he runs well, and a horse who thinks of the fun of drinking from a cold stream beside female horses in a field of rich grass.

The Greek "moral" system is also strange to us. For us, things are good or bad in themselves. For the Greeks, what a human did was not so important as how he did it. "Good and bad" become for them "appropriate and inappropriate." To kill a man in was is a good thing to do, but to take advantage of the same man when he is a guest is a very bad thing to do (see the incredible discussion between Glaucos and Diomedes in the _Iliad_). Drinking is fine when it is time to drink, but bad when it is time for fighting. In short, in the course of his life, a human must at the appropirate time honor with all his heart Aphrodite, Hera, Ares, Dionysios, and Artemis. Man must make his cities as beautiful as he can, knowing that eventually Poseidon with an earthquake or Zeus with a storm will destroy them.

Perhaps we can understand them better if we remember that these Greeks invented sports as we know them, things we know to be absurd, but which we like to do for their sakes. All people play--but Greek sports are something particular to them. They loved to do all the things that humans do and loved to do them well, whether it be having a party, having a family or having a war.

Now for some background for the story. Homer spoke to listeners or readers who knew Greek religion (or "myth-ology") as we know "Ford," "Chevrolet," or"Cadillac" (our "religion"). Therefore, Homer does not explain who his characters aren nor how they came to be at Troy. Modern readers might need a little more introduction.

First, the background--when Peleus, a mortal, was to marry Thetis, an immortal (and a daughter of one of the rulers of the sea), all the gods wore invited to the party except Eris, the goddess of discord (of anger, argument, and bad behavior). Here we must note that the goddess and the thing (Eris and discord) are the same thing, so the gods did not want "discord" at their party. But "discord" came anyway, because Eris threw into the party an apple which said, "This apple is for the most beautiful woman at the party." The apple was claimed by three powerful and beautiful goddesses--Hera, wife of Zeus and the one who gives people happy home lives; Athena, goddess of wisdom and thought; and Aphrodite, goddess of sex and fun. No one would judge the contest because the judge would make a friend of one goddess, but he would, for the rest of his life, be without the other two--the judge would either have no sex, no home, or no brains.

Eventually, the goddesses found a man stupid engough

to make the choice. This was Paris, or Alexandros, a child of the king and queen of Troy. Because it was foretold that he would cause trouble, Paris had been sent away from Troy to be a shephard. He was not very intellegent, but a lust young man, and so he gave the apple to Aphrodite if she would give him, as a lover, the most beautiful women in the world.

But there was a complication. The most beautiful woman in the world was Helen, the daughter of Leda. Leda was married to Tindareus, and by him she had a daughter, Clytemnestra. Zeus saw Leda one day and raped (or seduced) her in the farm of a giant swan (many painters have tried to picture the mechanics of this act). The result was Helen; a great many suitors wanted to marry Helen and Clytemnestra and almost went to war over them. Odysseus worked out a plan that suited everyone. Odysseus married Penelope, and Helen and Clytemnestra married two brothers, Menelaus and Agamemnon, sons of a powerful king named Atreus. To quiet the feelings of the suitors who lost out, those who were involved agreed to help out any of the group who was attacked by any one from the outside, in an attempt to maintain the balance of power.

So Aphrodite had to take Helen from her husband Menelaus and give her to Alexandros. Aphrodite arranged for him to visit Menelaus, and then made Helen fall helplessly in love with him, and they ran away to Troy. This angered the friends of Menelaus, because Paris had not only stolen Menelaus' wife but had behaved very badly--the Greeks took the duties of a host and guest seriously. So all the members, after a good many delays, got together and attacked Troy. They all also hoped to make money by taking home the riches of the city of Troy.

Now for the characters--the mortalsamong the Greeks are:

Odysseus--a strong wrestler, farmer, and king of Ithaca, son of Laertes, husband of Penelope and father of Telemachus. At first he did not want to leave his wife and infant son to go to Troy, but when he had to he fought with great strength and clever mind. He is called "wily" because he is good at out-smarting everyone. He is the samartest of the Greeks, but not always

too honest. Homer's audience admired his skill in
lying. Today he would be a used-car salesman.

Achilleus (Achilles). The son of Peleus and Thetis (whose
marriage began the whole thing), he is the strongest,
fastest, most violent, and most sentimental of the
Greeks. He had a choice between a long, dull life and
a short, action-filled one, and he chose the short
one. Achilleus is proud of himself, but a true friend
to Patroclos. Like many strong men, he saw the world
in simple forms fo loyalty. Today he would be a line-
backer in the National Football League.

Ajax--a large, gruff simple soldier.

Nestor--an old soldier, now important for his advice and
skill in helping the army stay together. He is the
best s½ealer a,pmg tje Greeks.

Agamemnon--Somehow, he seems to have more "clout" than
the rest of the Greeks. He rules Mycenae, Is married
to Helen's sister, Clytemnestra, is only a pretty
good soldier, and is the worst of the Greeks. He
does not behave himself well, is disloyal to his wife
(very unusual), is short-tempered and the least liked
of the Greeks. Today he would be a Snaor or President
of the United States.

Menelaus--the husband of Helen, and brother to Agamemnon,
he is a nice fellow about whom we know little. He is
a brave and strong soldier, who offers to settle the
was by single combat with Paris. Today he would be a
successful insurance salesman.

The Trojans:

Priam--the old king of Troy. Unlike the Greeks, he has
many wives, but his queen is Hecuba.

Hector--son of Hecuba and Priam, the smartest and most
sillful warrior among the Trojans, a general and a
good hand-to-hand fighter. He is a dedicated family
man, a man who sees his duty and does it. Today he
would be the president of General Motors.

Andromache--the wife of Hector, a beautiful woman, good
   wife and good mother. All of her relatives have
   been killed in raids by Achilles. The infant son of
   Andromach and Hector is Astyanax (nicknamed Scamandrios, after the river which runs beside Troy).

Alexandros (Paris)--also a son of Priam and Hecuba, he
   is handsome and proud of his beauty, a bit dull, a
   bit of a coward, not very strong in morals as in war.
   No one seems to liek him, even Helen. Today he would
   be a rock and roll singer.

THE ILIAD

O goddess! sing the anger of Peleus son,
Achilles; sing the deadly anger that brought
Woes numberless upon the Greeks, and swept
To Hades many a brave soul, and gave
Their limbs as food to dogs and buzzards--
For so had Zeus arranged it-- from the time
When the two chiefs, sons of Atreus, king of men,
And great Achilles, ended their friendship.
    Which of the gods put hatred between the chiefs,
That they should thus have trouble. It was Apollo.
Angered by Agamemnon, Apollo sent
A deadly disease among the army, and the men dying.
For Agamemnon had insulted Chryses the priest, who to
The Grecian fleet came to pay ransom for his daughter,
And he offered uncounted money. In his hand he carried
The sign of Apollo, the archer-god, upon a white staff,
And he asked of all the Greeks, but especially of the
Sons of Atreus, Agamemnon and Menalaus, the leaders:
    "You sons of Atreus, and you other chiefs, well-
                                                  armed
Achaians, may the gods who live upon Olympus allow
You to overthrow the city of Priam, mighty Troy, and
Allow you in safety to reach your homes; but give me
My beloved child, and take her ransom, for the sake of
The god who sends his arrows far, Apollo, son of Zeus."

    Thus said Apollo's priest Chryses, and then
All the Greeks cheered, asking Agamemnon to honor
The priest, and to take the liberal gifts he
Offered, but the advice did not please Agamemnon.
He dismissed the priest with scorn, and added
Vicious, threatening words. Agamemnon said,
    "Ole man, let me not find you hanginging around here,
Beside my roomy ships, or coming back later, because
The sign of Apollo which you carry will not protect you.
This girl I will never release--she will see old age
In my Argive hom, far from her native country, for
In my palace she will weave, and she shall fill my bed.
Go, anger me not, if you want to go in safety."

65

Thus spoke Agamemnon, and the old man in fear obeyed
The order, and in silence walked apart, along the
Many-sounding ocean-side, and he prayed as hard as
He could unto the monarch-god Apollo, Latona's son--
"Hear me, Apollo of the silver bow, who guards
Chrysa and the hold island of Cilla, and who are lord
In Tenedos; O Smintheus! If I ever helped to decorate
Your glorious temple, if I ever burned upon thy altar
The fat thighs of goats and bulls, grant me my Prayer,
And let your arrows avenge upon the Greeks the
Tears I have been forced to shed for my lost daughter."

So spoke he in prayer, and to him Phoebus Apollo
Listened. Down came Apollo, down from the summit of
The Olympian mountain, angry in his heart; his shoulders
Carried the bow and hollow quiver. There the arrows
Rang upon the shoulders of the angry god as he moved.
He came as comes the night, and seated above the ships,
Sent forth an arrow; terrible was the sound of that
Beautiful bow. At first he hit the mules and the dogs,
And then on man he turned his deadly arrows. All around
Burned the funeral pyres. Nine days already had his
Shafts been rained among the hosts, and now, upon the
Tenth, Achilles called the people of the camp to talk.
Hera of the snow-white arms had moved his mind to this,
For she saw with sorrow that the men were dying.
And when the assembly was full, swift Achilles stood
In the middle of the group and said:
"To me it seems, Agamemnon, that it would be a good
Idea, since now we are in trouble, to return home, if
Death take us not; for war and disease at once destroy
The Greeks. But let us first ask some seer or priest .
Or some dream-interpreter--for even dreams are sent
By Zeus--and ask him by what cause Phoebus Apollo has
Been angered thus. If by bad religious service we have
Made a mistake, perhaps by the burning of fat bulls and
Goats we can move the god to stop the disease."

He spoke, and took again his seat; and next got up
Calchas, son of Thestor, and chief of seers, on to whom
were known things past and present and to come. He,
Through his art of forecasting, which Apollo gave, had
Guided to the shore of Troy the Greek ships. With
Words well thought out and very courteously he spoke:

"Achilles, loved of Zeus, you tell me to explain the
Anger of Phoebus, monarch-god, who sends from afar his
Arrows. Willingly will I make known the cause; but
Promise me that, by word and hand, to protect me. For
My mind is upset that he who rules the Greeks, and to
Whom the Achaian race is subject, will be angry."
A king is too strong for poorer men, and though he
Keep his anger down awhile, it grows until he gets even.
Ao now think about this: will you keep me safe?"

Achilles the swift-footed answered Calchas thus:
"Fear nothing, but speak boldly out whatever you know
and say the will of Heaven. For by Apollo, dear to
Zeus, You Calchas, need not pray to the sacred oracles,
For no man, while yet I live, and see the light of day,
Shall lay a violent hand on you. Among our roomy ships,
No man of all the Grecian armies, though you name the
name of Agamemnon, whose high boast it is to stand
In power and rank above them all."

Encouraged thus, Calchas said:
"It is not neglected religious service or the sacrifices
Of bulls that move him, but the insult shown his priest,
Whom Agamemnon kicked out when he refused to set his
Daughter free, and to recieve her ransom. Therefore
Sends the archer-god these horrors, and still will send
Them on the Greeks, and he will never withdraw his
Heavy hand from our destruction until Chryseis freely,
And without ranson, is restored to her beloved father,
And with her a sacred offering to Chrysa be sent.
Only in this way can we make peace with the god."

Thus having said, Calchas took his seat. And then
Agamemnon got up, greatly angered. His gloomy heart
Was full ow anger, his eyes sparkled like fire; he
Fixed a menacing look full on Calchas, and said;
"Prophet of evil! never have you yet a cheerful
Word for me. To mark the signs of coming mischief is
Your only delight. Good do you never foretell nor
Bring to pass. And now you say, in your fortune-telling,
Before the Greeks, how the archer-god hurts us thus,
Because I would not take the costly ransom offered to
Get the young child of Chryses. It was my choice to
Keep her with me, for I like her more than Clytemnestra,

67

My bride of my young years. And I think her not less
Nobly graced than she, in form and feature, her mind
And pleasing arts. Yet will I give her back,if that
Is best; For gladly would I see my people saved from
This destructuion. But not for free! I will not be
Left, alone of all the Greeks, without my prize.
That would not be proper. All of you see that now my
Share of the prizes has been taken from me."

To him the great Achilles, swift of foot, replied:
"Famous Agamemnon, greediest of all men, where will
Find another prize among the Greeks, since none is set
Apart, a common store? The trophies brought from town
Which we have sacked have all been shared among us,
And now we could not without shame make every warrior
bring his portion back. Yield then, the maiden to the
God, and we, the Achaians, freely will give to you
Three or four times what you would get from the
Loot we shall get from this well-defended Troy."

Then the king Agamemnon answered his thus:
"Nay, use no cleverness, brave as you are, godlike
Achilles. You have not the power to change my mind.
Do you think that, while you keep safe your share
I shall sit idly down, deprived of mine? You tell me
To give the maiden back. It is well, if to my hand
The noble Greeks shall bring the worth of what I lose,
And in a shape that pleases me. Else will I come
Myself, and seize and bear away your prize, or that
Of Ajax or Odysseus, leaving him from whom I take his
Share with cause for anger. Another time we will
Think of this. Now come, and forth into the great
Salt sea launch a black ship, and muster on the deck
Men skilled to row, and put a large sacrifice on the
Ship, and let the fair-cheeked maid leave. Send
A prince to do the job, either Ajax Idomeneus, or
Odysseus--or yourself, Achilles; you soothe the anger
Of the archer god."

Achilles the swift-footed with stern look, thus
Answered: "Ha, your armed in impudence and loving
Money! Who of all the Greeks can willingly obey you,
On the march or bravely battling with the enemy?
I came not to this war because of wrong done to me

By the valiant sons of Troy. No feud had I with them;
They never took my cows or horses, nor, in Phthia's
Land spoiled my harvest fields. For many a shadowly
Mountain between us lies, and waters of the wide-sounding
Sea. Man shameless! We follow you so that you may
Glory in avenging upon Troy the grudge of Menelaus and
Your own, you shameless one. And yet you have for this
Neither thanks nor care. You threaten now to take
From me the prize for which I fought hard in battle;
And the Greeks gave it to me. I never take an equal
Share with you of treasure when the Grecian hosts
Have sacked some populous Trojan town. My hands perform
The harder labors of the fieldin all the tumult of the
Fight; but when the treasure is shared, the largest
Share of all is yours, while I content with little,
Seek my ships, weary with combat. I shall now go home
To Phthia; better is it to return with my beaked ships;
But here, where I am held in little honor, you will
Fail, I think, to gather, in large measure, wealth."

     Him answered Agamemnon, king of men:
"Desert, the, if you want to. I will not ask you to stay
For my sake. There will bo others left to do me honor,
And, best of all, the all-powerful Zeus is still with me.
You I hate most of men that I govern. You delight in
Causing trouble. If you are brave, some god, no doubt,
Has made you so. Hence, then, to your home, with all
Your ships and men! There be a big shot among your
Myrmidons; I heed you not, nor care I for your fury.
Thus, in turn, I threaten you--since Phoebus takes away
Chryseis, I will send her in my ship and with my friends,
And coming to your tent, I will bear away the fair-cheeked
Maid, your prize, Briseis, that you may learn how far I
Stand above you and that the other chiefs may fear
To test their strength with me, and doubt my power."

     The rage of Achilles , as he thus spoke, grew
Fiercer; in that shaggy breast his heart wondered
Whether from his thigh to draw his sharp sword, and,
Thrusting back the rest, to strike down Agamemnon, or
Whether he should try to control his and master his
Furious spirit. While he thus debated with himself,
And half drew out his sword from its sheath,
Pallas Athene came, sent from on high by Hera, the
White-armed, who loved both warriors and made both her

Special worry. Athene came behind him, seen by him and
Him alone, and she held his yellow hair. Achilles
Turned in wonder, and at once he knew the look of
Pallas and the awful-gleaming eye, and thus said
To her with winged words:
  "Why cme you here, daughter of the great Zeus who
Carries the Aegis? Are you here to see the insolence
Of Agamemnon, son of Atreus? Let me tell you what I
Think will be the outcome of all this--that men may
Lose his life, and quickly too, for such arrogance."
  Then thus the goddess, blue-eyed Pallas, spoke--
"I came from heaven to pacify your anger, sent by Hera
The white-armed, to whom you both are dear, and who
Ever watches over you both. Don't use violence;
Let not your hand take out the sword, but utter with
Your tongue insults, as you feel necessary. For I
Declare what time shall bring to pass; you will get
Even, and you will get three times the gifts of great
Value for this day's wrong. Now calm your angry
Spirit and obey the will of the gods."

  Achilles the swift footed- answered thus--
"O goddess, be the word you bring obeyed, however
Fierce my anger; for to him who hearkens to the gods,
The gods give in return their ear."
  So speaking on the silver hilt he stayed his strong
right hand, and back into its sheath put his good sword,
Obeying. She meantime returned to heaven, where
Aegis-carrying Zeus lives with the other gods. And
Now again Achilles spoke, showing his great anger:

  "Drunkard! with the face of a dog and the heart
Of a deer! You never yet have dared to arm yourself
For battle liek the rest of us, not to join the other
Chiefs who prepare to fight a battle. Such is your
Craven fear of death. Better it suits you among the
Greeks to rob some warrior of his prize who dares
Withstand you. King you are, and yet a ruiner of your
People. You rule a spiritless race, else this day's
Insolence were your last. And now I say, and I
Bind my saying with a mighty oath: By this staff,
Which can never bear a leaf or twig, since first it
Left its stem among the mountains, for the steel
has Cut away it boughs and bark, to sprout no more,

And now the Achaian judges bear it--they who guard
The Laws, received from Zeus--such is my oath: The
Time shall come when all the Greeks shall long to see
Achilles back, while many are dying by the hand of
Hector, the man-killer. You, meanwhile, although you will
Be sorry, shall have no power to help, and you shall
Rage against yourself to think that you have scorned
The bravest of the Greeks, the man who helped you most."

As thus he spoke, Achilles flung to the ground
The gold-studded wand, and took his seat.
Fiercely Agamemnon raged; but now uprose
Nestor, the master of persuasive speech, the clear-toned
Speaker from Pylos, whose tongue dropped words more
sweet than honey. He had seen two generations that
Grew up and lived with him on sacred Pylos pass away,
And now he lived with the third generation. With
Wise words he thus spoke to the assemby of chiefs--

"Look down, O gods, on what new misfortunes threaten
Greece! How Happy Priam and his sons would be, and
All the people of Troy, if they could know how furiously
You fight among yourselves. You who in council and in
Fight are greater than the other Greeks. Now listen
To your words--You who are younger than myself--for
I have lived with braver men than you, and yet they
Thought me very worthwhile. Such men as you I never
Saw for wasting your own powers. Such was not the
Case with men like Pirithous and like Druas, lord of
Nations, Caeneus and Exadius, and the great Polypheme,
And Theseus, son of Aegeus, in for similar to immortal
Gods. Strongest of the earth-born race they fought,
The strongest men of their times--with Centaurs, the
Wild dwellers of the hills, and the beat them. With
Those men did I talk, coming to their camp from Pylos
To a distant land. They sent to ask me to join with
Them in war, and by their side I fought my best, but
No man now living on the wide earth would dare to
Fight with them. Great were they, and they listened
To my words. You should listen also, and let my
Words perwuade you for the best.
You, Agamemnon, powerful as you are, take not from him
The maiden; suffer him to keep the prize given him by
The sons of Greece. And you, Achilles, squabble no

Longer with the king, since never Zeus gave anyone such
Power as a king as he has. Though you are braver,
Achilles, and goddess born, yet he has greater power and
Wider rule. Agamemnon, calm your anger. It is I who
Ask it of the most powerful ruler in Greece."

To him the kingly Agamemnon said,
"The things which you have said, aged chief, are
Well-spoken; but this man would stand above all others;
He wants to be the master, the boss of all others,
And to direct in all things; Yet, I think, there may
Be one who will not allow this. For if by favor of the
Immortal gods he was made brave, have they for such
A reason given him liberty of insolent speech?"

At this point the great Achilles broke in, saying,
"Yes, well might I deserve the name of coward and of
Wretch if I should submit in all things to your
Bidding. Such commands you lay on others, not on me.
Nor should you think I will obey you any longer.
This I say--and bear it will in mind--I shall not
Lift my hand to keep the maiden whom you first gave
And then took back from me; but whatever else may be
On board that swift black ship of mine,
Beware you carry not away the least without my
Permission. Come, if you wish, and test me now,
So that these may see your black blood bathe my spear."

Then, rising from that war of words, the two
Dissolved the assembly of the Greek Chiefs. Achilles,
Went with Patroclus and his warrior friends, while
Agamemnon ordered that a swift ship be launched
With twenty chosem men to ply the oars, and he put a
Sacrifice upon it for the god. He then led the
Fair-cheeked Chryseis on board. He sent with
Them the wise Odysseus, and they went forth upon
Their watery path. Agamemnon himself made a sacrifice
To Apollo in his camp. Then Agamemnon made worse his
Quarrel with Achilles. Thus he said to Talthybius
Eurybates, two of his most faithful ministers:
"Go to where Achilles holds his tent and take the
Fair-cheeked Briseis by the hand, and bring her to me.
If he does not yield her, I shall come forth to claim her
With a band of warriors, and it shall be worse for him."

He spoke and sent them forth with added words of hate.
With unwilling steps they went beside the ocean until
They reached the camp of Achilles sacker of cities.
They found Achilles seated by his tent, and their
Coming pleased him not. They, moved by fear and
Reverence for the king, stopped and did not speak to
Him, not told of their errand. He saw their worry
And said to them:

"Hail, heralds, messengers of Zeus and men. Come,
I don't blame you. I blame only Agamemnon, who has
Sent you for the maid. Noble Patroclus! Bring the
Girl here, and let them lead her away. My witnesses
Are you, before the blessed gods and mortal men, and
This wicked king, that I have done as he wished."

Therefore the goddess-born Achilles, swift of foot,
Sat beside his ships and brooded over his anger.
He did not come to the assembly of the chiefs,
Nor did he come to the war, but allowed idleness
To eat his heart away; for well he loved was and
Combat. But then now, at length, came the Twelvth
Day, and the ever-living gods returned to the
Olympian mountain with Zeus their leader. Thetis,
The mother of Achilles, kept in mind her son's
desire, and with the early morn, emerging from the
Depths of the ocean, climbed to the great heaven
And high mountain, and found all-seeing Zeus, who
From the rest of the gods was seated apart on one
Of the highest peaks of Olympus. She sat down before
The son of Uranos, clasped his knees with her left
Arm, and lifted up her right in begging of the
King of the gods, and said in supplication:

"O Zeus, my ruler, if among the immortals I have
Ever given you aid by word or act, deny not my request.
Honor my son, whose life is doomed to end so soon;
For Agamemnon, king of men, has done hime shameful
Wrong; he takes from my son the prize he won in war.
But you, Olympian Zeus, supremely wise, please honor
Him and give the Trojan host the victory, until the
Humbled Greeks heap many honors on my son."

She spoke, but cloud-gathering Zeus answered her

Not; In silence long he sat. But Thetis, who had
Held his knees at first now hugged them harder still,
And begged him yet again, saying,
"O promise me, and grant my plea, or else deny it,
For you need not fear that I will complain, for then
I will know that you do not honor me highly among
The gods." After she spoke, the Cloud-Gatherer
Sighed heavily and answered her thus: '
"Hard things do you ask of me, for by asking this you
Will force me into new disputes with Hera, who will
Make me angry yet again with her nagging words; she
Is always doing that kind of thing, among the immortals
Making arguments, saying that I aid the Trojans in
Their battles. Now go away and do not let her see
Us talking together. Leave the rest to me; and you
May be sure that I will do as you ask. Behold, I
Give the nod; for this, with me, the immortals
Know gives the highest certainlty. No word of mine
Which once my nod confirms can be revoked, or prove
Untrue, or fail to be fulfilled. It will be so."

As thus he spoke, the son of Chronosgave the nod
With his stormy brows. The lovely curls upon the
Sovereign One's immortal head were shaken, and with
Them the mighty mountain Olympus trembled. Then
They parted, she plunging from fright Olumpus to the
Ocean, and Zeus returning to his palace home.
All the gods were there, and when he entered, they
Rose from their thrones and came to meet him.
Zeus then took his seat at his place at the head,
But Hera knew--for she had see--that Thetis of the
Silver feet had talked seriously with her husband.
Therefore she spoke to the son of Chronos harshly:
"O sneaky one, with whom, among the gods, do you
Plot now? This is the way it has alwsys been. It is
Your pleasure to plot, apart from me, and make plans
In secret. You never willingly reveal to me your
Purposes, nor let me help you with your schemes."

Thus replied the father of all the gods and many
mortals:

"Hera, do not think to know all my plans, for

You will find the job too hard for you, even though
You are my wife. What is fit for you to know, no
One of the immortals or of men shall know sooner than
You; but when I make plans apart from all the gods,
Do not ever question me or try to pry into my mind."

    Hera of the large eyes replied quickly,
"What words, stern son of Chronos, have you said.
It never was my habit to question you or to
Pry into your plans, and you are usually left to
Form them as you wish. Yet Now I fear the silver-
                                    foote
Thetis, that daughter of the sea-ruler, has fooled you.
I am afraid she has convince you to do something
Bad, for at early morning I saw her sitting with you
And hugging your knees. And you have promised her.
I have no doublt, to give Achilles honor and to
Cause mny of the brave Greeks to die by their ships."

    Then Zeus, the gatherer of storm clouds, spoke
To his wife with harsh words, saying:
"Bitching woman! You always suspect me in this way,
Nor can I act without your watching me; and yet all
This gains you nothing, for it only serves to breed
Disgust in me, and it is the worse for you. But even
If it were as you think, it is enough that such has
Been my pleasure. Sit down, woman, in silence, and
Obey me, because if I decide to use my mighty fist
Upon you, none of these gods on Olympus will be
Able to stop me, and none will dare to help you."

    Thus ho spoke, and Hera tho largo oyod was
Afraid, and curbing her high spirit, sat down in
Silence; meanwhile, all the gods of heaven within
The walls of Zeus were upset. But Hephaistos,
The maker of things, tried to help his mother in
Her grief--so thus he said:
    "Great evil will it be and hard to bear, if, for
The sake of mortals, you are moved to such argument
Before the assembled gods. Even the pleasant feast
Will lose its flavor when we argue. Let me warn
You, my dear mother Hera, to remember that Zeus
Has greater power than us all._, Speak to him with

Gentle speeches, so that my eyes will not see you
Beaten with stripes. If Zeus punishes you I
Cannot help you even though I love you, for you
Will remember that once when I tokk you side, Zeus
Took me by the foot and threw me over the edge of
Heaven and I fell all day and with the setting sun
I struck the earth on Lemnos. Little life was left
In me then and I do not want to try the patience of
Zeus a second time."

Hephaistos spoke, and Hera the white-shouldered
Smiled and smilling took the cup her son had brought
Her; and next he poured to all the other gods sweet
Nectar from the jar, beginning first with those at
The right hand. As they beheld lame Hephaistos
Laboring over the palace floor, a great laughter
Broke from the blesse gods. So feastey they all
Day until sunset. From the feast none stood apart,
And Phoebus Apollo touched his wonderful harp,
And all the Muses sang sweetly in their turn.

At this point Homer ends Book One. Book Two tells
of the continuing debate ttween the Greek chiefs and the
stubborn Agamemnon. Homer begins Book Three with a
battle scene.

Now when both armies were arrayed for war, each
With its chiefs, the Trojan army moved on with
Shouts and noise of arms, as when the cry of cranes is
In the air, cranes which, flying south from winter
And the cold, wing their way over ocean, and at dawn
Bring fearful battle to the pygmy race, bloodshed and
Death. But silently the Greeks went forward, breathing
Valor, mindful still to aid each other in the coming
Battle. The marching armies raised a dust like an
Early morning fog which fills the rural valleys.

Now drew they near each other, face to face, and
Paris in the Trojan army pressed on, in appearance
Like a god. A leopard's skin was thrown across his

Shoulders, and he carried a crooked bow and spear,
Brandishing these weapons, he defied to mortal fight
The bravest of the Greeks. Menelaus. loved of Ares,
Saw Paris advancing with large strides before the rest;
As a hungry lion who has made a prey of some large
Beast--a horned stag or a mountain goat--rejoices, and
With speed devours it, so Menelaus felt great joy when
Paris, of the godlike form, appeared in sight, for
Now he thought to get his revenge on the guilty one,
And immediately sprang from his car to earth with his
Arms. But when the graceful Paris saw the chief come
Toward him from the foremeot ranks, his heart was
Troubled, and he turned and passed among his fellow
Warriors and avoided death. As one who meets within
A mountain pass a serpent and starts aside with sudden
Fright, and takes the backward way with trembling
Limbs and cheeks all white--the graceful Paris thus
Before the son of Atreus,Menelaus, shrank in fear.
Hector beheld and thus chided him harshly:
"O luckless Paris, nobly formed, yet woman-follower
And seducer! You should never have been born, or
Else at best have died unwedded; better it would be
Than thus to be a scandal and a scorn to all who look
on you. The long-haired Greeks, how they will laugh
Who for your handsome looks are thought a hero,
When there dwells in you no spirit and no courage.
Were you such when, crossing the great deep ocean in
Your strong ships with chosen comrades you did make
Your way among a stranger-people and bear off a
Beautiful woman from that distant land, allied by
Marriage ties to your father and to us and all the
People , to our foes a joy and a disgrace to you?
Why could you not await Menelaus? Then you would
Have been taught from what a gallant warrior you did
Take his lovely wife. Your harp will not help you
In battle, and neither will the gifts of Aphrodite,
And neither your curly hair, nor your graceful body.
It must be that the sons of Troy are faint of heart,
Else you would be, for the evil you have caused,
Been laid beneath a cover of stone."

    Thus spoke Hector, tamer of horses; Then answered
Paris of the godlike appearance to him: "Hector, your

Rebuke is just; you do not wrong me. Fearless is
Your heart; it is like an axe when, used by the
Hand that hacks a shipwright's plank, it cuts right
Through, doubling the user's force. Such a tameless
Heart lives in your chest. Yet reproach me not with
The fair gifts which golden Aphrodite gave. Whatever
In their grace the gods give us is not to be rejected.
It is not ours to choose what they shall give us. But
If you desire to behold my skill shown in combat,
Cause the Trojans and Greeks to pause from battle,
While, between the hosts, I and the warlike Menelaus
Strive in single fight for Helen and her wealth.
Whoever shall prevail and prove himself the better
Warrior, let him take with him the woman, and depart;
While all the other Trojans, having made a faithful
Treaty of friendship shall live on Troy's fertile
Plain, and all the Greeks return to Argos, famous for
Beautiful horses, and to Achaia, famous for women."

   He spoke, and Hector, hearing him, rejoiced, and
Went between the armies, and with his spear, held
By the middle, pressed the front lines of the Trojans
Back, and made them all sit down. The long-haired
Greeks, meanwhile, with bended bows, took aim against
Him, just about to send arrows and stones at him; but
Agamemnon, king of men, beheld, and thus he cried:
   "Wait a moment, friends; let not fly your arrows
You Achaians; Hector asks--Hector of the shiing
Helmet--asks to speak."
   He spoke, and the armies stopped, all at once,
And were silent. Hector then stood and said:
   "Listen, you Trojans and you nobly-armed Achaians,
To what Paris says by me. Paris bids the Trojan
And the Greeks to lay down their shining arms upon
The fertils earth, and let him and Menelaus, loved of
Ares, fight in single combat on the ground between
the two armies, for lovely Helen. And he who shall
Win and prove himself the better man, to his home
Shall go the woman, while the rest shall sign a
Solemn treaty of peace."

   Thus spoke Hector, and both the armies in silence
Listened. Then Menelaus, great in battle, said:
   "Now hear me also--me whose spirit feels the wrong

Most sharply. I propose that now the Greeks and Trojans
Separate, for greatly have we all suffered for the
Sake of my quarrel, and the original fault of Paris.
Whomsoever fate ordains to perish, let him die; but
Let the rest be from this moment reconciled, and
Part and bring an offering of two lambs--one white
And the other black--to Earth and Sun, and we ourselves
Will offer one to Zeus. And let the mighty Priam
Come here so that he may sanction this agreement--
For his sons are arrogant and faithless--lest some
Hand wickedly break the covenant of Zeus. The younger
Men of this time are rather silly people. But when
The elder shares the act, he looks both to the past and
Future, and provides what is most fitting for all."
   He spoke, and both the Greeks and Trojans heard
His words with joy, and hoped the hour was come to
End the hard-fought war. They stopped their horses,
Got off and removed their armor, which they laid upon
The ground near them in piles, each separate.
Then Hector sent two heralds forth with speed into the
Town, to bring the lambs and to call King Priam.
Meanwhile Agamemnon told Talthybius to seek the hollow
Ships and find a lamb for the altar. He obeyed the
Words of Agamemnon, king of men.

   Meanwhile to white-armed Helen came Iris, goddess
Of the rainbow and messenger of the gods. She took
The form of Laodice, the sister of Paris, whom
Antenor's son, King Helicaon, wed. Iris in the form of
Laodice came to where Helen was weaving a robe. She said;
"Dear lady, come and see the Trojan knights and
The brazen-armed Achaians doing things to wonder at.
They who, in this sad war, eager to kill each other,
Lately met in murderous combat on the field, are now
Seated in silence, and the war has stopped. They
Lean upon their shields, their massive spears are
Near them, planted in the ground upright. Paris
And Menelaus, loved of Ares, with their long lances
Will fight in single combat for you, and you will
Be declared the victor's wife."
Iris thus spoke, and in the heart of Helen awakened
Dear memories of her former husband and of her home

And kin. Instantly she left her chamber, robes and
Veiled in white, and shedding tender tears. Yet not
Alone, for two maidens, Aethra and Clymene, went with
Helen to the Scaean gates. When the arrived, King Priam
Called to Helen and said: "Come, dear daughter of mine,
And sit by me. You can see your former husband from
Here, your kindred and your friends. I blame you not.
The blame is with the immortals who have sent these
Pestilent Greeks against me. Sit and name for me this
Mighty man, the Greek chief, Gallant and tall. True,
There are taller men, but of such noble and dignified
Form I never saw. In truth, he is a kingly man."

And Helen, fairest among women, thus answered:
"Dear second father, whom at once I fear and honor,
I wish that cruel death had overtaken me before I left,
To wander with your son, from my marriage bed. But
That was not to be. And now I pine and weep. Yet I
Will tell you what you ask. The hero whom you see is
The wide-ruling Agamamnon, son of Atreus. He was once
Brother-in-law to me, if I may speak--lost in shame as
I am--of such a relationship."
      She spoke, and the aged Priam admired, and then
He spoke to her: "O son of Atreus, born under a happy
Fate, and fortunate among the sons of men! A mighty army
Of Greek youths obey your rule. I went to Phrygia once,
And there saw many Phrygians, heroes on swift horses,
The troops of Otreus, and of Mygdon, shaped like one
Of the immortals. Then I was an ally. Yet never before
This did I see such a large army assembled. Yet who
Is that, dear daughter, standing by Agamemnon, who,
Though less tall than he, is broader in the shouders
And chest. His armor lies on the teeming earth, but
Still he walks among the soldiers as a shepherd walks
Among the sheep, with an air of command."

And Helen, daughter of Zeus, answered thus:
"That is Odysseus, man of many arts, son of Laertes,
Raised in Ithaca, that rugged island, and skilled in
Every clever device and in planning actions wisely."
      Hearing what Helen said, the aged and wise Antenor
Spoke, saying: "You are right about Adysseus, Fair Helen.
Once he and Menelaus cme to Troy to ask for your re-

lease,

And while they were here they were guests in my palace,
Menelaus spoke well and we all respected him greatly.
But when Odysseus arose to speak, he seemed unused to
Public speaking, embarrassed, almost like an idiot.
But when forth he sent from his full lungs his mighty
Voice and words came like a fall of winter snow, no
Mortal man then would dare to strive with him for
Mastery in speech. We less admired the aspect of
Odysseus than the brilliance of his words."

Beholding then Ajax, the aged King Priam asked yet
Again of lovely Helen, "Who is that other chief of the
Achaians, tall, and large of limb, taller and broader
In the chest than the rest?"

Helen answered: "You see the mighty Ajax there, the
Bulwark of the Greeks. On the other side, among his
Cretans, stands Idomeneus, the godlike in aspect.
Two princes I do not see, and I wonder why they are not
Present. I do not see my brothers, twins born of the
Same mother as I, Castor, the fearless horseman, and
Pollux, theskillful boxer. Can it be that they have
Left the war because of my reproach and shame?"

Thus Helen wondered. She did not know that already
Castor and Pollux lay in the earth in Lacedaemon, their
Dear native land.

The heralds of both sides then conducted the offering
To the gods and made ready the field for tho single
Combat. Then Priam, of the line of Dardanus, said:
"Hearme, you Trojans, and you well armed Greeks! I
Must return to wind-swept Troy, for I cannot bear ,
With these old eyes, to look on my dear son engaged
In fierce struggle with Menelaus, the beloved of Ares.
Zeus and the ever-living gods alone know which of them
Shall meet this day with the doom of death."

So spoke the godlike man, and stepped into his
Chariot along with Antenor. Then they turned their
Horses and returned to Priam's palace.

Then Hector, son of Priam and the great Odysseu
Measured off a fitting space, and in a bronze helmet
They placed the lots, to shake and cast them to see which

Warrior first should hurl the brazen spear. Hector of
The shining helmet shook the lots, and out leaped the lot
Of Paris. Then they took their seats in ranks beside
Their swift horses, next to their rich armor. Paris the
Divine, husband of bright-haired Helen, there put on his
Well-made armor--upon his legs fair greaves, with silver
Clasps, and on his breast his brother's mail, fitting
Well his form. Around his shoulders then he hung his
silver-studded sword, and stout, broad shield, and gave
His glorious brows the dreadful helmet, dark with a horse-
Hair plume. A massive spear filled his right hand.
Meanwhile Menelaus, son of Atreus, clad himself in
Worthy armor.

And now when both were armed for fight, and each
Had left his army, and coming forward, walked between
The Trojans and the Greeks, and frowned upon the other,
A mute wonder held the Trojan soldiers and well-greaved
Greeks. There near each other in the measured space
They stood in angry mood with lifted spears.

First Paris hurled his massive spear; it struck the
Round shield of Menelaus, but the brass broke not
Beneath the blow. the weapon's point was bent on that
Strong shield. The next assault Menalaus made, but first
Offered this prayer to Father Zeus:
"O sovereign Zeus! allow that I avenge on guilty Paris
Wrongs which he was first to offer; Let him fall
 Beneath my hand, that men may learn not to repay
The kindness of a host with terrible injury."
He spoke, and threw his sharpened spear; it struck
The round shield pf Paris; right through the shining
Buckler went the rapid steel, and, cutting the soft
Tunic near the flank, stood fixed in the fair vest. Paris
Bent sideways before it and escaped death. Menelaus
Drew his sword, lifted it high, and hit his enemy's
Helmet. The weapon shattered into four fragments.
Menelaus looked to the broad heaven, and thus cried:
"O father Zeus! you are of all the gods the most un-
                                        friendly.

I had hoped to avenge the wrong by Paris done to me, but
My sword is broken in my grasp, and from my hand the
Spear was vainly flung and gave not wound."

He spoke, and rushing forward, seized the helmet of
Paris by its hore-hair crest, and turned and dragged
Him toward the well-armed Greeks. Beneath his tender
Throat the strap that held the helmet to the chin was
Choking Paris. And now had Menelaus dragged him this
Way, and earned the victory, if the daughter of Zeus,
The beautiful goddess Aphrodite, had not seen his
Trouble in time. She broke the ox-hide strap; an empty
Helmet followed the powerful hand. The hero saw,
Swung it aloft and hurled it toward the Greeks, and
There his comrades seized it. He again rushed with his
Brazen spear to slay his foe. But Aphrodite rescued
Paris yet again, by wrapping him in a thick fog, and
In this fog bore him safe to his chamber inside the
Walls of Troy. Then she took her way to call Helen.
On the lofty tower, she found her, amid a throng of
Trojan ladies. The goddess plucked at Helen's robe.
She took the form and feature of a spinner of the wool,
An aged woman who often worked with Helen. Aphrodite said;
"Come with me, Aleandros sends for you. He is now
In his chamber and at reat on his bed. He looks not like
One who comes from battle, but one who comes from a
Choral dance."

But Helen recognized the goddess Aphrodite even in
Her disguise, and said thus to the goddess:
"Strange Being! Why do you mislead mc still? Paris is
In disgrace. I will never go to Paris again to
Decorate his bed. If I did so, the Trojan womon would
Tease and taunt me without mercy. O, my griefs are many."

Displeased, the goddess Aphrodite said:
"Bitch, anger me not, let I abandon you in anger, and
Hate you with a fury as great as my love, and lest I
Cause Trojans and Greeks to hate you so that you shall
Die miserably." Thus the goddess spoke, and Helen,
Struck with awe, wrapped her robe around her and went.
When she reached the room the lovely daughter of Zeus,
Helen, nagged her husband thus: "Do you come from battle?

83

I wish rather that you had died by the mighty hand of
Him who was my husband. It was once, I know, your boast
That you were more than peer in strength and power of
Hand and skill with the spear, to warlike Menelaus.
Go then now, defy him and to the combat once again.
And yet I advise you to stand apart nor seek a combat
Once again, for he will certainly hit you with his
Sword and kill you."
     Then Paris answered" "Woman, do not nag me thus
Harshly. True it is, that, with the aid of Pallas
Athena, Menelaus has obtained the victory; but I many
Conquer him in turn, for we ahve also gods with us in
Trou. Now, let us give the present time to sex; never
Yet have I so strongly proved the power of love--not
Even when I took you from your home in Lacedaemon,
Sailing over the deep ocean in my good ships, and in
The island of Cranae made you mine for the first time.
Such a glow of love and sweet desire now possess me."
     He spoke, and to the bed went; his wife followed,
And that fair couch received them both.
     Meanwhile, Menelaus raged among the Trojan soldiers
Looking for Paris. When after a long search he could
Not find him, Agamemno, king of men, spoke:
"You Trojans, and Achaians, hear; The victory belongs
To Menelaus. The Trojans must restore the Argive
Helen and pay the fitting fine, which shall remain
A memonry and a lesson to men in future times."

     Thus Homer ends Book Three. In book Four, Zeus for-
bids any of the god or goddesses to take any further
part in the war. With the outside influences removed
the battle becomes even more bloody, and Homer reports
the bloodshed and carnage in great detail. The Greeks
do not miss Achilles and his army of Myrmidons very
greatly, for the Trojans suffer great losses, and Hector
returns to the city to city to ask for help by making
special sacrifices to the gods. We begin with an interesting encounter just before Hector returns to the
city.

84

When Diomed saw the warlike skills of his foe, he
Spoke to his, asking if perhaps he was the son of a god
Who had granted him such strength. Diomed's foe said:
    "I am Glaucus, the son of Hippolochus, and the
Grandson on great Bellerophon. My father sent me forth
To Troy with the command to bear myself like a brave
Man, and to bring credit to my family. I spring
From the bravest stock in Ephyra and the wide realm
Of Lycia. I boast to be os such a race and blood."

    He spoke. The warlike Diomed was glad, and planting
In the fertile earth his spear, addressed Glaucus thus"
"Most surely you are my ancestral guest; for the noble
Oenesu is my grandfather, and I have heard him tell
Of the days when he recieved the blameless chief
Bellerophon within his palace and kept him for twenty
Days. When they parted, they gave each other gifts
Such as host and guest exchange; a purple sword-belt
Oeneus gave, and Bellerophon a double golden cup.
This cup I left within my palace when I came to Troy.
So your grandfather and mine were host and guest!
From this time on I will be your host and friend in Argos;
You shall be the same to me in Lycia when I visit
Lycia's shores. When in the confusion of battle,
Let us avoid each other's spears, for there will
Be plenty of Trojans and their allies for me to kill
When some god brings them my way, and likewise for
You there will be many Greeks for you to kill if
You can catch them. Let us exchange our armor, that
Even these may see that you and I regard each other
As ancestral host and guest from this time forth."
    Thus having said, they leaped from their cars,
And clasped each other's hands and pledged their faith.

    Meanwhile, inside the city, Hector searched for his
Beautiful wife Andromache. Not finding hor in their
Rooms, he asked of the maidens there if she had gone
To the temple of Athena to ask the aid of the goddess.
One of the maidens thus replied:
"No Andromache has not gone to the temple of Athena;
But to the lofty tower of Troy she went when it was
Told to her that the Trojan troops lost heart, and that
The valor of the Greeks prevail~d. She is now hurrying

85

Toward the walls, like on gone mad, with her son."
    So spoke the maiden. Hector left in haste the rooms
And went back the way he came, between the rows of
Stately buildings, running across the mighty city.
When at length he reached the Scaean gates, his wife,
The nobly given Andromach came forth to meet him--she
Was the daughter of Eetion who, among the woody hills
Of Placos, in the Hypoplacian town of Thebe, ruled
Cilicia and her sons, and gave his child to Hector .
They had one son, Hector's only child, beautiful as
A star, whom Hector called Scamandrios, but who was
Named Astyanax, which means "lord of the city." Hector
Now looked on his child with a silent smile. Andromache
Pressed to his side meanwhile, and, all in tears,
Hugged her husband and thus beginning said:

    "You are too brave! Your great bravery will cause
Your death! Have you no pity on your tender child,
Nor pity for me, your unhappy wife, who soon must be
Your widow? All the Greeks will rush on you, to take
Your life. A happier lot would be mine, if I must lose
You, to go down to earth, for I shall have no hope when
You are gone--nothing but sorrow will be left. Father
Have I none, and no dear mother. Great Achilles has
Killed my father when he sacked the town of the
Cilicians--Thebe of the high gates. It was there that
Achilles killed Edtion, yet did not take his armor
As part of his spoils. Achilles respected him so much
That he burned the body with his bright armor on, and
Raised a mound above him. Seven brothers had I in my
Father's house, but all went with Hades in one day;
Achilles the brilliant killed them all . My mother,
Princess of the woody hills of Placos, with his spoils
Achilles took away, and only gave her back for a large
Ransom--then Artemis struck her down in her own home.
Hector, you are father and dear mother now to me,
And brother and my youthful husband besides. In pity
Keep within the fortress here, and do not make your
Child an orphan nor your wife a widow. Put your army
Near the place of the wild fig-tree, where the city's
Walls are low and may be climbed. You can stay there
And be of more use than in the forefront of the battle."
    Then answered Hector, great in war:

86

"All this I bear in mind, dear wife; but I should stand
Ashamed before the men and long-robed women of Troy if
I, like a coward, kept apart from the war. This is not
The way my heart makes me act, for I have learned to dare
And to strike among the foremost of the sons of Troy,
Upholding my great father's name and my own. Yet well in
My certain mind I know that the day will come in which our
Sacred Troy, and Priam, and the people over whom Priam
Rules, the people of Troy, shall all die by the swords
Of the Greeks. But the sorrows of the Trojan race, and
The sorrows of my mother Hecuba, and the sorrows of
My brothers and the many brave men in the army are not
The most important to me. None of these things grieve
Me so much as the thought that one day some armored Greek
Shall lead you weeping from here, and take from you your
Day of freedom. You in Argos then shall, at another's
Orders, work the loom, and from the fountains of the
Greek lands draw water. Heavy will be your burden then,
And cruel your lot. And then shall some one say who sees
You weeping, 'this was the wife of Hector, most famous
Of the horse-taming Trojans, when there was the war around
Troy.' So shall someone say, and you shall grieve the
More, sorrowing for me, who kept from you your day of
Slavery. My only consolation is that the earth will
Be heaped upon my head in death before that happens,
And I will not hear your cries as you are taken away."

So speaking, the mighty Hector reached his arms
To take his son from the nurse. The boy shrank crying
Back into his nurse's bosom, frightened to see his father
In his helmet of shining brass with the awful bobbing of
The horse-hair plume. At this both parents in their
Love for the child laughed, and quickly Mighty Hector
Took the helmet from his brow and laid it down upon the
Ground, and having kissed his darling son and held him
Up in play, Hector prayed thus to Zeus and all the gods:
"O Zeus and all you gods, Allow that this my son may
yet become among the Trojans great and famous like me,
And may he nobly rule over Ilium. May everyone say,
'This man is greater than his father was!' when they
Behold him coming from the battle field. Let him bring
Back to his home the bloody armor of his slaughterd enemy,
So that he can delight and make glad the heart of his
mother."

So speaking, to the arms of his dear wife he gave the
Boy; she on her lovely breast received him, weeping as
She smiled. The chief saw, and moved with tender pity,
Smoothed her forehead gently with his hand and said:
　　"Sorrow not thus, beloved one, for me
No man living can send to the shades of death fefore
My time; no man of woman born, coward or brave, can
Change his fate and destiny. But go you home, and tend
To your labors there--the weaving and cloth-making--and
Command the maids to speed the work. The cares of war
Are for men born of Troy, and most of all to me."
　　Thus speaking, mighty Hector took again his helmet,
Shadowed with the horse-hair plume, while homeward his
Belove wife went, often looking back, and shedding many
tears.

　　After this incident, the fortunes of the war change ,
and the Trojans begin to have more success. They drive
the Greeks back past the light defense line the Greeks
made just in front of the ships, and the Trojans at night-
fall find themselves on the plain far from the safety of
the walls of the city. Hector thinks over the situation
very carefully, trying to decide whether it would be best
to return to the city and give up the territory they had
won, or to expose themselves to danger by remaining outside the walls at night. He decides to remain camped,
but sends for supplies to maintain the army at full
strength and readiness. Meanwhile, the Greek chiefs have
become very angry with Agamemnon's stubborness, and do
all they can to force him to apologize to Achilles so
that Achilles will return to the war. At last Agamemnon
gives in, and, placing the blame for his actions on the
gods who took away his senses when he insulted Achilles,
offers Achilles many gifts. Agamemnon tells Odysseus to
go to Achilles and to offer him a great deal of gold and
silver, many slave-girls, and one of Agamemnon's daughters
as a bride. Homer does not say that Agamemnon offered to
return Briseis, but Odysseus assures Achilles that he will.
When Odysseus finds him, Achilles is playing his harp and
singing for his friend Patroclus. This is in Book Nine.

When Achilles had heard Odysseus tell of the offer
Of Agamemnon, he answered and thus said;
"Odysseus, son of Laertes, nobly born and silled in
Wise devices, let me frankly speak just as I think, and
Just as I shall act, and then you will not ask me any
More to agree to these terms. Hateful to me, as are the
Gates of Hades, is a man who, hiding one thing in his
Heart, says another. I shall speak as it seems to me
Best. For me there is no store of treasure put aside
From all that I have gathered by exposing myself to
Danger in battle. As a bird brings to her newly-hatched
Children all the food she finds, even though she herself
Is starving, so have I had many a night without sleep,
And have spent many a bloody day in combat fighting
Beside Menelaus and Agamemnon for their families.
I have destroyed twelve strong cities with my fleet of
Ships, and have marched over land to destroy eleven
More with my army. After sacking these twenty-three
Cities, I have brought all the loot to Agamemnon, and he,
Loitering beside his ships, received them all. Few he
Gave away to the troops, and many he kept. To chiefs
And princes he gave prizes, which they still keep. From
Me alone he takes my woman. This woman I loved very much,
And I thought of her as my wife, even though I took her
With the might of my spear. This is the most important
Point--let me ask you a question--For what reason did we
All come over the sea to Troy in the first place? Was it
Not to preserve the sanctity to the marriage of Menelaus?
Was it not to return the lovely Helen to her proper home?
Answer me this--Are the sons of Atreus, then, the only
Men on earth who love their wives? No every good man
Loves and cherishes his own wife; and mine I loved
Tenderly, even if she was my captive. And now, since he
Has taken away my reward, let him not try again, for I
Am now warned of his treachery. He will never persuade
Me to return and help him to fight the man-killing
                                                    Hector.
I will wed no child of Agamemnon, even though she is
As beautiful as golden Aphrodite in her charms, and
Be as skillful as blue-eyed Pallas Athena in her skill.
Let him choose among the Greeks a fitter husband--one
Whose rule is wider than my own. For if the gods
Preserve me, and I reach my home again, my father
Peleus will bestow on me a wife. There are many

Beautiful Achaian maids, and of these I will make my
Well-beloved wife. My soul has longed earnestly, with
A fitting wife married in proper form to make my home
In Phthia and there to enjoy my life. However, I know
This can never be. For, years ago, my mother said to me--
My goddess-mother, the silver-footed Thetis said--
That I could choose between two fates. If I remain to
Fight beneath the walls of Troy, I will die young, but
My fame will live forever. If I return to my dear
Homeland, my glory will be nothing, but long my life.
Now I think more and more of returning home, for I
Do not think we will every overthrow Troy, because Zeus
Seems to protect the lofty city. Anyway, I cannot
Accept the offer you have brought; but stay with me
Tonight and be my guest here within my tent."

His mission to patch up the quarrel between Achilles
and Agamemnon a failure, Odysseus leaves. But Achilles is
forced to return to the war by a strange series of events.
When the Trojans continue to press the Greeks almost into
the sea, Patroculus, Achilles' friend who grew up in
Achilles' home tries to persuade Achilles to return to the
battle. Achilles refuses, but does allow Patroclus to us
the armor which Achilles' mother Thetis has had made for
him by the craftsman-god Hephaistos. The armor makes the
Trojans think that Achilles has returned, and the Greeks
make great advances. But Hector challenges Patroclus,
thinking he is Achilles, and kills him, taking the armor
as a just prize of victory. The armies fight fiercely for
the body of Patroclus, and the Greeks finally rescue it.
Achilles is insanely angry over the loss of his dear friend,
and returns to the war with a vengeance. Achilles and
Agamemnon make up, and Achilles accepts all of Agamemnon's
gifts, including the return of Briseis. Before he can
return to the battle, however, he must have a new suit of
armor. For this he asks his mother Thetis, who convinces
Hephaistos, the craftsman of the gods, to rush through a
new suit for her son. The gods miraculously preserve the
corpse of Patroclus from decay so that his funeral can be
delayed. Achilles talks to the horses of Patroclus,asking

why they allowed their master to be killed, and one horse, Xanthus, tells Achilles of his forthcoming doom. This takes Homer through Book Nineteen.

Earlier, Zeus had forbidden the gods to interfere in the war. Hera hoodwinks Zeus with the help of Aphrodite. From Aphrodite Hera gets a special belt or sash which inspires in Zeus a greater sexual drive than usual, and as a results of his extreme sexual labors Zeus sleeps soundly and Hera is able to do as she pleases for a time. After this, Zeus removes his restriction. In Book Twenty and Twenty-one the gods and the soldiers on both sides fight with great enthusiasm, especially around the River Scamander. In Book Twenty-two, Hector, against all the advice of his parents and friends, goes against Achilles. Although Hector behaves bravely and fights well, he is no match for the mighty Achilles. After Achilles kills Hector, he abuses the corpse by tying it to his chariot and dragging it around the outside of the walls of the city three times. Homer gives us vivid and touching pictures of the news of Hector's death being brought to Priam and Andromache. The gods are so moved by the tragic nature of the death that they preserve the body miraculously, as they had done with the corpse of Patroclus.

Book Twenty-three deals in great detail with the funeral of Patroclus. Achilles prepares a very elaborate pyre of logs from the close-by mountains. Achilles provides prizes for a series of races and athletic events to honor his lost friend, and Homer gives lovingly elaborate descriptions of the contests and the disputes arising during them. It is then that Achilles makes the third of his great mistakes. First, Achilles should not have rejected Agamemnon's generous offer of reconciliation (he should not hold a grudge); second, he should not have abused the corpse of Hector; at the funeral of Patroclus Achilles makes a human sacrifice of twelve captured Trojan young men (human sacrifices always seem to get Greeks into great trouble).

In Book Twenty-four, the last, the gods move to restore the body of the brave Hector to his father. Iris assists Priam in getting through the Greek lines to the tent of Achilles.

Unnoticed the royal Priam came in, and moving
To Achilles, clasped his knees, and kissed those fear-

full
Man-killing hands, hands by which so many of his sons
Had died. And as, when some bloo-guilty man, whose
Hand in his own land has slain a fellow-man, flees to
Another country, and the house of some great chief, all
Men look on him astonished--so, when godlike Priam first
Was seen, Achilles was amazed, and all looked at each
Other, wondering at the sight. And thus King Priam spoke:

"Think, Achilles, of your own father, an old man like

me;
He too is on the sad edge of closing life even now.
Yet his heart is happy when he hears that you still live,
And every day he hopes that his dear son will come again
From Troy. My lot is hard, for I was the father of the
Bravest sons in of all wide Troy, and none are left me now.
Fifty were with me when the men of Greece arrived upon
Our coast; nineteen of these came from the same mother.
The rest were born within my palaces. Pityless Ares, god
Of war already had laid lifeless most of these, and Hector
Whom I cherished most, whose arm defended both our city
And ourselves, him did you lately slay while fighting
For his dear country. For his sake I come to the Greek
Fleet, and to ask for my son's body. In payment, I bring
A great ransom. O, respect the gods, Achilles, and be
Merciful, calling to mind your father. He is happier
Than I am, for I have had to bear the heaviest burden
A human can bear--I have had to kiss the hands that
Killed my son."
Thus spoke Priam, and Achilles in sorrow thought of
His own father. By the hand he took the begging Priam
And with gentle force removed the old man from him.
Both in memory of those they loved were weeping.
The old king, with many tears and rolling in the dust
Before Achilles, mourned his gallant son. Achilles
Sorrowed for his father's sake, and cried for the loss
Of Patroclus. The sound of mourning filled the tent.
At last Achilles rose from his seat and lifted the old
Man, pittying the white head, and spoke these winged words:

"Great have been your sufferings, unhappy king!

How could you stand to approach alone the Greek fleet,
And show yourself to the man who killed so many of your
Brave sons? You must have an iron heart. But sit down,
And let us allow our grief to sleep for a while, for too
Much love of grief is bad. The gods have made it so
That it is the lot of man to suffer, while they themselves
Are free from care. Beside Zeus' throne stand two jars
Of gifts for man. One jar contains the evil, and one
The good, and he to whom the Thunderer gives them mixed
Together sometimes has good luck, and sometimes bad luck;
But the man to whom he gives only the evil spends all
His life exposed to wrong, and he is chased from one
Terrible misfortune to another misfortune, wandering
Over the earth in misery, unloved by man and the gods.
On my father Peleus the gods rained blessings, giving
Him rule over the Myrmidons, wealth, and even a goddess
For a wife. Yet the gods add evil to the good, for not to
Him was born a family of kingly sons within his house.
One short-lived son is his, nor am I with him to cherish
Him in his old age, but here do I stay, far from my native
Land, causing trouble and grief for you and your people.
You too, Priam, were once famous for your wealth and power.
But now the gods have brought you endless war and sorrow.
Yet be firm of heart. Sorrow for your son will do no
good;
Weeping cannot bring him back, and while you are thus
Punishing yourself, new griefs may fall on you."

    Thus spoke Achilles, and Priam made his answer:
"Bid me not be seated here, godlike Achilles, while Hector
Lies among your tents unburied. Let me ransom him at once,
That I may look on him once more with my own eyes. Take
The many gifts we bring you, and possess them long, and
I give you my blessing to return to your native shore,
Since by your grace and permission I still live and
Behold the light of day."

    Achilles heard, and, frowning, thus replied:
"Anger me not, old man; It was my thought to let you
Ransom Hector, for my mother has asked me to do so.
Besides, I know that you could not have come through
The Greek lines and into my tent unless the gods helped.
But you must no longer remind me of my griefs, for I

May forget that you are both a guest in my house and a
Beggar, and if I forget and lose my temper and do you
Harm, I will break the laws of Zeus. Go with your son."

Thus Achilles spoke, and the aged man in fear obeyed.
Two trusted Greeks, Automedon and Alcimus, put the corpse
On a wagon and helped Priam to take it to Troy.

The trojans have a funeral for Hector which is
appropriate to the service he has given the city.   The gods
and goddesses also attend and pay their respects.   Homer
closes the _Iliad_ with these lines:

Now when the early rosy-fingered Dawn
Looked forth, the people gathered round the pile
Of glorious Hector. When they all had come
Together, first they quenched the funeral fires,
Wherever they had spread, with dark-red wine,
And then his brothers and companions searched
For the white bones. In sorrow and in tears,
That streaming stained their cheeks, they gathered them,
And placed them in a golden urn. Over this
They drew a covering of soft purple robes,
And laid it in a hollow grave, and piled
Fragments of rock above it, many and huge.
In haste they reared the tomb, with sentries set
On every side, lest all too soon the Greeks
Should come in armor to renew the war.
When now the tomb was built, the multitude
Returned, and in the halls where Priam dwelled,
Nursling of Zeus, were feasted royally.
Such was the mighty Hector's burial rite.

THE END

700 B.C. - 500 B.C.: EMERGENCE OF CLASSICAL GREECE

We know more about the 7th and 6th centuries B.C. (700
500 B.C.) than we do about any earlier period. There is an
increasing amount of archaeological knowledge available. In
addition, beginning around 600 B.C., we can draw up a fairly
clear outline of Greek development for the first time. Written evidence provides us with our first flesh and blood characters in this period. At the same time, such written evidence remains rare. No detailed study is possible until
close to 500 B.C. Our chief written source, the work of the
historian Herodotus from the mid-400's B.C., takes up its
story in the mid-500's B.C. Herodotus himself did not know
a great deal about what had happened before that time. We
also have a number of literary sources, but these are still
limited before 500 B.C.

The Greek world was continuing to develop swiftly in all
fields of activity. In this period the Greek world reached
the limits of its expansion for the time being and developed
many of the elements which are recognizable later as characteristic of Classical Greece. In the 600's B.C. Corinth and
Ionia still led the way. Athens emerged rapidly in the 500's
B.C. and in that same century Sparta became the chief Greek
military power.

POLITICAL DEVELOPMENT, 700 B.C. - 500 B.C.: ARISTOCRACY,
TYRANNY, OLIGARCHY, DEMOCRAT

It is the political development of the Greeks in this
period that we are most familiar with. This is no accident.
As we have noted before, Greeks attached enormous importance
to their political obligations. They did not see individualism or self-development as independence, as "doing your own
thing." As a result, when they examined the world about them,
they naturally directed a good deal of their attention to
public affairs. Greek philosophy, religion, art, literature,
were very political. This attitude helps to explain why
early historians, like Herodotus and Thucydides, naturally
concentrated upon public events, mostly politics and war.
They assumed that these were the most important things. It
is also no surprise that one of the most important and
characteristic of Greek developments came in politics. This
was democracy.

The Age of Tyrants.

In 700 B.C., as we saw, the customary Greek political
form was an aristocracy of some sort existing in a small
unit known as the polis. The next generations produced
challenges to these aristocracies in many city-states. The
aristocracies often offended many groups--the poor, the
middle class, the rich non-aristocrats, and even aristocrats
who felt ignored or rejected. Most important was the pressure from the rich, as the growth of commerce and urbanization around the Greek world produced a challenge by money
against birth.

In less developed areas, such as Thessaly, the old
land-based aristocracies survived, but elsewhere political
conflict led to a widening of the circle of power. This
widening usually occurred through the device of TYRANNY, so
that the period from about 650 B.C. to about 550 B.C. is
often called the Age of Tyrants. Tyrants xercised one-man
rule, but it was in the name of "the people," which meant
all free Greeks who were not aristocrats, from rich to poor.
Often this meant that the tyrants opened things up to the
rich. Many tyrants were actually "renegade" aristocrats,
men who carried grudges against their class or were simply
ambitious for their own family. Such men seemed like
"natural" leaders to the rich. There were tyrants of all
descriptions, good and bad. The word tyranny originally
had no necessary pejorative (bad) meaning, although the
Greeks did later use the word in this way, as we still do,
as they got rid of their tyrants.

Tyranny may have had its beginnings in the Ionic and
Aeolic Greek areas on the eastern side of the Aegean. These
were developed, commercial areas, and they were close to the
influence of the civilized non-Greek world in Asia Minor,
where powerful kings still flourished. Greeks believed that
the word tyranny came to them from Lydia, the strongest
of the non-Greek kingdoms in Asia Minor. Certainly, tyranny
was widely found in the Ionic and Aeolic Greek areas in the
600's B.C. One famous tyrant there was Pittacus of Mytilene,
on the island of Lesbos. Mytilene was the greatest of the
Aeolic cities. Pittacus around 600 B.C. sent into exile two
poets, Alcaeus and the woman Sappho, both of them champions
of the old aristocratic society. Pittacus won a reputation
for both efficiency and reasonableness. Despite the claims

of Alcaeus that he was a commoner, Pittacus seems to have been an aristocrat, although his father was a non-Greek from Thrace. In Ionia, the most prominent tyrant produced was Thrasybulus of Miletus, also around 600 B.C.

Corinth, the leading commercial city on the Greek mainland, became a tyranny about 650 B.C. The old aristocracy in Corinth was very restricted, being made up of a single clan or extended family, the Bacchiads. The Bacchiads were seen as Dorians (they claimed to be descended from Hercules), and as the family which earlier had provided the kings of Corinth. They were not allowed to marry outside their clan. The tyranny at Corinth was established by Cypselus, who was a "renegade" Bacchiad. His mother, a Bacchiad, was lame, so that no member of the clan would marry her. On his father's side, Cypselus claimed a non-Dorian background supposedly going back further than the Bacchiads. He claimed to represent the (non-Dorian) "people" against the Dorian aristocrats descended from the conquerors of the Dark Ages--a tactic we find other tyrants using elsewhere. Cypselus, according to Herodotus, killed widely among the Bacchiads. The tyranny he set up lasted in his family through three generations, until about 580 B.C., and it was in this period that Corinth was at the peak of her economic and cultural power. The son of Cypselus, Periander, built a three-mile route of grooved tracks across the isthmus at Corinth over which small ships could be dragged by oxen.

The feeling against the aristocracies at this time, which often led to the appearance of tyranny, can be seen in the poem Work and Days of around 700 B.C. by Hesiod of Boeotia, who was a substantial middle class farmer. Another source is the poetry of Archilochus, who was himself a "renegade" aristocrat, from the mid-600's B.C. Examples of the economic and social shifts which were undermining the power of the aristocrats are:
1. the introduction of coinage from Lydia in the late 600's B.C. -- an indication of the growing commercialization of Greek society.
2. the shift in warfare in the 600's B.C. away from the expensive and prestigious cavalry, drawn from the aristocracy, to the heavily armed infantry (HOPLITES), drawn from the growing substantial middle class. In the Classical Period, the hoplites, armed with spears which were for thrusting rather than for throwing, made up the core of a Greek

army, cavalry and archers being then little used. The hoplites fought together in a mass formation known as the phalanx. Aristotle argued in the 300's B.C. that the rise of the middle class, reflected in the switch to hoplites, undercut the aristocrats and led to tyranny. It is perhaps as likely that the tyrants, after coming to power, built up or switched to hoplite troops in order to keep themselves in power.

The most important characteristics of this period of tyranny were:

1. codification (writing down) of the laws, so that the non-aristocrats at least knew what their "rights" were. Hesiod in Work and Days was very critical of the unwritten laws of Boeotia in his day. This process of writing down the laws was going on across the Greek world at this time, even where tyranny did not flourish, as part of the process of taking power away from the aristocrats who had always supplied the judges.

2. material prosperity, the idea being that prosperity would bind the "people" (rich, middle class, and poor) to the tyrant. This belief that full bellies mean empty heads has always been a favorite of tyrants. Since an efficient dictatorship has enormous advantages over other systems in organizing and getting people to work, it is not surprising that many of the tyrants were able to win popularity for a while through promoting prosperity. The best-known example is at Corinth. There, in addition to such big public works as the route across the isthmus, the tyrants eagerly promoted colonization.

3. civic propaganda, as the tyrants promoted civic pride (pride in the polis) and "people's rights," as in writing down the laws. This increased the self-confidence of the non-aristocrats. The rich were used extensively by the tyrants to man their governments, even though aristocrats often kept much influence once they became reconciled to the tyrants. The middle class provided the hoplites. While it offered security to the tyrants against the aristocrats, this kind of line also tended over time to undercut tyranny itself by encouraging the self-assertiveness of the non-aristocrats.

4. promotion of Pan-Hellenism, the sense of oneness among Greeks. This can be seen in the encouragement of major, all-Greek, religious elements: the oracle of Apollo at

Delphi; the great religion of Dionysius, the god of fertility); the introduction of further Games around 600 B.C. (the Pythian Games to Apollo at Delphi, the Isthmian Games to Poseidon at Corinth, the Nemean Games to Zeus at Nemea). One idea behind Pan-Hellenism may have been to reduce the influence which the aristocrats obtained from their control of the old local worships of the polis; of course, Pan-Hellenism also appealed to a genuine emotion among Greeks regardless of political opinion. Tyrants, and other Greek politicians for that matter, spent a great deal of money patronizing these all-Greek centers. The tyrants of Corinth, for example, were very generous with the oracle at Delphi (which had backed them) and with the priests at Olympia, where they provided the money for a colossal gilded statue of Zeus. The Olympian Games had by this time an enormous significance; winners could count on becoming rich and famous. A great favorite of the tyrants, at Corinth and elsewhere, was Dionysius, whose worship had a non-aristocratic, common, touch about it which suited the purposes of the tyrants.

The Age of Tyrants was generally over by 500 B.C. Often, tyranny fell victim to the success of its own work in encouraging self-assertiveness and the widening of power and the economic growth which was revolutionizing Greek society. Tyranny usually was replaced by oligarchy, which means government by the few, the few normally being the wealthy. This is what happened at Corinth, where the family of Cypselus was followed by a stable oligarchy which lasted for 200 years. Democracy, meaning government by many people, was known, but it met with little success until it flourished in the 400's B.C. under the influence of Athens. Tyrants, however, continued to appear in some numbers through the Classical Age (to 300 B.C.). Sometimes the efficiency they could offer and their style of siding with the "people" proved attractive. Syracuse, the greatest overseas Greek city and by 400 B.C. the greatest of all Greek cities, was commonly a tyranny throughout the Classical Period.

THE DEVELOPMENT OF SPARTA AND ATHENS TO 500 B.C.

Neither Sparta, which became much the strongest Greek state in the 500's B.C., nor Athens, which was of growing importance in many areas by 500 B.C. and which was to be the great state of the 400's B.C., went through the usual stages of political development. This is a warning of the distortions involved in drawing up a scheme of development to fit the large number of independent Greek states.

SPARTA

The growth of the military power of Sparta was the great political event of the 500's B.C. in the Greek world. A very large state in itself by Greek standards, Sparta then dominated the entire Peloponnesus through its Peloponnesian League and exerted a great deal of power north of the isthmus. By that time, already, Sparta had long been an oddity in the Greek world from virtually every point of view.

In Homer, Sparta is the kingdom of Menelaus, brother of Agamemnon and husband of Helen. The Spartans, however, saw themselves as descendants of the conquering Dorians of the Dark Ages. At some point, they merged a number of their villages into a sizable state (polis) centered on Sparta. Sparta, however, never became a town of any considerable size--Spartans were not inclined to trade. Along the way, these Spartans also conquered neighboring groups of Dorian newcomers. Such people, called PERIOECI or "those who dwell around," were allowed some self-government, supplied soldiers, but could not become Spartan citizens. The two groups together, the Spartans and the Perioeci, made up the LACEDAEMONIANS (or people who lived in Laconia), which was the name by which Greeks referred to the state. The third group in the population, and probably a very large majority of the whole, were the HELOTS or slaves. They are assumed to have been the descendants of those who had lived in the area before the Dorian invasions. Conquered by the Dorians, they had come to speak Doric Greek. They belonged to the Spartan government and were leased out to citizens and to perioeci.

Long before 500 B.C., the Spartans were famous for toughness, bravery, simplicity, and discipline. These are the qualities we understand by the word <u>Spartan</u>. They spoke little,
and were known for the brief, sensible style we call <u>laconic</u>.

What we do know of their social system is strange and
impressive. Sons of Spartan citizens could be <u>exposed</u> (put
out to die) as infants at the decision of the state if they
were deformed or ill. If allowed to live, and if not bastards
or physically infirm, they were taken from their homes at the
age of seven to begin training. The training included periods
of complete isolation from the world with other youths and
ordeals such as whipping. Through much of this they went
naked or thinly clothed, in the coldest weather. A satisfactory performance would get them into the army at 20. Perhaps
at that time they also became citizens. Failure in the training meant that they could not become citizens. Those admitted
into the army continued to eat together and to sleep in dorm-
itories. They were allowed to marry, perhaps in a transves-
tite ceremony in which the bride cut her hair short and wore
male clothes and submitted to a ritual rape. The young women
involved would themselves have gone through a less rigorous
semi-military training, much of it also done nearly naked.
The young man at first would be allowed to visit his wife only
occasionally and under controlled circumstances. At 30,
probably, the soldier obtained full citizenship rights. These
rights he kept for life, unless he failed in some part of his
duty to the state. He had to continue to eat together with
other men in a common "mess"; failure to pay his share of the
costs of this would lose him citizenship rights. He lived
at home now, though, with his wife and family. Spartan women
seem to have been freer and more assertive than was usual in
Greek society. They had a great reputation for chastity, but
it seems that they could be loaned out and perhaps shared with
a husband's brothers. The state seems to have had the right
in emergencies to compel breeding outside marriage in order
to produce citizens. The Spartan citizen family received a
piece of state-owned land for its use, along with helots to
work the land. The family was entitled to a fixed amount of
produce from the land, with the helots keeping the rest. A
family could also own other land in its own right.

There perhaps never were many full adult male citizens,
and the number declined because of losses in war and the fail-

ure to breed. Among such a group, homosexuality was very common, the Spartans being well-known among other Greeks for such preferences. <u>Herodotus</u> says that there were about 8,000 in 480 B.C. Our estimates, as are all our population estimates for Greece, are not much more then guesses. The decline in the number of Spartan citizens, however, is unmistakeable. It became cirtical after 400 B.C. and was surely a great factor in the amazing decline of Sparta at that time.

Citizenship at age 30 for the males included the right to attend the <u>Assembly</u>. This met once a month to <u>listen</u> to business and to <u>vote</u> (by shout, but by vote if necessary). It did not discuss business, and in any case the officials seem to have been entitled to ignore its decisions. The Assembly chose the five EPHORS or leading officials, as well as the civil judges and the officials who controlled the perioeci. Any citizen over 30 could be an <u>ephor</u>, and the election of those officials by the Assembly was virtually by <u>lot</u>. The five ephors could settle things among themselves by a majority vote. The Assembly also chose the 30 members of the <u>Council</u> <u>of</u> <u>Elders</u>, a very important body which served as the chief criminal court and prepared business for the Assembly. Members of the Council of Elders had to be over 60 and had to come from certain noble families. There were <u>two</u> <u>kings</u> <u>of</u> <u>Sparta</u>, who descended independently from two families. The origins of this arrangement are not known. In typical Dorian fashion, both royal families claimed to be descended from Hercules. The kings, who cannot be traced back beyond 775-750 B.C., lost most of their powers long before the Classical Period. However, they continued to sit on the <u>Council</u> <u>of</u> <u>Elders</u> automatically and they normally served as commanders of the Spartan armies until 500 B.C., and frequently after that. Thus they were much more important than was usual in Greece at this time. Around 500 B.C. a law provided for <u>one</u> king only to be selected at a time by the Assembly to command in the field. This led frequently to great rivalry between the two kings. The king was accountable for what he did in the field.

Sparta was a fine example of a <u>mixed</u> constitution, with <u>democratic</u> elements (the Assembly and the Ephors), <u>aristocratic/oligarchic</u> elements (the Council of Elders), and <u>monarchical</u> elements (the kings). Spartan citizens, seeing

102

themselves as free men, won a reptuation in the 500's B.C. for leading the fight against tyrants in Greece. Both Herodotus and Thucydides admit this role.

The Spartans claimed that their political system had been introduced by a king named Lycurgus around 900 B.C. Lycurgus was also said to have divided up at least some of the land equally among the citizens, land which they owned but which they could not sell or exchange. Spartans explained their unusual lack of written laws, a lack which helped them to protect the secrecy of some parts of their system, by claiming that Lycurgus had forbidden written laws. Lycurgus is for us a legendary figure. The origins of the constitution are not known, but it is likely that it dates from around 700 B.C. As such, it is the oldest and longest lasting of the Greek constitutions.

This system rested on the support of the perioeci and the helots. The perioeci, the second-class free men, seem to have been used very confidently by the Spartans. Long before the Classical Period was over they must have provided a large majority of the "Spartan" army. They were reliable. Even in the great revolt of the 460's B.C. by the helots, the perioeci gave very little trouble. This is worth pondering when we talk about the Greeks and freedom. So, too, is the role of the helots, who greatly outnumbered everyone else. The helots were said to be treated harshly. It was claimed that the ephors each year declared war on the helots, so that they could be killed without fear of punishment even though they were the property of the state. Aristotle in the 300's B.C. said that young Spartans spent one period of their training roaming around at night indiscriminately killing helots. Since they belonged to the state, only the state could free the helots. While there were many helot revolts, the most dangerous that we know about being the one in the 460's B.C., the system seems to have been secure enough normally. Helots were used regularly in support of the army, and even sometimes as troops, the latter perhaps in exchange for their freedom.

The reason behind this very savage and disciplined system is often supposed to lie in the need of the small ruling class to control closely a large subject class. This argument does not explain why the system had such few counterparts elsewhere. The closest approach is found in Crete, which was heavily Dorian also. Many of the city-states there had military training programs and subject populations like the helots. The perioeci are missing, though, as are the kings, and the helots seem to have been treated much better than in Sparta. In general, the situation in Crete seems to have been closed to aristocracies such as existed in Thessaly on the mainland than it was to Sparta. It is also difficult to understand why the Spartan system was so resistant to change.

The system may have been encouraged by the Spartan conquest of Messenia in the late 700's B.C. This was a great and difficult undertaking, one not completed until the failure of the great revolt by Messenia in the mid-600's B.C. It made Sparta an unusually large state. The population of Messenia became helots. Harshness may have been adopted as a way of handling the new, subject population. The political structure which Sparta was to keep for centuries may also have been worked out at much the same time.

Over the next two centuries (700-500 B.C.), as Sparta resisted the changes which were affecting Greece, it became more and more of an oddity. It may have reacted deliberately to this situation by strengthening the very elements which made it odd. In some ways, the impression we get is of Sparta drying up and turning more within itself. In trying to stand still in a rapidly changing world, it strengthened the military values which affected all parts of Spartan life, becoming more harsh and determined. Political change, which must have produced over generations the constitution which existed by 700 B.C., largely stopped. The Spartan economy remained agricultural, the towns small. The Spartan attitude toward economic change is expressed in the refusal to accept the new gold and silver coinage until around 400 B.C. City life, and great private wealth, were regarded as threats to the discipline and toughness which seemed necessary. The life of the Spartan citizens, with all the slave labor avialable, must have been comfortable, but by the standards of a Corinth or an Athens Sparta by the 400's B.C. was not a wealthy state. We can see that this affected Sparta's ability to wage war. Culturally, Sparta's early achievements in pottery and in poetry, which are not negligible, had no successors. In poetry, Sparta produced two early names: Tyrtaeus, in the early 600's B.C., who recorded in patriotic style the continuing wars against the Messenians (and provides us with the knowledge that the hoplite phalanx was already in use); and Alcman, around 600 B.C., who is our finest source for the songs for girls of good families for which Sparta was then famous.

By the 400's B.C. Sparta, by its own choice, was a cultural wasteland, an economic relic, and a political oddity. It had willed upon itself a reputation for a bitterly determined and grimly old-fashioned stability and conservatism. Many Greeks admired Sparta's orderliness, discipline, and sense of duty; some made fun of its backward and simple ways; all feared Sparta's strength and courage on the battlefield.

ATHENS

Athens in the Classical Period, with its urbanization, its wealth, its variety, its love of change, its great cultural achievements, offered a sharp contrast to Sparta. The city-state of Athens (ATTICA) was about 40 miles by 25 miles (1000 square miles) in size—large for a Greek state, but much smaller than Sparta. The city of Athens was about five miles from the sea, its port being at the Piraeus.

We know nothing about the union of towns and villages into Attica. In legend it was the work of the king Theseus, of Minotaur fame, in the 1200's B.C. It may have begun that early as a defensive measure at the beginning of the Dark Ages; certainly it was largely completed by the 700's B.C.

The Athenian kings, whatever their origins and early powers, lost most of their powers very early, earlier probably than was usual elsewhere. Their decline continued, until by the 400's B.C. the king at Athens was only a minor religious official. Probably long before the 700's B.C. power had passed from the king to the MEDONTID clan, which provided the chief official or archon and the army commander or polemarch. These two, along with the kings, who were no longer hereditary, made up the group of high officials. In this way Athens was a narrow aristocracy similar to the Corinth of the days of the Bacchiads, although of course in Athens there is no suggestion of Dorian rulers.

Athens had achieved prominence during the Dark Ages. It remained important in the Archaic Period (800-500 B.C.), although others, Ionia and Corinth particularly, moved ahead of Athens by the 700's B.C. Only in the 500's B.C. did Athens regain great significance.

By the 600's B.C. the Medontids had lost their monopoly on high office. The right to hold office had been extended to the group of aristocratic families known as the EUPATRIDS (which means high-born). The Eupatrids were probably a closed group (that is, others, such as the new rich, could not get in). By that time, also, the offices of polemarch and archon had become elective, by the citizens in Assembly, and were restricted to one year. At first, the archon at least had held office for life. A man could serve as polemarch only once. This was also true of the office of archon by the 400's B.C., although by that time the archons had lost most of their powers; it may not have been so earlier. The king, too, now was elected each year, and his powers were fewer than those of the other two chief officials. In the 600's B.C. a further six lesser officials, elected yearly, were added. These officials, drawn from the Eupatrids, also were to be called archons. All nine officials together made up the executive Council of the state.

There was in addition by the 600's B.C. a Council of Elders. This body is also known as the Council of the Areopagus, a name taken from the hill of Ares where it met to hold murder trials. The Council of the Areopagus included the nine officials certainly, and perhaps other ex-officials, although its early composition, and the way of selecting these members who were not among the nine officials, are not known. Nor, apart from the fact that it was the highest court of the state, do we know what its duties were. All the members probably belonged to the Eupatrid families.

Concerning the Assembly, the "popular" element in the system, we cannot say much except that it elected the officials. The greatest likelihood is that all adult male citizens could attend from its earliest days, although it is possible that some, such as the poor, were excluded. There was also some sort of people's court, an extension of the Assembly.

This closed aristocratic system in Athens created the usual situation in a Greek commercial area in the 600's B.C. in which a tyrant could appear. Tyranny did in fact come to Athens, but only after an interesting and very famous attempt to avoid it.

632 (?) B.C.: an attempt at tyranny by the Eupatrid Cylon fails. This is our first closely dated event for Athens. Cylon, a winner of the middle-distance race at the Olympian Games in 640-639 B.C., made his attempt after consulting the oracle at Delphi. His motive seems to have been simple ambition.

Megacles, a member of the great Eupatrid family of the ALCMEONIDS, was the archon of the year. With Cylon's supporters trapped on the Acropolis, the sacred hill in the center of the city, Megacles lured them into surrender on a promise of safe treatment (Cylon himself had already escaped). It would have angered the gods to have starved the rebels to death or to have killed them in any way on the sacred Acropolis. Megacles killed them anyway, after they surrendered. This action caused great ill-feeling against his clan. Its male members were exiled for a while, their property confiscated. They were allowed to return by <u>Solon</u> in the 590s B.C.

The Cylon episode was a warning to the aristocrats. They responded, trying to head off tyranny by offering some of the things a tyrant usually supported.

620's B.C.: the <u>laws</u> of Athens are <u>written down</u> by DRACO, the archon. These laws have a reputation for being severe and savage (giving us the word <u>draconian</u>). Even so, they should be seen as an attempt to please non-aristocrats by listing their "rights" before the judges, who were all Eupatrids. Writing down the laws was also a part of the process across Greece by which the society moved beyond a "do-it-yourself" justice to something more organized.

594 B.C.: SOLON, a Eupatrid of the clan of the <u>Medontids</u>, was given the job of redrawing the constitution. His name provides us with the word <u>solon</u>, or wise legislator. The Athenians were impressed by his clever attempt to head off tyranny, even though it did not work. <u>Solon</u> was also a famous poet, and his poems are our main source of knowledge for what he did. He is perhaps the first Greek who is something of a real person to us.

Solon understood that the key problem in preventing tyranny was to satisfy the <u>rich</u>, who were excluded from office under the aristocracy. To achieve this, Solon abandoned aristocracy and based power on <u>wealth</u> instead of <u>birth</u>. Thus the Eupatrids lost their monopoly of office.

The free population was divided into four classes by wealth. It is likely that the four divisions were related to the type of military service a citizen was expected to supply. Citizens still provided their own equipment. The top two wealth classes were perhaps the cavalry; the third perhaps the <u>hoplite</u> infantry class; and the fourth perhaps those who

were normally exempt from service as unable to equip themselves. (We do not know how many there were in these classes.
It is assumed that the lowest class (called THETES) was much
larger than the others.)

A citizen's rights depended now upon his wealth. Only
the top two classes, probably a small proportion of the whole
number, could be elected to the high offices. It is likely
that the thetes could hold no office at all. The aristocrats, of course, ranked high in wealth; but they did now
have to compete for office with the rich. Plutocracy is the
name for a government based on wealth.

The two lower classes, hoplites and thetes, certainly now
could attend the Assembly, although it is likely that they
had possessed that right earlier. Solon made the Assembly
a court of appeal from the decisions of the judges (who were
now drawn from the top wealth classes). He may also have
provided for selecting the officials in some way by lot instead of by election, although if he did do so this change
was dropped under the later tyranny. Aristotle in the
300's B.C. said that Solon created a Council of 400, for
which the thetes were not eligible, to prepare business for
the Assembly and so limit the Assembly's power. If such a
Council of 400 did exist, we know nothing of it.

To the poorest citizens, who got very little from these
political changes, Solon offered the ending of bondage/
slavery (the hektemoroi) for being in debt. Solon himself
refers to people "sold and fastened in their terrible chains."
Precisely what was involved we do not know. Many believe
that sharecropping was common in Athens at this time and
that the hektemoroi referred to in the documents were share-
croppers who owed 1/6th (hektemorion) of their produce either
as an hereditary payment to their landlord or as a penalty
to their creditors for falling into debt. Such debts may
have included back taxes, rents, etc., as well as loans. The
idea of widespread sharecropping is at odds with the image
of Athens as a society of small farmers, but Aristotle says
that the small farmer did not flourish until after, and
because of, Solon. Existing debts were cancelled, and it
seems that those already "enslaved" (the hektemoroi) for
debt were freed and that those who had been "sold" abroad
or had fled were allowed to return. Whatever happened, it

seems likely that the change was substantial and that the poor at Athens now had a greater degree of economic protection than was common then or later elsewhere in the Greek world.

Solon's reforms did not work. The next generation saw a great deal of trouble in Athens. In two years in the 580's B.C. no archons could be elected (our world anarchy, meaning without government or lawlessness, indicates literally being without archons). There was also a two-year mini-tyranny under Damasias in the same decade. It is likely that the rich were still unhappy, as the Eupatrids, not accepting the spirit of the new arrangement, continued to dominate with the aid of their prestige and expertise and connections. The result was tyranny.

The tyrant was PEISISTRATUS. Born around 600 B.C., Peisistratus belonged to the old Eupatrid aristocracy. His family, it seems, had come to Athens from Messenia, but he actually related to Solon on his mother's side. He seized power twice for short periods (561-556, 550-549 B.C.)before his final success about 540 B.C. When he died in 527 B.C. he was succeeded by his sons, Hippias and Hipparchus. The tyranny was overthrown in 510 B.C.

This was a successful tyranny in most ways. It was under the tyrants that Athens again became very important in economic and cultural development. The tyrants followed a peaceful foreign policy, avoiding trouble, particularly with Sparta. They beautified Athens with large-scale public building. This was part of the tyrant's usual role of promoting prosperity, as it provided good contracts for the wealthy and employment for the ordinary citizens. Extensive colonization was encouraged for the same purpose, and the exploitation of the silver mines at Laurion, which would do much to fuel Athenian prosperity over the next century, probably began now. There was some land redistribution and the land tax was reduced from 10% to 5%. In addition, the tyrants introduced a 5% property tax on the wealthy, which was meant to provide money for handouts to poor families--a typical example of a tyrant appealing to the poor. The Athenian tyrants also, and again typically of their kind, actively patronized culture and religion, looking to get a favorable image for themselves and to reduce the aristocracy's influence over these things. In construction, culture, and

religion alike, the tyrants of Athens appealed to both
local pride and Pan-Hellenism against the aristocrats.

We can note the following:
-the promotion of Theseus, the hero-king of Athens, on vases.
-the promotion of ATHENA as the great champion of all Athens.
On silver coins she is a helmeted figure, with an owl (for
cunning or wisdom) on the reverse side. An early temple of
Athena on the Acropolis from about 600 B.C., of which some
traces have survived, was rebuilt, with some of the work
being done in marble.
-as part of the worship of Athena, the tyrants built up the
Great Panathenaic ceremonies every four years (they had perhaps begun in the 560's B.C.). An important part of these
occasions was the reading aloud of Homer's Iliad and Odyssey.
It is perhaps to Peisistratus that we owe these works in
the form in which we have them. This was a clever combination of local pride with panhellenism.
-the promotion of the panhellenic cult of Dionysius, the
god of all the people, a cult not controlled by the old
aristocracy. To judge from the pottery of the day, Dionysius
was the most popular of all the gods.
-as part of the worship of Dionysius, great encouragement
was given to the development of Athenian drama, which was to
be so important in the next century. The drama was produced
for the worship of Dionysius. Peisistratus built a theater
for the dramas.
-a new Hall of the Mysteries was built at Eleusis, as the
tyrants honored a popular but secret religion which seems to
have promised immortality.
-money was made available for work on the home of Apollo on
the island of Delos in the Aegean, which was, as we have
seen, a great shrine for all Ionians.
-money was made available for a great temple of Zeus at Athens.

Peisistratus seems to have been a "reasonable" tyrant,
in the sense that he did not kill many or rule with a heavy
hand. He left the constitution of Solon intact for the most
part, although he got rid of the selection of officials by
lot. It was enough for Peisistratus to know that he had the
controlling power. Many aristocrats went into exile at first,
but with time a good number came over to the tyranny.

The sons of Peisistratus were not equal to their father.

They continued the attempt to reconcile the aristocracy to the tyranny. For a while even the Alcmeonids, who ever since the Cylon episode a century earlier had been seen as the most determined enemies of tyranny, came over for a while. The leader of the Alcmeonid clan, CLEISTHENES, returned from exile to become archon in 525-524 B.C. This did not last. Cleisthenes soon went back into exile, and the aristocracy remained the heart of the opposition.

Hipparchus was assassinated in 514 B.C. in a homosexual love quarrel. Hippias was overthrown and sent into exile in 510 B.C. The Spartans, wishing to extend their power north of the isthmus and polish their image as the enemies of tyranny, sent troops to help overthrow Hippias, even though they had long been friendly to the Athenian tyranny. Their price was that Athens join the Peloponnesian League, which was a Spartan club. The Spartans worked with Athenian aristocrats led by Cleisthenes. Cleisthenes had spent money to rebuild part of the temple at Delphi--in return, the oracle told the Spartans to free Athens.

With the tyranny gone, there remained the question of what to put in its place. The choice lay between oligarchy, government by the few, perhaps of the kind established by Solon a century earlier, and a moderate democracy such as was appearing already in some places in the Greek world. Both sides were led by aristocrates. The struggle between oligarchy and democracy caused much disturbance over the next decade (510-500 B.C.). Those favoring oligarchy, who were led by Isocrates, had the support of Sparta. Sparta intervened twice, in 508 and 506 B.C., on behalf of the groups wishing oligarchy, but each time it was only in very half-hearted fashion and to no lasting effect. In 504 B.C. the annoyed Spartans even made a bid, similarly half-hearted, to restore the ex-tyrant Hippias. It was the democrats who won out. Their leader was the great aristocrat Cleisthenes, who in the words of Herodotus "took the people into partnership." The democracy now established in Athens was to last for almost 200 years—years in which Athens became great, so great that her political system was widely copied.

Why was tyranny replaced in Athens by democracy rather than, as was more frequently the case elsewhere, by oligarchy? Did the Athenian upper class, a mixture of the aristocracy

112

and the rich by 500 B.C., realize, as admirers of Athena, goddess of cleverness, that they could dominate a democracy and be secure in such domination since the "people" would think that the government was theirs? The democracy was dominated by the upper class. Especially apparent in the 400's B.C. was the great continuing power of the aristocrats, the traditional rulers. Even so, why should the upper class have preferred democracy of any sort to oligarchy? Corinth was already demonstrating that oligarchy could provide a reasonably stable government in a commerical environment. Was the self-confidence of the middle and lower classes in Athens so great by this time as to make oligarchy impossible? It became habitual with Athenians to suggest that democracy, and only democracy, suited their high opinion of human nature (that is, of themselves) — they were "fit" to rule themselves, as was to be expected of Greeks who had survived the Dark Ages. What the Athenians thought of themselves, and whether they were different from other Greeks, are matters we will look at later.

Constitutionally and psychologically, the centerpiece of the democracy of Athens was the Assembly of all adult male (over 20) citizens. There was nothing new about this body except its prestige: it had long been open to all citizens as a body which debated and adopted laws and policies and elected the officials. The Assembly now was encouraged to assert itself by:
1. The reorganization of the tribes. Whatever their origins, the four old tribes were probably territorial units by this time. Cleisthenes got rid of these old tribes and introduced 10 new ones, which were theoretically equal in size. Attica, the city-state of Athens, long had been divided into 100-200 small administrative districts called demes. Cleisthenes separated these demes into three groups: those in the city of Athens, those along the coast, and those in the interior. He divided the demes in each of these three geographical groups into 10 units or sections called trittyes. There were 30 trittyes in all, there being 10 in each of the 3 geographical groups. The demes were in theory grouped haphazardly into these trittyes. Each of the 10 new tribes contained one trittys from each of the three large geographical groupings of city, coast, and interior. In theory, then, a tribe was now representative in its composition, containing demes from all over Attica and with many different interests. The new tribes, lacking any distinct geographical

113

base, were obviously intended to reduce regionalism, an old divisive force, and also to offset the local influence of the old families. All of this would encourage the Athenian citizen to see himself as an individual rather than as the member of some local or class group. A citizen kept his deme, and thus his tribal identification, no matter where he moved to in the state; the same identifications were hereditary. Over time, deme and tribal tags would become increasingly artificial.

2. On the basis of these new tribes, a new group of officials called generals were introduced by Cleisthenes to take over many of the duties of the archons and to command the army. The army now was reorganized into 10 infantry regiments, one taken from each of the new tribes. The army, too, no longer had any kind of regional base. One general was elected yearly from each tribe although possibly the 10 were elected by the entire Assembly. At first, a general commanded his tribe's regiment, but the generals quickly became ordinary officials and commanders.

3. Ostracism was introduced, either by Cleisthenes or at some point soon after his changes. The first ostracism we know of did not take place until 488-487 B.C. Each year the Assembly met on a particular day to decide whether it wanted to ostracize anyone that year, ostracizing involving a 10-year sentence of exile, but without any confiscation of property. If the decision was taken to ostracize, the Assembly met at a fixed date later to make a choice; whoever "won" got to leave Attica. No reason or justification was required at any point in the proceedings. As a way of scaring politicians, this system has its obvious advantages. It clearly assumes that all politicians are necessarily corrupt and deserving of punishment, a condition which makes it reasonable for the people in Assembly to punish at random if they so decide.

At the same time, to hold the Assembly in check, Cleisthenes introduced a number of checks:

1. Limitations on the right to hold office. The lowest of the four classes set up by Solon, the thetes, possibly a majority of all citizens, could hold only very low offices. The high offices, the 9 old officials and the · new generals, could be held only by men from the top two census classes, who were possibly only a small minority of all citizens.

2. A Council of 500 was established. Each year, each of the
10 new tribes elected 50 of its members from the top three
census classes, the 50 being allotted among the demes of the
tribe according to their size. A citizen also had to be aged
30 to be eligible. The election was by lot; a man might serve
only two terms. These 10 groups of 50 from the tribes made
up the Council of 500. They did not, however, function as
a body of 500. Instead, each tribal group of 50 did the
Council's work for 1/10th of the year. During that time, the
50 lived in Athens and met daily (selecting a different chair-
man each day). Their job was to make policy, control the
agenda for the Assembly, supervise the officials. Inevitably, the Council soon became a very important body, being
particularly useful for manipulating the Assembly.

These limitations are actually mild oligarchic elements,
but in Greek terms they made the system introduced by
Cleisthenes at Athens a moderate democracy. They did not
offend the normal Greek view of democracy, which meant power
to many not to all. The Greeks were not nearly as capable
of fooling themselves about human nature as we are.

115

THE PERSIAN INVASIONS, 500-B.C. - 480 B.C.

In the 500's B.C. the Greek world reached the limits of its expansion. It then came under pressure from several directions, as the Greeks found for the first time that they could not just go their own way. In the West, the Greeks in south Italy found themselves challenged by the Etruscans, while those in Sicily were restricted to the eastern portion of the island by the Carthaginians, a Phoenician people. In both areas the Greeks could do little beyond hold their own. We will look at these events when we discuss Italy from the Roman viewpoint. In Asia Minor, to the east, the Greeks also began to encounter trouble, trouble which led eventually to the Persian invasions, the first serious threat to the very existence of the Greek world. These invasions produced some of the most famous episodes in Greek history. They are known to us in great detail from the history of them written by the Greek Herodotus, who lived in the generation following them. This was the first surviving work of its kind produced by our civilization.

As Greece came out of its Dark Age in the 700's B.C., the great power in the East was the ASSYRIAN Empire. Centered in northern Mesopotamia, the Assyrians controlled most of the Near East from Asia Minor to Egypt. They did not, however, threaten the Greek world, although they took control of Cyprus, which had been in the hands of a number of Greek and Phoenician cities.

Toward 600 B.C. the Assyrian Empire fell apart. Egypt became independent for a while; another kingdom (of the Babylonians) arose in southern Mesopotamia which soon grabbed Phoenicia, Israel and then Egypt. Most importantly, the Medes, an Indo-European people from the northern part of modern-day Iran, who had already established their independence of the Assyrians a century earlier, took southern Iran (Persia) and northern Mesopotamia stretching into Asia Minor.

In the 580's B.C. the Medes fought an inconclusive war against the powerful kingdom of Lydia in western Asia Minor. Lydia was not Greek, but it was extensively Hellenized (under

Greek cultural influence). It was also a place of fabled
wealth (the phrase "rich as Croesus" comes from the name of
a king of Lydia in the mid-500's B.C.); the Greeks had obtained the idea of coinage from Lydia a little earlier. It
was in this war that the scientist Thales of Miletus predicted an eclipse of the sun. Lydia was successful enough
to obtain security for 40 years.

Lydia used this period to do some expanding of its own.
King Croesus in the 550's B.C. conquered the Ionian cities
on the coast of Asia Minor except for Miletus. Since the
area was still the cultural leader of the Greek world, this
was a notable blow to the Greek world, even though Croesus
liked to pass himself off as a friend to the Greeks.

Croesus did not flourish for long. The security he
had looked for by marrying into the royal family of the
Medes disappeared when a revolution brought to power CYRUS
of the Persian Achaemenid family. This family was to rule
what we will now call the PERSIAN Empire for more than 200
years. The Medes and Persians seem to have been closely
related peoples, both Indo-Europeans, with a common culture
and religion.

Under Cyrus, the Persians now began a great era of conquest:
--540's B.C. Lydia was conquered. Croesus had been told by
the oracle at Delphi that if he crossed the Halys river
(his border with the Persian Empire) he would "destroy a
mighty empire." Croesus went ahead and attacked the Persians. He did destroy an empire -- his own. The Persians
also obtained control of all the Greek cities on the coast of
Asia Minor. They ruled them through puppet Greek tyrants.
The Persians at this time did not have a navy to use in the
Aegean, where the chief Greek power was the tyrant Polycrates
of Samos.
--530's B.C. Persians conquered southern Mesopotamia and
the coast of the Near East, destroying the Babylonian Empire.
-520's B.C. Persians conquered Egypt.
The possession of Phoenicia and Egypt allowed the Persians to build up their power at sea. Since they had every
thing else, Europe was their obvious next target:
--512 B.C. The Persian King DARIUS, who had succeeded to
the throne in 521 B.C. entered Europe. He conquered Thrace

117

and campaigned north of the Danube river.

It is likely that an attack upon Greece would have come sooner or later. In 499 B.C. the Ionian Greek settlements in Asia Minor revolted against the Persians and their puppet tyrants. Sparta, the great Greek military power, refused to help, but Athens and Eretria sent troops. The revolts were crushed. Miletus, the leading Greek city in Asia Minor, was sacked (494 B.C.), and the great temple of Apollo at Didyma was destroyed. This time, though, anxious to avoid more trouble, the Persians established puppet democracies in the Greek cities of Asia Minor.

The Persians were determined to obtain revenge for the help sent to the rebels from mainland Greece:
--492 B.C. A Persian army campaigned briefly in Macedonia, immediately to the north of mainland Greece.
--490 B.C. The Persians sent a small (by their standards) expedition to Greece to punish Eretria and Athens, winning control of the Aegean islands on the way. They took Eretria, while Athens did nothing. Then they landed on the east coast of Attica. Hippias, the former tyrant, was with the Persians -- they intended him to be their puppet in Athens. The Persians were beaten by the Athenians at the fabled battle of MARATHON. The 9000 Athenians, with 1000 allies from Plataea, launched a successful attack on the much larger Persian army (20-30,00?) before the invaders moved inland from the coast. 192 Athenians were killed, including the commander (polemarch) Callimachus and a brother of the great writer of tragedies Aeschylus. A mound was put up to commemorate the Athenian dead which can still be seen. Simonides, the great poet, defeated Aeschylus in the contest to write the poem of praise to the dead (an elegy) of Marathon. A new temple was put under construction on the Acropolis to give thanks.

Athens had done a great thing, and had done it almost alone. Sparta, which had dragged its feet all the way through the crisis, had played no part. The victory was a tremendous boost to the self-confidence of the young democracy of Athens, as well as to Greeks everywhere, even if on the Persian side little more had been involved than a big raiding party.

It was very likely that the defeat would only make the Persians more determined to attack Greece. Athens showed some interest in carrying the war to the enemy, but for a while the democracy seemed to be bent upon causing trouble for itself, for there was much political unrest in the state. The hero of the hour at Marathon had been Miltiades, who won the credit for talking Callimachus and the other commanders into attacking. Even before the battle there had been attempts, allegedly by the jealous Alcmeonid family, to prosecute Miltiades into exile. Herodotus claims that the Alcmeonids secretly supported the Persians and tried to betray the city to them after the battle. After the victory, Miltiades was given a force to "liberate" Paros, one of the Aegean islands. His failure there brought on his condemnation by the Assembly; Miltiades died soon afterwards. In 486 B.C., Megacles, a nephew of the great Cleisthenes (now dead), was ostracized. This was the second use of Ostracism, the first having occurred the previous year. Both men who were exiled may have been suspected of sympathizing with the Persians (which is called medizing). A connection with the suspect Alcmeonids may also have been behind the ostracism of Xanthippus in 484 B.C. In the late 480's B.C. large new deposits were discovered in the silver mines at Laurion. The Assembly wisely decided to spend this money on a new fleet and on defenses for Athens and its port the Piraeus rather than to share it out among the citizens. This decision was taken at the urging of THEMISTOCLES. The opposition to it was led by ARISTIDES the Just, who found himself ostracized in 482 B.C. There is a story that Aristides met a citizen outside the Assembly who intended to vote to ostracize him. When Aristides asked the reason, the citizen replied, "I am tired of hearing him called 'the Just.'"

In truth, the need to spend the new silver wisely was apparent by this time; we can only wonder at why the idea of a large fleet caused such an uproar. For the Persians were plainly making ready to attack Greece, this time in great force. Darius died in 485 B.C. and was succeeded by XERXES. While revolts occupied his attention for a while, Xerxes was anxious to settle the Greek matter.

In the face of this great threat, the Greeks of the mainland managed to act together much more efficiently than usual, although they could never totally overcome their jealousies. In 481 B.C. a congress was held at the Isthmus of Corinth to decide upon the manner of the resistance to the Persians. Many of the north Greeks, who expected to be the first to feel the weight of the Persians, were absent; they were already thinking of medizing. A Spartan presided at the congress and Sparta, the chief Greek military power, dominated the proceedings. A Spartan general (King LEONIDAS) was appointed to command the joint army which it was intended to put into the field. More absurdly, a Spartan was appointed to command the sea forces of the Greeks. Syracuse, the major Greek city in Italy, was asked for help, but sent none. The whole project promised much more on paper than the quarrelsome Greeks were capable of in practice.

In 480 B.C. Xerxes invaded Greece. Herodotus has a wonderful description of the Persian army crossing the Hellespont from Asia to Europe on a bridge of boats, with Xerxes watching from on high seated on a marble throne. The Persian army numbered perhaps 200,000 men. As this army proceeded across Thrace into Greece, the north Greeks, in- cluding Thessaly and Thebes, did indeed medize. The Spartans, to whom everyone on the Greek side looked for leadership, were not at all sure that they wanted to commit troops north of the isthmus. They wanted to hold the isthmus and keep the Persians out of the Peloponnesus, looking out for themselves rather than for Greeks as a whole.

In the event, the Spartans sent only a few of their troops north of the isthums. At THERMOPYLAE, a narrow spot between mountains and the sea which led into central Greece, King Leonidas tried to hold up the Persians. There were 7,000 men with him, but only 300 of them were Spartans. There is a tale of a Spartan soldier, being told that the arrows of the Persian multitude would darken the sun, replying "So much the better, we shall fight in the shade." The Spartans failed gloriously when the Persians found a mountain path which led them in behind the Greeks. This path was revealed to them by Greek traitors for money. Allowing most of the Greek troops to slip away, Leonidas and the Spartans stayed to die to the man. Two brothers of Xerxes were killed. In honor of this event, Simonides wrote his most famous lines:

Tell them in Lacedaemon, passer-by
That here obedient to their laws we lie.

The bravery of Leonidas should not hide the fact that the
Spartans were effectively giving everything north of the
isthmus to the Persians.

The Persians now occupied that area. Athens was abandoned, as the population fled or took to ships. The city
was devastated. The Greek fleet, which was mostly Athenian
thanks to the building program recently undertaken with the
proceeds from the silver mines, had been withdrawn into the
Bay of Salamis following action against the Persians around
Artemisium in support of Leonidas. Many Greeks wished to
withdraw before the larger Persian (actually mostly Phoenician and Egyptian) fleet, but Themistocles convinced them
to fight. There followed the sea battle of SALAMIS, a very
big affair with more than 400 triremes on each side. The
Greeks won an astounding victory.

Xerxes then went home for the winter (480-479 B.C.),
making no attempt to force his way into the Peloponnesus
against the Spartans. His army spent the next months in north
Greece. Themistocles wanted at this point to attack the
Hellespont, which would cut off the Persian army, but he could
not win acceptance for this plan.

In 479 B.C. the combined Greek army moved north from
the isthmus. It was about 100,000 strong, certainly the
largest army the Greeks ever put into the field at any point.
There were about 8,000 Athenians in the army. The heart of
the force, however, were the Spartans. There were perhaps
30,000 from Sparta, 5,000 citizens, 5,000 perioeci, the rest
helots. The 5,000 citizens almost surely represented virtually every able-bodied citizen Sparta had. Sparta was no
longer skimping, as it had the previous year. Now it was
gambling everything -- even risking arming very large numbers
of slaves. The enormous size of the army, and the decision
to move north, indicate a very different attitude from that
taken by the Greeks the year before.

The Greek army, commanded by <u>Pausanias</u>, a member of one of the Spartan royal families, defeated the larger Persian army (120,000?) in a great battle at PLATAEA in 479 B.C. Herodotus tries hard to make the Spartans look bad here, but it is clear that they carried the bulk of the fighting and delivered the victory. The 8,000 Athenians, commanded by Aristides, who had been allowed to return from exile in this emergency, failed embarrassingly to get involved.

The Persians withdrew from Greece for good, so that this episode marks a great moment in the development of an independent Western civilization. Greece was never again threatened from the East. In the matter of settling the credit for the Greek victory, the Spartans found to their annoyance that the Athenians walked off with the lion's share of the praise -- a result of the considerable Athenian talent for advertising themselves. The Spartans, perhaps, had only themselves to blame; a mighty effort on land a year earlier, in 480 B.C., might have settled the outcome then.

LITERATURE IN THE ARCHAID PERIOD

Between Homer's time (whenever that was) and what is
called the Age of Drama in Athens, there is a period we call
the <u>Lyric Age</u>, dominated by <u>Ionic Greece</u>. Ionic Greece grew
rich in trade during that era (600-500 B. C.), and seems to
have produced a great deal of excellent literature as well
as philosophy. Unfortunately, almost all of it has been
lost. We must remember that when we say something is "lost,"
we do not mean that it was lost soon after it was written.
The writers we are going to discuss were well-known and
widely read in Roman times. In early Christian times, partly
through neglect and partly through intentional destruction,
most of these works disappeared. The things which were
allowed to survive either were thought of as consistent with
Christianity or as valuable in leading toward it. Much that
has survived is nearly worthless, and much that was lost was
priceless.

First we must take note of <u>Hesiod</u> of <u>Boeotia</u>. What he
wrote and when he wrote is not certain, but probably he
lived and wrote around 700 B. C. He, like Homer, loves elaborate descriptions and complicated comparisons in verse.
We know little of his life except what he mentions in the
poetry, but tho personality we see in his work is that of an
old-fashioned , landed farmer who dislikes women and who sees
himself as living in an age when things are going from bad
to worse, as living in the midst of degeneracy which will get
even worse as time goes along, through seven stages, the
Golden Age, the Silver Age, and so forth.

In addition to giving advice about lucky days and months,
especially for agricultural projects (Hesiod loves farming),
he introduces into Greek thought many near-eastern (oriental) concepts. Unlike Homer, he makes much of nature myths
and creation myths. He tells of the castration of Uranos by
his son Chronos (the resulting blood drops do all kinds of
things), of the subsequent overthrow of Chronos by his son
Zeus, and of the imprisonment of the old forces, the Titans,
by the new ruling forces of the earth (their struggles to get
free causes typhoons and earthquackes). In his <u>Theogny</u> and
<u>Works</u> <u>and</u> <u>Days</u> he goes into great detail about the genera-

tion of hundreds of gods from the original procreative forces, Chaos, Earth, and Eros (sex). He emphasizes the oriental goddess Hecate (a fertility goddess and protectress of witches who is not mentioned in Homer). Hesiod, like Homer writes in Hexameter verse, but Hesiod's verse is clumsy and mechanical. In spite of his shortcomings, he gives us a very valuable insight into the daily life of his time.

Sappho (born about 612 B. C. on the island of Lesbos) was very much admired by later Greek and Roman poets, who knew a good many poems by her, but what has come down to us are mostly lines quoted by admirers. However, the poetry we have is of very high quality. Her poems are personal, usually written to members of her family, or for the weddings of girls whom she seems to have taught in school. There are also poems about sexual yearning, including a conversation between a bride and her maidenhood (a common subject) and one about a tirl who is kept from sexual activity by her weaving duties. Because of her "sexiness" (one fragment says, "Eros, you make me burn"), Christians later tried to destroy all of her poems, and almost succeeded. Our words for female homosexuality, "sapphic" and "Lesbian" come from their association with her, but maybe unjustly.

Archilochus is very important for his experiments in poetic metrics, but we have only a few fragments of his poems. He is thought to have been born on Paros, but when we do not know. He mentions an eclipse in his work, so he was a grown man either in 648 or 711 B. C. Unlike most of the older poets, he was not an aristocrat (his mother was a slave but his father may have been well placed), and he seems to have supported himself as a professional soldier ("I am supported by my spear," he says in one poem, " for it brings me wine "). He also wrote some poetic fables about foxes, eagles and hedgehogs, some poems about his troubles with his in-laws, and some victory songs for athletes.

Perhaps the greatest and most universally admired of Greek poets of all time is PINDAR, a Theban aristocrat. Although he lived well into the dramatic age (518-438 B.C.), the kinds of poems he wrote and his themes are typical of the earlier era. Because we tend to think of poems as being about trees and flowers, his subject matter might strike us as strange--

he wrote poems to winners in athletic contests, and his
poems are arranged according to the place of the games,
Pythian, Isthmian, or Olympics. His poems praise the victorious athletes, but use the occasion to make observations about life in general, often using a part of a mythological story in an unusual way as background. He ex-
perimented with many metrical forms, but usually wrote
"odes," songs of praise on a special event. Of all the
Greek poets, Pindar is the hardest to translate. His most
famous line comes out in English to be something like,
"Water is the finest of all things." But Pindar goes on to
explain that humans really need the simple things even if
the things are often forgotten. Pindar's view of the world
is similar to Homer's--a man must fight for athletic victories, knowing all the while that, being human, he will
lose in the end. In one of his greatest lines, Pindar
says that "a man is but the shadow of a dream." His philosophy is summed up in his statement that "whimsy rules all."

Because Pindar comes later than the other great lyric
writers, we can better understand his relationship to the
historical events around him. He first was in favor of the
Theban policy of neutrality in the Persian Wars, but later
changed hiss mind. In many of his poems, he speaks of the
standard Greek belief that the gods punish pride or self-
love (hubris), so he later spoke against the Athenians'
treatment of the members of the Delian League.

Other famous lyric poets include Alcman (674-611 B. C.),
who lived in Sparta, but may have been a slave there, having
been born in Lydia. Alcaeus (620-560 B. C.) wrote drinking
songs and political verses, as did Solon the Athenian
politician and reformer; Theognis of Megara (about 564-520
B. C.) sang beautifully of good drink and good parties.

125

ATHENS: EMPIRE AND DEMOCRACY, 480-430 B.C.

Empire.

The Athenians took much more than prestige from the defeat of the Persians. By grabbing a leading role in following up the victories at Salamis and Plataea, they made themselves a great power in the Greek world. At the same time, Athenian civilization flourished on a scale never seen before in the world. Over the next three generations, Athens produced an unbelievable variety of great cultural achievements, achievements which together constituted the climax of the Classical Greek world. All of this took place as Athens extended its democracy, moving from a moderate toward a radical form of that type. It is a great pity that we know relatively little about what was happening though most of this period. The work of Herodotus ends with the defeat of the Persians; for the years from then until the outbreak of the Peloponnesian War around 430 B.C., when the work of Thucydides takes up, we have only the outline of what went on.

The defeat of the Persian fleet at Salamis in 480 B.C. cleared the way for the Greeks to reassert themselves in the Aegean once they had turned back the Persian army. The fight was taken to the Persians at once. For a few years, Sparta played a role in the Greek advances, but it was not long before the Spartans lost interest. In their isolation and conservatism, they were unconcerned about building up overseas possessions and unwilling to build up the kind of large and expensive navy which would have been needed. It is also possible that the tremendous effort at Plataea had made the Spartans reluctant to risk further great manpower losses for the time being. In fact, the Spartans even lost ground in the Peloponnesus in the 470's B.C. and their old League became a very ramshackle thing. The disgusted Pausanias, hero of Plataea, "medized," plotted to seize power at Sparta, and was killed.

The Spartan attitude allowed the eager Athenians to take the lead against Persia. Athens made the very best of the opportunity. In 479 B.C., following Plataea, Athens, with her ships commanded by Xanthippus, another who had been allowed to return from exile, led the way in recapturing control of the Aegean and "liberating" the islands. In the following year, 478 B.C., Athens set up the Confederation of Delos, an alliance of itself with the liberated cities. The league's name came from the fact that the common warfund or treasury was kept on the sacred Ionian island of Delos. The official purpose of the league was to keep the Aegean free and to continue to carry the war to the Persians in Asia Minor. From the beginning, the alliance was dominated by Athens: Athens provided the military commanders and the treasurers for the league; Athens decided which states supplied ships and which supplied money to the league; Athens decided how the money burden was to be shared out among the member states (which numbered eventually more than 150). The league in theory was run by an assembly in which each member had one vote, but Athens, backed by its powerful navy and the prestige of the victory of Salamis, was in control from the start.

This was the Athenian Empire, the other members of the league being little more than Athenian satellites:
472 B.C. Athens decided in the case of Carystus on Euboea that a state could be compelled to join the league against its will.
469 B.C. Athens decided in the case of the island of Naxos that a state could be refused permission to leave the league. As punishment, both Carystus and Naxos actually were annexed by Athens.
465-463 B.C. Thasos, an island member of the league, was devastated by Athens for refusing to sacrifice its own interests to those of Athens in a local dispute.

By the 450's B.C., virtually all pretense that the league was at all a voluntary agreement among equals had been dropped. The league's assembly had disappeared--Athens simply issued orders. The league's treasury was moved to Athens in 454 B.C. Athens used the money for whatever purposes it chose, so that the forced contributions demanded each year of the members were just tribute. By that time, only three other members, the islands of Lesbos, Chios, and Samos, were allowed to supply ships rather than money for the league. The Athenians were using the members' money to build up their own navy. It also seems that Athens controlled the coinage of the members and had extensive rights to supervise and intervene in their legal affairs. By the 440's B.C. some of the League members were being forced to accept and provide land for colonies of Athenian citizens, an arrangement which gave Athens a military reserve across the Aegean.

Whatever the structure of the league, against the Persians it enjoyed great success. The campaign reached its climax in the victories at Eurymedon in southern Asia Minor in 468 B.C. At that point, only a dozen years after the Persian occupation of Athens, virtually all of the Greek settlements save for those on Cyprus had been "freed."

All the leading politicians at Athens seem to have supported the league and the war against the Persians. Themistocles, the hero of Salamis, remained the dominant figure until he was ostracized about 472 B.C. Themistocles wandered eventually into the Persian service and did good duty as a Persian governor in Asia Minor. Themistocles lost out to CIMON, the big new figure of the 470's B.C. Cimon was the son of Miltiades, hero of Marathon; he married into the Alcmeonids. He was the most successful general in the war against the Persians; he won the great victories at Eurymedon in 468 B.C.

Over the next few years after 468 B.C., Cimon, remaining the dominant figure, followed a generally peaceful policy. Such a policy could not be maintained for long. Substantial elements in the city wanted to keep on against the Persians—and also to adopt a more aggressive attitude toward the Spartans. Swollen with their successes in the Aegean over the previous 20 years, some Athenians thought that it was time for their city to assert itself on the mainland. All common sense indicated, however, that this should be done in a way calculated to avoid annoying the Spartans into a major military effort; Athens certainly had no way of defeating the Spartan army.

In the late 460's B.C., Cimon played into the hands of his opponents by actually sending 4000 Athenian troops to Sparta to help put down a helot rebellion. Cimon was ostracized in 461 B.C. The new dominant figures were Ephialtes and PERICLES. Ephialtes was assassinated that same year, but Pericles, a great-nephew of Cleisthenes, the architect of the democracy, was able to dominate the Athenian state for the next 30 years, until 430 B.C. In this period, the Age of Pericles, Athens reached the peak of its power.

Pericles took up a very aggressive foreign policy. The
money from the league members was a great help in this connection:
459-454 B.C. Athens mounted a large-scale attack on Persian-
held Egypt, a remarkable step for a Greek state to take.
While Memphis, the capital, was occupied for a while, the
campaign produced nothing over the long run except very
heavy losses and expenses.
459-453 B.C. Athens asserted itself in all directions on
the mainland. The Athenians enjoyed much success. The
entire area from Phocis southwards to the Saronic Gulf came
under their control, as well as extensive areas on the north
side of the Gulf of Corinth.

In the face of this new Athenian aggression on the mainland, Sparta was very restrained, although it did occasionally
supply a little aid to the enemies of Athens. In 452 B.C.
Athens arranged a 5 Years' Truce with Sparta. Cimon, who was
known as a friend to Sparta, was brought back from exile to
achieve this. The purpose was to allow Athens to concentrate
on a further big effort against Persia, in Cyprus and Egypt.
Nothing much came of the renewed fighting in the East. When
Cimon died on campaign in Cyprus in 450-449 B.C., the
Athenians decided to settle definitely with the Persians.
This settlement was the Peace of Callias of 449 B.C., named
for the Greek negotiator, who was Cimon's brother-in-law.
The Persians accepted their losses, but they kept Cyprus.

Now the Athenians could look to Greece itself. They
needed to, for there were plenty of signs of trouble.
Awareness of this situation may have encouraged the Athenians
to settle with the Persians and scrap their plans for the
East. The years 449-446 B.C. saw a series of revolts in
Greece and the islands against Athens. Athens lost control
of many of the mainland states, including Euboea, Locris,
Boeotia, Phocis, Megara, and the Gulf of Corinth; the
Athenians had to halve the tribute from the league in order
to ride out the storm. All of this had little to do with
Spartans; it was an expression of the desire for independence
of the Greek states. Accepting most of the setbacks, Athens
agreed to a 30 Years' Peace in 446 B.C. with Sparta and the
other Greek states. Athens had very little to show for all
its efforts on the Greek mainland since 460 B.C.

The failure of his foreign policy weakened Pericles for a while. An opposition arose, under the leadership of Thucydides, a relative of the dead Cimon. Pericles managed to survive, however, something which under the circumstances is a great tribute to his hold on the citizens. Thucydides was ostracized in 443 B.C. From then on, Pericles was beyond serious challenge. His foreign policy, though, was now much more cautious.

And yet by 434 B.C. Athens was again at war, the quarrel being with Corinth, the chief Dorian trading city and the closest competitor on the mainland to Athens in terms of wealth and culture. This time, the Spartans were unwilling to stand idly by. In 431 B.C. Sparta declared war on Athens, claiming that it did so reluctantly and against its will, and only because the Athenians had shown that they could not keep themselves from causing trouble. In light of the behavior of both Sparta and Athens since 480 B.C., it is very difficult not to sympathize with the Spartans on this occasion.

Athens, and the Greek world generally, now had on their hands a great war, the PELOPONNESIAN WAR. Lasting for a generation (431-404 B.C.), this conflict exhausted all sides. Neither of the two major powers involved, Athens and Sparta, would ever be as strong again.

Democracy.
The wonderful success of Athens in all areas in the 400's B.C. lent an enormous prestige to its democratic system. It was impossible even for anti-democrats to claim that democracy did not work. We can see this resentful admiration in the essay known as The Old Oligarch, which was written around 440 B.C. under Pericles. Its unknown author rejects as contrary to all good sense the principles on which democracy was based while agreeing that it worked. The democratic system established by Cleisthenes a little before 500 B.C. was not standing still: it was undergoing constant alteration, generally in the direction of a more radical democracy. We need to look at how the system worked, and at the changes it was experiencing.

We do not know what the population of Attica was in the

400's B.C. An estimate of 300,000 or more is a representative figure, with up to half of them living in the city.
Slaves made up a large share of this population: 25% is
probably conservative, 50%, is not unreasonable. Greeks
considered these slaves irrelevant to the discussion of
democracy--with Aristotle, they accepted slavery as natural
for inferior or unlucky types. There was no point to asking
a Greek to agree that all men were fit to be citizens.
Barbarians (non-Greeks) were slave material; with Greeks
there was a potential problem, at least for some Greeks.
Could members of the superior race be enslaved? Spartans
answered with a clear yes (the helots). In the case of the
Athenians, it is often claimed that, being amongst the "most
civilized" of Greeks, they:
-treated their slaves reasonably well. Comments from outsiders, notably Spartans, lend some support to this claim.
As we have seen, though, the Spartan line on this issue was
hardly a moderate one.
-kept few native Athenians, and few Greeks of any description,
as slaves. It is common to suppose that Athenian slaves came
mostly from abroad, as captives in war, etc.
-practised only a small-scale slavery, the typical slave being
attached to a single-family farm rather than to a large (impersonal) enterprise.

The purpose in all this is, obviously, to have Athenian
democrats look good: they like their slaves, treat them as
members of the family, refuse to enslave people of their
own kind, etc. In fact, we do not know enough to say much
about slavery anywhere in the Greek world, outside Sparta.
Slavery probably was usually small-scale, but if so it must
have been very widespread (the family of Hesiod the poet,
around 700 B.C., owned slaves). Thucydides says that in
413 B.C. during the Peloponnesian War 20,000 slaves escaped
to the Spartans (a forbidding prospect!). Many of these may
have come from the Laurion silver mines, which were the
biggest employer in the state. We do not know how the mines,
which were state-owned, were worked in the 400's B.C.; in the
300's B.C. the right to work the mines was leased out to
private businessmen for short periods.

Another group omitted by the democracy were the aliens,
those born outside the city. Aliens were allowed to live
permanently in Attica, but they could not own land and they

could be represented in court only through a citizen. They paid a special tax and they were liable for military service. Such aliens must have been very numerous in the Greek world, where a short trip down the road often took you into a different state (polis). They will have been especially numerous in trading centers such as Athens. We have some information about the construction of one of the holy buildings on the Acropolis, the <u>Erechtheum</u>, from the late 400's B.C., which shows aliens outnumbering citizens on the payroll three to one. Both groups received the same pay--as did those slaves who were employed at the same work. Aliens could be admitted to citizenship. Then, in 451 B.C., under Pericles, a law required two native-born parents in order to qualify for citizenship. After that, save for special cases, citizenship was not available to the aliens. This law is usually seen as an example of selfishness on the part of the existing citizen body; they wished to keep the benefits of citizenship for themselves. Of course, if there were large numbers of aliens in Athens, many citizens will have worried about the effect on the nature of the city of granting citizenship freely.

There is a good likelihood that slaves and aliens made up a substantial majority of the population of Athens, with the proportion increasing over time, with the aid of such steps as the citizenship law of 451 B.C. Further, among the citizen body, only <u>men</u> had political rights. In the most general terms, women held a very weak position in Greek society, although they were much freer than women in the East. Within this context, our general impression is that Athenian women were unusually depressed. A Spartan woman, for example, could own land--in fact <u>Aristotle</u> complained that they held 40% of all the land in Sparta. An Athenian woman could not inherit or hold property, nor could she enter into any deal involving a value greater than that of a bushel of grain. Upper-class women in Athens were not expected to go out unattended; they are conspicuous by their absence from our descriptions of social events such as dinners, discussions, etc. We have the impression that Athenian men liked to enjoy themselves alone. There is some doubt about whether they were allowed to attend the plays put on by the state.

All of this means that the active citizen group in Athens made up only a very small proportion of all adults.

And, of course, among the active citizens property restrictions kept the poorer citizens out of office. We are not looking at our conception of democracy. There is some evidence that toward the end of the 400's B.C. a more generous attitude toward both slaves and women began to make itself felt. The cunning slave who is smarter than his master had probably been a stock part of Greek comedy from the start; by the 300's B.C. there was some outright questioning of the validity of slavery. There are also signs of a "women's lib" movement, our best evidence of this coming from Greek literature. By the 300's B.C., also, it had become acceptable to show the female body naked in sculpture. We do not know much at all about this sort of thing, but such a change toward a more generous attitude is what we would expect of an operating democracy as time passes and things "improve." We have seen the same thing in our own civilization in the last 200 years.

In any event, for the Athenian democracy of the 400's B.C., only the adult male citizens counted. There were perhaps 30-40,000 of these. This fits with the figure of 10,000 or so which seems to have been the maximum size for the Athenian hoplite army, as at <u>Marathon</u>, <u>Plataea</u>, and later at <u>Syracuse</u>. Older male citizens and the thetes, the lowest wealth class, will have made up the rest. All could attend the Assembly, which gradually became more important at the expense of the Council of 500. The Assembly more and more freely altered Council proposals and took initiatives of its own. The Assembly met on 40 days plus special occasions, or roughly once a week. It is accepted that attendance generally was low. Ostracism, a major undertaking, required a quorum of 6,000, which suggests that such a figure was well above the usual attendance. 5,000 may be a generous figure for an average meeting. Many citizens may never have attended. Those who did attend may have come heavily from the poor, the old, the idle, those who lived in the city. The further a man lived from the city, where the Assembly met, and the busier he was, the less likely he may have been to attend. As a result, the Assembly may have been in a degree <u>unrepresentative</u> of the total body of citizens. This point was often made by Athenians, as we shall see. On the other hand, our general impression of Athenians is that they were very highly political, with a strong sense of their responsibilities toward the state.

133

Virtually from the time the democracy was established at Athens by Cleisthenes a little before 500 B.C. the privileges and powers of the citizens were being extended-- the democracy steadily became more "radical." Again, this is what we should expect, as the citizens grow more sure of themselves, more willing to assert themselves. The intro- duction of ostracism, a powerful weapon, may have been the first of these steps, since we do not know about it until just after 490 B.C. By the 480's B.C. all the archons, the ancient high officials, were being chosen by lot from a group (of perhaps 100) previously elected. This change made the position of archon unattractive for an ambitious man, since chance controlled the outcome. The archons now tended to be obscure, second-rate figures (from the two top wealth classes, of course). The same change made it necessary to take the job of commander-in-chief away from the polemarch, since there could be no assurance that the person produced by the lot for that position would be a man of high talent. The 10 generals, the officials introduced by Cleisthenes and drawn from his new tribes, now became the chief officials, commanding the army and navy and being the chief executive body. By the 470's B.C., at the latest, the 10 generals were being elected by the whole citizen body in Assembly instead of by the individual tribes, although there was still one general from each tribe. It was as general, reelected year after year, that Pericles for a generation ran Athens. In Pericles' day, one tribe was allowed to supply two generals: this was to make it possible for the ambitious men in Pericles' own tribe to get ahead--although, of course, it left one other tribe with no general whenever it was applied. The Assembly decided which generals got which military commands.

It is clear enough that throughout this period the old aristocracy, with all the advantages of its prestige, its experience, its self-assurance, and its money, continued to supply the political leadership for Athens. Pericles himself is the clearest possible indication of this. There were no political parties in our sense, but there were factions and more or less organized groups. Some groups claimed to be more firmly for "the people" than others; they would be the "reformers" or "radicals," their opponents the "conservatives." This is what we would expect in an expanding democracy--it is the situation adopted by Democrats and Republicans in our society. Nor is it surprising that in this scheme of things the "reformers" have certain advantages, in making promises at least, over their opponents.

Themistocles, for example, the great figure from 485–475 B.C., was on the "reform" side. The ships of the navy he built up provided well-paid employment as oarsmen for the thetes, the lowest wealth class of citizens, who were not used for service in the hoplite army, where a man had to provide his own equipment. In addition to jobs, the navy provided the thetes with a sense of accomplishment and service--and also with a very real political power, since Athens became very dependent on its great fleet. In a real sense, the thetes were the backbone of the state in the 400's B.C. This point is made very clear in the essay The Old Oligarch. Promoting the navy, and thus promoting an aggressive foreign policy, became a standard way of identifying oneself as a champion of "the people." The ships were maintained at the expense of designated groups of private rich citizens; this was an Athenian substitute for taxation.

Cimon, who displaced Themistocles as the dominant force in the state in the late 470's B.C., is seen as a "conservative." Although he had made his name in war, he became associated with a peace-policy in the 460's B.C. This meant specifically friendship with Sparta. Since Sparta was widely admired among anti-democrats and conservatives, friendship for Sparta was always a risky proposition for an Athenian politician. Cimon seems to have had an attractive personal style, friendly and out-going. He had a clever touch, as for example when he claimed to have found the bones of the hero-king Theseus on the island of Scyros and brought them back to Athens. A home for the remains, the Theseion, was built in the 460's B.C. Cimon also knew the value of patronizing the arts. He brought to Athens the greatest of Greek painters, Polygnotus of Thasos. Polygnotus painted a number of life-size frescoes on the Acropolis, including those on the walls of the Painted Portico. The ability to appear "religious," for which Cimon was also known, became a standard tactic on the "conservative" side in Athenian politics. In Cimon's case, however, he was accused of too close a relationship with his step-sister, the wife of Callias, who much later negotiated the peace of 449 B.C. with Persia. Callias, an Olympic winner, eventually divorced his wife, who had a bad reputation. In the sexual area, Athenian politicians were allowed wide freedom, certainly much more than are ours today, but they had to have some care: the citizens liked an occasional sex-scandal.

Ephialtes and Pericles built up a new "reform" group against Cimon in the late 460's B.C. He played into their hands by sending troops to help the Spartans against their helots, something any reasonable orator could project as the act of an anti-democrat. Once in, Ephialtes and Pericles (the former survived only briefly) offered war, which was identifiable as a "reform" element, and a further widening of the scope of the democracy:
—around 460 B.C., the old Council of the Areopagus, the body of archons and (probably) ex-archons, lost nearly all its powers, specifically its control over justice. Justice was now placed directly in the hands of the people. Each year those wishing to serve as jurors gave in their names. 6,000 names were selected by lot, being 600 from each tribe. These men made up the juries, large bodies whose size depended upon the importance of the case being considered. The jurors were paid 2 obols a day, an amount perhaps equal to the wage of an unskilled worker. The new arrangement was criticized in its day, as it has been since, both as instituting a bad system of justice, one which gave the power of decision to large groups of ignorant, biased men, and as introducing the principle of bribery into the state, with thousands of the old, the poor, the unemployed, becoming beholden to the state for these grants of money. With attendance at the Assembly itself often perhaps low, as we have seen, this may have been an important change. Certainly, with its emphasis upon well-meaning amateurishness, it looks strange to us, but it is fully in accordance with the view of man which is necessary to democracy——he is reasonably good and reasonably intelligent.
—in the 450's B.C., under Pericles, the process of selecting the archons became entirely one of lot, the initial vote for 100 from whom to choose by lot being abandoned. This completed the decline of the office of archon. Salaries were now introduced for the archons. At the same time, the office was thrown open to the third wealth class, leaving only the thetes ineligible. The purpose of a salary may have been to make it possible for men from the third wealth class to hold the position.
—in the 450's B.C. also the members of the Council of 500, the important body which prepared business for the Assembly and existed to discuss matters every day, began to receive

a salary from the state.

-in 451 B.C., as we saw, Pericles also put through a law
which kept aliens from becoming citizens. It is possible
that as citizenship became profitable, thanks to the salaries,
those who were already citizens became unwilling to allow
others in at the table.

These changes are a part of the reason why some people
accuse Pericles of "buying" the citizens. Thucydides the
historian, an admirer of Pericles, said as much in the next
generation. The money for this, and for the wars and much
more, was available from the tribute maney paid in by the
members of the Confederation of Delos. A great deal of the
tribute money was spent on a gigantic public works program
in Athens under Pericles, the biggest of its kind in Greek
history, and certainly the most famous. He had justification
enough, since the city and its public buildings had been
destroyed by the Persians in 480 B.C. Some rebuilding had
been done already. As a way of creating contracts for the
wealthy and jobs for others, of course, public works programs
had a long history; they had been a favorite device of
tyrants. Few, however, had enjoyed the advantage of Pericles,
who could spend the money in Athens and collect it somewhere
else. So it is that the noble architectural monuments of
the Age of Pericles are wrapped up in sordid questions of
political purpose--the Parthenon, too, in its way, was an
attempt to "buy" the citizens. We can note the following
items in the program:

On the Acropolis:

--the great temple of Athena on the Acropolis called the
Parthenon. Such a temple had been begun after the victory
at Marathon in 490 B.C., but it had come to nothing when the
Persians had destroyed the city in 480 B.C.

--a great bronze statue of Athena by Phidias on the west brow
of the Acropolis looking southwest.

--a small temple of Victory (Athena Nike), with a frieze
showing the Greeks fighting the Persians.

--a great entrance to the Acropolis was designed and begun.
It was not completed, for it would have interfered too much
with some of the buildings already on the Acropolis.

Elsewhere in Athens:

--the temple of Hephaestus, the god of handicrafts, was
restored. This is the only Greek temple which is not now a
ruin.

--a Hall of Music (Odeon) was built.
--many baths and gymnasia (places for exercise) were built.
Elsewhere in Attica:
--the old stone temple of Poseidon at Sunion was rebuilt in marble.
--the temple at Eleusis, home of the Mysteries, was rebuilt.
--the port of Athens, the Piraeus, was rebuilt on a rectangular block plan, the first such town plan. This was the work of Hippodamus of Miletus.
--the defences of Athens and the Piraeus, including the walls connecting the two, were completed.

We do not know in any detail how Pericles ran Athens, but it is clear enough that he was well organized. Personally, he seems to have been reserved, aloof; he went out little and did not put himself to too much personal bother in the line of pleasing the people. Once he had survived the ruins of his foreign policy in the mid-440's B.C. he was very secure, being open only to embarrassments rather than to any strong opposition. Phidias the sculptor was brought to trial in 438/437 B.C. He was acquitted of mishandling the funds for the statue of Athena in the Parthenon, but he was found guilty of putting himself and Pericles in the battle against the Amazons which was depicted on Athena's shield. In any case, it wasn't long before Phidias went off to Olympia to produce the mighty statue of Zeus seated, the finest work of Greek sculpture. In the same period, Anaxagoras, the leading scientist-philosopher of his day, a friend and teacher of Pericles, was convicted on a charge of undermining public faith in the gods and was exiled. Even Pericles' long-time mistress, Aspasia, was brought to trial on a similar charge of lack of piety; she, however, was acquitted. These were pinpricks rather than challenges. So were Pericles' occasional troubles with the comedy writers of his day, who naturally used political ridicule as a major part of their humor. A Pericles propaganda device of establishing Thurii in south Italy as a panhellenic colony, a new idea, moved Cratinus, the chief comic writer of the day, to ask if Pericles wished to be a second Theseus (the man who in legend had united Attica into one state) and unite all Greece. In a sense, this was what was being aimed at--the claim to represent, to speak for, all Greece. The idea did not work. A revolt on Samos in 440 B.C., imitated elsewhere in the Aegean by Athens' unhappy "allies," prompted Pericles for a while, after he had personally crushed the rebels, to censor the comedies (we do not know the details).

138

None of this amounted to much. Pericles was secure in his control of the city until the outbreak of the Peloponnesian War in 431 B.C. Then he entered on very hard times.

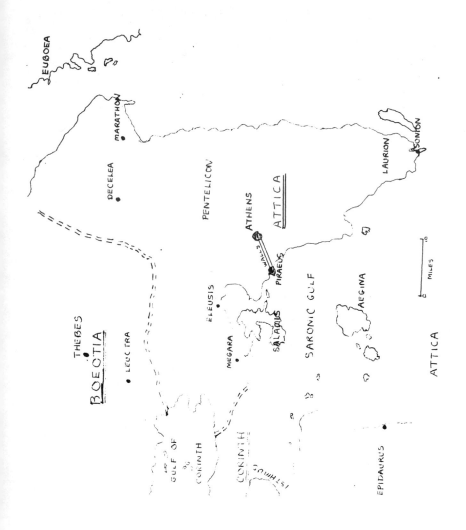

140

INTRODUCTION TO THE DRAMAS

About the beginnings of the drama we know almost nothing, but scholars have come up with a lot of speculation. Much of what we know is based on self-contradictory statements by Aristotle which he made one hundred fifty years after the drama was well established. All scholars since Aristotle agree that the drama began in the dithyramb, but no one knows what a dithyramb was. The dithyramb was a composition devoted to Dionysius, a type of poem which existed at least as early as 600 B.C. But Dionysius was, in different places and at different times, the god of growing things, of fertility (in plants, animals and men), of wine, of good times and parties, and of the dark, irrational side of the human mind. No one knows which characteristic is the most important for the drama. We also know that the word "tragedy" (and all serious dramas are tragic) means "goat-song," but we do not know whether this means that the actors originally dressed in goat skins, imitating goats at a sacrifice, or whether the word refers to the suffering of the people in the play as like that of goats at a sacrifice, or whether it refers to goats being given as prizes for the best dramas.

Probably we can get a good idea about what the early drama was like if we think of it as something like a presentation of the "Messiah," the musical composition by Handel which many churches attempt at Christmas. A chorus sings the words from the Bible which deal with Christ's birth, with occasional solo passages by individual singers. The classical Greeks did not distinguish between poetry and singing, and the early drama was probably a long, chanted poem in honor of some god with short passages by single speakers. Gradually, the solo parts grew longer, the chorus grew smaller and less important, and the "story" more important. In the Greek drama, the parts of the chorus talked to other parts of the chorus, or to single actors. The chorus may have been either fifteen, fifty or twelve people. The chorus could represent the elders of a town, the spectators of an event, or a group in the story. At first, there was only one solo speaker, and even very late, never more than four characters with solo parts.

The Greek dramas are a great challenge to the modern viewer or reader, for they are totally without the five elements we think of as most important to "drama." (1) Because the Greek drama had to deal with a wel-known story from literature or history, there could be no suspense about the ending, no concern for "who done it." In order to do away with any such concern about the outcome, some plays open with a brief plot summary, as if to get such un-important things out of the way. (2) Because the dramas were all written in very elaborate, high-flown language, the meaning is difficult to follow; then as now, the reader or viewer must pay attention and work to understand and appreciate the complex poetry. The Greeks like to hear even ordinary things said in a pretty way--many times the chorus simply says, " life is difficult," but it is always said in a new and lovely way. (3) because all speakers spoke in poetry and because all speakers spoke from behind masks (which may have been megaphones also), there was no "characterization." No individual actor could be identi-fied by his dialect, personal differences or physical appearance (by contrast, all TV characters are strikingly characterized by being old, fat, thin, etc., so that they can be easily identified). Probably female characters were played by males from behind the same type of mask as the male characters. (4) Because a tragedy was a sep-arate thing from comedy, there was no "relief." There were no comic passages, no "flashbacks" to happier times, but only uninterrupted progress to destruction. (5) Because (and this is most important for us) the Greek stage was bare and most of the players did not move, there was no "action." Today, it is possible to eliminate all other elements of the drama if there is enough action, enough car wrecks or motor-cycle accidents. The Greeks thought that this kind of violence would both interfere with the seriousness of the drama and distract the audience from the important ideas under discussion. In the course of these dramas, many very horrible things happen (things unmatched even in recent movies about murders committed with chain saws), but these things happen off-stage and are reported to the audience.

What then remains? The Greek tragedy is almost com-pletely controlled by theme. Modern movies and TV dramas always have some theme, asking whether or not Clint Eastwood

142

is justified in killing evil people with his .38 magnum or whether he should let the courts release them. However, instead of showing the murders and the police in action, the Greek drama always examines an action with which the audience is familiar and tries to decide who is responsible for what, and asks to what extent humans are responsible at all.

The Greek Drama was very formal, and each part had a name and came in a certain place. The chorus came on stage with a parados, proceeds to a stasimon, introduces the actor in the epesode, toes through other parts and leaves to the exodus. Each part had its own verse form, but the writers were free to make variations and changes, so there are as many exceptions as rules about this.

Furthermore, thinkers since Aristotle have written on what tragedy means and how good tragedies can be divided from bad ones. We must make some consideration of these thinkers on tragedy before we try own own interpretation. Aristotle said that there were three possible types of stories which might be tragic, but that only one of them really was. First, there could be a story about a bad man who gets what he deserves, a bad fate. This is what happens in all of the police shows on TV--a criminal does something bad and the police punish him for it. Or, said Aristotle, a good man could have something bad happen to him through no fault of his own--this is what happens on all soap operas on TV, in whihc nice people come down with horrible diseases over which they have no control. Aristotle said the first showed us mere legality, and the second one was merely sad, not tragic, for the people suffered as animals suffer, without self knowledge.

Aristotle concludes that the best tragedy is about an essentially good man who, because of a shortcoming or "flaw" in his personality, commits a wrong action, suffers as a result, and eventually comes to accept the justice of his punishment. We in the audience see that the punishment is just, even if extreme for the crime, and that the univers is a good and fair place. The most common sin, or "hamartia" that Aristotle saw in dramatic characters was "hubris," a special sin for Greeks. "Hubris" means "pride," or the belief by humans that they are very important. A

143

person who thinks he is a "big shot" is guilty of "hubris." The Greeks thought that if we brag about ourselves, the gods become jealous and put us into our place, and Greek drama and other literature is filled with the sentences like "Call no man happy until he carries that happiness into the grave.'' No matter how happy you are, the gods can always get you if they want. We show this Greek feeling when we brag on our good luck and then suddenly knock on wood. We don't want some god to overhear us bragging and get even with us to show us we are only human.

Aristotle thought that when we saw this essentially good man punished, we experienced something called"catharsis" or a cleansing, a purification. Going to the tragedy, then, was like taking a strong laxative or having a good cry--the experience itself is not nice, but we feel better afterwards. Thus Aristotle explained the experience of "tragic pleasure."

All considerations of "tragic" from 300 B.C. until today have taken Aristotle for a starting point, and many, many volumes have been written to clarify and expand Aristotle. Let us keep an open mind and see how Greek Tragedy appears to us.

The first great playwright whose plays have survived is Aexchylus, who began to write about 500 B. C., the time just before the great victories of the Greeks over the Persians; in fact, he wrote a play about the Persians, and his tombstone tells us that he fought at Marathon, beating the "longhaired Persians" (his tombstone does not mention his plays). Aeschylus is the earliest of the playwrights we read, and, according to whether we see the drama as decaying or improving, either the best or the worst. His plays are ruled by the chorus and ist long, long speeches. In Aeschylus, we find few individual characters, and the speeches are the most formal--and therefore for us the most boring. There were even in his own time many jokes about the dullness of the plays of Aeschylus, and the charaters in the plays themselves comment on the dullness of the speeches of the other characters.

Aeschylus wrote three plays about the family of Agamemnon, and the theme seems to be that people get what they deserve because the gods are careful to give it to them.

In these plays about Agamemnon's family, bad hosts and bad guests are punished by Zeus. Virtue is rewarded and vice punished by the gods.

In _Prometheus Bound,_ however, there are several powerful scenes which seem to deny cosmic justice. We seem to be more in the world of Homer, in which the gods are vicious and immoral. Prometheus in Greek mythology is a complicated figure. He gave fire to mankind, to help preserve them when Zeus thought of destroying them altogether. His name, Pro, meaning before, and metheus, meaning thought or knowledge, means that he alone among the god knows the future clearly. He knows the "moira," the fate of men and gods. One of the things he knows is when Zeus will die (although the gods are called the "athanoi," the undying ones, they do die time.) Zeus wishes to know his fate, more exactly, who will kill him. Zeus has the idea that if he knows his fate he can change it. Prometheus explains that his ability to know it means that he, Zeus, cannot change it. To know your fate is to be paralyzed by the knowledge that you cannot change it, and that it is therefore better not to know it. Then, at least, you have the thing that makes human life possible--hope. The one mortal who is denied this wonderful hope is Cassandra, a character with whom Aeschylus deals in _Agamemnon_. She was cursed by Apollo by being shown what would happen to her before it happened, and she therefore had to suffer all of her difficulties long before they actually happened. For instance, she knew the Trojan Horse would bring destruction to Troy, but she could not stop the Trojans from bringing it into the city. She could only repeat, "Beware of Greeks bearing gifts." In the same way, she must watch her own death coming closer and closer, powerless to stop it.

In _Prometheus Bound,_ we have the opposite type of character in Io. She has done nothing at all except to attract the attention of the lustful Zeus. To hide his lover from Hera, Zeus turned her into a cow. But Hera see through the scheme, and sends a swarm of tireless biting insects to torture her, and sets upon her a guard with a thousand eyes, Argus, to see that no one rescues her. The scene in which the two innocent victims, onethe victim of Zeus' lust and the other the victim of his anger, meet is a very powerful one. Prometheus refuses to tell Io when her suffering will end, only that it will end, for to tell her would take away the frail prop on which human beings rely so heavily--hope.

Prometheus, on the other hand, can stand his punishment because he knows when and how his suffering will end, and he almost enjoys his situations, knowing he is torturing Zeus, who, like us, cannot know what will happen next. Thus, for the people watching the drama, the normal roles are reversed, and Zeus worries about his fate like a mortal, while the mortal in the audience knows that Io will be the mother of Heracles' (Hercules') family, and the ancestor of the destroyer of Zeus. Although the gods can torture individual men, mankind will outlive and conquer the gods, the random, mindless forces of nature. As in Homer, we note that the mortal Io and the pro-mortal Prometheus are finer and more admirable characters than Zeus or Hera.

Sophocles follows Aeschylus in the history of the drama, but does not appear in out test. Everyone is familiar with his tragedies about the family of Oedipus, who killed his father and married his mother. Sophocles emphasized, however, that since many oracles had foretold that Oedipus would do this, he was not responsible for having done it. At the same time, Oedipus himself, in the plays, accepts the responsibility for his actions. To be human, he seems to say, is to accept responsibility for what you cannot change. Parents accept the resonsibility for their children, but cannot really control their actions.

In this complex view of the human mind which we see in Sophocles, we note a strange but important concept in the Greek attitude. They saw the mind in two parts, the psuche, the part of the mind which could learn. That part of the mind learns that when one touches a hot stove, one gets burned. But there is another important part, the demon. The demon makes us do things that we know will hurt us. No matter how many times a drunk suffers from drink, he continues to drink--he cannot learn from experience and seems controlled by forces within him over which he has no control. Today the alcoholic says, "I don't want to drink, but I can't help it." The Greek drunk says, "I want to stay sober, but my demon forces me to drink." Yet we must remember that for the Greek the demon was neither good nor bad. The Greek word for fortunate is good-demoned (lucky), and unfortunate was bad-demoned (unlucky). The ultimate bad-demoned person was the epileptic, who obviously could not control the forces within himself. We have no better explanation for the phenomenon.

The last of our playwrights is Euripides, whose dramas in his own time were looked upon as "advanced" or "degenerate" according to the critic. His plays have shorter speeches, more dialogue, less chorus, more lyrical metrics, less "moralizing" and more "characterization" than earlier plays. His plots almost always deal with insanity or obsession. "Hippolytus" deals with a step-mother's sexual attraction to her son, and "The Bacchaie" with mad women. He wrote about Heracles, the hero whom Hera cursed with insanity. Instead of assuming that man must try to control his destiny although he cannot, Euripides merely pictures man as a sick creature, a very modern view. "One Flew Over the Cuckoo's Nest" is quite Euripidean.

So is Medea, for it deals with divorce and re-marriage much as we see it today. Jason in Greek mythology is the center of many stories about his quest for the "golden fleece" (gold dust?). Many heroes, including Helen's brothers Castor and Pollus, went with him and enjoyed adventures of their own. The boat on which they voyaged was the Argo (thus the sailors were the argonauts). Jason went to Scythia (Russia) in his search, and would not have been able to accomplish his tasks and would have died had it not been for the "witch" Medea. In gratitude, Jason married her and gave her that greatest of blessings, life as a Greek. For a while, all went well.

Euripides had an uncanny grasp of the human mind, its femininity and its masculinity. In this play, Jason, a typical male, decides on purely selfish and emotional bases what he wants to do, and then thinks up rational and logical excuses ("rationalizations") for what he wants to do. Medea, a typical female, judges all actions by their public appearances ("what will people think?"). In the end, the male proves sensitive but stupid, the female the more cruel and calculating. The male seeks a sexy mistress and a practical wife, separating sex and love. The woman demands that sex and love be the same. Is there more to say?

147

PERSONS OF THE DRAMA

Strength and Force	Io.
Hephaistos	Hermes
Prometheus	CHORUS.
Oceanus	Nymphs of the Ocean

STRENGTH, FORCE, HEPHAISTOS, PROMETHEUS

STRENGTH. Here we have come to the wide earth's extreme
    bounds,
To Scythia are we come, those pathless wilds
Where human footstep never marked the ground.
Now,Hephaistos, to your task; at Zeus' command,
Fix to these high-projecting rocks this vain
helper of man; each huge link
Draw close, and bind his adamantine chains.
Your radiant pride, the fiery flame, that lends
Its aid to every art, he stole, and bore
The gift to mortals; for which bold crime
The gods assign him this just punishment;
That he may learn to reverence the power
Of Zeus, and moderate his love to man.
HEPHAISTOS. Stern powers, your harsh commands have here
Nor find resistance. My less hardy mind,   [an end,
Averse to violence, shrinks back, and dreads
To bind a kindred god to this wild cliff,
Exposed to every storm; but strong necessity
Compels me; I must steel my soul, and dare:
Zeus' high commands require a prompt performance,
High-thoughted son of truth-directing Themis,
You with unbreakable chains,
Must I now rivet to this savage rock,
Where neither human voice, nor human form,
Shall meet your eye, but parching in the beams,
Unsheltered, of that fervid sun, your bloom
Shall lose its grace, and make your wish th' approach
Of grateful evening mild, whose dusky cloak
Spangled with gems shall veil his fiery heat;
And night upon the whitening ground breathe frost,
But soon to melt, touched by the sun's ray.
So shall some present ill with varied pain
Afflict you; nor is he yet born, whose hand

148

Shall set thee free: thus your humanity
Receives its reward, that you, a god, regardless
Of the gods' anger, anger, honoured mortal man
With gifts, which justice not approves.
Therefore the joyless station of this rock
Unsleeping, unreclining, shall you keep,
And many a groan, many a loud lament
Throw out in vain, nor move the rig'rous breast
Of Zeus', relentless in his youthful power.

  STR. No more; why these delays, this foolish pity?
Do you not hate a god by gods hated,
That prostitutes your radiant boast to man?
  HEPH. Strong are the ties of kinship and long friendliness.
  STR. Well; but to disobey your lord's commands,
Dare you do that? Is not that fear more strong?
  HEPH. Soft pity never touched your ruthless mind.
  STR. Will your vain pity bring relief? Forbear,
Nor waste yourself in what will not help him.
  HEPH. Hated be all the fine skill of my hands.
  STR. And why hated? For of these present orders
You art, in very truth, is not the cause.
  HEPH. Yet wish I it had been some other's job.
  STR. All have their job appointed, save to reign
In heaven, for liberty is Zeus' alone.
  HEPH. Truth guides your words, nor have an argument.
  STR. Why thus reluctant then to bind his chains?
Let not your lord observe these slow delays.
  HEPH. The manacles are ready, you can see them.
  STR. Bind them around his hands; with all your force
Strike, nail them fast, drive them into the rock.
  HEPH. Thus far the work is finished, and not poorly.
  STR. Strike harder, strain them, let them not relax;
His skill will work new ways t' escape.
  HEPH. This arm too firmly bound.
  STR. And now clasp this secure, that he may learn
How impotent his craft, opposed to Zeus,
  HEPH. This work he only can with justice blame.
  STR. Across his breast draw now this stubborn bar
Of stone, fix firm its sharpened point.
  HEPH. This work he only can with justice blame.
  STR. Across his breast draw now this stubborn bar
Of stone, fix firm its sharpened point.
  HEPH. Thy miseries, Prometheus, I regret
  STR. Why do you linger? Still regret the laws of
Zeus? Take heed lest you kill yourself.

149

HEPH. You see, an object horrible to sight.
STR. I see him honoured as his deeds deserve.
But haste, fix this strong chain on him.
HEPH. I'm slow to do it; urge not its rigour.
STR. Urge you? I will, and in a higher tone.
Downwards; with all your force chain his legs.
HEPH. This too is finished, with no slowness,
STR. Strike hard, drive deep their penetrating points.
Zeus wants his orders carried out.
HEPH. Your voice is harsh, and rugged as your form.
STR. Now fair befall your softness, yet don't ridicule
My ruder and unpitying ruthlessness.
HEPH. Let us be gone; the horrid task is done.
STR. Now, Prometheus, triumph in pride now steal
The glory of the gods, and bear the gift
To mortal man; will they relieve you now?
False is the boasted prudence of your name,
Or wanted now to free you from fate.
PROMETHEUS (alone). Ethereal air, and your swift-winged
Your rivers springing from fresh founts, your waves, [winds,
That o'er th' interminable ocean wreathe
Your crisped smiles, your all-producing earth,
And you, bright sun, I call, whose flaming orb
Views the wide world beneath, see what, a god,
I suffer from the gods; with what fierce pains,
Behold, what tortures for revolving ages
I here must struggle; such unseemly chains
This new-raised ruler Zeus, of the gods made
Ah me! That groan bursts from my breaking heart,
My present woes and future to bemoan.
When shall these suff'rings find their necessary end?
But why that vain question? My clear sight
Looks through the future; unforeseen no ill
Shall come on me; I must then bear
Patient my destined fate, knowing how
To struggle with necessity's strong power.
But to complain, or not complain, alike
Is pointless. For favours shown
To mortal man I bear this weight of woe;
Hid in a hollow cane the fount of fire
I privately conveyed, of every art
Productive, and the noblest gift to men.
And for this slight offence, woe, woe is me!
I bear these chains, fixed to this savage rock,

150

Unsheltered from the pains of th' air.
Ah me! what sound, what softly breathing odour
Steals on my sense? Be you immortal gods,
Or mortal men, or of th' heroic race,
Whoe'er have reached this wild rock's extreme cliff,
Spectators of my woes, or what your purpose,
You see me bound, a wretched god, hated
By Zeus, and every god that walks his courts,
For my foolish love to man. Ah me! again
I hear the sound of wings close by; the air
Pants to the soft beat of light-moving wings:
All, that approaches now, is dreadful to me.

PROMETHEUS, CHORUS.

  CHOR. Don't be afraid: a friendly train
        On busy wings flutt'ring light,
        We come, our not asked in vain,
        And reach this promontory's height.
        The clanging iron's horrid sound
        Re-echoed through our caves profound;
 And though my cheek glows with shame's crimson dye,
 Thus with unsandalled foot with winged speed I fly.
  PRO. Ah me! ah me!
Ye virgin sisters, who come from
Fruitful Thetis, and th' embrace
Of old Oceanus, your fathers, that rolls
Around the wide world his unquiet waves,
This way turn your eyes, behold
With what a chain fixed to this rugged steep
Th' hated place of the rock I keep.
  CHOR. I see I see; and o'er my eyes,
        Overrun with sorrow's tearful rain,
        Dark'ning the misty clouds arise;
        I see your unbreakable chain;
        In its strong grasp limbs confined,
        And withering in the drying wind:
 Such the stern power of heaven's new-sceptred lord,
 And law-controlling Zeus' harsh word.
  PRO. Beneath the earth,
Beneath the gulfs of Tartarus, that spread
Endless o'er the dead,
Had his stern fury fixed this rigid chain,
Nor gods nor men had triumphed in my pain.

151

Butt hanging in th' ethereal air
The pageant gratifies my ruthless foes,
That gaze, insult, and glory in my woes.
   CHOR.   Is there a god, whose sullen soul
          Feels a stern joy in your despair?
          Owns he not pity's soft control,
          And drops in sympathy the tear?
          All, all, save Zeus; with fury driven
          Severe he tames the sons of heaven;
 And he will tame them, till some power arise
 To take from his strong hand the sceptre of the skies.
   PRO. Yet he, e'en he,
That o'er the gods holds his terrible reign,
And fixes this disgraceful chain,
Shall need my aid, the counsels to tell of
The destruction to his honour and his throne.
But not the honied begging, that flows
From his alluring lips, shall aught avail;
His rigid menaces shall fail;
Nor will I make the fatal secret known,
Till his proud hands this galling chain unbind,
And his remorse soothes my angry mind.
   CHOR.   Bold and brave is your soul,
          Fired with resentment's warmest glow;
          And your free voice disdains control,
          Disdains the tort'ring curb of woe.
          My softer bosom, thrilled with fear
          Lest heavier ills await you here,
 By milder counsels wishes you repose;
 For Zeus' relentless rage no tender pity knows.
   PRO. Stern though he be,
And, in the pride of power terrific dressed,
Rears o'er insulted his power,
Yet gentler thoughts shall mitigate his soul,
When o'er his head this storm shall roll;
Then shall his stubborn indignation bend,
Submit to suc, and court me for a friend.
   CHOR. But say, relate at large for what offence
Committed does the wrath of Zeus inflict
This punishment so shameful, so severe:
Tell us, if the tale shocks not your soul.
   PRO. 'Tis painful to relate it, to be silent
Is pain: each circumstance is full of woe.
When stern debate among the gods appeared,

And discord in the courts of heaven was raised;
While against Chronos some conspiring willed
To pluck him from the throne, that Zeus might reign;
And some, against, with strong belief opposed
Zeus' rising power and empire o'er the gods;
My advice, though quiet, wisest, best,
Moved not the Titans, those impetuous sons
Of Ouranus and Terra, whose high spirits,
Disdaining milder measures, proudly tried
To take by force the sceptre of sky.
Oft did my goddess mother, Themis now,
Now Gaia, under various names designed,
Herself the same, foretell me the event,
That not by violence, that not by power,
But gentle arts, the royalty of heaven
Must be obtained. While thus my voice advised,
Their headlong rage gave me not e'en a look.
What then could wisdom dictate, but to take
My mother, and with voluntary aid
Help the cause of Zeus? Thus by my advice
In the dark deep Tartarean gulf enclosed
Old Chronos lies, and his friendly powers.
For these good deeds the tyrant of the skies
Repays me with these dreadful punishments.
For foul mistrust of those that serve them best
Breathes its black poison in each tyrant's heart.
Ask you the cause for which he tortures me?
I will declare it. On his father's throne
Scarce was he seated, on the chiefs of heaven
He showered his various honours; thus confirming
His royalty; but for unhappy mortals
Had no regard, and all the present race
Willed to destroy, and to form anew.
None, save myself, opposed his will; I dared;
And boldly pleading saved them from destruction,
Saved them from sinking to the realms of night.
For this offence I bend beneath these pains,
Dreadful to suffer, piteous to behold:
For mercy to mankind I am not deemed
Worthy of mercy; but with ruthless hate
In this horrible way am fixed here
A spectacle dishonourable to Zeus.

  CHOR Of iron is he formed and stone,
Whose heart with social sorrow does not melt

At your afflictions: I never wished to see them,
Nor see them but with anguish at my heart.
　　PRO. It is a sight that strikes my friends with pity.
　　CHOR. But had th' offence no further aggravation?
　　PRO. I hid from men the foresight of their fate.
　　CHOR. What couldst you find to remedy that ill?
　　PRO. I sent blind Hope to live in their hearts.
　　CHOR. A blessing have you given to mortal man.
　　PRO. Nay more, with generous spirit I gave them fire.
　　CHOR. Do mortals now enjoy the blazing gift?
　　PRO.And by it shall give birth to various arts.
　　CHOR. For such offences does the wrath of Zeus
Thus punish you, relaxing nought of pain?
And is no bound set to your sorrow?
　　PRO. None else, but when his own will shall force
　　　him.
　　CHOR. Who shall force his will? Have you no hope?
Do you not see that you have much offended?
But to point out th' offence to me were painful,
And might sound harsh to thee: forbear we then;
Think how your sorrow might end.
　　PRO. How easy, when the foot is not entangled
In misery's thorny maze, to give monitions
And precepts to th' afflicted! Of these things
I was not unadvised; and my offence
Was voluntary; in man's cause I drew
These evils on my head: but ills like these,
On this aerial rock to waste away,
This desert and unsocial precipice,
My mind foresaw it not. But cease your grief,
Wail not my present woes; on the rough point
Of this firm cliff descend, and there observe
What further may betide me, e'en the whole
Of my hard fate; indulge me, O indulge
This my request, and sympathize with me
Thus wretched; for affliction knows no rest,
But rolls from heart to heart its flowing way.
　　CHOR. Not to th' unwilling we are hoping to hear what
will happen.
With light foot now this nimble-moving seat,
This pure air, through whose liquid fields the birds
Fly their easy way, I leave; and now
Alight I on this rude and craggy rock,
Anxious to hear all thy unhappy tale.

154

OCEANUS, PROMETHEUS, CHORUS.

OCEANUS. Far distant, through the great expanse of air,
To you, Prometheus, on this swift-winged horse
Whose neck unreined obeys my will, I come,
In social sorrow sympathizing with you
To this the near closeness of blood
Moves me; and be assured, except for that,
No one can tax my dear regard
Deeper than you: believe me, this is truth,
Not the false talk of a flatt'ring tongue.
Tell me then in what my power may serve you,
For never shalt you say you have a friend
More firm, more constant, than Oceanus.
  PRO. Ah me! What draws thee hither? Have you come
Spectator of my toils? How have you ventured
To leave the ocean waves, from you so called,
Thy rock-roofed cares arched by nature's hand,
And land upon this iron-teeming earth?
Come you to visit and bewail my ills?
Behold this sight, behold this friend of Zeus,
Th' friend of his empire, bending here
Beneath a weight of woes by him inflicted.
  OCEA. I see it all, and wish to advise you,
Wise as you are, to milder measures: learn
To know yourself; new model your behaviour,
As the new monarch of the gods requires.
What if your harsh and pointed speech should reach
The ear of Zeus, though on his distant throne
High-seated, might they not inflame his rage
T' inflict such tortures, that your present pains
Might seem a recreation and a sport?
Cease then, unhappy sufferer, cease your bravery
And think about the means of your salvation
To you perchance this seems the cold advice
Of silly age; yet, trust me, woes like these
Are earnings of the lofty-sounding tongue.
But your unbending spirit refuses to yield
E'en to afflictions, to the present rather
Ambitious to add more. Yet shalt you
If my voice may be heard, lift up your heel
To kick against the harness; so rough, you see
So uncontrolled the monarch of the skies.
But now I go, and will exert my power,

If haply I may free you from your pains.
Meanwhile be calm; forbear this nasty tone;
Has not your copious wisdom taught you this,
That mischief still attends the nasty tongue?
  PRO. I praise your fortune, that on you
No blame hath lighted, though a friend to me
In all, and daring equally. But now
Give up, of my condition take no care;
You will not move him; nothing moves his rigour;
Take heed then, lest to go brings harm on you.
    OCEA. Wiser for others than yourself I find
Your thoughts; yet shalt you not withhold my speed.
And I have hopes, with pride I speak it, hopes
T' obtain this grace, and free you from your sufferings.
  PRO. For this you have my thanks; Your courtesy
With grateful memory ever shall be honoured.
But think not of it, the attempt were useless,
Nor would your labour help me; cease then,
And leave me to my fate: although miserable,
I wish not to impart my woes to others.
  OCEA. No; for your brother's fate, th' unhappy Atlas,
hurts me: on the western shore he stands,
Supporting on his shoulders the heavy pillar
Of Heaven and Earth, a weight of heavy carrying.
Him too, the dweller of Cilicia's caves,
I saw, with pity saw, Earth's monstrous son,
With all his hundred heads, subdued by Force,
The furious Typhon, who' gainst all the gods
Made war; his horrid jaws with serpent-hiss
Breathed slaughter, from his eyes the gorgon-glare
Of awful lightnings flashed, as his proud force
Would take from Zeus his empire of the sky.
But him the vengeful bolt, instinct with fire,
Hit hard, and dashed him from his proud boast,
Pierced through his soul, and withered all his strength.
Thus stretched out huge in length beneath the roots
Of Aetna, near Trinacria's narrow sea,
Weakened, blasted, spiritless he lies;
On whose high summit Hephaistos holds his seat,
And forms the glowing mass. In times to come
A volcano of torrent fire with hideous roar
Shall burst, and with its wasteful mouths ruin
All the fair fields of fruitful Sicily.
Such rage shall Typhon, weakened as he is

With Zeus' fierce lightning, pour endless forth
In smoking whirlwinds and tempestuous flame.
  PRO. You are not unexperienced, nor have need
Of my instruction; save yourself, how best
Your wisdom shall direct you. I will bear
My present fate, till Zeus' harsh anger relents.
   OCEA. Know you not this, Prometheus, and soft
     speech
Is to nasty tempers soothing?
  PRO. When seasonably the healing medicine is applied;
Else it makes worse the swelling heart.
   OCEA. But in the fair attempt, in th' attempt,
What disadvantage, tell me, do you see?
   PRO. Unfruitful labour, and light-thoughted folly.
   OCEA. Be that my weakness then. Oft when the wise
Appears not wise, he works the greatest good
   PRO. This will be deemed my simple policy.
   OCEA. These words indeed force me to my care.
   PRO. Cease to bewail me, lest make Zeus angry.
   OCEA. What, the new monarch's of heaven's potent
     throne?
   PRO. Take care his indignation be not awakened.
   OCEA. Your misery shall be my guide.
   PRO. Go then, be cautious, hold your present judgment.
   OCEA. Your words add speed to my learning. Already
My plumed horse his levelled wings displays
To fan the liquid air, through strong desire
In his own lodge his wearied speed to rest.

PROMETHEUS, CHORUS

   CHOR. For you I lift the heart-felt sigh,
     My bosom melting a your woes
  For you my tear-flowing eye
     In streams of tender sorrow flows:
  For Zeus' imperious ruthless soul,
  That scorns the power of mild control,
  Chastens with horrid burning pain
Not known to gods, before his iron reign.

  E'en yet this large area over
    Hoarse sounds of sullen woe resound,
  Your state, your brother's state deplore,
    Age-honoured glories ruined round.

Your woes, beneath the sacred shade
Of Asia's pastured forests laid,
The chaste inhabitant bewails
Thy weeping re-echoing through his plaintive vales.

The Colchian virgin, whose bold hand
   Undaunted grasps the warlike spear;
On earth's last verge the Scythian band,
   The stale lake Maeotis near;
Arabia's warlike race, that wield
The sharp lance in th' embattled field,
Through all their rock-built cities moan,
The crags of Caucasus return the groan.

One other, before your painful chain,
   Of heaven's high sons with tortures quelled,
That rack each joint, each sinew strain,
   Titanian Atlas I beheld;
His giant strength condemned to bear
The solid, vast, and pond'rous sphere.
The springs whose fresh streams swell around,
The hoarse waves from their dephs profound,
And all the gloomy realms below,
Sigh to his sighs, and murmur to his woe.

PRO. It is not pride; think better of me, virgins;
It is not pride, that held me silent thus;
The thought of these harsh chains, that hang me here,
Cuts to my heart. Yet who, like me, advanced
To their high dignity our new-raised gods?
But let me spare the tale, to you well known.
The ills of man you've heard: I formed his mind,
And through the cloud of barb'rous ignorance
Sent the beams of knowledge. I will speak,
Not taxing them with blame, but my own gifts
Showing, and kindness to them.
They saw indeed, they heard; but what availed
Or sight, or sense of hearing, all things rolling
Like the unreal imagery of dreams,
In wild confusion mixed? The lovely wall
Of finer masonry, the raftered roof
They knew not; but, like ants still buried, dug
Deep in the earth, and scooped their sunless caves.
Unmarked the seasons changed, the biting winter,

The flower perfumed spring, the ripening summer
Fertile of fruits. At random all their works,
Till I instructed them to mark the stars,
Their rising, and, a harder science yet,
Their setting. The rich train of ordered numbers
I taught them, and the true pattern of letters.
T' impress these ideas on their hearts I sent
Memory, the active mother of all wisdom.
I taught the patient ox to bear the yoke,
In all his toils joint-labourer with man.
By me the harnessed horse was trained to pull
The rapid car, and grace the pride of wealth.
The tall ship, lightly sailing o'er the waves,
I taught its course, and winged its flying sail.
To man I gave these arts; with all my wisdom
Yet want I now one art, that useful art
To free myself from these afflicting chains.
   CHOR. Improper are your sufferings, sprung from error
And impotence of mind. And now enclosed
With all these ills, as some unskilful doctor
That sinks beneath his malady, your soul
Saddens, nor seeks medicinal relief.
   PRO. Hear my whole story, you will wonder more,
What useful arts, what science I invented.
This first and greatest; when the bad disease
Preyed on the human frame, relief was none,
Nor healing drug, nor cool refreshing drink,
Nor pain-killing drug; but they suffered
Without hope, and wasted, till I taught them
To mix the balmy medicine, of power
To chase each pale disease, and soften pain.
I taught the various modes of prophecy,
What truth the dream tells, the omen what
Of important things, what the casual sight
That meets us on the way, the flight of birds,
When to the right, when to the left they take
Their airy course, their various ways of life,
Their feuds, their fondnesses, their social flocks.
I taught th' priest to inspect the intestines
Their smoothness, and their colour to the gods
Grateful, the gall, the liver streaked with veins,
The limbs involved in fat, and the long cow
Placed on the blazing altar, from the smoke
And mounting flame to mark the accurate omen.

159

These arts I taught. And all the secret treasures
Deep buried in the bottom of the earth,
Brass, iron, silver, gold, their use to man,
Let the vain tongue make what high boasts it may,
Are my inventions all; and, in a word,
Prometheus taught each useful art to man.
  CHOR. Let not your love to man o'erleap the bounds
Of reason, nor neglect your horrid state;
So my silly hope suggests you shall be free
From these base chains, nor less in power than Zeus.
  PRO. Not thus, it is not in the Fates that thus
These things should end; crushed with a thousand wrongs,
A thousand woes, I shall escape these chains.
Necessity is stronger far than art.
  CHO. Who then is ruler of necessity?
  PRO. The triple fates and unforgetting furies.
  CHOR. Must Zeus then yield to their superior power?
  PRO. He no way shall escape his destined fate.
  CHOR. What, but eternal empire, is his fate?
  PRO. You may not know this now; forget about asking.
  CHOR. Is it of moment what you keep thus close?
  PRO. No more of this discourse, it is not time
Now to tell that which requires the seal
Of strictest secrecy; by guarding which
I shall escape the misery of these chains.

CHORUS.

Strophe.

    Never, never may my soul
    Zeus' all-ruling power defy;
    Never feel his harsh control,
    Sov'reign ruler of the sky.
    When the hallowed cow has bled,
    When the sacred feast is spread,
    'Midst the crystal waves below,
  Whence father Ocean's boundless billows flow,
    Let not my foot be slow;
    There, th' ethereal guests among,
    No rude speech disgrace my tongue.
    May my mind this rev'rence keep;
    Print it strong, and grave it deep.

Antistrophe.

When through life's lengthened scene
Hope her sure light throws,
Swells the soul with peaceful joy,
With highest triumph glows.
See you this pure light shine?
Are these heart-felt raptures yours?
My cold blood curdles in my veins,
To see your hideous woes, thy tort'ring pains,
And iron chains.
Your free soul, untaught to fear,
Scorned the danger threat'ning near;
And for mortals dared defy
Zeus, monarch of the sky.

Epode.

Vain your ardour, vain your grace,
They nor force nor aid repay;
Like a dream man's feeble race,
Short-lived reptiles of a day.
Shall their weak devices move
Th' ordered harmony of Zeus?
Touched with pity of your pain,
All sad and slow I pour the moral strain;
Changed from that melting vein,
When the light melodious measure
Round your bath, and round your bed
For our sea-nymph sister spread,
Awoke young love and bridal pleasure
And poured the soul of harmony,
To greet the bright Hesione.

IO, PROMETHEUS, CHORUS.

IO. Where, oh, where am I now?
To what rude shore, what barb'rous race? O you,
Whoe'er, that chained to that bleak rock,
The seat of sorrow, worries of your crime,
Say on what shore my painful footsteps walk.--
Again that sting! -- Ah me, that sting again! --
With all his hundred eyes the earth-born Argus --
Cover it, Earth! See, how it glares upon me,

The horrid sight! -- Will you not, O Earth,
Cover the dead, that from your dark abyss
He comes to haunt me, to pursue my steps,
And drive me foodless o'er the barren land?
Hoarse sounds the reed-compacted pipe, a note
Sullen and drowsy. -- Miserable me!
Where will these wide-wand'ring errors lead me?
How, son of Chronos, how have I offended,
That with these stings, these tortures you pursue me,
And drive to madness my frightened soul!
Hear me, supreme of gods, O hear my prayer,
Blast me with lightnings, bury me in th' earth,
Or cast me to the monsters of the sea;
But spare these pains, spare these wide-wand'ring errors,
Which drive me round the world, and know no rest.
  CHOR. Hear you the voice of this lamenting virgin?
For such she is, though she seems now a cow.
  PRO. I hear her griefs, that whirl her soul to madness,
Daughter of Inachus, whose love enflames
The heart of Zeus; hence Zeus' jealous rage
Drives the poor wanderer restless o'er the world.
  IO. Whence is it that I hear my father's name?
Speak to my misery, tell me who you are;
What wretch are you,that to a wretch like me
Says these truths, naming the the sickness,
Which, heaven-inflicted, stings my tortured soul
To maddness? Hence with hurrying steps I go
Foodless, pursued by never ceasing anger.
Ah me! What child of misery ever suffered
Misery like mine? But tell me, clearly tell me,
What woes await me yet, what ease, what ease, what cure?
Say, if you know, speak, tell a wand'ring virgin.
  PRO. All, you can wish to learn, I'll tell you clearly,
Wrapped in no veil of words; but in clear terms.
As friend to friend. Your eyes behold Prometheus,
Whose warm kindness gave fire to men.
  IO. O you, the common blessing of mankind,
Wretched Prometheus, Why are these sufferings?
  PRO. Scarce have I ceased lamenting my misfortunes.
  IO. And will you not allow me that sad office?
  PRO. Ask what you will, you shall learn all from me.
  IO. Say then, who bound you in that solid rock?
  PRO. The ruthless will of Zeus but Hephaistos hand.
  IO. In what offending are you punished thus?

PRO. It is enough for you to know who has done it.
IO. Say then what time shall end my wretched wand'rings.
PRO. Better stay in ignorance, than know.
IO. Whate'er my woes to come, hide them not from me.
PRO. That favour unreluctant could I grant thee.
IO. Why this delay then to declare the whole?
PRO. Ungrateful task to tear your soul with anguish.
IO. Regard not me more than is pleasing to me.
PRO. Asked thus strongly, I must speak. Hear then.
CHOR. Not yet; this mournful pleasure let me share:
Let us first learn the story of her woes;
Her lips will teach us each sad circumstance
Of misery past; the future by your task.
      PRO. Indulge their wish; they merit it;
And are besides the sisters of your father.
Nor light the payment, when they, who hear,
Melt at the melancholy tale, and drop,
In pity drop, the sympathizing tear.
      IO. Ill would excuse become me, or denial;
Take then the plain simple tale
Ye wish to hear; though sad the task you beg
And hard; for how to tell the heaven-sent tempest
That burst upon my head, my form thus changed
And all the weight of woe that overwhelms me?
Still, when retired to rest, air-bodied forms
Visit my slumbers nightly, soothing me
With gentle speech, "Blest maid, why hoard for ever
Thy virgin treasure, when the highest nuptials
Await thy choice; the flames of soft desire
Have touched the heart of Zeus; he burns with love:
Delay not, gentle virgin, ah! delay not
The couch of Zeus; to Lerna's deep recess,
Where graze your father's herds the grass along,
Go, gentle virgin, crown the god's desires."
The night returns, the visionary forms
Return again, and haunt my troubled soul,
Forbidding rest, till to my father's ear
I dared disclose the visions of the night.
To Pytho, to Dodona's talking grove
He sent his seers, anxious to know what best
Was pleasing to the gods. Returned they bring
Dark-uttered answers of double talk.
At length one oracle distinct and plain
Pronounced its necessity, charging Inachus
To drive me from his house and from my country.

To walk at large o'er earth's extremest bounds:
Should he refuse, the vengeful bolt of Zeus,
Winged with red flames, would all his race destroy.
Obedient to the Pythian god he drove me
Unwilling from his house, himself unwilling
Compelled by Zeus, and harsh necessity.
Straight was my sense disordered, my fair form
Changed into a cow, disfigured with these horns;
And tortured with the wasps' horrid sting,
Wild with my pain with frantic speed I hurried
To Cenchrea's land with silver-winding streams
Irriguous, and the fount whence Lerna spreads
Its wide expanse of waters; close behind
In wrathful mood walked Argus, earth-born herdsman,
With all his eyes watching my steps.
Him unawares a sudden fate deprived
Of life; whilst I, stung with that heaven-sent pest,
Am driven with devious speed from land to land.
You have my tale. If anything of woes to come
Your knowing mind sees, tell them freely;
Nor through false pity with lying words
Soothe my vain hopes, my soul hates as base
The tongue of flattery.
   CHOR. No more, no more, stop. Ahnever, never
Conceived I that a tale so strange should reach
My ears; that miseries, woes, distresses, terrors,
Dreadful to sight, intolerable to sense,
Should shock me thus: woe, woe, unhappy fate!
How my soul shudders at the fate of Io!
   PRO. Already do you sigh, already tremble!
Check these emotions till the whole is heard.
   CHOR. Speak, show us: to the sick some gleam of
comfort
Flows from the knowledge of their pains to come.
   PRO. Your first request with ease has been obtained;
For from her lips you wished to hear the tale
Of her afflictions. Hear the rest; what woes
From Hera's rage await this suff'ring virgin.
And you with deep attention mark my words,

Daughter of Inachus; and learn from them
The traces of your way. First then, from hence
Turn to the orient sun, and pass the height
Of these uncultured mountains; thence descend

To where the wandering Scythians, trained to bear
The distant-wounding bow, on wheels aloft
Roll on their cottages; to these
Approach not close, but turn your devious steps
Along the rough edge of the murm'ring sea
And pass the barb'rous country; on the left
The Chalybes inhabit, whose rude hands
Temper the glowing steel; beware of these,
A savage and horrid race.
Thence shall you reach the banks of that proud stream,
Which from its roaring torrent takes its name;
But pass it not, tempt not its dangerous depths
Unfordable, till now your weary steps
Shall reach the distant bound of Caucasus,
Monarch of mountains; from whose extreme height
The bursting flood rolls down his power of waters.
Passing those star-aspiring heights, descend
Where to the south the Amazonian tents,
Angry at men, stretch o'er the plain; whose troops
In after times shall near Thermodon's banks
Fix in Themiscyra's towers their strict rule,
Where Salmydesia points her cruel rocks,
And glories in her wrecks. this female train
With courteous zeal shall guide thee in thy way.
Arriving where the dark Cimmerian lake
Spreads from its narrow mouth its vast expanse,
Leave it, and boldly plunge your wandering foot
In the Maeotic straits; the voice of fame
Shall eternize your passage, and from you
Call it the Bosphorus: there shall you quit
The shores of Europe, and bravely reach
The continent of Asia -- Seems he now,
This tyrant of the skies, seems he in all
Of fierce and headlong violence, when his love
Sinks a mortal in such deep troubles?
A rugged lover, virgin, have your charms
Won you; for be assured what I have told you
Is but a prelude to the woes untold.
    IO. Ah, miserable me!
    PRO. Again that exclamation, that deep groan!
What will you do, when you shall learn the rest?
    CHOR. Remains there anything of ills yet to be told?
    PRO. A wide tempestuous sea of baleful woes.
    IO. What then has life desirable? Why rather
From this rude cliff leap I not headlong down,

And commit suicide? Better to die at once,
Than linger out a length of life in pain.
  PRO. Ill would you bear my miseries, by the Fates
Exempt from death, the refuge of the cured.
But my afflictions know no bounds, till Zeus
Falls from th' imperial throne of heaven.
  IO. Shall he then fall? Shall the time come, when Zeus
Shall sink dethroned? I think I should rejoice
To see the tyrant's ruin. Should I not,
Since from his hands I suffer all these ills.
  PRO. Then be you well assured it shall be so.
  IO. And who shall take th' imperial sceptre from him?
  PRO. Himself, destroyed by his stupid acts.
  IO. Oh say, if harmless what I ask, say how.
  PRO. Urging a marriage he shall dearly regret.
  IO. Heaven-sprung, or mortal? If permitted, say.
  PRO. What matters which? It may not be told.
  IO. Shall then a wife deprive him of the throne?
  PRO. She greater than the father shall bear a son.
  IO. Has he no means of power to change this fate?
  PRO. None, till from these vile chains I shall be free.
  IO. And who, 'gainst Zeus' high will, shall set you
    free?
  PRO. One, of necessity, from you descended.
  IO. From me! My son release you from your pains?
  PRO. Third of your race, first numb'ring ten generations.
  IO. Strange this, of difficult thought.
  PRO. Check then your wish, nor seek to know your toils.
  IO. Do not hold forth a grace, then snatch it from me.
  PRO. Of two relations I will grant you either.
  IO. Propose the two, then leave the choice to me.
  PRO. Shall I declare the rest of your misfortunes,
Or do you wish to know him that shall free me?
  CHOR. The first to her, to me this other grace
Tell, nor my request treat with contempt
To her tell what toils remain; to me
Him that shall free you; this I most desire.
  PRO. This your request I shall not be slow
To fill, and tell you all you wish.
First for your various wand'rings: Mark my words,
And put them on the tablet of your heart.
When you shalt pass the flood, the common bound
Of either continent, direct your steps
Right to the fiery doors of the east,

The sun's bright walk, along the roaring beach,
Till you shalt come to the Gorgonian plains
Of Cisthine, where dwell the swan-like forms
Of Phorcys' daughters, bent and white with age;
One common eye have these, one common tooth,
And never does the sun with cheerful ray
Visit them darkling, not the moon's pale orb
That silvers o'er the night. The Gorgons nigh,
Their sisters these, spread their broad wings, and wreathe
Their horrid hair with serpents, fiends abhorred,
Whom never mortal could behold, and live.
Be therefore warned, and let it profit you
To learn what else detestable to sight
Lies in your way, and dang'rous. Shun the Gryphins,
Those dumb and rav'nous dogs of Zeus. Avoid
The Arimaspian troops, whose frowning foreheads
Glare with one blazing eye; along the banks,
Where Pluto rolls his streams of gold, they stop
Their foaming horses; approach them not, but seek
A land far distant, where the tanned race
Dwell near the fountains of the sun, and where
The Nigris river pours his waters; wind
Along his banks, till you shalt reach the fall
Where from the mountains with Papyrus crowned
The old Nile angry pours
His headlong torrent; he shall guide your steps
To those fruitful plains, whose triple sides
His arms surround; there have the Fates decreed
You and your sons to form the lengthened line. --
Is anything imperfect, anything obscure? Resume
Th' inquiry, and be taught with greater clearness:
I have more leisure than I wish to have.
   CHOR. If you have anything remaining, anything omitted,
To tell her of her woeful wand'rings, speak it:
If all has been declared, to us tell
The grace we ask; what, you remember well.
   PRO. Her wand'ring in full measure has she heard,
That she may know she has not heard in vain,
Her labours passed, ere these rude rocks she reached,
Will I recite, good argument that truth
Stamps my predictions sure: nor shall I use
A length of words, but speak your wand'rings briefly.
Soon as your foot reached the Molossian ground,
And round Dodona's rocky heights, where stands

The seat oracular of Thesprotian Zeus
And, wondrous child, the talking groves,
These in clear, plain, unquestionable terms
Called you "Illustrious wife of Zeus that shall be,"
If that may soothe your soul. The tort'ring sting
Thence drove you wand'ring o'er the wave-washed strand
To the great gulf of Rhea, thence your course
Through the angry waves hither. But know this,
In after times shall that deep gulf from you
Be call'd th' Ionian, and preserve to men
The memory of your passage. This to you
Proving the brilliance of my mind, that sees
More than appears: the rest to you and her,
Resuming my speech, I speak in common
On the land's extreme edge a city stands,
Canobus, proudly raised, nigh where the Nile
Rolls to the sea his rich stream: there shall Zeus
Heal your distraction, and with gentle hand
Soothe you to peace. Of his high race a son,
The dusky Epaphus, shall rise, and rule
The wide-extended land o'er which the Nile
Pours his broad waves. In the fifth line from him
Fifty fair sisters shall return to Argos
Unwillingly, to fly the kindred beds
Of fifty brothers; these with eager speed,
Swift as the falcon's flight when he pursues
The dove at hand, shall follow, nor obtain
The nuptials, which th' angry gods deny.
These shall Pelasgia see by female hands
Swimming in blood, the night's convenient gloom
Fav'ring the daring deed; each female draws
The sharpened sword, and in her husband's blood
Stains the broad blade. Thus fatal to my foes
Be love! Yet one shall feel its softer flame
Melting her soul, and from the general murder
Preserve her husband, choosing to be deemed
Of base degenerate spirit, rather than stain
Her gentle hands with blood. From her shall Argos
Receive a long imperial line of kings.
The full distinct relation would be dull.
From her shall rise the hero, strong to wing
The swift arrow; he from these tort'ring pains
Shall set me free: this my age-honoured mother,
Titanian Themis, with truthful voice

7

Foretold; but when, or how, requires a length
Of story, which known would nothing help you.
   IO. Ah me! ah wretched me! That pang again!
Again that fiery pang, whose madd'ning pain
Corrodes and rankles in my breast! With fear
My heart pants thick; widly my eyeballs roll;
Distraction drives my hurried steps a length
Of weary wand'ring; my helpless tongue
Utters weary ravings, that roll high
The floods of passion swollen with horrid woes.

PROMETHEUS, CHORUS.

CHORUS.

Strophe.

  Was it not wisdom's kingly power
  That beamed her brightest, purest flame,
T' show her sage's soul the thought to frame,
  And clothe with words his heaven-taught ideas?
  "Whoe'er you are, whom young desire
  Shall lead to Hymen's holy fire,
Choose, from your equals choose your humble love:
  Let not the pomp of wealth attract your eye,
Nor high-traced lineage your ambition move;
  Ill suits with low degree t' aspire so high."

Antistrophe.

  Never, oh never may my fate
  See me a splendid victim led
To grace the mighty Zeus' imperial bed,
  Or share a god's mighty state.
  When Io's miseries meet my eyes,
  What horrors in my soul arise!
Her virgin bosom, aiming high,
  In man delights not, and his love disdains;
Hence the awful pest by angry Zeus sent,
Her wide wild wand'rings hence, and agonizing pains.

169

Me less ambitious thoughts engage,
  And love within my humbler sphere:
Hence my soul rests in peace secure from fear,
  Secure from danger's threat'ning rage.
Me may the powers that rule the sky
Ne'er view with love's resistless eye:
Ah! never be th' unequal conflict mine,
  To strive with their strange love:
Might not my heart against itself combine?
  Or how escape the powerful arts of Zeus?

PRO. Yet shall this Zeus, with all his self-willed pride,
Learn humbler thoughts, taught by that fatal marriage,
Which from the lofty throne of kingly rule
Shall sink him to a low, slave-like state,
And on his head fulfil his father's curse,
The curse of Chronos, vented in that hour
When from his ancient royalty he fell.
Of all the gods not one, myself, except,
Can warn him of his fate, and how to shun
Th' impending ruin. I know all, and how.
Let him sit, and glorying in his height
Roll with his red right hand his rolling thunder
Falsely secure, and wrap his angry flames.
Yet nothing shall they avail him, nor prevent
His abject and dishonourable fall.
Such rival opposite forms he now
Against himself, huge in his might,
And unassailable; whose rage shall roll
Flames that surpass his lightnings, fiercer bolts
That quash his thunders: and from Neptune's hand
Dash his mace, that from the bottom stirs
The troubled sea, and shakes the solid earth.
Crushed with this dreadful ruin shall he learn
How different, to command, and to obey.
  CHOR. Your fearful tongue gives utterance to your
    wish.
  PRO. It is my wish, and shall be ratified.
  CHOR. What, shall high Zeus bend to a greater lord?
  PRO. And to a collor more galling stoop his neck.
  CHOR. Do you not fear, hugging this bold discourse?

PRO. What should I fear, by Fate exempt from death?
CHOR. But he may add fresh tortures to your pain.
PRO. Let him then add them, I await them all.
CHOR. Wise they, who reverence the stern power of
    vengeance.
PRO. Go then, with prompt servility fall down
Before your lord, fawn, cringe, and suc for grace.
For me, I value him at less than nothing.
Let him exert his brief authority.
And lord it while he may; his power in Heaven
Shall vanish soon, nor leave a trace behind. --
But see, his messenger hastes on always
Th' dog'like slave of this new-made king:
He comes I know, bearer of fresh news.

    HERMES, PROMETHEUS, CHORUS.

  HERMES. To you grown old in craft, deep soaked
      bitterness,
Repulsive to the gods, too careless
Of unlawful gifts to mortal,
Thief of the fire of Heaven, to you my message.
My father bids you say what marriage these
Your tongue thus brags as threat'ning his high power;
And clearly say, spoken in no riddling phrase,
Each several circumstance; talk not to me
Ambiguous terms, Prometheus; for you see
Zeus allows not such, unfit to win his favour.
  PRO. You say your message proudly, in high terms,
Becoming well the servant of such lords.
Your youthful power is now; yet vainly seek you
Your high-raised towers above all pain:
Have I not seen two kings of the sky
Sink from their glorious state? And I shall see
A third, this present lord, with sudden ruin
Dishonourably fall. What, seem I now
To dread, to tremble at these new-raised gods?
That never shall their force extort from me.
Hence then, the way came return with speed:
Your vain inquiries get no other answer.
  MER. Such nastiness before, so fiery fierce,
Drew on your head this dreadful punishment.
  PRO. My miseries, be assured, I would not change

171

For your gay servitude, but rather choose
To live a slave to this dreary rock,
Than lackey the proud heels of Zeus These words,
If nasty, your nastyness returns.

   MER. I think you are delighted with your woes.
   PRO. Delighted! Might I see mine enemies
Delighted thus! And you I hold among them.
   MER. And why blame me for your troubles;
   PRO. To tell you in a word, I hate them all,
These gods; of them I deserved well, and they
Ungrateful and unjust work me these ills.
   MER. Your sickness, I find, is no small madness.
   PRO. If to detest my enemies be madness,
It is a malady I wish to have.
   MER. Where it well with you who could stand your
    pride?
   PRO. Ah me!
   MER. That sound of grief Zeus does not know.
   PRO. Time, as its age advanceth, teaches all things.
   MER. All its advances have not taught you wisdom.
   PRO. I should not else waste words on you, a slave.
   MER. Nothing will you answer then to what Zeus asks.
   PRO. If due, I would repay his courtesy.
   MER. Why am I checked, why rated as a boy?
   PRO. A boy you are, more simple than a boy,
If you have hopes to be informed by me.
Not all his tortures, all his arts shall move me
T' unlock my lips, till this cursed chain be loosed.
No let him hurl his flaming lightnings, wing
His whitening snows, and with his thunders shake
The rocking earth, they move not me to say
What force shall wrest the sceptre from his hand.
   MER. Weigh these things well, will these unloose your
    chains?
   PRO. Well have they long been weighed, and well con-
    sidered.
   MER. Subdue, vain fool, subdue your temper,
And let thy miseries teach you juster thoughts.
   PRO. Your counsels, like the waves that dash against
The rock's firm base, disquiet but not move me.
Think not of me that, through fear what Zeus
May in his rage do, my fixed contempt
Shall e'er relent, e'er suffer my firm mind
To sink to womanish softness, to fall prostrate,

To stretch my begging hands, asking
My hated foe to free me from these chains.
Far be that shame, that weakness from me.
  HERMES. I see you are stubborn, unsoftened
By all the mild entreaties I can urge;
But like a young horse reined that proudly struggles,
And champs his iron curb, your haughty soul
Weakens not of its useless fierceness.
But pride, disdaining to be ruled by reason,
Sinks weak and valueless. But mark me well,
If not obedient to my words, a storm,
A fiery and inevitable rain
Shall burst in threefold vengeance on your head.
First, his fierce thunder winged with lightning flames
Shall tear this rugged rock, and cover you
With hideous ruin: long time shall you lie
Buried in its rifted sides, till dragged
Again to light; then shall the bird of Zeus,
The rav'ning eagle, lured with scent of blood,
Tear your body, and each day returning,
An uninvited guest, plunge his beak,
And feast and riot on your black'ning liver.
Expect no pause, no respite, till some god
Comes to relieve your pains, willing to pass
The dreary realms of ever-during night,
The dark descent of Tartarus profound.
Weigh these things well; this is no fiction,
No fantasy, but words of serious truth.
The mouth of Zeus knows not to utter falsehood,
But what he speaks is fate. Be cautious then,
Look out for yourself; let not pride
Overcome the friendly voice of prudent counsel.
  CHOR. Nothing amiss we think his words, but full of
Reason, who but wills you to relax
Your haughty spirit, and by prudent counsels
Pursue your peace: be then advised; what shame
For one so wise to go on in error.
  PRO. All this I knew ere he declared his message.
That enemy from enemy should suffer
Extreme indignity is nothing strange.
Let him then work his horrible pleasure on me;
Wreathe his black curling flames, tempest the air
With volleyed thunders and wild warring winds,
Tear from its roots the firm earth's solid base,

173

Heave from the roaring main its boisterous waves,
And dash them to the stars; me let him hurl.
Caught in the fiery tempest, to ghe gloom
Of deepest Tartarus; not all his power
Can destroy th' ethereal breath of life in me.
  HERMES. Such ravings, such wild counsels might you hear,
From moon-struck madness. What is this but madness?
Were he at ease, would he stop his frenzy?
But you, whose gentle hearts with social sorrow
Melt at his suff'rings, from this place get out,
Get out with speed, lest the tempestuous roar
Of his fierce thunder strike your souls with horror.
  CHOR. To other themes, to other counsels turn
Your voice, where pleaded reason may prevail:
This is ill urged, and may not be allowed.
Would you solicit me to deeds of evil?
Whate'er betides, with him will I endure it.
The vile betrayer I have learned to hate;
There is no fouler stain, my soul hates it.
  MER. Remember you are warned; if ill o'ertake you
Accuse not Fortune, lay not the blam on Zeus,
As by his hand sunk in calamities
Unthought of, unforeseen: no, let the blame
Light on yourselves; your folly not unwarned,
Not unawares, but 'gainst your better knowledge,
Involved you in th' unbreakable chains.
  PRO. He is not lying; I feel in very deed
The firm earth rock; the thunder's deep'ning roar
Tolls with redoubled rage; the bick'ring flames
Flash thick; the eddying sands are whirled on high,
In dreadful opposition the wild winds
Tears the vexed air; the boist'rous waves rise
Confounding sea and sky; th' impetuous storm
Rolls all its terrible fury on my head.
See you this, awful Themis; and you AEther,
Through whose pure azure floats the general stream
Of liquid light, see you what wrongs I suffer!

MEDEA

NURSE OF MEDEA'S CHILDREN.
CHILDREN'S GURADIAN.
MEDEA.
CHORUS OF CORINTHIAN LADIES.
CREON, KING OF CORINTH.
JASON.
AEGEUS, KING OF ATHENS.
MESSENGER.
CHILDREN OF MEDEA.

The Scene is in front of JASON'S *house*
at Corinth.

Enter NURSE OF MEDEA'S CHILDREN
  NURSE. I wish to God that Argo's hull
    had never flown
Through those blue Clashing Rocks to
    Colchis-land,
Nor that the axe-hewn pine in Pelion's
    glens
Ever had fallen, nor filled with oars the
    hands
Of hero-princes, who at Pelias' hest
Quested the Golden Fleece! My mis-
    tress then,
Medea, ne'er had sailed to Iolcos' towers
With love for Jason thrilled through all
    her soul,
Nor had on Pelias' daughters been made to
    slay
Their sire, nor now in this Corinthian
    land
Dwelt with her lord and children glad-
    dening
By this her exile them whose land re-
    ceived her,
Yes, and in all things serving Jason's
    desires,
Which is the chief salvation of the home,
When wife does not argue with
    her lord.

Now all is hatred: love is sickness-
     stricken.
For Jason, traitor to his babes and her,
My mistress, marries a child of
     kings,
Daughter of Creon ruler of the land.
And, castaside thus, Medea, hapless wife,
Cries on the oaths, invokes that mightiest
     pledge
Of the right hand, and calls the Gods
     to witness
What payment from Jason she re-
     ceives.
Fasting, with limbs in grief's abandon-
     ment
Flung down, she weeps and wastes
     through all the days
Since first she knew her lord's wrong
     done to her,
Never uplifting eye, nor turning ever
From earth her face. No more than rock
     or sea-wave
Listens she to friends that talk to
     her;
Saving at times, when lifting her white
     neck,
To herself she weeps her father once
     beloved,
Her land, her home, forsaking which she
     came
Hither with him who holds her now
     contemned.
Alas for her! she knows, by affliction
     taught,
How good is fatherland not lost.
She hates her babes, joys not seeing
     them.
And what she may plan I dread to
     think.
Grim is her spirit, one that will not
     bear
Mishandling: yea, I know her, and I
     fear

176

Unless to her bridal bower she softly steal,
And through her own heart thrust the
    sharpened knife,
Or slay the king and him that weds his
    child,
And get herself some curse yet worse
    thereby;
For dangerous is she: who begins a feud
With her, not soon shall sing the
    triumph-song.
But lo, her boys, their racing-sport put by,
Draw near, all careless of their mother's
    wrongs,
For the young heart loves not to mope
    in grief.
Enter CHILDREN'S GUARDIAN *with boys*
 CHILDREN'S GUARDIAN. O ancient
    property of my mistress' home,
Why at the gates thus lonely stand
    you,
Yourself unto yourself talking of ills?
How wills Medea to be left of you?
  NURSE. O grey attendant you of
    Jason's sons,
The hearts of faithful servants still are
    touched
By ill-betiding fortunes of their lords.
For I have sunk to such a depth of
    grief,
That yearning took me hitherward to
    come
And tell to earth and heaven my lady's
    wrongs.
  CHILDREN'S GUARDIAN. Stops not
    yet the hapless one from moaning?
  NURSE. Stop!--her pain scarce be-
    gun, far from its height!
  CHILDREN'S GUARDIAN. Ah fool!--if
    one may say it of his lords--
Little she knows of the latest blow.
  NURSE. What is it, old man? Grudge
    not you to tell me.
  CHILDREN'S GUARDIAN. Nothing: I
    am sorry of the word that 'scaped
    me.

NURSE. Nay, but your beard, hide not
    from fellow-servant--
Silence, if need be, will I keep.
    CHILDREN'S GUARDIAN. I heard one
    saying--feigning not to hear,
As I drew near the old stone seats,
    sit
The ancients round Peirene's sacred
    fount,--
"Creon, this land's lord, is about
    banish
Mother and sons from soil Corinthian.
Howbeit, if the tale I heard be true
I know not: I wish I had not heard.
    NURSE. Will Jason brook such
    dealing with his sons,
Though from their mother he be
    how estranged?
    CHILDREN'S GUARDIAN. Old bonds of
    love are outrun by feet
Of new:--no friend is he unto this house
    NURSE. Ruined we are then, if we
    add fresh ill
To old, before lightened be our ship
    this.
    CHILDREN'S GUARDIAN. But you
    for 'tis not right that you lady
Should know--keep silence, and speak
    not the tale.
    NURSE. Hear, babes, what father this
    is unto you!
I curse him--not: he is my master still;
But to his friends he shows his evil side.
    CHILDREN'S GUARDIAN. What man
    is not? Have you learned this only now,
That no man loves his neighbour himself?
Good cause have some, with most it is
    greed of gain--
As here: their sire for a bride's sake
    loves not these.
    NURSE. Pass in, dear children, for
    it shall be well.
But you keep these apart to the
    trouble;

178

Bring them not night their mother angry
    souled.
For late I saw her glare, as glares a bull
On these, as 'twere for mischief; not
    her anger
I know, shall not stop, until its lightning
    strike.
To enemies may she work ill, and not to
    friends!

MEDEA *(behind the scenes)*.
O hapless I! O miseries heaped on
    my head!
Ah, me! ah me! would God I were
    dead!
NURSE. Lo, darlings, the things that I
    told you!
 Lo the heart of your mother astir!
And astir is her anger: withhold you
 From her sight, come not nigh
    unto her.
Haste, get you within: O beware
    you
Of the thoughts as you would a wild-beast
Of the nature too ruthless to spare
    you
    In this desperate mood.
Pass you within now, departing
 With all speed. It is plain to
    see
How a cloud of lamenting, upstarting
From its viewless beginnings, shall
    burn
In lightnings of fury yet fiercer.
 What deeds shall be dared of that
    soul,
So proud, when wrong's stings
    hurt her,
    So hard to control?
(Exeunt CHILDREN *with* GUARDIAN.)
MEDEA *(behind the scenes)*.
Woe! I have suffered, have suffered,
    foul wrongs that may waken,
    may waken

179

Mighty lamentings full well! O you
        children accursed from the
        womb,
Then to destruction, you children of a
        hated one forsaken, forsaken!
So with your father, and perish our
        home in the blackness of doom!
  NURSE. Ah me, in the father's wrongs
        What part have the babes, that
        you hate
      Should blast them? -- poor innocences,
       How much I fear for your fate!
      How terrible princes' moods are! --
       Long ruling, untaught to obey, --
      Unforgiving, unsleeping their hatred is:
      It's better not to be powerful.
       If I cannot be great, let me
      In quiet and peace to grow old.
      Sweeter name than "The Poor"
          shall you say not,
       And to taste it is sweetness
          untold.
      But to men never money more than
          enough
        On its perilous height
      The Gods in their hour of displeasure
          The strongest destroy.

ENTER CHORUS OF CORINTHIAN LADIES

  CHORUS. I have listened to the voice
    of the daughter of Colchis, the sound
    of the crying
Of the misery-stricken; nor yet is she
quiet. Now the tale of her tell,
Grey woman; for moaned through the
    porch from her chamber the wail of her
    signing;
And I cannot, I cannot be glad while the
    home in sorrow is lying,
      The house I have loved so well.

NURSE. Home?--home there is none:
    it hath vanished away:

    For my lord to a bride of the princes
        is a slave;
And my lady is wasting the livelong day
In her room, and for nothing that her
        friends' lips say
    On her heart may the dews of comfort
    fall.
MEDEA *(behind the scenes)*
I wish to God that the flame of the light-
        ning from heaven descending, de-
        scending,
Might burn through my head!--for
        in living is there any more
        gain
Alas as, and alas! I wish to God I might
        bring to an ending, an ending,
The life that I hate, and behind me
        might cast all its burden of pain!
CHORUS. O Zeus, Earth, Light, did ye
                hear her,
    How waileth the woe-laden breath
        Of the bride in unhappiest
            plight?
        What yearning for vanished de-
            light.
        O passion-maddened, should
            have might
    To cause you to wish death nearer--
        The ending of all things, death?
Take thou not for this supplication!
        If thine husband hath turned
            and adored
        New love, that estranged he
            is,
        O harrow thy soul for this:
        It is Zeus that shall right
            this mess.
    Ah, weep not in worry
        Of spirit, bewailing your lord!
MEDEA   *(behind the scenes)*
Lady of Justice, O Artemis' Majesty,
    see it, O see it--
Look on the wrongs that I suffer, by
    oaths everlasting who tied

181

The soul of my husband, that ne'er from the curse
                         he might free it, nor free it
From your vengeance. O may I behold him at last, even
                         him and his bride,
Them, and these halls where I stand, all shattered in
                         ruin, in ruin--
Wretches, who dare to do Medea unprovoked hurt.
O father, O city, whom first I left for undoing,
And for shame, when the blood of my brother I spilled
                         on my flight!
Nurse. Do you hear what she says, and uplifteth
                         her cry
Unto Themis and Zeus; to the Suppliant's King,
Oath-steward of men that are born but to die?
O my lady will not end her anger so
Soon, making her vengeance a great thing.

Chorus. If she would but come forth where we wait her,
If she would but give ear to the sound
Of our speech, that her spirit would learn
From its fierceness of anger to turn
And her lust for revenge not to burn!
O ne'er many my love prove traitor !
Never false to my friends be I found!

But go you andout of the house
Your mistress out to here lead.
Say to her that friends we are all.
O hurry, before trouble begins.
  The lords of the palace-hall
For her grief, like a tempest is swelling,
Resistless shall go toward ruin.

Nurse. I will do it: but almost my spirit is depressed.
To win her; yet labour of love shall it be.
But my queen on her slaves as a bull stares,
Or as a lioness laying mid her cubs. No one should
Dare draw near her, so angry is she.
People were right who said that the old poets in poetry
Were not clever, but left-handed bards, for their poems
They made for the happy times, the festive times,
Times of wine and the feast, when the harp strings are
                         ringing

182

To sweeten with melody life's sweet days

However, the fear of death of mortals, the
  painful heart-breaking --
Never poet by music has breathed on them peace,
Nor by song with his harp-notes in harmony blending;
Even if after comes death's dark ending.
Unto many a house that is wrecked by these.

And yet it was surely a gift to bring healing
of sorrow to mortals with song; but in vain
Amid the fulness of feasting ring voices
  clear pealing,
And the banquet itself has a glamour,
  concealing
From mortals their doom, flinging spells over pain.
                              (EXIT NURSE)
CHORUS. I have heard it, the sighing cry of the
  daughters
Of Cholcis, the woe-thrilling anguish of wailing.
For the traitor to love who with false vows
  caught her
Who in strength of her wrongs awakes Heaven,
  assaulting
The Oath-queen of Zeus, who with
  ropes all-prevailing
Carried her and brought her o'er
  star-litten water,
Wher the brine-mists hover o'er
  Pontus' Key,
Unto Hellas far over the boundless
  sea.

Enter MEDEA

  MEDEA. Corinthian dames, I have
    come out of my doors
Lest you condemn me. Many I know are held
Too proud--some, since they shrink from public gaze;
Some, from their bearing to their fellowmen;
Some quiet lives for laziness are talked about.
For justice lives not in the eyes of man,
Who, ere he hath looked into his neighbour's heart,

183

Hates him at sight, although nowise wrong
A stranger must conform to the city's habits.
Nor citizens uncondemned may so against their fellows,
Like mannerless bums, a law unto themselves.
But me--the blow you know of suddenly fell
Soul-shattering. 'Tis my ruin: I have lost
All grace of life: I long to die, O friends.
He, whom to serve well was my all in all,
My lord, of all men lowest has my become!
Surely, of creatures that have life and wit
We women are of all unhappiest,
Who, first, must buy, as buys the highest bidder,
A husband--nay, we do but win for our lives
A master! Deeper depth of wrong is this.
Here too is great risk--will the lord we gain
Be evil or good? Divorce?--'tis infamy
To us: we may not even reject a suitor?
Then, coming to new customs, habits new,
One need be a seer, to know the thing unlernt
At home, what manner of man her mate shall be.
And if we learn our lesson if our lord
Dwell with us, plunging not against the yoke,
Happy our lot is; else--no help but death
For the man, when the home-yoke galls his neck,
Goes forth, to ease a weary sickened heart
By turning to some friend, some kindred soul:
We to one heart alone cal look for comfort.
But we, say they, live an unperilled life
At home, while they do battle with the spear--
Unreasoning fools! Thrice would I under shield
Stand, rather than bear childbirth-peril once.
But ah, thy story is not one with mine!
Thine is this city, thine a father's home,
Thine bliss of life and fellowship of friends;
But I, lone, cityless, and outraged thus
Of him who kidnapped me from foreign shores,
Mother nor brother have I, kinsman none,
For port of refuge from calamity.
Wherefore I fain would win of thee this boon:--
If any path be found me, or device,
Whereby to avenge these wrongs upon mine husband,
On her who weds, on him who gives the bride,
Keep silence. Woman quails at every peril,
Faint-heart to face the fray and look on steel;

But when in wedlock-rights she suffers wrong,
No spirit more bloodthirsty shall be found.
   CHORUS. This will I; for it is right that you, Medea,
Pay back your lord: no marvel that you grieve.
But I see Creon, ruler of this land
Advancing, herald of some new law.

          ENTER CREON

   CREON. Black-lowering woman, angry against your lord,
Medea, forth this land I bid you go
An exile, taking your two sons with you
And make no delay: enforces of the law
Am I, and homeward go I not again
Ere from the land's bounds I have sent you forth.
   MEDEA. Ah me! undone am I in utter ruin!
My foes crowd sail pursuing: safe place
Is none from trouble and terror.
Yet, howso wronged, one question will I ask--
For what cause, Creon, do you exile me?
   CREON. I fear you--I don't need to hide my fears--
Lest you wreak cureless vengeance on my child.
And to this fear do many things came
Wise you are, cunning in much evil troubled
Of your husband angry you are bed bereft:
I hear thou threatenest, so they bring you word,
To wreak on sire, on bridegroom, on bride
Mischief. I guard mine head ere falls the blow.
Better be hated, woman now of thee,
Than once relent, and sorely groan too late.
   MEDEA. Not now first, Creon,--many a time before now
Rumour hath wronged and wrought me grievous harm.
Ne'er should the man whose heart is sound of wit
Let teach his sons more wisdom than the herd.
They are burdened with unprofitable lore,
And spite and envy of other folk they earn.
For, if thou bring strange wisdom unto dullards,
Useless shalt thou be counted, and not wise:
And, if thy fame outshine those heretofore
Held wise, thou shalt be odious in men's eyes.
Myself too in this fortune am partaker.
Of some my wisdom wins me jealousy,
Some count me spiritless; outlandish some;
Unsocial some. Yet no deep lore is mine.

And thou, thou fear'st me, lest I work thee harm.
Not such am I--O Creon, dread not me--
That against princes I should dare transgress.
How hast thou wronged me? Thou hast given thy child
To whomso pleased thee. But--I hate mine husband;
So, doubtless, this in prudence hast thou done.
Nay, but I grudge not thy prosperity.
Wed ye, and prosper. But in this your land
Still let me dwell: for I, how wronged soe'er,
Will hold my peace, o'ermastered by the strone.
    CREON. Soft words to hear!--but in thine inmost heart,
I fear, thou plottest mischief all the while;
And all the less I trust you than before.
The vehement-hearted woman--yea, or man--
Is easier watched-for than the silent-cunning.
Nay, set out with all speed: ask me no more.
For this is set: no device have you
To live with us, who are a foe to me.
    MEDEA (clasping his feet). Nay,--by
your knees, and by the bride, your child!
    CREON. You waste words; you never shall prevail.
    MEDEA. Wilt drive me forth, respecting not at all my
    prayers?
    CREON. Ay: more I love not you than mine own house.
    MEDEA. My country! O, I call you now to mind!
    CREON. Ay, next to my children, dear to me is Corinth.
    MEDEA. Alas! to mortals what a curse is love!
    CREON. Blessing or curse, I know, as fortune falls.
    MEDEA. Zeus, Zeus, forget not him who is cause of this!
    CREON. Hence, passionate fool, and rid me of my trouble.
    MEDEA. Troubled am I; new troubles need I none.
    CREON. Soon shalt you be by servants' hands out.
    MEDEA. Nay--nay--not this, O Creon, I beg you.
    CREON. So woman, you, it seems, will make trouble.
    MEDEA. I will flee forth:--not this the favor I ask.
    CREON. Why restive then? --why rid not Corinth of you
    MEDEA. Allow me yet to tarry this one day,
And somewhat for our exile to take thought,
And find my babes a refuge, since their father
Cares naught to make provision for his sons.
Compassionate Creon--a father too you are
Of children--it is proper for you to show them grace.
Not for myself I ask, if I be banished:
For them in their calamity I mourn.
    CREON. My spirit least of all is tyrannous.

Many a plan have my relentings ruined:
And, woman, now I know I am making a mistake.
Yet shall you win this favor. But I forewarn you
If you the approaching Sun-god's torch behold
Within this country's confines with thy sons,
You die: --the word is said that shall not lie.
Now, if remain you must, remain one day--
Too short for you to do the thing I dread

(EXIT.)

CHORUS. O hapless woman!
Woe's me for your misery, woe for the
    trouble and anguish that meet you!
Wither will you go?--what welcoming hand mid the
    strangers shall greet you?
What home or what land to receive you,
deliverance from evils to give you?
How mid surge of despair to o'erwhelm you in ruin
God's hand on your ship
Have steered, O Medea, your course!

MEDEA. Wronged--wronged by God and man! Who shall
    help?
But is it mere despair?--think not so yet.
Bridegroom and bride grim wrestlings yet await;
Nor troubles light await for these marriage-makers.
Do you think that I had begged from that man ever,
Except to gain some gain, or work some wile?
Nor word nor touch of hand had I saved him!
But to such height of folly has he come,
That, when he might forestall my every plot
By banishment, this day of grace he grants me
To stay, wherein three foes will make dead,
The father, and the daughter, and my husband.
And having for them many paths of death,
Which first to take in hand I know not, friends--
To fire yon palace midst their marriage feast,
Or to steal softly to their bridal-bed
And through their two hearts stick on sharp knife.
Yet one thing bars the way--if I am found
Crossing the threshold of the house and plotting,
Die shall I mid the mocking laughter of my foes.
Best the sure path, wherein my nature's cunning
Excels, by poisons to destroy them
Now, grant them dead: what city will receive me,

What host give me a land of refuge, a home
Secure, and from the avenger shield my life?
There is none. Wait then a little space,
If any tower of safety shall appear,
These deaths by guile and silence will I make happen.
But if misfortune drive me quickly forth,
Myself will grip the sword,--yea, although I die,--
And slay, and dare the strong and reckless deed.
Ah, by the Queen of Night, whom I love
Above all, and for fellow-worker chore,
Hecate, dweller by my fire's dark shrine,
None, none shall worry my soul, and not regret it.
Bitter and sorry wedding will I give them,
Bitter wedding-vows and the exile of me.
Up then! I won't forget any of my witches' tricks,
Of my knowledge of plotting of deceiving
On horrible deeds! Now is the time for daring.
Look at my wrongs. I must make trouble
For the sons of Sisyphus, for Jason's bride.
I know how to do it. I be a woman indeed.
Men say we women are not very good at doing good,
But that we are of evil deeds the best workers.
   CHORUS.
The sacred rivers are flowing upward and backwards to
   their fountains;
Justice has become injustice, the order of the world become
   confusion.
The dreams in the hearts of men are all evil only, and
   going
From the old foundations, and the old faith has become a
   delusion.
Everywhere, change: Even me shall men honor as a goddess!
My life shall be sunlit with glory; for woman the old story
Is ended, the nasty talk of the old days shall be chains upon
   women.
And the melody of the singers of the old times shall be heard
   no more,
For these songs were always of bad women, of their faithless-
   ness.
Alas, that our lips are not touched with the fire of song
   with the help
Of Phoebus, the Harper-king, of the inspiration-giver!
Else had I lifted my voice in challenge of song high-ringing
Unto men: for the roll of the ages shall find for the poet-
   sages
Proud woman-themes for their pages, heroines worthy their

singing.

But you from the ancient home did sail over miles of sea,
On-sped by a frenzied heart, and the seagates saw dispart,
The Twin Rocks. Now, in the land of the stranger, your
doom is to waken
To a widowed bed, and forsaken
Of your lord, and woe-overtaken,
To be cast forth shamed and banned.

Disannulled is the spell of the oath: no shame
  for the broken vow
In Hellas the wide do remain, but heavenward its flight
  hath it ta'en.
No home of a father have you for your haven when trouble-
  storms lower.
He has left your bed for that of another, in pride of her
  power,
Ill-starred, mocking you now.

ENTER JASON

  JASON. Not now first, nay, but oft-times have I noticed
What desperate mischief is a high tempered woman.
You might stay in Corinth, in these halls,
Bearing with a calm spirit your rulers' pleasure,
But for wild whirling words banished you are.
Me they vex not—cease never, if you wish,
Saying, "Jason is of men most evil!"
But, for your railing on your rulers, count it
All gain, that only exile punished you
For me—I have worked hard to ease the anger
Of kings: rather would I you should stay.
But you rein'st not your folly, speaking still
Evil of kings; you are therefore banished.
Yet, for all this, not wearied of my friends,
With so much forethought come I for
  you wife,
That, banished with your babes, you lack
  not gold,
Nor anything beside; for exile brings with it
Hardships full many. Though you hate me,
Never can I bear malice against you

MEDEA. Caitiff of caitiffs!--blackest of reproaches
My tongue for your unmanliness can frame--
You came to me most hateful proved
To heaven, to me, to all the race of men?
This is not daring, no, nor courage this,
To wrong your friends, and shrink not from their eyes,
But, of all plagues infecting men, the worst,
Is shamelessness. And yet 'tis well you came
For I shall ease the burden of my heart
Hating you, and you be angered to hear.
And with the first things first will I begin.
I saved you: this knows every son of Greece
That stepped with you aboard your Argo's ship,
You, sent to stop the flame-outbreathing bulls
With yoke-bands, and to sow the seeds of death.
The dragon, warder of the Fleece Gold,
That sleepless kept it with his many coils,
I killed, and raised deliverance for you.
Myself forsook my father and my home,
And I to Ioleos under Pelion came
With you, more zealous in you cause than wise.
Pelias I slew by his own children's hands--
Of all deaths worst,--and dashed the house to ruin.
Thus dealt with, basest of all men by me,
For a new bride have you forsaken me
Though I had borne you children
. If you were childless,
Not past forgiving were this marriage craving.
But faith of oaths have vanished
   I know not
Whether you think the olden Gods yet rule,
Or that new laws are now ordained for men;
For your heart speaks you unto me as a liar
Out on this right hand, which you aft would clasp,--
These knees!--I was polluted by the touch
Of a base man, thus frustrate of my hopes!
Come, as a friend will I commune with you
Yet what fair dealing should I hope for you?
Yet will I: questioned, baser shall you show
Now, whither turn I?--to my father's house,
My land?--which I betrayed, to flee with you
To Pelias' hapless daughters? Nicely
   Their father's killer they'd welcome home!

Their father's killer they'd welcome home!
For that's the way it is--I am now an enemy
To my own home! No argument did I have with those
With whom I have now a death-feud for your sake.
For all this have you made me very blessed
Among the daughters of Greece! Oh, in you have I--
O, miserable person I am--a devoted wife and partner,
Since from the country of my birth I went into exile,
Alone without friends, with my children alone,
A great recommendation for the new bridegroom, this--
"In poverty are his children, his wife a beggar!"
Oh, Zeus, why have you given to men
Plain sign to help us tell what is gold and what fool's gold.
But there are no marks by which women can tell what man is
  decent and what are not.
    CHORUS.
Terrible is your anger, and part all healing,
Terrible it is when those who once loved hate each other.

    JASON.
Many people have told me often that I have skill in speech
But it seems I cannot make myself clear to you.
You will not listen, but just let your foolish tongue
  run on.
This is how it was with us: it was Aphrodite,
Goddess of love who saved me. She forced you to
Do for me what you did, not you yourself. I
Do not like to say it, but you could not
Resirt what Aphrodite wanted you to do for me;
Therefore she deserves the credit for saving me, not you.
Yet take I not account too strict thereof;
For, in that you did save me, you did well.
Howbeit, more have you received than given
From my deliverance, as my words shall prove:--
First, then, in Hellas you now live, instead
Of land barbaric, know justice, learned
To live by law without respect of force;
And all the Greeks have heard wisdom's fame.
Renown is yours; but if on earth's far edge
You lived yet, you had not lived in story.
Now you are famous.
If my fair fortune be to fame unknown.
Thus far of my great labours have I spoken,--

This challenge to debate did you fling down:--
But, for your railings on my royal marriage,
Herein will I show, first, that wise I was;
Then,temperate; third, to you the best of friends
And to my children--nay, but hear me out.
When I came hither from Iolcos-land
With many a desperate fortune in my train,
What hapier treasure-trove could I have found
Than to wed--I, an exile--with a princess?
Not--where it galls you--that I leave your bed
And for a new bride smitten with desire,
Nor eager I to multiply my offspring:--
Enough are these born to me: no fault in them:
But that and this is my first goal--we might live in
    honour,
And be not poor,--for I know full well
How all friends from the poor man stand aloof,--
And I might nurture as is good for my house
Our sons, and to these born of your father
Brethren, and, knitting in one family all,
Live happy days. You, what would you of children?
But me if profits, through sons to be born
To help the living. Have I planned so ill?
Not you would say it, save for jealousy's sting.
But ye-ye women--so unreasoning are
That, if you get enough sex, all's well;
But, it once your sole tenure be infringed,
With the best, fairest lot are you at feud
Most bitter. Would that mortals otherwise
Could get them babes, that womankind were not,
And so no curse had been put upon men.
    CHORUS. Words, Jason, words, tricked out
full cunningly!
Yet to me--though I speak not to your mind--
Unjust you seem, betraying thus your wife.
    MEDEA. Nt as the world thinks think I;
Nay, to my thought, a villain's artful tongue
Doubles the hurt his villainy does to him:
So sure his tongue can gloze the wrong, he grows
Reckless in sin--a mere fool's wisdom this.
Then be not you, as touching me, fair-seeming
And crafty-tongued: one word shall overthrow you;
You should, were you not base, wed this bride

With my consent, not hid it from your friends.

JASON. Ay, this my purpose nobly have you helped.
Had I a marriage named, who even now
Can not refrain your heart's great anger!

MEDEA. Not this your problem but the alien wife.

JASON. Now know this well--not for the woman's sake
I wed the royal bride whom I have won.
But, as I said, of my desire to save you, and
Beget seed royal, to my sons
Brethren, and for mine house a tower of strength.

MEDEA. No prosperous life under sorrow's cloud for me,
Nor wealth, with thorns aye rankling my heart!

JASON. Do you know how to change your prayer, and wiser
show?
May your good never seem to you your grief;
Nor in fair fortune make your misfortune.

MEDEA. O yea, insult! You have a refuge by yourself.
But desolate I am banished from land.

JASON. Yourself have chosen this blame, none beside.

MEDEA. I?--in truth, by wedding and betraying thee!

JASON. By cursing princes with impious curse.

MEDEA. Ay--and to your house have you found me a curse!

JASON. With you no more I argue touching this.
But if, or for the children or yourself
For help in exile you will take my gold
Speak: ready am I to give with hand ungrudging,
And send guest-tokens which shall find you friends.
If you will not, foolish shall you be:
Forsake anger, and advantaged shall you be

MEDEA. Your friend!--nothing will I of friends of yours.
Nothing will I receive, nor offer you.
No profit is there in a villain's gifts.

JASON. In any case I call the Gods to witness
That all help would I give you and your sons;
But your good likes you not: your stubborn pride
Denies you friends: the more your grief shall therefore be.

MEDEA. Away!--impatience for the bride new-trapped
Consumes you loitering from her bed afar!
And: for maybe--and God shall speed the word--
Yours shall be bridal you will regret

CHORUS.
Love bring neither honour nor profit to men when it comes
inpart. Its unscanted excess: but if Aphrodite in measure
raining her joy, comes down, there is none other Goddess so

winsome as she.
Not upon me, O Queen, do you aim from your bow all-golden
The arrow desire-envenomed that none may avoid--not on me!

But let Temperance shield me, the fairest of gifts of the
Gods ever-living: nor ever with passion of jarring contention,
nor feuds unforgiving, in her terrors may Love's Queen visit
me, smiting with maddened unrest for a bed mismated my soul;
but the peace of the bride-bed be holden in honour of her,
and her keen eyes choose for us bonds that be best.
   O fatherland, O my home, not mine be the exile's doom!
Into poverty's pathways hard to be trod may my feet not be
   guided! Most piteous anguish were this. By death--O by
ere then may the conflict of life be decided, ended be
life's little day! To be thus from the home-land dived--
   No pang more bitter there is.

We have seen, and it needeth naught that of others
herein we be taught: for thee not a city, for thee not a
friend hath compassionated when affliction most awful
is thine. But he, who regardeth not friends, accursed
may he perish, and hated, who opes not his heart with
sincerity's key to the hapless-fated-- never such shall
be friend of mine.

                    ENTER AEGEUS

   AEGEUS. Medea, joy to you!--for fairer greeting
None know to meet his friends ever.
   MEDEA. Joy to you also, wise Pandion's son.
Where are you going through this land?
   AEGEUS. Leaving the ancient oracle of Phoebus.
   MEDEA. Why did you go to earth's prophetic navel?
   AEGEUS. To ask how I might have children.
   MEDEA. 'Fore Heaven!--aye childless is your life till
now?
   AEGEUS. Childless I am, by chance of some God's will.
   MEDEA. This, with a wife, or knowing not the bed?
   AEGEUS. Nay, not unyoked to wedlock's bed am I.
   MEDEA. Now what to you spake Phoebus about children?
   AEGEUS. Deep words of wisdom not for man to figure out.
   MEDEA. Might I know the God's reply?
AEGEUS. O yea--good sooth, it asks a wise wit to understand.
   MEDEA. What said he? Sav, if it is good for me to hear.

                        194

AEGEUS. "Loose not the wine-skin's forward-jutting foot"--
MEDEA. Till you should do what thing, or reach what land?
AEGEUS. "Till to the hearth ancestral back thou come."
MEDEA. And you, what would you sailing to this shore?
AEGEUS. There is one Pittheus, king of Troezen he,--
MEDEA. A man most pious, Pelops' son, they say.
AEGEUS. With him the God's response I wanted to talk.
MEDEA. Yea--a wise man, who has much skill therein.
AEGEUS. Yea, and my best beloved friend in war.
MEDEA. Now prosper you, and win your heart's desire.
AEGEUS. Why droops your eye?--why this pale color?
MEDEA. Aegeus, of all men basest is my husband.
AEGEUS. What do you say? Clearly tell me your heart's
    pain.
MEDEA. He wrongs me--Jason, never wronged by me.
AEGEUS. What has he done? More plainly tell it out.
MEDEA. Another wife he takes, his household's queen.
AEGEUS. Ha! hath he dared in truth this foul deed?
MEDEA. Yea: I am now dishonoured, once beloved.
AEGEUS. Another love was this?--or hate of you?
MEDEA. LOVE?--deep and high his love is!--traitor in love!
AEGEUS. Away with him, if he be evil as this!
MEDEA. His love was of being with princes.
AEGEUS. Who gives him his daughter? Tell me all.
MEDEA. Creon, who ruleth all Corinthian land.
AEGEUS. In truth, lady, reason was that you should
    grieve.
MEDEA. 'Tis death to me! Yea also am I banished.
AEGEUS. Of whom? A huge wrong you name now!
MEDEA. Creon from Corinth drives me an exile.
AEGEUS. Does Jason suffer this--I count it shame!
MEDEA. In pretence, no--yet O he bears it well!
But I beseech you, lo, your bearly touch,--
I clasp your knees, your suppliant as now:--
Pity, O pity me the evil-starred, and see me not cast forth
to homelessness:
Receive to a home in your palace.
So by heaven's blessing fruitful be love
In children, and in death yourself be blest.
You know not what good fortune you have found;
For I will end your childlessness, will cause
Your seed to grow to sons; such charms I know.
    AEGEUS. For many causes am I minded, lady,
This grace to grant you: for the God's sake first:

195

Then, for your promise of a seed of some
For herein Aegeus' name is like to die.
But thus it is--if to my land you come,
I will protect you all I can: my right is this;
but I forewarn you of one thine-- not from this land
to lead you I consent; If you reach of yourself my
halls safe shall you bide; to none will I yield thee.
But from this land you must yourself escape;
For even to strangers blameless will I be.
   MEDEA. So be it. Yet, were oath-pledge given for this
To me, then had I all I would to you.
   AEGEUS. Ha, you don't trust me?--or at what do you stumble?
   MEDEA. I trust you; but my foes are Pelias' house
And Creon. Oath-bound, you could never yield me
To these, when they would drag me from the land.
Had you but promised, to the Gods unpledged,
You might turn their friend, might lightly yield
To herald-summons. Strengthless is my cause:
Money is on their side, and a princely house.
   AEGEUS. Foresight exceeding, lady, in your words.
If this be your will, I draw not back.
Yes for myself is this the safest course,
To have a plea to show unto your foes;
And firmer stands your cause. The Oath-god's name.
   MEDEA. Swear by Earth's plain, and by my father's father,
The Sun, and join the Gods' whole race thereto.
   AEGEUS. That I will do or not do--what? Say on.
   MEDEA. Never yourself to cast me from your land.
Nor, if a foe of mine would hale me thence,
To yield me willingly up, while you do dost live.
   AEGEUS. By Earth, the Sun's pure majesty, and all
The Gods, I swear to abide by this you have said.
   MEDEA. Enough. For broken contrast what penalty?
   AEGEUS. The worst that scourges God-despairing men.
   MEDEA. Pass on your way rejoicing: all is well.
I too will come with all speed to your town;
When my intent is worked out, my wish attained.
                     (EXIT AEGEUS.)

   CHORUS. Now the son of Maia, the Wayfarer's King,
Bring you safe to your home, and the dream of your heart,
The sweet visions that wing your feet, may bring
To accomplishment, AEgeus, for now this thing
Has taught me how noble you are.

MEDEA. O Zeus, Zeus' daughter Justice, Light of the Sun!
Over my foes triumphant now, my friends,
Shall we become: our feet are on the path.
Now is there hope of vengeance on my foes.
For this man, there where my chief weakness lay,
Has for my plots a haven in storm appeared.
To him my ship's anchor make I fast,
To Pallas' home and fortress when I go.
And all my plots to you will I tell now;
Nor look I that my words should pleasure you:--
One of my household will I send to Jason,
And will ask him to my sight to come;
And soft words, when he comes, will I speak,
Saying, "Your will is mine, and, "It is well";
Saying his royal marriage, my betrayal,
Is good for us, and right well devised.
I will ask that my sons may stay--
Not for that I would leave on hostile soil
Children of mine for foes to trample on,
But the king's daughter so by lying to slay.
For I will send them bearing gifts in hand
Unto the bride, that my children may not be banished,
A robe fine-spun, a golden diadem.
If she receive and don my ornaments,
Die shall she horribly, and all who touch her;
With drugs so evil will I soak my gifts.
Howbeit here I pass this story by,
And wail the deed that yet for me remains
To bring to pass; for I will kill my children,
Yea, mine; no man shall pluck them from my hand.
Then, having brought all Jason's house to ruin,
I leave the land , fleeing my dear babes' blood
And having dared a deed most hideous.
For unbearable are mocks of foes.
Bt all go; what is life to me? Nor country
Nor home have I, nor refuge from mine ills.
I made my first mistake the day when I left
My father's house, by yon Greek's words decieved,
Who with God's help shall render me payment.
For never living shall he see henceforth
The sons I gave him, nor shall he beget
A son of his new bride, that girl destined
In agony to die by drugs of mine.
Let none account me impotent, nor weak,

Nor spiritless!--O nay, of other sort,
Grim to my foes, and kindly to my friends.
Most glorious is the life of such as I.
   CHORUS. Since you have made us partner of this tale,--
Wishing to help you, and yet loving
The laws of men, I say, do not do this.
  MEDEA. It cannot be but so: yet reason is
That you say this, who are not wronged as I.
   CHORUS. Woman, will you have the heart to slay your
     sons?
  MEDEA. Yea: so my husband's heart shall most be broken.
 CHORUS. But you of wives most wretched should become.
  MEDEA. So be it: wasted are all hindering words.
But ho! (ENTER NURSE) go you and Jason bring to me--
You whom I use for every deed of trust
And look you tell none anything of my intent,
If yours is loyal service, you a woman.
                 (EXEUNT MEDEA AND NURSE)

   CHORUS. O happy the race in ages past
Of Erechtheus, the seed of the Gods' line,
In a land unravaged, peacefully.
Þe drinking of Wisdom's glorius wine,
Ever though air clear-shining brightly
As on wings uplifted pacing lightly,
Where Harmonia, they tell, of the golden hair,
Åre the Pierid Muses, the stainless Nine.

And the streams of Cephisus the lovely flowing
They tell how Aphrodite drew,
And in Zephyr-winds sweet blowing
Breathed far over the land their dew
And she sends her Loves which throned in glory
By wisdom, fashion all virtue's story;
And over her hair is she throwing, throwing,
Roses in odorous wreathes aye new.

        RE-ENTER MEDEA

How then should the hallowed city,
The city of sacred waters,
Which shields with her guardian hand
All friends that would fare through her land,

Receive a murderess banned,
Who had slaughtered her babes without pity,
A pollution amidst of her daughters?
In thine heart's thoughts set it before you--
To murder the fruit of your womb!
O think what it means to slay your sons--what
a deed this day you would do! By your knees
we pray, by heaven and earth we ask you deal not to
your babes such a judgement.

What, oh, what will you gain by such desperate doings
That for spirit so fiendish shall serve,
That shall strengthen your heart, that shall nerve
Your hand, that it shall not swerve from the ruthless
deed that shall stain you with horror of children's blood?

O how, when your eyes you are turning on your little
ones, will you the motherhood in you to feel No upwelling
of tears? Can thou steel your breast when your children
kneel, bloody your hand, with unyearning heart for
your darlings killed?

ENTER JASON

  JASON. I at your bidding come: although my foe,
This grace you shall not miss; but I will hear
What new thing, lady, you wish of me.
  MEDEA. Jason, I ask you to forgive the words
Late-spoken. Well you may gently bear
With my wild mood, for all the old love's sake.
Now have I called myself to account, and railed
Upon myself--"idiot, why am I mad?
And why rage against good counsellors,
And am at feud with rulers of they land,
And with my lord, who works my truest good,
Wedding a royal house, to raise up brothers
Unto my sons? Shall I not cease from anger?
What is wrong with me, when the Gods give presents?
Have I not children? Know I not that we are exiles
from our own land, lacking friends?"
Thus thinking, was I aware that I had nursed
Folly exceeding, anger without cause.
Now then I praise you: wise you seem to me
In gaining us this kinship, stupid I,

Who in these plans should have been your friend,
Have furthered all, have decked the bridal bed,
And joyed to give help to the bride.
But we are--women: needs not harsher word.
Yet should you not for evil give back evil,
Nor pit against my folly folly of yours.
I yield, confessing mine stupidity then,
But unto better thoughts now am come.
Children, my children, come here; have the house;

ENTER CHILDREN

Come forth, greet your father, and with me
Bid him farewell: be reconciled to friends
You, with your mother, from the hate now healed
Truce is between us, hatred has given place.
Clasp you his right hand. Woe for ambushed ills!
I am haunted by the shadow of hidden things!
Ah children, will you thus, through many a year
Living, still reach him loving arms? Ah me,
How swift to weep am I, how full of fear!
Feuds with your father ended--ah, so late!--
Have filled with tears these soft-relenting eyes.
  CHORUS. And from my eyes start tears of pale surprize.
Ah, may no evil worse than this befall!
  JASON. Lady, I praise this mood, yet blame not that:
'Tis nothing strange that womanhood should rage
When the spouse move it into an alien marriage.
But now to better thoughts your heart hath turned.
And you, though late, have seen which policy
Must win: a prudent woman's part is this.
And for you, children, not unheedfully
Your father has taken much forethought, to help heaven.
For ye, I know, in this Corinthian land
Shall with your brothers stand the foremost yet.
Grow ye in strength: the rest shall by your father,
And whatso God is gracious, be given you.
You may I see to goodly stature grow
In manhood's prime, triumphant over my foes.
You, why with sad tears thus bedew your eyes,
Turning away from them your pale cheek?
Why bear you not with gladness my speech?
  MEDEA. 'Tis nothing; but over my children broods my heart.
  JASON. Fear not: all will I order well for them.

MEDEA. I will be brave--will not mistrust your words;
But woman is but woman--born for tears.
   JASON. Why hapless one, do you sigh over these?
   MEDEA. I bare them. When you prayed life for them,
Pity stole o'er me, whispering, "Shall this be?"
But that for which you came to speak of me
In part is said; to speak the rest is mine.
Since the king pleaseth forth the land to send me,--
Yea, for me too 'tis best, I know it well
That I bide not, a stumbling block to you
And the land's lord, whose house's foed seem,--
Lo, from this land I go to exile.
But, that my sons by your body may be raised,
I ask you Creon that they be not exiled too.
   JASON. Prevail I may not, yet I must try.
   MEDEA. Nay then, your bride bid them to pray her father
That your sons be not banished from the country.
   JASON. Yea surely; and, I know her shall I win.
   MEDEA. If of her sister women she is one.
I too will bear a part in your attempt;
For I will and her gifts better far
In beauty sanything in these days seen, I know,
A robe fine-spun, a golden diadem;
Our sons to bear them. Now must an attendant
With all speed hither bring the ornaments. (HANDMAID GOES.)
Lucky things shall hers be, not one, but untold,
Who wins you for a husband, a wonderful spouse,
Who owns ornaments which once the Sun,
My father's father, to his offspring gave!

                ENTER HANDMAID WITH BOX

Take in your hands, my sons, these bridal gifts,
And to the happy princess-bride bear you
And give--my gifts she shall not lightly value!
   JASON. But, fond one, why give away these?
Do you think a royal house has lack of robes,
Or gold? Keep these and give them not.
For, if my wife loves me at all, my wish
Will she prefer to treasure, wll I know.
   MEDEA. Nay, speak not so: gifts sway the Gods, they say.
Gold weigheth more with men than countless words.
She's the lucky one; God favours now her cause--
Young and a queen! Life would I give for ransom

                          201

Of my sons' banishment, not gold alone.
Now, children, enter you the halls of wealth.
Unto your father's new wife, my lady-queen,
Beg to enter, pray you be not exiled.
And give my presents--most important this,
That she in her own hands receive my gifts.
Haste ye, and to your mother bring glad tidings
Of good success in that she longs to win.   (EXEUNT JASON
                                                AND CHILDREN)
    CHORUS.   Now for the life of the children my hope hath
    been turned to fear.
No hope any more!   On the slaughterward path even now are
    they going.
The bride shall receive it, the diadem-garland that
    carries folded
Doom for the unlucky mid glittering sheen:
And to set the adorning of Hades about her curls
She shall take it her hands between.
For its glamour of beauty, its splendour unearthly, shall
    swiftly persuade her
To bedeck her with robe and with gold crown; she shall soon
    have arrayed her
In attire as a bride in the presence of phantoms from Hades
    uprisen; In such dread shall the hapless be whelmed, and
    from Doom's dark prison
Shall she steal forth never again.
And you sad bridegroom accurst, who are thinking of princely
    alliance,
Blasting you bringest--unknowing, unthinking!--
Of life on your sons, and your bride shall to foul death
    say her marriage vows
How far from your fortune of old are you sinking!
And amidst my lamenting I mourn for your anguish,
O hapless mother
Of children, who make you ready to slaughter
Your babes, to avenge you on him who whould lawlessly wed
    with another,
Would forsake you to live with a prince's daughter.

            ENTER CHILDREN'S GUARDIAN, WITH CHILDREN

    CHILDREN'S GUARDIAN.   Mistress, remission for your sons
    of exile!
Your gifts the princess-bride with joy received

In hand; and there is peace unto your sons.
Ha!
Why do you stand confounded mid good luck?
Now wherefore turn you your face away,
And do not hear with gladness this my speech?
  MEDEA. Wo's me!
  CHILDREN'S GUARDIAN. Can I have brought ill news
Unwitting--erred in thinking these glad tidings?
  MEDEA. As they are, are your tidings: you I blame not.
CHILDREN'S GUARDIAN. Why down-drooped is your eye? Why
  flow your tears?
  MEDEA. I must say, old friend, for these things the Gods
And I withal--O fool!--have put together poorly.
  CHILDREN'S GUARDIAN. Fear not: your children yet shall
  bring you home.
  MEDEA. Others before then shall I send home--ah me!
  CHILDREN'S GUARDIAN. Not you alone art separated from
  your sons.
Submissively must mortals bear sorrows.
  MEDEA. This will I: but within the house go you,
And for my children's daily needs prepare.
                     (EXIT CHILDREN'S GUARDIAN.)
O children, children, yours a city is,
And yours a home, where, forgetting poor me,
You shall abide, for ever motherless!
I shall go exiled to another land,
Ere I have joyed in you, have seen your bliss,
Ere I have decked for you the bed, the bride,
The bridal bower, and held the torch on high.
O me accurst in this my desperate mood
For nothing for nothing, my babes, I nurtured you,
And all for nothing I laboured, travl-worn,
Bearing sharp anguish in your hour of birth.
Ah for the hopes--unhappy!--all my hopes
Of helping hands about my time
Of dying folded round with loving arms
All men's desire! But now--'tis past--'tis past,
That sweet imagining! Forlorn of you
A bitter life and woeful shall I waste.
Your mother never more with loving eyes
Shall you behold, passed to another life.
Woe! woe! why gaze your eyes on me my darlings?
Why smile to me the latest smile of all?
Alas! what shall I do? My heart is falling

As I behold the light in my sons' eyes!
Women, I cannot! farewell, purposes
O'erpast! I take my children from this land.
What need to sting their father's heart with ills
Of these, to gain myself ills twice so many?
Not I, not I! Ye purposes, farewell!
Yet--yet--what ails me? Would I make a fool of myself,
Letting my foes slip from my hand unpunished?
I must dare this. Away with my coward mood
That let words of relenting touch my heart!
Children, pass yet within.
Sinless be present at my sacrifice,
On his head be it: my hand stops not.
Oh! oh!
O heart, my heart, do not--do not this deed!
Let them be, sorrowful heart, spare you my babes!
There living with me shall they gladen you, my heart.
No! by the hellish fiends that dwell with Hades,
Now shall this betide, that I will leave
My children for my foes to trample on!
They must die. And, since it must be,
Only I will kill them, I, who gave them life.
If this is simple fate:--she shall not 'scape!
Yes, on her head the diadem is: in my robes
The princess-bride is dying--I know it!
But--for I so on journey must unhappy,
And shall speed these on one yet unhappier--
I would speak to my sons.

RE-ENTER CHILDREN

Give, O my babes, Give to your mother the right hand
    to kiss.
O dearest hand, O lips most dear to me,
O form and noble feature of my children,
Blessings be on you--there!--for all things here
Your father has stolen. Sweet, O sweet embrace!
O children's roseleaf skin, O balmy breath!
Away, away! I have no strength to look
On you, but I am overcome of evil   (EXEUNT CHILDREN.)
Now, now, I learn what horrors I intend:
But passion overmasters sober thought;
And this is cause of all ills to men.

CHORUS. Full oft before this my soul has scaled
Lone heights of thought, empyreal steeps,
Or plunged far down the darkling deeps,
Where woman's feebler heart hath failed:--
Yet why failed? Should woman find
No inspiration thrill her breast,
Nor welcome ever that sweet guest
Of song, that sings Wisdom"s mind?
Alas! not all! Few, few, are they,--
Perchance amid a thousand one
You shouldest find,--for whom the sun
Of poetry makes an inner day.
Now this I say--calm bliss, that ne'er
Knew love's wild fever of the blood,
The pains, the joys, of motherhood,
Passeth all parents' joy-blent care.
The childless, they that never prove
If sunshine comes, or cloud, to men
With babes--far lie beyond their ken
The toils, the griefs, of parent-love.
But they whose halls with little babies sweet
Of childhood bloom--I mark them aye
Care-fretted, working always
To win their loved ones needed food.
One toils with love more strong than death:
Yet--yet--who knows whether he
A wise man or a fool shall be
To whom he shall his money give?
But last, but worst, remains to tell:
For though you get you wealth enough
And though your sons to manhood grow,
Fair sons and good;--if Death
To Hades vanishing, bears down
Your children's lives, what profit is
That Heaven hath laid, with all else, this
Upon mankind, this worst of all sorrows?
  MEDEA. Friends, long have I, waiting to see what
  happened,
Expected what from yonder shall befall.
And lo, a man I see of Jason's train
Hitherward coming: his wild-fluttering breath
Shows him the hearald of strange ills.

ENTER MESSENGER

MESSENGER. O you who has done an awful deed and lawless,
Run, O Medea, run, nor once leave
The ship, or the carriage that moves across the plain.
     MEDEA. Now what has happened that calleth for such flight?
     MESSENGER. Dead is the princess even now, and dead
Creon her father, by your poison-drugs
     MEDEA. A glorious tale you tell henceforth
Are you of my benefactors and my friends.
     MESSENGER. What say'st? Of sound mind are you, and
     not mad,
Who, hearing of the havoc of the hearth
Of kings, all glad, and have no fear in this?
     MEDEA. O yea: I too with words of argument
Could answer you:--yet, don't worry, friend,
But tell how died they: you shall make me happy
Doubly, if these most horribly have died.
     MESSENGER. When, with their father came your children,
And passed into the halls, for marriage decorated,
Glad were we slaves who sorrowed in your woes;
And straightway buzzed from ear to ear the tale
Of truce to old feuds between your husband and you.
One kissed the hand, and one the golden head
Of those your sons: myself by joy moved
Followed your children to the princess' room.
Ere she beheld your two sons
Upon Jason turned her yearning look.
But then before her eyes she cast the veil,
And swept aback the scorn of her white neck,
Hating your sons' approach; but your husband
To turn the maiden's anger and spite aside,
Thus spoke: "Nay, be not hostile to your friends:
Cease from your anger, turn your head again,
Accounting friends whomso your husband says is a friend
Their gifts receive, and ask your father
To pardon these their exile--for my sake.
Then when she saw the attire, she could not hold back
But yielded her lord all. And before their father
For from her room with those your sons had gone,
She took the rich-made robes and clad herself,
Putting on her head the golden crown,
And by a shining mirror ranged her hair,
Smiling at her own phantom image there.

206

Then, rising from her seat, down the halls
She walked on with ivory feet,
Happy in the gifts, and oftentimes
Moving her glance from neck to ankle-hem.
But then was there a horrid sight to see.
Suddenly changed her colour: reeling back
With trembling limbs she goes; and scarce in time
Falls on the bed to fall not on the ground.
Then a grey handmaid, thinking perhaps
That frenzy was of Pan or some God sent,
Raised the prayer-cry, before she saw the foam
White frothing from her lips, or marked how rolled
Her eyeballs, and her face's bloodless color;
Then a long cry of horror, not of prayer,
She sent forth. Straight to her father's chambers the maid
Hurried, and unto her new-made spouse,
To tell the bride's pains; all the room
Sounded with multitudinous-hurrying feet.
And a swift athlete's straining limbs had paced
By this the full length of the long course,
Then she from trance all speechless of closed eyes
In anguish woke with horrible-shrilling shriek;
For like two charging horses her torment came:--
The golden crown that on her head she had
'Can spurt a marvellous stream of ravening fire:
The delicate robes, the gift your children brought,
Had fangs to gnaw her delicate tortured flesh!
Upstarting from her seat she flees, all flame,
Shaking her hair, her head, this way and that,
To cast from her the crown; but firmly fixed
The gold held fast its grip: the fire, whene'er
She shook her locks, with doubled fury blazed.
Then by pain overcome, falls she on the floor,
Marred past all knowledge, save for a father's eyes.
No more was seen her eyes' Queenly calm,
No more her comely features; but the gore
Dripped from her head's crown flecked with blended fire.
The flesh-flakes from her bones, like the pine's tears,
'Neath that mysterious drug's devourings melted,--
Horrid sight! and came on all folk fear to touch
The corpse: her hideous fate had frightened us very much.
But, ignorant of all, her poor father,
Suddenly entering, falls upon her corpse,
And straightway wailed and clasped the body round,

And kissed it, crying, "O my poor child,
What God thus horribly has wounded you?
Who makes my old soul give up
My child? Ah, me would I might die with you!"
But when from wailing and from groans he ceased,
He would have liked to upraise his aged frame,
Yet stuck, as ivy sticks to laurel trees,
To the robes: then was a ghastly wrestling;
For, while he strained to upraise his knee, she seemed
To upwrithe and grip him; if by force he try to set free,
Torn from the very bones was his old flesh.
Life's light at last put out, he gave up the ghost.
Ill-starred, down-sinking 'neath destruction's sea.
There lie the corpses, child by grey old father
Hugged;--such horror tears, not words, must mourn.
And of your part no word be said by me:--
Yourself from punishment will find escape.
But man's lot now, as oft, I count a shadow,
Nor fear to say that such as seem to be
In mind most keen of men, most subtle of speech,
Even these pay heaviest penalty of all;
For among mortals happy man is none.
In fortune's flood-tide might a man become
More prosperous than his neighbor: happy?--no!   (EXIT.)
   CHORUS. Fortune, it seems, with many an ill this day
Does catch Jason,--yea, and rightfully.
But O the pity of your calamity,
Daughter of Creon, who to Hades' halls
Has passed because with you would Jason wed!
   MEDEA. Friends, my oath is taken, with all speed
To kill my children, and to leave this land,
And not to linger and to give up my sons
To death by other hands more mercyless.
They must die: and, since it must be so,
I will give them death who gave them life.
Up, get ready to kill,
Why loiter
To do the evil deeds that must be done.
Come, horrid hand of mine, the sword;
Grasp!--on to the starting-point of a hated life!
Oh, turn not coward--think not on your babes,
How dear they are, how you did bear them: nay,
For this short day you must forget your sons,
Thereafter mourn them. For although you kill them,

Yet dear they are, and I--am sorrowful!   (EXIT MEDEA.)
CHORUS. O Earth, O all showing splendour
Of the Sun, look down on a woman damned,
Or ever she get rid of the blood thirst
Of a mother whose hands would kill the tender
Fruit of her womb.
Look down, for she sprang of the Sun;s golden family.
Men's vengeance threatens--she's in trouble.
But Sun, O heaven-begotten flory,
Restrain her, refrain her: the gory, the horrid,
Erinys by demons dogged. we ask you
Snatch her from yon home!
For nothing was the childbirth-pain wasted;
For nothing di you bear them, the near and the dear,
Others who have fled through the Pass of Fear,
From the dark-blue Clashing Crags who have run.
Alas for her!--wherefore hath grim anger stirred her
Though depths of her soul, that ruthless murder
Her wrongs must pay for
Too hard upon mortals the vengeance falls
For human blood spilt; from the earth it calleth,
A voice from the Gods, and teh killers worry
On whose homes it shall light.
        (CHILDREN'S CRIES BEHIND THE SCENES.)
  CHILD 1. What shall I do?--how flee my mother's hands?
  CHILD 2. I know not, dearest brother. Death is here!
  CHORUS. Ah the cry!--do you hear it?--the children's cry!
Horrors!--woman of cursed destiny!
Shall I enter? My heart crieth, "Rescue the children from
  murder!"
        (THEY BEAT AT THE BARRED DOORS.)
  CHILD 1. Help!--for the God's sake help! Great is our
  need!
  CHILD 2. The sword's death-net is closing round us now!
        (SILENCE WITHIN. BLOOD FLOWS OUT BENEATH THE DOOR.
        THE WOMEN SHRINK BACK.)
  CHORUS. Witch! of what rock is your heart?--of what steel
  is the heart inside you made?
That the babes you have borne, with the selfsame hands that
  with love have enfolded
These, you have set yourself to kill?
Of one have I heard that laid hands on her loved ones of
  old, one only,
Even Ino distraught of the Gods, when

209

Zeus' bride drove her, lonely
And lost, from her home to stray;
And she fell--ah wretch!--on the brink as she stood
Of the sea-scaur: guilt of children's blood
Dragged downwards her feet to the salt sea-flood,
And she died with her two children
What ghastlier horror remains to be done?
O bride-bed of women, with anguish overrun
What horrors upon mortals before now have you brought,
What hideous things.

ENTER JASON, WITH SERVANTS

    JASON. Women, which stand close to this roof--
Is she within the halls, she who has done these
Deeds, Medea, or in flight passed thence?
For either must she hide her 'neath the earth,
Or lift on wings her frame to heaven's far depths,
Or taste the vengeance of a royal house.
How, trusts she, having murdered the land's lords.
Unpunished herself from these halls forth to flee?
Yet not for her care I, but for her sons,
Whom she has wronged shall repay her wrong:
But I to save my children's life am come,
Lest to my grief the kinsmen of the dead
Take out on them their mother's impious murder.
    CHORUS. Poor man, you know not how deep you are sunk in sorrow,
Jason, or you wouldn't say such words.
    JASON. What now?--and is she going to kill me too?
    CHORUS. Your sons are dead, slain by the mother's hand.
    JASON. Ah me!--what are you saying?
You have killed me, woman!
    CHORUS. Your children are no more: so think of them.
    JASON. How?--Killed them? Where--within, without, the halls?
    CHORUS (pointing to pavement before doors). Open, and you
Shall see your children's corpses.
    JASON. Burst in the bolts with all speed, serving-men--
Force hinges!--let me see this twofold horror,--
The dead, and her,--and in her blood avenge me!

MEDEA APPEARS ABOVE THE PALACE ROOF IN A CHARIOT
DRAWN BY DRAGONS

MEDEA. Why do you shake these doors and try to enter,
Seeking your dead and me who did the deed?
Stop trying. If you want anything of me,
Say what you want: your hand shall touch me never.
Such chariot has my father's father, the Sun,
Given me, a defence from foeman's hand.
  JASON. O thing abhorred! O woman hatefullest
To Gods, to me, to all the race of men,
You that could thrust the sword into the babes
You save life, and me have made a childless ruin!
Thus have you done, yet look you on the sun
And earth, who has dared a deed most hideous?
Now ruin seize you!--clear I see, who saw not
Thee, when from halls and land barbarian
To a Greek home I bare thee, utterance,
Traitress to sire and land that nurtured thee!
Thy guilt's curse-bolt on me the Gods have launched;
For thine own brother by his hearth thou slewest
Ere thou didst enter fair-pprowed Argo's hull.
With such deeds thou beganest. Wedded then
To this man, and the mother of my sons,
For wedlock-right's sake hast thou murdered them.
There is no Grecian woman that had dared
This:--yet I stooped to marry thee, good sooth,
Rather than these, a hateful bride and fell,
A tigress, not a woman, harbouring
A fiercer nature than Tyrrhenian Scylla
But--for untold revilings would not sting
Thee, in thy nature is such hardihood:--
Avaunt, thou miscreant stained with thy babes' blood!
For me remains to wail my destiny,
Who of my new-wed bride shall have no joy,
And to the sons whom I begat and nurtured
Living I shall not speak--lost, lost to me!
  MEDEA. I might have lengthened out long controversy
To these thy words, if Father Zeus knew not
How I have dealt with thee and thou with me.
'Twas not for thee to set my rights at naught,
And live a life of bliss, bemocking me,
Nor for thy princess, and thy marriage-kinsman.
Creon, unscathed to banish me this land!

211

Wherefore a tigress call me, an' thou wilt,
Scylla, haunter of Tyrrhenian shore;
For thine heart have I wrung, as well behoved.
   JASON, Ha, but thous sorrowest too, dost share mine
Ills!
   MEDEA. O yea: yet grief is gain, so thou laugh not.
   JASON. O children mine, what miscreant mother had ye!
   MEDEA. O sons, destroyed by your own father's lust!
   JASON. Sooth, 'twas no hand of mine that murdered them.
   MEDEA. Nay, but thine insolence and thy new-forged bonds.
   JASON. How, claim the right for wedlock's sake to slay
Them!
   MEDEA. A light affliction count'st thou this to a wife?
   JASON. A virtuous wife:--in thy sight naught were good!
   MEDEA. These live no more: this, this shall cut thine
Heart!
   JASON. They live--ah me!--avengers on thine head.
   MEDEA. The Gods know who began this misery.
   JASON. Yea, verily, thy spirit abhorred they know.
   MEDEA. Abhorred art thou: I loathe thy bitter tongue.
   JASON. And I thine:--yet were mutual riddance easy.
   MEDEA. How then?--what shall I do?--fain would I this.
   JASON. Yield me my dead to bury and bewail.
   MEDEA. Never: with this hand will I bury them,
To Mountain Hera's precinct bearing them,
That never foe may do despite to them,
Rifling their tomb. This land of Sisyphus
Will I constrain with solemn festival
And rites to atone for this unhallowed murder.
But I--I go unto Erechtheus' land,
With Ægeus to abide, Pandion's son.
You, as is right, foul man, shall foully die,
By Argo's wreckage smitten on the skull;
Who hast seen this new bridal's bitter ending.
   JASON. Now the Fury-avenger of children strike you.
And Justice that looks on murder pay you!
   MEDEA. What God or what spirit will listen to you?
Who betrays the guest?
   JASON. Get out lying bastard, foul thing by whose deed
Your children have died!
   MEDEA. Go hence to thy halls, thence lead to the grave of
Your bride!
   JASON. I go, a father forlorn of the two sons reft from
His home!

MEDEA.   Not yet do you truly mourn: abide till your old
Age come.
   JASON.   O children beloved above all!
   MEDEA.   O their mother beloved, not of you.
   JASON.   Yet she killed them!
   MEDEA.   That you might fall in the net that you spread for
me.
   JASON.   Woe's me! I yearn with my lips to press
My sons' dear lips in my hopelessness.
   MEDEA.   Ha, now you are calling upon them, now would you
Kiss, who rejected them then?
   JASON.   For the God's sake grant me but this,
The sweet soft flesh of my children to feel!
   MEDEA.   No--wasted in air is all your begging.
   JASON.   O Zeus do you hear it, how spurned I am?--
What outrage I suffer of yonder hatred
Child-murderess, yonder tigress-dam?
Yet out of mine helplessness, out of my shame,
I bewail my beloved, I call to record
High heaven, I bid God witness the word,
That my sons you have killed and withhold me,
That mine hands may not touch them, nor bury their clay!
Would God I had gotten them never, this day
To behold them destroyed of thee!
   CHORUS.   All dooms be of Zeus in Olympus; 'tis his to
Reveal them. Manifold things unhoped-for the Gods to
Accomplishment bring.
And the things that we looked for, the Gods deign not to
Fulfil them;
And the path undiscerned of our eyes, the Gods unseal them.
So fell this marvelous thing.   (EXEUNT OMNES.)

THE PELOPONNESIAN WAR, 431-404 B.C.

The Peloponnesian War which began in 431 B.C. is known to us in great detail through the writings of Thucydides. Thucydides was an unsuccessful Athenian general in the early years of the conflict. He was sent into exile as punishment for failure and there devoted himself to writing a history of the war. Thucydides did not use the term Peloponnesian War, but that is what we have come to call it. There were, in fact, two distinct wars, separated by the Peace of Nicias (421 B.C.). Broadly, the conflict was between Athens and its Confederation of Delos, with a few allies on the mainland, and Sparta and its allies, including most of the Peloponnesus and some areas north of the isthmus, among them Boeotia and Phocis. Few places in the Greek world were neutral.

431-421 B.C.

The very first stages of the war made it clear that the conflict would be a strange one. Pericles decided not to try to match or to challenge the Spartan army. This decision was never reversed. As a result, Athens could do little more than raid along the coast of the Peloponnesus or mount campaigns against Sparta's allies. Sparta, lacking a navy, was similarly unable to deliver any great blow against Athenian power, which rested upon the Athenian fleet. This tended to produce a stalemate, a situation which was not altered until Sparta finally made the decision to build up its power at sea.

In the first year of the war, the Spartan army ravaged Attica, destroying the spring grain crop. With the Athenian army incapable of matching the Spartans, the population of Attica took refuge in Athens and between the walls which connected Athens to the Piraeus. For Athens, this was embarrassing, but no more than that. Athens had the strength at sea to ensure itself a supply of food from abroad. At the end of the year, the Spartans withdrew for the winter. Pericles delivered the famous Funeral Speech in praise of the Athenian style and spirit. We have this from Thucydides; it is often used as an example of what the Athenian democracy was about.

214

The Spartans came again in the spring of 430 B.C.
This time, the crowded population within the walls at
Athens was swept by a disease of some kind which is usually
called the plague (the Spartans escaped). The humiliation
and the suffering produced a reaction against Pericles.
He was deposed briefly as general in 430 B.C. Soon, however, he was restored, only to die, of natural causes, in
429 B.C. His two legitimate sons had died in the plague,
so the Assembly, anxious to show that it honored his
memory, legitimized his bastard by Aspasia. No figure
of comparable stature could be found to take the place of
Pericles.

The Spartan army occupied Attica in five of the first
seven years of the war, forcing the population to live
within the city from spring to fall. The Spartans did
little else for several years, however, lacking both the
means and the inclination to tackle Athens at sea. They
ignored the opportunity to support the rebellions which
soon broke out among the unhappy "allies" of Athens across
the Aegean. The war revealed how unpopular the Confederation of Delos was with many of its members. In 428 B.C.
almost the entire island of Lesbos revolted, under the
leadership of Mytilene. The island was captured by Athens
the following year. By order of the Assembly at Athens,
the adult male population of Mytilene was killed, with the
women and the young being made slaves. The land was given
to Athenian "colonists"--who were allowed to stay at Athens
and lease it out. Increasingly, both sides engaged in acts
of this kind.

Having much the largest navy available, the Athenians
could maintain their hold upon the Confederation and at the
same time engage in raids upon the Peloponnesus and larger
attacks upon Sparta's allies. From 429 to 426 B.C. this
fighting centered upon Corcyra and the north shore of the
Gulf of Corinth. The Athenians triumphed repeatedly at
sea and scored some successes on land; here, too, there
was a great deal of nastiness in the fighting on both sides.
The Athenians produced no great general; Demosthenes, the
leading military figure on their side, does not seem to
have amounted to much.

These Athenian successes in the west came to a climax
in 425 B.C., when Pylos in Spartan territory in the southern
Peloponnesus was captured. Rebelling Messenians helped in
this victory. In thanks to the gods, the Messenians
dedicated at Olympia a famous statue of Victory by Paeonius,
in which Victory is seen in the air, with an eagle below
her. The Greek world was stunned by the surrender at
Pylos of 300 Spartan soldiers, including 120 Spartan
citizens. Men wondered what the world was coming to when
Spartans were not ready to die. The Athenians cleverly
kept the prisoners as hostages: one immediate result was
that the Spartan army stopped occupying Attica on its
spring jaunts. Little else came out of the victory for
Athens, though. In 424 B.C., made rash by success, the
Athenians attacked the Spartan ally, Boeotia, a rare
venture into large-scale land fighting. The Athenians were
defeated at Delium. Elsewhere, too, things were going
badly. In 425 B.C. Sparta had sent a general, Brasidas, to
attack the Athenian allies along the coast of Thrace. The
army Brasidas took with him contained some helots, but no
full Spartan citizens. Over the next three years (425-422
B.C.), Brasidas did very well, establishing himself as the
major military talent produced by the war so far. It was
against Brasidas that poor Thucydides failed.

The military situation slightly favored the Spartans,
but the desire of the latter to obtain the release of the
hostages from Pylos counted for something too. A one-year
truce arranged in 423 B.C. broke down in Thrace, where
Sparta hoped for further advantage. Brasidas won more
victories, but his death in battle in 422 B.C. cleared the
way for an end to the fighting. This came with the Peace
of Nicias of 421 B.C., which was supposed to last for 50
years. Generally, both sides went back to what they had
had before the war; the Spartans also got the hostages
from Pylos back.

The fighting may have been inconclusive, but the effect
on Athens had been substantial. The countryside was devastated, the income from the allies made undependable. Above
all, perhaps, Athens was damaged in its sense of self-
esteem, experiencing a great let-down after the wonders of
the Age of Pericles. One development of these years in
Athens which drew much attention at the time, and which may

have been linked to the pressures of the decade, was the emergence of a new kind of leadership. New men came to power, men who were wealthy but who were not aristocrats. These men were disliked by many in the aristocracy and the intelligentsia (the thinking classes, men such as the philosophers and the writers), who saw them as the wrong "types." To explain how such men flourished without inherited privilege, it became common to accuse them of corruption and lack of principle, a willingness to promise and to do anything to stay in power. Thucydides and the comedy writer Aristophanes are two of our major (and critical) sources of information about these men. In addition to the perils of the war years, the emergence of such types is likely to have been encouraged by the death of Pericles, which created something of a vacuum. For us, in a more general way, such men are an inevitable product of a democracy which lasts for any length of time; it seems natural to us that in such a system the aristocracy will lose power as the citizens gain in self-assurance and show a preference for men with a more "common" touch. The success of Pericles, a most skillful aristocrat, may have held such men back before 430 B.C., but during the Peloponnesian War it was more reasonable to criticize the aristocratic leadership which had produced the war.

The outstanding example of these new men in the 420's B.C. is CLEON, who came from a family of leather-merchants. Cleon won prominence as a leader in the Assembly; he was not a military figure like many of the old leaders (even Pericles had campaigned personally). He did, however, consistently support a vigorous war effort, something which was very much in the tradition of Athenian "reformers."

In 428 B.C., allegedly at Cleon's urging, Athens introduced a special war tax on all property of all citizens except the poor. With expenses up, and income from the allies perhaps less available, there may have been little alternative to such a tax. The idea of exempting the poor seems in no way objectionable to us. The normal absence of such a tax, and the way in which its introduction at this time was criticized as an attack upon the "better" elements in Athens, indicate the strength of the "oligar-chic" element in the democracy. Similar criticism greeted Cleon's leadership in 425 B.C. in raising the pay for

citizens on the juries from 2 obols to 3 obols. This looks
like the sort of "bribe" that Pericles had been accused of.
It may not have been much more than an attempt to protect
the poorer citizens from the inflation brought on by the
war and the loss of income from the farms.

The desire to push on with the war and to maintain
the income from the allies led Cleon to adopt a harsh
attitude toward the members of the Confederation of Delos.
In 427 B.C., he is said to have been responsible for the
Assembly's vote to wipe out the entire population of rebel
Mytilene. The Assembly soon altered its mind, limiting the
murders, as we have seen, to the adult male population.
Thucydides tries very hard to make Cleon look bad in this
episode. He attributes the Assembly's change of mind to a
speech of one Diodotus, who argued that good sense and self-
interest demanded that Athens go easy with Mitylene, in
order to please the other allies. Thucydides is much
attracted at all times to this kind of "cleverness." His
version of the episode gives him a wonderful opportunity to
criticize Cleon for mixing cruel barbarism with stupidity.
In fact, of course, Mitylene hardly got off easy. Apart
from the massacres, the island was turned into an Athenian
colony. Athenians were sent out there to live in ease off
the rents from the inhabitants who were allowed to go on
working the land.

In 425 B.C., with similar harshness, Cleon greatly
increased the tribute demanded by Athens of its allies. It
was easy to claim that this kind of thing caused more
trouble with the allies than it was worse. The increased
tribute also coincided suspiciously with the increased
payment to the juries. Aristophanes, the writer of comedies,
seized on this, accusing Cleon at once of stupidity and
double corruption--corruption in bribing the citizens,
corruption in accepting payments from allies in order to
"fix" their assessments. Cleon hauled Aristophanes into
court.

That year, 425 B.C., was Cleon's finest. He took his
first military command and managed to produce the capture
of Pylos and the Spartan surrender. Thucydides makes fun
even of this, claiming that Cleon was really a coward and
that he was tricked into taking the command by his enemies,
who called his bluff when he was criticizing the generals
for their efforts.

Cleon's luck turned sour the following year, when the invasion of <u>Boeotia</u> failed. He lost favor for a while. He came back into the limelight in 422 B.C., when the war picked up again after the short-lived truce of 423 B.C. He was sent with an expedition to <u>Thrace</u>. Cleon failed against Brasidas, and he got himself killed, but the death of the Spartan general at the same time cleared the way for the Peace of Nicias of 421 B.C.

This peace was named for the man chiefly responsible for it. <u>Nicias</u> was the leader of the conservative "aristocratic" opposition to Cleon. He had a good popular touch and a reputation for integrity and devotion to the gods. In the tradition of Athenian "conservatives," he also favored ending the war and establishing friendship with Sparta. In much of this, Nicias reminds us of Cimon, although he lacked the great military talents of the latter. Nicias it was, according to Thucydides, who tried to catch Cleon off-guard in 425 B.C. by offering him the command at Pylos. Opportunity for Nicias came in 424 B.C. when the invasion of Boeotia failed; he then arranged the brief truce with Sparta. Although this did not last, he did not miss the second opportunity, after the deaths of Cleon and Brasidas. The Peace of Nicias was the result.

421-413 B.C.
The Peace of Nicias did not last long. Many of Sparta's allies resented the failure of the Spartans to exert themselves much in the 420's B.C. Those allies had suffered much more than Sparta, and they were angry to see Athens escape unpunished. The Peloponnesian League fell apart. Minor fighting soon broke out between some of the old friends of Sparta and Athens, but the Spartans stayed out of it for a while.

A new "radical" and pro-war party emerged in Athens, in opposition to Nicias. One of its leaders was <u>Hyperbolus</u>, a manufacturer of lamps, a man of the type of Cleon. His name gives us our word (hyperbole) for misleading, exaggerated talk. The other leader of this group was ALCIBIADES, the most fascinating political figure of the period. <u>Alcibiades</u>, of the family of Pericles, was a young aristocrat of great beauty, attractiveness, and talents. He was much admired by the philosopher <u>Socrates</u>, who had saved his life in the defeat at <u>Delium</u> against the Boeotians in the unsuccessful invasion of 424 B.C. Sadly, Alcibiades was also indisciplined, unprincipled, and scandalously licentious. At this stage he was, in the style of Pericles, associating himself with the "reform" party and the supporters of war.

The early fighting went badly for Athens, which was never very sure of itself on land. In 418 B.C. Sparta entered the fighting for a while, inflicting a clear defeat at <u>Mantinea</u> on an Athenian force which was combined with some of Sparta's old friends in the Peloponnesus. These setbacks improved the position of Nicias at Athens. Alcibiades went over to Nicias and together in 417 B.C. they secured the <u>ostracism</u> of Hyperbolus. Hyperbolus was later murdered in exile. This proved to be the last ostracism.

The new combination of Nicias and Alcibiades was an odd and uneasy one. Nicias remained without enthusiasm for the war, but he lacked both the force of will to hold back the young Alcibiades and the talent to win military fame for himself. In 417 B.C. he failed on an expedition to <u>Thrace</u>. In 416 B.C. it was probably the excitable Alcibiades who was behind the decision to kill the adult male population of the island of <u>Melos</u> and enslave the rest of its population. Melos had stood bravely outside the Confederation of Delos all through the century. The island now paid a terrible price for its independence. This episode is one of the most famous in Thucydides. The Athenian writer uses it as another demonstration of his admiration for cleverness.

It was also probably Alcibiades who, in the same year of 416 B.C., talked Nicias and the Assembly into the idea of a major expedition to <u>Syracuse</u> on the island of Sicily to the west. Under the guise of aiding its friends among the Greek cities of Italy against the pro-Spartan states headed by Doric Syracuse, Athens was responding to the call of greed—a bandit greed for the riches of Sicily. This was an attractive chance to make up for the economic losses brought on by the war, but it was a most indirect way of getting at Sparta and it can hardly be said to have been part of a war policy at all. Above all, it was a tribute to the ability of Alcibiades that he could promote such an untraditional idea.

Syracuse was the wealthiest Greek city in Italy, and possibly it was already the largest and wealthiest city in the entire Greek world. It had played very little part in affairs in the Aegean so far. Between 427 and 424 B.C., during the earlier fighting, Athens had already given some help to the Ionic cities in South Italy and Sicily against Syracuse. The famous philosopher <u>Gorgias</u> had gone to Athens from Italy on that occasion to ask for support. The Athenian effort then had been a minor one, and even now the desire to offer such help was hardly the main reason for the intervention of Athens.

The expedition left Athens for Sicily in 415 B.C. There were about 30,000 troops involved, including 5,000 hoplites, with 130 triremes. This was much the biggest effort Athens had ever put out on land. Nicias was cold to the idea, but he was appointed one of the commanders, along with Alcibiades and <u>Lamachus</u>. Alcibiades soon had to drop out. Just before the expedition left there was a religious scandal in Athens. The <u>Hermae</u>, the stone figures at the entrances to houses and public buildings which were intended to protect travellers (Hermes was the god of travelers), were mutilated. Alcibiades and his wild friends were accused of this stunt. They were also accused of having put on a private show mocking the Mysteries of Eleusis. His enemies waited until Alcibiades had left with the expedition to bring him to trial on these charges. Rather than face a jury, Alcibiades escaped into exile.

Without Alcibiades, the expedition lacked aim or vigor. Nicias overruled Lamachus, a lesser figure, and refused to attack Syracuse. There is little question that the city could have been taken. By 414 B.C. the Athenian army had settled into a more or less aimless siege of Syracuse. Sparta sent some aid to Syracuse. The Spartans were encouraged to this step by Alcibiades, who went to Sparta, where he criticized democracy as "admitted foolishness." Lamachus was killed in the siege operations. In this year of 414 B.C. <u>The Birds</u> by <u>Aristophanes</u> appeared, an expression of hope that peace could be made. It was not to be.

The Assembly at Athens rejected a request from the unhappy Nicias that he be recalled. Instead, in 413 B.C. a further expedition was sent out, with 70 triremes and 5,000 more hoplites. Two more undistinguished generals,

Demosthenes and Eurymedon, went with these reinforcements.
The Athenian commanders could not decide what to do.
Demosthenes urged that the siege of Syracuse be given up.
Nicias refused, then agreed, then postponed any decision
for a month. Before the month was up, the Syracusans,
with help from the Spartans, broke up the siege in heavy
fighting. Eurymedon was killed, and Nicias and Demosthenes
surrendered what was left of the Athenian army. The
soldiers were enslaved, the two commanders were executed.
Syracuse commemorated this victory by issuing the most
brilliant of all its silver coins, an art in which it was
already famous.

413-404 B.C.

This unprecedented disaster greatly weakened the
military position of Athens. In the same year, 413 B.C.,
Sparta seized and fortified Decelea as a permanent base in
Attica. The Spartan army would now be on the scene all
the time: no crops could be grown, runaway slaves now had
a refuge, and most important of all, the silver mines at
Laurion had to be closed. The Spartans allegedly did this,
too, on the advice of Alcibiades. Thucydides is always
ready to make the Spartans look stupid, but this time it is
reasonable to ask why they had not taken this step earlier,
instead of going home each winter.

Many of the members of the Confederation of Delos
rebelled against Athens and Sparta began to get the upper
hand. By 412 B.C. Sparta could put out a fleet of 100
triremes, although only 25 of them were Spartan. Syracuse
sent a few ships. At the same time, the two Persian
governors in Asia Minor began (on their own initiative) to
supply money to the rebels and the Spartans. The Persian
government allowed this to go on. The Persians, wanting
to regain control of at least the Greek cities on the mainland of Asia Minor, had decided that it was the part of
common sense to support Sparta for the time being against
the sea-power Athens. Sparta in return agreed to allow
the Persians to retake the Greek cities on the Asian mainland. Alcibiades, forced to leave Sparta after seducing
the wife of one of the kings, had moved on to Persia to look
for further prospects. All the signs were that the Spartans
were finally becoming serious about the war and that they
had decided to build up a fleet.

Inside Attica, the disaster in Sicily and the setbacks elsewhere hurt the democracy. In 413 B.C. a group of 10 men was introduced to replace the Council of 500. At the beginning of 411 B.C., Aristophanes' play Lysistrata was out on. This play, which was a strong plea for peace, has become the best-known of that author's works. Later in 411 B.C. there was an oligarchic revolution. The Assembly "agreed" to hand power over to a group of 400 men. 5 men were named; these 5 picked 95 more; the 100 picked a further 300. There was also supposed to be an Assembly of 5000. Significantly, payment for public duties such as jury service was abolished. The anti-democrats claimed that they could carry on the war more efficiently; it was also possible that by giving up democracy, Athens would better be able to rival Sparta for the friendship of the Persians. Alcibiades was encouraging the oligarchic revolution, hoping to find himself a new career in Athens. The oligarchs, however, included men of many varieties of opinion. The "extreme" oligarchs were led by Antiphon, the "moderate" oligarchs by THERAMENES. After three months, Theramenes and the "moderate" oligarchs overthrew the 400 and replaced them with the 5,000, a figure which may have included all the remaining men above the thetes (the hoplite class). Antiphon was executed.

The oligarchy was not to survive in any form. The Athenian fleet at Samos, in which the lowest wealth class, the thetes, was very heavily represented, refused to recognize either version of oligarchy. The democratic elements in the fleet were led by THRASYBULUS and Thrasyllus. Alcibiades, that most notable bell-weather, was allowed to join the fleet on the democratic side. Clearly, he had decided that the democrats were going to win. The fleet twice defeated the young Spartan navy near the Hellespont, in 411 and 410 B.C., and then returned to Athens. The 5,000 were overthrown and democracy was re-established.

The outstanding political figure in the restored democracy at Athens over the next several years was CLEOPHON, from a family of lyre-makers, a man from the mold of Cleon and Hyperbolus. Payments for public duties were restored. Cleophon also introduced a further payment of 2 obols a day, which was probably a simple handout to the poor. He engaged in a new burst of public building at

Athens, which didn't make the best financial sense under the circumstances. The most notable artistic achievement at this time was the Erechtheon on the Acropolis, with its graceful Porch of the Maidens. It had been begun after the disaster at Syracuse, when fear seems to have prompted a religious revival in Athens, but work had been stopped during the political troubles of 411-410 B.C. The same revival of religion had produced a temple to the healing-god Asclepius and the introduction of a small special tax to maintain the services at Eleusis (which had been mocked by Alcibiades).

In the tradition of democratic "reformers," Cleophon pressed on with the war. The Athenians continued to do well at sea until 406 B.C., although the very existence of a naval threat to them showed how much the terms of the war had shifted against them. Athens rejected weak Spartan peace offers in 410 and 406 B.C. Alcibiades won some victories at sea for Athens, but, being as unreliable as ever, he was back in exile by 406 B.C. (we do not know why). The Athenian successes reached their climax at Arginusae in 406 B.C. Even in victory, though, the Assembly was so nervous by this time that it condemned to death the 8 generals who had been present at Arginusae for failing to try hard enough to rescue Athenian sailors from the water after the battle. Socrates objected to this remarkable step. Of the 8 generals, 2 fled into exile, but the other 6 were killed. Those executed included the legitimized son of Pericles and Thrasyllus.

It was taking the Spartans a long while to become skillful at sea fighting, but they were always ready to come back for more. The tide turned strongly in their favor in 405 B.C. when the Persian king stepped in directly and put his younger son Cyrus in charge of relations with Sparta. The flow of materials and money to the Spartans now increased sharply. In 404 B.C. the Spartan LYSANDER won an overwhelming sea victory at AEGOSPOTAMI in the Hellespont. In knocking out the Athenian fleet, Lysander delivered the blow which ended the war. He proceeded to Athens and starved it into surrender. Cleophon favored resisting to the last, but the Athenians executed him in order to clear the way for peace.

While the Spartans' victory was a tribute to their
determination, success had come only with Persian help
and at the expense of reintroducing Persia into the Greek
world for the first time since the 470's B.C. Neither
Athens nor Sparta, in fact, was ever able to recover fully
from the losses of money and manpower brought on by the war.
Other Greek states, as well as the Persians, soon realized
that they could turn this situation to their advantage.

In 404 B.C., in the wake of defeat, and with Spartan
encouragement, oligarchy again raised its head in Athens.
The Assembly agreed to hand power to a group of 30 and a
new Council of 500. The oligarchs, though, were as divided
as ever. The "extreme" oligarchs were led by Critias, a
pupil of Socrates. Critias belonged to the aristocratic
family of the great Solon. He engineered the execution of
Theramenes, who was again the chief figure among the
"moderate" oligarchs.

Like the earlier one in 411-410 B.C., this flirtation
with oligarchy also lasted only a few months, from 404 into
403 B.C. Critias obtained a Spartan garrison for Athens
to help protect him, but the Spartans, true to their
behavior a century before when they had overthrown the
tyrant Hippias, were not willing to make much of an effort
to control Athenian politics. Thrasybulus, one of the
heroes of 411-410 B.C., led the democratic forces in 403
B.C. in fighting in which Critias was killed. The Spartan
army mediated the civil war and agreed to allow the restoration of the democracy.

The democracy was to survive at Athens for 80 years
until Greece passed into the control of foreign conquerors.
Many of the aristocrats and the most distinguished minds
at Athens (such as Plato) continued to have little good to
say about democracy, but there was nothing they could do
beyond complain. There is little doubt that Athenians in
general cherished the democracy.

FROM THE PELOPONNESIAN WAR TO THE MACEDONIAN EMPIRE, 404-336 B.C.

The Supremacy of Sparta, 404-386 B.C.

Victory in the Peloponnesian War (431-404 B.C.) left Sparta predominant in the Greek world. The new situation tempted the Spartans into departing from their careful and conservative traditions. They applied a heavy hand throughout Greece and the islands, assuming for themselves the right to speak for the Greek world. While the city was not devastated, Athens lost its fleet and its empire, as well as the vital walls which connected Athens with the coast at the Piraeus. Across the areas "liberated" from Athenian control, the Spartans established garrisons and puppet oligarchies. They also exacted large amounts of tribute. The new wealth, a novelty in Sparta, in time damaged the simplicity of the state's old country life-style. Outside observers commented on the growth of a wealthy class in Sparta and of the love of material things, along with the decline of the old values of the acceptance of sacrifice and hardship.

Sparta used some of the wealth to move against Persia. The Spartans had allowed the Persians to regain the Greek cities in Asia Minor (which had been allies of Athens) in exchange for the aid they had received from the Persians in the closing stages of the Peloponnesian War. Ashamed of their action, the Spartans soon went back on the deal with the Persians.

A civil war broke out in Persia in 401 B.C. Cyrus, who had worked closely with the Spartans in the last years of the Peloponnesian War, challenged his older brother, who had just become king of Persia. Cyrus's strength rested on a force of some 13,000 Greek soldiers he had hired for pay (mercenaries). Of course, with the Peloponnesian War over, there were numbers of such soldiers looking for employment. Some were actually recruited from the Spartans. The Greek troops won the battle of Cunaxa in 401 B.C. in Mesopotamia for Cyrus, but the prince threw away his life in a foolish little attack after the outcome had been settled. The remaining Greek troops had no choice but to march home. They went north through eastern Asia Minor to the Black

Sea and then back to Greece in 399 B.C. (the March of the 10,000). This episode is well known to us through the description in the Anabasis (Going Up) by Xenophon of Athens, another of the pupils of Socrates and one of the commanders of the expedition. Xenophon gives us one of our best looks at Greeks on a day-to-day basis, providing an impressive picture of a democratic unit in which the individuals were not afraid to speak up for themselves or to accept responsibility. The expedition also had a great significance for the future. It demonstrated the superiority of Greek troops over Persian and indicated that an organized Greek effort might well be capable of overthrowing the Persian Empire.

The 6,000 Greek soldiers who survived the return from Mesopotamia were able to sign on for more fighting for the Spartans. In 400 B.C., trying to turn the rebellion of Cyrus to advantage, Sparta sent an army into Asia Minor to "liberate" the Greeks there from the hold which Sparta itself had given to the Persians. The contrast between this invasion and the Spartan reluctance to carry the war to the Persians 80 years earlier after the battle of Plataea is very obvious.

In the fighting over the next few years, the Spartans did reasonably well. They were not able, however, to match the Persians (really the Phoenicians still) at sea. The Persian fleet was commanded by Conon, a renegade Athenian, one of the 8 generals who had been disgraced after the defeat of Athens at Aegospotami. Lysander, the Spartan hero who had won that battle (404 B.C.) and ended the Peloponnesian War, had himself been in disgrace since 403 B.C. Sparta was always suspicious of its successful men as potential tyrants. To win his way back into a power, Lysander tried to promote a plan to make the kings of Sparta elective from among all the citizens--a proposal intended obviously to produce his own election to the position. This plan got nowhere. In 398 B.C. AGESILAUS, a figure of some talent, became one of the kings of Sparta. Lysander hoped that his friend Agesilaus would allow him to return to prominence, but such hopes were soon deceived. Agesilaus campaigned efficiently in Asia Minor in 396-395 B.C. The Spartans seemed to be getting the upper hand, and Agesilaus may have been thinking of conquering the entire Persian

227

Empire.

It was at this point that trouble began in Greece.
Annoyed by Spartan harshness, encouraged by the absence of
the Spartan army in Asia Minor, some of the Greek states
rebelled against Spartan control. The rising was begun
and was led by Thebes, with Athens following along.
Lysander, given a command in these difficulties, was killed
attacking Thebes. This setback prompted many more Greek
states to join the rebellion, including Corinth and Argos
in the Peloponnesus.

Such a war on two fronts was too much for Sparta.
Sparta lost the big sea battle of Cnidus to Conon and the
Persians in 394 B.C. and had to accept renewed Persian
control of the Greeks in Asia Minor. All the bother since
400 B.C. had produced nothing. In Greece, Sparta defeated
the rebel states at the battle of Corinth in 394 B.C.
(this defeat has left us with a fine funeral monument outside one of the gates of Athens to a cavalryman killed in
the battle). Sparta, however, could not force the isthmus.
Even the army which Agesilaus brought back overland from
Asia Minor in 394 B.C., while it defeated Boeotia and Thebes,
crossed into the Peloponnesus by sea, avoiding the task of
forcing the isthmus. The Spartans were restricted to the
Peloponnesus, with some minor fighting at the isthmus,
while north Greece was lost and Athens reasserted itself
to some extent in the Aegean and rebuilt the walls of the
Piraeus. The Persians aided Athens in these endeavors.

Then, as the years passed, the Spartans, still strong
in endurance, began to do better. In 390 B.C. they won
control of the isthmus and were then able to carry the
fighting into north Greece. They also enjoyed a limited
revival in Asia Minor, again under the leadership of
Agesilaus. At sea, too, the Spartans' position improved,
with the aid of some ships sent by Syracuse from Sicily.
Conon died and Thrasybulus, one of the most successful
Athenian generals,was killed.

The fighting ended in 386 B.C. with the King's Peace.
The Persian ruler supervised the settlement at the urging
of Sparta. The Persians were annoyed by the growth of
Athenian power in the northern Aegean; they always saw

Sparta, a land-power, as less of a threat to them than
Athens. Persian control of the Greeks in Asia Minor was
recognized by all. Athens lost the Hellespont area but
kept most of the north Aegean islands. Within Greece, the
independence of all Greek states was recognized. Spartan
overlordship disappeared and in theory all the leading
Greek states swore off the idea of picking up satellites
or forced allies. The Boeotian cities, for example,
became independent of their leader Thebes. The Persian
role in this peace was a great humiliation to the Greeks,
especially at a time when the Greeks were aware that they
were militarily superior to the Persians. The settlement
dramatized the Greeks' inability to work together.

A notable feature of this war was the heavy use of
mercenaries. This was not a principle the Greeks could
sustain for long. The mercenaries often came from the
northern, primitive fringes of the Greek world, although
there was at the same time an increase in the habit of
fighting for pay among Greeks themselves (as we saw in the
case of Xenophon and the soldiers hired by Cyrus the
Persian). The non-Greeks mercenaries were usually light-
armed infantry rather than the hoplites who were the basis
of the citizen armies. Was civic pride (pride in serving
the polis), the basis of traditional Greek life, declining?
Some people think so, and they often link this decline to
the increase in individualism, to the selfishness of putting oneself first, which seems to have marked the 300's
B.C. The mercenary generals were professional military
leaders, a new phenomenon in Greece. They were voted
funds with which they raised their own armies. The most
famous of such generals at this time was Iphicrates the
Athenian.

Attempted Spartan Revival, 386-371 B.C.
     Sparta could not reconcile itself to its reduced
condition. It caused trouble in the Peloponnesus, refusing to allow a full independence to the other states in
that area. Elsewhere, just as selfishly, the Spartans
encouraged the fragmentation ordered by the King's Peace.
In 382 B.C. a Spartan army seized Thebes in a surprise
attack; between 382 and 379 B.C. Sparta crushed a new
confederation in Chalcidice which was friendly to Athens.

Once more, Spartan aggression produced reaction. In 378 B.C. Thebes challenged Sparta successfully. Athens joined Thebes after a Spartan general who failed in an attempt to capture Athens in a surprise attack was left unpunished by Sparta. Athens now put together against Sparta a second confederation of the islands, just as it had a century earlier against Persia. In this second empire, Athens took steps to avoid some of the problems of the first. The confederation was an arrangement between two equals, Athens and the other members. There were two separate assemblies, one of Athens, one of the allies, each with a veto over any decision. The Athenians also agreed not to impose Athenian colonies on their allies. Both assemblies, however, met at Athens, and the confederation's military and common fund were under Athenian control.

The chief Athenian politician at this time was CALLISTRATUS. He usually favored peace with Sparta and hostility toward Thebes, since it was Thebes, rather than Sparta, which blocked Athenian power in north and central Greece. This opportunity to embarrass the Spartans, though, was too attractive even for Callistratus to pass it up.

Callistratus was the nephew of Agyrrhius, who in the 390's B.C. had introduced payment for attending the Assembly at Athens. This "reform" is a target for the comedy writer Aristophanes in the play Women in the Assembly. The extension of the principle of payment for public service is often taken, along with the increased use of mercenaries, as a sign of the decline of public spirit. It was perhaps also at about this time (although the change may go as far back as Pericles between 460 and 430 B.C.) that the practice of paying the public to attend the theater performances which were associated with the great religious festivals was introduced. With time, these hand-outs grew in scale, losing much of their connection with the festivals and becoming straightforward giveaways. This money, the so-called Theoric Fund, was put under the control of a special official, and the program was important enough that often this official was the dominant figure in the state. A diminished Athens was increasing the hand-outs to its citizens, a process which made it necessary for the state to cut corners elsewhere, particularly in military matters. One way to do this was to hire mercenaries, omit to pay them, and so encourage them to pillage and live off the land as they campaigned. For the war in the 370's B.C., the war property tax of Cleophon from the 420's B.C. was revived. The rich themselves, rather than the state, were made responsible for its collection.

378-371 B.C.

Thebes managed to hold off Sparta and then, flourishing, went on to the offensive, conquering the rest of Boeotia. Thebes was led by the great EPAMINONDAS. Epaminondas developed the tactical innovation known as the Theban wedge, which involved strengthening the left wing of an army and pushing it forward as the leading, and decisive, element. A Greek phalanx tended to crowd together to the right, as men looked to protect their unprotected right arms with the shields of the next in line: the wedge aimed to drive into this concentrated area. At the core of the army of Thebes was the Sacred Band of 300 aristocrats in 150 pairs. The decline of Spartan military strength in these years was widely noted. Spartan armies lacked the discipline and the will of old and they were much reduced in size, there being fewer and fewer full citizens available.

At the same time, Athens and its new alliance did well at sea against the Spartans. The most prominent Athenian general was Timotheus, the son of Conon. Under the influence of Callistratus, however, Athens was wary of Thebes and jealous of that city's increasing success. A peace was actually arranged between Athens and Sparta in 374 B.C., but it did not last long. In 373 B.C. Timotheus, who favored the war, was driven out of Athens after a trial for fraud. Callistratus was then able to reach a settlement with Sparta in 371 B.C., the Peace of Callias. Since the basis of the peace was the independence of Greek states promised in the King's Peace of 386 B.C., Athens had to give up its new confederation, a very considerable concession under the circumstances. Neither side on paper had anything to show for its efforts. Since, however, this peace did not end the war, both sides took their precautions.

The Supremacy of Thebes, 371-362 B.C.

The Athenian withdrawal from the war left Thebes in head-to-head conflict with Sparta. Thebes did amazingly

well. Epaminondas won a great victory over the Spartans
at Leuctra in 371 B.C. 1,000 Lacedaemonians were killed,
including 400 Spartans. A Spartan king was killed there,
the first to fall in battle since Leonidas at Thermopylae
in 480 B.C. Sparta abandoned the attempt to resist
Thebes in Boeotia and fell back into the Peloponnesus.
Thebes now received the aid of the briefly-powerful tyrant
Jason of Pherae, who had just united Thessaly under his
control. Jason, whose power rested on a strong mercenary
army, was assassinated in 370 B.C. His army, and Thessaly,
fell apart. Jason had talked openly about attacking the
Persian Empire, another reminder to the Greeks of the
opportunities they were ignoring.

Epaminondas of Thebes carried the war into Sparta in
370 B.C., right to the gates of the city. The Peloponnesus
was in uproar, as Spartan influence there collapsed.
Messenia broke away once more, and in the interior a Pan-
Arcadian Union came into effect with its capital at the
new city of Megalopolis (Great City). Sparta survived,
arming 6,000 helots with the promise of citizenship in
return for their help, but the humiliation of the Spartans
must have been a thing of amazement to Greeks.

Thebes now was all-powerful on the Greek mainland.
Boeotia perhaps was united under Thebes in one state.
To the north Thebes conquered Thessaly (364 B.C.). This
was to keep that area out of the hands of the Macedonians
even further north, who were friendly to Athens. As
guarantees of their good behavior, the Macedonians sent
to the powerful Thebes a number of hostages, including the
future king Philip. To the south, Epaminondas campaigned
through the Peloponnesus three more times (in 369, 366,
362 B.C.), as the Spartans remained too weak to offer much
resistance. The city of Sparta, however, was never taken.

The success of Thebes produced the inevitable reaction
in the Greek world. The Peloponnesian friends of Thebes
began to fear the outsider more than the now-humbled Sparta.
Repeated attempts to produce a peace failed, since Thebes
was unwilling to settle. Persia once more played a part
in these peace bids. Athens, seeing that it had dropped
out of the war only to find that Thebes did even better on
its own, cautiously aided Sparta in the Peloponnesus, but

without trying at any point to block the path of the army of Thebes across the isthmus. The Athenians knew that they could not match Epaminondas in the field. Thebes built up something of a navy of its own and encouraged revolts against Athens across the Aegean. The Athenians, relying still on Iphicrates and the recalled Timotheus, more than held their own.

In the 4th invasion of the Peloponnesus by Thebes (but only the second into Laconia itself), in 362 B.C., Epaminondas won the great battle of Mantinea against the Spartans, the supreme achievement of the Theban wedge. Epaminondas, however, was killed in the battle. The power of Thebes, which had rested on his military skill, quickly collapsed.

Stalemate and Exhaustion, 362-353 B.C.

In the years after the death of Epaminondas, no Greek state was predominant. Sparta was humbled and bankrupt: King Agesilaus died in 361-360 B.C. in Egypt where he had hired out a Spartan army as mercenaries to make some money for his poor country out of a civil war. He was 84. Thebes was leaderless, and once more was not even really a country, as the Boeotian cities reclaimed their independence.

By default, Athens became the strongest single state, although this Athens was only a shadow of its own former self. The peaceloving Callistatus, who had dominated Athens for 20 years, fled into exile in 361 B.C. to escape the death sentence. He returned some years later and was indeed executed. Athens now flourished on land and at sea, but predictably overreached itself. In Asia Minor Athens ran up against the tyrant Mausolus of Caria, a semi-independent figure who in theory was governor of southwestern Asia Minor for the Persians. Mausolus is best-known to us now for the tomb at Halicarnassus which he shares with his wife. The great Scopas did some of the friezes for this tomb, which gives us our word mausoleum, or large tomb. In the 350's B.C., Mausolus encouraged the Greek allies of Athens in the southeastern Aegean to revolt; the revolt spread as far as Corcyra. Athens was defeated. Timotheus and Iphicrates were both disgraced—the former was sent into exile (355 B.C.).

Another state which benefited briefly from the general exhaustion was Phocis. The Phocians in 356 B.C. siezed Delphi, claiming that the Boeotians were using the oracle against them. With the temple treasures the Phocians hired mercenaries, making themselves strong for a day. This episode was called the Sacred War.

The Rise of Macedonia, to 336 B.C.

It was into this vacuum that the Macedonians came in the 350's B.C. The Macedonians were kin to the Greeks in race and speech. They had been important since the 400's B.C., when they had begun to conquer the tribes to the interior and to play a role in the affairs of the Greek cities on the northern coast. The Macedonians showed the greatest respect for Greek culture, on an almost pathetic scale, but the Greeks continued to regard them as barbarian, backward types. One piece of evidence the Greeks could use along this line was the Macedonian political structure, which was centered upon kings in the way Greeks generally had done away with centuries earlier. It did not matter much that the power of the kings was limited in theory, or that each new king was chosen by the army; the kings in Macedonia dominated the state. Among the Greek states, the Macedonians' closest relations were with the Athenians, since it was Athens which generally controlled the Greek coastal settlements in the north after 500 B.C. It was primarily through Athens, too, that Macedonia received Greek culture; Euripides had spent his last years and had written his last plays in Macedonia a little before 400 B.C.

Before 360 B.C., Macedonia was largely promise, with little performance. The transformation in Macedonia's position after that time was mostly the result of the driving ambition and talents of one man, Philip of Macedon. Philip it was who threw out all of the old political rules of the Greeks.

King Perdiccas of Macedonia was killed in battle against the Illyrians from the mountains to the west of Macedonia in 359 B.C. His son, Amyntas, a child, succeeded him under the supervision of the dead king's brother, Philip. Philip, then 24, had spent some time as a hostage to Thebes under Epaminondas, and he may have picked up up there an insight into how easily the Greek world could be overturned, as well as a knowledge of the military tactics which underlay the power of Thebes. He soon got rid of Amyntas and made himself king. The capital of Macedonia was moved to Pella in the lowlands, a symbolic "looking-outward" toward the Greek world.

By 356 B.C., Philip had defeated the Illyrians. He was experimenting with a modified phalanx, more open in formation than the traditional Greek unit, with the men carrying very long spears. He was also developing a much heavier use of cavalry than was usual among Greek armies. Because of the great gold mines which were being opened up in Macedonia, Philip could afford large military expenditures, far beyond the scale of any Greek state.

Philip now made ready to move into Greece. In 353-352 B.C. he was defeated by the Phocians as he tried to take Thessaly, his first target to the south. In 352 B.C., however, Philip defeated the Phocians and occupied Thessaly. Athens and Sparta sent troops to hold Philip at Thermopylae, keeping him out of Phocis and Boeotia.

Philip turned aside for a while, in 352-351 B.C., to conquer Thrace. This success put him in a position to threaten the Athenian position at the Hellespont, the lifeline to the grain supplies of the Black Sea. The Macedonian conquest of Thrace moved the Athenian orator-politician DEMOSTHENES to the first in his series of famous attacks on Philip (the Philippics, giving us a word we use for bitter criticism). Demosthenes, born in 384 B.C., the son of a wealthy manufacturer at Athens, of a mother who had some barbarian (Scythian) blood, had made his name earlier in the 350's B.C. speaking on foreign policy, always his main interest. Generally, as here, he had supported an aggressive foreign policy, although not with entire consistency. On the Macedonian matter, Demosthenes was staking out a position against the chief Athenian political figure of the day, Eubulus. Eubulus normally followed the peaceful line which had been favored by Callistratus in the 370's and 360's B.C. He had been concerned enough about Macedonia, though, to send troops to help Phocis in 352 B.C. Demosthenes demanded a stronger line.

Encouraged by Demosthenes, Athens soon went to war
with Philip, a limited war which lasted from 351 to 346
B.C. This was a mismatch, an indication of the nonsense
which lay at the heart of Demosthenes' insistence that
Athens should and could resist Philip. Philip conquered
Chalcidice, encouraged to independence the people of
Euboea, right off the coast of Athens, and generally handled
the Athenians easily. Athens at least had the good sense
to avoid a major battle. Since Philip was staying out of
Greece proper, the other Greek states sat out the struggle.

Peace was made between Athens and Macedonia in 346
B.C., the Peace of Philocrates. Athens accepted the setbacks it had suffered and recognized the preeminence of
Philip. That year, Philip finally came into Greece; he
broke up the league of Phocian cities, posing as the
liberator of the temple of Delphi. Philip was given the
Phocian seat on the Amphictionic Council which supervised
the shrine at Delphi, the greatest of all the Panhellenic
religious places. He was also elected president of the
Pythian Games for 346 B.C.

Demosthenes criticized these concessions to Philip,
arguing that more resistance should have been offered.
Enough of the Athenians disliked seeing the Macedonians
lording it over the Greeks to permit Demosthenes to establish
himself as the chief political figure in the city from this
time. Philocrates, who had made the peace, went into exile
after he was condemned to death in 343 B.C. Demosthenes
did not, however, intend to do more than talk against Philip
for a while, and he had to be careful to hold in check
those who responded too eagerly to his arguments. Having
watched Athens fare badly on its own against Philip in 351-
346 B.C., at a time when Philip was hardly trying,
Demosthenes had decided to look for allies against the
Macedonians among the other Greek states. He aimed particularly at Thebes, which traditionally had been hostile to
Athens. The Thebans, much reduced from the glories of the
days of Epaminondas, had been treating Philip carefully;
indeed, they had taken the initiative in inviting Philip
into Greece in 346 B.C. under the pretense of settling
the Phocian problem. With the Thebans having a head-
start on good relations with Philip, the prospects for the
chance of a mutual suicide-pact with the Athenians against

Macedonia should have been slim.

There was an uneasy peace from 346 to 341 B.C. Philip added further conquests in Thrace and Epirus and became chief official (archon) of the confederated state of Thessaly. Then, with Demosthenes finally ready to make the great challenge, Athens reestablished its position in Euboea and went to war with Philip, citing the Macedonian threat to the Hellespont. The Athenians scored some encouraging successes at first in the northern Aegean and they seem to have been putting out a major effort. Eubulus himself, although favoring peace, had been slowly building up the city's strength at sea. Demosthenes pushed on with this. He won approval for diverting the Theoric Fund for entertainment expenses to military purposes. That fund had become large enough that it was a source of great influence for whoever managed it, an official being elected every four years for that purpose. Eubulus had directed the fund from 354 to 350 B.C., and perhaps until 346 B.C.

It remained true, however, that Athens and the rest of Greece were hopelessly vulnerable to a major attack from Philip's army whenever the Macedonian should decide to make his move. Since this was apparent to most, the Greeks again refused to support Athens. Then, in 338 B.C., the Amphictionic Council asked Philip to come into Greece to settle another argument about the sacred site at Delphi. Having now his excuse, so that he could look like a deliverer rather than a conqueror, Philip finally moved toward Greece. Few of the Greeks were willing to resist: the Peloponnesians, including the Spartans, intended only to watch. Incredibly, though, and for the mere price of recognizing Thebes' claim to dominate Boeotia, Demosthenes was able to get Thebes to join Athens in the war. Philip defeated the army of Thebes and Athens without problem at the battle of CHAERONEA in 338 B.C. The Athenians, including Demosthenes as one of the generals, fled, but the Sacred Band of 300 remained to perish to the man and are commemorated in the famous Lion of Chaeronea.

Philip treated Thebes, the last-minute convert to resistance, harshly, giving all the cities of Boeotia their independence. Athens, however, and Demosthenes got off very lightly, an indication of Philip's genuine admiration

237

for Athenian culture and his desire to associate himself
with the same. Philip continued south. Except for Sparta,
the Pelopennesus offered no resistance. Sparta was devastated and lost much of its territories to surrounding
states: it was quite beyond the Spartans by this time to
halt Philip.

Philip decided to keep several garrisons in Greece.
He also called a Congress of the Greek states at Corinth.
He presided personally over this, claiming the right to
speak for all Greeks. Only Sparta, weak enough now to be
ignored, refused to attend.

At a second Congress of Corinth, in 337 B.C., Philip
announced his intention to invade Asia Minor and attack
the Persians. The Greek states would help; they would be
told how much help would be needed. Jealous of the
Macedonians, and tied to their old ways of looking at
things, the Greeks were very unenthusiastic about this
project.

Philip's army entered Asia Minor in 336 B.C. under the
command of his chief general Parmenio. It is likely that
at first Philip intended only to "liberate" the Greek
areas of Asia Minor; but it is just as likely that victory
would have led him further afield. The king did not live
to face the temptation. That same year, aged 47, Philip
was assassinated at home in Macedonia.

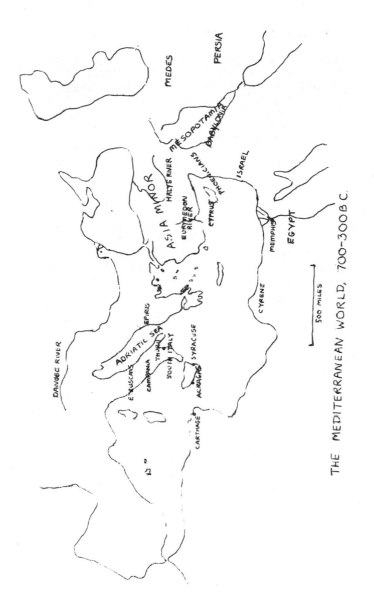

THE MEDITERRANEAN WORLD, 700-300 B.C.

ALEXANDER THE GREAT, 336-323 B.C.

ALEXANDER, the 20-year old son of Philip, became
ruler of Macedonia when his father was murdered in 336 B.C.
Alexander, and more particularly his mother Olympias,
daughter of a king of Epirus, were suspected of being
involved in the assassination. Philip had put Olympias
aside to take a second wife; by this second wife he had a
young son, who obviously threatened Alexander's position.
Certainly, Alexander had been on bad terms with his father.
The young boy, and his mother, were killed after the
assassination.

What Alexander achieved in his brief life made him a
wonder of the world. He took aim at conquering what was
to him the entire civilized world. The obvious first step,
and much the biggest step, in this direction was to conquer
the Persian Empire. That empire had fallen on hard times
since the 400's B.C., with weak, corrupt rulers, a loss of
control over its provinces (as we have seen with Caria),
and many local rebellions, most prominently in Egypt.
Even so, and for all the known superiority of Greek soldiers over the Persian, the conquest of such an enormous
area seemed to be a wild undertaking. Alexander conquered
the Persian Empire with bewildering speed, convinced that
he had, like Achilleus, only a brief time to live as the
price of his mighty talents, and supremely confident of his
own abilities and of the favor of the gods. He did it,
too, as the champion of Greek civilization, a position
which was far more than a pose to Alexander. He shared
this attitude with his father, who had always taken the
greatest of pains with the Greeks. The same attitude had
led Philip to hire Aristotle, the greatest Greek intellectual figure of the day, as a teacher for Alexander.
Aristotle's father had been a physician to earlier kings
of Macedonia. The Greeks, however, remaining unwilling to
adapt, were generally hostile to the whole business,
preferring to go on seeing the Macedonians as barbarians.

Alexander's first job, in fact, was to keep the Greeks
in line before going off to the East:
336 B.C. Alexander brought a Macedonian army into Greece
at once. The Assembly at Athens had passed a resolution

240

honoring the murderers of Philip—a play which, under the
circumstances, was doubly nasty. No blood was shed, the
Greeks not wishing to go beyond words at this stage.
Another Congress of Corinth was held. It elected Alexander
general to invade Asia. From this Congress we have the
famous story of Alexander meeting the Cynic philosopher
Diogenes, who was sitting in the barrel which he used as
his home. Alexander asked Diogenes if he could help him
at all and received the reply, "Stand out of the sun."
"If I were not Alexander," said the king, "I should want
to be Diogenes." Beyond showing Alexander's admiration
for Greek culture, the story indicates the predicament of
the Greeks of the late 300's B.C., pitting Diogenes' mad-
cap individualism and irresponsibility against the armed
might of the Macedonians.

335 B.C. Alexander campaigned feverishly in Thrace and
Illyria, winning brilliant victories as he worked to bring
those areas, too, to accept his power before going East.
During his absence, supplied with Persian money and encouraged by reports that Alexander had died during the
northern campaigns, Thebes revolted. Almost all of the
other Greek states this time provided some aid and encouragement. The appearance of the Macedonian army, however,
worked wonders in clearing men's minds. Athens and the
other Greek states got off lightly once more, but a
terrible example was made of Thebes. The entire population
was enslaved and with a single exception the whole city was
destroyed. The exception was the house of Pindar, the
great poet—another expression of Alexander's respect for
Greek culture. The brutality of this proceeding indicates
how anxious Alexander was to get off to the East. Duly
impressed, the Athenian Assembly, which had supported
Thebes, congratulated Alexander on what he had done!

334 B.C. Alexander could now go ahead with his plans. He
crossed the Hellespont into Asia Minor to join the
Macedonian general Parmenio, who had been there since 336
B.C. The Macedonian army may have numbered about 35,000.
The Persians, absurdly since it was no secret to anyone
what Alexander was intending, were not organized to meet
him. A new emperor, DARIUS, had taken office the year
before in 335 B.C. Darius, very much a weak figure, was
far away in Mesopotamia watching and slowly putting

together an enormous army. The Persian forces on the spot
in Asia Minor, perhaps 40,000 in number, were defeated at
Granicus by Alexander. The Macedonians now "liberated"
the Greek cities on the coast of Asia Minor. As a further
indication of his admiration for Greek processes, Alexander
established democracies in these cities, something he knew
better than to allow in Macedonia.

333 B.C. Alexander next crossed Asia Minor, looking for
battle with the main Persian army. At Gordian, where the
Macedonian army assembled after the winter's camp,
Alexander solved the riddle of the Gordian Knot. Legend
said that the man who untied the knot would conquer all
Asia: Alexander cut through the knot with his sword. He
defeated the Persian army, commanded by Darius in person,
at Issus in a very hard-fought battle. The Persian army
was much bigger than Alexander's, although we have no good
idea of its size, but it is notable that its most dependable unit was a phalanx of 15,000 Greek mercenaries.
Everything indicated what had been noticeable since at
least 400 B.C.--that the Greeks were the clear military
superiors of the Persians. Darius fled shamefully, and
his family was captured.

332 B.C. Allowing Darius to run off to the East and raise
another army, an indication of his sense of security,
Alexander moved south from Issus to capture the Phoenician
cities. There was a great siege at Tyre, the chief
Phoenician port. This step deprived the Persians of their
navy and made it much easier for Alexander to supply his
forces. Up to this point, he had been embarrassed by his
lack of strength at sea, a weakness which owed much to
the refusal of Athens to supply to the Macedonians the
ships which had been asked of it. By the end of the year,
Alexander had gone on into Egypt, where there was no
serious resistance at all.

331 B.C. Alexander spent much of the year in Egypt. He
founded Alexandria, intending it to replace Tyre as the
great trading city of the eastern Mediterranean. Alexandria
grew to enormous size and importance over the next several
centuries, becoming the chief center of Greek culture and
the largest city of the Roman Empire outside Rome itself.
Alexander also took Cyrene to the west of Egypt, which

brought him into contact with the <u>Carthaginian</u> territories in the central Mediterranean. Late in 331 B.C. Alexander entered <u>Mesopotamia</u>, and in October he defeated Darius in a second big battle at <u>Gaugamela</u> near <u>Nineveh</u>. He took Babylon and by year's end was at <u>Susa</u>, the summer capital of the Persian Empire.

In this year Sparta and some of the other states in the Peloponnesus revolted. They were easily defeated, being treated leniently afterwards. <u>Demosthenes</u> convinced the Athenians not to get involved.

330 B.C. Alexander took <u>Persepolis</u>, the Persian capital, and burned the palace of <u>Xerxes</u>, a symbolic act of revenge against the man who had invaded Greece 150 years before.

By this time it was clear that Alexander intended to try to secure his position, at the head of a single army very far from home with a gigantic area to administer, by adopting a generous attitude toward those he conquered. He was allowing a lot of self-government under the supervision of Macedonian officials. He also was generous toward the cultures he encountered. He won popularity in Egypt by freeing the ancient religions from the restrictions the Persians had put upon them. Toward the Persians themselves, he was similarly open-handed. He appointed Persian governors, sometimes wore oriental clothes, and allowed Persians to lie down in front of him (the prostration) as they had before their kings.

Some of this annoyed the Macedonians, and it was never far from their minds that the gods might have demanded madness as well as a short life from Alexander in trade for his wonderful talents. The great general <u>Parmenio</u> and his son were killed at this point, with Alexander being perhaps a little worried about the Macedonians. It gave the Greeks the opportunity to hit Alexander from both sides: resenting his success in spreading Greek influence and culture, they could also criticize him for permitting too much non-Greek influence to survive. It could be made to seem that Alexander was trying to "homogenize" the different traditions of the areas he conquered, something very different from trying to extend Greek civilization to them all.

Later in 330 B.C., Alexander followed the Persian army,
what there was left of it, to the east. Darius was
murdered by his own men.

329-327 B.C. Alexander campaigned through Afghanistan and
then north into the plains of Bactria and Sogdiana in
Central Asia. There he overcame the last organized
resistance on the part of the Persians. The Persian
governor of Bactria, who had been behind the murder of
Darius although related to the emperor, was executed by
Alexander in distinctly eastern manner: his nose and ears
were cut off and he was then crucified.

In 327 B.C. Alexander married a Sogdian princess,
Roxane. There were several conspiracies against him by
his followers, who were more and more unsettled. Among
others, Alexander killed for conspiracy a nephew of
Aristotle, Callisthenes, who was along as historian of the
campaign. Callisthenes objected to prostrating himself
in front of Alexander. In 327 B.C. Alexander murdered
his foster-brother, who had insulted him while drunk.

In Sogdiana Alexander believed that he was near the
edge of land, the great continent, with only the territories of the barbarians before him. Therefore, he turned
back to the south, to push toward the limits of the
continent in another direction.

327-325 B.C. Alexander took his army into northwest
India, the valley of the Indus. Here his favorite horse
Bucephalus died, and he founded a city in its honor.

In 326 B.C., as he prepared to move across the desert
from the valley of the Indus into the valley of the Ganges
(which he believed bounded the continent in that direction)
the Macedonians in his army finally mutinied. They
thought that Alexander had enough. Against his will, the
troops forced him to turn back.

325-324 B.C. Returning to Susa and later Ecbatana,
Alexander occupied himself putting his possessions back
into order. Most of the veteran Macedonian troops he
allowed to go home; replacing many of them with men drawn
from the old Persian Empire, his army must have had a
very different appearance now, although the new men were
still trained and still fought in the Macedonian manner.
He promoted racial mixing in marriage as well as in the

service, forcing his remaining Macedonian soldiers to take
wives locally. He himself, in oriental style, took a
second wife, a daughter of Darius; later, he took a third
wife. He also required the Greek states to recognize
that he was a god: all of them, Sparta included, did so.
Despite the Greek traditions of heroic men who became
gods, such as Heracles, Alexander's order was another
example of eastern influence.

Alexander found that he had to replace most of his
governors and administrators, who had flourished mightily
in corruption during his absence to the east since 330
B.C. The man he had left in charge of the finances in
Persia, Harpalus, fled with a great deal of booty as
Alexander returned in 325 B.C. Harpalus ran off to Greece,
hoping to use his money to tempt the Greeks into rebellion
against Alexander. His best prospects were at Athens,
which was involved already in a dispute with Alexander.

Athens had stayed out of trouble since 335 B.C.
Demosthenes was discredited by the total failure of his
policy of resistance, but the chief figure of the period,
Lycurgus, was himself cautiously anti-Macedonian. The
other leading politician at Athens was Phocion, who was
even more cautious. Phocion, with a great reputation for
honesty but no other mark of note, was so unobjectionable
that he had been elected general a record 45 years without ever doing much. The city engaged in a last burst of
public building at this time. The great architect Philo
built a new naval storehouse; a stadium was constructed
for the Panathenaic Games; and, most importantly, the
theater of Dionysius was rebuilt at the foot of the
Acropolis—its ruins can still be seen today. No challenge
to Macedonia was dared, but a mild form of the Spartan
youth training was introduced at this time, a sort of token
show of determination. Crisis threatened in 324 B.C. when
Alexander was reshaping his possessions. Alexander ordered
that all Greek exiles should be allowed to return home; for
Athens, this meant that the inhabitants of Samos, who had
been turned out a century earlier after the revolt of 440
B.C., would be allowed to return and reclaim their lands
from the Athenian citizens who had displaced them.
Athens refused.

245

It was at this point that Harpalus showed up. After
a little hesitation, Athens decided not to get involved.
Harpalus was arrested, but he escaped into exile before
he could be handed to the Macedonians. Athens seized
his money to keep for Alexander. When it came time to
hand the money over, though, only half of it could be
found. Demosthenes was at the center of the corruption
scandal which followed. He was one of those appointed to
watch over the money, and he had definitely pocketed some
portion of it. Demosthenes was convicted and fined, then
imprisoned for nonpayment of the fine; he escaped into
exile, the usual course for Athenian prisoners.

324-323 B.C. In 324 B.C., Alexander's favorite boy-friend,
Hephaestion, died. He was provided with an enormously
lavish funeral, Alexander having cared much more for him
than for any of his wives. Alexander intended as his next
step an expedition into Arabia to the south, which he
thought would bring him to the edge of the continent in
that direction. He died at Babylon in the summer of 323
B.C. during the preparations for this expedition, shortly
after the tremendous funeral ceremonies for Hephaestion
had been completed. As he had expected, Alexander had only
a brief life.

The news of Alexander's death moved some of the Greek
states to rebel against the Macedonians. Athens was the
leader, with most states north of the isthmus going along
save for Boeotia. After scoring some early successes, the
rebellion was put down by the Macedonians in 322 B.C.
without any great trouble. Demosthenes, who had been
allowed to return from exile to aid this last attempt at
resistance, now poisoned himself to escape Macedonian
anger. The generals of Alexander, not sharing his admiration for Athenian culture, dealt severely with the city.
They replaced the old democracy with a moderate oligarchy,
allowing about 40 per cent of the adult male citizens to
have political rights. A Macedonian garrison was to be
stationed at Athens; the Athenian landowners were thrown
out of Samos. The last shreds of independence and glory
had been taken from Athens. Fittingly, Aristotle, the
last of the great names, died in this same year of 322 B.C.

Had Alexander survived some years longer, he probably would have returned to the conquest of northern India. This would have left him with only the central and western Mediterranean to take in order to complete the conquest of what was to him the civilized world. The Greeks believed that there was one great continent. Its limits, they supposed, ran from Gibraltar across north Africa to Egypt, past Arabia and the coasts of Persia to north India, turning north at the Ganges and connecting on the north side via Sogdiana and the Caspian Sea with the Black Sea and the barbarian lands north of Greece, reaching finally out across more barbarian lands beyond Italy and the western Mediterranean to Gibraltar. The prospect of a Macedonian army campaigning under Alexander in the western Mediterranean, with all that it would have meant for the Romans, is a fascinating one.

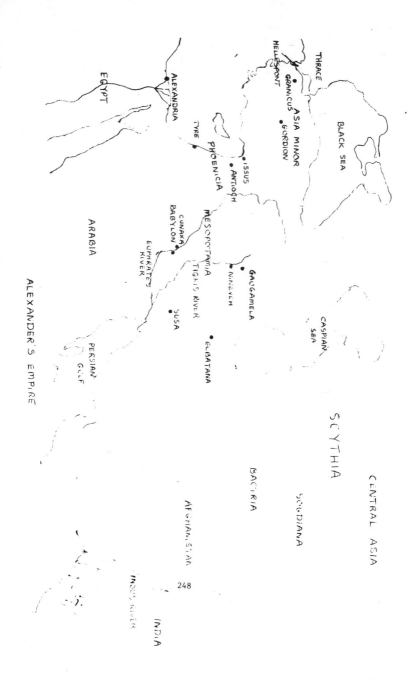

ALEXANDER'S EMPIRE

248

The effects of Alexander the Great's conquests were enormous. Although his empire was not able to survive as a single unit, most of the area he conquered remained under Macedonian control for several generations. Alexander's young son was murdered not long after his death (322 B.C.); the leading Macedonian generals and advisors carved out pieces for themselves. Three main blocs soon emerged, all ruled by kings in the Macedonian fashion (the successor—states): the Ptolemies (founded by Ptolemy), in Egypt; --the Seleucids (founded by Seleucus), centered at Antioch in Syria, holding Asia Minor, Mesopotamia, and for a while the possessions further east; --the Antigonids (founded by Antigonus), in Macedonia and Greece. These three blocs fought one another frequently; in the Aegean, where all had claims; in Thrace, where the Seleucids and Antigonids were at odds; in the Near East, around present-day Israel, where the Seleucids and Ptolemies were in conflict. The Antigonid and Ptolemaic areas were much more compact and stable than the Seleucid. The Seleucids lost just about everything east of Mesopotamia after a few decades--much of this was regained by Antiochus the Great in the late 200's B.C. for a further brief while. The richest of the three was Egypt, which the Macedonians exploited successfully, taking direct control of most of the Egyptian economy in the most thorough-going example of its kind in the ancient world. In Asia Minor, particularly, other lesser independent states emerged in the 200's, playing off the great states against each other. The most important of these was Pergamum, whose Macedonian king ruled the whole coast of Ionia and a good piece of the interior of Asia Minor. The area all around the eastern Mediterranean was Macedonian until the Romans came along. By 200 B.C. the Romans were in Greece and the Antigonids were living on sufferance. A few bare years later the Seleucids were defeated (Antigonus the Great was not great enough to begin to match the Romans; the Ptolemies fell into line without being pushed. So by soon after 200 B.C. the entire eastern Mediterranean area was under Roman influence. The Seleucid kingdom fell apart, although it remained in control of Antioch, but little more, until the 60's B.C. when it ended. The Ptolemies existed as Roman "friends" even longer, keeping Egypt, but nothing else, until 31 B.C. The last Ptolemaic ruler of Egypt was the famous Cleopatra.

The cultural effects of the Macedonian victories were also tremendous. Give-and-take among the Greek and other civilizations increased greatly, but, inevitably under the circumstances, the most important part of those exchanges was the spreading of Greek civilization around the Near East. Over time, many of the dominant groups in the area from Greece around the eastern Mediterranean to Egypt moved toward a common civilization, one which was heavily Greek in its orientation. Of course, as the price of such success, Greek civilization had to do a good deal of adapting of its own. This wal already to be seen in Alexander's day, and the price increased with the years. Because of all the changes they brought, Alexander's conquests are used to mark the end of Classical Greece and of Classical Greek civilization. The term used for the new age, of the extended and altered Greek civilization, is HELLENISTIC. We speak of the Hellenistic Age, a period lasting from Alexander (died 323 B.C.) to the conquest of the Near East by the Romans (by the 1st century B.C.).

The great oddity in all that happened was that Greece itself, disliking the Macedonians, was such an unwilling party to the extension of Greek influence and benefitted so little from it. Ever since the Peloponnesian War, when the suicidal instincts of the Greek states became clear, and when it also began to become clear that they were ignoring the opportunity to take advantage of their superiority against the Persians, there had been appeals to Greeks to unite, to forget thier old quarrels, to turn together agair.st the Persians. The great Sophist Gorgias had urged this at the Olympian Games of 408 B.C. The most prominent supporter of this line was the Athenian orator of the 300's B.C., Isocrates, the greatest name in the art of talking until Demosthenes came along. Isocrates' most famous speech urging a common effort against Persia came at the Olympian Games of 380 B.C. (of course, these all Greek affairs provided a natural setting for this kind of argument). Isocrates explained that the rise of Athens, the name of Greek should be thought no longer a matter of race but one of intelligence; and should be given to those who share our culture rather than just our common origin. Later, when Phillip became military marter of the era, Isocrates, consistent with his position on this matter, urged Greeks to accept his leadership. There were few to pay attention to these arguments; they were too much at odds with Greek

tradition. It was Demosthenes' futile plan which carried
the day.

From the Greeks' very local point of view, the
important thing about Alexander's success was that it put
the era of the city-state beyond recall. Athens and the
others learned this to their expense in 323-322 B.C.
Democracy was intolerable, and so it largely disappeared;
traditional philosophy was superfluous, and so it went
through a radical change in its nature. Little of what
had counted traditionally in the city-states made any sense
at all in the world of the god-kings in the generations
after Alexander.

It is not surprising that many Greeks were ill-equipped
to deal with what happened and that they took little
advantage of the tremendous opportunities opened up to them
by Alexander. The system of the city-state had been losing
its way since 400 B.C., as we have seen, but Greeks had
become skilful in ignoring that fact. This was not just
men like Demosthenes, preaching patriotism in a slave-ridden,
welfare, mercenary-dependent Athens; Aristotle, Alexander's
own teacher, centered his political system on the polis just
as if nothing was happening--as had Plato. With this kind
of attitude, it was asking a lot for Greeks to accept the
eastern-style Macedonian absolute monarchy, something much
closer to the old Persian system than to anything in their
experience. Greece devoted a good part of its energy to
fighting the Macedonian (Antigonid) control in the 200's B.C.,
but there was no future in this. The evident weaknesses of
the old, fragmented city-states encouraged a limited movement
toward larger, federated units, called Leagues. There were
two important such leagues in the 200's B.C., the Achaean in
the Peloponnesus and the Aetolian north of the isthmus. Even
so, the Macedonians were far too strong.

The idea of consciously trading influence with the East
in philosophy, literature, art, and science was not much
less objectionable. As a result, most strangely, Greece
itself became over the next two centuries something of a
backwater in Greek civilization, which now included the
entire Near East. Athens remained much honored, but its
active reputation was limited, extending to little beyond
a continuing mastery of public speaking, so that the city's
image was one of cynical cleverness. Intellectual and

cultural leadership lay elsewhere in the Greek world, usually at <u>Alexandria</u> in Egypt, which soon became the biggest city of the entire region. Greece proper even became an economic backwater, as the natural advantages of other areas in such things as food production and mineral wealth were exploited more vigorously by those who went with the Macedonians. In every way, the Greece which the Romans entered around 200 B.C. was just a shadow of its old self.

Actually, the richest part of the Greek world remained independent, untouched by the Macedonian conquests. This was the area of south Italy and Sicily, "Great Greece" as it was called. From the beginning, the Greek cities set up there in the 600's B.C. had grown quickly, taking advantage of the superior farm land and the precious metals they enjoyed. The native tribes were not much of a problem. The <u>Carthaginians</u>, who won control of the <u>Phoenician</u> colonies in the East, were more bothersome. They competed against the Greeks in trade in the western Mediterranean and they held the western part of Sicily. Even before 600 B.C. there had been trouble betweens the Greeks and the Carthaginians in Sicily and south Italy (in the latter area, the Carthaginians helped the <u>Etruscans</u> of centeal Italy against the Greeks). Things worked out to the advantage of the Greeks. Around 500 B.C., the Etruscans were defeated in south-central Italy, and a little later the Carthaginians were beaten in Sicily and were pinned to the western part of the island. Here, in the West, was a counterpart to the defeat and turning back of the Persians in the Aegean at much the same time. There was no serious further threat to the Greeks in this area for almost a century.

In the 400's B.C. the wealth of south Italy and Sicily became legendary. The Greek cities there took a full and active part in the cultural life of mainland Greece, the games, etc. The chief Greek city to the West, already, was <u>Syracuse</u>. Syracuse was controlled in the early 400's B.C. by the tyrant <u>Gelon</u>, who won credit for the defeat of the Carthaginians. Gelon, like most tyrants, was himself an aristocrat--but, unusually for a tyrant, he was very favorable to the aristocrats and no friend to the poor. The conservative poets of the last stage of the Archaic Period liked Gelon, and Syracuse, a great deal. Both

Simonides and Pindar praised the city to mainland Greeks.
The other major Greek city in Sicily was Acragas, the home
of the great philosopher Empedocles. It, too, was a
tyranny around 500 B.C. Gelon, tyrant of Syracuse, died
in 478 B.C. The tyranny remained in his family, but the
system was overthrown in 465 B.C. and a democracy was
established. Tyranny gave way to democracy in other
Greek cities in the area (including Acragas) at about the
same time--the pattern of the mainland was being followed.

The Greek cities of Sicily and south Italy kept themselves to themselves politically, taking little part in the
affairs of the Greek mainland. To some extent, this hid
their power. Ignorance and greed tempted Athens into
attacking Syracuse in the Peloponnesian War (415-413 B.C.)--
the victory of Syracuse must have made everyone much more
aware of how power had shifted in the Greek world. In 409
B.C., on the heels of the Athenians, came the Carthaginians,
moving out of the western part of the island, the first
time they had caused much trouble since the 470's B.C.
The Carthaginians did well, capturing Acragas (which had the
biggest of all Greek temples, the unfinished temple to
Olympian Zeus) and other Greek cities and defeating Syracuse.
Failure hurt the democracy at Syracuse much more than the
Athenian democracy was hurt by the Peloponnesian War. In
405 B.C. DIONYSIUS seized power at Syracuse as tyrant.

Dionysius of Syracuse became with time the greatest
political figure in the entire Greek world. A product of
an ordinary family, he played the line of friend of the
people in the way common with tyrants. As at Athens under
Peisistratus, the democratic constitution remained in theory
in effect. In a series of wars Dionysius drove the
Carthagininas into the western tip of the island, leaving
them with much less than they had started with. He also
grabbed control of the other Greek cities on the island.
Dionysius also helped himself to a good chunk of south
Italy. This was much the largest piece of territory any
Greek state ever controlled directly in the Classical Period;
it was the biggest step away from the city-state (an Empire
of Syracuse). Elsewhere in south Italy, and up the
Adriatic, Dionysius had allies/satellites among the Greek
cities. He did not control the Greek cities of Campania.
They fell at this time into the hands of native tribes.

Still, he did not bother much with Greece politically, although sometimes, as we saw, he helped Sparta against Athens. Plato visited Syracuse in 388 B.C. He found that Dionysius made poor material for a philosopher-king.

The great Dionysius died in 367 B.C. In a nice touch, he died partying after he received the word that one of his tragedies had finally won a first prize at Athens. He had been fancying himself in this line for a long time. It would be nice to know what his work was like. His feeble son held on for about a decade. Then turmoil and revolution followed, with a variety of figures setting themselves up as dictators. Plato made two more trips to Syracuse in this period, but still found that the city was no place to test his ideas. The Empire of Syracuse broke up.

In 344 B.C. the trouble was brought to an end for a while. Syracuse and the other Greek towns were turned into moderate democracies. This was the work of Timoleon, an aristocrat sent out from Corinth (the mother-city) to get the job done. This gave Timoleon a great reputation as a political wizard; he retired once his job was done and lived to enjoy a much-honored life.

Syracuse and south Italy avoided the threat of Macedonia. But another, and a much greater, threat was already in sight. This was Rome. The experience of the next half-century revealed how weak militarily the Greek states here were, with their mercenary armies, their lack of public spirit, their lack of ability to work together. Everything we saw in mainland Greece in the period of Demosthenes held true across the Adriatic as well. The cities of south Italy were no longer even able to protect themselves against the backward tribes in the interior. The Greek cities in Campania fell to the tribes around 400 B.C. Those further south picked up the sad habit of calling in outside Greek help. A Spartan king was killed there in the 330's B.C. fighting with a Spartan army for money against the tribes. An uncle of Alexander the Great, called Alexander of Epirus, died in the same line of work in 330 B.C. All of this made easy pickings for the Romans. As we shall see, they had a hard time with the tribes; with the Greek cities, they had no real problem at all. By the 270's B.C. the Romans had conquered all of south Italy;

once again, the best idea the Greeks here had come up with was to bring in mercenaries from the mainland. In the 250's B.C., with just as much ease, the Romans took control of Syracuse and the other Greek towns on Sicily. It would not be long before the rest of the Greek world followed.

Introduction to Plato

It has been truly said that all western philosophy is merely footnotes to Plato. He has indeed had more influence than any other philosopher, and even much of what we call "Christian" is actually Platonic.

We mus remember, however, that we know much more of Plato than the philosophers who came before him. We must try to see how Plato fits with the philosophers who came before himm philosophers we have already looked at.

Plato, coming late into the philosophic complexity of the debate between Heraclitus and Parmenides, decided to reconcile the two by using the dualism of Pythagoras, the body and the soul . Plato said that there was a place where all was flux, the world the non-philosophical call the "real" world, and a place where all was stasis, the ideal world, the world of ideas. As plato saw it, we know a cat when we see one because we see that it partakes of the idea of cat-ness, and a dog when we see one because it partakes of the idea of dogness. We never mistake a large cat for a small dog. Thus, Plato argued, the individual cats and dogs which we see are obviously imitations of an "ideal" cat and dog, an ideal which does not change. We also distinguish ugly cats and dogs from beautiful cats and dogs by comparing them, unconsciously, with an ideal cat and dog, an ideal we are aware of in our minds, and an ideal which is there from birth. Plato did not say this, but we might grasp what he was saying if we notice that all the girls in magazines like <u>Playboy</u> and in beauty contests are very nearly the same shape, like 38-20-38; none are 20-8 8-38 or 40-40-40. Probably, then, the ideal girl, of which these girls are pale approximations, would be 50-10-50. This ideal, of course, is not to be seen in the Heraclitean world of flux*

From this concept of the relationship between the

---

*Many Platonists object to such illustrations as this because they deal with shape, not form, an important Platonic distinction.

ideal and the real flow many consequences. First, only a foolish person would be interested in the "real" world, ... trees and people and food, for its own sake, but only as an avenue to the ideal world. All things in what we erroneously call the real world fade away, die, and disappear. Intelligent people should be interested in the eternal world of ideas, the "ideals." And if the concept of "Catness" is hard to grasp, the concept of "justice," "goodness," or "righteousness" is that much harder. We cannot judge whether a given act is "just" or not unless we can define justice, and to do that we must appeal to a constant, unchanging standard. To discover this "abstract" or ideal standard, we must examine many acts, decide whihc comes closest to an ideal ofjustice, and compare the individual act with the dieal.

Most men, the vast majority, cannot grasp the difference between the real and the ideal. They are foolishly more interested in tonight's supper and not in man's true nourishment, ideas. Only those who through study grasp the fact that what most men call "real" is actually an illusion and that what most men call "ideal" is actually real can make "true" judgments. The foolish majority concern themselves with money, which can be lost, and social status, which depends on the whim of other people. The intellegent minority concorn themselves with the ideas of value.

Obviously, then, the majority should be rules and guided by the intellegent minority. In his Republic, Plato explained this oligarchic scheme at great length. Those capable of going by absolute, "ideal" standards are to be identified early in life and trained to rule a society governed by such standsards. Since they, the rulers, know the standards and others do not, and since (obviously) all who "know" see the same absolute, there must be no deviation. All who disagree with the oligarchs in any was are to be elaborately "brainwashed" and if they still disagree, are to be killed.

Let us make an important observation here. First, the treatment of dissenters in Plato's republic is harsh and repressive. Yet Plato's mentor, Socrates, had been such a

dissenter; Socrates had, as we have seen, been very well
and fairly treated by the oligarchs of Athens, but finally executed. Had Plato learned nothing from the experience? This has caused Plato scholars no end of
difficulty. In reality, the answer is simple: Socrates
was not a realist byt an "idealist," and he existed in a
"realist" society: the opposite would obtain in Plato's
republic--Socrates would do the executing.

Secondly, we must note that Plato wishes to have a
state in whihc there is no conflict, no difficulty, no instability. This kind of state is very different from the
system of government in the Iliad and Odyssey, for in those
societies debates, conflict and disagreement were highly
desired. Nestor and Odysseus were much admired for their
skill in degates and oratory. Arguing was not only tol-
erated but part of the fun. All good men, in seeking the
best for their families, would come into conflict with other
good men. Turmoil, uncertainty, and upheaval were for the
Homeric people interesting. Whereas Homer's heroes could
tolerate anything but boredom, Plato's citizens would pay
ny price for stability.

Plato cannot, of course, be held responsible for the mis-
understandings and misinterpretations of his disciples, for
the next five hundred years. However, inherent in Plato's
scheme is the antipathy between those who think and those
who do, between hydraulic engineers and plumbers, exalting
thinkers (that is, professors) over doers. Moreover, Plato
tends to equate "good" with "soul and bad with "body." The
Homeric Greek loved booze, sex, poetry, friendship and war,
all at the appropriate times and places. The Platonist
opposes body and soul, and prefers the soul. Thus the
Platonist dislikes the pleasure of the flesh in order to
do good for the soul. From this reasoning, it is only a
step to punishing the body to enhance the soul (ascetisism).

Plato filled his writings with analogies for the body-
soul relationship. In one place, the male yearning for the
female mirrors the division in the "real" world for what is
one person in the "ideal" world. Ideally, there was a four-
legged, four-armed androgynous creature whihc in the "real"
world is a divided creature yearning for the "true" union,
often confused with the "real" union of the sexual organs

Our reading contains the most famous of these analogies of the real with the ideal, the allegory of the cave.

Plato's relationship to Greek "science" thus becomes extremely important and extremely comples. Our view is generally Platonic, for we see the scientiest as one interested in knowledge for its own sake, never thinking of himself or any practical results. Plato inscribed over the door of his Academy (for that was the name of his school) this motto:"Enter here none who do not know geometry and music." This would seem to show his interest in science and mathematics. But his interest tended to be Magical and Pythagorean, not scientific. These subjects for him re-inforced his idea that order existed in nature, the mark of all bad scientists (there are not many good ones). It seems to be that Plato encouraged philosophers to reject experimental science and industrial techniques as things beneath the interest of the philosopher. In the final analysis, Plato's philosophy is not a system but a method, and thus leads to no helpful conclusions. It is a procedure, not a paradigm.

Convinced by Plato and his followers, the Greeks abandoned astronomy, the belief that the earth is a random planet in a random system, for astrology, the belief that the earth is the central focus of a system of intricate meaningful connections (when the moon is in the seventh house, we are in the age of Aquarius). Of what is this significant?

The Euthyphro

Euthyphro. Why have you left the Lyceum, Socrates?
and what are you doing in the porch of the King Archon?
Surely you cannot be engaged in an action before the
king, as I am.

Socrates. Not in an action, Euthyphro; impeachment
is the word which the Athenians use.

Euth. What! I suppose that some one has been prosecuting you, for I cannot believe that you are the prose-
cutor of another.

Soc. Certainly not.

Euth. Then some one else has been prosecuting you?

Soc. Yes.

Euth. And who is he?

Soc. A young man who is little known, Euthyphro; and
I hardly know him: his name is Meletus, and he is of the
deme of Pitthis. Perhaps you may remember his appearance;
he has a beak, and long straight hair, and a beard which
is ill grown.

Euth. No, I do not remember him, Socrates. But
what is the charge which he brings against you?

Soc. What is the charge? Well, a very serious
charge, which shows a good deal of character in the
young man, and for which he is certainly not to be
despised. He says he knows how the youth are corrupted
and who are their corruptors. I fancy that he must be
a wise man, and seeing that I am anything but a wise
man, he has found me out, and is going to accuse me of
corrupting his young friends. And of this our mother
the state is to be the judge. Of all our political men
he is the only one who seems to me to begin in the right
way, with the cultivation of virtue in youth; like a
good husbandman, he makes the young shoots his first
care, and clears away us who are the destroyers of them.
That is the first step; he will afterwards attend to
the elder branches; and if he goes on as he has begun,
he will be a very great public benefactor.

Euth. I hope that he may; but I rather fear, Socrates,
that the reverse will turn out to be the truth. My
opinion is that in attacking you he is simply aiming a

blow at the state in a sacred place. But in what way does he say that you corrupt the young?

Soc. He brings a wonderful accusation against me, which at first hearing excites surprise: he says that I am a poet or maker of gods, and that I make new gods and deny the existence of old ones; this is the ground of his indictment.

Euth. I understand, Socrates; he means to attack you about the familiar sign, which occasionally, as you say, comes to you. He thinks that you are a neologian, and he is going to have you up before the court for this. He knows that such a charge is readily received by the world. I can tell you that, for even when I myself speak in the assembly about divine things, and foretell the future to them, they laugh at me as a madman; and yet every word that I say is true. But they are jealous of all of us. I suppose that we must be brave and not mind them.

Soc. Their laughter, friend Euthyphro, is not a matter of much consequence. For a man may be thought wise; but the Athenians, I suspect, do not trouble themselves about him until he begins to impart his wisdom to others; and then for some reason or other, perhaps, as you say, from jealousy, they are angry.

Euth. I am never likely to try their temper in this way.

Soc. I dare say not, for you are select in your acquaintance, and seldom impart your wisdom. But I have a benevolent habit of pouring out myself to everybody, and would even pay for a listener, and I am afraid that the Athenians know this; and therefore, as I was saying, if the Athenians would only laugh at me as you say that they laugh at you, the time might pass gaily enough in the court; but perhaps they may be in earnest, and then what the end will be you soothsayers only can predict.

Euth. I dare say that the affair will end in nothing, Socrates, and that you will win your cause; and I think that I shall win mine.

Soc. And now what is you suit Euthyphro? are you the pursuer or the defendant?

Euth. I am the pursuer.

Soc. Of whom?

261

Euth. You will think me mad when I tell you.

Soc. Why, has the fugitive wings?

Euth. Nay, he is not very volatile at his time of life.

Soc. Who is he?

Euth. My father.

Soc. Your father! my good man?

Euth. Yes.

Soc. And of what is he accused?

Euth. Of murder, Socrates.

Soc. By the powers, Euthyphro! how little does the common herd know of the nature of right and truth. A man must be an extraordinary man, and have made great strides in wisdom, before he could have seen his way to this.

Euth. Indeed, Socrates, he must have made great strides.

Soc. I suppose that the man whom your father murdered was one of your relatives; if he had been a stranger you would never have thought of prosecuting him.

Euth. I am amused, Socrates, at your making a distinction between one who is a relation and one who is not a relation; for surely the pollution is the same in either case, if you knowingly associate with the murderer when you ought to clear yourself and him by proceeding against him. The real question is whether the murdered man has been justly slain. If justly, then your duty is to let the matter alone; but if unjustly, then even if the murderer is under the same roof with you and eats at the same table, proceed against him. Now the man who is dead was a poor dependent of mine who worked for us as a field labourer at our farm in Naxos, and one day in a fit of drunken passion he got into a quarrel with one of our domestic servants and slew him. My father bound him head and foot and threw him into a ditch, and then sent to Athens to ask of a diviner what he should do with him. Meantime he had no care or thought of him, being under the impression that he was a murderer; and that even if he did die there would be no great harm. And this was just what happened. For such was the effect of cold and hunger and chains upon him, that before the messenger returned from the diviner, he was dead. And my father and family are angry with me for taking the part of the murderer and prosecuting my father. They say that he did not kill him, and that if he did, the dead man was but a murderer, and I ought not to take any notice, for that a son is impious who prosecutes a father. Which shows, Socrates, how little they know of the opinions of the gods about piety and impiety.

Soc. Good heavens, Euthyphro! and have you such a precise knowledge of piety and impiety, and of divine things in general, that, supposing the circumstances to be as you state, you are not afraid that you too may be doing an impious thing in bringing an action against your father?

Euth. The best of Euthyphro, and that which distinguishes him, Socrates, from other men, is his exact knowledge of all these matters. What should I be good for without that?

Soc. Rare friend! I think that I cannot do better than be your disciple. Then before the trial with Meletus comes on I shall challenge him, and say that I have always had a great interest in religious questions, and now, as he charges me with rash imaginations and innovations in religion, I have become your disciple. You, Meletus, as I shall say to him acknowledge Euthyphro to be a great theologian, and sound in his opinions; and if you approve of him you ought to approve of me, and not have me in to court; but if you disapprove, you should begin by indicting him who is my teacher, and who is the real corruptor, not of the young, but of the old; that is to say, of myself whom he instructs, and of his old father whom he admonishes and chastises. And if Meletus refuses to listen to me, but will go on, and will not shift the indictment from me to you, I cannot do better than to repeat this challenge in the court.

Euth. Yes, Socrates; and if he attempts to indict me I am mistaken if I do not find a flaw in him; the court shall have a great deal more to say to him than to me.

Soc. And I, my dear firend, knowing this, am desirous of becoming your disciple. For I observe that no one appears to notice you—not even this Meletus; but his sharp eyes have found me out at once, and he

has indicted me for impiety. And therefore, I adjure
you to tell me the nature of piety and impiety, which
you said that you knew so well, and of murder, and the
rest of them. What are they? Is not piety in every
action always the same? and impiety again, is not that
always the opposite of piety, and also the same with
itself, having, as impiety, one notion which includes
whatever is impious?

Euth. To be sure, Socrates.

Soc. And what is piety, and what is impiety?

Euth. Piety is doing as I am doing; that is to say,
prosecuting any one who is guilty of murder, sacrilege,
or of any similar crime—whether he be your father or
your mother, or whoever he may be, that makes no difference—and not prosecuting them is impiety. And please
to consider, Socrates, what a notable proof I will give
you of the truth of what I am saying, which I have
already given to others:—of the principle, I mean, that
the impious, whoever he may be, ought not to go unpunished. For do not men regard Zeus as the best and most
righteous of the gods?—and yet they admit that he bound
his father (Cronos) because he wickedly devoured his
sons, and that he too had punished his own father
(Uranus) for a similar reason, in a nameless manner.
And yet when I proceed against my father, they are angry
with me. So inconsistent are they in their way of
talking when the gods are concerned, and when I am concerned.

Soc. May not this be the reason, Euthyphro, why I
am charged with impiety—that I cannot away with these
stories about the gods? and therefore I suppose that
people think me wrong. But, as you who are well informed
about them approve of them, I cannot do better than
assent to your superior wisdom. For what else can I
say, confessing as I do, that I know nothing about
them? I wish that you would tell me whether you
really believe that they are true.

Euth. Yes, Socrates; and things more wonderful
still, of which the world is in ignorance.

Soc. And do you really believe that the gods fought
with one another, and had dire quarrels, battles, and
the like, as the poets say, and as you may see represented in the works of great artists? The temples are

full of them; and notably the robe of Athene, which is carried up to the Acropolis at the great Panathenaea, is embroidered with them. Are all these tales of the gods true, Euthyphro?

Euth. Yes, Socrates; and, as I was saying, I can tell you, if you would like to hear them, many other things about the gods which would quite amaze you.

Soc. I dare say; and you shall tell me them at some other time when I have leisure. But just at present I would rather hear from you a more precise answer, which you have not as yet given, my friend, to the question, What is "piety"? In reply, you only say that piety is, Doing as you do, charging your father with murder.

Euth. And that is true, Socrates.

Soc. I dare say, Euthyphro, but there are many other pious acts.

Euth. There are.

Soc. Remember that I did not ask you to give me two or three examples of piety, but to explain the general idea which makes all pious things to be pious. Do you not recollect that there was one idea which made the impious impious, and the pious pious?

Euth. I remember.

Soc. Tell me what you mean, and then I shall have a standard to which I may look and by which I may measure the nature of actions, whether yours or any one's else, and say that this action is pious, and that impious.

Euth. I will tell you, if you like.

Soc. I should very much like.

Euth. Piety, then, is that which is dear to the gods, and impiety is that which is not dear to them.

Soc. Very good, Euthyphro; you have now given me the sort of answer which I wanted. But whether what you say is true or not I cannot as yet tell, although I make no doubt that you will prove the truth of your words.

Euth. Of course.

Soc. Come, then, and let us examine what we are saying. That thing or person which is dear to the gods is pious, and that thing or person which is hateful to the gods is impious. Was not that said?

Euth. Yes, that was said.

265

Soc. And that seems to have been very well said too.

Euth. Yes, Socrates, I think so; it was certainly said.

Soc. And further, Euthyphro, the gods were admitted to have enmities and hatreds and differences—that was also said?

Euth. Yes, that was said.

Soc. And what sort of difference creates enmity and anger? Suppose for example that you and I, my good friend, differ about a number; do differences of this sort make us enemies and set us at variance with one another? Do we not go at once to calculation, and end them by a sum?

Euth. True.

Soc. Or suppose that we differ about magnitudes, do we not quickly put an end to that difference by measuring?

Euth. That is true.

Soc. And we end a controversy about heavy and light by resorting to a weighing machine?

Euth. To be sure.

Soc. But what differences are those which, because they cannot be thus decided, make us angry and set us at enmity with one another? I dare say the answer does not occur to you at the moment, and therefore I will suggest that this happens when the matters of difference are the just and unjust, good and evil, honourable and dishonourable. Are not these the points about which, when differing, and unable satisfactorily to decide our differences, you and I and all men quarrel, when we do quarrel?

Euth. Yes, Socrates, that is the nature of the differences about which we quarrel.

Soc. And the quarrels of the gods, nobile Euthyphro, when they occur, are of like nature?

Euth. They are.

Soc. They have differences of opinion, as you say, about good and evil, just and unjust, honourable and dishonourable: there would have been no quarrels among them, if there had been no such differences—would there now?

Euth. You are quite right.

· Soc. Does not every man love that which he deems

noble and just and good, and hate the opposite of them?

Euth. Very true.

Soc. But, as you say, people regard the same things, some as just and others as unjust; about which they dispute; and so there arise wars and fightings among them.

Euth. Yes, that is true.

Soc. Then the same things, as appears, are hated by the gods and loved by the gods, and are both hateful and dear to them?

Euth. True.

Soc. And upon this view the same things, Euthyphro, will be pious and also impious?

Euth. That, I suppose, is true.

Soc. Then, my friend, I remark with surprise that you have not answered what I asked. For I certainly did not ask you to tell me that which is both pious and impious: and now what is loved by the gods appears also to be hated by them. And therefore, Euthyphro, in thus chastising your father you may very likely be doing what is agreeable to Zeus but disagreeable to Cronos or Uranus, and what is acceptable to Hephaestus but unacceptable to Here, and there may be other gods who have similar differences of opinion.

Euth. But I believe, Socrates, that all the gods would be agreed as to the propriety of punishing a murderer: there would be no difference of opinion about that.

Soc. Well, but speaking of men, Euthyphro, did you ever hear any one arguing that a murderer or any sort of evil-doer ought to be let off?

Euth. I should say rather that these are the questions which they are always arguing, especially in courts of law: they commit all sorts of crimes, and there is nothing which they will not do or say to escape punishment.

Soc. But do they admit their guilt, Euthyphro, and yet say that they ought not to be punished?

Euth. No; they do not.

Soc. Then there are some things which they do not venture to say and do: for they do not venture to argue that the guilty are not to be punished, but they deny their guilt, do they not?

Euth. Yes.

Soc. Then they do not argue that the evil-doer should not be punished, but they argue about the fact of who the evil-doer is, and what he did and when?

Euth. True.

Soc. And the gods are in the same case, if as you assert they quarrel about just and unjust, and some of them say that there is unjustice done among them, and others of them deny this. For surely neither God nor man will ever venture to say that the doer of evil is not to be punished?

Euth. That is true, Socrates, in the main.

Soc. But they join issue about particulars; and this applies not only to men but to the gods, who, if they dispute at all, dispute about some act which is called in question, and which some affirm to be just, others to be unjust. Is not that true?

Euth. Quite true.

Soc. Well then, my dear friend Euthyphro, do tell me, for my better instruction and information, what proof have you that in the opinion of all the gods a servant who is guilty of murder, and is put in chains by the master of the dead man, and dies because he is put in chains before his corrector can learn from the inter- preters what he ought to do with him, dies unjustly; and that on behalf of such an one a son ought to proceed against his father and accuse him of murder. How would you show that all the gods absolutely agree in approving of his act? Prove to me that, and I will applaud your wisdom as long as you live.

Euth. That would not be an easy task, although I could make the matter very clear indeed to you.

Soc. I understand; you mean to say that I am not so quick of apprehension as the judges: for to them you will be sure to prove that the act is unjust, and hateful to the gods.

Euth. Yes indeed, Socrates; at least if they will listen to me.

Soc. But they will be sure to listen if they find that you are a good speaker. There was a notion that came into my mind while you were speaking; I said to myself: "Well, and what if Euthyphro does prove to me that all the gods regarded the death of the serf as unjust, how do I know anything more of the nature of piety and impiety? for granting that this action may be hateful to the gods, still these distinctions have no bearing on the definition of piety and impiety, for that which is hateful to the gods has been shown to be also pleasing and dear to them." And therefore, Euthyphro, I do not ask you to prove this; I will suppose, if you like, that all the gods condemn and abominate such an action. But I will amend the definition so far as to say that what all the gods hate is impious, and what they love pious or holy; and what some of them love and others hate is both or neither. Shall this be our definition of piety and impiety?

Euth. Why not, Socrates?

Soc. Why not! certainly, as far as I am concerned, Euthyphro, there is no reason why not. But whether this admission will greatly assist you in the task of instructing me as you promised, is a matter for you to consider.

Euth. Yes, I should say that what all the gods love is pious and holy, and the opposite which they all hate, impious.

Soc. Ought we to enquire into the truth of this, Euthyphro, or simply to accept the mere statement on our own authority and that of others? What do you say?

Euth. We should enquire; and I believe that the statement will stand the test of enquiry.

Soc. That, my good friend, we shall know better in a little while. The point which I should first wish to understand is whether the pious or holy is beloved by the gods because it is holy, or holy because it is beloved of the gods.

Euth. I do not understand your meaning, Socrates.

Soc. I will endeavour to explain: we speak of carrying and we speak of being carried, of leading and being led, seeing and being seen. And here is a difference, the nature of which you understand.

Euth. I think that I understand.

Soc. And is not that which is beloved distinct from that which loves?

Euth. Certainly.

Soc. Well; and now tell me, is that which is carried in this state of carrying because it is carried, or for some other reason?

Euth. No; that is the reason.

Soc. And the same is true of that which is led and of that which is seen?

Euth. True.

Soc. And a thing is not seen because it is visible, but conversely, visible because it is seen; nor is a thing led because it is in the state of being led, or carried because it is in the state of being carried, but the converse of this. And now I think, Euthyphro, that my meaning will be intelligible; and my meaning is, that any state of action or passion implies previous action or passion. It does not become because it is · becoming, but it is in a state of becoming because it becomes; neither does it suffer because it is in a state of suffering; but it is in a state of suffering because it suffers. Do you admit that?

Euth. Yes.

Soc. Is not that which is loved in some state either of becoming or suffering?

Euth. Yes.

Soc. And the same holds as in the previous instances; the state of being loved follows the act of being loved, and not the act the state.

Euth. Certainly.

Soc. And what do you say of piety, Euthyphro: is not piety, according to your definition, loved by all the gods?

Euth. Yes.

Soc. Because it is pious or holy, or for some other reason?

Euth. No, that is the reason.

Soc. It is loved because it is holy, not holy because it is loved?

Euth. Yes.

Soc. And that which is in a state to be loved by the gods, and is dear to them, is in a state to be loved by them because it is loved of them?

Euth. Certainly.

Soc. Then that which is loved of God, Euthyphro, is not holy, nor is that which is holy loved of God, as you affirm; but they are two different things.

Euth. How do you mean, Socrates?

Soc. I mean to say that the holy has been acknowledged by us to be loved of God because it is holy, not
to be holy because it is loved.

Euth. Yes.

Soc. But that which is dear to the gods is dear to
them because it is loved by them, not loved by them
because it is dear to them.

Euth. True.

Soc. But, friend Euthyphro, if that which is holy
is the same as that which is dear to God, and that which
is holy is loved as being holy, then that which is
dear to God would have been loved as being dear to God;
but if that which is dear to God is dear to him because
loved by him, then that which is holy would have been holy
because loved by him. But now you see that the reverse
is the case, and that they are quite different from one
another. For one is of a kind to be loved because it
is loved, and the other is loved because it is of a
kind to be loved. Thus you appear to me, Euthyphro,
when I ask you what is the essence of holiness, to offer
an attribute only, and not the essence—the attribute
of being loved by all the gods. But you still refuse
to explain to me the nature of holiness. And therefore, if you please, I will ask you not to hide your
treasure, but to tell me once more what holiness or
piety really is, whether dear to the gods or not (for
that is a matter about which we will not quarrel).
And what is impiety?

Euth. I really do not know, Socrates, how to say
what I mean. For somehow or other our arguments, on
whatever ground we rest them, seem to turn round and
walk away.

Soc. Your words, Euthyphro, are like the handiwork
of my ancestor Daedalus; and if I were the sayer or
propounder of them, you might say that this comes of
my being his relation; and that this is the reason why
my arguments walk away and will not remain fixed where
they are placed. But now, since these notions are
your own, you must find some other gibe, for they
certainly, as you yourself allow, show an inclination
to be on the move.

Euth. Nay, Socrates, I shall still say that you are
the Daedalus who sets arguments in motion; not I,

271

certainly, but you make them move or go round, for they would never have stirred, as far as I am concerned.

Soc. Then I must be a greater than Daedalus; for whereas he only made his own inventions to move, I move those of other people as well. And the beauty of it is, that I would rather not. For I would give the wisdom of Daedalus, and the wealth of Tantalus, to be able to detain them and keep them fixed. But enough of this. As I perceive that you are indolent, I will myself endeavour to show you how you might instruct me in the nature of piety; and I hope that you will not grudge your labour. Tell me, then,—Is not that which is pious necessarily just?

Euth. Yes.

Soc. And is, then, all which is just pious? or, is that which is pious all just, but that which is just, only in part and not all, pious?

Euth. I do not understand you, Socrates.

Soc. And yet I know that you are as much wiser than I am, as you are younger. But, as I was saying, revered friend, the abundance of your wisdom makes you indolent. Please to exert yourself, for there is no real difficulty in understanding me. What I mean I may explain by an illustration of what I do not mean. The poet (Stasinus) sings—

"Of Zeus, the author and creator of all these things,
You will not tell: for where there is fear there is
    also reverence."

And I disagree with this poet. Shall I tell you in what I disagree?

Euth. By all means.

Soc. I should not say that where there is fear there is also reverence; for I am sure that many persons fear poverty and disease, and the like evils, but I do not perceive that they reverence the objects of their fear.

Euth. Very true.

Soc. But where reverence is, there is fear; for he who has a feeling of reverence and shame about the commission of any action, fears and is afraid of an ill reputation.

Euth. No doubt.

Soc. Then we are wrong in saying that where there is
fear there is also reverence; and we should say, where
there is reverence there is also fear. But there is
not always reverence where there is fear; for fear is
a more extended notion, and reverence is a part of fear,
just as the odd is a part of number, and number is a
more extended notion than the odd. I suppose that
you follow me now?

Euth. Quite well.

Soc. That was the sort of question which I meant
to raise when asking whether the just is the pious,
or the pious the just; and whether there may not be
justice where there is not always piety; for justice
is the more extended notion of which piety is only a
part. Do you agree in that?

Euth. Yes; that, I think, is correct.

Soc. Then, now, if piety is a part of justice, I
suppose that we should enquire what part? If you had
pursued the enquiry in the previous cases; for instance,
if you asked me what is an even number, and what part
of number the even is, I should have had no difficulty
in replying, a number which represents a figure having
two equal sides. Do you agree?

Euth. Yes.

Soc. In like manner, I want you to tell me what
part of justice is piety or holiness, that I may be
able to tell Meletus not to do me injustice, or indict
me for impiety, as I am now adequately instructed by
you in the nature of piety or holiness, and their
opposites.

Euth. Piety or holiness, Socrates, appears to me to
be that part of justice which attends to the gods, as
there is the other part of justice which attends to
men.

Soc. That is good, Euthyphro; yet still there is
a little point about which I should like to have further
information, what is the meaning of "attention"? For
attention can hardly be used in the same sense when
applied to the gods as when applied to other things.
For instance, horses are said to require attention,
and not every person is able to attend to them, but
only a person skilled in horsemanship. Is not that true?

Euth. Quite true.

Soc. I should suppose that the art of horsemanship is the art of attending to horses?

Euth. Yes.

Soc. Nor is every one qualified to attend to dogs, but only the huntsman?

Euth. Yes.

Soc. As the art of the oxherd is the art of attending to oxen?

Euth. Very true.

Soc. And as holiness or piety is the art of attending to the gods?—that would be your meaning, Euthyphro?

Euth. Yes.

Soc. And is not attention always designed for the good or benefit of that to which the attention is given? As in the case of horses, you may observe that when attended to by the horseman's art they are benefited and improved, are they not?

Euth. Certainly, not for their hurt.

Soc. But for their good?

Euth. Of course.

Soc. And does piety or holiness, which has been defined as the art of attending to the gods, benefit or improve them? Would you say that when you do a holy act you make any of the gods better?

Euth. No, no; that is certainly not my meaning.

Soc. Indeed, Euthyphro, I did not suppose that this was your meaning; far otherwise. And I asked you the nature of attention, because I thought that you could not mean this.

Euth. You do me justice, Socrates; for that is not my meaning.

Soc. Good: but I must still ask what is this attention to the gods which is called piety?

Euth. It is such, Socrates, as servants show to their masters.

Soc. I understand—a sort of ministration to the gods.

Euth. Exactly.

Soc. Medicine is also a sort of ministration or service, tending to the attainment of some object— would you not say health?

Euth. Yes.

Soc. Again, there is an art which ministers to the

ship-builder with a view to the attainment of some
result?

Euth. Yes, Socrates, with a view to the building of
a ship.

Soc. As there is an art which ministers to the
house-builder with a view to the building of a house?

Euth. Yes.

Soc. And now tell me, my good friend, about the
art which ministers to the gods: what work does that
help to accomplish? For you must surely know if, as
you say, you are of all men living the one who is
best instructed in religion.

Euth. And that is true, Socrates.

Soc. Tell me then, oh tell me—what is that fair
work which the gods do by the help of us as their
ministers?

Euth. Many and fair, Socrates, are the works which
they do.

Soc. Why, my friend, and so are those of a general.
But the chief of them is easily told. Would you not
say that victory in war is the chief of them?

Euth. Certainly.

Soc. Many and fair, too, are the works of the
husbandman, if I am not mistaken; but his chief work is
the production of food from the earth?

Euth. Exactly.

Soc. And of the many and fair things which the gods
do, which is the chief and principal one?

Euth. I have told you already, Socrates, that to
learn all these things accurately will be very tire-
some. Let me simply say that piety is learning how to
please the gods in word and deed, by prayers and
sacrifices. That is piety, which is the salvation of
families and states, just as the impious, which is un-
pleasing to the gods, is their ruin and destruction.

Soc. I think that you could have answered in much
fewer words the chief question which I asked, Euthyphro,
if you had chosen. But I see plainly that you are not
disposed to instruct me: else why, when we reached
the point, did you turn aside? Had you only answered
me I should have learned of you by this time the nature
of piety. Now, as the asker of a question is necessarily
dependent on the answerer, whither he leads I must

275

follow; and can only ask again, what is the pious, and
what is piety? Do you mean that they are a sort of
science of praying and sacrificing?

Euth. Yes, I do.

Soc. And sacrificing is giving to the gods, and
prayer is asking of the gods?

Euth. Yes, Socrates.

Soc. Upon this view, then, piety is a science of
asking and giving?

Euth. You understand me capitally, Socrates.

Soc. Yes, my friend; the reason is that I am a
votary of your science, and give my mind to it, and
therefore nothing which you say will be thrown away
upon me. Please then to tell me, what is the nature of
this service to the gods? Do you mean that we prefer
requests and give gifts to them?

Euth. Yes. I do.

Soc. Is not the right way of asking to ask of them
what we want?

Euth. Certainly.

Soc. And the right way of giving is to give to them
in turn what they want of us. There would be no meaning
in an art which gives to any one that which he does
not want.

Euth. Very true, Socrates.

Soc. Then piety, Euthyphro, is an art which gods and
men have of doing business with one another?

Euth. That is an expression which you may use, if
you like.

Soc. But I have no particular liking for anything
but the truth. I wish, however, that you would tell me
what benefit accrues to the gods from our gifts. There
is no doubt about what they give to us; for there is
no good thing which they do not give; but how we can
give any good thing to them in return is far from
being equally clear. If they give everything and we
give nothing, that must be an affair of business in
which we have very greatly the advantage of them.

Euth. And do you imagine, Socrates, that any benefit
accures to the gods from what they receive of us?

Soc. But if not, Euthyphro, what sort of gifts
do we confer upon the gods?

Euth. What should we confer upon them, but tributes

of honour; and, as I was just now saying, what is grateful to them?

Soc. Piety, then, is grateful to the gods, but not beneficial or dear to them?

Euth. I should say that nothing could be dearer.

Soc. Then once more the question is repeated that piety is dear to the gods?

Euth. Certainly.

Soc. And when you say this, can you wonder at your words not standing firm, but walking away? Will you accuse me of being the Daedalus who makes them walk away, not perceiving that there is another and far greater artist than Daedalus who makes them go round in a circle, and that is yourself; for the argument, as you will perceive, comes round to the same point. I think that you must remember our saying that the holy or pious was not the same as that which is loved of the gods. Do you remember that?

Euth. I do.

Soc. And are you not saying that what is loved of the gods is holy, but this is the same as what is dear to them - do you see that?

Euth. True.

Soc. Then either we were wrong in our former assertion; or, if we were right then, we are wrong now.

Euth. I suppose that is the case.

Soc. Then we must begin again and ask, What is piety? That is an enquiry which I shall never be weary of pursuing as far as in me lies; and I entreat you not to scorn me, but to apply your mind to the utmost, and tell me the truth. For, if any man knows, you are he; and therefore I shall detain you, like Proteus, until you tell. For if you had not certainly known the nature of piety and impiety, I am confident that you would never, on behalf of a serf, have charged your aged father with murder. You would not have run such a risk of doing wrong in the sight of the gods, and you would have had too much respect for the opinions of men. I am sure, therefore, that you know the nature of piety and impiety. Speak out then, my dear Euthyphro, and do not hide your knowledge.

Euth. Another time, Socrates; for I am in a hurry, and must go now.

Soc. Alas! my companion, and will you leave me in despair? I was hoping that you would instruct me in the nature of piety and impiety, so that I might have cleared myself of Meletus and his indictment. Then I might have proved to him that I had been converted by Euthyphro, and had done with rash innovations and speculations, in which I had indulged through ignorance, and was about to lead a better life.

The Republic

And now, I said, let me show in a figure how far our nature is enlightened or unenlightened:—Behold! human beings living in an underground den, which has a mouth open towards the light and reaching all along the den; here they have been from their childhood, and have their legs and necks chained so that they can not move, and can only see before them, being prevented by the chains from turning round their heads. Above and behind them a fire is blazing at a distance, and between the fire and the prisoners there is a raised way; and you will see, if you look, a low wall built along the way, like the screen which marionette players have in front of them, over which they show the puppets.

I see.

And do you see, I said, men passing along the wall carrying all sorts of vessels, and statues and figures of animals made of wood and stone and various materials, which appear over the wall? Some of them are talking, others silent.

You have shown me a strange image, and they are strange prisoners.

Like ourselves, I replied; and they see only their own shadows, or the shadows of one another, which the fire throws on the opposite wall of the cave?

True, he said; how could they see anything but the shadows if they were never allowed to move their heads?

And of the objects which are being carried in like manner they would see only the shadows?

Yes, he said.

And if they were able to converse with one another, would they not suppose that they were naming what was actually before them?

278

Very true.

And suppose further that the prison had an echo
which came from the other side, would they not be sure
to fancy when one of the passersby spoke that the
voice which they heard came from the passing shadow?

No question, he replied.

To them, I said, the truth would be literally nothing
but the shadows of the images.

That is certain.

And now look again, and see what will naturally
follow if the prisoners are released and disabused of
their error. At first, when any of them is liberated
and compelled suddenly to stand up and turn his neck
round and walk and look towards the light, he will suffer
sharp pains; the glare will distress him, and he will
be unable to see the realities of which in his former
state he had seen the shadows; and then conceive some
one saying to him, that what he saw before was an
illusion, but that now, when he is approaching nearer
to being and his eye is turned towards more real existence, he has a clearer vision,—what will be his reply?
And you may further imagine that his instructor is pointing to the objects as they pass and requiring him to
name them,—will he not be perplexed? Will he not fancy
that the shadows which he formerly saw are truer than
the objects which are now shown to him?

Far truer.

And if he is compelled to look straight at the light,
will he now have a pain in his eyes which will make
him turn away to take refuge in the objects of vision
which he can see, and which he will conceive to be in
reality clearer than the things which are now being
shown to him?

True, he said.

And suppose once more, that he is reluctantly dragged
up a steep and rugged ascent, and held fast until he
is forced into the presence of the sun himself, is he
not likely to be pained and irritated? When he approaches
the light his eyes will be dazzled, and he will not be
able to see anything at all of what are now called
realities.

Not all in a moment, he said.

He will require to grow accustomed to the sight of

the upper world. And first he will see the shadows best, next the reflections of men and other objects in the water, and then the objects themselves; then he will gaze upon the light of the moon and the stars by night better than the sun or the light of the sun by day?

Certainly.

Last of all he will be able to see the sun, and not mere reflections of him in the water, but he will see him in his own proper place, and not in another; and he will contemplate him as he is.

Certainly.

He will then proceed to argue that this is he who gives the seasons and the years, and is the guardian of all that is in the visible world, and in a certain way the cause of all things which he and his fellows have been accustomed to behold?

Clearly, he said, he would first see the sun and then reason about him.

And when he remembered his old habitation, and the wisdom of the den and his fellow prisoners, do you not suppose that he would felicitate himself on the change, and pity them?

Certainly he would.

And if they were in the habit of conferring honours among themselves on those who were quickest to observe the passing shadows and to remark which of them went before, and which followed after, and which were to-gether; and who were therefore best able to draw conclusions as to the future, do you think that he would care for such honours and glories, or envy the possessors of them? Would he not say with Homer, "Better to be the poor servant of a poor master, " and to endure anything, rather than think as they do and live after their manner?

Yes, he said, I think that he would rather suffer anything than entertain these false notions and live in this miserable manner.

Imagine once more, I said, such an one coming suddenly out of the sun to be replaced in his old situation; would he not be certain to have his eyes full of darkness?

To be sure, he said.

And if there were a contest, and he had to compete
in measuring the shadows with the prisoners who had never
moved out of the den, while his sight was still weak,
and before his eyes had become steady (and the time which
would be needed to acquire this new habit of sight might
be very considerable), would he not be ridiculous?
Men would say of him that up he went and down he came
without his eyes: and that it was better not even to
think of ascending; and if any one tried to loose
another and lead him up to the light, let them only
catch the offender, and they would put him to death.

No question, he said.

This entire allegory, I said, you may now append,
dear Glaucon, to the previous argument; the prison-
house is the world of sight, the light of the fire is
the sun, and you will not misapprehend me if you interpret the journey upwards to be the ascent of the soul
into the intellectual world according to my poor belief,
which, at your desire, I have expressed—whether rightly
or wrongly God knows. But, whether true or false, my
opinion is that in the world of knowledge the idea of
good appears last of all, and is seen only with an
effort; and, when seen, is also inferred to be the
universal author of all things beautiful and right,
parent of light and of the lord of light in this visible
world, and the immediate source of reason and truth in
the intellectual; and that this is the power upon which
he who would act rationally either in public or private
life must have his eye fixed.

I agree, he said, as far as I am able to understand
you.

Moreover, I said, you must not wonder that those who
attain to this beatific vision are unwilling to descend
to human affairs; for their souls are ever hastening
into the upper world where they desire to dwell; which
desire of theirs is very natural, if our allegory may be
trusted.

Yes, very natural.

And is there anything surprising in one who passes
from divine contemplations to the evil state of man,
misbehaving himself in a ridiculous manner; if, while
his eyes are blinking and before he has become accustomed to the surrounding darkness, he is compelled to

fight in courts of law, or in other places, about the
images or the shadows of images of justice, and is
endeavouring to meet the conceptions of those who have
never yet seen absolute justice?

Anything but surprising, he said.

And one who has common sense will remember that the
bewilderments of the eyes are of two kinds, and arise
from two causes, either from coming out of the light or
from going into the light, which is true of the mind's
eye, quite as much as of the bodily eye; and he who
remembers this when he sees any one whose vision is
perplexed and weak, will not be too ready to laugh;
he will first ask whether that soul of man has come out
of the brighter life, and is unable to see because
unaccustomed to the dark, or having turned from darkness
to the day is dazzled by excess of light. And he will
count the one happy in his condition and state of being,
and he will pity the other; or, if he have a mind to
laugh at the soul which comes from below into the
light, there will be more reason in this than in the
laugh which greets him who returns from above out of
the light into the den.

That, he said, is a very just distinction.

But then, if I am right, certain professors of
education must be wrong when they say that they can put
a knowledge into the soul which was not there before,
like sight into blind eyes.

They undoubtedly say this, he replied.

Whereas, our argument shows that the power and
capacity of learning exists in the soul already; and
that just as the eye was unable to turn from darkness
to light without the whole body, so too the instrument
of knowledge can only by the movement of the whole
soul be turned from the world of becoming into that
of being, and learn by degrees to endure the sight of
being, and of the brightest and best of being, or in
other words, of the good.

Very true.

And must there not be some art which will effect
conversion in the easiest and quickest manner; not
implanting the faculty of sight, for that exists already,
but has been turned in the wrong direction, and is
looking away from the truth?

Yes, he said, such an art may be presumed.

And whereas the other so-called virtues of the soul seem to be akin to bodily qualities, for even when they are not originally innate they can be implanted later by habit and exercise, the virtue more than anything else contains a divine element which always remains, and by this conversion is rendered useful and profitable; or, on the other hand, hurtful and useless. Did you never observe the narrow intelligence flashing from the keen eye of a clever rogue—how eager he is, how clearly his paltry soul sees the way to his end; he is the reverse of blind, but his keen eye-sight is forced into the service of evil, and he is mischievous in proportion to his cleverness?

Very true, he said.

But what if there had been a circumcision of such natures in the days of their youth; and they had been severed from those sensual pleasures, such as eating and drinking, which, like leaden weights, were attached to them at their birth, and which drag them down and turn the vision of their souls upon the things that are below—if, I say, they had been released from these impediments and turned in the opposite direction, the very same faculty in them would have seen the truth as keenly as they see what their eyes are turned to now.

Very likely.

Yes, I said: and there is another thing which is likely, or rather a necessary inference from what has preceded, that neither the uneducated and uninformed of the truth, nor those who never make an end of their education, will be able ministers of State; not the former, because they have no single aim of duty which is the rule of all their actions, private as well as public; not the latter, because they will not act at all except upon compulsion, fancying that they are already dwelling apart in the islands of the blest.

Very true, he replied.

Then, I said, the business of us who are the founders of the State will be to compel the best minds to attain that knowledge which we have already shown to be the greatest of all—they must continue to ascend until they arrive at the good; but when they have ascended and seen enough we must not allow them to do as they do now.

What do you mean?

I mean that they remain in the upper world: but this must not be allowed; they must be made to descend again among the prisoners in the den, and partake of their labours and honours, whether they are worth having or not.

But is not this unjust? he said; ought we to give them a worse life, when they might have a better?

You have again forgotten, my friend, I said, the intention of the legislator, who did not aim at making any one class in the State happy above the rest; the happiness was to be in the whole State, and he held the citizens together by persuasion and necessity, making them benefactors of the State, and therefore benefactors of one another; to this end he created them, not to please themselves, but to be his instruments in binding up the State.

True, he said, I had forgotten.

Observe, Glaucon, that there will be no injustice in compelling our philosophers to have a care and providence of others; we shall explain to them that in other States, men of their class are not obliged to share in the toils of politics; and this is reasonable, for they grow up at their own sweet will, and the government would rather not have them. Being self-taught, they cannot be expected to show any gratitude for a culture which they have never received. But we have brought you into the world to be rulers of the hive, kings of yourselves and of the other citizens, and have educated you far better and more perfectly than they have been educated, and you are better able to share in the double duty. Wherefore each of you, when his turn comes, must go down to the general underground abode, and get the habit of seeing in the dark. When you have acquired the habit, you will see ten thousand times better than the inhabitants of the den, and you will know what the several images are, and what they represent, because you have seen the beautiful and just and good in their truth. And thus our State, which is also yours, will be a reality, and not a dream only, and will be administered in a spirit unlike that of other states, in which men fight with one another about shadows only and are distracted in the struggle for power, which in their eyes is a great good. Whereas the truth is that the

State in which the rulers are most reluctant to govern
is always the best and most quietly governed, and the
State in which they are most eager, the worst.

Introduction to Aristotle

Aristotle and Plato have survived as the two Greek philosophers and western philosophers since have seen them as the two possible choices of philosophical position. We have perhaps seen the differences as too great, and the similarities as too small. Perhaps we should note more carefully what they had in common. Aristotle lived well into the end of the Greek decline--he was the teacher of Alexander the Great.

We usually see Aristotle as the practical, down-to-earth philosopher, less interested in the ideal than Plato. Aristotle's method was to set up extremes, both of which are "bad," and to define the "good" as the mid-point between them. This is sometimes called the "Golden Mean" approach. Aristotle applied the method in the two realms in which he specialized, natural philosophy ("biology" to us) and ethics.

In discussing Aristotle, we have a bit of a problem. A great deal survives of his thought, but it may be that what we possess are student notes, or perhaps Aristotle's notes for class discussion. Like notes, the texts seem to lack connective tissues, being mostly concise statements which might have been added to in the classroom. Occasionally, it seems that Aristotle may be joking, or speaking in a satirical way when we take him seriously. Perhaps he hoped that the students would object to certain over-statements. In any event, much of what we have is quite absurd. Of course, we are now trying to judge from a distance of twenty-three centuries.

In the realm of ethics, Aristotle argued that, for in-stance, Valor was mid-way between foolhardiness and coward-ice. The soldier should not be "brave" when he knows for certain that he will die without being able to aid his cause. He should save himself to fight another day. However, he should not desert his post to preseve himself. Similarly, one should not drink too much, nor should one absolutely avoid wine--one should drink moderately.

A great deal of Aristotle, as we have noted, concerned

biology and physics and his method served him poorly in these areas. How many teeth should a horse logically have? Should an object which weighs twice as much as another object fall twice as fast?

The trouble with this method is obvious, both in ethics and in physics. If adultery is bad and celibacy is bad, then the proper approach must be a little fooling around. Maybe. Then is not a little murder not good? Not hardly. Can one be almost a virgin, almost pregnant, almost a thief? Likewise, the world of physics happens not to be logical--heavy objects fall at exactly the same rate of speed as light ones.

Here is where Aristotle and Plato share assumptions which did not mislead earlier thinkers--they both assume that the world was created, designed by a rational intellegence. Thus, there is a reason for everything which exists and for all parts of the universe. Both philosophers, quite consciously and deliberately, moved between mad-made objects and natural objects in their illustrations. "Why do horses have teeth?" is the same as "Why do chairs have arms?" "What is cat-ness?" is the same as "What is chair-ness?" To both philosophers, nature provided laws to be discovered (the bad scientiest's attitude), not random data to be organized as best one can (the good scientiest's attitude).

Aristotle gave Western philosophy the theory of logic, induction and deduction, with iron-clad rules for distinguishing true from false deduction and induction, with very elaborate ways and names for going wrong. The old and much loved syllogisms ("Man is mortal; Socrates is a man; therefore, Socrates is mortal") still are popular in freshman logic and English. Aristotle's extreme relience on cause and effect made western philosophy and logic unduly concerned with it ("What causes cancer?" we constantly ask--but even if we knew, we might not be able to prevent it). God for Aristotle became the "first cause" after which all other events were effects of previous causes.

But do not the conclusions we reach by logic depend upon the definitions we use for the categories? What does "fool-hardy" mean? Maybe the earlier philosophers had a point.

ARISTOTLE

Tragedy

Tragedy, then, is an imitation of an action that is serious, complete, and of a certain magnitude; in language embellished with each kind of artistic ornament, the several kinds being found in separate parts of the play; in for form of action, not of narrative; through pity and fear effecting the proper purgation of these emotions. By "language embellished," I mean language into which rhythm, "harmony," and song enter. By "the several kinds in separate parts," I mean, that some parts are rendered through the medium of verse alone, others again with the aid of song.

As the sequel to what has already been said, we must proceed to consider what the poet should aim at, and what he should avoid, in constructing his plots; and by what means the specific effect of Tragedy will be produced.

A perfect tragedy should, as we have seen, be arranged not on the simple but on the complex plan. It should, moreover, imitate actions which excite pity or fear, this being the distinctive mark of tragic imitation. It follows plainly, in the first place, that the change of fortune presented must not be the spectacle of a virtuous man brought from prosperity to adversity: for this moves neither pity not fear; it merely shocks us. Nor, again, that of a bad man passing from adversity to prosperity: for nothing can be more alien to the spirit of Tragedy; it possesses no single tragic quality; it neither satisfies the moral sense nor calls forth pity or fear. Nor, again, should the downfall of the utter villain be exhibited. A plot of this kind would, doubtless, satisfy the moral sense, but it would inspire neither pity not fear; for pity is aroused by unmerited misfortune, fear by the misfortune of a man like ourselves. Such an event, therefore, will be neither pitiful nor terrible. There remains, then, the character between these two extremes, that of a man who is not eminently good and just, yet whose misfortune is brought about not by vice or depravity, but by some error or frailty. He must be

288

one who is highly renowned and prosperous,—a personage like Œdipus, Thyestes, or other illustrious men of such families.

A well constructed plot should, therefore, be single in its issue, rather than double as some maintain. The change of fortune should be not from bad to good, but, reversely, from good to bad. It should come about as the result not of vice, but of some great error or frailty, in a character such as we have described, or better rather than worse. The practice of the stage bears out our view. At first the poets recounted any legend that came in their way. Now, the best tragedies are founded on the stories of a few houses,—on the fortunes of Alcmæon, Œipus, Meleager, Thyestes, Telephus, and those others who have done or suffered something terrible. A tragedy, then, to be perfect according to the rules of art should be of this construction. Hence they are in error who censure Euripides just because he follows this principle in his plays, many of which end unhappily. It is, as we have said, the right ending. The best proof is that on the stage and in dramatic competition, such plays, if well worked out, are the most tragic in effect; and Euripides, faulty though he may be in the general management of his subject, yet is felt to be the most tragic of the poets.

In the second rank comes the kind of tragedy which some place first. Like the Odyssey, it has a double thread of plot, and also an opposite catastrophe for the good and for the bad. It is accounted the best because of the weakness of the spectators; for the poet is guided in what he writes by the wishes of his audience. The pleasure, however, thence derived is not the true tragic pleasure. It is proper rather to Comedy, where those who, in the piece, are the deadliest enemies—like Orestes and Ægisthus—quit the stage as friends at the close, and no one slays or is slain.

Ethics

Now what the genus of Virtue is has been said; but we must not merely speak of it thus, that it is a state, but say also what kind of a state it is.

We must observe then that all excellence makes that whereof it is the excellence both to be itself in a good state and to perform its work well. The excellence of the eye, for instance, makes both the eye good and its work also: for by the excellence of the eye we see well. So too the excellence of the horse makes the horse good, and good in speed, and in carrying his rider, and standing up against the enemy. If then this is universally the case, the excellence of Man, i.e. Virtue, must be a state whereby Man comes to be good and whereby he will perform well his proper work. Now how this shall be it is true we have said already, but still perhaps it may throw light on the subject to see what is its characteristic nature.

In all quantity then, whether continuous or discrete, one may take the greater part, the less, or the exactly equal, and these either with reference to the thing itself, or relatively to us: and the exactly equal is a mean between excess and defect. Now by the mean of the thing, i.e. absolute mean, I denote that which is equidistant from either extreme (which of course is one and the same to all), and by the mean relatively to ourselves, that which is neither too much nor too little for the particular individual. This of course is not one nor the same to all: for instance, suppose ten is too much and two too little, people take six for the absolute mean; because it exceeds the smaller sum by exactly as much as it is itself exceeded by the larger, and this mean is according to arithmetical proportion.

But the mean relatively to ourselves must not be so found; for it does not follow, supposing ten minae is too large a quantity to eat and two too small, that the trainer will order his man six; because for the person who is to take it this also may be too much or too little: for Milo it would be too little, but for a man just commencing his athletic exercises too much: similarly too of the exercises themselves, as running or wrestling.

So then it seems every one possessed of skill avoids excess and defect, but seeks for and chooses the mean, not the absolute but the relative.

Now if all skill thus accomplishes well its work by keeping its eye on the mean, and bringing the works to this point (whence it is common enough to say of such works as are in a good state, "one cannot add to or take ought from them," under the notion of excess or defect destroying goodness but the mean state preserving it), and good artisans, as we say, work with their eye on this, and excellence, like nature, is more exact and better than any art in the world, it must have an aptitude to aim at the mean.

It is moral excellence, i.e. Virtue, of course which I mean, because this it is which is concerned with feelings and actions, and in these there can be excess and defect and the mean: it is possible, for instance, to feel the emotions of fear, confidence, lust, anger, compassion, and pleasure and pain generally, too much or too little, and in either case wrongly; but to feel them when we ought, on what occasions, towards whom, why, and as, we should do, is the mean, or in other words the best state, and this is the property of Virtue.

In like manner too with respect to the actions, there may be excess and defect and the mean. Now Virtue is concerned with feelings and actions, in which excess is wrong and the defect is blamed but the mean is praised and goes right; and both these circumstances belong to Virtue. Virtue then is in a sense a mean state, since it certainly has an aptitude for aiming at the mean.

Again, one may go wrong in many different ways (because, as the Pythagoreans expressed it, evil is of the class of the infinite, good of the finite), but right only in one; and so the former is easy, the latter difficult; easy to miss the mark, but hard to hit it: and for these reasons, therefore, both the excess and defect belong to Vice, and the mean state to Virtue; for, as the poet has it,

"Men may be bad in many ways, But good in one alone."

Virtue then is "a state apt to exercise deliberate choice, being in the relative mean, determined by reason, and as the man of practical wisdom would determine."

It is a middle state between two faulty ones, in the way of excess on one side and of defect on the other: and it is so moreover, because the faulty states on one side fall short of, and those on the other exceed, what is right, both in the case of the feelings and the actions; but Virtue finds, and when found adopts, the mean.

And so, viewing it in respect of its essence and definition, Virtue is a mean state; but in reference to the chief good and excellence it is the highest state possible.

But it must not be supposed that every action or every feeling is capable of subsisting in this mean state, because some there are which are so named as immediately to convey the notion of badness, as malevolence, shamelessness, envy; or, to instance in actions, adultery, theft, homicide; for all these and such like are blamed because they are in themselves bad, not the having too much or too little of them.

In these then you never can go right, but must always be wrong: nor in such does the right or wrong depend on the selection of a proper person, time, or manner (take adultery for instance), but simply doing any one soever of those things is being wrong.

You might as well require that there should be determined a mean state, and excess and defect in respect of acting unjustly, being cowardly, or giving up all control of the passions: for at this rate there will be of excess and defect a mean state; of excess, excess; and of defect, defect.

But just as of perfected self-mastery and courage there is no excess and defect, because the mean is in one point of view the highest possible state, so neither of those faulty states can you have a mean state, excess, or defect, but howsoever done they are wrong: you cannot, in short, have of excess and defect a mean state, nor of a mean state excess and defect.

It is not enough, however, to state this in general terms, we must also apply it to particular instances, because in treatises on moral conduct general statements

have an air of vagueness, but those which go into detail
one of greater reality: for the actions after all must
be in detail, and the general statements, to be worth
anything, must hold good here.

We must take these details then from the Table.

I. In respect of fears or confidence or boldness:

The Mean state is courage: men may exceed, of course,
either in absence of fear or in positive confidence:
The former has no name (which is a common case), the
latter is called rash: again, the man who has too
much fear and too little confidence is called a coward.

II. In respect of pleasures and pains (but not all,
and perhaps fewer pains than pleasures):

The Mean state here is perfected Self-Mastery, the
defect total absence of Self-control. As for defect in
respect of pleasure, there are really no people who are
chargeable with it, so, of course, there is really no
name for such characters, but, as they are conceivable,
we will give them one and call them insensible.

III. In respect of giving and taking wealth (a):

The Mean state is Liberality, the excess Prodigality,
the defect Stinginess: here each of the extremes
involves really an excess and defect contrary to each
other: I mean the prodigal gives out too much and takes
in too little, while the stingy man takes in too much
and gives out too little. (It must be understood that
we are now giving merely an outline and summary, inten-
tionally: and we will, in a later part of the treatise,
draw out the distinctions with greater exactness.)

IV. In respect of wealth (b):

There are other dispositions besides these just
mentioned; a mean state called Munificence (for the
munificent man differs from the liberal, the former
having necessarily to do with great wealth, the latter
with but small); the excess called by the names either
of Want of taste or Vulgar Profusion, and the defect
Paltriness (these also differ from the extremes connected
with liberality, and the manner of their difference
shall also be spoken of later).

V. In respect of honour and dishonour (a):

The Mean state Greatness of Soul, the excess which
may be called Braggadocia, and the defect Littleness
of Soul.

VI. In respect of honour and dishonour (b):

Now there is a state bearing the same relation to
Greatness of Soul as we said just now Liberality does
to Munifidence, with the difference that is of being
about a small amount of the same thing: this state
having reference to small honour, as Greatness of Soul
to great honour; a man may, of course, grasp at honour
either more than he should or less; now he that exceeds
in his grasping at it is called ambitious, he that falls
short unambitious, he that is just as he should be has
no proper name: nor in fact have the states, except
that the disposition of the ambitious man is called
ambition. For this reason those who are in either
extreme lay claim to the mean as a debateable land, and
we call the virtuous character sometimes by the name
ambitious, sometimes by that of unambitious, and we
commend sometimes the one and sometimes the other. Why
we do it shall be said in the subsequent part of the
treatise; but now we will go on with the rest of the
virtues after the plan we have laid down.

VII. In respect of anger.

Here too there is excess, defect, and a mean state;
but since they may be said to have really no proper
names, as we call the virtuous character Meek, we will
call the mean state Meekness, and of the extremes, let
the man who is excessive by denominated Passionate, and
the faulty state Passionateness, and him who is deficient Angerless, and the defect Angerlessness.

There are also three other mean states, having some
mutual resemblance, but still with differences; they
are alike in that they all have for their object-
matter intercourse of words and deeds, and they differ
in that one has respect to truth herein, the other two
to what is pleasant; and this in two ways, the one in
relaxation and amusement, the other in all things
which occur in daily life. We must say a word or two
about these also, that we may the better see that in
all matters the mean is praiseworthy, while the extremes
are neither right now worthy of praise but of blame.

Now of these, it is true, the majority have really
no proper names, but still we must try, as in the other
cases, to coin some for them for the sake of clearness
and intelligibleness.

I. In respect of truth:

The man who is in the mean state we will call Truthful, and his state Truthfulness, and as to the disguise of truth, if it be on the side of exaggeration, Braggadocia, and him that has it a Braggadocio; if on that diminution, Reserve and Reserved shall be the terms.

II. In respect of what is pleasant in the way of relaxation or amusement:

The mean state shall be called Easy-pleasantry, and the character accordingly a man of Easy-pleasantry; the excess Buffoonery, and the man a Buffon; the man deficient herein a Clown, and his state Clownishness.

III. In respect of what is pleasant in daily life:

He that is as he should be may be called Friendly, and his mean state Friendliness: he that exceeds, if it be without any interested motive, somewhat too Complaisant, if with such motive, a Flatter: he that is deficient and in all instances Unpleasant, Quarrelsome and Cross.

There are mean states likewise in feelings and matters concerning them. Shamefacedness, for instance, is no virtue, still a man is praised for being shamefaced: for in these too the one is denominated the man in the mean state, the other in the excess; the Dumbfoundered, for instance, who is overwhelmed with shame on all and any occasions: the man who is in the defect, i.e. who has no shame at all in his composition, is called Shameless: but the right character Shamefaced.

Indignation against successful vice, again, is a state in the mean between Envy and Malevolence: they all three have respect to pleasure and pain produced by what happens to one's neighbour: for the man who has this right feeling is annoyed at undeserved success of others, while the envious man goes beyond him and is annoyed at all success of others, and the malevolent falls so far short of feeling annoyance that he even rejoices (at misfortune of others).

But for the discussion of these also there will be another opportunity, as of Justice too, because the term is used in more senses than one. So after this we will go accurately into each and say how they are mean states: and in like manner also with respect to the Intellectual Excellences.

Now as there are three states in each case, two
faulty either in the way of excess or defect, and one
right, which is the mean state, of course all are in a
way opposed to one another; the extremes, for instance,
not only to the mean but also to one another, and the
mean to the extremes: just as the half is greater if
compared with the less portion, and less if compared
with the greater, so the mean states, compared with the
defects, exceed, whether in feelings or actions, and
vice versa. The brave man, for instance, shows as rash
when compared with the coward, and cowardly when compared
with the rash; similarly too the man of perfected self-
mastery, viewed in comparison with the man destitute of
all perception, shows like a man of no self-control,
but in comparison with the man who really has no self-
control, he looks like one destitute of all perception:
and the liberal man compared with the stingy seems
prodigal, and by the side of the prodigal, stingy.

And so the extreme characters push away, so to speak,
towards each other the man in the mean state; the brave
man is called a rash man by the coward, and a coward
by the rash man, and in the other cases accordingly.
And there being this mutual opposition, the contrariety
between the extremes is greater than between either
and the mean, because they are further from one another
than from the mean, just as the greater or less portion
differ more from each other than either from the exact
half.

Again, in some cases an extreme will bear a resemblance to the mean; rashness, for instance, to courage,
and prodigality to liberality; but between the extremes
there is the greatest dissimilarity. Now things which
are furthest from one another are defined to be contrary, and so the further off the more contrary they
will be.

Further: of the extremes in some cases the excess,
and in others the defect, is most opposed to the mean:
to courage, for instance, not rashness which is the
excess, but cowardice which is the defect; whereas
to perfected self-mastery not insensibility which is
the defect but absence of all self-control which is the
excess.

And for this there are two reasons to be given; one

from the nature of the thing itself, because from the one extreme being nearer and more like the mean, we do not put this against it, but the other; as, for instance, since rashness is thought to be nearer to courage than cowardice is, and to resemble it more, we put cowardice against courage rather than rashness, because those things which are further from the mean are thought to be more contrary to it. This then is one reason arising from the thing itself; there is another arising from our own constitution and make: for in each man's own case those things give the impression of being more contrary to the mean to which we individually have a natural bias. Thus we have a natural bias towards pleasures, for which reason we are much more inclined to the rejection of all self-control, than to self-discipline.

These things then to which the bias is, we call more contrary, and so total want of self-control (the excess) is more contrary than the defect is to perfected self-mastery.

Now that Moral Virtue is a mean state, and how it is so, and that it lies between two faulty states, one in the way of excess and another in the way of defect, and that it is so because it has an aptitude to aim at the mean both in feelings and actions, all this has been set forth fully and sufficiently.

And so it is hard to be good: for surely hard it is in each instance to find the mean, just as to find the mean point or centre of a circle is not what any man can do, but only he who knows how: Just so to be angry, to give money, and be expensive, is what any man can do, and easy: but to do these to the right person, in due proportion, at the right time, with a right object, and in the right manner, this is not as before what any man can do, nor is it easy; and for this cause goodness is rare, and praiseworthy and noble.

Therefore he who aims at the man should make it his first care to keep away from that extreme which is more contrary than the other to the mean; just as Calypso in Homer advises Ulysses,

"Clear of this smoke and surge thy barque direct;"

because of the two extremes the one is always more, and the other less, erroneous; and, therefore, since to hit exactly on the mean is difficult, one must take the least of the evils as the safest plan; and this a man will be doing, if he follows this method.

INTRODUCTION TO THE CLOUDS

Greek tragedy, it is true, requires the modern viewer of reader to make a great many adjustments, but Greek comedy is much like our own. We feel right at home at a well-translated presentation of a Greek comedy, for all the devices are familiar. We recognize the sarcastic servant (see any TV "family" show), the fat-thin and clever dull stereotypes, the lyric quality of musical comedy, and the spoofing of current political and social events. Greek comedy was a good bit more "gross" than ours, resembling more the crudeness of old-time burlesque than movies today. For sexy scenes (and there were many), the players wore over-sized organs, and public officials were in the comedy ridiculed as homosexuals, transvestites, or other kinds of deviants. Although they occasionally got into trouble, comedy writers seem to have enjoyed a free hand in dealing with public figures, and they made the most of it.

In spite of all thes comic aspects, the Greek comedy was very serious about its political and social satire, and every one respected the talents of the comic writers. Only one has survived at all, Aristophanes, but we think he was probably the best of the four hundred writers whose names have come down to us as comedians.

Aristophanes' ideas and attitudes are comples and difficult. He is often mistaken for a pacificist because he opposed the Peloponessian Wars. True, he wrote several plays, like Peace and The Birds, which make fun of the conduct of the war. In his most famous play, Lysistrata, a woman organizes all the women--wives, prostitutes and mistresses--on both sides into a coalition. The women deny their men any sexual satisfaction until the men end the war. Needless to say, this arrangement gives Aristophanes the opportunity to get off a lot of excellent dirty jokes, while the sex-starved males provide classic material for comedy. The play was often produced in conjunction with protests against the Viet Nam war by peace advocates.

However, Aristophanes actually has much more in common with ultra-right wing Republicans. For all his naughtiness (even by Greek standards), he recommends the old virtues of self-control, military strength, family duty, and narrow morality. In Women Celebrating the Thesmos (a holiday allowing women to do anything they liked), Aristophanes makes fun of the women's rights movement of his day and attacks "immoral" x-rated modern plays by Euripides. In The Frogs, Aristophanes contrasts the decadent, degenerate, selfish and loose values of the Athenians of his day with those of the age of Marathon, and he sees the modern plays as reflecting the decadence. While Aeschylus is moral, formal, and dull, Euripides is, according to Aristophanes, immoral, sloppy, and pornographic. Although he is aware of Aeschylus' long-windedness, Aristophanes at the end of the play recommends the old values.

Aristophanes' values are clearest in the little known play Women in the Assembly. Here his crusty reactionary sympathies show themselves in his opposition to women's rights and "progressive" economics and morality. Women in Aristophanes usually have absurd ideas, and in this play they have an especially bad one. They think that wealth should be distributed equally according to need. To accomplish this socialist scheme, assemblymen's wives all make extreme demands of their husbands' sexual powers the night before the assembly meeting and then take their husbands' places in the assembly when the men cannot get out of bed the next day. The women then pass legislation requiring that all goods be collected into a single pot and then redistributed equally to all citizens. All but a few of the citizens are in favor of this idea because of its "justice." When questioned, however, they admit that they really figure that they will get more by the division, for they can only see what they do not have that others do. Their motive is greed, not equality. After the division, strangely enough, everyone has less--the ones who were rich have less than even the poor used to have.

By this method, Aristophanes ridicules the popular philosophers of his time who insisted that the whole was the sum of its parts. To show how this is not the case with economic and social issues, Aristophanes his idea that "equality" is a foolish goal by having the women introduce a bill for sexual equality. As society had been run, young pretty women had many lovers, while old or ugly ones had few. To make things equal and just, all women were given by the government a rating of ugliness. Any woman who found a sexual act about to be commetted could demand to see the rating of the woman involved, and if she were rated uglier, could insist that she be served first. (Is this not the way that beaurocrats solve our problems today?) The older men, of course, were the most opposed to this proposal. But the law was passed and the play closes with a striking scene. A beautiful young girl and a virile young man are about to consumate their love when a group of hags appear. They argue about who is the ugliest, each grabbing for the young man. He is torn to pieces, and no one gets anything.

We must remember Aristophanes' bias toward the old virtues when we look at The Clouds. Perhaps no generation is better prepared to read the play than the generation of college students since the 1960's. The generation gap always exists, but rarely so markedly as in Aristophanes' time and ours. The brave, out-numbered Greeks nobly defeated the better-prepared Persians between 500 and 480 B. C. The heroes of Marathon could not understand how Athenians could lose to Egyptians, just as the heroes of Iwo Jima and Normandy in World War II could not see how the United States could lose to North Viet Nam. More importantly, the heroes of Normandy, who had no choice but to spend four or five years in the Army under combat cond itions, had difficulty understanding why anyone would object to the minor inconvenience of an easy two year hitch. The older generation had always accepted work, duty and morality as a necessary part of life. Suddenly, their children questioned the validity of marriage, duty to country, and even wealth. Certainly, for students today there must be a familiar ring to the conversations between Strepsiades and Pheidipides.

Aristophanes attributes the "decline" of the Greek attitude to Socrates and his disciples, the "Sophists." Scholars have hotly debated his conclusion for a long time, expecial ly in the last three hundred years. A "sophist" is a philosopher who questions the assumptions of all systems, leading all arguments into deeper mazes of definitions, always making matters more and more confused. The sophist always says to his opponent, "Yes, but what do you mean by that word?" Almost all modern psychologists ("What do we really mean by happiness?"), lawyers "What do we really mean

301

by guilty?"), and economists ("What do we really mean by depression?") are really sophists who prefer to define problems out of existence rather than solve them. Plato and subsequent friends to Socrates have denied that Socrates was a sophist, and Plato thought that the unjust portrait of Socrates in The Clouds caused his trial and execution. But then Aristophanes knew a younger Socrates as an equal, and Plato knew an older one as a teacher. Certainly, Socrates did use the favorite technique of the sophists, that of calling for definitions of things which cannot be defined but which are necessary assumptions ("What is truth? What is guilt? What is evil?"). The reasoning used by Strepsiades in the last of The Clouds is a well-known Socratic technique. Strepsiades argues that since money is the root of evil, to pay money that is owed would corrupt the recipient, and would then be evil. Socrates asked if we should return what we had borrowed from a friend if we knew the friend were going to commit suicided with it.

We will never be able to say how accurate Aristophanes' portrait is, but we can see what the playwright meant Socrates to represent. In the debate about Zeus and Vortex, about "dipper and dipperess," Socrates attempts to modity language to fit patterns which Socrates thinks exist in nature. Strepsiades, the anti-intellectual, thinks language and society are convenient assumptions which must be accepted without question ("That's the way it has always been"). Which is the better way of seeing things?

The Greek comedy, like the tragedy, had many conventions, of whihc we will ignore all but one, the agon. This is the central debate between the opposing forces in the comedy. In The Clouds, the debate is between the old logic and the new logic. We must note that the old logic stands for dullness, military duty, Fourth of July oratory, and Greek nationalism. The new logic (whihc is also named the bad logic) stands for cleverness, ease, sarcasm, pleasure and selfishness. Does the last scene make it clear which side Aristophanes is on?

STREPSIADES is discovered in his chamber, PHEIDIPPIDES
sleeping in his bed. Time, before break of day.

Strep. *(stretching and yawning.)* Ah me, ah me! will this
    night never end?
Oh kingly Zeus, shall there be no more day?
And yet the cock sung out long time ago;
I heard him - but my people lie and snore,
Snore in defiance, for the rascals know
It is their privilege in time of war,
Which with its other plagues brings this upon us,
That we mayn't rouse these vermin with a stick.
There's my young son too, he sleeps it through,
Snug under five fat blankets at the least.
I wish I could sleep so sound! but my poor eyes
Have no sleep in them; what with debts and bills
And stable-keepers' bills, which this fine son
Heaps on my back, I lie awake the whole night:
And what cares he but to put curlers in his hair,
Ride, drive his horses, dream of them all night,
While I, poor devil, may go hang - for now
The moon in her last quarter goes on,
And my usurious creditors are gaping.
Heavens! a light! bring my me tablets, boy!
That I may set down all, and sum them up,
Debts, creditors, and interest upon interest-
               (Boy enters with a light and
               tablets.)
Let me see where I am and what the total-
$500 to Pasias - Hah! to Pasias $500!
Damn, and for what? A horse, of all things,
Right noble by the brand - Curse on such brands!
I wish I had giv'n this eye from out this head,
Ere I had paid the purchase of this nag!
Pheidip. Watch what you're doing, Secretariat! - Keep
    within your ring.
Streps. There 'tis! that's it! the end of all my peace-
He's racing in his sleep.
Pheidip. A time trial! a trial!
How many records for the lap?
Streps. More than enough;
    You've giv'n me laps enough - I am worn out.
But to my list - What name stands next to Pasias?
Man o' War - still for the race-
A chariot mounted on its wheels complete.

Pheidip. Dismount! unharness and away!
Streps. I thank you;
   You have unharness'd me: I am dismounted,
   And with a vengenace - All my goods in pawn,
   Fines, forfeiture, and penalties all over the place.
Pheidip. *(wakes)*. My father! why so restless? who has
   irritated you?
Streps. The sheriff irritates me; he breaks my rest.
Pheidip. Oh, nuts, let me sleep!
Streps. Sleep on!
   But take this with you; all these debts of mine
   Will double on your head: a plague confound
   That cursed match-maker, who drew me in
   To wed, forsooth, that precious dam of yours.
   I liv'd at ease in the country, coarsely clad,
   Rough, free, and full withal as oil and honey
   And store of stock could fill me, till I took,
   Clown as I was, this rich man's daughter,
   This vain, extravagant, high-blooded dame:
   Rare bed-fellows and dainty - were we not?
   I, smelling of the wine-vat, figs and fleeces,
   The produce of my farm, all perfumes she,
   Saffron and harlot's kisses, face-creams and lip-sticks,
   A pamper'd bitch - Idle I'll not call her;
   She took due pains in faith to work my ruin,
   Which made me tell her, pointing to this cloak,
   Now threadbare on my shoulders - see, goodwife,
   This is your work - in truth you toil too hard.
                (Boy re-enters.)
Boy. Master, the lamp has drunk up all its oil.
Streps. Aye, 'tis a drunken lamp; the more fault yours;
   Dog, you shall howl for this.
Boy. Why? for what fault?
Streps. For cramming such a greedy wick with oil.
                (Exit boy.)
   Well! in good time this hopeful heir was born;
   Then I and my beloved fell to arguing
   About the naming of the brat - My wife
   Would dub her colt some "hokey-set" name,
   Or it might be Callipides, she car'd not
   So 'twere equestrian the name - but I
   Stuck for his grandfather Pheidonides;
   At last when niether could prevail, the matter
   Was compromis'd by calling him Pheidippides:
   Then she began to fondle her sweet babe,

And taking him by th' hand — Lambkin, she cried,
When thou art some years older thou shalt drive,
Megacles-like, thy chariot to the city,
Rob'd in a saffron mantle — No, quoth I,
Not so, my boy, but thou shalt drive thy goats,
When thou art able, from the fields of Phelle,
Clad in a woollen jacket like thy father:
But he is deaf to all these thrifty rules,
And drives me on the gallop to my ruin;
Therefore all night I call my thoughts to council,
And after long debate find one chance left,
To which if I can lead him, all is safe,
If not — but soft: 'tis time that I should wake him.
But how to soothe him to the task — *(speaking in a soft
gentle tone)* Pheidippides!
Precious Pheidippides!

Pheidip. What do you want, dad?

Streps. Kiss me, my boy! reach me thine hand —

Pheidip. Come on, what do you want?

Streps. Dost thou love me, sirrah? speak!

Pheidip. Oh, yes equestrian Neptune!

Streps. *(angrily)*. Name not him,
Name not that charioteer; he is my curse,
The source of all my sorrow — but, my son,
If thou dost love me, prove it by obeying.

Pheidip. In what must I obey?

Streps. Reform your habits;
Quit them at once, and what I shall ask,
That do!

Pheidip. And what is it that you want?

Streps. But wilt thou do't?

Pheidip. Yea, by Dionysus!

Streps. 'Tis well: get up! come hither, boy! look out!
Yon little hut right there —
Dost see them?

Pheidip. Clearly. What of that hut?

Streps. Why that's the council-chamber of all wisdom:
There the choice spirits dwell, who teach the world
That heav'n's great concave is one mighty oven,
And men its burning embers; these are they,
Who can show lawyers how to twist a cause,
If you'll but pay them for it, right or wrong.

Pheidip. And how do you call them?

Streps. Well, I know not that,
But they are men, who take a world of pains;

Wondrous good men and able.

Pheidip. To hell with them!
Poor idiots, I know them now; you mean those scabs,
Those squalid, barefoot, beggarly impostors,
The mighty hippies of whose sect
Are Socrates and Chaerephon. Not me!

Streps. Hush, hush! be still; don't vent such foolish
prattle;
But if you'll do what I say, join their college
And quit your riding-school.

Pheidip. Not I, so help me
Dionysus our patron! though you brib'd me
With all the racers that Leogaras
Breeds from his Phasian stud.

Streps. Dear, darling lad,
Prythee be rul'd, and learn.

Pheidip. What shall I learn?

Streps. They have a choice of logic; this for justice.
That for injustice: learn that second style,
And all these creditors, that now beset me,
Shall never touch a dollar that I owe them.

Pheidip. I'll learn of no such masters, nor be made
A scare-crow and a may-game to my comrades;
I have no zeal for starving.

Streps. No, nor I
For feasting you and your fine pamper'd cattle
At free cost any longer - Horse and foot
To the crows I send you. Just get out!

Pheidip. Well, sir, I have an uncle rich and noble;
Megacles will not let me be unhors'd;
To him I go; I'll trouble you no longer.   (Exit.)

Streps. (alone). He has thrown me to the ground, but I'll
not lie there;
I'll up, and, with permission of the gods,
Try if I cannot learn these arts myself:
But being old, sluggish, and dull of wit,
How am I sure these subtleties won't pose me?
Well! I'll attempt it: what avails complaint?
Why don't I knock and enter? - Hoa! within there! -
                        (Knocks violently at the door.)

Student (half-opening the door). Go, hang yourself! and
give the crows a dinner -
What noisy fellow art thou at the door?

Streps. Strepsiades of Cicynna, son of Pheidon.

306

Student. Whoe'er thou art, 'fore Heaven, thou art a fool
    Not to respect these doors; battering so loud,
    And kicking with such vengeance, you have marr'd
    The ripe idea of my pregnant brain,
    And brought on a miscarriage.
Streps. Oh! the pity! –
    Pardon my ignorance: I'm country bred
    And far a-field am come: I pray you tell me
    What curious thought my luckless noise has killed,
    Just as your brain was hatching.
Student. These are things
    We never speak of but amongst ourselves.
Streps. Speak boldly then to me, for I am come
    To be amongst you, and partake the secrets
    Of your profound academy.
Student. Enough!
    I will impart, but set it down in thought
    Amongst our mysteries – This is the question,
    As it was put but now to Chaerephon,
    By our great master Socrates, to answer –
    How many of his own lengths at one spring
    A flea can hop – for we did see one vault
    From Chaerephon's black eye-brow to the head
    Of Socrates.
Streps. And how did he
    Figure to measure this?
Student. Most accurately:
    He dipped the insect's feet in melted wax,
    Which, hard'ning into sandals as it cool'd,
    Gave him the space by rule infallible.
Streps. Imperial Zeus! what brilliance of thought!
Student. But there's a deeper question yet behind;
    What would you say to that?
Streps. I pray, impart it.
Student. 'Twas put to Socrates, if he could say,
    When a gnat humm'd, whether the sound did issue
    From mouth or tail.
Streps. My, my. What said he?
Student. He said your gnat doth blow his trumpet backwards
    From a sonorous cavity within him,
    Which being filled with breath, and forc'd along
    The narrow pipe or rectum of his body,
    Doth vent itself in a loud hum behind.
Streps. Hah! then I see the foot print of your gnat
    Is trumpet-fashion'd – Oh! the blessings on him

307

For this discovery; well may he escape
The law's strict punishment, who thus develops
The anatomy of a gnat.
Student. Nor is this all;
Another grand experiment was blasted
By a damned cat.
Streps. As how, good sir; discuss?
Student. One night as he was gazing at the moon,
Curious and all intent upon her motions,
A cat on the house ridge was at her needs,
And urinated in his face.
Streps. Damn her for it!
Yet I must laugh no less to think a cat
Should so bespatter Socrates.
Student. Last night
We were rooked out of our supper.
Streps. Were you so?
What did your master substitute instead?
Student. Why to say truth, he sprinkled a few ashes
Upon the board, then with a little pin,
Crook'd for the purpose, pretending to describe
A circle, neatly filch'd away a cloak.
Streps. Why talk we then of Thales? Open to me,
Open the school, and let me see your master:
I am on fire to enter - Come, open up!
        (*The door of the school is unbarred. The Socratic
        scholars are seen in various grotesque situations
        and positions. Strepsiades, with signs of
        astonishment, draws back a pace or two, then
        exclaims:*
O Hercules, defend me! who are these?
What kind of cattle have we here in view?
Student. Where is the wonder? What do they look like?
Streps. Methinks they're like our Spartan prisoners,
Captur'd at Pylos. What are they in search of?
Why are their eyes so glued to th' earth?
Student. There their researches centre.
Streps. 'Tis for onions
They are looking for - Come, lads, give it up;
I'll show you what you want, a noble plat,
All round and sound - but wait! what mean those people,
Who dip their heads so low?
Student. Well, because
Their studies lead that way: They are now diving
To the dark realms of Tartarus and Night.

Streps. But why are all their rear ends mounted up?
Student. To practise them in star-gazing, and teach them
    Their proper elevations - but no more:
    In, fellow-students, in: if chance the master come
    And find us here -
        *(addressing himself to some of his fellow-students,
        who were crowding about the new-comer.*
Streps. No, no, let 'em stay,
    And tell me about my business.
Student. Impossible; they cannot give the time.
Streps. Now for the love of Heav'n, what have we here?
    Explain their uses to me.   *(observing the apparatus.*
Student. This machine
    Is for astronomy -
Streps. And this?
Student. For geometry.
Streps. As how?
Student. For measuring the earth.
Streps. Indeed!
    What, by the acre?
Student. No, faith, sir, by the lump;
    Ev'n the whole globe at once.
Streps. Well said, in truth.
    A cute device, and made for general use.
Student. Look now, this line marks the circumference
    Of the whole earth, d'ye see - This spot is Athens -
Streps. Athens! got to, I see no courts are in session;
    Therefore I can't believe you.
Student. Nay, in truth,
    This very spot is Attica.
Streps. And where,
    Where is my own Cicynna?
Student. Here it lies:
    And here's Euboea - Look! how far it runs -
Streps. How far it runs! Yes, Pericles has made it
    Run far enough from us - Where's Lacedaemon?
Student. Here; close to Athens.
Streps. Ah! how much too close -
    Please, good friends, take that bad neighbour from us.
Student. That's not for us to do.
Streps. The worse luck your's!
    But look! *(casting up his eyes)* who's this suspended in
    a basket?   *(Socrates is discovered.*
Student. *(with solemnity).* HIMSELF. The HE.
Streps. The HE? what HE?

Student. Why, Socrates.
Streps. Hah! Socrates! - *(to the scholar)* Make up to him
    and roar,
    Bid him come down! yell loud!
Student. Not I;
    Do it yourself; I've other things to mind. *(Student
    leaves).*
Streps. Hey! Socrates - Hey, my little Socrates!
Socrates. Mortal, how now! Thou insect of a day,
    What do you want?
Streps. I would like to know what you are doing.
Socr. I tread in air, contemplating the sun
Streps. Ah! then I see you're basketed so high,
    That you look down upon the Gods - Good luck;
    You'll lower a peg on earth.
Socr. Sublime in air,
    Sublime in thought I carry my mind with me,
    Its cogitations all assimilated
    To the pure atmosphere, in which I float;
    Lower me to earth, and my mind's subtle powers,
    Seiz'd by sickening dullness, lose their spirit;
    For the dry earth drinks up the generous sap,
    The begetating vigour of philosophy,
    And leaves it a mere husk.
Streps. What do you say?
    Philosophy has sapped your vigour? Fie upon it.
    But come, my precious fellow, come down quickly,
    And teach me those fine things I'm here to look for.
Socr. And what fine things are they?
Streps. A new way
    To send off my creditors, and cheating them
    By the art logical; for you shall know
    By debts, pawns, pledges, usuries, executions,
    I am ruined, torn to pieces.
Socr. Why put up with it?
    What strange infatuation seiz'd your senses?
Streps. The horse-consumption, a devouring plague;
    But so you'll enter me among your scholars,
    And tutor me like them to hood-wink my creditors,
    Name your own price, and by the Gods I swear
    I'll pay you the last dollar
Socr. By what Gods?
    Answer that first; for your Gods are not mine.
Streps. How swear you then? As the Byzantians swear
    By their worthless iron coin?

Socr. Art thou ambitious
    To be instructed in celestial matters,
    And taught to know them clearly?
Streps. Yes, Yes, I am.
    If they be useful in getting out of debt.
Socr. What, if I bring you to a conference
    With my own proper Goddesses, the Clouds?
Streps. 'Tis what I wish devoutly.
Socr. Come, sit down;
    Repose yourself upon this bed.
Streps. 'Tis done.
Socr. Now take this cap for sacrifices.
Streps. Why this cap?
    Would'st make of me another cow,
    And sacrifice me to a cloud?
Socr. Fear nothing;
    It is a ceremony necessary
    At OUR initiations.
Streps. What to gain?
Socr. *(instead of the sacred meat, which was thrown on
    the sacrificed victim, a basket of stones is showered
    on the head of Strepsiades).*
    'Twill sift your faculties as fine as powder,
    Bolt 'em like meal, grind'em as light as dust;
    Only be patient.
Streps. Truly, you'll go near
    To make your words good; an' you pound me thus,
    You'll make me very dust and nothing else.
Socr. *(assuming all the magical solemnity and tone of
    voice of an adept).* Keep silence, then, and listen
    to a prayer,
    Which fits the gravity of age to hear –
    Oh! Air, all powerful Air, which dost enfold
    This pendant globe, thou vault of flaming gold.
    Ye sacred Clouds, who bid the thunder roll,
    Come faith, approach, and cheer your suppliant's soul!
Streps. Wait, keep 'em off awhile, till I am ready.
    Oh! luckless me, wou'd I had brought my umbrella,
    So I could keep from getting wet.
Socr. Come, come away!
    Fly swift, ye Clouds, and give yourselves to view!
    Whether on high Olympus' sacred top
    Snow-crown'd ye sit, or in the blue vales
    Of your own father Ocean sporting weave
    Your misty dance, or dip your golden urns

In the seven mouths of Nile; whether ye dwell
On Thracian Mimas, or Moeotis' lake,
Hear me, yet hear, and thus invok'd approach!
    (Chorus of Clouds. (The scene is at the remotest
    part of the stage. Thunder is heard. A large
    and shapeless Cloud is seen floating in the air;
    from which the following song is heard.)
Ascend, ye watery Clouds, on high,
Daughters of Ocean, climb the sky,
And o'er the mountain's pine-capt brow
Towering your fleecy mantle throw:
Thence let us scan the wide-stretch'd scene,
Groves, lawns, and rilling streams between,
And stormy Neptune's vast expanse,
And grasp all nature at a glance.
Now the dark tempest flits away,
And lo! the glittering orb of day
Darts from his clear ethereal beam,
Come let us snatch the joyous gleam.
<u>Socr</u>. Yes, ye Divinities, whom I adore,
    I hail you now propitious to my prayer.
    Didst thou not hear them speak in thunder to me?
<u>Streps</u>. *(kneeling, and, with various acts of clowning,*
    affecting terror and embarrassment.)
    And I too am your Cloudships' most obedient servant;
    No *(turning to Socrates),* take it how you may, my
        terror and fears
    Have pinch'd and choked my poor bowels so,
    That I can't choose but treat their holy nostrils
    With smelly farts,
<u>Socr</u>. Stop
    These gross stupidities, for low clowns,
    And con-men more fitting. Hush! be still,
    Listen to the chorus of their heavenly voices,
    For music is the language they delight in.
<u>Chorus of Clouds</u> *(approaching nearer).* Ye Clouds replete
    with fruitful showers,
    Here let us seek Athena's towers,
    The cradle of old Cecrops' race,
    The world's chief ornament and grace;
    Here mystic rituals, and rites divine
    And lamps in sacred splendour shine;
    Here the Gods dwell in marble domes,
    Feasted with costly sacrifices,
    That round their votive statues blaze,

While crowded temples ring with praise;
And pompous sacrifices here
Make holidays throughout the year,
And when gay spring-time comes again,
Bromius gathers his sportive train,
And pipe and song and choral dance
Hail the soft hours as they advance.

Streps. Now, in the name of Zeus, I want you to tell me,
   Who are these ranting dames, that talk in stilts?
   Of the Amazonian cast no doubt.

Socr. Not so,
   No dames, but clouds celestial, friendly powers
   To men of sluggish parts; from these we draw
   Sense, apprehension, volubility,
   Wit to confuse, and cunning to ensnare.

Streps. Aye, therefore 'twas that my heart leapt within
   me
   For very sympathy when first I heard 'em:
   Now I could talk shrewdly of first causes,
   And spin out metaphysic cobwebs cutely,
   And dogmatise most rarely, and argue
   And paradox it with the best of you:
   So, come what may, I must and will behold 'em;
   Show me their faces, I beg you.

Socr. Look,
   Look towards Mount Parnes as I point - There, there!
   Now they go down the hill; I see them plainly,
   As plain as can be.

Streps. Where, where? Please, show me.

Socr. Here! a whole troop of them thro' woods and hollows,
   A byway of their own.

Streps. What is wrong with my eyes,
   That I can't catch a glimpse of them?

Socr. Behold!
   Here at the very entrance -

Streps. I'll be damned,
   If yet I see them clearly.

Socr. Then you must be
   Sand-blind or worse.

Streps. Nay, now by father Zeus,
   I cannot choose but see them - precious creatures!
   For in good faith here's plenty and to spare.
               (Chorus of Clouds enter.

Socr. And didst thou doubt if they were goddesses?

Streps. Not I, so help me! only I'd a notion
    That they were fog, and dew, and dusky vapour.
Socr. For shame! Why, man, these are the nursing mothers
    Of all our famous sophists, fortune-tellers,
    Quacks, med'cine-mongers, bards long-winded,
    Chorus projectors, and star interpreters,
    And wonder-making cheats - The gang of idlers,
    Who pay them for their feeding with good store
    Of flattery and mouth-worship.
Streps. Now I see
    Whom we may thank for driving them along
    At such a furious dithyrambic rate,
    Sun-shadowing clouds of many-colour'd hues,
    Air-rending tempests, hundred-headed Typhons;
    Now rousing, rattling them about our ears,
    Now gently wafting them down the sky,
    Moist, airy, bending, bursting into showers;
    For all which fine descriptions these poor knaves
    Dine daintily on scraps.
Socr. And proper fare;
    What better do they merit?
Streps. Tell me this,
    If these be clouds (d'you get me?) very clouds,
    How came they metamorphos'd into women?
    Clouds are not such as these.
Socr. And what else are they?
Streps. Well, I can't rightly tell, but I should guess
    Something like flakes of wool, not women, sure;
    And look! these dames have noses. -
Socr. Hark you, friend,
    I'll put a question to you.
Streps. Out with it!
    Be quick: let's have it.
Socr. This it is, in short -
    Have you ne'er seen a cloud, which you could think
    Shap'd like a centaur, leopard, wolf, or bull?
Streps. Yea, of course, have I, and what then?
Socr. Why then
    Clouds can assume what shapes they will, believe me;
    For instance; should they spy some hairy clown
    Rugged and rough, and like the unclean child
    Of Xenophantes, straight they turn to centaurs,
    And kick at him for vengeance.
Streps. Well done, Clouds!

But should they spy that thieving crook,
Simon, that public theif, how would they treat him?
Socr. As wolves – in character most like his own.
Streps. Aye, there it is now; when they saw Cleonymus,
That bastard runaway, they turn'd to deer
In honour of his cowardice.
Socr. And now,
Having seen Cleisthenes, to make fun of his sassyness,
They change themselves to women.
Streps. Welcome, ladies!
Imperial ladies, welcome! If it please
Your Highnesses so far to grace a mortal,
Give me a touch of your celestial voices.
Chor. Hail, grandfather! who at this late hour of life
Wants go to school of lying; and all hail,
Thou prince pontifical of hair-splitting.
Speak thy full mind, make known thy wants and wishes!
Thee and our worthy Prodicus excepted,
Not one of all your sophists have our ear:
Him for his wit and learning we esteem,
Thee for thy proud acting and high looks,
In barefoot beggary strutting up and down,
Content to suffer mockery for our sake,
And carry a grave face while others laugh.
Streps. Oh! mother earth, was ever voice like this,
So reverend, so portentous, so divine!
Socr. These are your only deities, all else
I say, to hell with them.
Streps. Wait! Olympian Zeus –
Is he no god?
Socr. What Zeus? what god?
Prythee no more – away with him at once!
Streps. Say'st thou? who gives us rain? answer me that.
Socr. These give us rain; as I will demonstrate:
Come on now – When did you e'er see it rain
Without a cloud? If Zeus gives rain,
Let him rain down his favours in the sunshine,
Not ask the clouds to help him.
Streps. You have hit it,
'Tis so; heav'n help me! I did think till now,
Then 'twas his godship's pleasure, he urinated
Into a screen and gave the earth a shower.
But, hark'ye me, who thunders? tell me that;
For then it is I tremble.

<u>Socr</u>. These, these thunder,
  When they are tumbled.
<u>Streps</u>. How, blasphemer, how?
<u>Socr</u>. When they are charg'd with vapours full to th'
    bursting,
  And bandied to and fro against each other,
  Then with the shock they burst and crack apart.
<u>Streps</u>. And who is he that bangs them thus together
  But Zeus himself?
<u>Socr</u>. Zeus! 'tis not Zeus that does it,
  But the airy vortex
<u>Streps</u>. What is he?
  I never heard of him; is he not Zeus?
  Or is Zeus put aside, and Vortex crown'd
  King of Olympus in his state and place?
  But let me learn some more of this same thunder.
<u>Socr</u>. Have you not learnt? I told you how the clouds,
  Being supercharged with vapour, rush together,
  And, in the conflict, shake the poles with thunder.
<u>Streps</u>. But who believes you?
<u>Socr</u>. You, as I shall prove it:
  Look at the Thanksgiving, where you cram
  Your belly full of turkey; if you shake
  And stir it lustily about - what then?
<u>Streps</u>. Well, why then it gives a desperate mess;
  It bounces like a thunderbolt, the dressing
  Makes such a gas within me - At the first,
  Pappax it cries - anon with double force,
  Papappax! - when at length *Papappapax*
  From forth my sounding entrails thund'ring bursts.
<u>Socr</u>. Think then, if so your belly bursts out;
  How must the vasty vault of heaven resound,
  When the clouds crack with thunder!
<u>Streps</u>. Let that pass,
  And tell me of the lightning, whose quick flash
  Burns us to cinders; that, at least, great Zeus
  Keeps in reserve to launch at liars?
<u>Socr</u>. Idiot! Moran! were you born before the flood
  To talk of lying, whilst Simon breathes,
  Theorus and Cleonymus, whilst they,
  Thrice-perjur'd villains, brave the lightning's stroke,
  And gaze the heavens unscorcht? Would these escape?
  Why, man, Zeus' random fires strike his own people,
  Strike Sunium's guiltless top, strike the dumb oak,

Who never yet lied or falsely swore.

Streps. It may be so, good sooth! You talk this well:
  But I would like to be taught the natural cause
  Of these appearances.

Socr. Mark when the winds,
  In their free courses check'd, are penned and blown up
  As 'twere within a balloon, stretching then
  And struggling for expansion, they burst forth
  With crack so fierce as sets the air on fire.

Streps. The devil they do! why now I see something:
  So was I serv'd with a damn'd paunch, I broil'd
  On Zeus' day last, just such a dirty trick;
  Because, forsooth, not dreaming of your thunder,
  I never thought to give the rascal an opening,
  Boom! goes the bag, and covers me all over
  With filth and ordure till my eyes struck fire,

Chor. The envy of all Athens shalt you be,
  Happy old man, who from our lips dost suck
  Into thy ears true wisdom, so thou art
  But wise to learn, and studious to retain
  What thou hast learnt; patient to bear the blows
  And buffets of hard fortune; to persist,
  Doing or suffering; firmly to abide
  Hunger and cold, not craving where to dine,
  To drink, to sport and trifle time away;
  But holding that for best, which best becomes
  A man who means to carry all things through
  Neatly, expertly, perfect at all points
  With head, hands, tongue, to force his way to fortune.

Streps. You can bet on it; I'll be a student
  With a tough heart, watchful as I can be,
  A thrifty, pinching fellow, that can dine
  Upon a piece of celery and to bed;
  I am your man for this, hard as an anvil.

Socr. 'Tis well, so you will ratify your faith
  In these our deities - CHAOS and CLOUDS
  And SPEECH - in these and only these believe.

Streps. If from this hour henceforth I ever waste
  A single thought on any other gods,
  Or give them sacrifice, libation, incense,
  Nay, even common courtesy, you can beat me.

Chor. Speak your wish boldly then, so shall you prosper
  As you obey and worship us, and study
  The wholesome art of making money.

Streps. Gracious ladies,
    I ask no mighty favour, simply this –
    Let me but out-lie every tongue in Greece,
    And run 'em out of sight a hundred yards.
Chor. Is that all? there we are your friends to serve you;
    We will endow thee with such powers of speech,
    As henceforth not a politician in Athens
    Shall spout such popular lies as thou shalt.
Streps. To hell with powers of lying! give me powers
    Of out-witting my creditors.
Chor. A trifle –
    Granted as soon as ask'd; only be bold,
    And show yourself obedient to your teachers.
Streps. With your help so I will, being undone,
    Stript of my money by these high-blooded cattle,
    And a fine woman, the torment of my life.
    Now let them work their wicked will upon me;
    They're welcome to my carcass; let 'em claw it,
    Starve it with thirst and hunger, fry it, freeze it,
    Nay, beat the very skin off; 'tis their own;
    So that I may but hood-wink my creditors,
    Let the world talk; I care not though it call me
    A bold-faced, loud-tongued, overbearing bully;
    A shameless, vile, lying cheat;
    A tricking, quibbling, double-dealing bastard;
    A prating, pettyfogging limb o' th' law;
    A sly old fox, a perjurer, a hang-dog,
    A raggamuffin made of shreds and patches,
    The leavings of a manure-pile – Let 'em rail,
    Yea, marry, let 'em turn my guts to fiddle-strings,
    May my bread be my poison! damned if I care.
Chor. This fellow hath a prompt and daring spirit –
    Come hither, sir; do you perceive and feel
    What great and glorious fame you shall acquire
    By this our schooling of you?
Streps. What, I pray you!
Chor. You will live the envy of mankind
    Under our patronage?
Streps. When shall I see
    Those wonderful days?
Chor. Then shall your doors be jammed
    With clients waiting for your coming out,
    All eager to consult you, pressing all
    To catch a word from you, with abstracts, briefs,

318

And cases ready-drawn for your opinion.
But come, begin and lecture this old fellow;
Sift him, that we may see what meal he's made of.
Socr. Hark ye, let's hear what principles you hold,
That these being known, I may apply such tools
Fit your needs.
Streps. Needs! Heaven's sakes;
Are you about to confuse me?
Socr. Not so, but simply in the way of practice
To try your memory.
Streps. Oh! as for that,
My memory is of two sorts, long and short:
With them who owe me anything it never fails;
My creditors indeed complain of it,
As mainly apt to leak and forget to pay.
Socr. But let us hear if nature hath given you
With any grace of speaking.
Streps. None of speaking.
But a most apt tendency to cheating.
Socr. If this be all, how can you hope to learn?
Streps. Fear me not, never break your head for that.
Socr. Well then be quick, and when I speak of things
Mysterious and profound, see that you don't
Get confused, but −
Streps. I understand your meaning;
You'd have me wholesale philosophy by mouthfuls,
Just like a hungry dog.
Socr. Oh! brutal, gross
And barbarous ignorance! I must suspect,
Old as thou art, thou must be taught with beatings:
Tell me now, when thou art beaten, what dost feel?
Streps. The blows of him that beats me I do feel;
But having breath'd awhile I lay my action
And cite my witnesses; then more cool,
I bring my cause into the court, and sue
For damages.
Socr. Take off your cloak! prepare.
Streps. Prepare for what? what crime have I committed?
Socr. None; but the rule and custom is with us,
That all shall enter naked.
Streps. And why naked?
I come with no search-warrant; fear me not;
I'll carry nothing away with me.
Socr. No matter;
Conform yourself, and strip.

Streps. And if I do,
    Tell me for my encouragement to which
    Of all your scholars will you liken me.
Socr. You shall be call'd a second Chaerephon.
Streps. Ah! Chaerephon is but another name
    For a dead body - excuse me.
Socr. No more words:
    Get up your courage; answer not, but follow:
    Get to work and get perfect.
Streps. Give me my first lesson
    Of learning in hand, and pass me on;
    Ne'er trust me if I do not quake and tremble
    As if the cavern of Trophonius yawn'd,
    And I were stepping in.
Socr. What ails you? enter!
    Why do you halt and loiter at the door?
        (Socrates and Strepsiades enter the mansion of
        the former.
Chor. Go, brave adventurer, proceed!
    May fortune crown the gallant deed;
    Tho' far advanc'd in life's last stage,
    Spurning the infirmities of age,
    Thou canst to youthful labours rise,
    And boldly struggle to be wise.

    You, who are here spectators of our scene,
    Give me your patience to a few plain words,
    And by my patron Dionysius, whose I am,
    I swear they shall be true ones - Gentle friends,
    If I may prosper in your fair esteem,
    As I declare in truth that I was mov'd
    To give you my former comedy,
    Thinking it the best of all my works,
    And you its judges worthy of that work,
    Which I had wrought with my best care and pains:
    But fools were found to thrust me from the stage,
    And you, whose better wisdom should have sav'd me
    From that most nasty bunch, permitted it;
    For which I must complain, yet not so sharply
    As to break off from such approv'd good friends:
    No, you have been my patrons from all time,
    Ev'n to my first-born issue: when I dropt
    My plays at your door to hide the shame
    Of one, who call'd herself a youthful poet,

You charitably took the stuff in,
And gave it worthy training. Now, behold,
This sister comedy, Electra-like,
Comes on the search if she perchance may find
Some recognition of a brother lost,
Though but a bit of his well-known hair.
Seemly and modest this play appears before you;
Not like our stage clowns in shaggy hide
To set a mob a roaring; she will vent
No foolish jests at baldness, will not dance
Th' indecent strip-tease; we have no old man
Arm'd with a staff to practise manual jokes
On the by-standers' ribs, and keep the ring
For them who dance the chorus: you shall see
No howling madmen burst upon the stage
Waving their torches; other weapons
Than the muse gives us we shall not employ,
Nor let *ah me, ah me!* sigh in your ears,
The way the big-shot dramatists do
To play for your tastes out of scraps
At second or third hand, but fresh and fair
And still original, as one, who knows,
When he has done a good deed, where to stop;
And, having levell'd Cleon to the ground,
Not to insult his corpse, like to those
Who, having once run down Hyperbolus,
Poor devil! beat and mangle without mercy
Him and his mother too; foremost of these
Was Eupolis, who stole from my stuff,
And pass'd it for his own with a new name,
Guilty the more for having ruined his theft
With the obscene junk about an old hag
Dancing the drunken burlesque in her cups,
Like her Phrynichus feign'd to be devour'd
By the sea-monster – Shame upon such pornography!
Hermippus next *Hyperbolis* wrote,
And now the whole pack open in full cry,
Trying to catch the rabbits I scared out.
If there be any here, who laugh with such clowns,
Let such not smile with me; but if this night
Ye crown these scenes with deserved applause,
The gods shall praise your taste.
<u>Semichorus</u>. Great Zeus, supreme of Gods, and heav'n's
    high king,

First I ask; next to him, Poseiden,
Whose mighty stroke strikes the wild waves in two,
And makes the firm earth tremble; thee from whom
We draw our being, all-inspiring Air,
Parent of nature; and thee, radiant Sun,
Thron'd in thy flaming chariot, I ask to come,
Dear to the gods and by the world loved.

Chorus of Clouds. Most grave and wise judges, hear the
   charge,
Which we shall now prefer, of insults not pleased
By us your wrong'd friends: for whilst we
The patronesses of your state, the Clouds,
Of all the powers celestial serve you most,
You graceless mortals worship us not at all;
Neither smoke, nor sacrifice comes from you,
But blank ingratitude and cold neglect.
But if you'll learn of us the ready mode
To forget your past errors, and ensure
Fame and good-fortune for the public weal,
You have nothing else to do, but stop the eating
Of that wide-gaping buzzard, that thief
Convicted and admitted, with a neat noose
Drawn tight and fitted to his lousy throat.

*Socrates (coming out of the house in violent
indignation), Strepsiades, Chorus*

Socr. A living breath, empty air,
And thou profoundest chaos, witness for me
If ever wretch were seen so gross and dull,
So stupid and foolish as this old clown,
Whose shallow intellect can entertain
No image no impression of a thought;
But ere you've told it, it is lost and gone!
'Tis time however he should now come forth
In the broad day - What wait! Strepsiades -
Take up your bed; bring yourself and it
Into the light.
Streps. Yes, if the bugs would let me.
Socr. Quick, quick, I say; set down your load and listen!
Streps. Lo! here am I.
Socr. Come, tell me what it is
That you would learn besides what I have taught you;
Is it of measure, verse, or modulation?

322

Streps. Of measure by all means, for I was robbed
    Of two days' work i' th' measure of my food
    By a damn'd theiving crook.
Socr. Pish! who talks
    Of food? I ask which metre you prefer,
    Tetrameter or trimeter.
Streps. I answer –
    Give me a pint of beer.
Socr. Yes, but that's no answer.
Streps. No answer! stake your money, and I'll wager
    That your tetrameter is half my pint.
Socr. Go to the gallows, half-wit, with your pint pot!
    Will nothing stick to you? But come, perhaps
    We may try further and do better with you –
    Suppose I spoke to you of modulation;
    Will you be taught of that?
Streps. Tell me first,
    Will I make money? will I be paid
    The food that I was beaten out of? tell me that.
Socr. You will be profited by being taught
    To watch your manners at table in some sort
    After a decent fashion; you will learn
    Which verse is most proper and fit
    To the chorus in the dance of war,
    And which with most harmonious song guides
    The poetic finger in his course poetical.
Streps. The finger? Sure I know that well.
Socr. As how? discuss.
Streps. Here, at my fingers' end;
    This is my finger, and has been my finger
    Since I could count my fingers.
Socr. Oh! the idiot.
Streps. I wish to be no wiser in these matters.
Socr. What then?
Streps. Why then, teach me no other art
    But the fine art of cheating.
Socr. Granted; still
    There is some primary matter, as for instance
    The sexes male and female – Can you name them?
Streps. I were a fool else – These are masculine;
    Ram, bull, goat, dog, and chicken.
Socr. There you're wrong:
    Chicken is male and female.
Streps. Tell me how?

323

<u>Socr.</u> Rooster and hen – So they should be nam'd.
<u>Streps.</u> And so they should, by the empty air!
  You've hit it; for which rare discovery,
  Take all the gold this dipper can hold.
<u>Socr.</u> Why there again you sin against the genders.
  To call it your "dipper,"
  Making that masculine which should be fem'nine.
<u>Streps.</u> How do I make my dipper a male?
<u>Socr.</u> Did you not call it dipper? As well
  You might have call'd Cleonymus a man,
  He and your dipper alike belong
  To t'other sex, believe me.
<u>Streps.</u> Well, my dipper
  Shall be a dipper-ess and he Cleony-miss
  Will that content you?
<u>Socr.</u> Yes, and while you live
  Learn to distinguish sex in proper names.
<u>Streps.</u> I do; the female I am perfect in.
<u>Socr.</u> Give me the proof.
<u>Streps.</u> Lysilla, she's a female;
  Philinna, and Demetria, and Cleitagora.
<u>Socr.</u> Now name your males.
<u>Streps.</u> A thousand – as for instance,
  Philoxenus, Melesias, and Amynias.
<u>Socr.</u> Call you these masculine, stupid clown?
<u>Streps.</u> Are they not such with you?
<u>Socr.</u> No; pretend this happens:
  You and Amynias meet – how will you greet him?
<u>Streps.</u> Why, thus for instance – Hip! holla! Amynia!
<u>Socr.</u> There, there! you make a wench of him at once.
<u>Streps.</u> And fit it is for one who is so sissy;
  A coward ought not to be call'd a man;
  Why teach me what is known to all the world?
<u>Socr.</u> Aye, why indeed? – but come, calm yourself.
<u>Streps.</u> Why so?
<u>Socr.</u> For meditation's sake: lie down.
<u>Streps.</u> Not on this cot I ask you, sir;
  But if I must lie down, let me lie
  On the bare earth and think.
<u>Socr.</u> Away!
  There's nothing but this bed will help thought.
<u>Streps.</u> It helps, alas! a host of bugs,
  That show no mercy on me.
<u>Socr.</u> Come, begin,

Beat your brains and turn yourself about;
Now think awhile, and if you start
A thought that puzzles you, try t'other side,
And turn to something else, but not to sleep;
Don't sleep to close your eyes one moment.

Streps. *(after a considerable pause).* Ah! woe is me; ah,
  woeful, Heavens!

Socr. What ails you? why this moaning?

Streps. I am lost;
  I've waked up the bugs from their hiding holes;
  A colony of bugs in ambush
  Have fall'n upon me: belly, back, and ribs,
  No part is free: I feed a whole nation!

Socr. Take not your sufferings too much to heart,

Streps. How can I help it? - a wretch made up of wants!
  Here am I penniless and spiritless,
  Without a skin, Heav'n knows, without a shoe;
  And to complete my miseries here I lie,
  Like a starv'd sentinel upon his post,
  At watch and ward, till I am shrunk to nothing.
                 (A pause of some duration.

Socr. How now; how are you getting along? Have you
  sprung a thought?

Streps. Yes, yes, so help me Poseidon!

Socr. Hah! what is it?

Streps. Why I am thinking if these cursed bugs
  Will leave one fragment of my body free.

Socr. A plague confound you!

Streps. Spare yourself that prayer;
  I'm plagued already to your heart's content.

Socr. Don't be so careful of your skin;
  Tuck yourself up and buff it like a man:
  Keep your skull under cover, and depend on't
  'Twill make your brain bring forth some precious idea
  For furthering your good-fortune with
  A little dishonesty and injustice.

Streps. Ah! would to Heav'n some friendly soul would help
  me
  To a fine idea how to cheat the bugs
  With a little bugspray.   *(A long pause.*

Socr. Whereabouts, I wonder,
  Sits the wind now? What ails you? are you sleeping?

Streps. Not I, by Heaven!

Socr. Can you think nothing yet?

<u>Streps</u>. Nothing, so help me.
<u>Socr</u>. Will your head breed no project,
  Though primed so well!
<u>Streps</u>. What should it breed?
  Tell me, sweet Socrates; give me some hint.
<u>Socr</u>. Say first what 'tis you wish.
<u>Streps</u>. A thousand times,
  Ten thousand times I've said it o'er and o'er –
  My creditors, my creditors – 'Tis them
  I want to cheat.
<u>Socr</u>. Go to! get under cover,
  Keep your head warm, and spark your wits
  Till they shall grow some fine idea,
  Some scheme of happy promise: sift it well,
  Divide, abstract, compound, and when 'tis ready,
  Out with it boldly.
<u>Streps</u>. Miserable me!
  Would I were out!
<u>Socr</u>. Lie still, and if you strike
  Upon a thought that baffles you, break off
  From that tangle and try another.
  So shall your wits be fresh to start again.
<u>Streps</u>. *(not attending to what Socrates is saying)*. Hah!
  my dear boy! My precious Socrates!
<u>Socr</u>. What would'st thou, idiot?
<u>Streps</u>. I have sprung a thought,
  A plot upon my creditors.
<u>Socr</u>. Discuss!
<u>Streps</u>. Answer me this – Suppose that I should hire
  A witch, who some fair night shall raise a spell,
  Whereby I'll snap the moon from out her sphere
  And bag her.
<u>Socr</u>. What to do!
<u>Streps</u>. To hold her fast,
  And never let her run her courses more;
  So shall I 'scape my creditors.
<u>Socr</u>. How so?
<u>Streps</u>. Because the addition of their interest
  Are made from month to month.
<u>Socr</u>. A gallant scheme;
  And yet methinks I could suggest a hint
  As practicable and no less ingenious –
  Suppose you are arrested for a debt,
  We'll say $5,000, how will you find a way

To cancel at a stroke both debt and note?
Streps. Heavens! I can't tell you how off hand;
   It needs some thinking.
Socr. Were you apt,
   Such thoughts would not be to look for;
   They would be present at your fingers' ends,
   Buzzing alive, like bees in a string,
   Ready to slip and fly.
Streps. I've hit the nail
   That does the deed, and so you will confess.
Socr. Out with it!
Streps. Good chance but you have noted
   A pretty toy, a trinket in the shops,
   Which being rightly held produceth fire
   From things combustible –
Socr. A burning glass,
   Vulgarly call'd –
Streps. You are right; 'tis so.
Socr. Proceed!
Streps. Suppose now your bastard bill collector comes,
   Shows me his warrant – I, standing thus, d'ye mark me,
   In the sun's stream, measuring my distance, guide
   My focus to a point upon his warrant,
   And up it goes in smoke!
Socr. Heavens!
   That's really smart.
Streps. The very thought
   Of his $5,000 cancelled at a stroke
   Makes my heart dance for joy.
Socr. But now again –
Streps. What next?
Socr. Suppose yourself in court, surpris'd
   Into a suit, no witnesses at hand,
   The judge prepar'd to sentence you –
   How will you get out of it?
Streps. As quick as thought –
Socr. But how?
Streps. Hang myself,
   And get even with the suitor –
Socr. Come, you are joking.
Streps. Serious, by all the gods! A man that's dead
   Is out of the law's reach.
Socr. I've done with you –
   Teaching is wasted upon you; your idiot jokes
   Put me beyond all patience.

327

<u>Streps</u>. Nay, but tell me
What is it, my good fellow, that irritates?
<u>Socr</u>. Your horrible lack of memory.
Why how now; what was the first rule I taught you?
<u>Streps</u>. Say'st thou the first? the very first - what
was it?
Why, let me see; 'twas something, was it not?
About the meal - Out on it! I have lost it.
<u>Socr</u>. Oh you stupid, old doating blockhead,
Can hanging be too bad for thee?
<u>Streps</u>. Why there now,
Was ever man so abused? If I can't make
My tongue keep pace with your's, teach it the tricks
And quibbles of your sophistry at once,
I may go hang - I am fool forsooth -
Where shall I turn? Oh gracious Clouds, befriend me,
Give me your counsel.
<u>Chorus</u>. This it is, old man -
If that your son at home is apt and docile,
Put him in your place, and send him hither.
<u>Streps</u>. My son is well endow'd with nature's gifts,
But stubborn against learning.
<u>Chorus</u>. And do you suffer it?
<u>Streps</u>. What can I do?
He's a fine full-grown youth, a dashing fellow,
And by the mother's side of noble blood:
I'll feel my way with him - but if he kicks,
Befall what may, nothing shall stop me;
I will kick him headlong out of doors,
And let him graze ev'n where he will for me -
Wait only my return; I'll soon get him.   (*Exit*.
<u>Chorus</u>. "Highly favour'd shalt thou be,
With gifts and graces kept in store
For those who our divinities adore,
And to no other altars bend the knee:
And well we know th' obedience shown
By this old clown came only
From lessons taught by thee.
Wherefore to swell thy lawful gains,
Thou soon shalt skin this silly dog,
Whom thou hast put in such a stir,
And take his plunder for thy pains:
For mark how often dupes like him devise
Projects that only serv t' enrich the wise."

Strepsiades *(coming out of his house to his Son, who
    stands at the door),* Pheidippides.

Streps. Out of my house! I call the Clouds to witness
    You shall not set a foot within my doors.
    Go to your Lord Megacles! Get out of here,
    And gnaw his posts for hunger.
Pheidip. Ah, poor man!
    I see how it is with you. You are mad,
    Stark mad, by Zeus!
Streps. You swear by Zeus!
    Why then, I swear by Zeus there's no such god –
    Now who is mad but you?
Pheidip. Why do you turn
    Such solemn truths to ridicule?
Streps. I laugh
    To hear a child talk of such old men's tales;
    But listen to what I'll tell you, learn of me,
    And from a child you shall become a man –
    But keep the secret, do you hear me, secret;
    Beware of babbling.
Pheidip. Heyday! what is coming?
Streps. You swore but now by Zeus –
Pheidip. I did.
Streps. Mark now what 'tis to have a friend like me –
    I tell you at a word there is no Zeus.
Pheidip. How then?
Streps. He's off; I tell it you for truth;
    He's out of place, and Vortex rules instead.
Pheidip. Vortex indeed! What freak has caught you now?
Streps. Brilliant Socrates the Melian,
    And Chaerephon, the flea philosopher.
Pheidip. And are you so far gone in idiocy, Dad,
    As to be fooled by men like them, fellows
    Whose philosophy has driven them nuts.
Streps. Keep a good tongue;
    Take heed you slander not such worthy men,
    So wise and learned – men so pure
    And cleanly in their morals, that no razor
    Ever cut their beards; their unwash'd skins
    Ne'er stooped to a bath, no sweet odor
    Of perfumes as they pass'd along.
    But you, a prodigal fine punk, make waste
    And havoc of my means, as I were dead
    And out of thought – but come, turn in and learn.

329

Pheidip. What can I learn or profit from such teachers?
Streps. You can learn everything that turns to profit;
    But first and foremost you can learn to know
    Yourself how totally unlearn'd you are;
    How mere a blockhead, and how dull of brain –
    But wait awhile with patience –   *(Enters the house*
                                            hastily.
Pheidip. Woe is me!
    How shall I deal with this old crazy father?
    What course pursue with one, whose reason wanders
    Out of all course? Shall I take out the statute,
    And call him a lunatic; or wait
    Till nature and his phrenzy, with the help
    Of the undertaker, shall provide a cure?
        (Strepsiades returns, with a cock in one hand
        and a hen in the other.
Streps. Now we shall see! Lo! what have I got here?
Pheidip. A chicken –
Streps. Well and this?
Pheidip. A chicken also.
Streps. Are they the same then? Have a care, good boy,
    How you expose yourself, and for the future
    Describe them rooster and hen.
Pheidip. Ridiculous! Is this the grand discovery
    You have just borrow'd from these sons o' th'
    manure-heap.
Streps. This, and a thousand others – but being old
    And lax of memory, I lose it all
    As fast as it comes in.
Pheidip. Yes, and methinks
    By the same token you have lost your clothes.
Streps. No, I've not lost them; I have laid them out
    Upon the arts and sciences.
Pheidip. Your shoes –
    They're vanish'd too. How have you laid them out?
Streps. Upon necessary things – Like Pericles
    I'm a barefooted patriot – Now no more;
    Do as thou wilt, so thou wilt but conform
    And humour'd thee, and in thy playful age
    Brought thee a little go-cart from the fair,
    Purchas'd with what my legal labours earn'd.
            (Going towards the house of Socrates.
Pheidip. You'll be sorry.
    I'd bet on it; you will be sorry for this.
                (Following reluctantly.

330

Streps. No matter, so you'll humour me – What, hey!
   Why Socrates, I say, come forth, behold,
   Here is my son!
   I've brought him, tho' in faith
   Sorely against his will.

Socrates enters.

Socr. Aye, he's a beginner,
   And knows not where the baskets hang yet.
Pheidip. I would you'd hang yourself instead of the
   baskets.
Streps. Oh monstrous impudence! this to your master!
Socr. Mark how the idiot quibbles upon *hanging.*
   Driv'ling and making mouths – Can he be taught
   The loopholes of the law; whence to escape,
   How to evade, and when to press a suit; –
   Or tune his lips to that soft rhetoric,
   Which steals upon the ear, and melts to pity
   The heart of the stern judge?
Streps. Come, never doubt him;
   He is a lad of parts, and from a child
   Took wondrously to dabbling in the sand,
   Whereof he'd build you up a house so natural
   As would amaze you, trace you out a ship,
   Make you a little cart out of the sole
   Of an old shoe mayhap, and from the rind
   Of a watermelon cut you out a frog,
   You'd swear it was alive. Now what do you think?
   Hath he not wit enough to learn
   Each rule both right and wrong? Or if not both,
   The latter way at least – There he'll be perfect.
Socr. Let him prepare: His lecturers are ready.
Streps. I will retire – When next we meet, remember
   I look to find him able to contend
   'Gainst right and reason, and outwit them both. *(Exit.*

True-Logic and False-Logic enter.

True. Come forth; turn out, thou bold nasty man,
   And face this company.
False. Most willingly:
   I do desire no better: take your ground
   Before this audience, I am sure to triumph.

331

True. And who are you that brag in this way?
False. Fashion itself - the very style of the times.
True. Aye, of the modern times, and them and you
    I say are worthless.
False. I shall bring down your pride.
True. By what most witty weapon?
False. By the gift
    Of cleverness.
True. Then I see
    You have your fools to back you.
False. No, - the wise
    Are those I deal with.
True. I shall spoil your market.
False. As how, good sooth?
True. By speaking such plain truths
    As may appeal to justice.
False. What is justice?
    There's no such thing.
True. How! No such thing as justice?
False. No; where is it?
True. With the immortal gods.
False. If it be there,
    How chanc'd it Zeus himself escap'd
    For castrating his own father, Chronos?
True. For shame, irreverent man, thus do you talk?
    I sicken at impiety so gross,
    My stomach kicks against it.
False. You are craz'd;
    Your wits, old gentleman, are off the hinges.
True. You are a vile blasphemer and clown.
False. Go on! you hit me - but it is with roses.
True. A scoffer!
False. Every word your hatred shows,
    Weaves a fresh crown for your nonsense.
True. A parricide!
False. Proceed, and spare me not -
    You shower down gold upon me.
True. Lead, not gold,
    Had been your pay in times past.
False. Aye, but times present cover me with glory.
True. You are too evil.
False. You are much too weak.
True. Thank your own self, if our Athenian fathers
    Coop up their sons at home, and fear to trust them

332

Within your schools, conscious that nothing else
But evil and sickness can be learnt of you.
False. Methinks, friend, your's is but a ragged trade.
True. And your's, oh shame! a thriving one, tho' late,
A perfect Telephus, you walked the streets
With beggar's cup cramm'd with hungry scraps,
Choice gather'd from – Pandeletus' garbage.
False. Oh! what rare wisdom you remind me of!
True. Oh, what rank folly their's, who rule this city,
And let it nourish such a pest as you,
To sap the morals of the present people.
False. You'll not inspire your pupil with these notions,
Old white-haired idiot.
True. I will inspire him,
If he has grace, to shun the sickness
Of your eternal foolishness.
False. Turn to me, youth!
And let him rant as he pleases.
True. Keep your distance,
And lay your hands upon him at your peril.
Chor. *(interposing)*. Come, no more arguing. – Let us
hear you both;
You of the former time produce your rules
Of ancient discipline – of modern, you –
That so, both weigh'd, the candidate may judge
Who offers most, and make choice between you.
True. That's OK by me.
False. 'Tis agreed.
Chor. But which of you shall start?
False. That shall he:
I yield him up that point; and in reply,
My words, like arrows levelled at a butt,
Shall pierce him through and through; then, if he
rallies,
If he comes on again with a rejoinder,
I'll launch a swarm of syllogisms at him,
That, like a nest of hornets, shall sting him,
Till they have left him not an eye to see with.
Chor. "Now, sirs, make your best effort,
And gravely for the charge prepare;
The well-rang'd hoard of thought explore,
Where sage experience keeps her store."

333

<u>True</u>. Thus summon'd, I prepare myself to speak
     Of manners primitive, and that good time,
     Which I have seen, when discipline prevail'd,
     And modesty was enforced by the laws,
     No babbling then was suffer'd in our schools; -
     The scholar's test was silence. The whole group
     In orderly procession went out
     Right onwards, without straggling, to attend
     Their teacher in harmonics; though the snow
     Fell on them thick as meal, the hardy kids
     Bested the storm naked: their harps were stung
     Not to ignoble strains, for they were taught
     A loftier key, whether to chant the name
     Of Pallas, terrible amidst the blaze
     Of cities overthrown, or wide and far
     To spread, as custom was, the echoing peal.
     There let no low clown use his tricks,
     Let no nonsense on a note,
     No running of divisions high and low
     Break the pure stream of harmony; no Phrynis
     Practising wanton warblings out of place -
     Woe to his back-sides that so was often spanked!
     Hard stripes and heavy would reform his taste.
     Decent and chaste their postures in the school
     Of their gymnastic exercises; none
     Expos'd an attitude that might provoke
     Bad behavior; their lips ne'er mov'd
     In love-inspiring whispers, and their walks
     From eyes obscene were sacred and secure;
     They ate meat and potatoes and drank milk.
     They hated french fries and hot dogs and coke.
<u>False</u>. Why these are ideas obsolete and stale;
     Worm-eaten rules, like the songs
     Of Stephen Foster.
<u>True</u>. Yet so were train'd the heroes, that won
     The field of Marathon with hostile blood;
     This discipline it was that braced their nerves
     And fitted them for conquest. You, in truth,
     At great Athena's festival produce
     Your martial dancers, not as they did,
     But safe underneath a cowardly suit
     Of heavy armour, till I sweat to see them
     Dangling their shields in such unseemly
     As spoils the sacred measure of the dance.

334

Be wise, therefore, young man, and turn to me.
Turn to the better guide, so shall you learn
To scorn the noisy forum, shun the bath,
And turn with blushes from pornography:
Then innocence shall make you bold
To spurn the injurious, but to respect older people
Meek and submissive, rising from your seat
To pay the respect due, not shall you ever
Or wrong the parent's soul, or stain your own.
In purity of manners you shall live
A bright example; vain shall be the lures
Of the strip-teasers floating in the dance,
Useless all her arts to snare you in her arms,
And rob you of your virtue and good name.
No nasty reply shall you oppose
To fatherly commands, nor give
Smart replies to him.
Poor thanks for all his fond parental care.
False. Aye, my brave youth, do, follow these fine rules,
    And learn by them to be just pigs,
    Driveller, and dolt, as any of the sons
    Of our Hippocrates; – I swear by Dionysius,
    Folly and foul contempt shall be your pay.
True. Not so, but fair and fresh in youthful bloom
    Amongst our young athletics you shall shine;
    Not in a disco fool the time away
    In dirty talk, like our gang of idlers,
    Nor yet in some foolish paltry lawsuit
    Wrangling and quibbling in our petty courts.
    But in the solemn academic grove,
    Crown'd with the modest reed, talk
    With your collegiate equals; there serene,
    Calm as the scene around you, underneath
    The fragrant foliage where the ivy spreads,
    Where the oak trees strews thin leaves,
    Where the tall elm-tree and wide-stretching maple
    Sigh to the fanning breeze, you shall inhale
    Sweet odours wafted in the breath of spring.
    This is the regimen that will insure
    A healthful body and a vigorous mind,
    A countenance serene, expanded chest,
    Heroic stature and a temperate tongue;
    But take these modern masters, and behold
    These blessings all revers'd; a pallid cheek,

335

Shrunk shoulders, chest contracted, sapless limbs,
A tongue that never rests, and mind debas'd,
By their vile sophistry perversely taught
To call good evil, evil good, and be
That thing, which nature spurns at, that disease,
A mere Antimachus, the house of evil.
Chorus. "Oh sage instructor, how sublime
These maxims of the former time!
How sweet this unpolluted stream
Of eloquence, how pure the theme!
Thrice happy they, whose lot was cast
Amongst the generation past,
When virtuous morals were the rage
And these grave institutes obey'd.
Now you, that vaunt yourself so high,
Prepare; we wait for your reply,
And recollect, or ere you start,
You take in hand no easy part;
Well hath he spoke, and reasons good
By better only are withstood;
Sharpen your wits then, or you'll meet
Contempt as certain as defeat."
False. Doubt not I'm ready, full up to the throat
And well nigh chok'd with this horse-manure.
Now, the mighty masters of the modern school
Call me the Lower Logic, so separated
From the old practice of the upper time,
By him personified; which name of honour
I gain'd as the inventor of that method,
Which can baffle and puzzle all the courts
Of law and justice - An invention worth
Money to them who practise it, whereas
It defeats all opponents. - Let that go.
Now take a sample of it in the ease,
With which I'll baffle this old professor
With his warm baths, that he forbids.
Harkye, old man, discuss, if so it please you,
Your excellent good reason for this rule,
That won't let us take warm baths.
True. Simply this -
I hold it a relaxer, rendering men
Sissy and feeble.
False. Hold awhile -
I have you on the hook. Answer me this -
Of all the heroes Zeus has father'd,

Which is for strength, for courage, and a bunch
Of labours most renown'd?
True.   I know of none
Superior in those qualities to Hercules.
False.   And who e'er heard Herculean baths were cold?
Yet Hercules himself you own was strong.
True.   Aye, this is in the very style of the times;
These are the ideas now in fashion
With our young sophists, who frequent the baths
Whilst the people starve.
False.   I grant you this;
It is the style of the times, by you condemn'd,
By me approv'd, and not without good cause;
For how but thus doth ancient Nestor talk?
Can Homer make errors? Were all his wise men fools?
They are my witnesses. – Now for this tongue,
This member out of use by the new ideas,
Not so by mine. – His scholar must be silent
And chaste also – damping prescriptions both –
For what good fortune ever did happen
The mute and modest? Give me an example.
True.   Many – Chaste Peleus so obtained his sword.
False.   His sword! and what did Peleus gain by that?
Battle and blows this modest Peleus gain'd;
Whilst mean Hyperbolus, whose wretched craft
Was lamp-making, by craft of viler sort
Got a lot of money, solid coin, not swords.
True.   But good work helped Peleus so,
As won the goddess Thetis to his bed.
False.   And drove her out of it – for he was cold,
Languid and listless: she was brisk and stirring,
And sought her sex elsewhere. Now are you answered?
Good sooth you're in your dotage. Mark, young sir,
These are the fruits of good work: you see
What pleasure you must give up to preserve it –
All the delights that woman can bestow;
No sexy flirting to catch the cute girl's smile,
No luscious dainties shall you then partake,
No cocktail parties, where the glass
With peals of laughter circulates around;
These you must give up, and without these
What is your life? – So much for your delights. –
Now let us see how stands your score with nature –
You're in some scrape we'll say – intrigue – adultery –
You're caught, convicted, crush'd – for what can save

you?
You have no powers of speech - but arm'd by me,
You're up to all occasions: Nothing fear;
Ev'n give your genius scope; laugh, frolic, sport,
And forget about shame; for should the spying wife
Detect you in the fact, you shall so argue
With her appeal, that nothing shall convict you;
For Zeus shall take the blame from off your shoulders,
Being himself an adulterous god,
And you a poor mortal - Why should you
Be wiser, stronger, purer than a god?

True. But what if this your scholar should get
    Th' adulterer's punishment, - pill'd and sanded,
    And garnish'd with a radish in the behind,
    The scoff of all beholders - What fine quirk
    Will clear him at that pinch, but he must pass
    For a most perfect Ganimede?

False. What then?
    Where is the harm?

True. Can greater harm befall a man than to be ridiculed?

False. What will you say if here I can prove you wrong?

True. Nothing - my silence shall confess your triumph.

False. Come on then - answer me to what I ask.
    Our lawyers - what are they?

True. Bastards.

False. Our tragic poets - what are they?

True. The same.

False. Good, very good! - our demagogues -

True. No better.

False. See there! See that you are beaten?
    Cast your eyes round this company! -

True. I do.

False. And what do you discover?

True. Numerous birds
    Of the same filthy feather, so Heaven help me!
    This man I mark; and this, and this fine fop
    With his curl'd locks. - To all these I can swear.

False. What say you then?

True. I say I am confuted -
    Here, wagtails, catch my cloak - I'll be amongst you.

Socr. *(to Strepsiades, just returned)*. Now, friend,
    what say you? who shall school your son?

Streps. School him and beat him, take him to yourself.
    And mind you sharpen him to an edge on both sides,

This for slight skirmish, that for stronger work.
Socr. Doubt not, we'll finsih him to your pleasure
    A perfect sophist.
Pheidip. Perfect skin and bone –
    That I can well believe.
Socr. No more – Away!   *(Strepsiades retires.*
                            Pheidippides follows
                            Socrates into the house.

            Chorus talks to the audience.

Now to our judges we shall tell
What payment they may expect from us,
If they indeed are careful to deserve it:
First, on your new-sown grounds in kindly showers,
Postponing other calls, we will descend.
The bearing branches of your vines shall sprout,
Nor scorch'd with summer heats nor chill'd with rain.

Strepsiades *(with a sack of meal on his shoulder, and*
            talking to himself).

Lo! here's the fifth day gone – the fourth – the third–
The second too – day of all days to me
Most hateful and accurs'd – the dreadful eve,
Ushering the new moon, that lets in the tide
Of happy creditors, all out to get me,
To rack and ruin me forever.
I, like a good debtor, who would like to
Soften their flinty hearts, thus say to them,
"Ah, my good sir, this payment comes upon me
At a bad time, excuse me – That bill's due,
But you'll extend your grace – This you will cancel,
And totally acquit me." – Not hardly;
All with one voice cry out, they will be paid,
And I must be rooked into the bargain,
And threaten'd with a suit to mend the matter –
Well, let it come! – They may ev'n do their worst;
I care not since my son hath learnt the trick
Of this new rhetoric, as will appear
When I have beat this door – *(knocks at the door)* –
    Boy, boy! come forth!

            Socrates *comes forth.*

Socr. Hail to Strepsiades!
Streps. Thrice hail to Socrates!

                        339

But first I pray you *(setting down the meal against the door)* take this bit of food
In token of the reverence I bear you;
And now, so please you, tell me of my son,
Your late beginner. Comes he along well?
Socr. He learns well.
Streps. Oh great news!
    How excellent is fraud.
Socr. Yes, you may set your creditors at nothing.
Streps. And their policemen too?
Socr. Had they a thousand.
Streps. *(singing and dancing).* Then I'll sing out my song,
    and sing aloud,
    And it shall be - Woe, woe to all your gang,
    Ye money-jobbing bastards, loan sharks!
    Hence with your accounts, your cents-per-cent;
    I fear you not; ye cannot hook me now.
    Oh! such a son have I in training for you,
    Arm'd with a two-edg'd tongue that cuts o' both sides,
    The stay, support, and pillar of my house,
    The scourge of my tormentors, the redeemer
    Of a most wretched father - Call him,
    Call him, I say, and let my eyes feast on him -
    What ho! My son, my boy - Your father calls;
    Come forth and show yourself. *(To them Pheidip.*
Socr. Behold him present!
Streps. My dear - my darling -
Socr. Lo! you have your darling.
Streps. Joy, joy, my son! all joy - for now you wear
    A face of a right character and cast,
    A wrangling, quibbling, contradicting face;
    Now you have got it neatly on the tongue -
    The very quirk o' th' time - "What's that you say?
    What is it?" - Shifting from yourself the wrong
    To him that suffers it - a clever idea
    To make a transfer of evil,
    When it has serv'd your turn - Yes, you will pass;
    You've the Attic stamp upon your forehead.
    Now let me see a sample of your service.
Pheidip. What irritates you, my father?
Streps. What! the moon,
    This day both new and old.
Pheidip. Both in one day?
    Ridiculous!

Streps. No matter — 'Tis the day
   Will bring my creditors upon my back
   All in a swarm together.
Pheidip. Let them swarm!
   We'll smother 'em if they dare so to miscall
   One day as two days.
Streps. What should stop them?
Pheidip. What, do you ask? Can the same woman be
   Both young and old at once?
Streps. They speak by law:
   The law says they're right
Pheidip. But they twist
   The spirit of the law.
Streps. What's that?
Pheidip. Time-honour'd Solon was the people's friend —
Streps. This makes not to the case of new or old.
Pheidip. And he appointed two days for the process,
   The old and new day — for citation that,
   This for discharge —
Streps. Why did he name two days?
Pheidip. Why, but that one might warn men of their debts,
   The other serve them to escape the payment;
   Else were they laid by th' heels, as sure as fate,
   On the new moon ensuing.
Streps. Why then
   Upon the former day do they start
   Collecting on the first of the month,
   And not at the new moon?
Pheidip. Because, in truth,
   They're hungry feeders, and make haste to thrust
   Their greedy fingers in the public dish.
Streps. Hence then, ye witless creditors, begone!
   We are the wise ones, we are the true sort;
   Ye are but blocks, mob, cattle, empty casks —
     "Therefore with ecstasy I'll raise
     My happy voice in fortune's praise,
     And, oh rare son! — Oh happy me!
     The theme of my song shall be;
     For hark! each passing neighbour cries —
     All hail, Strepsiades the wise!
     Across the market as I walk,
     I and my son the public talk,
     All striving which shall have to boast

341

He prais'd me first, or prais'd me most –
And now, my son, my welcome guest,
Enter my house and grace my feast." *(Exeunt.*

Pasias, *and a Witness.*

Pasias. Should this man be permitted to stay
    Out of jail? It must not be.
    Better for him to have brok'n up at once
    Than to be thus beset. Therefore it is
    That I am forc'd upon this hostile course,
    Empowering you to summon this my debtor
    To get back my money.

Strepsiades *re-enters.*

Streps. Who's this?
Pasias. The old and new day call upon you, sir.
Streps. *(to the spectators).* Bear witness that this man
    has nam'd two days –
    And for what debt do you want me to pay?
Pasias. For $100 that you took up at interest
    To pay for your son's racer.
Streps. I a racer?
    Do you not hear him? Can you not all witness
    How mortally and from my soul I hate
    All the whole racing season!
Pasias. What then?
    You took the gods to witness you would pay me.
Streps. I grant you, in my folly I did swear,
    But then my son had not attain'd the art
    Of the new logic.
Pasias. And have you now the face to stand it out
    Against all evidence?
Streps. Assuredly –
    Else how am I the better for my schooling?
Pasias. And dare you, knowing it to be a falsehood,
    Take the great gods to witness to your oath,
    When I shall put it to you?
Streps. What great gods?
Pasias. *(starting at the question).* Hermes, Poseidon,
    Zeus.
Streps. Yes, I will take the oath, so help me Zeus!
Pasias. Insolent wretch, you'll die for this evil!

342

Streps. Oh! that this madman was well scrubb'd with salt
    To save his brains from souring.
Pasias. Damn.
    Are you making fun of me?
Streps. Yes.
    He'll take at least six gallons for a dressing.
Pasias. So may great Zeus and all the gods deal with me
    As I will handle you for this clowning.
Streps. I thank you for your gods - They're pleasant
    fellows -
    And for your Zeus, the learn'd and wise
    Hold him a very silly thing to swear by.
Pasias. 'Tis well crazy man, 'tis well! The time will
    come
    When you shall wish these bragging words unsaid:
    But will you pay the debt or will you not?
    Say, and I'll go.
Streps. Set your mind at rest;
    You shall have satisfaction in a twinkling - *(Steps
                                                    aside.*
Pasias. What think you of this nut?
Witness. That he will pay you.

                Strepsiades *returns.*

Streps. Where is this creditor of mine? Come hither,
    friend,
    How do you call this thing?
Pasias. A baker's board,
    Or, as we say, a dipper -
Streps. Go to!
    Dost think I'll pay my money to a blockhead,
    That calls this baker's board a *cardopus?*
    I tell you, man, it is a *cardopa* -
    Go, go, you will not get a penny from me,
    You and your *cardopus.*
Pasias. Will you not pay me?
Streps. Assure yourself I will not - Hence, begone!
    Will you not get out, and quit my doors?
Pasias. I'm gone, but take this with you, if I live
    I'll sue you in the court before night.
Streps. You'll lose your suit, and your $100 besides.
    I'm sorry for your loss, but who can help it?
    You may ev'n thank your baker's board for that

(Exit Pasias and Witness.

Amynias *enters, followed by a Witness.*

Amynias. Ah me, ah me!
Streps. Who's that with his - "Ah me?"
Amynias. Alas!
    Would you know who I am? Know then I am
    A wretch made up of woes -
Streps. A woeful wretch -
    Granted! pass on.
Amynias. Oh unlucky day.
    Oh ye hard-hearted, chariot-breaking fates!
    Oh! Pallas my destroyer, what a crash
    Is this that you have giv'n me!
Streps. Hah! what ails you?
    Of what can you accuse Tlepolemus?
Amynias. Mock not my miseries, but bid your son
    Repay what he has borrow'd.
Streps. What do you mean?
    What should my son repay?
Amynias. The sum I lent him.
Streps. Is that it? Then you are in bad shape.
    Truly you're out of luck.
Amynias. I'm out of everything -
    I wrecked my chariot - By the gods
    That's being *out,* I take it, with a vengeance.
Streps. Say rather you are kick'd by an ass - a trifle!
Amynias. But, sir, my lawful money is no trifle;
    I shall not choose to be kick'd out of that.
Streps. I'll tell you what you are - Out of your mind.
Amynias. How so?
Streps. Because your brain seems very leaky.
Amynias. Look to't! By Hermes, I'll put you in jail,
    If you don't pay me.
Streps. Hark'ye, one short question -
    When Jove rains on us does he rain fresh water,
    Or only vapours that the sun exhales?
    Answer me that.
Amynias. I care not what he rains;
    I trouble not my cap with such nonsense.
Streps. And do you think a man, that has no brain
    To argue upon these rare points, will argue me
    Out of my money?

344

Amynias. Let your debt go on,
    And pay me up the interest.
Streps. What is that?
    What kind of thing is that same interest?
Amynias. A thing it is that grows from day to day,
    And month to month, swelling as time rolls on
    To a round sum of money.
Streps. Well said
    One question more - What think you of the sea?
    Is it not fuller now than it was?
Amynias. No, by the Gods! not fuller, but as full:
    That is my judgment of it.
Streps. Oh you miser!
    That so would stint the ocean, and yet cram
    Thy swelling coffers till they overflow -
    Fetch me a whip, that I may lash him hence:
    Take to your heels - begone!
Amynias. I will bring
    My witnesses against you.
Streps. Start! set off! -
    Away! you weasel, you!
Amynias. *(to the spectators).* Is not this outrage?
Streps. *(smacking his whip).* Will you not run? will you
    not buckle kindly
    Into your shoes, or must I mount and kick you
    In the behind, till you kick and wince
    For very madness? Oho! Are you off?
    A welcome riddance - All the devils drive
    You and your cursed chariot hence together!
                    (Strepsiades goes into his house.
Chorus. "Mark here how rarely it succeeds
    To build our trust on guilty deeds:
    Mark how this old crook,
    Who sets a trap to catch himself,
    Falsely believes he has found the way
    To hold his creditors at bay.
    Too late he'll curse the Sophists' school,
    That taught his son to cheat by rule,
    And train'd the modest lips of youth
    In the vile art of torturing truth;
    A modern logic much in use,
    Invented for the law's abuse;
    A subtle knack of spying flaws
    To cast in doubt the clearest cause."

Strepsiades *(rushing out of the house, in great
confusion, followed by his son)* Pheidippides, Chorus.

Streps. Hoa there! What hoa! for pity's sake some help!
 Friends, kinsmen, countrymen! turn out and help!
 Oh! my poor head, my cheeks are bruis'd to jelly –
 Help by all means! – Why, thou ungracious son,
 Thy father wouldst thou beat?
Pheidip. Assuredly.
Streps. There, there! he owns that he would beat his
 father.
Pheidip. I own it, good father!
Streps. Parricide!
 Impious assassin! Sacrilegious wretch!
Pheidip. All, all, and more – You cannot please me better;
 I glory in these names. Go on!
Streps. Monster of lying!
Pheidip. Crown me with roses!
Streps. Wretch, will you strike your parent?
Pheidip. Religiously,
 And will maintain the right, by which I do it.
Streps. Ah shameless villain! can there be a right
 Against all nature so to treat a father?
Pheidip. That I shall soon make clear to your conviction.
Streps. You, you convince me?
Pheidip. With the greatest ease:
 And I can work the proof two several ways;
 Therefore make choice between them.
Streps. What do you mean?
Pheidip. I mean to say we argue up or down –
 Take which you like. It comes to the same end.
Streps. Aye, and a precious end you've brought it to,
 If all my care of you must end in this,
 That I have put you in the way to beat me,
 (Which is a thing unnatural and profane)
 And after justify it.
Pheidip. That I'll do.
 By process clear and logically,
 That you shall fairly own yourself a convert
 To a most legal beating.
Streps. Come on!
 Give me your arguments – but spare your blows.
Chorus. How to restrain this headstrong son of your's
 Interests you now, old man, to find the means
 For sure he could not be thus confident

346

Without some cause; something there needs must be,
Some strong possession of himself within,
That buoys him up to this high pitch of daring.
Streps. So please you then I will the cause unfold
   Of this base treatment to your patient ears,
   And thus it stands – When we had supp'd together,
   As you all know, in friendly sort, I bade him
   Take up his lute and give me the good song
   Of old Simonides, – "the ram was shorn;" –
   He would not sit twanging the lute, not he;
   'Twas not for him to cackle o'er his wine,
   As if he were some woman working the loom.
   'Twas vulgar and unseemly –
Pheidip. Grossly so;
   And was it not high time that I should beat you,
   Who had no better manners than to set
   Your guest a chirping like a grasshopper?
Streps. These were his very words, and more than these;
   For by and by he told me that Simonides
   Was a very bad poet. This you'll own
   Was a tough morsel, yet I gulp'd it down,
   And pass'd it off with bidding him recite
   Some passage out of Æschylus, at least
   But he said,
   "I hold your Æschylus, of all our poets,
   First of the spouters, incoherent, harsh,
   Precipitous and turgid."
   I calmly said – "Call something else to mind
   More to your taste and from some modern bard,
   So it be good withal and worth the hearing –"
   Whereat, would you believe it? he began
   Repeating from Euripides – Great Zeus,
   Guard my chaste ears from such another dose!
   A perilous long-winded tale of incest
   'Twixt son and daughter of the same sad mother.
   Sick to the soul I spurn'd at such declaiming,
   Adding, as well I might, all that my scorn
   Of such vile trash could add! till, to be short,
   Words begat words, and blows too as it prov'd,
   For leaping from his seat he sprung upon me,
   Struck, buffeted, and bang'd me out of measure,
   Throttled me, pounded me well nigh to dust –
Pheidip. And what less does that heretic deserve
   Who will not praise Euripides, the first

347

In wisdom of all poets?
Streps. He the first!
    How my tongue itches! - but the rogue is ready;
    He'll beat me if I answer.
Pheidip. And with reason.
Streps. What reason, graceless son, will bear you out
    For beating me, who in your baby age
    Caress'd you, dandled you upon my knee,
    Watch'd every motion, humour'd all your wants?
    Then if you lisp'd a syllable I caught it -
    Bryn cried the child - right away I gave you drink:
    Mamman it mew'd - and that was bread:
    Nay, I perform'd the nurse's dirtiest task,
    And held you out before me at your needs;
    And now you beat me.
Chor. Now every young man's heart beats an alarm,
    Anxious to hear his advocate's appeal;
    Which if he can establish, the same right
    By him asserted will on all devolve,
    And beating then will be so much in vogue
    That old men's skins will be reduc'd to cobwebs.
Pheidip. Now gratefully the mind receives new lights,
    Emerging from the shades of prejudice,
    And casting old establishments aside!
    How right it is to punish this old sinner!
Streps. Mount, mount your chariot! Oh, that I could see you
    Seated again behind your favourite horses.
Pheidip. Now then I ask you, gathering up my thread
    Where it was broken off, if you, my father,
    When I was but a stripling, spanked my backsides?
Streps. No, for I studied all things for your good,
    And therefore I corrected you by spanking.
Pheidip. Agreed.
    I also am like studious of your good,
    And therefore I most lovingly correct you;
    If beating be a proof of love, you have it
    Plenteous in measure, for by what exemption
    Is your most sacred body freed from stripes
    And mine made subject to them? Am not I
    Free-born as you? If you beat me then,
    I should beat you now.
Streps. By what one rule
    Of equity?
Pheidip. What equity were that

348

If none but children are to be chastis'd?
And grant they were, the proverb's in your teeth,
Which says old age is but a second childhood.
Again, if tears are seen to follow blows,
Ought not old men to expiate faults with tears
Rather than children, who have more to plead
In favour of their failings?

Streps. Where's the law
That warrants this proceeding? There's none such.

Pheidip. And what was your law-maker but a man,
Mortal as you and I are? And tho' time
Has sanctified his statutes, may not I
Take up the cause of youth, as he of age,
And publish a new ordinance for leave
By the son's rights to correct our fathers?

Streps. If you are thus for pecking at your father
Like a young fighting-cock, why don't you peck
Your dinner from the dunghill, and at night
Roost on a perch?

Pheidip. The cases do not fit,
Nor does my master Socrates suggest
Rules so absurd.

Streps. Cease then from beating me;
Else you get your self in trouble.

Pheidip. How?

Streps. Because the right I have of beating you
Will be your right in time over your son,
When you shall have one.

Pheidip. But if I have none,
All my sad hours are lost, and you die laughing.

Streps. There's no denying that. - How say you, sirs?
Methinks there is good thought in his plea;
And as for us old sinners, truth to say,
If we deserve a beating we must bear it.

Pheidip. Hear me - there's more to come -

Streps. Then I am lost,
For I can bear no more.

Pheidip. Oh fear it not,
Rather believe what I have now to tell you
Will cause you to make light of what is past,
'Twill bring such comfort to you.

Streps. Let me have it:
If it be comfort, give it me.

Pheidip. Then know,

349

Henceforth I am resolv'd to beat my mother
As I have beaten you.
Streps. How say you? How?
Why this were to out do all you have done.
Pheidip. But what if I have not a proof in law,
To show the moral uses of this beating?
Streps. Show me a proof that you have hang'd yourself,
And with your tutor Socrates beside you
Gone to the devil together, both at once.
Those moral uses I will thank you for –
Chor. Evil events from evil causes spring,
And what you suffer flows from what you've done.
Streps. Why was I not warned? You saw me old,
and practis'd on my weak simplicity.
Chor. 'Tis not for us to warn a wilful sinner;
We hold him not, but let him run his course,
Till by misfortunes caught, his wakes up
And prompts him to pray to gods.
Streps. I feel my sorrows, but I own them just:
Yes, ye reforming Clouds, I'm duly punish'd
For my intended fraud. – And now, my son,
Join hands with me and let us forth together
To wreak our vengeance on those base deceivers,
That Chaerephon and Socrates the chief,
Who have ruined us both.
Pheidip. Grace forbid
I should hurt my masters!
Streps. Nay, nay, but rather dread avenging Zeus,
God of your ancestors, and him worship.
Pheidip. You're mad, methinks, to talk to me of Zeus
Is there a god so call'd?
Streps. There is! there is!
Pheidip. There is no Zeus, I tell you so;
Vortex has whirl'd him from his throne, and reigns
By right of conquest in the Thunderer's place.
Streps. 'Tis false, no Vortex reigns but in my brain.
Pheidip. Laugh at your own dull joke and be a fool!
(*Exit.*
Streps. (*striking his breast*). Stupid idiot that I was;
What ail'd me thus to court this Socrates,
Ev'n to the exclusion of the immortal gods?
O Hermes, forgive me; be not angry,
With fire and arson I will fall upon them,
And send their school up in smoke to the Clouds.

350

Hoa, Xanthias *(calling to one of his slaves)*, hoa!
  bring forth without delay
Your ladder and your shovel, climb to the roof,
Break up the rafters, tear down the house upon them,
And bury the whole bunch beneath the ruins.
        *(Xanthias mounts the roof and begins working
        with his mattock.*
Haste! if you love me, haste! Oh, for a torch,
A blazing torch new lighted, to set fire
To the infernal edifice. - I warrant me
I'll soon unhouse the rascals, that now carry
Their heads so high, and roll them in the dust.
                (One of the scholars comes out.
First Disciple. Woe! mischief! misery!
Streps. *(mounts the roof and fixes a torch to the joists).*
                Torch, do your stuff:
  And we shall muster up a conflagration.
First Disciple. What are you doing, fellow?
Streps. Chopping logic;
  Arguing a knotty point with your house-beams.
Second Disciple. Oh horror! Who has set our house on
  fire?
Streps. The very man whose clothes you stole so neatly.
Second Disciple. Undone and ruin'd - !
Streps. Heartily I wish it -

                Socrates *comes forth.*

Socr. Hoa there! What man is that?
  You there upon the roof - what are you doing?
Streps. *Treading on air - contemplating the sun -*
Socr. Ah me! I'm suffocated, smother'd, lost -

                Chaerephon *appears.*

Chaerephon. Wretch that I am, I'm melted, scorch'd,
  burned -
Streps. Blasphemers, why did you insult the gods?
  Dash, drive, demolish them! Their crimes are many,
  But their contemptuous treatment of the gods,
  Their impious blasphemies, exceed them all.
Chor. Break up! - The Chorus have fulfill'd their part.

                351

ART IN THE 400's B.C.

The Archaic Style in art lasted from around 600 B.C.
to the period of the Persian Wars (490-480 B.C.). Over that
time, the figures gradually lost some of their strange
stiffness and aloofness and relaxed into more human/natural
attitudes. Then, at the time of the Persian Wars, there
was a clear break from the Archaic into what is called the
Early Classical or Severe Style. The successful struggle
against the Persians may have done a lot for the Greeks'
self-esteem (although this was never a quality they lacked)
and for their view of the distinction between themselves and
the Easterners. We can see changes in hair-styles and in
dress at this same time. Greek men adopted short hair,
giving up the beards and long, curled hair which looked more
eastern; both sexes took up a simpler form of dress, simpler
in style and in materials. The Spartans are said to have
led the way in this kind of thing. It is possible that the
wars encouraged trends which were already under way in the
arts. We have to remember too that Greek society was developing very rapidly at this time, regardless of the Persian
affair.

EARLY CLASSICAL (SEVERE) STYLE, 480-450 B.C.

The Early Classical Style lasted for some 30 years, from
480 to 450 B.C. It has the name Severe from its simplicity
and seriousness. It is a long step toward naturalism or
realism, toward emotions and changeability, but at the same
time the controls remain tight, and the emphasis upon the
ideal, the type, is still very strong. It is a moment of
balance between realism and abstraction, between humanizing
and idealizing. This is what we mean by Classical. It is
a typical Greek dualism, tension, balance, such as we see
also in their philosophy. The glorification of humans continues, with the same emphasis on subduing nature and the
passions, on order and form, but now the humans are notice-
ably more human.

Pottery.
We can see the change in style in the pottery of the
period, but pottery was now giving way to the rapidly developing sculpture in terms of prestige, even though its standards remained wonderfully high. Red Figure pottery, which

had come in the late 500's B.C., continued to dominate in
the 400's B.C. Then, toward the end of the century, it gave
way to a new White Ground technique. In the White Ground,
the pots were given a slip (coat) of white clay and on this
were painted delicate single figures in pale colors.

Sculpture.
        We can see the change from Archaic to Early Classical
in the pediment sculptures (see below) of the Temple of
Artemis Aphaia on Aegina. The west pediment, done around
490 B.C., is a fine example of late Archaic work, with a
very lively Athena, still with the strange smile. The east
pediment, which was restored after damage in the 470's B.C.,
is very different. We have from each pediment a largely
complete figure of a fallen soldier; the one done in the
Early Classical Style in the 470's B.C. is much more human,
realistic--there is far more feeling and personality about
it.

        The most famous example of the new style in its first
days is the marble Kritios Boy (Kritios being the sculptor
credited with the work), which comes out of the Archaic
tradition of naked kouroi pieces. It is dated around 480
B.C. at Athens. There is a human and a slightly dramatic
air about the piece. The weight is placed on the left leg--
freeing the right one, which is bent a little, to move,
although the work still does not show motion. The weight
shift requires that the entire body adjust for balance: the
hips are no longer horizontal, the shoulders lean a little
the other way, the torso is not simply vertical, the head
turns and no longer looks flatly to the front. The subject
has at least some awareness of the world. The old Archaic
smile is gone--these Severe statues do not smile, they are
very serious. The Severe type is also blocky, square-looking,
more so than the Archaic. The Severe figure shows subtly
the bones beneath the flesh, muscles in tension and relaxed,
soft as well as hard areas of the body--whereas the Archaic
figures had looked more like just blocks of stone.

        We have also a marble head from the Acropolis at Athens
around 480 B.C., known as the Blonde Boy. It has the same
characteristics as Kritios Boy--moody, thoughtful, restrained.
In both pieces, the sculptors are plainly working with systems
of proportions--a predictable Greek way of looking for order,

of producing a type, indicating the belief that symmetry/
balance, is good/beautiful. The pieces are planned mathematically; almost every part is in some way a multiple or
an equal division of every other part. The search for the
most desirable system of proportions went on, with several
ratio systems being produced. At the end of the Early
Classical Period, about 450 B.C., <u>Polykleitos of Argos</u>, one
of the rare major figures not associated with Athens by this
time, created his canon (or rule) statue, the <u>Spear-Bearer</u>,
which was accepted widely as representing the best system
of proportion. We have this statue only in marble Roman
copies. The original was in bronze, which was more easily
worked. Bronze, rather than the marble of the Archaic
period, was to be the common medium for sculpture in the
Classic period of the 400's and 300's B.C. Polykleitos
wrote a book, lost to us, explaining his system. We can
only guess at the proportional system he recommended; it was
not a purely mechanical formula but allowed some flexibility
for movement, or angle, or impression. As in architecture,
the Greeks had decided that it was necessary to improve upon
nature in order to create the impression of order.

The range of approach in the Early Classical Period can
be seen in the contrast between the <u>Charioteer of Delphi</u> and
the portrait of the Athenian leader <u>Themistocles</u>, both from
about 470 B.C. The Charioteer, a bronze original which was
a part of a larger group, is very composed and aloof for
someone engaged in such a physical activity. The
Themistocles, of which we have the head in a marble Roman
copy, is vastly more realistic--an isolated example of a
style which was to get little attention for several more
generations, being too clearly tilted toward the human for
Greek taste generally in this period.

The second major name in sculpture in this period, after
Polykleitos, is <u>Myron</u>, the early master of movement. We have
a Roman copy of his most famous work, the bronze <u>Discus-
Thrower</u>, which he did about 460 B.C. It catches the athlete
at the point just before the movement gets under way; the
curved arms keep the work cleverly in a single plane. From
the same time, 460 B.C., we have a rare original, the wonderful bronze <u>Zeus</u> (or <u>Poseidon</u>) from <u>Artemisium</u>. It catches
the same moment before movement, with the same contrivance of
a single plane. The god is commanding, powerful--with a

"godlike" human build.

The best temple sculpture from the Severe Period comes from the Temple of Zeus at Olympia, 470-455 B.C. This Olympia work was done in the soft marble of Paros (Parian), a favorite medium. Creamy, translucent, with clearly visible crystals, Parian marble could be worked relatively easily and had a very appealing look about it. The pediment scenes at Olympia are varied, the subjects drawn from mythology, with a good deal of action and movement. Among the metopes (see below), one is very famous--Athena, reserved and aloof but full of human sympathy, as the helper of Herakles.

The Athena at Olympia indicates that the representation of women was caught up in the greater freedom of the Early Classical Period. We have the Aspasia type (falsely named for the mistress of Pericles) of around 460 B.C. from marble Roman copies. She is simple, cool, distant--the usual Severe face type. She also gives a blocky, heavy impression. We can note the simplicity of the dress, but also the mastery shown in its representation. Since women remained clothed, the sculptor faced the challenge of presenting the drapery. Over the next century more and more sculptors would work their way through drapery effects, becoming bolder with time, until they arrived at female nudity.

At the end of the Severe Period, 450 B.C., we have the presumed Athena Lemnia of the great sculptor Phidias in marble Roman copies. This piece was called "the beautiful"-- if a genuine copy, it was stunningly emotional and sentimental for its time, although still with the Severe feeling of detachment.

THE CLASSICAL STYLE: THE AGE OF PERICLES, 450-430 B.C.

The next generation is dominated by the Athens of Pericles, the wealthiest and most powerful Greek city of its day. It was a part of Pericles' plan to be "the school of Greece," in art as in other things, and with the money from the Confederation of Delos he succeeded wonderfully. Swelling self-confidence and optimism about man and his future was the order of the day. As Sophocles said in the Antigone (442 B.C.), "Many wonders are there, but none more wonderful than man." Yet this confidence was kept in check, to avoid hubris. For Sophocles said in the same play, "Great words of the proud are punished by big setbacks." The ideal remained one of balance, of order, of restraint. As Pericles said in the famous Funeral Speech, when he was trying to explain what Athens was about, the aim was "achievement without extravagance, cleverness without softness." We do not have much work from this period but most of what we do have is associated with Athens and is very famous.

The Parthenon.
The most famous expression in art of the Age of Pericles, when Athens set the standards for Greece, is the Parthenon. This was a temple to Athena, the clever one, who watched over the city. The temples on the Acropolis had been destroyed by the Persians in 480 B.C. The buildings destroyed included a new temple of Athena which had been begun in the 480's B.C. in thanks for the Athenian victory of 490 B.C. at Marathon against the Persians. In the 460's B.C. Callicrates, the greatest architect of the century, began a new temple to Athena on the Acropolis. Pericles halted work on this around 450 B.C. in order to make way for his own dream-child, the Parthenon.

We have little of Greek temple architecture before the Parthenon. Perhaps the first major work of the century was the Doric Temple/Treasury of Apollo at Delphi (around 490 B.C.). The most impressive remains are those of the temple to Zeus at Olympia, whose sculpture we mentioned. Outside Greece, there is the temple to Neptune (actually Hera) at Paestum in south Italy from about 460 B.C. The material for a large building (other than the roof) was marble. The support system was post and lintel (   ) rather than arches. This gave the buildings a blocky look (precise, ordered), so that they combined in the desired fashion beauty with restraint and order. The Greeks produced buildings which made themselves look good—not blending with nature but being arranged to please in a clever way. When they built homes for the gods, the Greeks had their eyes firmly on themselves.

The Parthenon was built between 447 and 432 B.C. The architects Ictinus and Mnesicles, along with Callicrates, planned the work; they are only names to us. The sculpture

356

was supervised, some of it perhaps done, by Phidias. The
material for the building was marble from nearby Pentelicon
(Pentelic marble), which was cream-colored. The wooden roof
was covered by marble tiles. The stylobate, the usual three-
stepped base on which it was built, was 228' by 101'. The
Acropolis itself is about 1000' by 450'.) This was the usual
rectangular shape, a little more than 2 x 1 (the measurements
at the Zeus temple at Olympia, for example, were 210' by 91').
There were 17 columns on each side, 8 at each end (compared
to 13 and 6 at Olympia). There was also an inner row of 6
columns at each end. The columns were 34' high. The central
building contained two rooms: the large home of Athena,
which contained her colossal statue, and a smaller western
room for Athena's handmaidens. The treasury of the Confederation of Delos was also kept in the smaller room. The building was not meant for worship--it was the home of Athena.
Services were held on altars outside the building.

It is well known what lengths the builders went to in
giving the impression of order, line, and symmetrical proportion. Being well aware that the eye can deceive, they
took some precautions; at other points, it seems, they
deliberately created tensions, being aware that symmetry
alone was not enough:
--the stylobate (the top step of the base) and the archi-
traves (the lintels which stretch across the columns) curve
upward (the stylobate 4" on the sides, 2" on the ends) to
make them look straight.
--each column has 20 flutes or grooves to make it look round
and to give a play of light and shade. Round columns look
flat.
--the columns, usually 14' apart, are closer together at the
corners (up to 1½" difference).
--no mortar is used in the columns. To protect the line, the
column sections are fitted together with square plugs.
--the corner columns are about 2" thicker than the others.
They can be seen isolated against the light, which makes
them look thinner than the others.
--the column shafts swell a little (11/16") then taper to
give the appearance of straightness.
--the column shafts lean in 3" (as do the outside, but not
the inside, walls of the temple itself).

The Parthenon is basically a Doric style (or Order)
building. The other, and newer, style was the more fancy

Ionic Order, named for the area where it began. These
terms refer particularly to the structure of the columns:
--A Doric column rested directly on the stylobate; an Ionic
had a fancy base.
--A Doric column was shorter and fatter (5.5 x their diameter
on the Parthenon; 4.7 at Olympia). Ionic columns were widest
at the bottom and had 24 flutings or grooves instead of the
16 or 20 of the Doric.
--A Doric column was connected to the architrave, or lintel,
by a much simpler and smaller capital than the Ionic. There
were 4 Ionic columns inside the little temple room (The
Parthenon proper). In addition, a Doric architrave was a
block, while an Ionic had 3 horizontal bands, the lower ones
pushed slightly inwards. On the frieze, the area for decoration which ran around the building above the architrave,
a Doric building had an alternating system of
   1. triglyphs--of standardized pattern, 3 grooves, 2 in
the center and a half-groove on each side. These pieces
carried the weight; usually there was one above each column
and one in between each pair of columns.
   2. metopes--each carrying a different sculpture. An Ionic
temple had a straight sculptured frieze all the way round.
There was such a continuous frieze around the actual temple
walls within the columns of the Parthenon. Above the frieze,
the cornices were much less fancy in the Doric style.

   A particular glory of the Parthenon is the sculpture,
which was planned by Phidias. This is in fact our major
source for the sculpture of the period. The marble was
tinted with bright paint colors, but the figures were left
cream. You should remember that all the sculpture was meant
to be seen in bright sunlight from about 35' below. The work
is simplified and distorted. The sculpture can be divided
into three groups:
1. the metopes of the Doric frieze above the columns. These
were done in high relief (sticking out), to take advantage
of the light. The metopes measure 3'11" by 4.2". They
present the usual scenes from myth: on the east side, the
battle of the gods for the world and the victory of the
Olympian gods; on the south side, the struggle of the Lapiths,
the legendary first inhabitants of Greece, and Theseus, the
hero-king of Athens, against the Centaurs, the man-beasts;
on the north side, the defeat of Troy; on the west side, the
Greeks beating the Amazons (for whom read Persians). This

represented the victory of the "good guys," the bringing of order, from the beginning to the present. The work is uneven in quality and very detached, aloof in spirit.
2. the continuous _Ionic frieze_ along the outside wall of the temple within the columns. This seems to have shown the Panathenaic festival and procession, the great panhellenic celebration held to Athena at Athens every four years. The choice of subject indicates the Athenians' interest in themselves; it is exceptional to find such a current, non-mythical subject. The frieze band is 3'9" by 500' with 600 figures. It is in low relief (cut shallowly). It stands out 1¼" at the bottom of the frieze, 2¼" at the top, so that it does not seem to fade away. All the human heads are at the same level, to stress the continuous procession element.
3. the free-standing _pediment_, or gable, figures, at each end of the building. The pediment space was 90' long, 11' high in the center. These figures were carved in the round and were more than life-size. Both pediments deal with Athena. On the west (facing the city), where little survives, was shown her victory over Poseidon for the friendship of Athens: on the east, her miraculous birth, with the famous _female group_ and the _Three Goddesses_. The females are clothed, in lavish drapes, but they are "sensual" in the way the effect of the _wind_ is shown on their clothes. The breasts are very prominent and there is a suggestive off-the-shoulder style. This effect is especially strong in the case of the _reclining goddess_. It is a cheap-looking effect.

Inside the temple was a colossal statue of Athena, the work of Phidias, a native Athenian and the greatest name in sculpture in this generation. It was about 40' high, an ivory body with gold drapery and accessories. Phidias made a great name for himself with these giant statues. He placed another one, of Athena also, out in the open on the Acropolis, and later he did one of Zeus seated at Olympia--the most famous of them all. We do not have them, but it is interesting to think what impression they could have created in this classical age.

Other Works.
The other glory of architecture at Athens under Pericles was the _Propylaea_, the grand entrance to the Acropolis from the east (the city). It may have bothered Pericles that the

Acropolis was such a clutter--it needed order. His planned
new entrance was a very substantial affair, extending into
galleries for pictures and statues along the north and south
flanks of the rock. Strong religious objections were raised
to the idea of moving gods to make way for the new structure,
and Pericles was forced to alter and cut back on his plan.
The Propylaea which resulted was constructed in the 430's
B.C. under the direction of Mnesicles. It is a mixed Doric-
Ionic work, of Pentelic marble except for some contrasting
dark stone from Eleusis in the frieze. The overall width
was 156', including the wings. The central porch had 6 Doric
columns, with more slendor Ionic columns in the open hallway
(vestibule).

An interesting architectural device which developed
around this time was the grid-street plan-the kind of thing
we take for granted in American (but not European) cities.
This was an invention of Hippodamus of Miletus. He applied
it first in his own town. The Piraeus, the port of Athens,
was rebuilt in this style under Pericles. The arrangement
says a good deal about Greek attitudes. It was copied
widely and was picked up by the Romans.

There is little else we need to note from this period.
We have a Roman copy of the head of a statue of Pericles
from the 430's B.C., the work of one Kresidas, originally
from Crete. It is very aloof, idealized, "unrealistic"--
much more so than the piece from 40 years earlier showing
Themistocles. Callicrates, in the 440's B.C. at the same
time as he was involved with the Parthenon, built a famous
Doric temple at Delphi to Hepheaston--who was, appropriately,
the god of skill.

THE PELOPONNESIAN WAR, 430-400 B.C.

The Peloponnesian War brought all kinds of troubles to
the Greek world, and to Athens particularly, but they seem
to have had very little effect in art at the time. The
general style is not distinguishable in any very important
way from that of the previous generation, the Age of Pericles.

Athens.
Naturally, the war meant less public construction. Two

360

small masterpieces, though, were added on the Acropolis at
Athens:
1. The Temple of Athena Nike (Victory--a theme for the
times) in the 420's B.C. This was the last major work by
Callicrates. It measured 17'9" by 26'10", in Pentelic marble
in the Ionic style. The temple perched right on the northeast edge of the Acropolis, jutting out beyond the Propylaea,
overlooking the city.
2. The Erechtheum, the work of Mnesicles, built between 421
and 409 B.C., mostly under Cleophon. It measured 37' by 66',
again in Pentelic marble in the Ionic style. This was a
complicated looking building, since it was to house a number
of things. Apart from its associations with several ancient
minor gods, the site contained--
--the place where Athena and Poseidon had competed for the
favor of Athens. There was the rock of Poseidon, which he
had struck with his trident to make a horse jump out--his
gift to humans. Athena had won the contest by offering the
olive to Athens. The sacred olive tree she had produced was
here.
--the tomb of Erechtheus, the mythical founder of Athens. He
was the son of Athena, born after she won control of the city.
In Homer, Erechtheus is "the light-hearted."
    The building was also meant to house the ancient wooden
statue of Athena, which was now homeless thanks to the
Parthenon. As a result of all this, the building has four
rooms on two levels, with one higher than the others, as well
as three porches.
    The most famous part of the structure is the southern
(smallest) porch, the Porch of the Maidens. This is 10' by
15'. On a 6' wall, the 6 maidens (9' high) are used as
substitutes for columns to cover the rest of the vertical
distance. They are in procession; those on the right lift
their left, inside leg, those on the left lift their right
leg. The drapery folds are a substitute for the flutes or
grooves of columns. They are cool and aloof in the usual
manner, but again sex is clearly suggested. The drapery is
"thin," with the legs and the breasts very apparent. Frieze
and pediment are left out on the Erechtheum. The carvings
on the wall of the temple, though, are much admired; they
represent fruits, plants, etc., in an unusual choice of
subject.

The Style.

The chief impression given by the Erechtheum is one of grace; a light touch, an elegant prettiness, which is at odds with the war which was going on and with the doubts which the Athenians were experiencing. The same impression is given by the relief sculptures from the small temple of Athena Nike, where we even see Athena leaning down to fix her sandal. The same is true of the famous Flying Nike which the Messenians dedicated at Olympia after the defeat of the Spartans at Pylos in the 420's B.C. One breast is naked and the appeal to the senses in the wind-swept drapery is very clear. In the Temple of Apollo at Bassae in Arcadia, built over the period 450-420 B.C., perhaps partly at least by Ictinus, there is the same clever prettiness. Here are our first Corinthian columns--a third style, more fancy than the Ionic, much more slender. The Corinthian style supposedly was introduced by Callimachus here in the late 400's B.C.--we know almost nothing about him.

The signs point toward an increasing humanity along with a growing liking for complicated, pretty things. These values are also typical of the new White Ground pottery of the day, with its delicate figures, elegant and pretty, and a much stronger interest in portraying women. This was pointing the way to the 300's B.C.

Painting.

We can say very little about painting at this point, or at any other period in the Classical Age (500-300 B.C.). The painting was a good deal less durable, lasting than the architecture, sculpture, and pottery. It is clear that the Greeks were fond of color and of painting; they used it on their sculptures to some degree, they covered the walls of their temples with it. We have some names and we know that the Greeks, as we would expect, made big technical advances in painting. But the work itself is missing. It seems that movement in painting had started by 500 B.C., as it had in sculpture. The great name of the 400's B.C., Polygnotus of Thasos, specialized in great wall paintings, now all lost (500-430 B.C.). Aristotle said that his paintings had "character"--meaning that he read into man, blended the human with the ideal, in the usual Classical way. Polygnotus is associated with the early development of perspectives in painting, the ability to portray the sense of distance, of fading away

and coming forward. Another name is <u>Mikon</u> <u>of</u> <u>Athens</u>. Both
came to notice in the 460's B.C. doing the paintings for the
buildings <u>Cimon</u> was putting up at Athens. Later, in the
second half of the 400's B.C., the chief name in painting
was <u>Apollodorus</u> <u>of</u> <u>Athens</u>. He was the "shadow" painter,
able to use <u>light</u> <u>and</u> <u>shade</u> with skill. He also developed
the smaller-scale easel painting. By 430 B.C., with some
command of perspective and shadow, the Greeks were able to
put three-dimensionality into their paintings--a great
achievement. It is a great pity that the work is gone.

PHILOSOPHY/SCIENCE/RELIGION IN THE 400'S B.C.

Over the century after 600 B.C., from <u>Thales</u> <u>of</u> <u>Miletus</u>
to <u>Pythagoras</u>, the way the Greeks looked at the world had
grown much more complicated. Still, they were headed in all
kinds of directions in their attempts to reduce the world to
order by explanation. The two giant figures in Greek thought
around 500 B.C., the age of the Persian invasions, were
HERACLITUS of <u>Ephesus</u> in <u>Ionia</u> (530-470 B.C.) and, just a
little later, PARMENIDES of <u>Elea</u> in <u>south</u> <u>Italy</u>--the same
two centers of thought, Ionia and south Italy, which had
been dominant since the beginning. We know more about these
men than the earlier figures and we have some bits of their
work.

Heraclitus.
       <u>Heraclitus</u>, the Ionian, was famous as an eccentric. He
stayed out of the public eye and had nothing but contempt
for other men and for all other philosophers. Here was
another non-democrat. Heraclitus was called "the Obscure."
From the 100+ fragments of his work that we have, it is easy
to see why. He wrote in short, strange phrases, hard to
understand but easy to remember--so that many of them became
famous.

1. Abandoning all earlier thought (in theory), he says "I
searched myself"--that is, trust absolutely your <u>senses</u>,
your <u>intuition</u>, rather than <u>reason</u>. This was a reasonable
slap at the Pythagoreans, but it risked further encouraging
Greeks to ignore the evidence.
2. <u>Everything</u> <u>is</u> <u>change</u>, motion. This is the most basic
mark of Heraclitus. "You cannot step into the same river
twice" is his most famous phrase. Rest, stability, cannot

exist--permanence is an illusion created by false senses.
3. Everything is conflict as well as change. "War fathers
everything."
4. That conflict is the conflict of opposites (hot/cold;
wet/dry; good/bad).
5. Harmony is a harmony of conflict and contrast, delicate
and easily upset. It is produced by opposing tensions, as in
a tightly-strained, well-tuned string; it is not produced by
compromise, or reconciliation, or bringing together.
Heraclitus aims here at those who looked for the unchanging,
the everlasting, the stable--which included the Pythagoreans.
6. There are no sides to take. In the conflict of opposites,
both sides are equally natural and necessary: "good and bad
are the same." There are no absolutes (since everything must
change).
7. This world of change is directed by a living principle of
order and measure, which Heraclitus calls Logos (a term used
later by Christians for the Word). He means the right
proportion of mixture which produces the harmony of opposing
tensions. This force is identified somehow, though, with the
Fire, something very material: "The Fire governs everything,"
he says. The Fire, which is controlled by the Logos, is
everything: "Fire can be traded for all things, and all
things for fire, like gold for goods and goods for gold."
The soul is made of the Fire and goes down/changes with the
body--in contrast to the Pythagorean idea.

We know too little of what Heraclitus has to say to
make sense out of his system as opposed to his simple insistence that change is everything. It is possible that in the
Logos/Fire he is offering an explanation which is non-
materialistic--which explains, approximately in the form we
would, the force behind matter. That force, living, lasting,
keeping all things in their place, is balance--it is not
right or wrong in our sense. It is much more of an attempt
than the Milesians made to establish what is in back of
matter. On a different level, the strong insistence of
Heraclitus on the instability of all things was to have a
great influence later among Greeks, Plato among them.

Parmenides.
        Parmenides lived in south Italy, where the Pythagorean
influence was very heavy. His town of Elea was the place
where Xenophanes had settled after leaving Ionia. Parmenides

was an active political figure. We have some long fragments
of a work he wrote in epic hexameter verse. In many ways--
and it is his chief claim to fame--Parmenides was the first
Greek philosopher to reason rather than to state, to suppose.
The great structure of Greek, and our, logical thought begins
here.

1. Trust reason/knowledge, not senses/opinion. The senses
are the source of all error. This is the opposite of
Heraclitus--although both men agree that reason and the
senses are separate.
2. All reality is one--which sounds like the Xenophanes
influence.
3. There is no change, since "That which is is." What
looks like change is an error of the senses. Not being is
not possible; things cannot be and not be (that is, be
changing, becoming, giving way).
4. Nothing can come out of nothing. There must be a single,
everlasting principle, unchanged and unmoved; nothing can
come out of it. This is the One, the Being, the same for all
time. This One is limited in size--it is a solid and has
the form of a sphere occupying all space. There is no void
(not being is not possible). The One is neither material nor
spiritual--it is mathematical, logical. It is not the single
stuff of the Milesians--that won't do.

Parmenides offers the first determined attempt to explain
everything from one principle (monism). He has the same deep
desire for unity, rest, order as the Pythagoreans, as well as
their objections to the material world. Thus his insistence
that the world our senses know does not exist and cannot
exist--which links him to the Pythagorean insistence on the
"badness" of the body, of matter. He describes a cosmogony,
the origins of the physical world, but it is only as it seems
to others--the gap between his One and what we see cannot be
bridged. Parmenides had to reject the traditional arguments
that an original stuff (a One) had evolved naturally into
the Many we see--he believed that this was impossible, since
there was no real change or development in a living thing.
What he had to say about the falseness of our senses, about
the irrelevance of the world as it seems to us, struck home
to Greeks. We will see its influence later in Socrates and
Plato. Compared to Heraclitus, and the Pythagoreans, though,
Parmenides was describing a world without any spiritual
purpose.

365

It was in general the thought of Parmenides and the south Italians which dominated in the Greek world between 475 and 425 B.C., the golden age of Athens. The preference for no change over the everything is change idea of Heraclitus indicates the Greeks' desire for order and predictability and type. The outstanding supporter of the standard or orthodox line of Parmenides was Zeno, also of Elea (490-430 B.C.). Zeno took to extremes the search for truth by reason only. He flatly refused motion, claiming that it could not exist, and to illustrate how the senses misled men into believing in such ideas he offered a series of famous paradoxes (something which seems to be nonsensical but which may be true). Insisting on the infinite divisibility of a line, Zeno argued that a things moves either
1. where it is—but it can't move there, because it is there, at rest; or
2. where it isn't—but it can't move there, because it isn't there at all.
Two of Zeno's paradoxes are:
1. The Arrow: So long as a thing is in a space equal to itself, it is at rest. An arrow is in a space equal to itself at every moment during its flight. Therefore the arrow is at rest.
2. Achilles and the Tortoise: If the tortoise has a head-start on Achilles, Achilles can never catch up with it. For, while Achilles covers the distance from where he was to where the tortoise was, the tortoise advances some distance more; while Achilles covers this distance, the tortoise covers a further distance, and so on and so on. So Achilles can run for ever without overtaking the tortoise.

More commonly, thinkers accepted the no change principle of Parmenides but tried to work around it by arguing that there are various combinations of unchangeable things (a special way of looking at the One) and that the combinations are made by a separate cause or causes. The former was an attempt to get around the weakness of always having to claim that commonsense was wrong; the latter was an attempt to throw in a spiritual element, in the fashion of Heraclitus and the Pythagoreans. The distinction between the things moved and the moving cause—a piece of two-world thought out of the Pythagoreans—was to have a lot of influence on Plato. The things moved (matter) were, of course, the inferiors in

366

this arrangement. The three big names associated with
these trends, the men who dominated the period from 450 to
425 B.C., were:
Empedocles of Acragas in Sicily (500-435 B.C.)
Anaxagoras of Ionian Clazomenae in Asia Minor (500-425 B.C.)
Democritus of Abdera in Thrace (460-370 B.C.)

Empedocles.

With Empedocles, we have all the weirdness of the Orphic/
Pythagorean tradition of south Italy, including the migrations
of souls among bodies. How he reconciled this with his
philosophy we cannot say. He was an eccentric, a great poet
(we have some of his work). He too was an active politicaian--
only he, unusually, was a democrat. He was a famous biologist
too, in the line of practical men of science who also looked
for the key which would explain everything: he produced a
description of the respiratory system.

We can note the following about his philosophy:
1. There are 4 roots or elementary substances--Fire, Air,
Earth, Water (the standard 4 of later Greek thought). The
One was gone. He took these separate elements from medicine
(see below)--the Greeks regarded him as one of the "fathers
of medicine."
2. There are 2 moving causes: Harmony/Love which unites,
Conflict which divides. Each is in control in turn in a
cycle which goes on for ever. These two causes are physical.
3. The cycle starts with the Sphere (the World-Egg again?)
in which the 4 roots are perfectly mixed under the complete
control of Love. Our universe is the intermediate stages in
the move from perfect Love to total Conflict--and then back
to Love. That is why the sexes are now separate (Strife--
bad); at first, in trees say, they were not (Love--good).
4. The idea of Harmony, which is good, as a balance or
mixture of opposing elements was very attractive to Greeks--
they took to it much more eagerly than to the idea of
Heraclitus that no mixture was possible.

Anaxagoras.

Anaxagoras the Ionian was clear-headed and a good deal
less interested in satisfying religious feelings. He moved
to Athens and became the chief intellectual figure there in
the age of Pericles--the first great intellectual name
associated with Athens. From this point, Greek intellectual
life centered on that city. Around 440 B.C. Anaxagoras was

condemned by a jury at Athens for teaching atheism (not
believing in gods). He was forced to leave--the first major
victim of a democracy which did not much like seeing the old
beliefs challenged. It scared and annoyed people that
Anaxagoras said that the sun was only a fiery stone. As a
professional astronomer, Anaxagoras developed the true
theory of eclipse.

Anaxagoras agreed with Parmenides that matter does not
change, but he too, like Empedocles, got rid of the One. He
has a moving cause also. This moving cause places seeds of
unchanging matter into various combinations. These seeds
are basic substances (flesh, bone, hot, cold). They cannot
be grouped into "more basic" elements such as the 4 roots of
Empedocles. We can say little about how Anaxagoras explained
change in the combinations. He said "There is a piece of
everything in everything." Orange juice contains everything,
but it has a certain color because it has more of some things
than of others.

The moving cause for Anaxagoras was Nous (Mind or
Intelligence), a word he introduced. Nous is matter, of the
finest kind. It is unmixed, it is in everything, it moves
constantly, ordering movement to everything else. Nous has
brought the elements out of chaos through a vortex into our
universe. Anaxagoras did not say why or how Nous ordered
everything. He may have believed that Nous ordered things
for the best, but if so he took this for granted without
making it clear. Many of his followers liked to say that
order just happened, but the way was open for men like Plato
to give to Nous a will, a desire to help the world, to order
things for the good.

Democritus.
Democritus was the most famous of the Atomists. Atomism
has won for Democritus and his associates a lot of attention
in this century, for obvious reasons. Atoms are the basic
bodies; they cannot be divided or analyzed; they are invisible
(which is what atom means) and they last forever. They come
in all shapes and sizes and they are on the move all the time.
There is no cause for the movement, no directing force. The
movement of atoms, he assumes, accounts for what we see. Our
sensations come from the shape (round=sweet) and texture or
position (rough, uneven=black) of the atoms. Empty space,
which Parmenides had flatly ruled out, is also assumed, to

give the atoms something to move around in. The body, the soul, the gods, are all such chance collections of atoms.

This atomism offers a distrust of the senses as great as that of Parmenides or Zeno--after all, things hardly look like atoms. Since it has no moving cause, it is a simple materialism, and one not of a very scientific kind--it is based on supposing, not observing. At the same time, Democritus, it seems, did have an ethical system (a way of calculating right and wrong)--it just didn't have anything to do with his atomism. It was practical. He urged peace of mind, a condition which arose from knowledge (i.e., atomism), rather than from pleasures of the body. Peace of mind came through moderation, in avoiding both too much and too little. The usefulness of this is obviously limited, although it is very Greek in assuming that knowledge is a good thing; that the senses are less important; that moderation, balance, proportion are the keys.

It is probably fair to say that nothing the philosophers had come up with since 500 B.C. put them in any very good light. Despite the small steps of Heraclitus and Anaxagoras, there was little to satisfy religious longings (as the public made clear in the case of Anaxagoras). The dominant tradition played down the senses and the material world, and so seemed to take something of a delight in being useless and irrelevant. It had nothing to say about how people should treat one another, let alone how they should deal with the supernatural. And the tradition which had been built up since Thales around 600 B.C. did not look with much favor on fact, on observation--on science. The philosophers, as Anaxagoras, remained professional scientists/mathematicians, but nearly everything they said pointed away from such work. There is a story from the 440's B.C. of a one-horned ram being brought to Pericles from his farm. A seer interpreted the deformity to mean that Pericles would defeat his political rival Thucydides--and so be the one man. Anaxagoras split the ram's head open and showed that the problem was a malformation. Well and good--but generally, we can suspect, Anaxagoras did not much bother with such problems. With some reason, the public may have thought that philosophers in the late 400's B.C. were a pretty useless bunch, handy only at bothering people to no good purpose. As Pindar the poet said in the early 400's B.C., the philosophers "got a poor

369

harvest from their cleverness."

In this kind of situation, different men continued to find different answers. For some, the need for religious satisfaction was the most important thing. To such people, philosophers were both annoying and offensive to the gods. Some reacted to the hard times of the Peloponnesian War by claiming that the Greeks (and the Athenians especially) had overreached themselves (hubris). Sophocles, in Oedipus the King (429 B.C.), showed a great man--an intellectual--being brought down by hubris; he can't solve the plague in this city (obviously Pericles). The old weird religions and religious customs benefitted: Orphism revived, and we can see that the great Oracle at Delphi still flourished despite a very tarnished record. The Oracle had been neutral in the first Persian attack upon Greece in 490 B.C. (which had ended at Marathon) and had actually advised giving in ("medizing") at the time of the great Persian invasion of 480 B.C. More recently, the Oracle had spoken against Athens at the beginning of the Peloponnesian War. The messages from Apollo were delivered by a woman in a state of trance. The priests (all males), who had the gift of understanding what the seer said at such times, wrote down the messages--the important ones in hexameter verse. Some of the messages we know indicate that attempts were made to provide answers that could be interpreted more than one way, but the Oracle's batting average must have been good--many of the questions she was asked involved very straightforward and down-to-earth matters which it would have been hard to fake. New weird offerings appeared. Aesculapius, a mystic man-god who healed, enjoyed great popularity. He was "brought" to Athens from Asia Minor in 420 B.C. For a while, he was "housed" at the home of Sophocles, who had had a vision of the healer.

Others went their own way, dealing with the world as they found it. A good example, particularly after mentioning Aesculapius, is medicine, the most advanced and the most genuinely scientific of the Greek sciences in the late 400's B.C. We have an enormous number of works credited to Hippocrates of Cos (born about 450 B.C.), the "father of medicine." Some of them probably were his work. He is said to have lived to be over 100 (perhaps an argument that he knew his business); certainly he was very famous in his own lifetime, running a sort of medical school. One thing associated with Hippocrates is the famous Doctor's Oath, still in use today.

Much of the tone in the writings credited to Hippocrates
is very sensible: superstition and magic are out, accurate
diagnosis, careful observation, and reliable proven treatment
are in. In the work On the Sacred Disease, for example,
epilepsy, which had wonderful implications in the ancient
world, is treated as just another disease. Diseases are
seen as disturbances in the balance of the 4 humors or
fluids of the body, which coincide with the 4 elements of
Empedocles (earth/black bile; air/blood; fire/yellow bile;
water/phlegm). Disturbances could result from all sorts of
causes, but the most common were diet and climate. Treatment
was limited, certainly in comparision to the careful checking
which went into finding out what was wrong. It was supposed
that nature would cure most ailments if given a chance.
Improved habits of diet and hygiene were the usual course;
few drugs were used, and surgery was a last resort. Most of
the writings show that medicine was going its own way,
resisting or ignoring the influence of philosophy. Some
pieces, though, do show signs of the influence of the
philosophers--there is an insistence sometimes that you have
to understand the universe before you can understand a man.
Often, too, the arguments are not experiments but construc-
tions--if you do such and such, you will find such and such.

Sophists.
Doctors could go their own way; many others were not so
lucky. In the confusion of a fast-changing world, about
which the philosophers so far had had little that was useful
to say, there grew up in the late 400's B.C. a willingness
to break new paths in concentrating on human relationships--
something relatively down-to-earth, but very practical.
This was the work of the SOPHISTS. The word then had no bad
sense, although we use it about misleading or false arguments.
The Sophists taught men how to get along in life, how to deal
with other people. They travelled around, charged a lot,
and naturally tended to concentrate at Athens, although they
were to be found all over. They taught people to bring
nature, their surroundings and associates, under control;
knowledge was important, a real key to getting ahead. They
concentrated on rhetoric (public speaking), grammar, and the
social graces and talents. They even encouraged a careful
attitude toward fact, something the philosophers sometimes

371

ignored--for the Sophists, it was a part of looking informed, impressive. They usually supported conservative, old-fashioned behavior and beliefs (again as ways of fitting in, looking good), but they were accused of undermining moral standards and producing immorality. For the Sophists argued that there were no absolute standards: religion and morals were just habits (conventions); so were the laws. A sensible man generally kept to the old habits--but only because it was to his interest to do so, not because he "believed" in them. It is easy to understand why this kind of moral relativity was disliked by many and won for the Sophists a bad name. It is just as easy to understand how it led many of the Sophists' students to think that they were entitled to break the law, the old rules of every kind, when it suited them--to believe in the right of the stronger, the more efficient, to believe that success was virtue (the good)--a harsh individualism. It was common in the late 400's B.C. to blame the behavior of men like Alcibiades and the oligarchs (Critias especially) on the "godless and unprincipled" Sophists who had taught them.

Many of the Sophists were not philosophers at all in the traditional sense. Even so, their existence showed what had been missing in the usual philosophical approach. The greatest of the Sophists was Protagoras. Like Democritus, he came from Abdera in Thrace, but he moved to Athens and became a prominent figure there in the period of the Peloponnesian War. Protagoras believed in a great controlling force (Forethought) which kept the material world in balance. To the man in the street, thought, he must have seemed a disturbing influence. "Man is the measure of all things" is his most famous phrase--a very typical Sophist feeling. "As to the gods," he said too, "I do not know if they exist or not." In 415 B.C. Protagoras was accused of attacking the gods--the same charge which had been brought against Anaxagoras. He fled Athens, but was lost in a wreck at sea. The particular practical achievement of Protagoras was to establish the science of grammar; he distinguished the different parts of speech. The use of words, obviously, was very important to the Sophists. Gorgias of Leontini in south Italy bacame famous for encouraging a new, clever style of argument which depended on an antithetical structure (contrasting pairs), a style very different from the old poetic imagery of previous generations. The historian

372

Thucydides is an outstanding example of this rational approach to making an argument. In many ways this was a characteristic Greek achievement--words had been reduced to order, to type--their secrets had been discovered.

SOCRATES, 470-399 B.C.

The Sophists performed a service in turning their attention to people, even if they concentrated on self-interest. It was natural that the attempt would be made soon to look at people in a way more in line with philosophical tradition--philosophy would capture the Sophists. This was the work of SOCRATES.

We do not know much about Socrates. He was an ugly little man, physically very tough--indifferent to his body, but not a freaky ascetic, just a man who took things like food and drink as they came. From a reasonably comfortable family, he spent his time, and perhaps made his living, teaching at Athens, his home, through conversation. By the time the Peloponnesian War began (431 B.C.) he was the most famous "thinker" of his day. The Delphi Oracle said he was the wisest man in Greece--Socrates answered this compliment with his famous explanation that his wisdom lay in the fact that he knew that he didn't know anything.

He was a loyal Athenian, taking his duties to the state very seriously in the usual Greek way (which means that he is not at all our kind of individualist). We have seen him in the army, and he may also have served on the Council of 500. He was his own man, though--in the last decade of his life he offended both the oligarchs and the democrats at Athens by refusing to help either camp murder its opponents. At the age of about 70 he was brought to trial under the restored democracy for attacking the old gods and for corrupting young men--another example of the people's dislike of the philosophers. The people must have seen him as more or less of a Sophist, throwing out the gods and teaching self-interest. His most famous pupil (at that time), the late Alcibiades, offered strong evidence against him in this connection. Socrates did not offer much of a defense. In a jury of 501, he lost by 60. Condemned to death, he refused to take the usual course and flee. Instead, he drank the poison and died.

373

Socrates wrote nothing. Our written evidence comes
from three chief sources:
1. The play Clouds, written by Aristophanes in the 420's
B.C. when Socrates was at the height of his reputation and
Aristophanes was a young comedy-writer just starting out.
Socrates is the chief character. He is shown as a Sophist,
a word-merchant, a man who specializes in teaching rich kids
how to get away with things--and at the same time one who
is mad, madly unrealistic. And what we have is a toned-down
version of the original script. Admirers of Socrates have
always held this play against Aristophanes; Plato said it
helped to get Socrates killed (20 years later). As we will
see, though, there is a good deal of the word-merchant in
Socrates.
2. The writings of Xenophon (he of the epic of the 10,000).
Xenophon was a pupil of Socrates. Much later, perhaps to
cash in on what he knew, he wrote some dialogues and a
memoir of Socrates. Little attention is paid to what
Xenophon has to say--it is usually claimed that he had never
known Socrates well and that time had dimmed (to put it
charitably) what little he did have to remember.
3. This leaves the writings of PLATO, another pupil of
Socrates who was nearly 30 when the old man died. We do
not know how close Plato was to Socrates while the latter
was alive (Plato, typically of the Sophists' pupils, was
from an aristocratic family). After the death of Socrates,
though, Plato dedicated himself both to the memory of his
teacher and to completing his philosophy. He wrote many
pieces, in the form of dialogues or conversations, in which
Socrates is the main character. Some of them were written
not long after 399 B.C. and have the appearance of more or
less faithfully reporting what Socrates had had to say. It
is clear that Plato had a very deep emotional attachment to
the dead man. This emotion, and Plato's wonderful ability
as a writer, produced in his various accounts of the trial
and death of Socrates (Apology, Crito, and especially Phaedo)
perhaps the greatest pieces of all Greek prose. Plato lived
50 years after the death of Socrates. He continued to use
Socrates as a mouthpiece in his writings, but less and less
convincingly and carefully--the dialogues become more
artificial as Plato, we assume, speaks increasingly for
himself. Plato is unique among Greek writers; we have
probably a great majority of all the things he wrote.

While there is no sure way to distinguish between
Socrates and Plato, we can say that Socrates believed that
1. A man's true job is to take care of his soul (psyche),
to make it as good as possible. He is the first man to
think of soul in the way we do—as the essential personality
of the human. This was a line of thought which became very
widespread among Greeks and which prepared the way more
than anything else for the much later acceptance of
Christianity.
2. A good soul makes a good (happy) man.
3. The world is controlled by intelligent powers which
order everything for the best. This was not a new idea. It
had become common even among believers in the traditional
gods to argue that they upheld justice; philosophers, in
stressing balance, often assumed the same thing.

This is a teleological world (one aimed at an end, a
purpose). The end for humans is to benefit their souls.
How do we do this? By helping the soul to know what good
is. Virtue, by which the Greeks also meant skill, is
happiness; it is knowing the good (by which he would mean
intuiting it, opening your eyes to it, as well as studying
it). We can be taught to know the good—by exercising our
minds, through discussion, pointing out mistakes, hinting
around at answers, etc. The good is all one (virtue is one)—
a great universal value, and very much the kind of thing
that we would say. The good never changes, holds everywhere
and at all times, and is objective—it can be known. Knowing
the good will lead to doing "right," which will improve the
soul, and to being happy. Here Socrates insisted that not
knowing the good, which is ignorance/wickedness, is not a
condition a person wants to be in. A human, he thinks, is
bound to respond to the chance to improve himself. This is
very optimistic—much good sense indicates otherwise, as
Christians, seeing man as a sinful creature, well know. He
had little beyond this to say about the good, and little
also to say about what this soul was. He may have believed
in immortality (the soul living forever). We cannot say;
in the Apology he is reported as denying a belief in
immortality.

This can all sound good and wonderful, and there is no
doubt that from a Christian point of view it is much more

attractive, much more "moral," than anything we have seen
so far. It points the way from shame (looking bad to others)
to guilt (looking bad to yourself). There are in it, though,
substantial elements from the Sophists--enough, surely, to
explain why Aristophanes and the public could be hostile.
Like the Sophists, Socrates was a rationalist (searching
for the truth through argument in the new style) and an
individualist (a person should concentrate on improving his
soul). Both things could easily be "misinterpreted":
knowledge as virtue, truth by argument and definition
(rationalism), could look dangerously "clever," snobbish
(anti-democratic), and unreligious; virtue as happiness,
and the fact that, while Socrates won't say much about what
the good is, he favors what is useful (utilitarianism),
could look like a Sophist encouragement of selfishness, of
doing what you wanted. His way of boasting that he was
willing to question anything cannot have helped, either.
The Euthyphro is a wonderful chance to see these "Sophist"
elements in Socrates--in many ways, he is not at all the
kind of Socrates we expect the admiring Plato to draw for
us.

ART IN THE 300's B.C.

Sculpture.

Sculpture in the 300's continued to move toward naturalism and realism. Idealism remained, but now it was associated
with a much clearer appeal to the senses. Sculpture inspired
less, it appealed to human sympathies more. It was more
personal, more individual; less tied to the spirit and
propaganda needs of the polis, less tied to religion. So it
was moving away from its ties with the old public architecture, such as temples--sculpture now could stand on its own,
some of it for private citizens to buy for their own houses.

The usual subjects for sculpture in the 300's B.C. were
still myths and the gods. The gods and goddesses now, though,
are human, with human emotions and personalities. There is
less stress on type, more stress on exploring emotions,
humanity. As a part of this, personification grew. We have
a Roman copy of Peace and Wealth, a work by Kephisodotos of
around 375 B.C., which was a public monument to go up in the
Agora or market-place at Athens. It shows a cool but tender-
hearted woman playing with a child. Tenderness was itself a
favorite and typical theme. We have, from about 340 B.C.,
again in copy, the Hermes with the Child Dionysius. This was
by PRAXITELES of Athens (390-330 B.C.), the greatest name
of the century in sculpture, and the son of Kephisodotos.
This piece was for the Temple of Hera at Olympia. These
gods are now very cute and human. Playing with children was
to be a favorite theme for a very long time.

Strain, tension, outright suffering, also came in as
favorite emotions. The horrors of violent death are shown
on the pediment sculptures at the Temple of Aesculapius
(the god of healing) at Epidaurus about 380 B.C. The spirit
is very different from the coolness of the previous century.
The head of Herakles (if that is who it is) from the Temple
of Athena at Tegea, about 340 B.C., shows the hero worried
and anxious--not in charge of the situation at all. This
piece was the work of Skopas of Paros, another great name,
a man who seems to have specialized in presenting emotion.
At the other extreme, humor, playfulness came into style.
This element is in the Hermes with the Child Dionysius by
Praxiteles. The most famous example of humor is the same
man's Apollo the Lizard Killer, again in Roman copy, from

377

the 330's B.C. Apollo is now soft, young, gay (?). The subject is a play on an old legend of Apollo killing a dragon.

The most startling sign of interest in emotions, the
senses, is the deliberate <u>sensuousness</u> of some of the work.
<u>Praxiteles</u> is the big name in this connection. His style
was soft, dreamy. He worked usually in marble, the soft
Parian marble, for a more appealing appearance, adding to
the impact by rubbing the surface with beeswax and using
painted tints. His statues look alive and real, with the
warmth and life of flesh and the appearance of actual hair,
skin, etc. His males are young, pleasant, able to enjoy
life; they are relaxed in his famous S-curve, an arrangement which has a strong effect on the viewer. The sensuousness is most obvious in the treatment of females, in the
eventual willingness to show the naked female form. The
great work here is the <u>Aphrodite</u> <u>of</u> <u>Cnidos</u> by Praxiteles
(330's B.C.), the most famous statue of the ancient world,
and one of which many copies were made. The work was
intended for a round temple or an enclosed courtyard where it
could be seen from all angles. The goddess is a distinct
individual, a woman, not a type or an abstract. She is
surprised by an intruder (the viewer) as she prepares to
bathe. She reacts with only a token sort of modesty, with
one hand almost in front of her. The effect is stunning,
psychologically and physically. Lucian, a Roman writer,
referred to her "soft" melting gaze."

In these works, the religious significance of the gods
has been lost--the subject is simply conventional. At the
same time, the growing interest of society, and art, in the
emotions, in the individual, made it certain that religions
which offered a personal or a weird/strange appeal would
flourish and would find their way into art. On the <u>personal</u>
side, for example, we have the sensitive marble head of the
healer man-god <u>Aesculapius</u> (23") from about 350-330 B.C.--
the figure is almost Christ-like in its mood of concern.
On the <u>fanciful/weird</u> side, the colossal head of the god
<u>Serapis</u> (an Egyptian import), a copy of an original by
<u>Bryaxis</u> <u>the</u> <u>Carian</u> from around 300 B.C., keeps only the
Greek insistence that the god has a human form. Everything
else is deliberately strange: silver and gold and jewels all
over it, a sacred bluish-black dye, a great beard and wild
hair, with a basket of grain on the head. The attraction
of the strange (the disorderly) was <u>increasing</u>; <u>Praxiteles</u>

did a famous piece, The _Satyr_, part-man, part-beast, part-god.

The last great name in sculpture of this period is
LYSIPPUS of _Argos_ (350-300 B.C.). He developed a new
system of proportions (a new canon), one with smaller
heads and more slender bodies. He worked usually in bronze,
and lacks the sensuousness of Praxiteles. His most famous
work, a marble copy of a bronze original, the _Youth_ _Scraping_
Himself (330 B.C.), is a clear expression of life-like
naturalism. Lysippus has the figure reaching out, moving
actively. He became the favorite of _Alexander_ _the_ _Great_ in
the 320's B.C. and began the chain of hero-god-king statues.
These represented a type but still expressed personality.
The well-known statue of Alexander from _Pergamum_ around 200
B.C., which shows the conqueror with plenty of problems,
may well be in the style created by Lysippus. He also
revived the old colossal style, perhaps as a way of appealing
to Easterners as Greek influence spread with the Macedonian
conquests. The most famous piece in this style, a much later
Roman version of the type produced by Lysippus, is the
Herakles _Farnese_ (10'5"); Herakles has quite a body, but he
is tired out, his old skin put aside.

Individual portraits, of which we have a few from the
400's B.C., such as the _Themistocles_ and the _Pericles_, began
to thrive with these new attitudes. The Alexander portraits
of Lysippus are an example. The great statue of _Mausolus_ _of_
Caria, from his famous tomb of the late 300's B.C., is force-
ful and vividly naturalistic. We have a copy of an
Aristotle from about 330 B.C.--realistic, but detached,
much as one would expect a philosopher to look.   We have a
less convincing copy of a _Socrates_ from around 340 B.C.
The most famous piece of this type is the _Demosthenes_, a
marble copy of a bronze from about 280 B.C. which was put in
the Agora at Athens. The great orator looks tired, tense,
upset, quarrelsome--reasonable enough in his predicament.
Such personal portraits had a fine future before them over
the next several centuries.

An odd expression of the growing emphasis on emotions
was the appearance of _deliberate_ _revivals_ of the art forms
of the 400's B.C. We see the same thing in the drama too.
A fondness for the past is often found in periods of emotional
art forms. We see the Romans doing the same thing endlessly,

and it was an important part of our Romantic Movement in the 1800's.

Painting.

We know little about <u>painting</u> in the 300's B.C. We can imagine that painting went through much the same changes in content as sculpture; Aristotle said that the painters of his day (late 300's B.C.), compared to the old, lacked character (the desire to abstract and improve). <u>Aristeides of Thebes</u> had a reputation for expressing human emotions; <u>Apelles of Cos</u> was said to be an erotic painter. They are only names to us. Perspective and shading became common, being very useful in appealing to the senses. We have some scraps of tomb (headstone) paintings. a famous one, that of <u>Hediste</u> from <u>Pagasai</u> (about 280 B.C.) shows the woman Hediste, dead in childbirth, lying worn-out on the bed, her face a mess—but her breasts sticking boldly out above the bedclothes. The <u>Battle of Alexander at Issus</u>, a wall painting from the ruins of Roman <u>Pompeii</u>, is assumed to be a copy of a painting of around 330 B.C. It is very lively, full of intense excitement.

Architecture.

In <u>architecture</u>, while the evidence is still slim, we can see a movement toward grace and the fanciful. The <u>Ionic</u> order largely replaced the more squat and simple <u>Doric</u> style, and found itself challenged by the even more fancy and light <u>Corinthian</u> style, which had first appeared in the late 400's B.C. A Corinthian column was much more ornately decorated and was higher and more slender (height 10 times the diameter). This produced an elegant look. A good example of the Corinthian style is the small round temple built by <u>Lysicrates</u> at Athens in 334 B.C. (the <u>Choragic Monument</u>). This was 21 1/2' high x 9' diameter, out of Pentelic marble. The older Doric style still continued though, as in the columns of the <u>Temple of Zeus at Nema</u> (330 B.C.), which at 34' are the same height as those on the Parthenon.

The Choragic monument is an example of other character-istics of the architecture of the 300's B.C.—the greater diversity of ground plans and the greater attention to interiors. <u>Type</u> was to some extent being abandoned here, too—we saw an early example in the <u>Erechtheum</u> (420-410 B.C.), although the diversity in that case came from the needs of the occasion. In the 300's B.C., the circular plan was popular. There is one at Delphi from 390 B.C., another at Epidaurus from 370-350 B.C. A well-known example is the Philippeion at Olympia, begun by Philip of Macedon in 339 B.C. near the end of his life. We do not know what these buildings were for; they were ornately worked, in the popular fashion of the day. Public temples, even when they kept the old rectangular shape, became more complicated in their interior plan--an early example is the temple to Apollo at Bassae from the late 400's B.C. (see above). Sometimes the ground plan was quite untraditional and very much directed toward the mystery that was in the interior. The extreme example is the shrine of Apollo at Didyma near Miletus--a very old holy place. This was begun around 300 B.C. One temple connected with another inside it through dark passages which ran downwards into a courtyard. The structure was Ionic, and very rich and fancy.

Theaters.

It is also from the 300's B.C. that we have our earliest theaters, where the plays were put on. One was built at Athens, at the foot of the Acropolis, perhaps not long after 400 B.C. The earliest well-preserved theater is at Epidaurus, probably from the late 300's B.C. The seats are arranged in ascending semi-circles, built into the receding hillside, looking down on to the open round space (orchestra) for the chorus and for the wilder activities, with beyond it the plat- form which the actors used (the latter with doors to be used as houses, etc.). Of course, this arrangement was traditional --building a theater was a matter of technique, of form, rather than of individual self-expression.

Music.

We cannot say much at all about music at any point in the Classical Period. It is clear that music was important to the Greeks, although usually it was used with some other art form, such as the drama. We still have this, in ballet (music and dancing) and opera (music and drama), etc. The enjoyment of music on its own, for itself, is a fairly new thing even with us.

We know that from a little before 500 B.C., thanks to
the Pythagoreans, the Greeks developed a scale system,
having discovered that the relations, the intervals,
between notes could be expressed mathematically. However,
we do not understand their system of musical notation. We
also know that they organized musical tones into patterns
or modes. Each mode had its ethos, its spirit or "moral"
value. The chief modes, we know from many discussions of
them, were
--the Dorian, older, manly, solemn, warlike. This mode was
associated with the chief traditional Greek instrument, the
lyre (a small string instrument which was cradled in one
arm and picked with the other hand). A kithara was a large
string instrument of the same nature.
--the Phrygian, newer (but already common in the 400's B.C.),
softer, exciting, sensuous. This mode was associated with
the aulos, a woodwind instrument. The name Phrygian
indicates an origin in Asia Minor, and the style was
criticized by many Greek conservatives as too uncontrolled
for Greek tastes. In legend, Athena had discovered the
aulos but she threw it away in disgust. The aulos was
picked up by a Phrygian satyr named Marsyas, who challenged
Apollo, who had given Greece the lyre, to a contest. The
contest between Marsyas with the aulos and Apollo with the
lyre was a favorite theme for Greek painting and sculpture.
Marsyas (naturally) lost, and in punishment was flayed alive.
--the Lydian (also indicating an origin in Asia Minor),
pleasant and sentimental, for girls.

    Both Plato and Aristotle believed that everyone would
be better off without the aulos--its emotional appeal seems
to have annoyed them. Plato criticized the Phrygian mode,
which was associated with the aulos, but was willing to
allow it under controlled circumstances as an encouragement
to relaxation. Aristotle criticized Plato on this point,
saying that the only sensible course was to get rid of the
whole thing. It is clear from this, as it is from many
other sources, that music was taken very seriously and
that, in the usual fashion, it was treated from the moral
viewpoint in the same way as the other arts. Enjoyment
alone was not a sufficient end. Despite all the criticism,
though, the Phrygian mode triumphed--by 300 B.C., and over
the next centuries, it was the dominant mode across the
Hellenistic world.

ART/PHILOSOPHY/LITERATURE IN THE HELLENISTIC AGE
300–100 B.C.

Inevitably, cultural forms were heavily influenced by
the different world which existed in the eastern Mediterranean after the conquests of Alexander of Macedon. The
spirit of those forms between 300 and 100 B.C. was very
different from the habits of the 400's B.C., the golden age
of Classical Greece. For all that, the cultural forms of
the dominant or ruling groups in the Hellenistic Age were
still obviously Greek, and often the spirit expressed had
its origins clearly in the world of the polis before
Alexander came along. There is not a single, sharp break
between the Classical and Hellenistic periods--the second
is the triumph of certain styles and preferences which
marked the later stages of the first. We can provide a
reasonably clear outline of Hellenistic culture--but in all
areas of activity, in fact, little has survived.

ART IN THE HELLENISTIC AGE, 300–100 B.C.

In sculpture and architecture the continuity from the
300's B.C., the late Classical Period, into the Hellenistic
age is very clear. Hellenistic art is an enlargement of
tendencies we have noted in the art of the 300's B.C., in
such men as Praxiteles and Lysippus--coupled with endless
revivals of the original early Classical style of the 400's
B.C., a habit which is also found in the 300's B.C. The
spirit is emotional, the style often excessive in richness.
It is not an art likely to appeal to us much. It was the
art picked up by the Romans as they came into control of the
eastern Mediterranean--it may not have appealed much to
them, though, either.

The principal art center of the Hellenistic age was
Pergamum, a wealthy kingdom which controlled the western
coast of Asia Minor. This state established its independence of the Antigonids and Seleucids, the great Macedonian
successor-states, in the mid-200's B.C. It won respect and
prestige with its defeat of the barbarian Gauls (a Celtic
people called Galatians--we will meet them again) who swept
into Asia Minor in the mid-200's B.C. from the Danube area,
pillaging Greece and the Antigonid kingdom on the way.

Pergamum (the Pergamene kingdom) penned the Galatians in the undeveloped interior of Asia Minor. For 100 years from the mid-200's B.C. Pergamum flourished, taking a leading role in sculpture and architecture. The state protected itself against the Antigonids and Seleucids by a deliberate policy of friendship toward Rome, which was already involved in the East by 200 B.C. Pergamum thus became a very important channel through which Greek/Hellenistic art influences made themselves felt in Rome.

Pergamum, the capital city, was laid out in the grid plan which had appeared in the 400's B.C. It was centered on an acropolis, but this was dominated, in fashion typical of the new age, by the residence of the kings. In Greek fashion, though, the royal palace was no splendid or gigantic thing--it was a rambling collection of buildings. The major architectural interest was still in the temples-- the homes of the gods. There were the normal public buildings of a Greek city--temples, gymnasiums, a theater (this built about 170 B.C. and seating some 10,000). There was also a great library, located predictably in an area dedicated to Athena, the friend of reason. Libraries are an important feature of the Hellenistic age, an age when knowledge was being collected and stored. With some 200,000 "volumes" (single scrolls), the library at Pergamum ranked second only to that at Alexandria, the capital of the Ptolemies and the intellectual center of the Hellenistic world (some 500,000 scrolls).

From Pergamum we have the two most famous works of sculpture of the Hellenistic age. The first is a set of figures, in marble copies of bronze originals, from around 225 B.C. which were part of a monument commemorating the victory of Pergamum over the Gauls/Galatians. The monument rested on a cylinder some 7' high, stood the men of Pergamum, the winners. On three steps below them were the defeated Gauls. The two best-known pieces are --the Dying Gaul: a trumpeter-warrior of the Gauls, with a great wound in his side, is making ready to die. Great care is given to realistic detail--the greasy hair, the collar around the neck, the bushy hair and moustache--in the individualizing fashion we saw in the 300's B.C. The emotional content is high--the invitation to feel sympathy with the suffering is also a style from the 300's B.C.

(remember that it is the enemy that is being shown).
--the Gaul and His Wife: the Gaul knows he is beaten and
that he and his family face slavery; he has killed his wife
and is now killing himself, looking over his shoulder at
the approaching enemy. This piece may seem too melo-
dramatic and too overdone for us: the sword in the neck,
the backward glance, the stunning body (very different
from that of the Dying Gaul). In these very respects,
though, the entire composition is typical of much of the
work of the Hellenistic age--and very untypical of the
400's B.C.

The other major Hellenistic work from Pergamum is the
Altar of Zeus, from about 180 B.C. (by which time a Roman
army already had campaigned through Pergamum). This we
have largely in its original materials. The work became
very famous across the Hellenistic world. The altar is
inside a courtyard (rather than outside the temple in the
old style)--we have seen this increasing concentration on
interiors already in the 300's B.C. The structure rested
on a platform with five steps, and was arranged in a U-
shape to add to the inward-looking feeling. The building
was aimed mostly at decorative effect. An enormous frieze
ran right around the building, 7' in height and 450' long.
But the frieze was put at the bottom, to be seen--it was
the most important element. Above the frieze were columns
in the Ionic order, hardly taller than the frieze. Free-
standing statues were placed along the outer edges of the
roof. The frieze showed the battles of the gods from the
Greek past. To fill up such a large space, a great many
scenes and figures were needed. The librarians must have
helped with this, searching out little known episodes. The
names of the unfamiliar figures were added. The carving is
in very high-relief style, the figures virtually standing
out on their own, allowing a great play of light and shade,
especially against the background which was painted blue.
The technical standard of the work is very impressive. The
style is thoroughly realistic and individualistic, with a
tremendous range of emotions being shown, and a heavy
emphasis on the weird,(snakes, monsters, etc.). The visual
impact is overwhelming, but tiring--there is too much of
everything, in a way that is very Hellenistic. The
melodrama of a clever and calculated emotionalism had taken
the place of classical restraint.

Sometimes Hellenistic emotionalism is simply absurd.
A fine example is the Laocoon Group of the late 100's B.C.
(Laocoon was a Trojan leader who was destroyed, along with
his two sons, by a snake sent by Athena). Sometimes the
effect is repulsive. An example is the Old Market Woman,
from the 100's B.C., where an appealing and very "realistic"
idea, and an interesting face, are turned to strange
purpose by the careful arrangement around the breasts.
The appeal of sex had produced, through Praxiteles, the
most famous works of the 300's B.C. The same vein continued to be heavily worked through the Hellenistic period.
It produced, around 100 B.C., the Venus de Milo (of Melos),
the well-known piece in the Louvre at Paris. A female nude
of very great beauty is the Aphrodite of Cyrene, very
clearly patterned after Praxiteles but a good deal more
brazen in her appeal. On the male side, the most famous
work is the Apollo Belvedere, a Roman copy of a statue from
about 300 B.C. The trade in colossal statues, another
phenomenon of the 300's B.C., also continued to flourish.
In this connection, the most famous Hellenistic work is the
Colossus of Rhodes, a statue (now lost) of the Sun--Rhodes'
patron--from not long after 300 B.C.

It remains impossible to say much to any good purpose
about Hellenistic painting or music. Assuming that, as is
usually the case, the Romans doggedly copied Hellenistic
art, often through Pergamum, we can take the Roman paintings from Pompeii and the other towns destroyed by the
eruption of the volcano Vesuvius in 79 A.D. as indicating
the Hellenistic style. It is what we would expect--
overdone, self-consciously clever. The well-known Hercules
Finding His Infant Son Telephus, which may be a copy of a
work from Pergamum (Telephus was supposed to have founded
Pergamum), is silly enough. Look at the child: it is
Hermes and the Child Dionysius gone mad. The Hellenistic
interest in nature, which is such a strong element in the
literature of the period (see below), could find more of a
place in painting than in sculpture. Demetrius, a painter
of Alexandria in the 100's B.C., was famous for his
paintings of natural scenes (landscapes).

PHILOSOPHY/SCIENCE IN THE HELLENISTIC AGE, 300–100 B.C.

The effect of what Alexander did may have been greater in philosophy than in any other area—it is common to say so. Certainly, he destroyed the universe of the Greek city-states, which most Greek thinkers traditionally had used as a basis for judging man. Long before Alexander, though, the Greek philosophical scene had been very diverse, with many claiming that the old concerns were a sham and/or a waste of time. We have seen this with the Sophists in the late 400's B.C. In their insistence that "Man is the measure" the Sophists had challenged both the traditional emphasis of Greek philosophy/science on the physical world rather than man and the usual argument that a man was only himself in acting as a citizen, in performing his public duties. <u>Plato</u> had tried to respond to this by in effect ignoring science to concentrate upon man while denying that man was important—an up-to-date Pythagoreanism. Men had gone on in the 300's B.C. pointing out that the philosophers had nothing useful to say. This is what Isocrates, the orator, said about Plato—it is hard not to agree with him. Revealingly, Isocrates, willing to look to common sense, was one of the few Greeks to argue in the 300's B.C. that the old age of the city-state and the active local citizenship was passing. Aristotle in effect made the same point about Plato—but his answer, which involved ignoring man except in a mad-cap way and accepting all the old cliches of the city-state, was hardly better.

A most important figure in the 300's B.C. was DIOGENES of <u>Sinope</u> in the Black Sea area. Diogenes died in 323 B.C., the same year as Alexander. He was the founder of the group known as <u>Cynics</u>. He did not offer a philosophy, an understanding of the world, but a <u>way</u> <u>of</u> <u>life</u>, a way of protecting yourself against the world. The key was to live according to nature. Now this can mean lots of things; to Diogenes, it meant an ascetic life, a life of doing without. If you don't want, you're well on the way to peace of mind. Diogenes knew how to advertise this style. He became famous for his poverty, his refusal to possess things. He lived in a "tub" in the street and he made the street his toilet (perhaps also masturbating there). This upset many Greeks, so that the name Cynic (meaning "like

dogs") was applied to the group--think of what dogs will
do in public. Bad manners, though, were only a part of
the problem. Diogenes made it plain that from his point
of view much in life was a put-on; dishonesty was everywhere; habits often were hypocritical as well as silly.
He wandered around with a lamp looking for one honest man--
a nice touch in his game. He seems to have had some
popular appeal--it's easier to do without when you don't
have--and there is no doubt that he bothered the people
at the top, including men such as Plato whom he despised,
who made up the rules. Diogenes attacked slavery, seeing
it as a typical example of society's evil; men talked a
lot of rubbish about "the people" while enslaving most of
human race. Plato, likewise, could write with endless
enthusiasm about the Good while keeping mankind in chains.

Diogenes was too extreme for his movement to survive
without alteration; but he had very great influence. After
him, thinkers were much more likely to keep man at the
center of things and to be conscious of the evils of
society. Diogenes was a much greater force for the good
in our sense of the word than were Plato and Socrates.
The next step was for men to tone-down Diogenes' message
and to integrate it with traditional philosophy/science.

This was the work of ZENO (336-264 B.C.). From Cyprus,
Zeno may have had some Phoenician (non-Greek) blood in him.
Around 310 B.C. he set up a school in Athens. The members
are called STOICS, after the covered walkway (stoa) by the
Agora where Zeno taught. In the same way, his system is
known as STOICISM. We have bare fragments of what Zeno had
to say, and hardly more from his followers for many generations. This is an odd situation--our knowledge of
Stoicism is mostly drawn from what Roman Stoics said about
it much later, and we cannot do much more than guess at
what the original system was like.

Zeno offered mostly a rule of life, but from the beginning he founded it on a grand interpretation of the entire
physical world in the old-fashioned Greek manner. He was a
great admirer of Diogenes, and early Stoics probably had
much sympathy with Cynic views and have been similarly
critical about society. Zeno was followed as head of the

movement by Cleanthes, of Assos in northwest Asia Minor, who was leader from 264-232 B.C. The next head (232-204 B.C.), was Chrysippus, from Tarsus in Cilicia (the city of St. Paul). Chrysippus seems to have played a big role in redirecting Stoicism, something reflected in his reputation as the "2nd Founder." It is likely that he made Stoicism much more ornately philosophical in the traditional Greek sense and that he played down the criticism of society. Certainly, with time, Stoicism became acceptable to and popular with the kings and their adivsors who ruled the eastern Mediterranean--and with the Roman Senate, which knew how to spot an undesirable idea from a great distance.

We can describe the Stoicism of, say, 200 B.C. in the following general manner:
--one energizing principle existed; this could be called God, Nature, the Divine Fire, etc. It was universal; it gave order to everything, entering into and giving life to passive matter like a fiery breath. The greatest works of this force are the sun and the stars. The Stoics talked about this principle, this Divine Fire, mysteriously, and with devotion, but it was a purely material thing (so that two bodies are in the same place--the energizing matter, from this Divine Fire, and the passive matter). The fiery breath, the Divine Fire, is in everything. It is the soul in man. That soul is blank at first (that is, we know nothing at first) but it has the power to reason, which power it uses to test the other things (pieces of matter) with which it comes into contact. This is all part of Stoic materialism: bodies, the Divine Fire, the soul, the mind--all are material. The Stoics also believed that this world was destroyed and then recreated--exact in every detail--endlessly in cycles; Socrates would exist again.

The interest to us of the Stoics lies in the way they handled the God, Nature, the one principle, and the lessons they drew from it. Everything was for the best, it seemed--an indication that the principle was predictable and served the good (and something that Diogenes would have found absurd). For this reason, man must obey Fate (the operations of the principle), but he can choose how to obey--he can be false to the principle. Such false action will result usually from following the senses (an honorable and long tradition behind that!); emotions are false reason--

389

ask people lower down to feel sorry for him. The Stoic
insistence that everything was individual, that everything
is one and distinct, emphasized a fragmentation, an
individualism, which was very much in the interest of the
kings of the day. This was close to the ultimate absurd-
ity--a brotherhood of all which left each human alone; a
sense of duty toward all which meant doing nothing for
anyone. We have seen this in the 300's B.C. It seems
likely that Stoicism had covered a lot of ground by 200
B.C.--that it had already gone most of the way toward
political respectability.

One other major line of thought picked up some of the
ideas of Diogenes in the years immediately following the
life of Alexander. This EPICUREANISM, named for its
founder EPICURUS (341-270 B.C.). Epicurus was the son of
an Athenian colonist on Samos. He moved to Athens and
eventually, around 310 B.C., opened up a "school" there,
winning a circle of followers. This group was heavily
Ionian in its early days, in contrast to the Stoics, who
were drawn from a wide area. Epicureans proved to be
more resistant to what was happening, less willing than the
Stoics to go along with the new world.

We have, for the entire Hellenistic period, only
scraps of Epicurean material. It is possible, though, to
construct an approximate outline of their system.
Epicureanism claimed to be independent, original, isolated,
something which took little from what had gone before.
There was one great exception to this rule--the atomism
which had come in the 400's B.C. and which we associate
particularly with Democritus. The aim of Epicureanism
was peace of mind. It came from within a person, and was
basically a negative freedom from pain, and trouble, and
above all fear--in particular, fear of the gods and of
possible punishment after death. Although it is common
to say that the elite of this period did not believe in
immortality or a reward/punishment system after death, it
is likely that such beliefs were widespread and that they
did affect many educated people--we have seen this kind of
thing in Plato. Epicureanism did not mean what the word
now means to us--a selfish delight in the senses (hedonism).
Rather it meant a refined enjoyment of quiet pleasures,
particularly friendship, with a high moral tone. For

they are to be wiped out. The man who is true to the
Divine Fire should be free from emotions, indifferent to
emotions. He should be above the run-of-the-mill things
of life. Such a man also will realize that he is associated with all other humans (including slaves, barbarians,
etc.), for all men have the spark of the Divine Fire
within them. A good man will not ill-treat other humans,
and he will engage in public activity in order to serve
other humans. He will not do this because he cares, but
because it is proper--it is his duty. The spark of the
Divine Fire, of God, is stronger in some people than in
others. All should do what is appropriate to their condition; there are some to lead and some to follow, some to
act properly in line with the principle and some to act
wrongly in defiance of the principle. A man who finds
that he cannot act properly should consider suicide. At
the other extreme, certain great men, kings and such have
cultivated the spark more carefully than others: they have
great responsibilities and so great privileges.

This is a very peculiar mixture. It has elements
which Diogenes could have agreed with. (1) All men are
brothers. This broke right out of the mold of the city-
state and offered sympathy to ordinary people and slaves.
This was the feeling of a "natural law" coming from the
principle and giving all men some basic rights and duties
in common. Stoics never lost the feeling of brotherhood,
but the expression of human solidarity fairly soon became
largely ritual--a thing to say and put away. (2) A man
should take care of himself and be above the material and
emotional cares of life. Of course, this tended to run
counter to the sense of human brotherhood. Indifference
to the emotions meant that a man would do his duty coldly,
as a matter of form, not "to do good." More noticeable,
though, are the elements which made Stoicism more and more
acceptable at the top: the belief that things must be the
way they are, that power should rest in the hands of a
certain few men. Indifference to material things had become
a reason for not changing rather than for rejecting society
and its values (save in the insistence on being a loner,
an individual, with the preferred style of criticizing the
baubles of the world). This was something a ruler could
live with and feel good with: he was rightly in charge,
he did not have to change anything, he was entitled to

391

Epicureans, most of the more blatant pleasures were more
bother than they were worth; they were not as desirable
as they looked. Incidentally, a minor <u>Hedonist</u> movement
did come along in philosophy in the 200's B.C., but even
the Hedonists soon found that fun, especially of the
physical kind, was a less reliable source of pleasure than
quiet contemplation. In the pursuit of peace of mind, it
recommended avoiding politics, public service, almost all
commitments. It had no absolute standards (which is people
came to accuse it of encouraging all sorts of pleasures),
but it supported customary rules as a way of avoiding
trouble, of preserving peace of mind.

Epicureans, like Stoics, were thorough materialists—
rejecting the tradition which had run from Pythagoras
through Plato. However, unlike the Stoics, they insisted
that the <u>senses</u> were always <u>right</u>—error came from judgment.
This was where atomism was involved. Sensation derived
from atoms thrown off things which penetrated the mind
(itself made of atoms). A thing was very likely to be as
it seemed to the senses. This led Epicurus into the famous
claim that the sun probably was about as large as it
appeared to the eye—a claim people have made fun of ever
since, but one certainly no sillier than a lot of things
Plato said. In any case, as a materialist, Epicurus'
claims could be judged in terms of fact—Plato, being an
idealist, always had an answer. Epicurus believed that
the gods exist. He reasoned that everyone believes in
them, that we can "picture" them (our senses at work). But
the gods do nothing, and they are not concerned with or
involved in man's activities. Nor is there any Fate, any
kind of supervising authority. All that is the heavens
are just chance collections of atoms, like man. A wise
man can "commune" with the gods in the sense of relating
spiritually to them, drawing example from them. Death,
though, for all men brings just a breaking up of the body.

Epicureans wanted to avoid the determinism of atomism—
that atoms had to follow patterns, laws, etc., of movement
and combination. This kind of argument, they thought, was
another way of introducing Fate and the fear which would
come with it. So they developed the doctrine of <u>swerve</u>.
Atoms veer, swerve, do crazy, unpredictable things. As
a result, no natural law, no consistent or predictable

rights of the Stoic Kind, can be established. No thing can
be taken for granted save what the senses tell us. To us
it is hard to see the attractiveness of this kind of
argument. Like Epicurus' insistence that there is no after-
life, it seems to cater to the opposite of what we would
think he would expect people to want—the assurance of
salvation, the idea that things are ordered and predictable.
Total uncertainty is a strange thing to rely on—but it
makes sense of Epicurus' suggestion that we withdraw from
the world into ourselves and our friends as best we can.

Under most circumstances, Epicureanism was not likely
to be much bother to anyone. Epicurus did allow women and
slaves into his group, and there seems to have a network
of such groups, as there was among the Stoics, but the
basic insistence on turning aside from the world was too
clear and strong to make the group troublesome. The state
could get away with anything, for the Epicurean answer to
evil was to turn aside from it. The Epicurean dislike
for the state and for public life as basically foolish and
meaningless might be annoying, but it could not be dangerous. Nor could the insistence that the gods had nothing
to do with anything—educated people had been saying that
for a long time.

What Cynics, Stoics, and Epicureans all had, each
group from its own vantage-point, was a turning away from
society to concentrate on the individual. This certainly
started with Diogenes and the Cynics as a way of protesting society and the futile traditions of the old ways.
With Stoics, however, at least after a while, and with
Epicureans from the start, the individualism was in large
part an escape, a way of ignoring reality and the obligations of active citizenship. It is common to accuse both
schools of deliberately seeking these purposes, in order
to provide a way to survive under the god-kings after
Alexander who did not want informed or active citizens. To
a degree, this is reasonable—as long as it is remembered
that we would hardly accuse Plato or Aristotle of encouraging any beyond a select few to assert themselves. The
Epicurean did this flatly, keeping a hint of religious and
social criticism; the Stoic did it much more indirectly
keeping up a line about public service and the brotherhood
of man and natural rights. From the point of view of a

slave or a peasant, it takes little imagination to realize
that duty and brotherhood could easily become knowing your
place and putting up with it--and that, after a while, that
is what they did become. There was little to either
Stoicism or Epicureanism to bother the state or enthuse
the people; their political content was very limited, their
emotional appeal was very weak.

Stoicism and Epicureanism were the great new schools
of the Hellenistic period. It is usual to see them as
inferior systems, the work of pygmies coming after giants.
There is no way to say, truly, the immediate evidence of
their founders being so slight--if we had to judge Plato by
his followers we would have a very slight opinion of him.
Stoicism, whatever it became with time, seems to have been
a serious effort in the grand Greek tradition, and certainly one that was a good deal more comprehensible and
coherent than what Plato had to say. Both systems were
influential, but they did not at all monopolize intellectual activity. Some, particularly those in the tradition of
Plato, tried to go their own way. We know little about
them but they seem to have spent a good deal of their time
in practice criticizing the newer schools, as well as those
who followed Aristotle. For this reason they are known as
Sceptics (doubters). They played a major part in the
Hellenistic age in giving Greek, and particularly Athenian,
philosophy a bad name for hair-splitting and word-mongering. Both Socrates and Plato had been geniuses at that.
The most famous of these Sceptic Platonists in Carneades
in the 100's B.C. (died 129 B.C.). Not until after 100 B.C.
did Platonism revive.

A good many of the educated during the Hellenistic
period took a form of escape which was even more direct
than Epicureanism. This was the path of science, which
had been pointed out by Aristotle in the late 300's B.C.
as he tired of Plato. This was a desirably inward-looking,
self-centered kind of pursuit--and one which was very safe.
So the Hellenistic age quickly became obsessed with
cataloguing and ordering knowledge--libraries, encyclopedias,
text-books, are all very typical characteristics of the
period. Alexandria quickly became the busiest center of
this kind of activity. Some of the intellectual achievements which resulted were very impressive. This was true

394

particularly in math; Euclid of Alexandria around 300 B.C. catalogued and explained his culture's knowledge of the subject in a work that kept its importance for many centuries. The emphasis on math was no accident. You should know by now that the subject held a special attraction for the Greeks. The scholars of the Hellenistic age generally had the same weaknesses as those of the earlier Classical period. They preferred the theoretical, the abstract, to the scientific, the experimental. They were often hardly scientists at all in our sense. Like Aristotle, they seldom bothered about whether their reasonings could be made to fit reality. They were encouraged in this attitude by the values of their society, which ranked thinking ahead of doing: philosophy (and thus math) was gentlemanly, acceptable; science, experimentation, engineering, were not.

As a result, the period is to us unsatisfying. It produced some tremendous increases in theoretical knowledge, but the practical consequences were in general disappointingly slim. The fascination with astronomy, a notable branch of math and one loaded with mystic implications for Greeks since Plato, produced the beginnings of spherical geometry and trigonometry (Apollonius, 260-170 B.C.). The discovery was made that tides were caused by the moon, not the sun; the first modern calendar was developed at Alexandria, complete with Leap Year. It was from Alexander that Caesar took his (and our) calendar in the 40's B.C. It was established that the world was definitely more or less round, and its diameter was calculated to within 50 miles (Eratosthenes of Cyrene, died 194 B.C.). Hipparchus in the 100's B.C. discovered the movement of the equinoxes. Aristarchus of Samos, 320-250 B.C., developed the heliocentric (sun at the center) theory of our universe. And yet, before many generations had passed, astronomy had picked up heavy doses of astrology (magical knowledge of the heavens) and had become bogged down in the problems of measuring the paths and relationships of the planets which revolved around the earth. Heliocentricity had simply been abandoned, for geocentricity—a revolving but otherwise stationary earth at the center of things. This was the greatest of all triumphs of theory over sense and fact—a victory for Aristotle and the insistence that the earth must be at the center because it is the most important. They were looking for "meaning" in the universe—

how the planets "related" to earth--rather than for knowledge. To serve their purposes, they had to invent endless
"eccentric" movements by the planets and the sun to explain
why they didn't behave the way they "should." It seems
to have bothered them hardly at all that their mathematical
systems of motion were not realized physically. They were
aware, for example, that little of what they said about the
sun made much sense; but they decided to "explain away"
the problem. For this reason, the great handbook of
astronomy by the Egyptian Ptolemy, produced in the 100's
A.D., is the most characteristic of all the products of
Hellenistic learning. A summary of all "progress" in
astronomy, it is a tragedy of lost opportunity.

Much the same thing seems to have happened in medicine,
the scientific pride of Classical Greece--although in
medicine our chain of evidence is a good deal less secure.
Alexandria became in the 200's B.C., the early Hellenistic
age, the center of a great school of medicine. The two
great names associated with that school in the 200's B.C.
are Herophilus of Chalcedon and Erasistratus of Antioch.
These two men gave a great boost to scientific medicine
and are often described as the founders of anatomy and
physiology. We know little about what happened after that
until the period of Galen in the 100's A.D. Galen is the
equivalent in medicine to Ptolemy, his near-contemporary,
in astronomy. He is the summarizer of knowledge. Much of
his work survived and gave Galen a reputation second only
to that of Hippocrates in Classical medicine. Galen was
from Pergamum, but after study in Alexandria he became a
society physician, looking after emperors and aristocrats.
He claimed that "experiment is tedious and hard but it
leads to the truth." Generally, experiment was too bothersome for Galen. He made some discoveries, particularly
that the arteries contained blood rather than air, but he
was dissecting animals rather than people (the latter being
illegal) and he was very much prone both to jump to conclusions and to flatly disregard the evidence if it did not
show what it "should." He was, in other words, a terrible
scientist. Galen also was convinced that all the parts
and functions of the body expressed some plan of the gods.
In treatment, unlike Hippocrates, Galen liked to recommend
a wild variety of drugs. One of his victims was the Roman
emperor Marcus Aurelius (161-180 A.D.), who was doped up

by Galen against probably an ulcer problem. Like astronomy, medicine was getting ready to turn itself into magic.

The same thing happened to what we can call engineering in the Hellenistic age. Early on, there were some
useful inventions. But practical progress tended to stop
here too. The most instructive career here is that of
ARCHIMEDES of Syracuse, the greatest name in science during
the 200's B.C. Archimedes was well known for both
contributions to theory and practical inventions. He
developed a careful method for determining areas and
volumes, laying the foundations of our calculus. He
established the idea of upward force against a body when
it is immersed in a liquid. He also worked out a system
for establishing the equilibrium rule of a lever. His
most famous practical devices were a water screw--a pump
to lift water from mines, and systems of compound pulleys
and levers to raise heavy objects. He is said to have used
his knowledge of light rays to work up a series of gigantic
concave mirrors with which he directed the sun's force
on to Roman ships which were attacking Syracuse, causing
them to burn. Plutarch reported, however, that Archimedes
was ashamed of his engines, seeing them as beneath the
dignity of a gentleman.

The other great name in Hellenistic mechanics was
Hero, who left Greece to establish himself at Alexandria
in perhaps the first Century A.D. Hero wrote a textbook
of engineering. He also made several important innovations:
a water clock, a screw cutter (which would have allowed
really sound machinery to be made), and most dramatically
a steam (turbine) engine--using heated water to provide
energy. Most practical progress was made in the study
and uses of water (hydrostatics) in the Hellenistic age
than in any other area of science. What became of Hero's
idea of steam power has served ever since as a case study
in what was "wrong" (for us) with the attitudes of the
Hellenistic period. Apparently no one could think of any
general use for the idea. It was employed for little
more than to provide a "magic" way of opening temple
doors when a fire was lit on the altar.

Hero himself seems to have had his doubts about what
he was doing. He noted that the force saved by a device

was negated by a proportional lengthening of the path over which force must be applied. With time, this grew into the argument that no economy of labor can be effected—that what you save on the swings, you lose on the roundabout. This is not much of an attitude for men involved in such lines of work.

What we notice about mechanics in this period is that such gadgets as were produced were not put to very good purpose—and that, by the time of Christ, the supply of new ideas and inventions had pretty well dried up. By then, of course, as in Ptolemy's and Galen's day (the 100's A.D.), the Romans ran the Mediterranean world. Many people have been struck by the slow rate of technological progress under a people allegedly so practical-minded as the Romans. It hardly seems surprising to find the Romans uninterested in theory, but we somehow expect them to have been eager to put knowledge (generally the knowledge of others, the Greeks) to good purpose. To some degree, they did. We can note:
—water mills, brought into general use from Greece or Asia Minor from about 100 B.C. Even here, though, the water wheel was not used to drive bellows or hammers (to serve industrial purposes).
—Glass-blowing, coming out of Syria in the 1st century B.C. The use of glass in general, for mirrors, windows, etc., grew as the Roman period went on;
—the introduction of concrete, and specifically the brick and concrete arch, in the 100's B.C.;
—the hypocaust, a system of under-the-floor heating, devised, like concrete, by the Romans themselves, around 100 B.C.

This list is not very substantial—and it ends well before the life of Christ. It is as if the Romans early on could benefit from the practical knowledge of the Hellenistic world, and found themselves motivated by it, but that after a while innovation petered out. Did the fault lie with the Hellenistic scientists, always ready to shun the practical? Or did it lie with the Romans, who found some way of discouraging initiative?

The Romans concentrated more and more, it seems, on bigness, on just adding in size to existing techniques.

398

This is the case with their aqueducts, their gigantic
cranes (which were just compound pulleys), their military
engines (the catapult dated from the 300's B.C. and was a
Greek invention). The list of things the Romans did
not follow up on, or which they simply failed to develop,
is a long one. They put to little use their knowledge of
insulation, which permitted them to develop thermos
flasks; the same was true of their knowledge of steam
power (from Hero) which allowed them to have plumbed hot
water on tap. They did nothing about their lighting,
using the old crude oil lamps; there was no street lighting. There was no soap; freezing was unknown; the old
double yoke, which suited oxen but was ill-adapted to
horses, was kept; they took no steps to increase labor
efficiency in agriculture; writing materials, parchment/
papyrus and the ink used (which was carbon black suspended in a gum solution), remained largely unchanged;
despite their knowledge of dye stamp, they did not go on
to printing; cotton was not developed much, and the entire
textile business remained a domestic (home-based) industry--
Augustus boasted that the women of his house made the
family's clothes; they had no blast-furnaces, and could
not produce pig-iron or liquid cast-iron--when they
stumbled on cast-iron by accident, they threw it away:
there was no important advance in shipping after the
jibsail, attached to the bowsprit, came in from the
Hellenistic world by 100 B.C. Over the centuries of Rome's
power, no big new raw materials, no really new methods of
production were developed. Even military technology and
equipment remained steady over very long periods of time.

Various explanations are offered for the slow rate of
change, for the "failure" of the Greek/Roman world to make
some sort of breakthrough into a high technology period.
The favorite is the prevalence of slavery, the availabil-
ity of a great labor supply, costing little and being
easily managed. There was less need for technology;
technology would leave the slaves with nothing to do.
Other favorites in way of explanation are the social
snobbery we have noted already--the hostility toward
practical knowledge on the part of the ruling class; and,
once the Hellenistic period began, heavy control of society
by government officials who knew little beyond administration, little about business and technology, and yet were

making the decisions that determined what happened in the
economy. Whatever their more general validity, none of
these explanations can account for why there was more
change at some times than at others--specifically, why
the Hellenistic age's scientific thrust ran out of steam
as the Romans secured control of the Mediterranean, and
why the Romans seem to have been progressively less
receptive to change. Slavery, for example, seems to have
been on the decline after Christ, at the time when the
Roman Empire was growing more resistant to change. And
were the Romans more snobbish than the Greeks, so that
they objected more strongly to empirical and practical
efforts? One possible answer is that Rome changed less
as the need to change became less; if necessity is the
mother of invention, this may serve, for by the life of
Christ there was no one for Rome to fear, no one for it
to compete with. At that time, Roman writers, busy
making up their encyclopedias and text-books in the
Hellenistic fashion, still had a sharp eye for technology.
We can note Pliny the Elder (23-79 A.D.) and his Natural
History; Vitruvius, the 1st century B.C. architect and
engineer; Varro (116-27 B.C.), writing on agriculture;
as well as the Greek geographer Strabo (65-25 B.C.).
For 200 years and more, from the 1st century B.C., Rome
stood unthreatened. A lack of initiative may have been
a part of the price for such a position.

THE ROMANS AND HELLENISTIC CULTURE.

The Romans had had extensive contact with Greeks in Italy since their early days, and they had always borrowed heavily from the Greeks. By 250 B.C., the Romans had control of all the Greek settlements of south Italy and Sicily. Contact with the Greeks picked up dramatically around 200 B.C., when in the space of a few years the Romans campaigned through Greece itself and on into Asia Minor. From then on, the Romans were the dominant influence across the entire Mediterranean, although they were very slow to take actual possession of the area. Rome was growing with tremendous speed in these decades, in power and in self-esteem. With that growth came the question of what attitude to adopt toward the Hellenized culture in the East.

In fact, the resolution of this question never was in doubt. As Horace the Roman poet said in the 1st century B.C., "Captive Greece captured her crude conqueror." The Roman state adopted the practices of Hellenistic culture, in art, architecture, philosophy, and literature. As a result, the arrival of the Romans made very little cultural difference across the eastern Mediterranean--this area was from the start the most advanced part of Rome's possessions, and it remained so to the end. Rome, on the other hand, became a pipeline through which Hellenistic culture was carried to the West. At the same, the Romans took some care with what they copied. This was particularly true in philosophy and religion, areas which the Romans considered politically troublesome. They did not want to copy undesirable ideas. As a result, Hellenistic philosophy experienced a considerable change and religion remained fragmented, under the careful supervision of the state.

What happened should not surprise us. As a relatively primitive people, the Romans had been copying from the Greeks and Etruscans for so long that it was second-nature--they had no separate or distinct set of cultural forms of their own. When, by say 200 B.C., they had become wealthy enough and developed enough to experience rapid cultural change, it was inevitable that they would copy from the Greeks. What else could they have done? Nor should it surprise us that the lavish and emotional styles of the Hellenistic age were copied

401

so easily by the Romans. It was, in fact, a style which
seems to have suited the Romans quite well. They found it
possible for a long time to combine toughness and efficiency
with lavish emotionalism--Germans in our century do the same
thing. Some even early Romans work is quite surprising in
its addiction to the fancier Hellenistic forms. This was
particularly so in art and literature. In addition, it
should be kept firmly in mind that from the Romans' point of
view copying, picking up a culture, was definitely very much
what they were doing. It did not enter their minds to claim
that they were a highly cultivated or original people; they
knew better. They needed the appearance of cultural achievement, as a great power does--so they went out and got it.
Sometimes they stole it, their armies bringing back great
hoards of Greek art treasures from the East in the 100's
B.C.; sometimes they hired it, establishing a dependence on
Greek intellectuals and artists which endured; sometimes
they copied it. In many ways, they never really got the
hang of it themselves, so that often their work looks or
sounds silly. We will meet plenty of examples of this. They
did, though, make some contributions of their own, particularly in the direction of the big and the useful. Only in
literature, perhaps, and then for only a short period, did
they attain genuine originality along with careful quality.
That originality made them uneasy; it did not seem right to
them. So they soon did away with it.

The thing did not come to pass without debate and disagreement, though. The Romans of 200 B.C., as we have seen,
knew surprisingly little about their past. They did know,
however, that they had a good deal to be proud of. They made
up a past which showed themselves as terribly brave, serious,
dedicated, unselfish men, loving truth and honor and caring
little for culture. The Greeks, so highly developed, so
easily conquered, were available as the opposites of each one
of these values. Copying from the Greeks was inevitable; but
many did not care for it much, and all perhaps were agreed
that it had to be done with some care.

This debate was largely settled in the 100's B.C. during
the first few generations of heavy contact with the Hellenized
world. It was settled in favor of those who wished to copy
(the "Hellenizers"), but with enough safeguards to satisfy the
other side. The oppositon to Hellenizing was headed by Cato

402

the Elder (the Censor) who, over the course of a long life, from 234 to 149 B.C., established himself as the champion of tradition. The tradition, of course, was in many ways a bogus one, made up for the purpose by Cato and his friends. It suited them to portray a Rome in which the virtuous simplicity of primitive early days was bing undermined by the influence of the decadent cultivated Greeks. There may have been something to this; we have no way to know-- nor, for that matter, did Cato. Romans commonly saw them- selves in this fashion, whether they agreed with Cato or not. We can call Cato's side the "conservatives," since they sometimes appeared as the particular champions of the Senate and the existing political and social structure. The Greeks by this time, quite in addition to weakness, long- windedness, dishonesty, and moral degeneracy, were iden- tified by the Romans with democracy, tyranny, and monarchy-- all things that the Senate, and probably most Romans of the day, hated.

The other side, the "Hellenizers," were centered in the 100's B.C. on the Scipios: on Africanus, who had defeated Hannibal; on Aemilianus, his adopted grandson and the de- stroyer of Carthage; and, oddly, on his daughter, Cornelia, the only woman to make her mark in the entire course of the Roman Republic. Both sides, naturally, were concentrated in the Senate. We must be careful not to exaggerate the differences between these groups. Roman public life, as we have seen, was generally surprisingly low-key. Both sides for long were united in support of the Senate oligarchy.

The argument developed toward 200 B.C., when Rome was tested severely by Carthage in the 2nd Punic War and when it found itself acquiring influence in the East. Scipio Africanus, we have seen, the great military hero of the day, was suspected of desiring an unreasonable amount of power for himself. His taste for things Greek was used to add to this impression--tyranny/dictatorship was something Greek. We cannot say much about Africanus or the charges against him (which included the claim that he shaved too closely, an apparent indication of moral decadence). Later generations of Romans wondered at the simple nature of Scipio's country home at Liternum (where, it will be remembered, he insisted on being buried). In his own day, his wife, of the Aemilii, was known for her oldfashioned virtues and her plain styles.

Scipio's daughter, Cornelia, is barely more than a name to us. She was a patron of culture. We know that she refused to marry the Ptolemaic king of Egypt after her husband, Sempronius Gracchus, died. But she was not a figure of scandal or of notorious decadence. Her role as the mother of the Gracchi brothers did something in later generations to put her on this side of the issue--"reformers" such as her sons could easily be made to look like another result of Greek influence, even though there was a long tradition of them in Roman public life. Scipio Aemilianus is a more substantial figure to us in this connection. A man of charm and wit in his own right, he actively supported the Hellenizing influence, surrounding himself with a "Greek circle" of admirers. Personally, though, he had a reputation for integrity, decency, and fairness, and in politics, as we saw, he was hardly a radical influence. In the next century, Aemilianus was described by Cicero as the ideal statesman. Cicero was a man who knew a threat to the system when he saw one; he was very critical of the Gracchi brothers. There does not seem to be much to any of this.

By the 180's B.C., Cato had emerged as the great anti-Hellenizer. Again, we must be careful not to exaggerate what this meant. Cato was a new man, from a wealthy Tusculum framing family. Puritanical in his own life style, he was also greedy, ruthless, and very vindictive; he could carry a grudge with a vengeance, most clearly in the case of Carthage. One thing which upset him was the growing prominence and freedom of Roman women--which Cato knew how to blame on the Greeks and which he represented as a sign of rot. Women were dressing too flashily, getting divorced too easily, attending public entertainments. Happily for Cato they couldn's get their hands on cigarettes. Cornelia may have had something to do with his anger in this connection. As censor of 184 B.C. he obtained a tax on extravagance. In 169 B.C. he secured a return to the old property laws, which were more severe on women. None of this seems to have had much effect. The laws against flashy tastes (sumptuary laws), of which several were passed, were simply ignored; the laws on property were easily evaded. Wealth, and women, continued their "advance." Cato also tried very hard to establish an independent Latin literature (not philosophy--for him, that was beyond contempt). He wrote a great deal, including a lost

404

history of Rome, the first in Latin (this must have been a wonderful thing). We have little beyond his work on agriculture, On Farming, made public about 160 B.C. toward the end of his life. In this, the earliest Latin prose work which still exists, the style is archaic, simple, consciously different from the flashy Hellenistic tastes of the day. He also had some influence on oratory in the same simple direction--at least for a while.

Cato won some victories (including the disgrace of Africanus)but he lost the war. By the 1st century B.C. Roman society was lavishly wealthy and extensively Hellenized. The surrender of the "traditionalists," however, was not total by any means. The Romans remained resistant to some of the style and a good deal of the content of the Hellenistic, and they made their own contributions.

ROMAN ART, FROM 200 B.C. TO AUGUSTUS.

Already by the 100's B.C., when we are first able to say something to purpose about Roman art, it was a hodgepodge of the various Hellenistic styles in combination with the Italian-Etruscan habits and preferences. It combined severity, which we may think of as Roman, with intense and brilliant coloring and a desire to decorate everything, to fill up space--a definite Hellenistic trait. The Romans put paint and statues everywhere.

Architecture.
The traditional Roman form for public buildings, temples specifically, was derived from the Etruscans. It featured raised podiums for the buildings, a strong directional basis, with the building facing flatly to the front and approached up a flight of steps, and a deep vestibule with many columns. The (Tuscan) columns were short and unfluted. Another architectural form which already flourished at this time was the free-standing monumental arch. The earliest we know about (two built in 196 B.C.) have not survived. This form had a great future before it. Early building materials were huge, hewn blocks of stone in layers. There was also already a common use of arches, made of wedge-shaped blocks. The arch was found in the East, but at Pergamum for example it was used primarily for gateways, for drains, etc. The Romans from the start were much less tied to the preferred Greek post-and-lintel pattern. In the 100's B.C. the Romans

discovered concrete, adding bits of broken stone to cement--
one of their great practical achievements. This may have
occurred early in the 100's B.C., although the use of
concrete was not widespread until the late 100's B.C. By
mixing concrete in among the blocks or bricks with which
they built their arches, the Roman could produce an arch
which exerted pressure downwards rather than to the side
and so could sustain great weight without needing to be
buttressed. This allowed them to build vaults and arches
of great size.

        Among the work of this period which survives we can
note the following:
--175 B.C.?: an Ionic temple at Rome, which included the
customary Roman features of a high podium, frontal direction,
and a large vestibule.
--144 B.C.: the first aqueduct at Rome with arched, high-
level sections of length. This is the 36-miles long Aqua
Marcia. The channel was lined with concrete; the material
was not yet used in the arches. There were aqueducts in
the East. Pergamum, for example, built one in the mid-100's
B.C.
--125 B.C.?: remnants of the Marcian Gate at Perugia.
This combined Corinthian columns with arches.
--120 B.C.?: the basilica at Pompeii. A basilica was a
public hall, for government business, etc. It was a Greek
idea. Cato the Censor built the first basilica at Rome in
184 B.C., during his censorship, but it has not survived.
--109 B.C.: the great Milvian Bridge across the Tiber at
Rome, with its wide-spanned arches.
--100 B.C.?: Doric temple at Cori, with the standard
Italian features. In this case, the vestibule actually was
largely than the temple walled-building (cella) itself, so
that the latter was wider than it was deep.
--100 B.C.: a circular Corinthian temple at Tivoli, with the
standard high podium and large vestibule.
--75 B.C.?: a circular Corinthian temple at Rome, of Pentelic
marble.
--70's B.C.: the Tabularium (Records Office) of Sulla, the
most important architectural remain of the Republic. It is
of hewn stone rectangular blocks. The front offered a series
of arcades, with Doric columns engaged in the walls. The
substructure, the floors, and the ceilings, are of concrete.
The inside rooms and the stairways are barrel-vaulted. Each

of the 11 bays of the main arcaded hall is spanned by a
cross-arched vault.
--25 B.C.?: the mighty aqueduct at <u>Tarragona</u> in <u>Spain</u>. It
was built in two tiers, the top one being 700 feet long.

There was a great amount of building, although we have
very little of it. We can note the <u>Theater</u> <u>of</u> <u>Pompey</u>, built
in the 50's B.C.--a victory for those who had wanted a
permanent building for the comedy and drama. This was
located in a kind of arts center which included a building
for Senate meetings (Caesar was murdered in this in 44 B.C.).
Caesar himself was a great builder. He built a basilica
which occupied much of the western part of the old Forum or
city-center. He built a Senate-House of his own too. He
began a great new Forum, a new center for the city, which
set the example for the later dictators. This included a
shrine to Venus the Mother, from whom, through Aeneas,
Caesar and his family claimed to be descended. Unhappily,
he put a statue of Cleopatra next to that of Venus.

<u>Sculpture.</u>
Very little relief sculpture, from temples and other
public buildings, survives from the Republican period. Most
pieces seem to be simple, single compositions, with figures
side by side or in parallel rows. Beginning around 100 B.C.
we have some portrait statues, which are the best work of
the period. The interest in such portraits seems to have
been very strong among the Romans. <u>Many of them have what
seems a distinctive Roman look about them; they are direct,
severe, even aggressive, although also melancholy and
individualized in the Hellenistic fashion.</u> They are
portraits rather than types, but the subjects are generally
not identifiable. The most famous piece in this group is the
<u>Roman</u> <u>Couple</u>, of 75-50 B.C., which may be Cato and his wife.
They are hard but sad--and they hold hands. We can also note
the severe <u>Old</u> <u>Woman</u>. By this time, the Romans had developed
the habit of doing heads more frequently than the entire
body--an interesting emphasis upon individual character. The
level of technique is uneven and far from brilliant. A copy
of the 1st century B.C. statue of Apollo with the cithara
indicates the limitations on skill at this time. The entire
concept of the piece is ridiculous.

Painting.

It is clear enough that the Romans were given to an extensive use of wall paintings in their public buildings and their homes. However, we have very little of such work from the Republican period. Early work seems to have been mostly patterns, changing in the first century B.C. toward the predictable Hellenistic subjects--nature, gods, myths, etc. One interesting device found even then was the trompe l'oeil (deceiving the eye)--a painting designed to give the appearance of being a window. This was to being a little sense of relief into the many windowless rooms in Roman houses. The basic house plan for the better off (the poor in the cities lived in tenement houses) was still the old atrium-plan, a house looking closed, like a fort, to the outside, without windows, and was centered on an atrium, a blend of front-hall and courtyard. The atrium also held the family statues and religious objects. Many of the individual rooms were small and without windows. Taking their lighting still from primitive oil-lamps (this was an area in which they did not advance), such rooms were bleak and can have been used for little except sleeping. Wall-painting was a way of giving life to such rooms. Some of these paintings were done on wood panels, with water colors or encaustic (a process of wax painting in which heat is used to fix the colors). Painting put directly on to the walls was done in watercolor on wet stucco (plaster), and was bound by a mixture of lime, milk, egg, and gum.

ROMAN PHILOSOPHY, FROM 200 B.C. TO AUGUSTUS.

The Romans copied Greek/Hellenistic philosophy as they copied art. They did it very unconvincingly, though, never being sure that it was worth the bother. It was beyond the Romans to generate "philosophies" on their own--something they seem to have been well aware of, and a quality they found quite admirable in themselves. Through the entire course of Rome's existence, no Roman philosophical system ever developed. Educated Romans, in so far as they felt the need for philosophy at all, got along by picking up a hodge-podge of Hellenistic ideas. The copying was by no means entirely mindless, however. More than art, philosophy was potentially dangerous--socially and politically. To be acceptable to Romans, philosophy had to be made useless and pointless. The Republic's ruling class did a wonderful job

of this in the last 200 years before Christ--often aided,
it must be said, by the eagerness of the philosophers to
undergo mind-cleansing (the Roman state was a very poor
place to be independent-minded). The job was done so
efficiently that in the great crisis of the 1st century B.C.,
when aristocracy gave way to tyranny, philosophy was not
involved at all--nor did it occur to Romans that it should
be.

Epicureanism found the going hardest, mostly because of
its insistence that the gods had nothing to do with anything.
This was offensive to tradition-minded Romans, and very
offensive to the Senate ruling class, which relied heavily
on the gods, old and new, to help it keep control in the
state. We have seen how the Senate used religion, kept it
under careful control, cleverly brought in new gods when a
booster was needed. As Polybius said in the 100's B.C.:

I dare to say that what all others make fun of is what
lies at the basis of Rome's greatness--superstition. This
thing can be seen everywhere in their public and private
lives, with every trick to impress the mind, in a way that
could not be improved on. Many people may not understand
this; I believe that it is done to impress the masses.

Epicureanism did produce in this period the one Roman
classic of philosophy, the On the Nature of Things by
LUCRETIUS (95-55 B.C. approximately). This very emotional
poem, which ranks with Virgil's Aeneid as the chief work of
Latin poetry, is in fact our main source of information as
to what Epicureanism was--even though it comes 200 and more
years after the system was founded. Lucretius puts heavy
stress on the abuse of religion, the evils of fear and superstition, in the usual Epicurean way.

He might as well not have bothered. By his day, already,
Epicureanism seems to have been on its last legs. As early
as 173 B.C. the Senate had made its preferences known by
expelling the Epicurean philosophers from Rome. By the 1st
century B.C. Epicureanism had for the most part, despite
Lucretius, either withered away or turned into the hedonism
with which its enemies liked to associate it. As hedonism,
it had a certain popularity in the Roman aristocracy in the
last decades before Christ. Sulla, a man with a wonderful

reputation for pleasing himself, was an Epicurean; so was Caesar (who gave himself lots of birthday parties because he liked birthdays). Nothing in this had anything to do with what Epicurus would have recognized as Epicureanism.

Stoicism did better, becoming a favorite with many Romans, so that it can be said that if Romans did have a philosophy in this period, it was Stoicism. We have seen already how well Stoicism had prepared itself by the 100's B.C. for approval by Romans. Panaetius of Rhodes, the chief Stoic of the 100's B.C., was a familiar figure at Rome and he seems to have played a major part in continuing to reshape the system to the requirements of Rome. In general terms, much of the philosophical content of Stoicism, its physical theory, etc., was deemphasized, even abandoned, and its "social" content (the brotherhood of man, the natural law, the sympathy with the downtrodden, etc.) was allowed to become very little more than a token. What was left was a moral code which seemed both hard and sympathetic (take care of yourself, do your duty, recognize the community of men) while it left things much as they were, and which sounded like a philosophy. The insistence that this was the best of all worlds, that the Roman power was inevitable and to be accepted, was the ultimate gift of Stoicism to Rome.

There were still hints of social criticism about Stoicism in the 100's B.C. Scipio Aemilianus was criticized for encouraging Stoicism (Panaetius was associated with him), and it was suggested that those around Scipio held an unfortunate belief in natural justice--that is, reform; Aemilianus clearly did not do much more than talk, if he did that. Similarly, men noted that Tiberius Gracchus, the first of the great friends of the people (133 B.C.), had had a Stoic teacher. As late as 161 B.C., the Senate ordered all teachers of philosophy out of Rome--the Stoics among them.

These strands of radicalism were relics. The next major Stoic, the Greek Posidonius (135-50 B.C.), a pupil of Panaetius at Athens, completed the process of making Stoicism acceptable at Rome. We have only fragments of his writings. Stoicism had become a gratifying system of mental training and moral conduct, now associated, thanks to Posidonius, with a good dose of Platonic idealism. So the Stoic could now talk on about the mystic link between man and the cosmos, between our

410

souls and the Divine Fire into which they will return.
There was now the possibility of immortality (joining the
Divine Fire, as it were personal), and the force watched over
things on earth almost as if it had a will. This left as
the major object in life the contemplation of the order and
truth (again personal) which the Fire brought into the
world--a substantial qualification of the old encouragement
of public activity. From now on, not surprisingly, Stoicism
had a substantial dose of superstition, of astrology (magic)
about it. This was diverse enough, and innocuous enough, to
appeal to a wide range of types, including the most bullheaded
opponents of change. Cato the Younger, for example, the
great champion of the late days of the Republic, was a Stoic--
he was attracted probably by both the sense of duty and the
assurance that duty was not much more than going seriously
about what you were going to do anyway. Self-interest was
fine--as long as you pushed it hard.

There was, so far as the Romans were concerned, nothing
left in Stoicism that was worth calling a philosophy--a
desirable state of affairs. The finest example of the Roman
Stoic type of the last decades before Christ is <u>Cicero</u>, who
lost his life in the civil wars which put an end to the
Republic. We have an immense amount of material from Cicero,
particularly his speeches and his letters. He was a noted
stylist, in both the spoken and the written word--a sort of
Roman Sophist, save that Cicero was strong on conscience.
He refers all the time to natural law, the universal brotherhood of man, the spark of the divine which is in us all--the
usual Stoic routine. He urges constantly that people should
do their duty and serve their fellow man. It takes a moment
to realize that it all amounts to very little besides a
device for convincing yourself that you are alright. Cicero
was a strong social and political conservative. He probably
did not believe in immortality (he discussed this in letters
after his daughter died in childbirth), and he could not
involve himself in the more superstitious elements of religion,
but he was keenly aware of the value of religious lies in
controlling the population and he does not bother to hide the
knowledge. Usually Cicero was willing to admit that he was
no philosopher--there was no room for one in Roman Stoicism.

Given the predicament of philosophy, men reasonably
tended to stay away from it. Cicero is an example. Posidonius

411

himself, interestingly, wrote a large history of Rome (from 146 B.C., where Polybius' work left off)--an odd way for a philosopher to spend his time, but a safe one. He was also a geographer. Many of Rome's best minds tended to go into such subjects, things practical and reasonably safe. The greatest intellectual of the late Republic perhaps was <u>Varro</u> (116-27 B.C.), who was primarily an antiquarian (one who studies old times and things). He, too, was a Stoic, and a strong supporter of the established order.

ITALY

The Roman Empire was the result of a most remarkable
achievement: the conquest, over a period of 500 years, of
the entire Mediterranean world by a single town, Rome. Rome
is in Italy, immediately to the west of Greece and squarely
in the middle of the Mediterranean. The area of mainland
Italy south of the Alps, the mountain chain which runs
around the northern end of Italy in a semicircle, is about
700 miles long and includes some 95,000 square miles--a
little less than twice the size of North Carolina or New
York.

Italy is more favored by nature than Greece. The climate is Mediterranean, except in the valley of the Po river
to the north. The winters are mild, usually bright and windy
(although it can snow at Rome); the summers are reasonably
wet, the summer drought short (in Rome it lasts about one
month). There is generally more vegetation and better soil
than in Greece. There are some sizable stretches of rich
soil,beyond anything to be found in Greece. As a result,
Italy was and is able to support a much larger population
than in Greece -- something that was very important in the
development of Rome. The best farming area is the valley of
the Po, which has something of a continental climate, with
sharper winters and more rainfall than the rest of the peninsula, as well as a constant supply of water from the Alps.
There is also a volcanic lowland district, with rich soil and
good rainfall, which reaches from southern Tuscany to the
Bay of Naples along the west coast. The volcanoes had long
been extinct in the age of Rome; the exception was Vesuvius,
the chief volcano in the region, which rumbled in 63 A.D. and
then erupted in 79 A.D., burying Pompeii and other towns
close by. Rome is in this volcanic district, in the small
region known as Latium, or land of the Latins, the people to
which the Romans belonged. Latium is an area some 30 miles
deep and 60 miles long between Tuscany to the north and
Campania to the south.

Italy has few mineral riches, except for copper and a
little iron in northern Tuscany. There are also few good
harbors, a point on which Italy is less fortunate than Greece.
The exceptions are Genoa, La Spezia, Brindisi, and Taranto --
none of them within easy reach of Rome. The river mouths are

413

dangerous; with no strong tidal movement to carry away the river deposits, they silt up. The two big rivers, the Po and the Tiber, have never been open to large ships. Ostia, the port for Rome, had to be built away from the mouth of the Tiber.

There is excellent pasturage in the Apennines, the mountain chain which makes the backbone of Italy. The Apennines provide the usual interior for the northern Mediterranean lands -- mountainous, rugged, difficult. While they do not reach to 10,000 feet, the Apennines are a substantial obstacle to movement. Their rivers, variable in volume and rapid in movement, also restrict rather than aid travel. Even so, it was easier to move around in Italy than it was in Greece. The Alps, in contrast, despite the several passes which thread them, were a very important barrier to the interior in ancient times and gave Italy a certain isolation from the more primitive north.

ROME

Rome is about 15 miles from the sea, 20 by the river, at the lowest practical crossing on the Tiber before the river enters a marshy coastal plain. The Tiber lay in a deep trough at this point, with an island to assist the crossing. The city of Rome grew on the higher land above the south bank of the river on what are called the Seven Hills, so that Rome is often called the City of the Seven Hills. Four of the "hills" are actually spurs jutting out from the plateau which stretches away to the east. Between 200 and 300 feet above sea level, the higher ground stood about 100 feet above the surrounding flat land, secure against floods.

This is a very valuable site, at the most convenient crossing of Italy's second river in a rich agricultural district. The site was occupied early, perhaps as soon as fear of volcanic activity faded. We have stone and copper tools from people who lived there perhaps around 2000 B.C. At that time, though, and for long afterwards, until around 700 B.C., the area around Rome, like all parts of Italy, was very backward compared to Greece and other regions to the east. We still know very little about Italy in this early period.

414

THE BRONZE AGE IN ITALY, 1800-1000 B.C.

The primitive peoples who lived in Italy in this period
were fragmented, localized, with no kind of unity of language
or race. The Bronze Age began in Italy around 1800-1600 B.C.
Traditionally, it has been thought that this change was
introduced by newcomers who came into Italy from the outside
and who were Indo-Europeans. Two major groups of sites for
Early Bronze Age society in Italy can be identified:
1. In the Po valley to the north. There the villages were
built on wooden piles on the edges of lakes. These people
cremated their dead and had Indo-European languages. It
is likely that these people came from north of the Alps and
that settlements in the area which belong to the Middle and
Late Bronze Ages (1500-1200 B.C.).
2. The Apennine Culture, spread over a large area from
Bologna to Apulia. This had developed by about 1500 B.C.,
with good bronze work and decorated pottery by that time.
The people here, though, remained semi-nomadic and pastoral
for a long time, although by about 1200 B.C. they had settled
down to farming. These people seem to have buried their
dead. It is possible that much of the population across
this area was descended from the old Neolithic (New Stone
Age) inhabitants, with smaller numbers of outsiders as newcomers. These newcomers, perhaps Indo-Europeans bringing
the use of bronze, may have come from the east, from the
Balkans, crossing the Aegean. They may also have brought
with them the mountain dialects (the Oscan-Umbrian-Sabellian
dialects of peoples such as the Samnites and Sabines) which
we meet later and which are related to Latin, the language of
the Romans. However, these languages may date from the next
stage, the Iron Age, and from later invaders.

By the Late Bronze Age (1400-1200 B.C.), these two
groups were merging. Cremating and burying, for example,
are found together. There are traces of Bronze Age culture
at Rome by this time, from about 1400 B.C., although we cannot say what was happening there. There is a chance that
from this point the area which became Rome was permanently
settled, without a break.

We do not know how, or if, these newcomers into Italy
after 2000 B.C. were related to the Indo-Europeans who
entered Greece at about the same time and who are known to
us as the Mycenaeans. Under the influence of Crete, and

because they were perhaps entering an area which was already more developed than they were, the Mycenaeans advanced much more rapidly than the Indo-Europeans who entered backward Italy.

Through the Bronze Age, there was definitely some trading contact between Italy and the Mycenaeans. There were possibly even Mycenaean settlements in southern Italy, for example at Cumae. Later Greek legends assumed this kind of contact. King Minos of Crete was said to have settled in southern Italy, and Italy was involved in the wanderings of Odysseus and of the Argonauts. Daedalus, who was supposed to have built the labyrinth of the Minotaur on Crete, was said to have escaped to Italy (on wings made of feathers and wax) when he was forced to flee from Crete.

THE IRON AGE IN ITALY, 1000-700 B.C.

We know very little about the long period which separates these Late Bronze Age cultures in Italy from the Iron Age cultures which developed later. The Iron Age in Italy may have begun soon after 1000 B.C.; it was well under way by 750 B.C. The main Iron Age culture in Italy is called Villanovan, after an archaeological site discovered in 1853 at Villanova, four miles from Bologna. Numerous sites have since been found in that area. A second concentration of Iron Age sites is in northern Latium, in the neighborhood of Rome.

The most common calculation is that the Villanovan settlements around Bologna were the work of a new group of Indo-Europeans from the north who brought iron with them into Italy. They may have entered Italy at much the same time as Indo-European invaders were pushing Greece into its Dark Ages. Such Indo-European newcomers from the north may have pushed into the area around Rome. There is some likelihood that at more or less the same time other Indo-Europeans once again came from across the Aegean into central and southern Italy, bringing the Iron Age from another direction. The archaelogical evidence indicates a movement of people into Latium at this time from southern Italy, perhaps Apennine peoples who had been in contact with the newer Indo-European groups from across the Aegean.

416

Cremation, followed by burial of the ashes in <u>urns</u>, which is a characteristic of the Villanovan settlements, is found at Rome, but from around 800 B.C. there are again burials (inhumations), which are more characteristic of the south. Any such newcomers, from north, or south, or both, mingled with the existing population, which already contained Indo-European elements from the Bronze Age invasions, to produce in Latium the people called <u>Latins</u>, who by the 700's B.C. definitely spoke an early form of Latin, an Indo-European language related to those which developed in the Apennines.

We can think of the population of Italy in the 700's B.C. as generally Indo-European, or at least mixed with Indo-Europeans, the peoples who had come into Italy since 2000 B.C. Some primitive, non-Indo-European groups still existed, especially in Liguria, but even they seem to have picked up Indo-European languages and they were perhaps under Indo-European control. Italy was still very undeveloped, and all the peoples in the peninsula remained illiterate. Rome, and Latium generally, though, were among the most developed areas, a tribute to the agricultural advantages of the area.

THE FOUNDING OF ROME (753 B.C.)

By tradition, the <u>Latins</u> who lived across <u>Latium</u> were divided into 30 groups. The <u>Romans</u> were one of these groups. The early Latin religious center was the <u>Holy Mountain</u>, the <u>Alban Mount</u>,13 miles southeast of Rome, a 3,000 feet high extinct volcano among the Alban <u>Hills.</u> Here was the holy place of JUPITER, who was already the greatest of the Latin gods. Jupiter, "the bright one," is the counterpart to the Greek <u>Zeus,</u> although in fashion characteristic of the Latins he was at first a <u>non-personal</u> force of the heavens. He is clearly an Indo-European god; <u>Mars</u>, a very popular god all over early Italy, about whose origins and associations we are ignorant, had already lost out.

<u>Alba</u> <u>Longa</u>, close by the Holy Mountain, had a religious priority among the Latin towns, but it probably had no important political priority, although it may have been at the head of loose league of Latin towns early on. Each Latin town was essentially independent.

417

In later Roman legend, Rome was founded from this holy city of Alba Longa. In the legend of AENEAS, which was already well-established in the 400's B.C., Alba Longa was founded by Aeneas, a refugee from fallen Troy (in the 1100's B.C., therefore). Aeneas married the daughter of a King Latinus and began the Latin race. There followed a long line of kings at Alba Longa, the last of them being the father of Rhea Silvia. Rhea Silvia had twin sons, Romulus and Remus, bastards born allegedly of the god Mars. ROMULUS AND REMUS were abandoned, being thrown into the Tiber. When they were washed ashore a wolf suckled them until they were found and raised by a shepherd. The twins wished to build a town to mark where the wolf had found them, but they disagreed about the spot. Romulus founded a settlement on the Palatine hill, Remus one on the Aventine hill to the south. In a quarrel over this matter, Romulus killed Remus. He went on to become the first king of Rome, but he left the Aventine outside the city he had founded. To solve the shortage of women in his new town, Romulus and his followers stole women from the Sabine people who lived on the nearby Quirinal hill (spur). This is the episode known as the Rape of the Sabine Women. The Sabines eventually became friendly toward the Romans and the two groups merged. Romulus disappeared mysteriously one day, being taken up into the sky by his father Mars to become the god Quirinus.

Around 500 B.C. a famous bronze sculpture of a wolf was put up on the Capitoline hill at Rome. The whole legend was well-known by that time. It was not until much later, though, that the Romans settled upon 753 B.C. as the year when Romulus had founded Rome (or rather the Palatine). Believing that there had been seven kings of Rome stretching back to Romulus from the end of the monarchy around 500 B.C., Roman historians gave a generation or so to each. This placed the founding of Rome in the 700's B.C. Various more specific estimates were made until, in the first century B.C., Varro fastened upon 753 B.C. April 21 was the day selected; it still is the "birthday" of the modern city. In ancient Rome, April 21 was also devoted to the honor of Pales, protector of shepherds and their animals. For many centuries, into the days of the Roman Empire, a shepherd's hut with a thatched roof was preserved on the Palatine hill as a reminder of Romulus' early years.

418

The year 753 B.C. was selected in an act of invention; it is far too late for the first settlements at Rome, too early for real urbanization. It is likely, though, that the Palatine hill was the earliest settlement at Rome. Later, each February 15, in the festival of the Lupercalia, men who were naked except for goatskin girdles ran around the base of the Palatine to mark out and bless the old boundary. It does seem also that the Quirinal hill was settled early (remember the story of the Sabines).

THE GREEKS AND ETRUSCANS IN ITALY, 800-500 B.C.

By 700 B.C. the development of Italy was being altered and much speeded up by the arrival of two advanced peoples, the Greeks and the Etruscans. The appearance of these two groups marks the beginning of civilization in Italy:
The Greeks.
    By 800 B.C., with the Greek Dark Ages ending, Greek traders were again in contact with Italy. From then until 600 B.C. the Greeks set up a chain of settlements in eastern Sicily and along the southern and western coast of Italy from Tarentum (Taranto) to Campania. The oldest, and for long the most important, of these Greek towns was Cumae in Campania. The Greeks had an enormous cultural influence on Italy, both directly and through the Etruscans. Their political influence, however, was much weaker; the usual chaos of their city-state system kept them, here as elsewhere, from having the impact they could otherwise have had. Syracuse, in its great days in the 300's B.C. under Dionysius, had outposts as far north as the mouth of the Po, but it still had only a negligible political impact upon Italy as a whole.
The Etruscans.
    The Etruscan city-states flourished between 700 and 500 B.C. in Tuscany, from the Arno river to the Tiber and inland to the backbone of the Apennines. The word Tyrrhenian Sea comes from the Greek word for Etruscans.

We do not know who the Etruscans were. The basic question concerning them is whether they were:
--native (and so backward) Italians who developed under Greek influence;
--backward newcomers who developed under Greek influence;

419

--advanced outsiders who brought with them a civilization of
their own.

The Etruscans took their alphabet at some point from the
Greeks; the Latins and many of the peoples of the Apennines
obtained their alphabets from the Greeks through these
Etruscans. Yet, while being able to read the letters of the
Etruscan alphabet and having a number of bilingual inscriptions which include Etruscan, we cannot tell the nature of
the Etruscan language or decide whether it was an Indo-European language, as Greek and Latin were. The likelihood is
that Etruscan is not an Indo-European language.

This language problem suggests that the Etruscans were
neither Italians nor backward Indo-Europeans coming into
Italy from the north or the Balkans. The alternative is that
they came to Italy from the East already a rather highly
developed (civilized) people. In support of this alternative
we can note:
--Herodotus, the first of the great Greek historians of the
400's B.C., believed that the Etruscans had gone to Italy
from Lydia in Asia Minor in 1100-1000 B.C. as part of the
movement of peoples in the Greek Dark Ages;
--Thucydides, the great Greek historian of the late 400's
B.C., believed that the Etruscans had once lived on Lemnos
in the Aegean Sea, perhaps on their way west. Inscriptions
from Lemnos do reveal a language like that of the Etruscans.
--Many areas of Etruscan life reveal what look like oriental
influences, often existing alongside heavy Greek influences
presumably picked up in Asia Minor and/or from south Italy.
For example:
religion: The Etruscans seem to have been very religious in
ways not usually found among Greeks and Romans. There is a
persistent note of the fantastic about them. In their tombs,
which have survived while most of their towns have disappeared,the Etruscans lavishly drew the horrors of hell.
Having a strong belief in the occult, they made heavy use of
interpreting signs, such as flashes of lightning and animal
livers and entrails. They were fond of human sacrifices,
often through gladiatorial contests, which they featured in
their funerals. Many of the victims were prisoners of war.
status of women: Women occupied an important role in Etruscan art, in a way characteristic of the Minoans on Crete
but definitely not of the Greeks or Romans.

luxuriousness and sensuality: Etruscan painting, particu--
larly in their tombs, stressed the pleasures of the senses,
showing feasting, dancing, hunting, fighting. Etruscan
music and dancing were famous among Italian peoples such as
the Latins for their sensuality. The Etruscans were much
attracted to gold, as in their splendid gold jewelry. Greeks
and Romans, in contrast, liked to see themselves as disciplined people who were capable of restraining their appetites.
art: Etruscan art was a strange combination of eastern and
Greek influences. This was the period of the "orientalizing"
style in Greek art itself. Oriental, or at least non-Greek,
elements in Etruscan art, beyond those already mentioned,
can be seen in architecture. The lofty platforms and roomy
colonnaded porches of Etruscan temples are clearly not Greek.
Nor are their big and showy rock-cut tombs, the best-known
of which are at Tarquinii and Caere. Etruscan houses were
of the atrium style which is well-known to us later at Rome,
with rooms leading off from a central entranceway (the atrium). Etruscan sculpture is far from brilliant, but there
is good, highly-colored terracotta (glazed clay) work. The
most famous is a group sculpture from Veii of around 500 B.C.
called "The Contest for the Sacred Hind." This piece centers
on Apollo; the life-size Apollo, while largely Greek in shape
and manner, is gross and lively, with an amount of individual
detail, in a style not characteristic of Greek work of the
period.

The combination of the fantastic, the feminine, and the
brutal gives to Etruscan civilization a distinctly un-Greek
look. At the same time, it is difficult to explain the
sudden appearance of the rich Etruscan work without believing that it was brought in from outside Italy; the Italians seem to have been then both incapable of such achievements and not inclined to a lot of the values expressed in
those achievements. Against this, it appears that in the
Etruscan areas of Italy there was no sharp break with the
past in settlement, and so it is likely that the mass of the
population under Etruscan control was native to Italy. Dionysius of Halicarnassus, a Greek historian who lived around
the time of Christ, believed that the Etruscans were native
Italians. It is very difficult to accept this opinion.

The most frequent conclusion is that from about 800 B.C.,

and heavily by 700 B.C., there came into Italy from somewhere in the East a non-Greek people who were already much
more highly developed than any of the Italian peoples, and
who already had a tradition of contact with Greek civilization. These people settled in Tuscany (land of the
Etruscans, or Etruria), perhaps attracted by the copper and
iron in the area. There they took over Villanovan Iron Age
sites, creating a number of city-states in the fashion of
the Greeks and Phoenicians.

By tradition, there were 12 city-states in Etruria.
There may have been 12 major ones, although we do not know
the names of the 12 at any one point. In any case, the
number of cities established or taken over by the Etruscans
was far greater than 12. Tradition also said that there
was once a single king over all the Etruscans. In fact,
each city seems to have been independent, at first under
the control of a king, many later under aristocracies. The
cities sent delegates once a year to a meeting at a religious
site not yet identified (probably not far from Lake Volsiniensis). Any political combinations by the Etruscans, however, seem to have been rare and weak. We saw the same kind
of thing among the Latins of the period. As with the Greeks,
the Etruscan refusal to combine politically reduced their
impact.

The Phoenicians.
The Phoenicians, too, the great trading people of the
Near East, were putting out settlements into the western
Mediterranean in the 700's B.C. These settlements ranged
from Spain across western North Africa into Sicily. The
Phoenicians challenged the Greeks for control of trade
across the western Mediterranean, and in Sicily particularly
the contest was more direct, the Phoenicians in the western
part of the island regularly fighting the Greeks to the east.
The Phoenicians traded freely with the Italians and the
Etruscans, but they had no settlements on the Italian mainland and their cultural influence there was hardly observable.
The one great advantage of the Phoenicians in the West was
that their settlements quickly passed into the control of
their chief colony in the area. This was Carthage, on the
coast of North Africa directly across the Tyrrhenian Sea
from Rome and very close to Sicily. Carthage, founded from

the Phoenician city of <u>Tyre</u> around 700 B.C., absorbed the other Phoenician colonies and built up interests and possessions which stretched from southern Spain to Sicily and north into Sardinia and Corsica. In moving beyond the concept of the independent city-states, the Carthaginians/Phoenicians assured themselves of a great future in the West, greater than those the Greeks and Etruscans were to enjoy; for a long time, though, the Phoenicians were of little signifiance to Italians.

ROME, 700-600 B.C.

It was impossible for Rome and the other Latin cities
to escape the influence of the Etruscans just to the north
and the Greeks just to the south. The appearance of the
much more developed Greeks and Etruscans must have speeded
up the economic and cultural growth of the Latin people a
great deal. It is possible that under this influence Rome
benefitted more than most and became prosperous and locally
important among the Latins rather than being just another
Latin town.

We can not say a great deal about Rome in the 600's B.C.
The city was probably beginning to develop rapidly. By 700
B.C. many of the settlements on various hills and spurs at
Rome had joined together for religious purposes, and probably
politically as well. We do not know how this kind of merging
took place. By 600 B.C. all of the seven hills of later
Rome were included in the city, with the single exception of
the Aventine, an exception which Romans explained by the
story of Remus. The rocky Capitoline hill became a fortress
for the city. About 600 B.C., perhaps, the low-lying Forum
or city-center was drained. Probably at this time the Great
Drain was dug, at first as an open trench. These engineering
efforts, however, may date from the period after the Etruscans took over Rome around 600 B.C.

Religion.
        Rome was a highly religious community, a heritage which
Romans prized greatly in later centuries. The Greek Dionysius of Halicarnassus said much later that "To understand
the success of the Romans, you must understand their piety."
Roman religion, though, was very distinctive and very different from that of the Etruscans. It was based on two major
values:
--fides, meaning mutual trust and good faith, keeping your
word, etc., among people and between people and the gods.
Later, for example many treaties with other states were not
written down. Fides was a goddess. Polybius, another Greek
historian, was still much struck in the 100's B.C. by the
importance which Romans attached to keeping their word.
Romans always made it very clear that one of the things they
disliked about the Greeks was the carelessness (dishonesty)
of the latter in this kind of matter.

--_pietas_, being the proper respect owed to superiors, whether
parents, aristocrats, the state, or the gods.
These values stressed _careful_ _ritual_ and _correct_ _procedure_,
knowing your place and doing as you were supposed, rather
than _good_ _behavior_. This was the attachment of a simple
people to "proper" conduct.

Religion, as a result, was highly _legalistic_; immense
importance was attached to using the right words and the
right procedures in worship. The correct procedures would
maintain _the_ _peace_ _of_ _the_ _gods_, a balance in which humans
and the divine forces were in harmony (so that the gods left
the world alone). One element in this balance was the _divine_
double (a sort of angel) which each Roman had, a _genius_ for
a man, a _juno_ for a woman. Reasonable care and correctness
would preserve the good favor of this spirit.

There was no prominent _moral_ _element_ as we would mean
it in the religion; the whole thing was very much a matter
of _sensible_ _self-interest_. The religion also was for _groups_
rather than for _individuals_, in a way that we are no longer
much used to. It was highly _social_, and _political_, in
character, providing a guide for acceptable behavior, tips
on how to get along with men and the gods, rather than a way
of relating to the supernatural, or of trying to find immortality, or of serving any absolute standards of right and
wrong. As a result, public success was admired much more
than goodness. Later inscriptions on the tombs of the great
very bluntly stress their political and social achievements
rather than ethical or religious concerns. The best man was
the one who had performed the greatest political and military deeds while working _within_ the system.

The emphasis upon _correct_ _behavior_ produced a heavy reliance on _precedent_ and _custom_. This was what Romans called
the _mos_ _maiorum_, which we can translate as the _old_ _ways_. It
strengthened conservatism and restricted individualism.
This had all kinds of political consequences later; the
Romans did not take easily to democracy. The great and the
powerful found much security in the admiration of which
they were the objects. The same value can be seen in the
respect for older men and the positions of fathers in the
family structure. In theory, the head of the family could

refuse to recognize his new-born children and have them exposed;   he could punish his children and his wife with death;   he could sell his children into slavery.

Because of these attitudes, the mysterious side of Roman religion lacked a great deal. One way of preserving this state of affairs was to keep religion squarely under the control of the government. There was no separate professional priesthood;   the holy men (there were no female religious leaders) were the aristocrats, the same people who controlled the state. Many of the priesthoods were hereditary in certain aristocratic families.

There were no sacred writings except prayers. There was little dabbling in magic in the Etruscan style, although there were holy men called augurs who specialized in looking for omens, particularly in the flight patterns of birds. Prophesying and the private interpreting of signs was much frowned on. The divine powers at first were <u>not</u> personalized (<u>anthropomorphism</u>) in the way that was habitual with the Greeks. They generally did not marry, have children, etc., and few myths grew up about them;   Romans were not "curious" about the gods in the way the early Greeks were. The Roman gods were vague and often less than overpowering, having usually only limited abilities. The chief gods of early Rome were:
--<u>Jupiter</u>:   the great god, the Zeus of the Romans, at first an impersonal force.
--<u>Juno</u>:   a female force, associated with birth, the moon, etc., originally independent but then seen as the wife of Jupiter.
--<u>Quirinus</u>: much less important. We hardly know who he was at all. Later, Quirinus was seen as Romulus-become-god. This promoting of men to be gods, a stock part of Greek religion, generally held little appeal for the Romans.

More typical was <u>Vesta</u>, the goddess of the hearth and home, guardian of the family and thus of the great family that was Rome. Vesta <u>was</u> the hearth itself;   she could not be portrayed. Her temple, which was at first a straw hut near the Forum, contained no image. Vesta was served by the <u>6</u> <u>Vestal Virgins</u>, who were selected in childhood from aristocratic families and served in seclusion, and as virgins, for 30 years. Similarly, Janus, who became the god of beginnings, of new things (and so our January), surely began as a personification of a gateway (ianus), something you pass through to get somewhere. Both Vesta and Janus express the Roman respect which a sensible and careful person will have for the unknown. They also indicate that many of the city's gods were in a way big household gods. The daily worship of the many gods of the house was under the control of the male head of the family.

Religion reflected the group emphasis and the downplaying of individuality which characterized Roman life. Even so, that religion can hardly have been satisfying, emotionally or spiritually, to many ordinary citizens. By 600 B.C., under the influence of the Etruscans and Greeks, Roman religion was being modified in some predictable ways. There was some personalization, with an increase in the use of statues. There was a wave of interest in stories about gods, the stories taking the convenient path in identifying Roman gods with Greek gods. This also served the purpose of making Roman gods more "respectable." Juno became the Greek Hera and was matched up with Jupiter/Zeus. Mars was identified with the Greek Ares as the god of war. Romans also took from the Etruscans some entirely new gods, such as Saturn and Vulcan, as well as an increased interest in the occult (the Etruscan specialty in this line was the reading of animal entrails--the auspices). There were limits to borrowings, however, and the peculiarities of early Roman religion were never overwhelmed. Vesta remained without a statue; personalization, where it occurred, often was not much more than a token gesture; the identifications with Greek gods, as with Mars, were similarly limited in number and in degree; the men-gods of the Herakles (or Roman Hercules) fashion, despite the example of Romulus-Quirinus, remained rare; the stranger copyings from the Etruscans were not extensive and were very much copyings, the Romans being generally content to consult the foreign experts as occasion arose; and religion, new and old, still was very firmly under the control of the state.

Public Affairs.
We know very little about Rome's relations in the 600's B.C. with the surrounding towns and peoples, Latin and other. The wars mentioned by much later writers and commemorated in

427

statues in the Forum during the Roman Empire are for the
most part surely inventions. In legend, Rome did become
locally important before 600 B.C.; specifically Rome
1. defeated Alba Longa, the religious center 12 miles away,
and its Latin League, and
2. expanded to the coast and established the port of Ostia
by the mouth of the Tiber.
All this would have made Rome the dominant Latin town. What
actually happened we cannot say.

All Romans later agreed that in these years before 600
B.C. Rome was ruled by kings. The first king was Romulus
himself. However, there are only three names for the period
from Romulus (who in legend founded Rome in 753 B.C.) to
600 B.C.:
  1. Numa Pompilius around 700 B.C. He is said to have
     been a Sabine -- a sign of the merger of the Sabines
     with the Romans under Romulus.
  2. Tullus Hostilius 673-642 B.C. He is said to have con-
     quered and destroyed Alba Longa.
  3. Ancus Martius 642-617 B.C. He is said to have extended
     Rome's power to the sea at Ostia.
It is likely that kings ruled the city, but everything else
about these men and about the kingship generally is open to
great doubt. This includes their names; Romulus itself
means only "the man of Rome." The title king (rex) survived,
as in Greece, to become the name of a religious official.
This official lived later in the Regia, an ancient place in
the Forum which perhaps had been, as its name suggests, the
residence of the kings. Religious tasks probably were an
important part of the duties of the early kings. Numa
Pompilius is associated in legend with drawing up the first
Roman calendar of religious practices -- a procedural thing
of the kind very important to the Romans. A new calendar
borrowed from the Etruscans may have been introduced at this
time to replace the old Roman lunar calendar.

There is little to be said about the powers of the
kings. Everything about the Romans suggests that they did
not think of their kings as divine, but the kings probably
had very great power, in the fashion of the high officials
(consuls) of the later Republic. Romans were not in the
habit of crippling their officials with restrictions as they
went about their business, just as the father was allowed
great power over his family. The symbols of the kings'

authority (imperium) were the _fasces_. These were bundles
of rods, of hard birch and elm, witnesses to the power to
scourge, surrounding an _axe_, witness to the power to _execute_.
These symbols survived into the Republic. Their revival in
this century, still as symbols of authority, gives us the
word _Fascism_. It is possible that the early kings were
elected, as was often the case in Greece, rather than hereditary. The legends support this idea by inserting the
Sabine name, Numa, into the list.

It is very likely that the mass of the population was
free and _property-owning_. Slavery became important only as
foreigners (non-Romans) were captured in war. Tradition
said that from the beginning Romans were divided into _three_
tribes. Of the origins of these tribes, whether they indicated racial or economic or geographical differences, we
can say very little. Each tribe was divided, we do not know
how, into 10 _wards_ (_curia_, plural _curiae_), meaning simply
collections of men. Each ward (curia) contained a number
of _clans_ or groups of families. These _tribes_ and _wards_ may
have been the bases for several of the institutions of
early Rome:
--_the army_: a _legion_ Of 3,000 infantry and 300 cavalry,
raised by drafting the better-off citizens (in the Greek
manner) 1/3 from each tribe, 1/30 from each ward.
--_the Senate_: possibly from early on 300 members, with 1/3
from each tribe, 1/30 from each ward. It is likely that the
kings _picked_ the senators from the important heads of families,
so that the Senate was a kind of council of elders. The
name given to the early senators, the _patres conscripti_
(conscript or drafted fathers), indicates both the idea of
age and the idea of forced service. We do not know what the
Senate did in this period, but presumably it was some sort
of advisory body.
--_the Assembly of Wards_ (_Comitia Curiata_): the wards met
together as the earliest Assembly of Rome. Here is the
principle, dear to Romans, of voting by unit rather than
individually -- an expression of their hostility to individuality. We do not know what the Assembly did. Perhaps
it approved decisions made by the king, or by the king and
the Senate; perhaps it helped to select the new king. It
was probably only an occasional body and almost surely not
important.

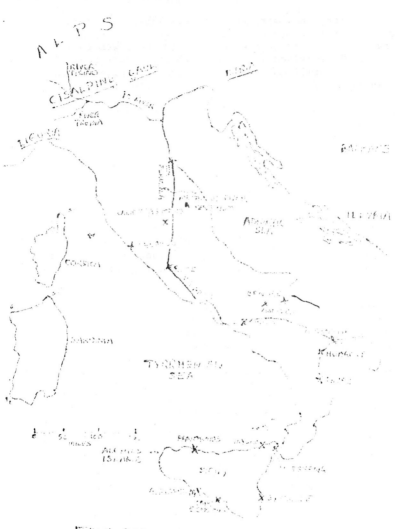

ITALY, 275 - 120 B.C.

ROME UNDER THE ETRUSCANS, 600-500 B.C.

Around 600 B.C., it is almost certain, Rome fell into the hands of the Etruscans. We do not know how this happened, or which Etruscan city was involved. The closest major Etruscan cities to Rome were Tarquinii (40 miles), Caere (20 miles), and Veii (12 miles). Veii was being established at about this time, around 600 B.C., perhaps to contest the control of the lower Tiber with Rome. For some 200 years Veii was to be more important than Rome.

The Etruscans may have been interested in Rome not so much for itself but to secure the passage across the Tiber toward the very fertile land of Campania to the south. The Greeks had been in Campania since the 700's B.C. Their biggest city was at Cumae, just north of the Bay of Naples. By 600 B.C., and perhaps a good deal earlier, the Etruscans had moved into Campania, although just how they did this we cannot say. The major Etruscan settlement in Campania was at Capua, which was founded around 650 B.C.

The Etruscan Kings.
On the traditional list of kings, the Etruscans took over at Rome after Ancius Martius (642-617 B.C.). They ruled Rome for 100 years, under 3 kings:
1. Tarquin the Elder   616-579 B.C.
2. Servius Tullius   578-535 B.C.
3. Tarquin the Proud (the Younger)   534-510 B.C.
The dating (616-510 B.C.) for the period of Etruscan control at Rome is very questionable. Many believe that the Etruscans took over a full generation later, around 575 B.C. The archaeological evidence puts some important early urbanization (draining the Forum, for example) around 600 B.C., during the period assigned by tradition to Tarquin the Elder, and it is tempting to believe that this was the work of the more advanced Etruscans.

Roman historians later were not at all happy talking about the Etruscan domination of Rome; the fact that they accepted an Etruscan period suggests that it had existed. Apart from the humiliation of foreign conquest, the Etruscan period made it more difficult for Roman writers to invent a glorious and ancient past for their city, something they

431

usually did by pushing every event and every development as
far back into the past as possible. One device to overcome
this problem was to place the introduction of things like the
tribes, the wards, the Senate, the Comitia Curiata, and the
new calendar to the period of the 600's B.C. before the
Etruscans took over. It is possible that in fact all of these
things were developed only in the 500's B.C. under the
Etruscan kings of Rome. At the same time, since pushing
back into the 500's B.C. things which may have occurred later
in Rome's development ran the risk of making the Etruscans
look good, later Roman writers relied on a series of assumptions about the Etruscan period to deny credit to the Etruscans.

Tarquin the Elder was said to have come from Etruscan
Tarquinii, although he was supposed to have had a Greek
aristocrat-adventurer from Corinth for a father. He was
said to have won power peacefully in Rome, a device which
avoided the shame of a conquest. In fact, we can say nothing about him or about the way the Etruscans came to power
in Rome. His very existence is in doubt.

The next king in the Etruscan period, Servius Tullius
(578-535 B.C.), has a Latin name and was said to have been
Latin (Roman). Servius Tullius was turned into a "good"
Latin king in a "bad" Etruscan period. He was given the
credit for a whole series of innovations, a thorough over-
haul of Roman institutions -- changes which may have been made
at some point under the Etruscans, but all of which may also
have been introduced only later, after the Etruscan period.
This device served the double purpose of pushing things
further back into the past and denying the Etruscans credit
for them. Virtually everything about Servius Tullius may
be invention, including his existence, (although we should
not flatly rule out the possibility that a Latin became king
of Rome during the Etruscan period. We do not know enough
about the politics of the day, including how kings were
selected, to say. One Roman historian, however, the man who
became the Emperor Claudius, knew a tradition which said
that Servius Tullius had been an Etruscan.

The third and last king of the Etruscan period, TARQUIN
the PROUD, was supposed to have been the son of the first

Tarquin. This is an odd scheme from every viewpoint. We
can say little about this second Tarquin. There is a suspicion that the two Tarquins may be one man, turned into two
in order to have one reasonably good Tarquin (good enough
to have won power peacefully at Rome) and one very bad Tarquin
(bad enough to have been thrown out of Rome).

There may have been only one Etruscan king, subdivided
into two by legend and stretched out over time, with an
imaginary good Latin king inserted in the middle. There may
have been other Etruscan kings, but if there were everything
about them, down to their names, is gone. We cannot know.

Political Conditions.
We can do little more than guess at how Rome was ruled
in this period. It seems that the kings in the 500's B.C.
left the Regia and lived in a fort they built on the steep
Capitoline hill next to the great temple to Jupiter, Juno and
Minerva. Certainly the Senate and the Comitia Curiata
existed at this time, if not earlier, although we still do
not know how they worked.

A number of changes were credited by tradition to
Servius Tullius, the good Latin king of the period. They
are usually placed in this period, although some or all of
them may have been introduced later:
1. The three tribes, which, although they had Etruscan names,
are usually believed to have existed before the Etruscan
takeover around 600 B.C., were replaced by 21 new ones,
4 being in the city and 17 in the surrounding country areas.
Later, we know,16 of the 17 country tribes were named after
famous families, and the names may go back to the 500's B.C.
These new tribes were geographical units. Their introduction
will have made it easier to collect taxes and raise troops.
The new tribes may also have been intended to reduce family
loyalties and indeed old loyalties of every kind, in order
to help Etruscan newcomers to fit in and move ahead socially
and politically.
2. A new military system was introduced. The infantry was
doubled in numbers to 6,000. The soldiers were now equipped
and trained in the Greek fashion, as heavy-armed hoplights
fighting in a phalanx. We find hoplite equipment appearing
in Etruria by 650 B.C. The new army was made up of property-
owners, graded by wealth. A census was taken to make the

/

property classifications. The wealthy men equipped themselves as cavalry (equites or knights). Many of these must
have been aristocrats. The infantry was divided into 5
classes, depending on what citizens could afford. The poor
citizens were not expected to fight regularly, being too
poor to equip themselves. they were called proletarii,
meaning those who can provide only children, and not taxes
or soldiers, for the state. From this we get proletariat,
being the poor, the working-class. All of this is the kind
of thing we have seen in Greece, including the attractive
principle that those with the least stake in the society
should not be taxed or drafted save in emergencies.

The new, larger army was not based on the old wards
(curiae) any longer, but on a unit called the Century, there
being 60 centuries of 100 men each.
3. Reflecting this change in the military, a new Assembly of
Centuries came into existence. This body largely replaced
the old Assembly of Wards (Comitia Curiata). The older
Assembly, however, did not disappear; it simply became
unimportant. This odd Roman willingness to have more than
one assembly will be seen again later. In the new assembly,
the Assembly of Centuries, as in the old, voting was by
units. Rome never had much interest in a one-man, one-vote
system. There were 193 units. Of these, 18 represented the
cavalry (equites). The top infantry class made up 80 units
and votes. This gave the top two census classes a majority
(98 of 193). Since voting by unit always began at the top
with the equites, a matter could be decided by these two
classes alone if they stuck together, with the rest not
even getting the chance to vote.

This is as blatant a system based on wealth (plutocracy)
as you could wish. While we do not know how many citizens
were in each class, it is very safe to assume that the top
two wealth classes, which had a voting majority in the new
assembly, made up only a small minority of the citizens.
The rest of the middle class, the remaining infantry classes,
had a much weaker voice. The poor, the proletarii, who may
have been numerous, had 5 votes out of the 193. The poor
did not normally have to fight; in return, they were ignored politically.

We do not know what powers this Assembly of Centuries
had in the Etruscan period. In fact, some think that it
was not even created until later, after the Republic had
displaced the kings, perhaps even as late as the 300's B.C.

/

In the Republic the Assembly of Centuries was the chief
assembly; it elected the chief officials and decided on
war and peace. If it existed in the 500's B.C. under the
kings, we do not know what its powers were, but it is likely
that the assembly was only asked to reject or accept, by vote
and without discussion, some measures brought to it by the
kings and/or the Senate.

Social Conditions.
        We do not know how "Etruscan" Rome became. There is
no way generally to distinguish Etruscan influence at this
period from that which already existed -- and of course the
source of much of the cultural influence was Greek anyway.
Inscriptions indicate that there was a Latin-speaking population under an Etruscan-speaking ruling class. It is not
impossible if Etruscan rule in Rome lasted for around a
century that large numbers of people from the Etruscan area
moved in to the city. Our general impression is that the
Etruscan influence in Rome was very heavy. It is significant
that the Romans finally agreed to take Aeneas of Troy as the
founder of the Latin people and so, at a remove, of Rome.
Aeneas received much attention from the Etruscans, who saw
him as one of their founders. Already in the 400's B.C.,
not long after the Etruscan period at Rome, Greek observers
recognized Aeneas as the founder of the Latins. Romans
themselves were more reluctant to do this, disliking the
idea of Etruscan influence. Still, Aeneas won out. His
position was cemented by the writer Virgil around the time
of Christ. Virgil himself was part Etruscan.

        It is reasonable to supposed that Rome grew and flour-
ished under the Etruscans in the 500's B.C. this is indicated by the archaeological evidence (quite apart from the
question of the Great Drain). A wall of earth was built to
protect at least the eastern part of the city, on the vulnerable open plateau, from the Quirinal hill toward the
Esquiline hill. This was is associated in tradition with
the king Servius Tullius, although it is not the so-called
(stone) Wall of Servius Tullius, which circles most of later
Rome and dates from no further back than the 300's B.C.
Here is a point at which tradition must be rejected.

        One great product of the Etruscan period at Rome was
the temple on the Capitoline hill which was divided into

435

three sections for the worship of Jupiter the Best and Greatest, Juno, and Minerva. This temple was for centuries the center of the chief Roman official cult. The temple was dedicated in 509 B.C. according to tradition, immediately after the fall of the Etruscan kings. It survived, with alterations, until it was destroyed by fire in 83 B.C. All three gods had Italian names, but each had an Etruscan counterpart and the idea of linking them together is Etruscan, as is the idea of subdividing a shrine. The temple was the work of the Etruscan outsider, Vulca of Veii, the only name we have among Etruscan craftsmen. The massive and vividly painted temple had a deep Etruscan porch with three rows of six columns, as well as a row of free-standing columns down each side. It was 180 feet wide and over 200 feet in length. The temple was built of wood, a characteristic Etruscan medium, on a stone platform 16 feet high. Much of the platform, but little eles, survives.

Another important temple built at this time, in legend by Servius Tullius, was the shrine of Diana on the Aventine hill, which lay just outside the city boundaries to the south. Diana was a "bright one," a sky goddess, one who also brought children. She is probably patterned after the Greek goddess Artemis, who was much favored by the large Greek colony at Massilia in southern France. Massilia surely had trade contacts with Rome by this time. The major center for the worship of Artemis was at the Ionian Greek city of Ephesus on the coast of Asia Minor; from the beginning the Roman shrine of Diana on the Aventine hill contained a statue of the many-breasted kind which existed at Ephesus. This is a good example of Greek influence in personalizing Roman religion. Close by the temple to Diana was an altar to Hercules (Herakles), another Greek god. One of Hercules' jobs was to watch over the marketplaces; the existence of his altar here, and that of the temple of Diana closeby, point to this being the place where the Greek traders did their business, just outside the city.

The most famous surviving example of art in Etruscan Rome is the great bronze Wolf on the Capitoline hill, which dates from around 500 B.C. This is thought to be the work of an Etruscan artist. We also have head sculptures of the period, male and female, many with the characteristic archaic smile of the Greek work of the period.

436

The Romans, who had probably just struggled to literacy with what is called proto-Latin, now took their alphabet, with some changes, from the Etruscans, a step which brought the appearance of Archaic Latin. Like the Etruscan writing, this Archaic Latin was short in vowels and redundant in the c, k and q group. From the Etruscans, too, came much later Roman ceremonial, many names, both of people and places, art and architectural themes and styles and talents (gateways, bridges, arches, the atrium house design).

Rome and the Latins.

Legend had it later that Rome had become important among Latin towns even before the Etruscan period began at Rome around 600 B.C. This is possible, but it may also mark an attempt to push further back developments which came under the Etruscans. There is little doubt that Rome under the Etruscans was one of the most important, perhaps the most important, of Latin towns (not, of course, that this amounted to much). It may have been under the Etruscans, rather than earlier, that Rome conquered Alba Longa and reached out to the coast at Ostia. The temple of Diana on the Aventine, for example, may have been an attempt to grasp the leadership of a league of Latin cities which centered on the worship of Diana at Aricia. This league (the Arician League) was headed by Tusculum, another leading Latin town. Building the new shrine outside the city limits of Rome may have been an attempt to reduce the obviousness of such an effort.

By 500 B.C. the early independent Latin towns had probably been reduced in number to about 10 or 12. Rome was among the biggest of these and it treated with the other chief Latin towns -- Praeneste, Tibur, Tusculum -- as equals. At the end of the Etruscan period (500 B.C.) Rome may have controlled an area of some 350 square miles. In a treaty with the Phoenician city of Carthage which may date from around 500 B.C. Rome seems to be a spokesman for Latin towns situated along the coast well southe of the Tiber river. This treaty may be only a renewal of an earlier and similar agreement.

437

THE END OF MONARCHY AT ROME: OVERTHROW OF THE ETRUSCANS, 500 B.C.

In tradition, <u>Tarquin the Proud</u>, the last Etruscan king, was thrown out by the Romans in 510 B.C. This revolution was led by <u>Brutus</u> and grew out of a sex-scandal, the rape of <u>Lucretia</u>, cousin of Brutus, by Tarquin's son. The spicy details encourage suspicion of the story, as does the year selected, since 510 B.C. is also the year in which the tyranny in Athens was overthrown.

Whatever the circumstances, it is likely that the monarchy did end in Rome around 500 B.C. A rival theory, that the kings lasted into the mid-400's B.C., has little support. Etruscan control was ended and the monarchy was replaced by the Roman <u>Republic</u>, which was dominated by the city's aristocracy. Etruscans generally, though, were not thrown out of Rome, and their influence remained.

Kings were losing out in other parts of Italy, including the Etruscans' own <u>Etruria</u>, at this time, and usually to such aristocracies as took power in Rome. In addition, the Etruscans generally in <u>Latium</u> and <u>Campania</u> were on the retreat. The Greeks of Campania were reviving. In the 520's B.C. <u>Aristodemus</u> of <u>Cumae</u>, which was the chief Greek city of Campania, defeated the Etruscans near his city. He may have beaten them again 20 years later, around 505 B.C., at <u>Aricia</u>. Certainly, many Latin towns besides Rome threw off Etruscan control in these years. This may have helped to revive the Latin league which had been centered on Aricia and its shrine of Diana, a revival which perhaps came at the expense of the Romans. While the details are not known to us, it seems that Rome's influence among the Latins declined in this period when Etruscan power collapsed.

<u>Tarquin the Proud</u> tried unsuccessfully to regain power at Rome. Then <u>Lars Porsenna</u> of <u>Clusium</u>, an Etruscan adventurer who was acting on his own behalf rather than for Tarquin, attacked Rome, perhaps around 505 B.C. In legend, Lars Porsenna was turned back at the bridge on the Tiber river by the hero <u>Horatius</u> and gave up when he discovered how determined the Romans were to resist him. In fact, it seems that Lars Porsenna <u>did</u> capture Rome. The Roman

historian Tacitus, writing around 100 A.D., mentioned "the surrender of the city to Porsenna." It is likely that Lars Porsenna had to give up Rome after an Etruscan army under the command of his son was defeated at Aricia by Aristodemus of Cumae and some of the Latin towns.

Despite this episode and other raids on Rome and Latium, the Etruscans do not seem to have made any great effort to recover what they had lost. A generation later, in 474 B.C., the Etruscans were defeated at sea off Cumae by the Greeks, who had help from Carthage. The Etruscans accepted their defeat as final. In compensation, perhaps, they moved north beyond the Apennines into the valley of the river Po. (Virgil, the great Roman poet, was descended from Etruscans who had founded Mantua at about this time.) Roman tradition had the Etruscans going north of the Po to the Alps, but we have no other evidence of this. The Etruscans did not hold their gains in the north for long; they lost them to the Gauls around 400 B.C.

The end of monarchy in Rome left a dislike for kings which lasted for centuries. The Republic which was founded around 500 B.C. lasted for over 400 years. Under it, Rome grew from being just an important Latin town to become the greatest power in all the Mediterranean world.

THE EXPANSION OF ROME, 500-350 B.C.: THE CONQUEST OF WEST-CENTRAL ITALY

510-490 B.C. Early Relations with the Latins.

Rome's important position among the Latin towns may have weakened as a result of the upheavals which drove the Etruscan rulers out of Latium. Rome and some other Latin towns stood alone, but many of the Latin settlements were grouped in the Latin League which grew out of the fighting against the Etruscans. This Latin League may have been jealous of the earlier influence of Rome in the Etruscan period, and some Latin towns seem to have used the troubles to escape from Roman control and join the League.

Rome fought the Latin League over a period of years following the end of the monarchy. The most famous episode is the battle of Lake Regillus about 496 B.C., which Roman legend claimed as a great victory for Rome. Around 490 B.C. this fighting was ended for the time being by a treaty (the treaty of Spurius Cassius) which made Rome and the Latin League allies. Rome and the League agreed to have their armies form one common army, with command of the force alternating yearly between the two parties. Cicero said that the bronze tablet on which the treaty was written still existed in his day, 50 years before Christ, and we have a summary of the terms from Dionysius of Halicarnassus around the time of Christ. It is not known how faithfully the terms were kept. It is clear that Rome was as strong as the League; of course, some other important Latin towns were not involved at all.

490-410 B.C. Wars against Neighboring Peoples.

Through many small wars, with many ups and downs, Rome and the Latin League established their power over the neighboring peoples, all at a time when Greece was experiencing its golden age. The peoples in the hills around Latium were related to the Latins but were more primitive:
1. The Hernici were soon forced into alliance with Rome and the League;
2. The Sabines were brought under control by the mid-400's B.C. In legend, a Sabine leader, Attus Clausus, brought his whole clan of 5,000 to settle on Roman territory very soon after the establishment of the Republic, around 500 B.C. This was seen as the beginning of the great clan of

Claudius (the Claudians). The story may cover up some sort
of capture of Rome in these early days by the Sabines. The
Sabines did raid Rome later, and about 460 B.C. they even
captured for a short time, until the League sent help to
drive them away, the fort on the Capitoline hill;
3. The Aequi, who penetrated well into Latium as they
came down from the hills, were brought under control or
were driven back into the mountains by the late 400's B.C.;
4. The Volsci, who moved into southern Latium from the
interior in the 500's B.C., were tamed by about 400 B.C.,
the process being completed when their port at Antium
(Anzio) was captured in 377 B.C.

It is clear that these wars were generally joint
efforts of Rome and the Latin League. In the areas brought
under control, Latin colonies were established, joint
projects also. The Roman members of such colonies lost
their citizenship and counted simply as Latins. More than
a dozen such colonies were created between 500 and 350 B.C.,
the earliest of them going back perhaps to not long after
500 B.C. Beyond this, almost nothing can be said about the
relationship between Rome and the League (and the other
Latin towns). It seems that toward the end of the 400's
B.C. Rome was asserting itself at the expense of the League.
Around 415 B.C. Rome got the right to organize the important Latin festival at the Alban Mount, and soon after that
Rome was signing treaties with individual Latin towns,
against the spirit of the League.

410-395 B.C. Roman Conquest of Veii.
Veii, a city larger and richer than Rome, was the
closest major Etruscan city-state (about 12 miles to the
north). Rome had been at odds with Veii for a long time.
In 476-475 B.C. Veii was able to occupy for a while land
right down to the Tiber river opposite Rome. Fighting
between the two increased from the 430's B.C. In legend,
the eventual Roman capture of Veii was the result of a
great 10-year siege (copied from Troy?). The capture was
seen as very important by later Romans, who regarded it as
the first big step in Rome's expansion. The Roman hero of
the war was Camillus; to thank the gods for victory,
Camillus was said to have sent a golden bowl to the great
Greek shrine of Apollo at Delphi.

441

However it came about, Rome's victory over Veii was a great military achievement for the Republic. It must have required much effort, even though the other Etruscan cities did very little to help Veii. The size of the effort is suggested by the traditional story that Camillus got Rome to adopt continuous military service and introduced pay for the soldiers, moving away from the more casual, part-time system which asked the citizen-soldiers to provide for themselves and gave them time off to work their land, etc.

Veii was destroyed, an early example of deliberate Roman brutality. Its land was given to Roman citizen-farmers. Although we do not know what the Latin League had contributed to the effort against Veii, the episode looks very much like a Roman affair, another sign that the city was growing away from the League.

390 B.C. Attack of the Gauls.
By 400 B.C. things were going well militarily for Rome and the Latins in all directions, even if there were per-haps growing problems in the alliance. Then came disaster. The CELTS were a barbarian people who had been on the move across Europe from the east since the 700's B.C. Eventu-ally they spread as far west as Spain and Britain. They spoke a common language but were divided into many tribes. In the 400's B.C. they came into Italy across the Alps from the north. The Celts in Italy, and also those in France, are called GAULS.

Having conquered and settled in north Italy in the 400's B.C., displacing the Etruscans in some places, about 390 B.C. some of the Gauls attacked central Italy. A fierce and primitive people, some of them fighting naked, the Gauls were a considerable military force, even if they were often not well organized. On this occasion, they defeated the Romans at the battle of the ALLIA river. With the figures involved reported as 10-15,000 Romans and/or Latins and 30,000 Gauls, this is very likely to have been much the biggest battle the Romans had experienced to that time.

Following the battle, the Gauls occupied Rome and de-stroyed much of the city. There is no doubt about this. In legend, the fort on the Capitoline hill held out, being

442

saved from surprise attack by the warning cries of the
geese which were kept there for religious sacrifices. The
Gauls were bought off. They moved back north (in legend
hurried along by Camillus) and did not return to the area
even to raid, it seems, for 30 years, concentrating
happily on fighting one another in north Italy in their
usual disorganized way. It was fortunate for the Romans
that the Gauls were too backward to have any interest in
cities beyond destroying them in passing. They did keep
north Italy, however, and for a very long time neither the
Romans nor anyone else could do anything about that.

One result of the attack by the Gauls was that Rome
built for protection the great stone Wall of Servius Tullius,
put up at this time but wrongly named for the earlier king.
The wall enclosed 1000 acres and all seven hills (including the Aventine).

390-350 B.C. Recovery and Domination of the Latins.
The attack of the Gauls hurt Rome's military position
and prestige. It was also followed by serious political
and economic troubles within the city which slowed Rome's
military recovery. On the other hand, other towns in the
area had suffered from the Gauls, although we do not know
how widespread the damage was or if it was as bad as that
in Rome. The Aequi and the Volsci tried to reassert themselves against the Latins, and some of the Etruscan towns
attacked from the north. The Latin League was still operating and against threats from the outside such as these
it could hold together and continue to cooperate with the
Romans. The Aequi and the Volsci were put down, the
Etruscans were defeated. The Latins even moved into southern Etruria and established two Latin colonies there.

With the military success returning, the tensions
between Rome and the League increased. In all likelihood,
Rome was again straining to alter the relationship with the
League to its advantage. In 381 B.C., for example, only a
decade after the invasion by the Gauls, Rome gave full
Roman citizenship to Tusculum, 15 miles south, which had
formerly been a prominent League member. There was a great
deal of trouble between Rome and the League, but we can
barely even guess at its outline. The final step came in
358 B.C. when Rome's treaty with the League ended. It is

likely that Rome, being more and more the dominant element,
refused to renew the treaty. In the next years Rome tried
instead to push the other Latin towns into individual
agreements with it--agreements which made these towns more
or less dependent allies of Rome. The common army of Rome
and the League became a Roman army to which these new
allies supplied troops. The Latins generally cannot have
been pleased at what was happening.

Summary.
       At this point, Rome was the chief power in west-
central Italy. This looks like no very big thing on a map,
but it meant that by Greek standards Rome already was a
very substantial city. Rome was, in fact, among the major
organized military forces in Italy. The topsy-turvy nature
of its experiences to this point matched the way the Romans
liked to see themselves later--as struggling through many
setbacks and hard times to final victory.

THE EXPANSION OF ROME, 350-270 B.C.: THE CONQUEST
OF CENTRAL AND SOUTH ITALY

Rome was willing to look for opportunities to expand
its influence and strong enough to take advantage of them.
It soon moved southwards, toward Campania. The tribes
which occupied the highlands of the southern Apennines in
the interior were known as the SAMNITES. Related groups,
known as Sabellians, had moved down from the highlands in
the 400's B.C. and had conquered Campania, including the
large cities there, Greek Cumae and Etruscan Capua. The
Sabellian conquests had come not long after the Greeks in
Campania had reasserted themselves against the Etruscans.
The Sabellians had become more developed in their new
environment in Campania and they were often themselves
threatened by the still primitive tribes which remained in
the interior.

343-340 B.C. 1st Samnite War.

Rome responded to a request for help from the
Sabellians holding Capua against the upland tribes. This
set the pattern for the Roman habit of using such an appeal
from a friend as a reason for getting into a war, a style
which the writer Cicero summarized 300 years later in the
phrase
"Our empire was acquired in defending our allies."

The Roman intervention brought on the 1st Samnite War.
While there is a possibility that the whole war is an invention of the historian Livy around the time of Christ, it is
generally believed that this war did take place. The fighting went in favor of the Romans, but then in 340 B.C. many
of the Latins rebelled against Roman control. Even Capua,
oddly, switched sides and supported the Latins. Since the
Latin rebellion directly threatened the Roman military
system, Rome called off the Samnite War in order to concentrate on putting the Latins into order.

340-338 B.C. Latin Revolt.

The Latins, along with the Volsci who joined them, may
have been protesting at the way they were now being used to
promote Rome's own ambitions. With the Romans in Campania,
the Latins would be hemmed in by Rome all around.

The revolt did not last long. The end, in 338 B.C.,
brought a final settlement of the Latin problem. The old
Latin League was broken up. Rome made a separate arrangement with each Latin city and with each of the surrounding
peoples such as the Volsci. A few places near Rome were
given full citizenship; now 'Rome' itself covered 4500
square miles. Most of the rest, Latins, Volsci, Sabines,
etc., became half-citizens or citizens without the vote
(called also Latin Rights). The same condition was extended to Capua and some other cities in Campania which had
come under Roman influence in the recent war. A half-
citizen could not vote in the Roman assemblies or hold
Roman office, but he did have the private rights of Roman
citizens, such as making contracts as an equal with Romans
under Roman law and marrying a Roman without giving up his
rights as a parent. Roman law normally discriminated
against aliens and prevented Roman property from passing
into their hands. The areas which were given half-citizenship did not have to pay the property tax which was required of Romans in emergencies, but they had to follow Roman
foreign policy and raise and pay for a quota of soldiers
for the Roman army. These soldiers served as separate and
distinct units, and some of their commanders were non-
Romans. This half-citizen status may have had its beginnings in the favors given by Rome to the Etruscan town of
Caere in the 380's B.C. in reward for the help given to
Rome by Caere against the Gauls. Although no permanent
Roman garrisons were put into the half-citizen areas, some
of the land there was taken by the Roman government and
Roman (not Latin) colonies were established.

This type of arrangement, clever, flexible, and reasonable, set out the way in which the future Rome would protect
its own identity while it worked up a confederation of
peoples bound to it in ways that would strengthen with age.
Rome already had the tools it would use to overcome the
Greek problem of localism.

327-304 B.C. 2nd Samnite War.
After a while Rome turned again to the south. This
time, the move was in answer to an appeal from the Greek
city of Neapolis (Naples) which was being attacked by
Samnites from the interior.

446

The big new war which resulted was won by Rome only
with great difficulty and after many setbacks. The tribes
in the uplands did not make easy victims. By the end of
the war Rome was putting an army of 100,000 into the field.
In addition, fighting fire with fire, the Romans built up
a reputation for deliberate brutality which would serve
them well in the future. Rome was now a very great military force, far stronger surely than any Greek state had
ever been, although it was Rome's good fortune to escape
attack from the Macedonians under Alexander who were
conquering the East at this same time.

The long fighting in bad, broken country against fierce
tribesmen contributed to the reorganization of the Roman
military system. The army became more professional: the
soldiers were paid, and standardized equipment was now
issued by the government. In addition, the war may have
encouraged the long-term move away from the old Greek
hoplite phalanx, with its heavily armed infantry in mass
formations using long spears. While we do not know when or
how it came about, the Romans were developing an open formation. Under the new system, a legion was divided into 30
maniples, each maniple containing two centuries of 80 men.
A maniple, under the guidance of the two centurions who
commanded the centuries, could fight independently. The
men stood in three lines several feet apart, each man in
each line being 4-5 feet from his immediate neighbor, those
in the back lines being posted to cover the gaps in the line
to the front of them. The chief weapons for these soldiers
were swords and shorter throwing spears about 6 feet long.
This style of fighting emphasized bravery and efficiency,
and so it matched the way Romans saw themselves. It also
guaranteed heavy casualties in hand-to-hand combat, but the
Romans do not seem to have been bothered by this. While
obviously useful in rugged areas where a phalanx might be
unmanageable, the new style later proved itself more than
a match in open field for the best phalanxes.

Early ambitious attempts to defeat the Samnite tribes
led to several disasters. The greatest setback came at the
Caudine Forks (location not certain) in 321 B.C., where a
Roman army surrendered in the Republic's biggest defeat
since the invasion by the Gauls at the beginning of the
century. Perhaps the Romans had not yet adapted enough.

447

Roman losses were enough to make Rome avoid further heavy engagements for a half-dozen years. The Samnites raided into Latium in this period.

Then, between 316 and 314 B.C., the Roman armies defeated the Samnites and occupied many of their territories in the interior. The outcome had been decided, even though the war dragged on in guerrilla style in the mountains for another 10 years.

It was at this time, soon after the Romans had won control of the situation, that the Etruscans and some others of Rome's old enemies, including the Aequi and the Hernici, entered the war on the Samnite side. Rome handled this problem with no great difficulty, annexing the territories of the Aequi as punishment and occupying Etruria. The last step brought the Republic's armies into contact with the Gauls to the north. Again, there is a possibility that this episode is an invention, a carryback from the story of the next war.

Victory in the 2nd Samnite War made Rome the great power in all Italy south of the area of the Gauls. Already Rome was pressing the large Greek cities in the far south, usually by offering "protection" against the hill tribes.

298-290 B.C. 3rd Samnite War.
Attempting to reassert themselves, the Samnites allied with the Etruscans and the Gauls against Rome for this war. The Romans, threatened on all sides, won a big battle at Sentinum in 295 B.C. against an army of Samnites and Gauls. After further victories over the Samnites the alliance against Rome fell apart.

Large areas of central and south Italy were taken into Roman possession as punishment. In vengeance finally won for the sack of Rome in 390 B.C., the largest amounts of land were taken from the Gauls, who were pushed well to the north. Campania, and some parts of Etruria, also lost their independence, as did many of the Samnite peoples. The inhabitants of these areas usually were made half-citizens.

The remaining areas, including most of the southern uplands, were left in the hands of the local tribes or

cities. Such areas were made "allies" of Rome. Each city
or tribe signed a separate treaty with Rome. The ally
normally could not ally itself to another ally of Rome; it
could deal only with Rome. The ally had to supply Rome
with soldiers if they were asked for, but it did not pay
taxes to Rome. Usually, officials of allied cities or
tribes were made Roman citizens after their term of office.
The most favored among these allies had private rights
similar to the half-citizenship which was common in Roman
territory.

To guard Roman interests, many new Latin colonies were
established all over the peninsula, from Ariminum (Rimini)
in the north to Venusia in the southern uplands. Almost
all of these were on a half-citizenship basis. At the same
time, some purely Roman colonies were established. These
were always on Roman territory and served obvious military
purposes. They were a lot smaller than the Latin colonies,
with about 300 families, and they had no powers of self-
government, being controlled directly from Rome. One of
the first of these Roman colonies had been built at Ostia,
perhaps in the 340's B.C. About a dozen were established
over the next century as Rome conquered central and south
Italy (compared to about 20 of the much larger Latin
colonies, which were much more diverse in purpose). The
colonies of both kinds established through this period
(350-270 B.C.), added together, amounted to about 60,000
individual holdings.

280-275 B.C. War with Pyrrhus of Epirus.
      The Greek cities on the south coast of Italy reason-
ably felt threatened by Rome; a Latin colony was begun at
Venusia in 291 B.C. Under the circumstances, incidents
were inevitable. Tarentum (Taranto), by this time the
chief Greek city in the south, made an agreement with Rome
in which Rome promised not to send its ships into the Gulf
of Taranto. In 282 B.C. the Greek city of Thurii (founded
by Athens in the 400's B.C. as a panhellenic colony), being
under attack from the tribes of the interior, appealed for
help to Rome--another case of the preferred formula. The
Romans came, with their fleet. An angry Tarentum attacked
and defeated this Roman fleet and occupied Thurii. War
was certain.

Tarentum and other Greek cities nearby looked for aid against Rome from across the Adriatic. Help came in the person of PYRRHUS, King of EPIRUS, the most famous soldier of his day in the Greek world. Pyrrhus, who claimed to be descended from Alexander the Great, who had been dead now for nearly half-a-century, brought with him 25,000 mercenaries, the bulk of them forming a great 20,000 men phalanx, and 20 Indian elephants. He meant to make money, win glory, and look good fighting for Greek civilization against the more backward Romans. An uncle of Alexander the Great had come over to Italy 60 years earlier on the same kind of mission, although on that occasion it had been to protect the Greek cities against the inland tribes.

Pyrrhus defeated a Roman army in a hard fight at Heraclea in 280 B.C., largely thanks to his elephants, a weapon the Romans had not seen before. He then raided northward toward Rome, but he found none of the tribes willing to rebel and join him against Rome. The next year, 279 B.C., Pyrrhus again defeated a Roman army at Asculum, in a battle that was bloody and very closely-fought. Pyrrhus did not want any more victories like these (which gives us our word pyrrhic, a pyrrhic victory being one that costs too much). He offered peace, but the Romans refused. In a famous speech of which the text still existed 300 years later, APPIUS CLAUDIUS THE BLIND conviced Rome "not to negotiate so long as an enemy remained on Italian soil." Pyrrhus went off to Sicily, looking for easier pickings there defending the Greek cities in the eastern part of the island against Carthage. When he returned to south Italy in 276 B.C., he was defeated by the Romans at the battle of Beneventum. Pyrrhus then went back to Greece. The legions of Rome had shown themselves to be superior to the best there was in the way of Greek phalanxes.

The Greek cities of the south now became allies of Rome. Later, a Latin colony was set up at Brundisium in the far south, to watch the Greeks--and to draw trade away from Tarentum.

Summary.
These wars had produced in 75 years an Italy which was completely under Roman control. Of the 50,000 or so square miles which were involved, 12,000 were Roman territory,

5,000 were in Latin colonies, and the rest, the very large
majority, belonged to allies of Rome. Perhaps about
2/3rds of the total population of about 4 millions lived
in the allied areas. Tarentum, with around 200,000 people,
probably was the largest city, with Capua and Rome itself
next with perhaps 150,000 each. None rivalled Syracuse,
the great Greek city on Sicily, which had perhaps 500,000
inhabitants. Carthage in North Africa may not have been
much smaller than Syracuse; certainly it was much bigger
than anything on the Italian mainland.

The free population on the Italian mainland which was
under Roman control can be divided into 4 groups:
1. Full Roman citizens   ⎫ living in Roman
2. Half-citizens (Latin Rights)   ⎬ territory
3. Allies with half-citizenship (Latin Rights) living in
4. Other allies   allied areas.
Under these circumstances, the Roman army was at this time
about half full citizen (category 1), the other half being
drawn from the remaining three groups.

Rome was now a very great power in terms of the entire
Mediterranean world, even though the Romans had not yet
waged war against another first-rate power and remained
little known outside Italy. Responding to Rome's emergence,
other governments were establishing contact with this new
force. Examples are the friendship arrangements made with
Rome in the 270's B.C. by the Egypt of the Ptolemies and
the important Greek trading state of Rhodes.

LAKE
VOLSINIENSIS

ETRURIA
(TUSCANY)

• TARQUINII

TIBER RIVER

SABINES

AEQUI

CAERE VEII

ROME

• TIBUR

LATIUM

LAKE REGILLUS

• PRAENESTE

TUSCULUM,

OSTIA

ARICIA

ALBAN MT.

HERNICI

VOLSCI

ANTIUM (ANZIO)

SAMNITES

TYRRHENIAN
SEA

BENEVENTUM

CAMPANIA

CAUDINE FORKS(?)

CAPUA

SABELLIANS

CUMAE

NAPLES

VESUVIUS

BAY OF
NAPLES

POMPEII

CENTRAL ITALY

ADRIATIC
SEA

0   25

MILES

452

DEVELOPING THE REPUBLICAN CONSTITUTION, 500-270 B.C.:
THE CONFLICT OF THE ORDERS

Not a great deal is known about the early Republic, in
the period from the overthrow of the Etruscan kings around
500 B.C. to about 350 B.C. Our chief sources are the
histories written much later, after 200 B.C. Many parts of
the broad outline which will be given here are more or less
generally accepted, but a great deal is in disupute and
some people are very suspicious even of the most basic
elements in the story.

Structure

The Republic which replaced the kings around 500 B.C.
was basically an aristocracy, controlled by certain families called the PATRICIANS. We do not know how certain
families had come to belong to this patrician class, but it
is clear enough that those which did belong knew who they
were and that they were distinguished by birth from the
rest of the population. Patricians could not be created:
They were born. In the very early Republic the patrician
class probably included both families which had long been
important and had held office under the kings and families
of much more recent importance. We have the names of about
50 patrician clans or great extended families for the 400's
B.C. in the early Republic. Portraits or busts of families
great men of the clan were kept in the houses of families
which belonged to the larger group. Among the 50 are names
which were to be powerful for centuries longer, names we
will meet repeatedly: the Fabii (plural of Fabius), the
Aemilii (Aemilius), the Cornelii (Cornelius), and the
Claudii (Claudius)--the Claudii being Samnites. The most
important clan in the very early Republic was that of the
Fabii. Their estates lay to the north and west of Rome,
toward Veii, and it is clear that in the generation after
500 B.C. the Fabii operated what was very much a private
army. How common this was, how such forces were linked to
the regular army of citizen draftees, we do not know. The
entire patrician class, divided into about 1,000 families
grouped into the clans, made up perhaps about 7-10% of the
total population.

Whatever the source of their membership in the patrician
class, it is very likely that these families had a monopoly

453

on high office not long after the establishment of the
Republic--and perhaps from the start. Some of the early
names we have for high officials soon after 500 B.C. appear
to be non-patrician (plebeian). If they were, it is an
oddity we cannot explain. Such non-patrician names soon
disappear; patricians then held all the major offices for
a long time.

The stronghold of the patrician class was the Senate,
although there, too, there were probably some important
non-patricians. Having begun as some sort of advisory
group to the kings, the Senate became in the early Republic
a powerful body of important citizens, almost all of them
from the patrician families. We do not know how individuals got into the Senate in the early Republic. Some were
probably the heads of the leading families; one important
way into the Senate was to go there after holding major
office. The size of the Senate may have been set at 300,
the later figure, already at this time. It is not likely
that there was any longer a rigid sharing out of the
Senate places among the curiae (wards) and the tribes.

It is possible that at first a single high official
was chosen each year to head the Republic, with the title
of praetor (leader; praeire = to march ahead, to go before).
Later, certainly, and perhaps most likely from the start,
there were two chief officials elected each year, the
CONSULS (=colleagues). The consuls inherited the symbols
of authority of the old kings--the fasces and the 12
attendants or lictors. In legend, Brutus, the hero of the
overthrow of the Etruscan kings, was one of the first two
consuls. Romans habitually used these principles, common
also among Greeks, of limiting an office to one year and
having more than one man holding an office. The consuls
had complete power (imperium) over the laws and the army.
They commanded the armies on campaign; if both were in
Rome, they alternated in power monthly. They were not
responsible to anyone and they were immune from prosecution
while they were in office. It was a distinctly Roman policy
to give freedom to act to the official while he was in
office. The consuls were elected by the Assembly of
Centuries, but they probably were selected and nominated by
the Senate from among its own members. Not long after the
foundation of the Republic, at the latest, all the consuls

454

belonged to the patrician class. The consuls had some
sort of control over the admission of new members to the
Senate, but, given their reliance on Senate advice and
experience and their family ties within the Senate, the
consuls ordinarily must have had a very cosy relationship
with the Senate.

As other, lesser officials were added over time, the
consuls remained at the top, and the principle was followed
that an official had the power to overrule the orders and
actions of any official he outranked. Officials were not
paid a salary. One office rated above the consulship.
This was the dictatorship, an emergency office which gave a
man full power for up to six months. We have the names of
many dictators during the early Republic, but most of them
are more or less legendary figures. The office of dictator
may not even have been introduced until well toward 400 B.C.
The religious duties of the old kings were transferred to
the Chief Priest, who held office for life; most of the
priesthoods, however, were co-opted and so beyond his control.

The Assembly of Centuries was the most important assembly of the early Republic. The older Curial Assembly was
used for little more than ceremonial purposes; long before
the end of the Republic it had become a purely symbolic body,
with certain officials being deputed to act as the ancient
assembly. The Assembly of Centuries passed the laws,
elected the officials, declared war and peace, and conducted
trials. Yet:
1. it met only when called by an official;
2. it voted, but did not discuss.
Beyond these limitations, the Senate commonly was allowed to
do things which were supposedly reserved to the Assembly; we
will see the Senate making war and peace, passing resolutions
which were to all intents and purposes laws, etc. And we
can be sure that the Senate supervised, had the right of
approval, over the Assembly's decisions.

In addition, the Assembly of Centuries was not in any
sense a democratic body. It was in fact very far from being
such. As we have seen, it voted by units (193 of them), and
the units were portioned out according to wealth, with the
wealthiest classes having a voting majority in the Assembly.

455

Obviously, the Assembly of Centuries was not a counter-part to the Assembly of Athens (or, for that matter, of Sparta). Of course, neither the Assembly nor any other body or individual in the state spoke for the growing numbers of people Rome was bringing under its control.

Conflict of the Orders.
In the most general terms, the early Republic was highly aristocratic (Senate and officials), with a weak oligarchic/plutocratic element (Assembly of Centuries) and negligible democratic elements. Over the first 200 years of the Republic (500-300 B.C.) this system was repeatedly challenged. These challenges make up the Conflict of the Orders--the orders being the 2 classes, the patricians (aristocrats) and the plebeians (everyone else). It is important to note that this was not rich against poor. The plebeians were not the poor--they were all who were not aristocrats, including many wealthy, educated, and talented people. Such plebeians provided the natural leaders for the class.

All plebeians could join in certain basic demands aimed at restricting the power of the aristocrats. On most matters, though, the plebeians had little in common with one another. Richer plebeians often had ambitions very different from those of the poor. In addition, as in Greece, political unrest against the aristocracy was often sharpest in times of economic difficulty. Demands for aid and relief by poorer citizens often found the richer plebeians much closer to the aristocracy in their sympathies.

The biggest threat the plebeians could make was to withdraw their military services (of course, this would involve the better-off plebeians, since the poor were virtually exempt from the draft). Later Roman writers listed 5 such cases, calling them secessions (withdrawals) because the plebeians symbolically went outside the city to dramatize their point. These secessions occurred in 494, 449, 448, 342, and 287 B.C. The first "strike" by the plebeians may be an invention; it is possible that the others are too, in some degree.

The early aims of the plebeians were to obtain offi-cials of their own and a new Assembly which would be less

thoroughly controlled by the patricians in the Senate.
Even the second part of these very general objectives would
not be so attractive to many of the richer plebeians
because of their importance in the Assembly of Centuries.
Equites, cavalrymen, is the word for the richest plebeians,
the name for the group being the Equestrians or the
Equestrian class.

494 B.C.? Tribunes. Perhaps as early as this date, as a
result of the first secession, the office of TRIBUNE of
the people was established. A tribune's job was to protect
the plebeians against the Senate and the officials and the
Assembly of Centuries. A tribune was not an official
(that is, he lacked imperium); he acted negatively, protesting and vetoing actions he considered to be contrary to
the interests of the plebeians. Such protests included
blocking moves to collect debts. Only plebeians could be
tribunes. At first there were perhaps only two tribunes;
soon, by 449 B.C., there were 10.

485 B.C. Spurius Cassius, three times consul and the
architect of the first treaty with the Latin League (490
B.C.), was executed by the patricians for proposing public
land distribution to the poor citizens. There is a good
chance that this story is a later invention.

471 B.C. Tribal Assembly. By 471 B.C. at the latest there
existed a new Assembly, called eventually the Tribal
Assembly. The tribunes summoned it and presided over it;
it, in turn, elected the tribunes (we do not know how
tribunes were chosen before this if it was by some different means). It could pass resolutions (plebiscites, a
word we use), but these were expressions of opinion, not
laws; it had some judicial powers. Probably only plebeians
could attend this Tribal Assembly. It voted in units,
a fixed Roman principle, the units being tribes. The
tribes numbered 21 in the early Republic, 33 by 265 B.C.,
and 35 eventually (by 241 B.C.). There were 4 city tribes,
the rest being in the countryside. However they had
originated, by the 300's B.C. these tribes were totally
artificial units, although we can say very little else
about them. The enrollment of new citizens in the tribes
was something easily manipulated. The simplicity of the
tribal units, compared to the 193 units of the Assembly

457

of Centuries, is obvious, and in theory at least the Tribal
Assembly was not organized on a wealth basis and so could
be more representative of the great body of citizens. The
origins and the early development of this Assembly are so
little known to us that we are still not decided whether
there was one such body or two of a similar nature. If
there were two, we do not know what were the differences
between the two in composition and duties. It is possible
that by 450 B.C. an assembly of all the citizens organized
along tribal lines existed. How distinct this was from
the original Tribal Assembly we cannot say. Here we will
refer simply to the Tribal Assembly as one body.

451 B.C. Code of the Twelve Tables. As in Greece, a
regular complaint against the aristocrats at Rome was that
they protected their own powers by refusing to reveal or
write down the law. As priests, the patricians monopoliz-
ed the interpretation of the unwritten laws. In 451 B.C.
all plebeians scored a great victory at Rome in forcing
the patricians to write down the laws--even though legal
procedures, so important to the Romans, remained secret.
The original written tablets (bronze or wooden) were
destroyed when the Gauls captured Rome in 390 B.C., but
we have excerpts and summaries which provide our best
source of information for the 400's B.C.

     In 451 B.C. the consulship (if it existed already)
was suspended to make way for a 10-man group called the
DECEMVIRS (= 10 men), who had the job of writing down the
laws. The decemvirs, all patricians, were headed by
Appius Claudius of the famous Sabine family. Tradition
later said that the 10 men went to Athens to study the
laws of that city. The laws the 10 men wrote down, which
are known as the Twelve Tables, are generally pretty grim.
There was imprisonment and some sort of bondage for debt,
for example. However, there are some bright spots. In
marriage, while a husband had the same rights over his
wife that a father had over his children, a wife aged 25
or above could keep possession of her own property, under
the formal control of her father or guardian; by passing
three nights in a year away from home, a wife could avoid
her husband's legal control. We get the definite impression that women were freer in Rome than they were in
Athens. With time, they became still more free. Eventually, in the late Republic. a system of free and equal

marriage developed, with easy divorce. One important
political element in the Twelve Tables was that only the
Assembly of Centuries could hear capital cases and impose
the death penalty; this restricted the officials and the
Senate.

Many legends surround the decemvirs. Some of the
stories look very much like fakes. The work on the law
codes carried over into 450 B.C. with a second set of
decemvirs. Five in the new 10 were plebeians, and only
Appius Claudius kept his place among the 10 from the
previous year. The new decemvirs acted very badly. They
confirmed a law, or made into law an old custom, banning
marriage between patricians and plebeians (which would
keep the aristocracy closed). Appius Claudius disgraced
himself by lusting after <u>Verginia</u>, so that her father
killed her to save her. The plebeians seceded for a
second time (assuming a first secession had taken place
in 494 B.C.); the decemvirs resigned, the consulship was
restored, and the angry plebeians obtained more concessions:
--449 B.C.: <u>The</u> <u>Laws</u> <u>of</u> <u>Valerius</u> <u>and</u> <u>Horatius</u>--
1. Something is done to increase the importance of the
   plebiscites passed by the Tribal Assembly. Perhaps
   they are given the force of law if they are accepted
   by the Senate.
2. Tribunes are given legal protection by the state
   (that is, the plebeians' champions are <u>recognized</u>
   by that state).
--445 B.C.: <u>Law</u> <u>of</u> <u>Canuleius</u>--allows plebeians and
patricians to marry. This reversed the decision of
the decemvirs. There is some doubt about the content
of the law and whether it actually passed.

444-367 B.C. <u>Consulship</u> <u>Abandoned</u>: <u>Military</u> <u>Tribunate</u>.
It was not long before the consulship was abandoned
again, this time for an extended period. In its place a
<u>military</u> <u>tribunate</u> was created. There were 3 military
tribunes until 427 B.C.; then 4 until 400 B.C.; then 6
until 367 B.C. The purpose behind this change was probably military, relating to changes in the size and structure of the army that we know little about. The military
tribunes were regular officials with the powers of consuls.
Consuls were actually reintroduced in 22 of the years
between 444 and 367 B.C., but from 391 to 367 B.C. there
were none.

It is barely possible that one of the ideas behind
the military tribunate was to create opportunity for
plebeians. If plebeians ever had been able to acquire the
consulship, they could no longer do so by 450 B.C. Changing the name of the chief official position and increasing
the number of men holding it might do the trick. Some
military tribunes were plebeians, including one of the
first 3 chosen in 444 B.C., but such a thing remained rare.
In 3 years between 444 and 367 B.C. one military tribune
was a plebeian; in 379 B.C. 3 of the 6 military tribunes
were plebeians; in 400 and 396 B.C. plebeians made up a
majority of the military tribunes.

443 B.C. Censor. In 443 B.C. the office of CENSOR (the
censorship) was established. It was held by a man of great
importance, usually an ex-consul, eventually for an 18-
month period every 5 years. The censor's job was to keep
the list of citizens up to date (thus our census) and to
assess taxes. Soon the censors were supervising the letting
of government contracts and serving as guardians of morals
(our censorship). They could throw people out of the
Senate, for example, for corrupt or scandalous behavior.
Many of these duties in the past had been handled by consuls; the introduction of censors was linked somehow to
the change from consuls to military tribunes, to free the
latter for military duties--or to reduce the importance
of an office which might become available to plebeians.

421 B.C. Quaestors. Twenty years later the old office of
the quaestors, who assisted the consuls/military tribunes,
was opened to plebeians. By this time there were 4
quaestors, who were in charge mainly of financial affairs.
They lacked imperium. This was a minor gain for the
plebeians.

     The great raid of the Gauls into Latin country (390
B.C.) and the sacking of Rome produced the most serious
economic and political strains the Republic had experienced.
There was a great deal of disorder, some anarchy (not being
able to elect officials), and two dictatorships by the
patrician military hero Camillus. Again, the plebeians
won concessions:
--367 B.C.: The Laws of LICINIUS and SEXTIUS. Licinius
     and Sextius were both plebeians. They had led the plebeian

forces for 10 years and perhaps were reelected tribunes
in each year through that troubled period.
1. The system of two consuls each year is restored.
   Some provision about plebeians and the consulship
   was passed. In 366 B.C. Licinius became the first
   plebeian consul (or at least the first since the
   very early days of the Republic). Perhaps one
   consul each year was to be a plebeian--although,
   if so, the law was ignored in 7 of the years down
   to 342 B.C.
2. A law was passed to limit holdings of public lands
   (lands which belonged to the state). Later, the
   limit was some 300 acres; we do not know what limit
   was used in 367 B.C.

With the plebeians definitely achieving the rank of
consul here, they soon were able to make their way into
the other high offices and to win other concessions. Over
the years from 343 to 264 B.C. some 60,000 family land-
holdings were carved out of the public lands in individual
plots and colonies. Most of these went to citizens, something which will have helped to relieve tensions. In
politics:
356 B.C.: 1st plebeian dictator.
351 B.C.: 1st plebeian censor.
342 B.C.: Law of Genucius: requiring definitely that
one consul at least each year be a plebeian. This was
enforced (although it was not until 172 B.C. that both
consuls were plebeians). Also, a 10-year interval was
required between terms in the same office; this provision
was often suspended.
339 B.C.: Laws of Publilius. Publilius was a plebeian
dictator. He carried a law that one censor at least must
be a plebeian. Not until 131 B.C. were both censors
plebeians. Another law of Publilius may have removed the
Senate's veto of actions of the Tribal Assembly.
336 B.C.: 1st plebeian praetor. This office of praetor
had been created in 366 B.C. to handle some of the duties
of the consuls, particularly legal and other civilian
business, when the consulship was being restored after
the crisis of 367 B.C. As the business of Rome and its
commitments in Italy increased, there was little choice
but to create more officials. The praetorship is an
example. Another device for responding to such needs, and

461

one much more to the liking of the patricians, was the
idea of a promagistrate, a man serving in the place of a
specific official. This system appears in 327 B.C. on
campaign at Naples in the 2nd Samnite War. A proconsul,
for example, was a man, usually an ex-consul, who served
in the place of a consul and enjoyed his powers. These
promagistrates were chosen by the Senate rather than the
Assembly.

326 ? (or 313?) B.C.: Law of Poetelius. This was a small
triumph for debtors, after many earlier attempts to help
them had achieved little. We do not know all the details
of the law. Probably it did not stop hereditary bondage
for debt, as was often claimed later, but it did require
a court judgment before bondage could begin. It may have
done away with bondage and imprisonment for some types of
debts. It may have allowed loans to be made against
property as well as persons, so that the lender would have
to accept whatever property the borrower offered in payment.

In 312 B.C. Appius Claudius the Blind, of the great
patrician Sabine family, became censor. He is the earliest
Roman about whom we know enough to make him something of
a flesh-and-blood character. As censor, Appius Claudius
planned and let the contracts for
1. The 1st great aqueduct at Rome, the Aqua Appia,
   the Appian Waterway;
2. the 1st of the great Roman roads, the Via Appia,
   the Appian Way. This covered the 130 miles from
   Rome to Capua, aiding the Romans in the 2nd Samnite
   War. The road was extended to Brundisium by 244
   B.C. These roads were built by private contractors
   to state specifications. They were narrow (just
   a few feet wide, for a few men or a wagon) and ran
   straight where they could--from the air this often
   looks like a series of zigzags. They were intended
   primarily for government and army use. Typical of
   old Roman roads, the Appian Way at first had a
   gravel surface, but by 295 B.C. it was paved. The
   preferred paving was heavy blocks of basalt lava
   on massive foundations.

Appius Claudius is also associated with a number of
"reforms." As censor in 312 B.C. he proposed to let
landless citizens (most of whom would be poor) register

in any tribe of their choice. This might allow the poor
in the city to win control of the country tribes, since
not many farmers would bother, we can suppose, to go to
the Tribal Assembly. The existing system, which confined
the city-dwellers to 4 of the 31 tribes, must have produced an odd Assembly in Rome. Appius Claudius also allowed
the sons of freedmen (ex-slaves) into the Senate if they
were otherwise qualified. Freedmen themselves were not
allowed even to vote, although their sons were. The
Senate threw out this concession to the sons of freedmen
the next year, 311 B.C. In 304 B.C. Appius Claudius made
public a handbook of correct forms of legal procedure,
opening to the plebeians a subject which had been kept
secret and thereby improving their standing before the
law.

We do not know enough to say why the patrician Appius
Claudius promoted such reforms. Later, he was sometimes
seen as the originator of the patrician "friend of the
people" type who finally overthrew the Republic. He was
a poet, the first known Latin literary figure. His biting
Proverbs were his most famous work. This reminds us of
Solon, the early politician-poet of Athens.

The revelation of legal procedures was a blow at the
aristocratic priests who interpreted the law. Soon afterwards, in 300 B.C., the religious offices were opened to
plebeians, and a requirement was introduced that half of
the religious officers were to be plebeians.

The Conflict of the Orders came to its conclusion in
287 B.C. in the law of HORTENSIUS. Hortensius was a
plebeian dictator for six months after the crisis of the
fifth, and last, secession by the plebeians. Plebiscites
of the Tribal Assembly were now accepted as having the
force of law; the Assembly had become a true legislature.
The constitution as it now was survived for almost 200
years.

Summary.
With the Tribal Assembly accepted as a legislature,
and the plebeians being eligible for all offices, Rome
could boast that it had elements of democracy. The Greek
historian Polybius in the 100's B.C. called it a mixed

463

constitution, of the kind much admired by the Greeks, with
all the right checks and balances:
--democratic elements, provided by the Tribal Assembly and
  the principle of access to high office for plebeians;
--oligarchic/aristocratic elements, provided by the Senate
  and the patricians;
--monarchical elements, provided by the imperium of the
  consuls.

In reality, the mass of the citizens had settled for
relatively little. The unit system in the Tribal Assembly
was easily rigged, and the right of plebeians to high
office benefitted only the wealthy--and only a few of
those. A small number of patrician families still ran
things, primarily through the Senate. The old patrician
families were much reduced in numbers. Of the more than
50 patrician clans of the 400's B.C., only 29 appear in
the 300's B.C., and they then surely made up less than
5% of the citizen population. Most of the old patrician
families had simply died out by 300 B.C. However, those
which survived continued to provide the heart of the system.
They also showed great skill and good sense in absorbing
the most aggressive elements in the plebeian class.
Between 366 and 265 B.C. we can see 36 plebeian clans holding 90 consulships (a little less than half of the total
number of consulships). The first member of a plebeian
family to obtain high office and then go into the Senate
was called a NEW MAN. The patricians and the new man
together made up the NOBILITY. The few new men generally
married into the grand patrician families and adapted
themselves to their new situations. Such alliances were
particularly useful for supplying offspring who could be
used as plebeian tribunes in the Tribal Assembly to keep
an eye on that body for the Senate.

The entire process provides strong evidence of the
conservatism and restraint of the Romans. The democratic
element, as opposed to the ambitious new men, was never
strong; a relatively few concessions to it were enough
to produce general acceptance of continuing domination by
the narrow group, the nobility. It was a proud Roman
boast later that the Conflict of the Orders had produced
a minimum of violence and no bloodshed. Even if the
claim was exaggerated, it too is revealing as an indication

464

of the limits on the struggle. The Roman experience had indeed been notably less violent and troubled than the kind of thing that was common in Greece; the "people" had asserted themselves much less vigorously. The life of a politician at Athens, for example, was very obviously much more trying and dangerous than that of his Roman counterpart. Tradition indicates three attempts at tyranny in the Greek fashion in Rome in these years (478, 431, 376 B.C.). While we do not know how well founded in fact these episodes are, the likelihood is that such tyranny was hardly a serious possibility in Rome at this period. It would have seemed to Romans to be contrary to good sense and tradition.

The influence of the patricians was bolstered greatly even in this early period by the system of clientship. Clientship can be traced back into the period of the kings; the system came to be very important in the late Republic. A client, who might be a wealthy, ambitious, talented friend or a poor dependent, attached himself hereditarily to a powerful family. He would receive help (for some, political advancement, as with a new man; for others, such as the poor, jobs and handouts). In return he identified himself with and supported the interests of that family. For the poor, this could mean doing odd jobs, voting right, turning out for street fights. The system was very deeply entrenched and it was taken very seriously, even though the mutual undertakings of clientship were not enforceable at law. A client was supposed to rate ahead of relatives by marriage. Clientship was the kind of thing that naturally had heavy religious overtones for the Romans, for it involved in very basic ways both fides and pietas.

One thing to remember is that few of the citizens at Rome seem to have worried much about telling other Italians what to do. The Conflict of the Orders, the idea of "power to the plebeians," which was limited enough in its application to citizens, did not apply at all to the non-citizens. It worried Athenians and other Greeks that Athens should tell its allies what to do; the Romans do not seem to have been able to invent much of a problem for themselves in this connection.

465

EXPANSION OF ROME, 270-200 B.C.: CONQUEST OF THE WESTERN MEDITERRANEAN COASTAL AREAS

This period is the first in Rome's development that is known to us in some detail. This knowledge we owe mostly to the writings of the Greek Polybius in the 100's B.C. and of the Italian Livy near the beginning of the Christian era.

There was only a brief pause after Rome's conquest of the Greek cities in south Italy in the 270's B.C. It was not long before Rome moved outside the Italian mainland. That movement brought Rome's first contest against a great power, the strong state of CARTHAGE in North Africa. From the Latin word for Phoenician (Carthage having been founded by Phoenicians), the wars of Rome against Carthage are known to us as the Punic Wars.

Carthage was a wealthy trading state. It had possessions stretching across the coastal areas of western North Africa, southern Spain, Corsica, Sardinia, and western Sicily. The only rivals at sea in the western Mediterranean to Carthage were Massilia, the Greek city in southern France, and the Greek cities in eastern Sicily, chief among them Syracuse. Trading interests had taken Carthage into early contact with the Italian mainland. Carthaginian settlements existed in the Etruscan cities in the 500's B.C., and Carthage may have established friendly relations with Rome almost as soon as Rome secured its independence around 500 B.C. Later treaties renewed Carthage's friendly connections with Rome through the period of the Roman conquest of Italy (500-270 B.C.). Carthage supported Rome against Pyrrhus of Epirus and sent help in that struggle, at least in the form of money. The rise of Rome put great strain on the tradition of friendship with Carthage, although Rome, land-bound and lacking a large navy, was not in any way necessarily a serious immediate threat to Carthage.

Politically, Carthage was a narrow oligarchy. A few families dominated the Council in which most power was concentrated. Carthage's traditional stability had been much admired by Aristotle and other Greeks. The city-state

relied heavily on mercenary soldiers recruited from the
more backward peoples it dominated, North Africans and
Spaniards particularly, and its ruling class had little of
the sense of military duty which was so evident at Rome.

1st Punic War, 264-241 B.C.

The war began when Rome responded to a plea from
Messana, in Sicily directly across from the toe of Italy,
for help against the Carthaginians. A group of veterans
from Campania had grabbed the city about 20 years earlier.
They had recently called in Carthaginian forces to protect
themselves against a threat from Greek Syracuse. It upset
the Greeks, including the Roman allies in south Italy, to
see Carthage secure such a hold in eastern Sicily.
Messana was "convinced" to change its mind and to appeal
for help to Rome instead (264 B.C.).

The Romans came, but only after some hesitation. The
Senate at Rome had difficulty making up its mind, and even
asked the Assembly to make the decision (foreign policy by
this time was almost entirely a matter for the Senate). It
is possible that Rome had promised to stay out of Sicily in
its most recent treaty with Carthage in 278 B.C. Attracted
perhaps by the prospect of booty, and by a false hope that
the campaign would be brief, the people decided in favor of
a step which meant removing the Carthaginians by force from
Messana. The outbreak of the war followed the pattern of
the response to Capua's appeal for help in 343 B.C., but
the decision to fight had no very clear objective at all;
it looks like Rome was just drifting along, aided by the
impetus from the recent wars of conquest in Italy.

The war turned into a very big affair. We can note
the following stages:
264-257 B.C.: At first things went well for Rome. The
Roman army pinned the Carthaginians into their great for-
tresses in the western part of Sicily. Panormus was the
biggest Carthaginian base. After the Romans stormed
Agrigentum the Carthaginians avoided any further major land
battle for the rest of the war. Syracuse, which at first
supported Carthage, quickly changed sides. In doing so, it
became Rome's first foreign "client," another extension of
the old idea of clientship. In 259 B.C. a Roman army under
L. Cornelius Scipio began to occupy Corsica and Sardinia.

467

All this was possible because at the same time Rome put together a large navy of Greek-style quinqueremes to match Carthage at sea. The Romans won the first big battle at sea at Mylae in 260 B.C. To offset Carthaginian naval skill, the Romans concentrated on grappling the enemy ships, looking for hand-to-hand fighting. They put heavy spikes or beaks at the prows of their ships to grip the enemy vessels and tied to their masts wooden "bridges" which could be dropped on to the enemy ships at close quarters. They found, though, that these bridges made their ships top-heavy and they suffered enormous losses in storms, etc. The war produced the greatest series of sea battles in the ancient world (all fought just off the coast, of course).

256-255 B.C.: Following victory off Cape Ecnomus in the biggest sea battle of the war, Rome put an army on to the North African coast to move against Carthage. The war seemed close to an end, but things did not go as planned. The Roman army commander in North Africa, Atilius Regulus, instead of following instructions to limit himself to holding a position through the winter (256-255 B.C.), tried to win the war himself. He was defeated, and surrendered. The Roman fleet was not able to rescue him; the fleet itself suffered terrible damage in a storm on the way home. Romans believed later that the captured Regulus was sent to Rome to work for peace, but that he refused to play this part once at Rome and went back voluntarily to Carthage to be tortured and killed.

254-242 B.C.: The Romans now withdrew from Africa and settled down to a drawn-out war at sea and in Sicily. They gradually obtained a decisive superiority at sea, despite repeated early setbacks. In Sicily, the Romans soon took Panormus, but there was occasional heavy fighting around other Carthaginian strong points in the western part of the island. Carthage found a very able young general, HAMILCAR BARCA, who caused the Romans great difficulties.

241 B.C.: Following a last great sea victory at the Aegates Islands, Carthage gave up.

Carthage agreed to surrender Sicily and to pay a large amount of money (an indemnity) to Rome. It was to remain a Roman principle to make enemies pay for its wars. No Carthaginian warships could enter Italian waters. Sicily became Rome's first overseas possession. The task of administering the new territory was tackled in a simple, straightforward, and profitable manner. Rome left some cities on the island, including Syracuse, free, and appointed a governor for the rest, although in the unfree areas also the towns were allowed some degree of selfgovernment. Since the island was intended to profit its new owner, only a small staff was provided for the governor. Much of the island was confiscated by the Roman state and then leased out to local towns or their inhabitants. Syracuse's idea of a direct tax of 1/10th of the crops was applied by Rome to the island, as a substitute for military service. Rome welcomed the opportunity to get at the island's wealth, but it had no use for Phoenician or Greek soldiers.

Interwar Period, 241-218 B.C.

Carthage: Carthaginian mercenary soldiers rebelled in North Africa after the war, threatening even the city of Carthage itself. The state was hard pressed to pay them. Rome supported Carthage against the rebels, but then, in 238 B.C., when mercenaries on Sardinia also rebelled and this time appealed to Rome, Rome took the opportunity to seize both Sardinia and Corsica. Following this blatant piece of aggression, Rome added insult to injury by increasing the indemnity required of Carthage, thereby recouping the costs of her land-grab. The two islands were placed together in a second province. The coastal areas won from Carthage paid the 1/10th tax which was used in Sicily. The interiors of the islands long remained more or less independent in the hands of various tribes.

Illyria: In 229 B.C. Rome moved east for the first time. A Queen Teuta, who ruled much of the semi-Greek Illyria directly across the Adriatic Sea, was raiding along the Illyrian coast, where there were independent Greek cities, and was disturbing trade with Italy. Finally, after Teuta allowed a Roman envoy to be murdered, a Roman army was sent across the sea to punish her. The Greek coastal cities were made protected friends of Rome. A number of them were put under the control of a Greek adventurer named Demetrius. Demetrius was put out by Rome 10 years later when he proved an unreliable client.

North Italy: A large army of Gauls invaded central Italy in 225 B.C. in the first upsurge of trouble from that direction since the early part of the century. The Gauls were defeated at Telamon by the two consuls of the year (one of whom was Atilius Regulus, son of the man who had been defeated in

North Africa in 256-255 B.C.). Rome then conquered north
Italy. The big name here was GAIUS FLAMINIUS, who led the
first Roman army across the river Po. Flaminius, a friend
to the "people" (see below), ignored a recall by the Senate
over bad signs (auguries). The Senate then opposed giving
him a triumph (the great procession which was given to a
successful general on his return from campaign), but the
people insisted on giving him one. Latin colonies were
placed in the north to begin the Romanization of the area.

2nd Punic War, 218-201 B.C.

The second war between Rome and Carthage was the great-
est war of the ancient world, as well as the most dramatic
and the best recorded. It grew out of events in Spain. The
Carthaginians conquered the southern and eastern areas of
Spain in the period between the two Punic Wars (241-218 B.C.).
They did this under the leadership of the Barcid family:
Hamilcar Barca, who had made his name in the first war
against Rome; then, after Hamilcar drowned in 229 B.C., his
son-in-law Hasdrubal (229-221 B.C.); and finally, after
Hasdrubal's assassination, Hamilcar's great son HANNIBAL
(from 221 B.C.). After Carthage lost almost all of its
holdings in Spain to the native tribes in the 1st Punic War,
Hamilcar convinced his state that by concentrating on Spain
it would secure enough revenue to pay off the Romans and to
regain its strength. There were also fine native soldiers
to be picked up in Spain, to use perhaps against the Romans
eventually. Certainly the Barcids were hostile to Rome.
There was a Roman story that Hamilcar made his son Hannibal
swear as a youth to oppose Rome forever.

The Barcids conquered more than half of Spain. They
placed their capital at New Carthage. The Barcids enjoyed a
great deal of independence from Carthage itself, and it is
possible that they used this freedom in Spain to hurry on
another conflict with Rome. There are some indications that
in the war which grew out of Spain, the 2nd Punic War,
Carthage, as distinct from the Barcids, did not have its
whole heart in the business.

Hasdrubal (not Carthage) made an agreement with Rome in
226 B.C. He seems to have promised not to go north of the
Ebro river; the Romans may have promised not to go south of
the same river. Half-a-dozen years later, Saguntum, a

native Spanish town south of the Ebro, appealed to Rome for help against Hannibal, who had just taken over from Hasdrubal. Rome had taken in Saguntum as a client-friend in 223 B.C. (after the agreement with Hasdrubal), although perhaps not in a formal treaty. Rome hesitated, being occupied in north Italy with the Gauls. It sent envoys to Spain to warn Hannibal to let Saguntum alone. He refused, and the town fell to him in 219 B.C. Rome decided upon war.

The Romans intended to carry the war to the Carthaginians as they had in the earlier war. For 218 B.C. Rome prepared armies to go to Carthage and Spain. Hannibal, then aged 29, the greatest military talent the Roman Republic ever faced, broke up the Roman plans by an attack of his own. 218 B.C.: Hannibal invaded Italy by land over the Alps. Of his 45,000 men, about 25,000 survived the long march from Spain and the fighting against the tribes they had to pass through. He also took with him 37 elephants; they did not last long.

This surprise move forced the recall of some of the Roman troops which were already on the march for Spain. These Hannibal defeated at the Ticino. The Roman commander, the consul P. Cornelius Scipio, then withdrew to await the other consul, who had been recalled from his original job of attacking Carthage. Hannibal defeated them both overwhelmingly in a major battle at the Trebia in December, 218 B.C. 217 B.C.: Hannibal next moved south. He had picked up enough men from the Gauls in north Italy to build his force up to 50,000. In April he defeated the consul Gaius Flaminius, the people's favorite, at LAKE TRASIMENE. Flaminius was killed; his army, surprised as it marched along the lake shore, was all but annihilated.

After Lake Trasimene, the Romans gave the dictatorship to Q. FABIUS MAXIMUS, of a great Senate patrician family. He was elected dictator by the Assembly: of the consuls who should have nominated him, one was dead and one was cut off from Rome. The selection of Fabius was a sign that Flaminius's failure had hurt the people's cause badly. Fabius shadowed Hannibal as the latter moved south. In avoiding battle, Fabius both acknowledged Hannibal's military talents and gave Roman manpower and morale a chance to recover from the series of defeats. He won the name the

Delayer (Fabius Cunctator), and the term Fabian in English means moderate, or slow, or piece-meal.

Hannibal needed another battle. He was disappointed to find that the Italians did not desert Rome to support him; his line about "liberating" Italy was not working. He did not have the strength or equipment to attack Rome itself, and could only move around the countryside. He advanced into south Italy.

216 B.C.: Then Rome played into Hannibal's hands by abandoning delaying tactics and going on to the attack again. It did this even though further minor attacks against Hannibal since Lake Trasimene had also only brought defeat. The two consuls, Terentius Varro, a people's favorite, and L. Aemilius Paullus, together confronted Hannibal at CANNAE with perhaps 60,000 men, the largest single field army the Romans had put forward to that time. They were badly beaten, as Hannibal managed to surround them even though he was outnumbered. Cannae was the most famous defeat ever suffered by a Roman army. Most of the Romans, once surrounded, chose to die fighting rather than give in. Paullus was killed. Varro fought his way out and rallied some of the survivors. The Senate thanked Varro for "not giving up on the Republic," but he was savaged by later Roman writers for having survived. Two legions which escaped destruction were sent to the disgrace of garrison duty in Sicily by a Senate which thought that they should have stayed to die.

The worried Romans freed 8,000 slaves and armed them to defend the city. Hannibal, however, still lacked the ability to attack Rome itself. He did find now, though, that many areas of south Italy joined him, including Capua and Tarentum and Syracuse, the three largest Greek cities. Central Italy continued to be loyal to Rome, which was something of a tribute to the city under the circumstances. Rome did not despair. In this hour of their crisis, the Romans went back to Fabius and his cautious, defensive tactics. By avoiding battle, they would gain time for their manpower supply to build back up. Hannibal, cut off from Carthage, with his own state showing little interest in making much of an effort to resupply him by challenging the Romans at sea, would be contained and worn down. The flat refusal of the Romans to consider giving in after this line of great defeats made nonsense of Hannibal's plans.

472

At this point, the Romans were at their best, in one of the proudest moments of their history. The atmosphere in the city is expressed in the following piece taken from a history written by APPIAN, a Greek of Alexandria who wrote in the 100's A.C., more than 300 years later:

Hannibal allowed the Romans he had captured to send messengers to Rome in their own behalf, to see if the citizens would ransom them with money. Three were chosen to go, of whom Sempronius was the leader. Hannibal required them to swear that they would return to him. The relatives of the prisoners, gathering around the Senate building, said that they were ready to pay the ransoms out of their own money and begged the Senate to let them do so. The public joined them with their own prayers and tears. Some of the senators thought that it was not wise, after such great defeats, to allow the city to lose so many more men, or to reject free men when liberty was being given to slaves. Others thought that compassion like this would teach men to flee a battle; instead, they should be taught to conquer or die in the field, knowing that even the friends of those who ran away would not be allowed to pity them. After many precedents had been cited on both sides, the Senate decided at last that the prisoners should not be ransomed by their relatives. The Senate believed that with so many dangers still hanging over the city softness now would produce harm in the future, while harshness, although painful, would be of advantage to the public in the future, and at the present would surprise Hannibal by its boldness. So Sempronius and the two prisoners who were with him went back to Hannibal. Hannibal sold some of his prisoners into slavery, put others to death in anger, and made a bridge of their bodies with which he passed over a stream. He made the senators and other distinguished prisoners in his hands fight with each other, as a spectacle for the Africans, fathers against sons, brothers against brothers. He did not miss any act of nasty cruelty he could think of.

Enormous armies were raised by Rome in the next years from the much reduced population which remained loyal. All free males aged 18 to 46 were used, serving an average of seven years. Even the proletarians, the poor, were drafted and then equipped at the public expense. In 212 B.C., Rome

473

had at least 250,000 men in the field. At this point, it could go cautiously on to the offensive again. Avoiding Hannibal in the field (although another consul was killed in 212 B.C. fighting Hannibal), the Romans struck at those who had abandoned them. Capua and Syracuse were taken in 211 B.C. Archimedes, the Greek scientist, was killed in the recapture of Syracuse. Hannibal was not strong enough to break up these Roman siege operations. He made a dash to Rome that year, circling the city in full view of the inhabitants standing on the walls. This attempt to draw the Roman troops off from Capua failed. In 209 B.C. Tarentum was retaken by the Romans and almost destroyed in deliberate brutality. Things were improving, although that year (209 B.C.) 12 of the 30 Latin colonies reported to Rome that they were unable to supply their quota of men.

Increasingly, Rome's attention turned to Spain. Even in the darkest days, Rome had not abandoned the troops sent out there in 218 B.C. at the start of the war. An army was built up in Spain under the command of P. Cornelius Scipio (consul of 218 B.C.) and his brother. They did well with limited resources against the Carthaginians, who were led by Hasdrubal, Hannibal's younger brother. One result was that Hasdrubal could not send fresh troops to his brother in Italy. Then, in 211 B.C., both of the Scipio brothers were killed in separate battles. 210 B.C.: P. CORNELIUS SCIPIO AFRICANUS, the son of the consul of 218 B.C., was named to command the Roman army in Spain. Aged only 25, and having held only minor office, Scipio was not legally eligible for the command. The Assembly chose him, as the people began to assert themselves once more, now that the worst of the crisis was over, after a period of lack of confidence following the defeat of their favorite Flaminius in 217 B.C. The Senate was reluctant to abandon Fabianism and to give in to the people. Fabius and his supporters opposed the appointment of Scipio, but in vain.

The patrician Scipio, the first private citizen to receive such imperium, embodied the people's traditional support of aggressive tactics. He was to prove the Roman answer to Hannibal, the greatest soldier the Republic had yet produced. 209 B.C.: Scipio at once engineered a successful surprise

attack on New Carthage, the Carthaginian capital in Spain.
208 B.C.: Scipio won a great victory at Baecula. In the
same year, his command in Spain was prolonged indefinitely.
207 B.C.: Following the defeat at Baecula, Hasdrubal seems
to have accepted that Spain could not be saved. He took
some of his troops to Italy to help his brother Hannibal.
The Romans discovered the brothers' plans and defeated
Hasdrubal and his army of 30,000 (many of them Gauls who had
been picked up in north Italy) at the Metaurus before
Hannibal could join him. The news of this defeat came to
Hannibal when his brother's head was thrown into the Carthaginian camp by the Romans.
206 B.C.: A victory at Ilipa gave Scipio and the Romans control of Spain.

Scipio went back at once to Rome. There he was elected
consul. He wanted a new command to attack Carthage itself,
but he found the Senate opposed to this. Apart from the
point that Hannibal was still loose in south Italy and the
old dislike of Scipio as a popular favorite, the Senate
objected to Scipio's style, believing that he might be
aiming at dictatorship. He is the first of such figures
among the great generals of the late Republic. Scipio had
put his own head on coins in Spain, and he may have been
hailed as imperator (great general, a word from which we get
emperor) by his troops; things which were against all custom.
He had a high and mighty manner, with the Spanish natives as
well as with his own troops, and a strange habit of regarding
himself as divinely inspired in the fashion of Alexander the
Great. There is no sign, though, that he wanted anything
more than great glory.

With the Assembly's help, Scipio secured a compromise
appointment from the Senate. He was given Sicily as his
area of operation, with the two legions which had been stationed there in disgrace ever since Cannae (216 B.C.). He
could go to Africa if necessary, and could use any volunteers
he was able to find for the army. In all, Scipio came up
with about 30,000 men.
204 B.C.: Scipio attacked Carthage. He had the help of
Masinissa, ruler of Numidia nearby, an arrangement which
Scipio had worked out during his stay in Spain.
203 B.C.: Scipio's victories made Carthage recall Hannibal
from Italy after he had been there for 15 years. Hannibal

got Carthage to refuse to accept terms which had already been worked out with Rome.
202 B.C.: Scipio defeated Hannibal at the battle of ZAMA in a tight struggle. The two men are said to have met before the battle.

Carthage now gave up. Rome took Spain and the usual large indemnity. Carthage had to surrender its navy, accepting a limit of 10 warships for the future, and became a Roman satellite in foreign policy. Masinissa obtained some land in western North Africa from Carthage, which was now limited to the area in its immediate neighborhood.

Those parts of Spain held by the Romans were divided into two provinces: Nearer Spain (administered from New Carthage), and Further Spain or Baetica. Being anxious to use the warlike and primitive Spaniards for soldiers, Rome required of Spain troops for its army; in return, the tax on crops was to be only 1/20th instead of the 1/10th taken in Sicily. Scipio had founded Italica in Spain for his veterans, a great break with tradition even though Italica was not given the status of a colony.

These two wars had tested Rome severely. They left Rome the strongest power in the entire Mediterranean world. From this point, everything else was Rome's for the taking. Some, Polybius among them, believed that Rome had a plan for domination of the Mediterranean by this time. It is difficult to believe this. The Romans stumbled along, responding to things as they arose. Their horizons grew bigger with their power, and certain things about them were highly predictable --their unwillingness to back down and their iron determination when aroused. Beyond this, there was little in the way of a plan.

Growing Roman power had already pointed the Republic in a new direction. Philip V of Macedon, ruling the closest of the major Macedonian successor-states to Alexander the Great's empire, came out in support of Carthage in 215 B.C. after Cannae. Philip at that time had recently secured control of Greece in alliance with the Achaean League of the Peloponnesus. He may have thought that with the defeat at Cannae the Romans were done for. This was something Philip would welcome, since the minor Roman involvement in Illyria before the war had indicated the beginning of a Roman

476

interest in the Greek world. Philip had already given
refuge to Demetrius when the Romans had thrown that unsat-
isfactory puppet out of Illyria around 220 B.C.

Philip's move brought on the 1st Macedonian War (215-
205 B.C.). There was little to the war. Rome was too busy
elsewhere to bother much; Philip did little for the Carthaginians, realizing soon that he had miscalculated. Philip
and his allies the Achaeans had the better of what fighting
there was in Greece. The Romans made an alliance with the
rival Aetolian League, and one with the kingdom of Pergamum
in Asia Minor. These were the first formal Roman alliances
to the East, but the Romans disappointed their new allies on
this occasion by their lack of interest. The war was ended
slightly to Philip's favor. Greece and Macedonia were sure
to be areas of concern as soon as Rome was free of Carthage;
Rome would not willingly look bad for long.

THE CONDITION OF THE ROMAN REPUBLIC, 270-133 B.C.

The extension of Roman power outside Italy in the generations after 270 B.C. raised many questions for the
Republic. Wealth and power brought inevitable social and
economic change. At the same time, the close contact with
the East, specifically with the Hellenistic civilization
which was predominant across that region, brought a challenge to the Roman way of life and to all the old Roman attitudes. Rome's political institutions also had to cope
with ever-increasing responsibilities.

It must be remembered that all the institutions and
habits of mind of Rome were those of a relatively unsophis-
ticated city-state. Even citizens had to be present in the
Assemblies at Rome to participate. Already, before 270
B.C., this was no longer practicable for most of the citizens, who lived too far away from the city. And Rome also
controlled even by that time Italy, a large area, with most
of its population simply receiving whatever terms the Roman
government decided to offer. In the most basic senses, the
power of Rome had already by 270 B.C. far outrun the city's
institutions--what came after 270 B.C. only made that fact
more and more obvious and more and more absurd. The Assemblies, which increasingly involved only a very small minority of citizens, not only had to speak for all citizens but
had also to deal with the multiplying non-citizen groups
and areas. In 270 B.C. this meant Italy; by 133 B.C. it
meant an area extending from Spain to Egypt.

This situation worked to the advantage of the Senate,
which could provide some of the knowledge and continuity
needed to look after Rome's interests. The Senate, which
was now the body of ex-high officials, contained men who
knew the problems and the areas involved. The Senate, too,
was a local body, containing only the leading citizen families, almost all of them from Rome or areas close by, but
the practical advantages of the Senate over the Assemblies
as Rome's empire developed were enormous. In a world in
which a grand phrase like "the people" often meant just
those Roman citizens, usually residents of the city, who
were willing or were able to attend the Assemblies, a body
of people unrepresentative of the mass of humanity under

478

Rome's control—and perhaps not even very typical of the general body of citizens, the cry of "power to the people" lost a good deal of its appeal and almost all of its good sense. We can imagine the same thing happening if the people living just in Washington, D.C. had conquered the United States and were denying political power to others and referring to themselves alone as "the people." Power would tend to fall into the hands of the administrators—of the equivalent of the officials and the Senate at Rome.

This happened the more easily in Rome because, as we saw, the democratic elements there had never been very strong. The powers of the Assemblies were always severely limited, their voting systems easily manipulated; the Senate always had enormous power. The result at Rome was that the circle of power actually <u>contracted</u> as Roman control expanded outside Italy after 270 B.C. More and more openly, a few families ran things through the Senate, as if the <u>Conflict</u> <u>of</u> <u>the</u> <u>Orders</u> had not taken place. For a long time the system seemed to work fairly well, but then it came under challenge, and in 133 B.C. there occurred the first major attack upon the Senate-centered system which had developed. That attack began a chain of events which resulted eventually in replacing the Republic with a dictatorship.

<u>270-220 B.C.: Further Concessions to the "People."</u>
For a while after 270 B.C. plebeian gains in the old style continued:
253 B.C.: <u>Coruncanius</u>, the first plebeian chief priest, admitted his <u>students</u>, and perhaps the general public, to his consultations with officials, thereby opening up the law a little more. He is the first in the line of great Roman law figures (<u>jurists</u>). Because of the Romans' willingness to identify rules and precedents with religion, it was natural for the priests to serve as legal advisors. Jurists gave legal advice, and even sat in on the courts to answer questions, because the officials who presided at trials were not allowed to lay down the law as they went along—they had to follow precedent and the written law. At all times, much of Rome's intellectual talent went into the law, which was the kind of practical and concrete thing which appealed to the Roman taste for administration and efficiency.
240-220 B.C.: The last two tribes were created in 241 B.C., making 35 in all. Around this time, the <u>Assembly of</u>

Centuries was adapted to the tribal unit system which had always been the basis of voting in the Tribal Assembly. This, of course, reduced in theory the importance of the wealthiest classes in the Assembly of Centuries, although experience had already shown that the tribal unit system could be effectively controlled under most circumstances by the Senate. With these Assemblies now organized on the same tribal basis there is less point to distinguishing between them. From now on the term Assembly will be used to indicate both, with a distinction being made only if there is some purpose to it.

The last great surge of the "people" for a long time is associated with Gaius Flaminius. A plebeian and a new man (see below), Gaius Flaminius is associated with a number of steps which indicate his style as a champion of the "people."
232 B.C.: As tribune, he had a law passed in the Tribal Assembly, against the objections of the Senate, to give the people public land which had been taken from the Gauls in northern Italy (south of the Ro river) half a century before. Only one Roman and one Latin colony had been established there, as the Senate and the wealthy apparently had kept the lands intact to exploit themselves. There were probably many farmer-citizens made poor by the 1st Punic War (264-241 B.C.) who wanted such land. Flaminius' enemies liked to claim later that his proposal had upset the Gauls and had led to the war in the 220's B.C. with them. His action in overruling the Senate objections to this law is said to have been without precedent.
223 B.C.: As consul, Flaminius won military glory in north Italy against the Gauls, but it was again, as we saw above, in circumstances which placed him against the Senate.
220 B.C.: As censor, Flaminius may have been the man who revised the Assembly of Centuries along tribal lines, a move in favor of the poorer citizens.
218 B.C.: Flaminius was the force behind a new law which kept senators out of international trade and money-lending. They were to concentrate on their landed estates instead of trying to make money out of Rome's expansion. By tradition, Flaminius was the only senator who voted for this law, as the Senate again found itself overruled.
217 B.C.: Given the consulship again, as the choice of the "people" in the emergency created by Hannibal's invasion of

Italy, Flaminius was killed and his army devastated at Lake
Trasimene.

2nd Punic War: Revival of the Senate
The failure of Flaminius was of great advantage to the
Senate. It was a Senate favorite, Fabius, who received the
dictatorship and led the Roman recovery over the next few
years in the 2nd Punic War. The Assembly was discredited
still more in 216 B.C. when another favorite of the "people," Varro, not only encouraged the aggression which led to
the further Roman defeat at Cannae but sadly managed to survive the battle. In a general way, the terrible experience
of the 2nd Punic War (218-201 B.C.) is usually seen as the
time when the Senate, by getting the credit for winning the
war and "saving" Rome, got the upper hand and became even
more secure than it had been before. From this time until
133 B.C. the Senate was more or less firmly in control. We
find the Senate suspending laws, declaring them null and
void, making war and peace, having virtually a complete control over foreign policy and relations with the subject peoples. The Senate controlled the Assemblies, determined the
choice of officials, controlled those officials (and through
them the army), appointed the governors of the provinces
which were being created. It had to approve the contracts
let by the censors for roads, aqueducts, buildings, monuments, etc. It controlled the courts by its ability to control the officials and by operating itself as a court of final appeal.

At the heart of the Senate were the patricians, the
ancient aristocratic families which went back to the establishment of the Republic around 500 B.C. and beyond. By
200 B.C., most senators, perhaps 3/4ths of the total number,
were not patricians; they belonged usually to families which
had appeared in the previous 200 years. Such families had
been marrying into the patrician class for generations, and
they tended to be very willing to accept the lead of their
more prestigious relatives. Patricians provided the operating leadership for the various groups and factions which
developed in the Senate. Some two dozen families had a near
monopoly of high office in the 100 years before 133 B.C.,
and the most important of these were patricians. Of the 200
consuls between 233 and 133 B.C., 99 came from just 10 families, 159 from 15 families. The family of Fabius was

patrician; so was the most famous and successful of all the families of this period, that of the Scipios, who obtained 23 consulships in less than 100 years. As the Senate became more secure in this period, as the challenge from below lost most of what little force it had had in the past, so those who controlled things had less need to admit newcomers to their ranks. New men (who had accounted over the previous several generations for most of the existing Senate families) became rare. Only 16 of 262 consuls between 264 and 134 B.C. were new men; only 5 of these came after 200 B.C. In the 100's B.C., in other words, it became almost impossible to break into the circle of power. The government of the Roman Republic was overwhelmingly aristocratic--it had not undergone the experience of the Athenian democracy, in developing the so-called "new leadership" of the wealthy (the class of equites in the Roman case).

The Senate's Approach

The Senate's approach to things remained "amateurish." This was most apparent in the armies, which were still commanded by the political officials, consuls and such. Military setbacks were frequent: a war often began with Roman defeats, until the Romans gave command to, or stumbled upon, a man of military talent. Often the impression is that the Senate squandered Rome's great military power. The worst area was Spain, where the rebellions of the mid-100's B.C. revealed tremendous military inefficiency. The Senate was very reluctant to experiment with irregular, extended commands such as those held by Scipio Africanus in the 2nd Punic War; it preferred to rely on the officials of the day. It was fortunate for Rome that war required relatively little professional skill and that commanders could often be rescued from their mistakes by the fine quality of the men, in particular of the centurions. Polybius described the centurions in the mid-100's B.C. as men who "stand their ground when battered and hard pressed, and are ready to die at their posts." Roman military efficiency definitely improved later as power passed from the Senate to the generals.

"Amateurishness" was also behind the Senate's refusal to build up a careful system of administration in the provinces which were being acquired. A governor of a province found himself very much on his own, with only a skeleton

staff and some soldiers. Usually he had only a year to
serve. A governor tended to leave things as they were in
his province, concentrating on avoiding rebellion and on
drawing out money—the latter as much for himself as for
the state. Often, since the governor was virtually unsuper-
vised, the temptations to corruption proved too strong. In
general, administration of the provinces in this period was
famous for its inefficiency and its corruption. The same
sloppiness and lack of supervision allowed generals away
from Rome to go their own way to an alarming degree. Repeatedly, orders were reinterpreted or disregarded—again,
Spain was the chief victim. Here were the seeds of the
later lack of discipline in the armies and the self-assertiveness of the generals. It was, by the nature of things,
very difficult for the Senate to take any serious steps to
keep members of its own leading families in line.

The same carelessness often marked the Senate's general attitude toward expansion. Politics in the Senate revolved around family groups. Some of those groups had reasonably clear ideas about foreign problems, at least on occasion, but mostly, it seems, the Senate had little interest
in developing coherent policies. The best example is the
Greek world, where Roman policy between 220 and 133 B.C. was
a bewildering mixture of indifference, generosity, and brutal aggression. We can think of the several wars with Macedonia; the strange withdrawal from Greece in the 190's B.C.;
the destruction of <u>Corinth</u> in 146 B.C. Perhaps this sloppiness was not entirely unfortunate. One of the few instances
when the Senate took up a definite policy, at the urging of
those who wanted consistency, led to the destruction of Carthage in 146 B.C. Once again, in many ways the development
of a planned foreign policy had to wait until dictators took
over from the Republic. We would suspect from our own experience that a sizable group of men such as the Senate was is
not very likely to be able to develop an ordered foreign
policy.

Still, whether because of or despite the Senate, Rome
was flourishing abroad. The Republic was wealthy and
strong, with a whole world to plunder. How were these gains
handled? How were the costs and the proceeds shared?

Rome expected its wars to pay for themselves—and then some. We have seen the repeated indemnities forced on defeated enemies. Generals were also expected to pillage widely, both to satisfy their soldiers and to bring home good things for the state. All of the Roman historians writing on this period take it for granted that large-scale looting went on all the time. For the provinces, this was a part of the terrible exploitative side of Rome. Rome seldom bothered to pretend that it came for the good of others—it came to protect, and help, itself. Our kind of humanitarianism was generally notably missing. The outstanding example of "helping" others, the "liberation" of Greece from Macedonian control, turned into a nightmare. From freedom the Greeks went to imprisonment; from prison they went to their deaths. Perhaps for the next several centuries, through the rest of the Republic and the Empire which followed, Greece did not recover from what the Senate did to it in the 100's B.C. War paid—and the provinces went on paying, once conquered, although except for the scourge of corrupt governors they were generally left alone as long as they remained quiet and handed over what money or men Rome wanted. There was enough resistance to the Romans, there were enough rebellions, to indicate that the people they conquered did not see them as deliverers. Only slowly were people broken to Roman rule so that the Romans came to be appreciated for their usefulness in providing stability and order.

This kind of thing can look very bad to us, but its repercussions in Rome were very limited. There was not much point at Rome to criticizing the Senate for abusing the provinces. Instead, the important questions involved the costs of the wars and the ways the proceeds were divided.

The Costs of Expansion: The Manpower Problem

The Roman government asked little money of its citizens; under the circumstances, it hardly needed to. But the manpower needs of the state were enormous. The Roman army was still very heavily _Italian_ even in 133 B.C. Of these Italians, about 1/3rd were _Roman_ citizens. The soldiers were raised by the draft. In the early Republic, service had been for a brief period. The better-off citizens had served, supplying their own equipment, with the

484

poorer citizens (the proletariat) being normally exempted.
Service often took a man a long way from home for a long
period--normally a 16-year term for a draftee. He had to
be equipped and paid by the state. It is likely that the
state also had to find various ways of forcing the proletariat into the service, although this is a process about
which we do not know very much.

The government was always short of soldiers. The male
citizens of draft age (ages 17-46) who had enough property
to qualify for the draft numbered as follows:

218 B.C.	280,000
209 B.C.	237,000
164 B.C.	337,000
136 B.C.	317,000
125 B.C.	395,000

The losses in the 2nd Punic War (218-201 B.C.) reduced the
manpower pool a great deal. The number available for service then recovered, but it collapsed again in the middle
of the 100's B.C. as the Spanish wars claimed heavy casualties. In the period 200-168 B.C. there were usually about
50,000 citizens in the army; both before and after that the
number was greater. A male citizen, in other words, could
expect to be drafted.

A man taken by the army and drawn out of Italy for a
long period was in no position to protect his family--or to
start one, as the case might be. Given the way the legions
fought, the soldier stood a good chance of not getting home
at all. The situation was bad enough from the soldiers'
point of view that, despite good pay and plenty of loot,
indiscipline of all kinds, up to outright mutiny, was common. The worst period was in the Spanish wars of 154-133
B.C. The Roman army was not a well behaved thing. Some
concessions to the soldiers were made by the Senate:
--the term of service was kept short where possible;
--in 198 B.C. soldiers were given the right of appeal
against scourging and the death penalty. Civilians had won
these privileges 100 years earlier;
--in 184 B.C. summary executions in the army were ended.
Among the techniques given up was the decimation, in which
10% of the names of the soldiers in a given unit were drawn
by lot for execution in the case of poor battlefield performance.

485

For the soldiers' dependents back in Italy, the consequences of service were often very bad, even if their men
survived. Many farming families found themselves unable to
protect their farms. Sometimes they would sell out, and
then become landless laborers or drift into the cities; decline into proletarian status at least brought a degree of
protection from the draft. Rome was the chief magnet for
such citizens. It grew rapidly in this period, having a
population of perhaps 500,000 by 150 B.C. Some of these
poor citizens could be taken on as clients by great families, but they were potentially a dangerous element, having
the right and now the opportunity to attend the Assembly.

For the free but non-citizen Italians, who provided
most of the soldiers, things were often worse. While pro-
portionately the demands of the draft fell less heavily on
the non-citizens, the Italians were being made to serve a
state which was not theirs. Their economic problems in
some ways were greater than those of the citizens. The
Italian soldiers were short-changed in sharing out the war
loot. A law of 177 B.C. gave non-citizen soldiers only
half of a citizen's share of movable loot. Much of the
land across southern Italy had been badly damaged during
the 2nd Punic War (218-210 B.C.); some of it does not seem
to have ever recovered. Many Italians also had been forced
off their lands when the Roman state seized large areas in
punishment for the support given to Hannibal in that war.
Dependents of the non-citizen Italian men were in a very
precarious position. Holders of Latin rights could attend
the Assemblies and vote if they drifted off the farms and
into Rome. To offset this, and to maintain the manpower
supply, a Roman law of the 180's B.C. required any person
with Latin rights who came to Rome to leave one son at home.
As early as 265 B.C., people leaving Latin colonies had been
subjected to the same requirement. Other free Italians,
lacking the half-citizenship of Latin rights, could only
hang around Rome, politically powerless but a possible
source of friction.

The Profits of Expansion
      Rome's wars produced enormous profits, in money, in
other property, and in the form of large numbers of human
beings brought into Italy as slaves. Some of the figures
we have defy belief, but there is no question that the number of slaves brought into Italy in this period was very

486

great, great enough certainly to change fundamentally the structure of Italy's population and economy. Some slaves were Italians: 30,000 from the destroyed Greek <u>Tarentum</u> in the 2nd Punic War, for example. Most were foreigners. The biggest bag came from <u>Epirus</u> in 167 B.C., when <u>Aemilius Paullus</u>, who was on his way home from the 3rd Macedonian War, picked up 150,000 people as slaves. He did this at the direct order of the Senate, which clearly had decided to make sure that Rome recouped the costs of the war. It was Paullus' boast that he kept nothing for himself of all the loot from the war except for the library of the king of Macedonia.

The flood of wealth could have been put to many purposes. Paullus' booty alone, for example, allowed the Senate to do away with all <u>direct</u> <u>property</u> <u>taxes</u>. Only <u>citizens</u> paid such taxes, which were regarded as a very bad thing to be collected only in emergencies. As <u>Cicero</u> said later, "it is a politician's duty not to make the people (that is, the citizens) pay a property tax." A heavy property tax had been used in the dark days of the 2nd Punic War, but in 190 B.C. the Senate had actually <u>repaid</u> to the citizens all or part of the tax collected during that war. Now, in 167 B.C., the direct tax disappeared, not to return for more than a century. Taxes, unlike death, are not inevitable. Still, if you lose your land, knowing that you do not have to pay a tax on what you no longer have is not a great consolation.

In any case, the wealth was used mostly to finance new wars, to enrich the State, and to benefit the wealthy and the ruling class. Senate families wound up with a big piece of the proceeds—since they commanded the armies, made the deals, and supervised the distribution and/or sale of the proceeds, this is not so surprising. Many senators became large-scale slaveowners and landowners. Being kept out of <u>trade</u> and <u>finance,</u> at least in theory, by the law of 218 B.C. (see above), the senators concentrated on the <u>land</u>, which was the most prestigious area of the economy. Land they could obtain by buying out poorer citizens and Italians. The wealth coming into Italy produced an <u>inflation</u> which worked to the benefit of the senators, hurting the poor and encouraging them to sell out at what looked like high prices. In addition, a great amount of land in Italy

487

was in the possession of the Roman government. The most
recent large chunks had come from the confiscations aimed
at those in south Italy who had sided with Hannibal in the
2nd Punic War (218-201 B.C.). In all, about 1/3rd of all
the land in Italy belonged to the government. This land
was generally held off the market and leased out in large
pieces to people with influence. The leases were little
more than formalities; the rents were often not collected.
It did not bother the Senate that under the Laws of
Licinius and Sextius of 367 B.C. such large holdings of the
public lands were illegal.

A new style of Italian farming resulted. The old,
small grain farms gave way to extensive olive and wine production and, especially, to cattle and sheep grazing, usually relying on slave labor. Cato, in his work On Farming in
the 100's B.C., reveals a sharp eye for profit and a very
cold attitude toward these slaves. He advised that they be
treated carefully, as you would your animals, but he made
them pay to have sex. Oddly, he made loans to some of his
slaves to help them buy slaves of their own. The large
ranches which developed are described in the 1st century
B.C. by Varro.

This kind of situation naturally produced a danger of
slave uprisings. The first serious outbreak came as early
as 198 B.C. The first very big slave rising was in Sicily
in 135-132 B.C. The slaves held much of the island of
Sicily for three years. They defeated an army commanded by
a consul in 134 B.C., and it took two more campaigns by consuls, in 133 and 132 B.C., to put them down. The rebellion
of Aristonicus at Pergamum after the Romans inherited that
kingdom in 133 B.C. was also in many ways a slave revolt
against Rome. Another great slave revolt broke out on
Sicily in 104 B.C. and lasted until 100 B.C.

The Senate's Answers
The Senate deliberately refused to adopt the most obvious and substantial way of fighting what was going on--
which would have been to put people, citizens and Italians,
back on the land by sharing out the public lands which belonged to the state. We saw in the case of Flaminius in the
230's B.C. the interest of the citizens in these public
lands. Instead, the state's lands were leased out to the

488

wealthy. No colonies at all were founded after about 180
B.C. Of course, as long as the draft continued to take
such numbers and the war-profits were so unevenly distributed, even putting people back on the farms would improve
things only temporarily; it would give them the chance to
go through the same cycle of decline a second time.

We have already seen, in such things as the ending of
the direct property tax, some of the steps the Senate took
to respond to the situation its own policies were creating.
We can also note further minor concessions to the Assemblies
and the plebeians:
1. By 150 B.C. the death penalty for citizens had been virtually done away with.
2. 149 B.C. Extortion Court. After many scandals the
Senate set up a court to look into abuses by Roman officials
in the provinces. This extortion court, as it is called,
was the state's first permanent court. All the judges,
though, were senators (as were the governors of the provinces), and there was no appeal against the court's verdict.
Not surprisingly, the court developed a reputation for protecting its own.

The establishment of this court was a victory for the
equites, the class of wealthy citizens who ranked just below the senators. The equites provided the leadership for
the plebeians, so they were potentially dangerous. They
were finding it harder to break into the circle of power as
new men, at a time when their numbers and their wealth were
expanding rapidly with the growth of the state. We do not
know the precise definition of the equites class, but it included the businessmen of Rome, and many of them were heavily involved with the state. The government did almost
everything through private contractors, providing many opportunities for the equites. Even the right to collect many
provincial indirect taxes (sales taxes, for example) was
leased out (farmed out) to the equites (tax-farmers); so was
the collection of rents from public lands. The law of 218
B.C., which barred senators from money-lending and trade,
opened the way for the equites, even though the law was not
always observed. The general sloppiness of the Senate's supervision of things allowed endless profiteering. Apart from
rooting out corrupt governors, the extortion court set up in
149 B.C. gave the equites a chance to bring charges against

governors who got in their way (that is, honest governors).
For the moment, the equites were satisfied, but their
wealth gave them the means to cause trouble and their exclusion from power tempted them to such a course. In the
future they would cause many problems for the Senate.
3. 139 B.C. A secret ballot was introduced in the election of officials in the Assembly of Centuries.
4. 137 B.C. A secret ballot was introduced for all proceedings in the Assembly of Centuries.

These changes came during the long Spanish wars, which
clearly increased tensions and reduced confidence in the
Senate; improvements in the terms of service in the military were made at the same time. At the same time, however, the Senate took a counterstep (150 B.C.) by obtaining for officials, who were usually under its control, the
right to obstruct Assembly business by announcing bad auspices (religious signs).

The client system was expanded greatly in Rome itself.
It is clear that by the end of this period (133 B.C.) the
chief Senate families could put what were virtually private
armies into the streets. Rome had no police force, so that
in one sense such private groups met a need. The dependen-
cy of the clients made it much easier for the Senate families to keep control of the Assembly. Of course, the poor
Italian non-citizens were not available generally for the
client system: as we have seen, steps were taken to discourage them from moving to the city.

At the same time, a number of social and cultural developments were allowed, to please the plebeians, particularly the poorer ones among them:
--handouts and entertainments in Rome. These included dis-
tributions of food and drink. The most spectacular element,
though, was provided by the public and private games, including gladiator and wild animal contests, which grew rapidly in these decades. Public games, at the state's expense, which were hardly known before the 2nd Punic War
(218-201 B.C.), became common later. Private games, which
were the same kind of thing put on by prominent men at
their own expense, also became common. Gladiators seem to
have been introduced, perhaps by copying Etruscan or
Samnite custom, around 260 B.C. In a 264 B.C. funeral, the

490

two sons of the dead man offered three gladiatorial contests to the public. The Circus Flaminius was built in 220 B.C. by the censor Gaius Flaminius, the people's friend, (see above) to house such attractions. This kind of program, feeding and entertaining the public, became a main feature of Roman life for many centuries. It is often described as a bread and circuses policy. The violent entertainments flourished until they ran afoul of the Christian Empire in the 300's A.D.

--a related development was the growth of the theater, particularly the broad comedy associated with men like Plautus and Terence (see below), presented, as in the Greek fashion, by the state or by privately wealthy men. The comedy was short enough of political comment to be "safe," but it was still regarded with suspicion by the ruling class. There was no permanent stage: a proposal to build one was defeated on moral grounds in 154 B.C.

--the careful encouragement of new, more exciting religions from the East, to catch the people's fancy. Religion, of course, was closely watched by the state. The Romans had been copying from Greek and Etruscan religion for centuries, taking up emotional or spiritual elements which were missing or only weakly developed in their own religious framework. Now they took from the eastern world in general. The copying was usually done reluctantly, when things were going badly, and under the careful eye of the government.

In the crisis surrounding the establishment of the Republic around 500 B.C., for example, the SIBYLLINE BOOKS were obtained from Greek Cumae. The Sibyl of Cumae was a mouthpiece of Apollo. The Books contained her predictions. Those books became the most famous source of revelations in Roman religion--but they remained distinctly foreign. The Roman priests who had charge of the books supervised all foreign religions as they were allowed later into Rome; the books could only be consulted at the instruction of the Roman government.

In 291 B.C. the Greek god of healing, Asclepius, was introduced at Rome. This step was recommended by the interpreters of the Sibylline Books as a way of checking a disease which was sweeping the city.

491

The great series of defeats by Hannibal at the beginning of the 2nd Punic War (218-216 B.C.), the most important challenge in the Republic's history, constituted a religious crisis for Romans. The Senate eagerly explored all ways of lifting the people's spirits as it used the setbacks to bolster its own power. The religious atmosphere in the city after Cannae (216 B.C.) is described by Livy:

The Romans were terrified not only by the great disasters they had suffered, but also by a number of marvelous events, and in particular because two Vestals, Opimia and Floronia, in that year had been convicted of losing their virginity. One of these had been buried alive, as is the custom, near the Colline Gate, and the other had killed herself. Lucius Cantilius, as assistant to the great priests—one of those who are now called lesser priests—was the man who had had sex with Floronia, and the Chief Priest had him scourged in the Assembly so severely that he died under the blows. Coming in the middle of so many calamities, this evil was, as does happen at such times, turned into a sign for the future. So the officials were ordered to consult the Sibylline Books, and Quintus Babius Pictor was sent to Delphi to ask the oracle what prayers and deeds were needed to make the gods happy again and what would be the outcome of all the evils the Romans were suffering. Meanwhile, by the direction of the Books of Fate, some unusual sacrifices were offered. Among them, a man and a woman of the Gauls and a man and woman of the Greeks were buried alive in the Cattle Market, in a place walled in with stone, which even before this time had been defiled with human victims, a sacrifice completely alien to the Roman spirit.

In 217 B.C. the government ordered a banquet of the gods at which statues were introduced to represent the gods rather than the traditional vacant places for their spirits—a significant movement toward personalization. In 204 B.C. the first major eastern (non-Greek) religious import arrived. The statue of the Great Mother was brought from Asia Minor. Naturally, this was done at the urging of the Sibylline Books. A temple for the Great Mother was built on the Palatine hill. Her priests, however, were all noncitizens (and eunuchs): the Senate remained very suspicious of this kind of thing, although it was ready to exploit it.

One very lively religious import which flourished in
these difficult years was the worship of the Greek god
Dionysius (Bacchus to the Romans). It did not take long
for the Senate to move against the orgies of drink and sex
which were reported to be associated with Bacchus. In 186
B.C. the Senate announced that no more than five people
could celebrate the religion at one time, and only then
with the approval of the officials.

The Senate was even more hostile toward one other eastern group. In 139 B.C. it ordered all Jews (there cannot
have been many of them in Italy at that time) out of Italy.
There were no orgies or indiscipline to hold against the
Jews: the Senate disliked their idea that religion should
not be something manipulated by the Roman state for its
convenience. Astrologers were ordered out along with the
Jews, the Senate wishing to keep the reading of signs very
much under its own control.

Fear of Dictatorship/Tyranny.
From its point of view, the thing the Senate had to
worry about most was the possibility of a dictator/tyrant
coming to power. This was a fear taken from the Greek experience, that an ambitious aristocrat (patrician) would
ally with the "people" to overthrow the aristocracy (the
Senate). Apart from this practical aspect, dictatorship,
the supreme act of individualism, was objectionable to the
many Romans who saw things in a group context, with men
knowing their places and following the rules. Such Romans
would have said that there was something very "un-Roman"
about dictatorship. The group leadership provided by the
Senate is a clear expression of this principle.

Talk about dictatorship became common for the first
time in reference to the career of Flaminius around 230 B.C.,
although in light of his status as a new man Flaminius hardly qualified as a potential dictator. The most important
case was that of Scipio Africanus, the chief hero of the
2nd Punic War (218-201 B.C.) and the biggest name in Roman
public life in this period. Although Scipio belonged to one
of the leading patrician families, many senators were
alarmed by his popularity with the Assembly and with his
troops and by the way he pushed himself ahead during the
war. There were about Scipio some of the signs the Senate

looked for in a potential dictator: his assurance of direct inspiration from the gods, his willingness to put his own head on coins he minted in Spain, his general love of splendor and show. Scipio's generosity toward Spaniards (mixed with brutality though it was) and his admiration for Greek culture were also used against him, the former as a sign of a craving for popularity, the latter as indicating a preference for such a Greek political form as tyranny.

Much of the criticism aimed at Scipio, of course, was only used as a matter of convenience to his rivals—it gave their arguments a high-sounding purpose. There was no evidence to speak of that Scipio aimed at the dictatorship.

Scipio's family dominated the Senate in the 190's B.C., the decade after the 2nd Punic War. The Scipio faction promoted a policy of aggression in the East, coupled with friendship to the Greeks. Africanus himself with his brother Lucius took the first Roman army into Asia and defeated Antiochus. Then came the reaction. In 187 B.C. Lucius Scipio was accused of embezzlement during the campaign in Asia. Africanus took the account books of the campaign into the Senate and tore them up, defying the Senate to proceed. The charge was not denied—we can suppose that embezzlement, a very common thing, had occurred. This fine gesture only delayed his opponents. In 184 B.C. Lucius was fined. At the same time, Africanus himself was charged with treason, specifically that he had worked out secret deals (money?) with Antiochus during the campaign. The charge was dropped, but an angry Africanus retired to his country estate at Liternum, where he died the next year. He left orders to be buried there rather than at Rome, "so that my funeral not be held in my ungrateful country."

All of this may have had a good deal more to do with factional struggles than with political principles, but at Rome it certainly did not help a man to be accused of aiming at dictatorship. The chief opponent of the Scipios in all this was the new man Cato, known to us as Cato the Censor or Cato the Elder. It was Cato, as censor of 184 B.C., who pressed the charges home.

494

To keep individuals from grabbing for power, the Senate took a number of general steps:
--the old, emergency dictatorship of six months was abandoned after the 2nd Punic War;
--in 180 B.C. a cursus honorum was set up. This established the order in which offices could be held and the minimum age for each: 1. quaestor, minimum age 25; 2. praetor, age 39; 3. consul, age 42. It was intended to prevent the kind of promotion that Africanus had obtained as a young man;
--around 150 B.C., reelection to an office was forbidden.

No person rivalling the achievements of Africanus emerged for a long time, there being no crisis comparable to that of the 2nd Punic War to force the Senate to rely so heavily on single individuals. Still, the Senate's suspicions were reasonable--it was to dictatorship that the Senate finally had to give way.

ITALY

496

EXPANSION OF ROME, 200-120 B.C.: THE ENTIRE MEDITERRANEAN
BECOMES "OUR SEA" (MARE NOSTRUM)

While the fighting was never on the scale of the 2nd
Punic War, a long series of campaigns over the next decades
brought further big gains to Rome and left the Republic
without any serious rival anywhere in the Mediterranean long
before the end. Rome's aims were not the same everywhere,
and sometimes they were far from clear, as Roman policies
remained unsettled and unpredictable. Rome's strength and
determination, however, were such that this did not matter;
whenever Rome applied itself, it could count upon success.

In the West, although the Romans often were lackadaisi-
cal about it, the objective was reasonably clear--the accum-
ulation of territories at the expense of the backward peoples who occupied the area stretching from Italy to Spain.
Because of the toughness of these tribal peoples, the fighting was sometimes hard and always mean.

1. The Conquest of North Italy.
200-190 B.C.: The Gauls south of the Po river were reconquered after the defeat of Hannibal. Then north Italy beyond
the river was taken. This process was completed in the
190's B.C. by another Scipio, P. Cornelius Scipio Nasica, a
cousin of Scipio Africanus. Much territory was seized outright by the Roman government, as some tribes of Gauls were
actually driven out over the Alps. The whole area is referred to as Cisalpine Gaul (Gaul on this side of the Alps).
It was not organized as a province until 100 years later.
187-180 B.C.: Conquest of Liguria. The Ligurians, who controlled the coastal area connecting Italy with France, were
a primitive, ancient people who have lived in Italy since
before the Indo-Europeans had entered the peninsula around
2000 B.C. L. AEMILIUS PAULLUS did well there in 181 B.C.,
completing the conquest. 40,000 Ligurians were moved to
south Italy where, since Hannibal's campaigns, there was
plenty of vacant land. Campaigns were needed later, especially in the 150's B.C., to keep Liguria in check.
181-176 B.C.: Conquest of Istria, the area connecting Italy
with the northeast.

2. Sardinia and Corsica.
As these conquests in the North were being completed,

rebellion broke out among the still independent native peoples in Corsica (181 B.C.) and Sardinia (177-176 B.C.) T. Sempronius Gracchus made his name crushing the trouble in Sardinia. The Romans slowly extended their influence over the islands, but they made very little use of them.

3. The Conquest of Spain.
        With the 2nd Punic War over, Rome looked to move further into Spain. The region was attractive for its precious metals (gold and silver) and because it was a good recruiting area for the military. The tribes, which were not anxious to exchange an old Carthaginian master for a new Roman one, moved Rome to quick action by rebelling in 197 B.C.
197-178 B.C.: The conquest of northern and central Spain. This came only with difficulty. The long war of conquest, so far from Rome, was a new kind of thing to Rome, and one that many of the soldiers did not like. Some great reputations began here:
        M. PORCIUS CATO, 195 B.C.
        L. AEMILIUS PAULLUS, 191-189 B.C., who served later in
            Liguria.
        T. SEMPRONIUS GRACCHUS, 179-178 B.C., who served next in
            Sardinia. Gracchus won a reputation for fair dealing
            in Spain as well as hard fighting, distinguishing
            himself from the general nastiness of the undertaking.

        There was relative order for the next quarter of a century, but then:
154-133 B.C.: War was renewed in Spain. The trouble began in the west with the Lusitanians, who were still independent, and spread into the north to the Celtiberians (the mixed population of Celtic newcomers and older inhabitants; Iberia is the Latin for Spain):
        Lusitanian War 154-138 B.C.
        Celtiberian War 153-151 and 143-133 B.C.
This fighting was the hardest Rome saw anywhere in the century. It earned for Spain a reputation as a graveyard, for soldiers and for military reputations. Spain was the horrida et bellicosa provincia (the rough and warlike province).

        The interior of Spain was mountainous and barren. The people, fierce and brave at all times, found a leader of genius in the Lusitanian Viriathus (146-140 B.C.), who was

498

able to overcome to some extent the unwillingness of the tribes to work together. Successive Roman generals campaigned badly and acted dishonorably toward the Spaniards. Regrettably, Gracchus, who had a good name in Spain, had died in 154 B.C. just as the trouble began. The war did much to make the Senate of Rome and the ruling class look both incompetent and dishonest.

The murder of Viriathus by Roman agents in 140 B.C., a typical undertaking of the period, broke the Spanish effort. The fighting was largely over by 139 B.C. Attention then centered on the attacks by the Romans against Numantia, the main Celtiberian base in the north. This siege produced further scandals of incompetence and bad faith. In 137 B.C. a consul surrendered a 20,000 men army to the rebels near Numantia, offering to win good terms for them at Rome in exchange for his life. The Senate, much embarrassed, turned down the agreement the consul made with the rebels and sent him back to the rebels for them to deal with as they wished. (This is the probable origin of the similar story involving Atilius Regulus in North Africa in 255 B.C.)

Finally, in 133 B.C., Numantia and its 4,000 remaining defenders fell to a 60,000 man Roman army. The defenders were starved out in an eight-month siege. The Roman commander was P. CORNELIUS SCIPIO AEMILIANUS, son of L. Aemilius Paullus, adopted grandson of the great Scipio Africanus.

Now, with the exception of the far west and northwest, all Spain was Roman. There was no further rebellion in Spain on this kind of scale.

4. The Conquest of the Southern Coast of France.
It made good sense to take the coastal area which connected north Italy with Spain. An excuse was available in the disorderliness of the tribes of Gauls which occupied the region. Greek Massilia, on the coast, long Rome's ally, conveniently asked for help against the tribes. Rome became active in the area (as opposed to just marching its troops through the area on the way to Spain) as early as the 150's B.C.

125-120 B.C.: The southern coastal area of France was
conquered. The major Roman figure involved was Cn. Domitius
Ahenobarbus, from whom the famous dictator Nero was descended. The major tribes of Gauls in the south, especially the
Arverni, were thoroughly defeated. Soon, a Roman colony was
founded at Narbo (now Narbonne), the first outside Italy.
For a while the area was left dependent on friendly Massilia,
but later it became a separate province (Gallia Narbonensis).
123 B.C.: As part of the same process of clearing the way
to Spain, the Balearic Islands were conquered at this time.

5. The Conquest of the City of Carthage.
     Rome was at peace with Carthage for half a century
after the 2nd Punic War (218-201 B.C.). Hannibal soon was
exiled from Carthage, and that city's ruling class tried
hard to get along with Rome. Rome was satisfied with the
situation, although some groups in Rome were strongly anti-
Carthaginian and were jealous of Carthage's reviving prosperity. The chief spokesman against Carthage was M. Porcius
Cato, who liked to dwell upon the theme that "Carthage must
be destroyed" (Delenda est Carthago).

     Carthage's desire to please Rome put the city at the
mercy of Rome's ally in western North Africa, King Masinissa
of Numidia. A long line of minor land grabs by Masinissa at
the expense of Carthage occurred. Under the terms it had
accepted after the 2nd Punic War, Carthage could deal with
Masinissa only through Rome. The Romans usually sided with
Masinissa.

     In 150 B.C. an exasperated Carthage, tired of appealing
to Rome, took up arms against Masinissa. It lost anyway
against the Numidian. Nonetheless, Rome, after some hesitation, fell in with Cato's line and decided to punish
Carthage.
149-146 B.C.: 3rd Punic War. Carthage was conquered by
Rome. The resistance was desperate, since Carthage correctly feared the worst. In 147 B.C. the frustrated Romans
gave the command to Scipio Aemilianus, then a young man
technically unqualified for the post. After its capture by
Aemilianus, the city was totally destroyed. Its 50,000
survivors were sold into slavery. The site was cursed and
salt was scattered there, to indicate that the land should
not again be used.

In this unnecessary and brutal attack the Romans were at their worst. The area was made into the province of Africa, with a few independent towns as clients. Numidia (Masinissa had died in 148 B.C. during the war, aged 90) was not rewarded.

In the East, Rome was much less interested in adding to its territories. At first, the Republic wanted only to punish Macedonia for the aid given Hannibal. This led on to other involvements. The Romans soon found that the opposition in the civilized East was so weak that they quickly became all-powerful across the entire area. They generally avoided acquiring territory, but they had no way of resisting the results of their power.

The Senate seems to have been determined to move against Philip of Macedon as soon as the 2nd Punic War was over. Since the Republic was also involved in north Italy and Spain at the same time, this meant a very substantial military effort. The Assembly, exhausted from the war against Carthage, resisted the idea of moving East. The first Assembly vote was against war, but in the end the Senate had its way.

Apart from the desire for revenge, the Senate used as justification for war a typical appeal from Rome's friends. In 203 B.C. a child had succeeded to the kingdom of the Ptolemies, the Macedonian successor-state in Egypt. This encouraged Philip and ANTIOCHUS III the Great, the Seleucid (the other major Macedonian successor-state), to make an arrangement to attack Egyptian interests in the Aegean and in Asia Minor. Rome's friends in the area, the Aetolian League, Rhodes, and above all Pergamum, appealed to Rome to protect them. Rome asked Philip to leave Greece alone and to compensate Rhodes and Pergamum for damage done to their interests. When Philip refused, the war began.

200-197 B.C. 2nd Macedonian War.
This ended with victory for Rome at Cynoscephalae in 197 B.C. The Roman conqueror was the consul T. Quinctius Flamininus, a 29 years old favorite of the Scipios. Obviously, Macedon was no match for Rome by this point. Philip of Macedon was forced to give up his fleet and his forts in Greece and to pay a large indemnity to Rome.

The Greeks, including the Achaeans, traditionally friends of Macedon (they had fought against Rome in the 1st Macedonian War), had supported Rome. In reward, they were now "liberated" from Macedon after 150 years. Flamininus made this announcement in spectacular circumstances at the Isthmian Games of 196 B.C. at Corinth. Of course, the Romans meant that the Greeks were now Roman clients, friendly dependents.
194 B.C.: All Roman soldiers were withdrawn from Greece.

Into the vacuum the Romans left in Greece stepped the Seleucid king, Antiochus the Great. From his capital at Antioch, Antiochus had already restored Seleucid control to the east in Iran and central Asia. He had then reasserted his power in Asia Minor. and moved into Thrace in Europe in 196 B.C. Pergamum and Rhodes, threatened once more, again appealed to Rome. This time, the Senate was not anxious to get involved. Rome had no cause of its own to oppose Antiochus. So Flamininus did not get involved with Antiochus after defeating Philip of Macedon; he did, though, warn Antiochus to keep his hands off Greece. Since Antiochus was already into Thrace, and had even given refuge to Hannibal, who had been forced out of Carthage in 195 B.C. by his political opponents, this was a strangely easy-going attitude on the Romans' part. Clearly there were divisions within the Senate about getting involved in the East. The Scipios stood out among those who favored involvement.

In 192 B.C., not long after the Roman army was withdrawn, Antiochus moved 10,000 men into Greece. They came at the invitation of the Aetolian League. The League was now twice disappointed with the Romans. Having received so little help from its Roman ally in the 1st Macedonian War (215-205 B.C.), the League had been angered at the end of the 2nd Macedonian War to find that the general "liberation" of Greece prevented it from picking up the territories it wanted. The League asked Antiochus in also as a champion of democracy in Greece against the oligarchies which were always favored by the Romans--an absurd role for a Macedonian king.

The Seleucid move into Greece made war all but inevitable. The Romans could strike for the "freedom" of Greece and honor the continuing pleas from their friends Rhodes and Pergamum. There seems to have been little doubt in anyone's

502

mind about the outcome. The Achaean League and Macedonia
sided with Rome and contributed a little to the fighting.

191-188 B.C. War against Antiochus.
191 B.C.: Consul Acilius Glabrio, another Scipio man, won
the battle of Thermopylae in Greece. Antiochus was forced
to get out of Greece.
190 B.C.: Victories at sea in the Aegean, the last big sea
battles Rome ever needed to fight, cleared the way for the
Roman army to enter Asia--a great moment in the Republic's
history.
winter 190-189 B.C.: Under the command of consul L.
Cornelius Scipio, and his brother Scipio Africanus, who was
along as an "advisor," the Roman army defeated the Seleucids
decisively at Magnesia-ad-Sipylum in Asia Minor. This ended
the war--the Seleucids had been even less of a match for
Rome than Macedonia.

Antiochus was compelled to give up his fleet and to
retire from Asia Minor. He also had to pay an enormous
indemnity. The Romans wanted to get their hands on Hannibal.
He escaped, but finding himself with no future he committed
suicide by posion. The Aetolian League was treated generously
and accepted the status of a Roman satellite.

Rome took nothing for itself. Its army rampaged across
Asia Minor showing the flag. The army along the way defeated
the Galatians. This was a Celtic people which had reached
central Asia Minor from the Balkans a century earlier after
raids through the Greek world which had netted them great
booty, including the treasure from the temple of Apollo at
Delphi. The Romans relieved the Galatians of these proceeds,
took what they wanted elsewhere, and went home. Pergamum and
Rhodes, particularly the former, received territory in Asia
Minor.

Roman influence now was supreme through the eastern
Mediterranean. The Seleucids were never again a problem;
their kingdom began to fall apart, particularly with the rise
of the PARTHIANS in Mesopotamia and Iran. Greece remained
quiet and Macedonia gave no trouble for some years.

Difficulties built up again in the late 170's B.C.
Philip of Macedon died in 179 B.C. He was succeeded by his
son, Perseus. Macedonia's enemies, Pergamum especially,

503

tried to turn Rome against Perseus. The king of Pergamum even went to the Senate in Rome in person to appeal for action against Perseus in 172 B.C. There was little enough to the accusations that Perseus was a troublemaker, but they did the trick. On this occasion, the Senate, having had no major recent campaigns, seems to have been willing to get involved for relatively little cause.

171-167 B.C. 3rd Macedonian War.
Another brief war ended in 167 B.C. with the victory of the consul L. Aemilius Paullus, whom we have met before, at PYDNA.

The terms were savage, out of all proportion to Perseus's behavior before the war. The kingdom of Macedon disappeared; Perseus himself was taken off to Rome to star in the triumph given Paullus. He soon died in prison there. The kingdom of Macedon was replaced by four republics. These were all Roman clients. They paid taxes to Rome, and the old royal mines and lands became the property of the Roman government (usually being leased out). The mines, however, which were the chief source of the wealth of Macedon, were ordered closed for the first years.

Illyria was divided in the same way into three republics. Nor did the Greeks, who had given some aid to Perseus in the war, get off lightly. There were big massacres in the Aetolian League and elsewhere. From the Achaean League Rome took 1,000 prominent citizens as hostages (among them was the historian Polybius). On its way home through Epirus, the Roman army, acting on the orders of the Senate, took very great numbers as slaves. All together, perhaps 1/4th of the entire Greek population was killed or carried off. It is clear that Rome was growing tired of coming into Greece--even if, this time, Rome had hardly needed to.

In the same ugly mood, Rome turned on its old friends Pergamum and Rhodes. Accusing Pergamum of having been luke-warm in a war it had done so much to cause, the Romans made it clear that they would no longer protect Pergamum against its enemies; they may even have encouraged attacks upon the kingdom. Even more bluntly, to hurt Rhodes, which had offered to mediate the quarrel with Perseus, Rome success-fully built up Delos as a rival trading power and slave center; Rome also took away the possessions of Rhodes on the mainland of Asia Minor.

This 3rd Macedonian War saw Roman policy at its most bizarre and unpredictable. Nevertheless, the war made clear to all in the East that Rome was not to be messed with. It was in this atmosphere that in the year of Pydna, 167 B.C., the king of Bithynia, entering the Senate at Rome to talk to the senators, knelt on the floor and addressed them with "Greetings, savior gods." Similarly, it was only a few weeks after Pydna that the incident of the circle in the sand occurred, an episode described by Polybius and much loved by later Romans as an example of their power and bluntness. Antiochus IV the Seleucid, son of Antiochus the Great, had attacked the Ptolemies in Egypt and had seized Alexandria. Rome sent any envoy, Popillius Laenas, to Egypt to stop Antiochus. The envoy did this in no uncertain manner. Here is Polybius's account of the incident:

When Antiochus came after Ptolemy and intended to take Pelusium, Caius Popilius Laenas, the Roman commander, appeared. Antiochus greeted him and held out his hand. Popilius handed to the king the copy of the Senate's order, which he had with him, and told him to read it first. He thought it wrong, it seems to me, to make the usual sign of friendship before he found out if the intentions of the man greeting him were friendly or hostile. But when Antiochus, after reading the order, said he would like to talk with his advisors about the matter, Popilius behaved in a way which looked offensive and very arrogant. He was holding a stick cut from a vine, and with the stick he drew a circle around Antiochus and told him he must remain inside the circle until he gave his decision about what was in the letter. The king was amazed at being ordered about like this, but, after hesitating a few moments, he said he would do all that the Romans demanded. Then Popilius and his men all shook him by the hand and greeted him warmly. The Senate's letter told Antiochus to stop the war with Ptolemy at once. So, as a fixed number of days were allowed him to withdraw, Antiochus led his army back to Syria, deeply annoyed and complaining a great deal, but giving in for the moment.

Of the period which had begun with the 2nd Punic War

(218 B.C.) and which ended here, Polybius wrote:

> There is, I trust, no one so slow and dull as not to
> wonder how, and from what causes in Roman government,
> almost the whole inhabited world in less than 53 years
> came completely under the control of Rome--the like of
> which, it will be seen, has never happened before.

Following this burst of energy, Rome withdrew for another extended period. There was little trouble until 150
B.C., when an adventurer, Andriscus, who claimed to be a
son of Perseus, seized Macedonia and put an end to the four
republics there.

150-148 B.C. 4th Macedonian War.
    The trouble was crushed in 148 B.C. by Q. Caecilius
Metellus. Macedonia became a Roman province. Rome had at
last decided that it had to annex areas to the east.

With a Roman army in Macedonia, and Rome upset that it
had had to act in the area once again, what came next made
little sense. In 146 B.C. the Achaean League rebelled
against Roman influence. The League's particular complaint
was that Rome had just allowed Sparta, which had been forced
into membership, to leave the League. Sentiment in the
League had also been excited by the return in 150 B.C. of
the 300 survivors of the 1,000 hostages of 167 B.C.

The Achaean League was not much of a match for Rome.
Caecilius Metellus came down from Macedonia and another
consul was sent over from Italy with more troops. The rebellion was crushed easily. The League was broken up. Corinth,
the capital of the League, was destroyed totally in the same
horrible manner that Carthage experienced in the same year
(146 B.C.). The Greek city-states remained independent, but
they were placed in the care of the nearby governor of
Macedonia. They were also made to pay taxes to Rome.

This was the end of Rome's difficulties in Greece. From
a beginning in which Rome claimed to champion Greek freedom,
a position which reflected Rome's debt to and its admiration
for Greek culture, the Republic moved to an end which saw
Greece laid waste and all but annexed. The process says a
great deal about the Roman attitude toward Greeks, which
mixed admiration and awe with outright contempt.

Rome had wound up with the province of Macedonia very much as last resort. That province remained the Republic's only territory in the East until 133 B.C. Then Rome acquired Pergamum, its old ally, by inheritance. The king of Pergamum, dying without an heir, left his territory in his will to Rome. Rome turned the kingdom into the province of Asia, the Republic's first Asian possession. First, though, Rome had to put down a rebel, Aristonicus, who claimed to be an illegitimate son of the last king of Pergamum. In the fighting one consul, P. Licinius Crassus, was killed.

Elsewhere in the East, Rome was content to promote its influence without fighting or obtaining land. It did not use troops in Asia after the defeat of Antiochus in 191-189 B.C. Rome intervened frequently all around the area, but that was all. Scipio Aemilianus, for example, went to Egypt in 140 B.C. to settle a quarrel over who should rule there, a type of question which gave the Senate a lot of trouble in these decades. Similarly, when the Jews began to rebel under Judas Maccabaeus against the collapsing Seleucid kings (160-130 B.C.), trying to obtain a new Jewish kingdom, Rome naturally was involved, making sure that things did not get out of hand.

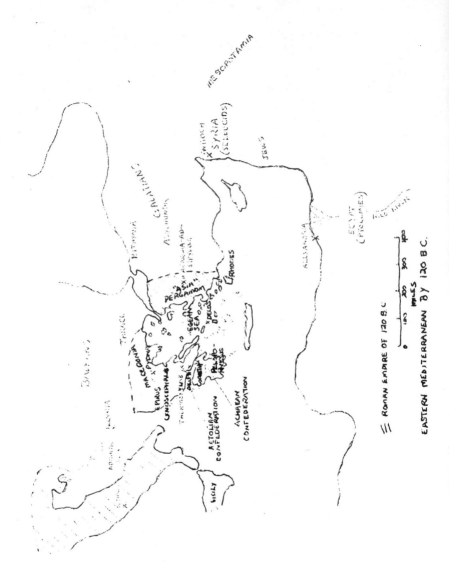

EASTERN MEDITERRANEAN BY 120 B.C.

≡ ROMAN EMPIRE OF 120 B.C

MILES
0   100   200   300   400

CHALLENGE TO THE OLD ORDER: THE GRACCHI BROTHERS, 133-120 B.C.

The first major challenge to the Senate came in 133 B.C. at the end of the troublesome Spanish wars. The prestige of the Senate then was lower than it had been at any point earlier in the century. Apart from the horrible war in Spain, the first of the great slave rebellions was dragging on in Sicily. The challenge was the work of a tribune of that year, TIBERIUS SEMPRONIUS GRACCHUS. Tiberius, aged 30, was the son of the hero of the same name from the earlier Spanish wars of the 170's B.C. The family had been prominent for several generations, but it was <u>plebeian</u> -- which was why the office of tribune, whose job it was to protect the people, was open to Tiberius. His mother was the patrician <u>Cornelia</u>, daughter of Scipio Africanus. Tiberius' wife came from the great patrician family of <u>Appius Claudius</u>, a family we have met many times already. Tiberius' father-in-law, Appius Claudius Pulcher, was the First Senator, the senior man in the Senate, the senator who spoke first in debate.

All this made an unlikely background for a champion of the people against the Senate. It also typifies the process by which the office of tribune had been efficiently neutralized. The patrician families which dominated the Senate selected tribunes from among their plebeian connections in the Senate. Only one tribune in a given year of the 10 chosen had to absolutely reliable, since each one could veto the actions of the others. In addition, tribunes were treated well. They had picked up the habit of sitting in the Senate, speaking to that body, even convening it if they wished -- all very cosy. Generally, they had come to see things from the Senate's point of view.

133 B.C.: Tiberius presented an <u>Agrarian Law</u>. This would enforce the old and long-neglected limit on <u>public land holdings</u>. It would leave the limit of some 300 acres to the sitting tenants (and perhaps a further 150 acres for each child, although this idea may have been dropped when the Senate got nasty). There would also be compensation for improvements which had been made on the public land taken back by the state. The law would redistribute public

lands to the poorer and landless citizens in small plots for
a small rent, the plots to be inalienable for a period of
years. A Land Commission of three men was proposed to put
the law into effect.

This was an attempt to put the poor citizens back on
the farms -- a step which would also increase the manpower
available to the legions. At the same time, Tiberius
offered a reduction in the length of military service.

Many prominent senators, including Tiberius' father-
in-law, seem to have supported the plan as a reasonable act
in the public interest (benefitting the army and therefore
the state). Tiberius, however, perhaps believing that the
Senate would not approve his proposal, took it directly to
the Tribal Assembly. He was entitled to do this; Flaminius
had done it a century before with his land law. In the
Assembly another tribune, acting for the Senate, vetoed the
proposed Agrarian Law, a step which was itself unusual.
Tiberius got the Assembly to throw the stubborn tribune out
of office. This step was without precedent. A little
violence occurred, and the Agrarian Law was then passed.

The Senate, now very upset, resisted voting money to
finance the plan and the proposed commission. Normally
the Senate controlled all financial matters. Tiberius had
the Tribal Assembly vote to accept the gift of Pergamum,
which was left to Rome by its last king at this time, and
to apply some of the money to the purposes of the Agrarian
Law. This was a clear blow at the Senate's domination of
all matters of financial and foreign policy. The three men
appointed to the Land Commission were Tiberius, his younger
brother GAIUS, and his father-in-law Appius Claudius Pulcher.

132 B.C.: Tiberius sought reelection as tribune for 132 B.C.
This was not illegal; it was unusual. The Senate, led by
Scipio Nasica, a member of the great family to which Tiberius' mother belonged, killed Tiberius and some 300 of his
followers. We do not know if this was deliberate or if
it was a riot which got out of hand. In tradition, this
was the first time blood had been shed in Rome in political
disturbances. Later, a Senate board was set up to try and
to execute more of Tiberius's followers, with no right
to the Assembly.

The _Agrarian Law_, however, was not abandoned. The
Senate wished to show that it loved the people but hated
Tiberius as a potential tyrant. Tiberius' place on the
commission was taken by his brother Gaius' father-in-law,
P. _Licinius Crassus_, a member of another great Senate family.
By 125 B.C. some 75,000 allotments had been shared out, and
the number of citizens eligible for military service had
increased from 319,000 to 395,000.

The land plan was reasonable enough, and surely was
in the public interest. Tiberius's methods were more
questionable, especially his own apparent willingness to
use violence. On the other hand, it is likely that the
Senate would have turned down his proposal. Many senators
may have been undecided as to what to do. The most instructive case is that of _Scipio Aemilianus_, the chief political
name of the day and of course a close connection of Tiberius.
He was in fact married to Tiberius' sister, although the
couple had separated. _Aemilianus_ himself had something of
a reputation as a friend of the people, as for that matter,
did the Scipios generally. In 140 B.C. one of his associates
had brought forward a bill to redistribute the public lands
much in the manner of Tiberius's bill of 133 B.C. This
earlier proposal had been dropped at the insistence of the
Senate; Aemilianus had no interest in challenging the
system. Tiberius and Aemilianus had become estranged in
137 B.C. when Tiberius, on service in Spain, was involved
in offering the truce to the rebels which the Senate rejected.
Aemilianus was still on service in Spain in 133 B.C.: he
captured _Numantia_ that year. When he returned, Aemilianus
strongly opposed the land commission and tried to get it
abandoned. He is reported to have said, "if Tiberius intended to seize the state, he was killed justly." Aemilianus died suddenly in 128 B.C. Some claimed that Tiberius'
friends had killed him.

Tiberius's land plan had two particular weaknesses:
1. Many citizens had no wish to return to a hard, lonely,
and uncertain life on the farm. In Rome, with the client
system and public entertainments, many poor citizens had
found a welfare life which suited them. Back on the farm,
there was a good chance that they would be drafted, leading
to a chain of circumstances they had already experienced
to their unhappiness.

511

2. Tiberius offered worse than nothing to the Italian non-
citizens. Not only did they get no share of the land redistribution; some of them were displaced to make way for the
plan and others found the commissioners challenging their
titles or their boundary rights. The Italians were angry,
and those in Rome were in a position to do something about
it when the fighting came. Latin rights holders, of course,
were able to attend the Assemblies in Rome.

Despite Tiberius' death, a wave of pressure against the
Senate had been set in motion. This produced more concessions:
131 B.C.: both censors were plebeians for the first time;
130 B.C.: the secret ballot was introduced in the Tribal
Assembly (it already was in use in the Assembly of Centuries);
129 B.C.: reelection of tribunes was legalized, removing
any doubt about Tiberius' reelection.
At the same time, though, nothing was done for the Italians--
in fact, they lost ground:
128 B.C.: Latin rights are altered. A man holding Latin
rights could no longer secure citizenship, and thus the
right to vote, simply by moving to Rome. Only Latin rights
holders who had been local officials could now do so;
126 B.C.: Allies (the lowest category of free non-citizen)
could no longer move to Rome at all. At the same time, at
least in theory, those already in the city were expelled;
125 B.C.: one of the men on the land commission, the tribune
Flaccus, proposed that any Italian who wanted citizenship
should be given it. This proposal was defeated. The Latin
colony Fregellae rebelled to protest this decision and was
brutally destroyed.

In 123 B.C. GAIUS GRACCHUS, the younger brother of
Tiberius and a veteran of the land commission, became a
tribune. Gaius offered a much more extensive reform program:
1. the public land program was reaffirmed;
2. a corn law was introduced, with the government selling
grain regularly to citizens at Rome at below market prices.
Bread, of course, was the overwhelming staple of the Roman
diet. This kind of thing had been common in Greek states
(which was not much of a recommendation at Rome);
3. a big public works program, including much road construction, was announced;
4. the conditions of military service were improved, including having the state supply free clothing to the soldiers;

512

5. many new colonies were to be established, providing even more opportunities to get back on the land. One of these was to be at Carthage. The idea of a Carthage colony was a dramatic and controversial one—it would be the first overseas colony and it would be on a site which had been cursed and condemned to barrenness after the destruction of Carthage. Some non-Roman Italians may have been among the colonists.

These proposals made up a much more solid attempt to win the support of the poor citizens of Rome. While the chance to go back to the land was expanded, those who found being in Rome attractive enough would now be taken care of through jobs and low food prices. The corn law, in particular, was potentially a heavy blow against the private client system. It offered the poor the chance to become clients of the state instead (public welfare instead of private welfare).

Along with all this, Gaius reached out for new and powerful allies against the Senate. The Equites, the rich business class, was given control of:
1. the extortion courts which had been set up under the law of 149 B.C. Several recent scandals had shown the Senate juries to be very partial to the governors. Control of these courts by the equites was a clear blow to the prestige of the Senate and promised to let the businessmen step up their sharp practices in the provinces;
2. the taxes of the province of Asia. Most of the tax exemptions which had been given to various towns in Asia were ended. Further, the taxes would now be collected not by the local government but by those who bid highest for the privilege in Rome. The idea was that a group of equites would hand over a large sum of money to get a monopoly right to collect the taxes of Asia for a certain time (a tax-farm). The taxes would actually be collected by the local communities themselves on shorter subleases. A governor of Asia who thought about interfering would be likely to find himself attacked in the exortion courts, which were now to be in the hands of the equites. Gaius was correct in calculating that many of the equites would line up with a "reformer" against the Senate. The price, however, was high; over the next decades, the administration of the provinces was to be more of a disgrace than ever.

513

At the same time, following here in the footsteps of the tribune Flaccus of 125 B.C., Gaius intended to do something to meet the problem of the Italians. This, too, would afford him some further protection against the Senate if violence came:
--full citizenship was offered to all the Latins and half-citizenship (Latin rights) to all other free Italians. This was no very great step. The large majority of Italians would still be unable to take part in politics at Rome and to share in the benefits of Gaius' reform program. Nonetheless, it caused great complaint. The poor citizens and the Italians were very jealous of one another.

Gaius was reelected tribune for 122 B.C., a step which was now definitely legal. He found, however, that he was losing ground in the city. Citizens disliked the idea of doing the Italians a favor (which meant that there were more to share the good things with) and many felt uneasy about the proposed colony at Carthage. Gaius did not help himself by going off for a while to inspect the site at Carthage.

The Assembly rejected the Italian bill. Encouraged, the Senate found a friendly tribune, Drusus the Elder, to offer a clever rival plan which:
1. gave the citizens more -- more colonies and at lower rents;
2. gave the Italians less -- no citizenship for any, but exemption for Latin rights holders from capital or physical punishment by Roman citizens.

In late 122 B.C. Gaius failed to win reelection to a third term as tribune, for 121 B.C. Once he was out of office, and so no longer immune, the Senate moved against him. As tribune, Gaius had obtained a law which had retroactively forbidden all courts with the power of the death penalty which were not set up by the Assembly. The idea had been to protect himself for the future and to gain revenge against the Senate court which had killed his brother's followers 10 years before. The consul of 132 B.C., who had headed that court, had been driven into exile under Gaius. The Senate did not allow Gaius' new law to frustrate it. When some scuffling broke out between the friends of Gaius and supporters of the Senate, the Senate declared

a state of emergency, which allowed the laws to be ignored.
Some 3,000 of Gaius' supporters were killed after token
trials. Gaius and Flaccus were killed.

Once again the Senate, with its private armies, had
triumphed. Violence had become a part of the way of things
at Rome; it was now up to the "reformers" to find some way
of matching the Senate's strength in this area. In its
emergency decree, the Senatus Consultum Ultimum, the Senate
seemed to have found a fine excuse for having its way by
force; this tactic became very common over the next two
generations.

"The Gracchi gave the state two heads." This was the
importance of Tiberius and Gaius Gracchus, the Gracchi
brothers (Gracchi is the plural of Gracchus). A serious
challenge had been delivered to the Senate on behalf of a
number of groups (the poor, the equites, the Italians -- but
not the slaves or the provinces), protesting that the benefits of empire were limited to too few. Things would never
be the same again.

The two heads in the state came to be called the OPTI-
MATES, the "best men," the Senate's side, and the POPULARES,
the "reformers," those in the tradition of the Gracchi. Both
groups in fact were run by Senate families. Following the
Gracchi, some Senate groups, either from ambition or because
they believed it would strengthen the state, supported the
cause of the Populares and provided that side's leadership.
We cannot guess at the motives of such men, any more than
we can in the case of the Gracchi themselves. We must be
careful not to draw too clear a line between the two sides.
The struggle would be violent. It would cripple the Senate's
ability to run things, leaving the state without an effective
government (two heads meaning no head) and clearing the
way in turn for the intervention of the military.

515

THE SENATE LOSES CONTROL: THE AGE OF MARIUS, 120-100 B.C.

Having shown that it was ready to use violence to keep its power, the Senate went on to give more evidence that it objected less to what the Populares demanded than to the way in which the demands were made. It showed great caution in whittling away at the reform program of Gaius Gracchus: --the corn subsidy was cut back but not given up; --the idea of a colony at Carthage was abandoned, but many other colonies were founded, the first in many decades; --the public land program went on for a while, but it was phased out over a decade. By 112 B.C. the land commission was done away with and public land redistribution was ended. In all, perhaps 7-10% of the public lands had been redistributed -- no very great share, but enough perhaps to create about 75,000 new farms. In 121 B.C., very soon after the death of Gaius Gracchus, a law was passed allowing holders of the new farms on the public lands to get rid of them if they wished (by selling them, for example). In 111 B.C. all public land holdings were recognized as private possessions, subject to no rent or other limitation. The Senate had won this fight. --the extortion courts were put back into the hands of the Senate in 106 B.C.

The important point to the Senate was not the question of welfare or reform but the desire to keep control of the state. This aim it advanced at once, in 120 B.C., by securing the acquittal of the consul L. Opimius for killing citizens without trial during the state of emergency which had been used to bring down Gaius Gracchus. With the principle of the Senatus Consultum Ultimum apparently established, the Senate was willing to be reasonably easy-going toward the reformers' program.

111-105 B.C. The Jugurthine War.
The Senate in its restored power did little to give the impression that it was capable of running Rome's affairs efficiently. By 110 B.C. Rome faced serious military difficulties on two fronts. One of these was in Numidia, Rome's old friend in western North Africa. When Masinissa's successor as king of Numidia died in 118 B.C. the kingdom was divided between his two sons and his nephew. The nephew, Jugurtha, got the least valuable section, the undeveloped

western area. He successfully fought his cousins for the
rest, ignoring Roman attempts to negotiate a settlement. His
supporters also massacred Italian traders in Numidia. Rome
finally went to war with Jugurtha in 111 B.C. amid charges
that the Senate had resisted such a step earlier because of
the bribes Jugurtha had been passing out. A consul of 111
B.C. failed to push hard against Jugurtha. This encouraged
further talk of bribery. The Tribal Assembly voted to ask
Jugurtha to go to Rome to explain what had been happening.
Jugurtha's presence in Rome prompted all kinds of allegations,
although the Senate blocked an actual investigation. Jugurtha left, allegedly calling Rome "a city for sale."

The next year's campaign against Jugurtha, in 110 B.C.,
produced a heavy defeat for the Roman army after the consul
in command had simply left to return to Rome. Talk of bribery picked up again; several senators were exiled. The
command in Numidia for 109 B.C. was given to consul Q.
Caecilius Metellus, whose uncle had won the 4th Macedonian
War (150-148 B.C.). The Metelli (plural of Metellus) had
been the chief Senate family since the fall of Gaius Gracchus
a decade earlier. They had links with the equites and liked
to appear vaguely as friends of the people. This was a
style that more and more of the great families would try as
things got more difficult.

Metellus was in command in Numidia from 109 to 107 B.C.
His failure to end the war upset the Populares, and in 107
B.C. his command was given to MARIUS, who was now elected
consul for the first time. Marius was one of that rare breed,
a new man. He came from a middle-class farming family of the
Apennines (citizens but not Latins). Marius had worked his
way ahead as an associate of the Metellus family, but he was
now ready to go on his own. Marius received the command in
Numidia from the Assembly after the Senate had voted to
leave it in the hands of Metellus. Metellus was given a
meaningless triumph in Rome as compensation.

Marius was a good general, in many ways the first professional general Rome had produced, since he was hardly a
politician at all but had risen through the army. He had
first come to notice at the siege of Numantia in Spain 30
years earlier. Between 107 and 105 B.C. Marius conquered
Numidia; he captured Jugurtha by treachery. The later

dictator, L. Cornelius Sulla, was prominent as an aide to
Marius in this campaign and played a big part in grabbing
Jugurtha. The Numidian was killed in prison at Rome; Numidia
was divided between two new princes who were willing to go
along with Rome.

We know this war well from a detailed work written by
the historian Sallust in the middle of the next century
(The Jugurthine War). Sallust, as a friend of the Populares,
may have exaggerated the corruption and incompetence on the
Senate's part, but there is little doubt that the Senate
was hurt by the episode. In addition, the Populares had
found a possible new champion, Marius. As a military man,
Marius had strengths as a friend of the people that were
quite beyond those of the Gracchi brothers.

111-101 B.C. War against the Germans.
There was trouble in the north at the same time. German
tribes which had earlier lived beyond the Celts had been on
the move in the Danube area for years. Roman armies were
not able to hold them as they moved around to the north of
Italy:
111 B.C.: The German tribes of the Cimbri and the Teutones
defeated a consul and his army in Yugoslavia. Then they
moved through the Alps into Rome's new possession of southern
France.
109 and 107 B.C.: The Cimbri and the Teutones defeated two
more Roman armies commanded by consuls.
105 B.C.: The Cimbri and the Teutones won the great battle
of ARAUSIO (Orange) in southern France. Both consuls of the
year were killed. This was the greatest Roman defeat since
Cannae in 216 B.C.

These German tribes were the most serious military problem Rome had faced since the 2nd Punic War (218-201 B.C.).
Because of their primitive character, however, it did not
occur to them to aim at destroying the Roman state or conquering Rome. They were roaming around, fighting the Romans
whenever they ran into them. After the battle at Arausio
(105 B.C.) the German tribes went raiding in Spain.

Marius, who had just returned from his victories in
North Africa, was elected consul for 104 B.C. and was given
the command against the Cimbri and Teutones -- again at the
wish of the Assembly over the objections of the Senate.

Marius was reelected consul every year from 104 to 100 B.C., five years in a row in all. This procedure, which was illegal and without precedent, indicates the very serious weakness of the Senate at this time,discredited as it was by the failures in North Africa and against the Germans.

The German tribes did not return to France until 102 B.C. This gave Marius two years to prepare to meet them (of course, the Roman forces in Spain were not strong enough to stop the Germans). In preparation, Marius raised a new kind of army, the first professional army Rome had had. Instead of relying on the draft of citizens with property, Marius called for volunteers for a short term of years from the poor and the landless. They volunteered to serve him, the great general, the friend of the people, rather than the state, the Senate. It was Marius' army more than it was Rome's. The volunteers expected Marius to bring them victory, booty, and then nice pensions and/or land grants; in a way, they were Marius' clients.

At the same time, Marius made a number of practical improvements in the army. His highly efficient soldiers were a far cry from the citizen armies of old. Because he made them carry their own equipment and entrenching tools, to make them more self-sufficient and mobile, his soldiers were called "Marius' Mules." Standardization increased, the troops being issued their equipment by the state so that the old variations in weapons which reflected the different classes of citizens disappeared. All the troops were equipped with the short spear and sword, and they were trained in the violent hand-to-hand combat of the gladiators. A wooden rivet was introduced for the spears, so that the shaft would snap on impact, making it impossible for the enemy to throw the spear back -- and difficult for an enemy soldier to pull out a spear head which found its mark. The old maniples gave way completely to the cohorts of six centuries, units big enough, at about 500 men, to look after themselves for most purposes.

There is great debate about just how much of all this was the work of Marius rather than of others before him, but it is clear that to Romans what he was doing was remarkable. It is also clear that from this point on with Marius' system being copied widely, the Roman armies were more efficient

than ever before. This was the advantage of a professional
army. The disadvantage was the political threat which such
an   army and its general posed. A general now had a sort
of private army which he might use against the government;
the army was divided in its loyalties between the general and
the government, and the soldiers, poor men mostly, had very
little stake in the society they were protecting.

Marius and his soldiers proved themselves when the
Germans returned from Spain:
102 B.C.: The Teutones were defeated by Marius at Aquae
Sextiae (Aix-en-Provence);
101 B.C.: The Cimbri were defeated by Marius at Vercellae,
which was perhaps near Ferrara.
These victories restored the situation in the north and
freed the troops for use elsewhere. The second great slave
revolt which had broken out in Sicily in 103 B.C. was now
crushed by Marius' soldiers. Mark Antony was able in 100
B.C. to seize Cilicia in Asia Minor and clean out for a while
the pirates who had been using the area for a base.

104-100 B.C. Saturninus.
The city of Rome saw in these years a second major
attack on the power of the discredited Senate in the name of
the Populares. Marius, of course, was being reelected consul
each year as one expression of this attack.
104 B.C.: The priesthoods were thrown open to election instead of being controlled by the Senate families.
SATURNINUS became prominent as the new friend of the
people. It is unfortunate that we know so little about this
man, for he did something very important -- he matched the
power of the Senate in Rome, something which had been beyond
the Gracchi brothers.
As a tribune of 103 B.C., Saturninus
--extended the corn subsidy
--offered a plan for many new colonies in Sicily and Greece
--established treason courts which were in the hands of the
equites
--obtained land in Numidia and southern France for the men
who had served with Marius in North Africa. These men probably included a majority of Italian non-citizens. This
program was at once a way of redistributing land and of doing
something for the Italians.

520

In addition to reviving the Gracchi appeal to the people (corn subsidy and colonies) and the equites (courts), Saturninus added two new elements:
1. A willingness to use violence regularly to get his way. In turning violence against the Senate, Saturninus became Rome's first street-fighting man, proving himself a much tougher nut to crack than the Gracchi. With hired groups of toughs at his disposal, Saturninus was willing to murder his political opponents, and he was very skillful at working up a riot.
2. Association with Marius and his armies. Saturninus must have hoped that this would give him protection against the Senate. Here was the potential danger of the private army. We do not know about the relationship between Marius and Saturninus. Obviously, it suited Saturninus to look after Marius' interests; for a while, it suited Marius to have Saturninus look after those interests.

The troubles in Rome increased in 102 B.C. when Saturninus, who wanted to become a senator, was not added to the roll of the Senate by the censor. Riots won Saturninus a place in the Senate.

In 100 B.C. Saturninus again became a tribune. This time he
--obtained land for the veterans of Marius' war against the German tribes
--required senators to swear an oath, under penalty of exile, to support his laws.
Saturninus also got himself elected to a third term as tribune for the following year (99 B.C.).
The Senate passed another Senatus Consultum Ultimum, declaring an emergency. The senators, however, did not have the strength to put Saturninus down; there could be no repeat of the Gracchi episodes. So the Senate appealed to Marius the consul. This was the critical moment, since it was in Marius' power to decide the outcome -- in favor of the Senate, or of Saturninus or of himself. The general went with the Senate. Saturninus and his friends were killed by Marius' men. The Senate then threw out most of the laws passed by Saturninus on the grounds that they were not valid because they had been passed under the threat of violence. Even the land grants to Marius' veterans, were reduced and the Italians were left out.

521

So Marius, the first great military figure of the late Republic, refused to impose himself upon the state. For him, as for <u>Scipio Africanus</u> a century earlier, it was enough to have won great fame and high office. Still, the future lay with the legions and their commanders. The Senate was losing control of Rome and of the army at the same time. All good sense suggested that the army eventually would prevail at the expense of the competing elements in the city. Saturninus could match the army. Sooner or later a general would intervene to help himself.

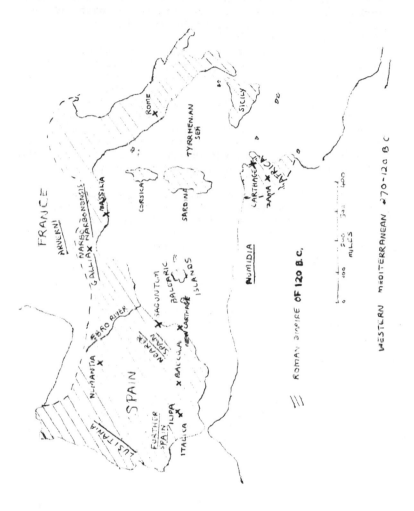

FRANCE

ARVERNI

NARBO
GALLIA NARBONENSIS

MASSILIA

CORSICA

SARDINIA

TYRRHENIAN SEA

ROME

SICILY

CARTHAGE

ZAMA UTICA

NUMIDIA

SPAIN

NUMANTIA

EBRO RIVER

SAGUNTUM

BALEARIC ISLANDS

NEW CARTHAGE

BAECULA

FURTHER SPAIN

ILIPA

ITALICA

LUSITANIA

ROMAN EMPIRE OF 120 B.C.

0   100   200   300   400
        MILES

WESTERN MEDITERRANEAN 270-120 B.C.

DICTATORSHIP APPEARS: THE AGE OF SULLA AND CINNA 100-82 B.C.

After the uproar over <u>Saturninus,</u> the 90's B.C. were relatively quiet. There were no serious military problems to give trouble. Marius was in retirement, the Populares were leaderless; both were a little embarrassed at what had happened. The Senate was generally in control.

Things were uneasy. In the biggest incident of the decade an ex-consul, <u>P. Rutilius Rufus</u>, was convicted of extortion in <u>Asia</u> and was sent into exile (92 B.C.). Since his crime was that he had tried to protect the people of the province of Asia against the tax-farmers, the conviction of Rufus was a major victory for the equites and a blow to the Senate. The episode is one of those used to show the evils of Rome's handling of the provinces; the convicted Rufus, one of the rare <u>new men</u> in Roman politics, was welcomed as a hero into exile in Asia by the people he was supposed to have plundered.

One old problem became very urgent as the decade went on: the question of the free Italian non-citizens. In addition to all the old complaints (and the Italians still had actually lost ground since the beginning of the troubles with Tiberius Gracchus in 133 B.C.), the Italians were upset because those among them who had volunteered for Marius' armies had failed to receive the lands they had been promised. As had always been the case, holding the line against the Italians was something on which Senate, equites, and poorer citizens were in general agreement. In the 90's B.C. the government refused to revive Saturninus's plan to give the Italian veterans land. It even ordered the Italians out of Rome so that the veterans would not cause trouble in the city. By the end of the decade some of the Italians were ready for rebellion.

In 91 B.C. another reformer emerged. This was the tribune <u>Drusus the Younger</u>, the man whose father had been used by the Senate against Gaius Gracchus 30 years before. Drusus offered the usual things to the people—an increased corn subsidy, some land redistribution, more colonies. He offered the Senate half of the places on the extortion courts, a sensitive issue following the conviction of <u>Rufus</u> the year before. All this was to pave the way for offering full citizenship to the Italians. If his plan gives Drusus the look of a statesmen, he was ready to follow Saturninus in marshalling gangs of thugs to get his way. The Senate threw out his laws and Drusus was murdered; the senators knew that no important group in Rome was interested in the Italians.

91-88 B.C. The Social War.

The overthrow of Drusus moved many of the Italians to rebellion. The rebels set up a government of their own, "Italia," in the Apennines. The war which followed is known as the Social War, or war against the allies, socius being the Latin for ally. The fighting was heavy, even though most Italians outside the southern Apennines did not desert Rome. One consul of 90 B.C., and one of 89 B.C., were killed.

Marius left his retirement to take part, but he soon dropped out when he found that he could not get a special overall command against the Italians. The biggest name to emerge from the war was that of SULLA, who had served with Marius in Africa. Other successful generals were Cn. Pompeius Strabo and L. Julius Caesar, each the father of a great man, the men we know in the next generation as Pompey and Caesar.

The Italian effort was undercut when Rome offered all the Italians south of the Po river full citizenship (this was the Julian Law of 90 B.C., named for L. Julius Caesar, a consul in that year). Having brought on the war by refusing to take this step earlier, the Romans at this point looked less than clever.

With all the Italians south of the Po now Roman citizens, the old idea of a city-state of Rome no longer made any sense. Rome made no change in its constitution, however, keeping all of its political institutions in the city, so that Italians could participate only if they were in Rome. Even then, Rome tried to control their influence. By placing all the new Italian citizens in only 8 or 10 of the 35 tribes, Rome intended to limit their influence in the Assembly, no matter how many of them came to Rome.

88-87 B.C. Sulla Uses the Army.

As a reward for his role in the Social War, and because he was known as a Senate man, Sulla was elected one of the consuls for 88 B.C. and was given the attractive command against King Mithridates VI of Pontus in Greece and Asia Minor. This was the first chance to make a great military reputation since Marius' war against the German tribes in 104-100 B.C. The family of Mithridates, which had ruled Pontus for 200 years, was descended from the royal family of the old Persian Empire which Alexander the Great had destroyed, but it was Hellenized. As king of Pontus since 120 B.C., Mithridates had done a great deal to build up the power of his country, while always taking care not to upset the Romans. He controlled the Caucasus and the Crimea and he dominated the Black Sea. Mithridates seems to have decided to take his chances in 88 B.C. Attacking Bithynia, he moved on through the Roman province of Asia, massacring the Italian traders and settlers, and into Greece.

Sulla's appointment to the command against Mithridates was contested by another violent reformer. A tribune, Sulpicius Rufus, a friend of Drusus the Younger, offered to allow the new Italian citizens into all 35 of the tribes. This ended the lingering resistance among the Samnites in the Apennines, but it was not so popular in Rome. Looking for a more popular move, and wishing to obtain for himself some armed support, Sulpicius got the Assembly to switch the command against Mithridates from Sulla to Marius. This was legal; Marius had benefitted from the same thing 20 years earlier in 107 B.C. Marius, now 68 years old, was still popular with both the Romans and the Italians. He was also willing to be used, being jealous of Sulla and eager for more glory for himself; he had been under something of a cloud since 100 B.C. Violence followed in Rome, with Sulpicius and Marius winning their way. Sulla lost the command he had been looking forward to, and indeed scarcely escaped death. Marius, reversing his 100 B.C. decision, had now used violence in the city to seize power from the Senate.

To reverse the outcome, Sulla had to increase the stakes. He was the man to do this. Hurrying off to the port of Nola, where the six legions (some 30,000 men) he had commanded in the Social War had been preparing to go east with him, Sulla persuaded them to support him against Marius. He marched with his soldiers on Rome. Sulpicius was killed, Marius fled into hiding in North Africa among his veterans from the Jugurthine War. Sulla threw out Sulpicius' law allowing Italians into all the tribes; he obtained a law requiring previous Senate approval of all matters presented to the Assembly; and he took back for himself the command against Mithridates of Pontus. Then Sulla left for the East.

526

This was the first such use of the army in Rome's history. It was done as a way of protecting the Senate, but even so it showed how insecure things had become. Sulla was acting on his own behalf as much as on the Senate's; it would not be long before generals picked up the habit of using their armies to protect themselves.

87-82 B.C. Cinna and the Populares in Charge.

With Sulla gone, it was impossible for the Senate to keep control. Violence had become the order of the day. CINNA, a patrician who had been elected a consul for 87 B.C. while Sulla was still at Rome, joined the Populares that same year. Cinna reintroduced Sulpicius' bill to allow the Italians into all the tribes. For this he was driven out of Rome by violence. Cinna raised an army among the Italians, got the aid of Marius, who was free now to come out of hiding, and fought his way back into the city. To resist them, the Senate could find only Pompeius Strabo, who was himself a law breaker. Sulla had taken away Strabo's command against the Italians in central Italy in 88 B.C. Waiting until Sulla left Italy, Strabo took a leaf from the bigger man's book and killed the general who had been sent to replace him. The Senate forgave Strabo when it needed his services against Cinna and Marius. Strabo, however, died in Rome before he could do anything for the Senate.

Cinna and Marius looted Rome, killing far more people than had died in any earlier violence. Both men were elected consuls for 86 B.C. Marius died in 86 B.C. in his 7th term as consul (107 B.C.; 104-100 B.C.; 86 B.C.). Sulla's laws were done away with; Sulla himself was outlawed and lost his command. The Italians were allowed into all the tribes, so that no distinction was made between them and the older citizens.

Now the Populares were finally in control. Cinna had himself reelected as consul each year. He lorded it over the Senate and the city, holding a position that was not much different from that of a dictator/tyrant. He did away with most existing debts (a step popular with the poor and debtors); he restored the currency (popular with the equities). Offering something for all save the Senate, he kept order after his own initial murders and may have deserved a better name than he had later.

But Cinna could not be secure as long as Sulla was at large. Sulla cleared Mithridates out of Greece and the province of Asia with no great problem. He pillaged widely (including Athens), picking up a lot of money for himself and building up his army. Obviously, that army was very much his army, particularly the new soldiers picked up after he left Italy. Not wishing to get tied down in Asia, he accepted a compromise settlement with Mithridates. This allowed Sulla to guard himself against Rome. Sulla and his soldiers simply ignored the orders from Cinna to give up the command again. Men sent out from Rome by Cinna to replace Sulla came to a bad end: the first was murdered, the second committed suicide.

In 84 B.C. Cinna prepared to take an army east himself against Sulla. He was murdered by his soldiers, who figured, surely correctly, that Sulla was going to win. In 83 B.C. Sulla returned to Italy with many of his soldiers. There was heavy fighting before Sulla won. The last big battle was in 82 B.C. at the Colline Gate just outside the city of Rome. The resistance was led by a son of Marius, a consul of 82 B.C., who finally committed suicide.

THE DICTATORSHIP OF SULLA, 82-79 B.C.

Sulla was <u>voted</u> the <u>dictatorship</u> for an <u>indefinite</u>
<u>period</u>. This was an entirely new thing in Rome, a long
step away from the Republic. Dictatorship, alien and Greek
as it had seemed, had arrived, and it flourished open and
unhidden. Sulla held the dictatorship only until 79 B.C.
Then he retired to enjoy private life on his country estates.
This suited his personality, for Sulla was self-centered,
eager for fame and money and enjoyment, an Epicurean. A
great believer in his star, having risen from an undistin-
guised and unimportant patrician family, Sulla took the name
<u>Sulla</u> <u>Felix</u> (Sulla the Fortunate). He had no desire to put
up with the daily chores of administration which faced a
dictator; he had used the army and had come to the dictatorship only to protect himself. His devotion to enjoying himself in his retirement gave rise to scandalous stories which
circulated long after his death, but Sulla secured only a
year of peace. He died in 78 B.C. at the age of 60.

As dictator, Sulla's aims were to:
1. <u>punish</u> <u>his</u> <u>enemies</u> <u>and</u> <u>enrich</u> <u>himself</u>. He killed many
and seized a great deal of property. This scared the op-
position and brought in a lot of money to Sulla and his
cronies. Some great fortunes were made in this way, including that of the <u>ex-slave</u> <u>Chrysogonus</u>, one of Sulla's political aides. Chrysogonus was the first ex-slave (freedman) to
reach such power. Sulla, for his own delight and protection,
kept a 10,000 man personal army of slaves who had been confiscated from his enemies.
2. <u>reward</u> his <u>soldiers</u>. Some 100,000 of Sulla's soldiers
were given land grants. The large amounts of land needed
were taken by force from peoples of Italy who had supported
the wrong side (Cinna's side) in the war. This step strengthened Sulla's hold upon his men and gave him the image of a
generous friend.
3. <u>promote</u> <u>a</u> <u>lot</u> <u>of</u> construction. A lot was needed, especially
in Rome, after the damage done in the civil war. A building
program also created the kind of image Sulla liked. We can
note:--a new <u>Record</u> <u>Office</u>. This is one of the great architectural inheritances from the past. It is used today as the
Rome City Hall.
--a rebuilt <u>Senate</u> <u>House</u>.
--a rebuilt <u>Temple</u> <u>of</u> <u>Jupiter</u> on the Capitoline hill, to re-

place the great ancient temple which had been destroyed.
--a shrine to Fortuna (Fortune, Sulla's favorite) at
Praebeste,
4. reestablish the power of a reorganized Senate. Sulla increased the size of the Senate from 300 to 600. Many of the
newcomers were Italians rather than Latins; most were equites
rather than patricians. This was an attempt to produce a
Senate which was a compromise between Optimates and Populares,
between Latins and Italians. It was the biggest change in
the distribution of power at the top in many generations.

To protect this Senate against other bodies and against
ambitious individuals, Sulla took various steps:
--censors lost their powers to censure the Senate and to
issue government contracts. These powers went to the consuls.
--tribunes could no longer suggest laws on their own initiative to the Assembly. They also lost most of their veto
powers over court cases. A man who served a term as tribune
was not eligible for any other office.
--a strict cursus honorum was established, in the order
quaestor (minimum age 30), praetor (at least 39), consul (at
least 42). A 10-year minimum was necessary between two consulships. All quaestors went into the Senate after completing their term.
--end of the corn law which dated back to Gaius Gracchus.
--all courts were placed in the hands of the Senate (which
now, of course, contained many equites). Sulla set up seven
permanent courts, a long step away from the arbitrary judicial power of the officials.
--control of the priesthoods was returned to the Senate, reversing the law of 104 B.C.
--governors of provinces were to be picked by the Senate
rather than the Assembly. Governors and army commanders
should be at least ex-praetors.
--governors were forbidden to start wars, or leave their
provinces, or use their soldiers outside their own provinces,
without Senate approval.
--no army was to be stationed in Italy.
Sulla was trying to guard against every possible source
of threat to the new Senate, and in particular against ambitious tribunes (the tradition of the Gracchi brothers,
Saturninus, Drusus, Rufus) and generals (Marius and Sulla himself). He must have known that what he was doing had very
little chance of lasting, and given his personality there is
some reasonable question about whether in fact he much cared--

otherwise, why did he retire? Neither the Assembly nor the generals could be controlled by the Senate any longer; this was why the program had to be introduced by a dictator. And the Senate, still dominated by the patricians and the old families for all Sulla's changes, continued to have very little interest in reforming the state. The future lay with the generals and the Populares. Since everyone could see this, it became increasingly common for elements in the Senate, including patricians, to side with the Populares against their own order, and for generals to play their own games.

Sulla himself, in fact, was not able to enforce his own laws against the most serious threat, the ambitious general. POMPEY THE GREAT, the son of Strabo, had raised a private army in Italy and had given very important help to Sulla in the fighting against Cinna's supporters in 83-82 B.C. Pompey married Sulla's step-daughter. Sulla rewarded the young man (Pompey was born in 106 B.C.) with a command in North Africa, even though Pompey was unqualified, being too young and not having held the office of praetor. Pompey in 79 B.C. demanded a triumph for his minor victories in North Africa, something else to which he was not entitled. By adopting a threatening attitude with his army, he was able to get his way with Sulla, who had at first refused. This did not promise well for the future.

79-70 B.C. THE RISE OF POMPEY AND CRASSUS

Most of Sulla's reforms were thrown out over the next
10 years:
78 B.C.: The consul M. Aemilius Lepidus tried to renew the
corn law and to restore the powers of the tribunes. Lepidus,
from a great patrician family, wished to identify with the
Populares, and many in the Senate seem to have been ready to
support him.
77 B.C.: Lepidus tried to overthrow the government, presumably to establish himself as dictator. The private army he
raised in Italy was defeated by Pompey, although Pompey was
still unqualified for such a task under Sulla's laws. Afterwards, Pompey again refused to disband his army. The Senate
bought him off with a command in Spain.
Pompey did well in Spain between 76 and 71 B.C. His task was
to overcome the rebellion of Sertorius, a Roman general who
had set up a government of his own in eastern Spain. Sertorius
was eventually murdered and his rebellion crushed.
75 B.C.: Tribunes were allowed to hold further offices.
73 B.C.: The corn law was reestablished.
73 B.C.: The greatest of all the slave revolts broke out in
southern Italy. This uprising was led by Spartacus, a man
from Thrace who had seen some service in the Roman army.
Spartacus defeated several Roman armies and for two years he
held most of south Italy. The slaves did not try to break
out of Italy to scatter to their homes, but instead stayed in
Italy to plunder.
72-71 B.C.: The slave revolt was put down by M. LICINIUS
CRASSUS. Crassus, from a family which had been prominent for
several generations, had been a close associate of Sulla and
had made an immense fortune out of the properties seized by
Sulla. 6,000 of the slaves were crucified along the Appian
Way south of Rome as an example. It was enough of an example
to make this the last of the great slave revolts. Since
Crassus had never been consul, he was not entitled under Sulla's
laws to the command against the slaves.
71 B.C.: Pompey came back to Italy from Spain at the Senate's
request to help fight the slaves, only to find that Crassus'
success had made his help unnecessary.

At this point, the two men, Crassus and Pompey, faced each other in Italy, each refusing to give up his army. For a moment it looked as if they might fight. Instead, they did a deal—two generals deciding together to control the Republic. 70 B.C.: <u>Pompey and Crassus</u> became the two consuls for 70 B.C. Crassus was eligible, but Pompey was still too young and he had not served as quaestor or praetor, so that he was not even a senator. The two consuls, both old associates of Sulla, threw out most of what was left of Sulla's reforms. Both men were passing as Populares:
--<u>tribunes</u> and <u>censors</u> are restored to all their old powers. The censors of 70 B.C. put 64 men out of the Senate.
--the Senate now filled only 1/3rd of the seats on Sulla's <u>courts</u>. Another 1/3rd went to the equites, the remaining 1/3rd to the class immediately below the Equites in wealth. This change was encouraged by the corruption trial of <u>Verres</u> in 70 B.C. on charges growing out of his term as governor of <u>Sicily</u>. It was in this trial that the young orator CICERO made his name, successfully prosecuting Verres on behalf of the people of Sicily. This was the latest in a series of corruption cases which placed Sulla's Senate juries and the Senate's handling of the provinces in very bad light.
--the approval of the Senate was no longer needed before bills could be presented to the Assembly.

Pompey and Crassus controlled the state at this point. Fortunately for the Republic, neither man had any serious interest in a dictatorship. Crassus was satisfied to stay in Rome, enjoying his wealth and playing a dominant part in politics. Pompey only wanted the chance for further military glory. This he got.

Pompey in the 60's B.C.
67 B.C.: <u>Gabinian Law</u>. A tribune got the <u>Assembly</u> to give <u>Pompey</u> a special three-year command against <u>pirates</u> in the Mediterranean. Rome had been struggling against these pirates for a decade. With 120,000 infantry and 500 ships, the largest command a Roman general had ever had, Pompey brought the problem under control in three months. Under Sulla's laws, such commands could be given only by the <u>Senate</u>.
66 B.C.: <u>Manilian Law</u>. Again a tribune got the Assembly to give Pompey command of the war in <u>Asia Minor</u>, with the power to settle the affairs of the Near East.

Rome had been at war in Asia Minor since 74 B.C. The problem was the same Mithridates of Pontus of Sulla's day. Mithridates had continued to cause trouble since the 80's B.C. He had conquered Cappadocia and Syria; he overwhelmed the remains of the kingdom of the Seleucids. He had obtained the kingdom of Armenia for his son-in-law. When Bithynia was left to Rome in the will of its king in 75 B.C., Mithridates made a grab for the place. L. Licinius Lucullus, another former associate of Sulla, was given the command against Mithridates in 74 B.C. Lucullus took Bithynia, drove Mithridates out of Pontus itself, and attacked Armenia. For the last, he had no orders. Lucullus had a great military talent, but over the years his discipline and honesty annoyed his troops, driving them to mutiny, and frustrated the interests of the greedy equites in Asia Minor. In 66 B.C. Lucullus was replaced by Pompey.

66-62 B.C. Pompey did very well in the East. He defeated Mithridates, who finally committed suicide. Pompey annexed Pontus, adding it to Bithynia in a single province. Armenia was left as an independent client, but it became a Roman client.

Moving on, Pompey annexed Syria and much of Judaea, organizing the area into the province of Syria. The rest of Judaea was left in the hands of a Jewish client king of the Maccabees. Pompey upset the Jews by attacking the Temple at Jerusalem and entering the Holy of Holies. Pompey had achieved great things, although the enormous size of his forces made success all but certain.

Crassus and Rome in the 60's B.C.

Things became unsettled in Rome while Pompey was away. Crassus grew jealous of the success of his rival, but found that he was strong enough in Rome to have things his own way. He failed to obtain citizenship for Italy north of the Po river, a proposal that would have given him many friends in that region. Above all, Crassus was aware that he might need an army to match Pompey's. As censor in 65 B.C. Crassus tried without success to carry a bill to annex Egypt (a questionable will of an earlier king of Egypt had left that kingdom to Rome). He had hoped to put in his young friend C. JULIUS CAESAR as governor of Egypt with an army. Caesar, was born around 100 B.C. of a patrician family, had grown up in association with Marius and the Populares. His aunt had

534

married Marius early in that general's career. Caesar himself as a teenager had married a daughter of Cinna. He was
very fortunate to have survived Sulla's purge in 82-79 B.C.
Caesar divorced Cinna's daughter at Sulla's order and
married Sulla's granddaughter. Now, as Crassus and Pompey
had given up Sulla's support of the Senate, it came very
easily to Caesar to return to the style of the Populares.
In the mid-60's B.C. he was working as an aide to Crassus,
while looking for the chance to move ahead. Of Caesar's
enormous talents, and his ability to play the game of politics, there was never any doubt.

Since this man is known to us as Julius Caesar, this is
a convenient point to explain the structure of Roman names.
The form C. Julius Caesar is one we have met many times al-
ready--it is the basic form of a Roman name. Caesar is the
family name, the equivalent of Smith or Jones, and it is the
form usually used here. The initial, C for Caius in this
case, is the first or given name, the equivalent of Thomas
or Henry. Julius is the clan or extended family name; it
is not his first name. It makes no sense to call him Julius
Caesar, but we do it. Caesar, or C. Caesar, is the appropriate form. This is the Latin form of his name, save that,
with no J in Latin, it was actually Iulius. Usually, it is
the Latin form of the name which we have wound up using, although there are exceptions. Pompey is an example, being an
English version of Pompeius. Female names in the patrician
families were usually simply the feminine form of the clan
name. Scipio Africanus' daughter, for example, was Cornelia
(from Cornelius). Caesar's daughter, similarly, was Julia
(from Julius). We have kept a great many of these female
names.

64-63 B.C. The Catilinarian Conspiracies.
The trouble in Rome came to a head in the Catilinarian
Conspiracies. These involved Catiline, a bankrupt patrician
of few scruples who was one of Crassus' less desirable and
more violent associates. Catiline wanted to be a consul,
but being under indictment for embezzlement he was barred
from running for 65 B.C. and again for 64 B.C. In 64 B.C.
he was allowed to be a candidate for consul of 63 B.C.
Crassus supported him, but Catiline lost. One of the successful candidates for consul of 63 B.C. was Cicero, who had
made his mark in the prosecution of Verres in 70 B.C. From

the same town as Marius, Cicero was probably the first new man to become consul since 94 B.C. Cicero was still friendly to Pompey (he had supported the Manilian Law of 66 B.C.), but he was at odds with Crassus. On this occasion, as the lesser evil, he was favored by most of the Senate against Catiline. It is from Cicero's own description of these events, and from Sallust's work on Catiline written a little later, that we know what happened.

Cicero was already dreaming of a great political compromise between the Senate and the equites, which he called the Concord of the Orders. This idea was to win him a reputation as one of the last champions of the Republic. Actually, what he proposed was not very different from what Sulla had tried already in his enlarged Senate. In any case, it was already clear that the Republic was entirely at the mercy of its soldiers.

Catiline was again a candidate in the elections held in 63 B.C. to select the consuls for 62 B.C. He ran as the candidate of the Populares, with Crassus' approval, offering land redistribution and a general cancellation of debts (something that would do Catiline himself no harm). When he lost once more, Catiline plotted to overthrow the state.

He intended to gather an army in Etruria and march on Rome. When the plot was discovered, the Senate declared an emergency. Cicero, as a consul, arrested five associates of Catiline, some of them men of very high rank. These men were executed immediately without trial. This caused many complaints, since those killed had not been actually engaged in rebellion and so were entitled to trial. Many thought that Cicero was grandstanding, posing as a savior of the Republic. Catiline was later caught and killed; his rebellion did not amount to anything, a fact which cast further suspicion on Cicero. Crassus, of course, cut loose from Catiline, but he could not escape all damage by association.

In the uproar which followed Cicero's actions, the Senate moved to head off complaints from the Populares by promoting a big extension of the corn law. It had the proposal introduced in the Assembly by one of its rising stars, the 29 years old tribune CATO, great-grandson of Cato the Censor. Hard and cold, Cato was to become the greatest champion of the Senate and the old constitution in the last years of the Republic.

On this occasion, he defended what Cicero had done. In contrast, Caesar criticized Cicero, adding to his reputation with
the Populares and winning the chance to move ahead. Caesar
had been elected Chief Priest (a life-time position) by the
Assembly in 63 B.C., when Sulla's law that the Senate should
control the selection of priests was overturned. This position
had given him control of much patronage, as well as the opportunity to throw his own money away to good purpose on splashy
religious/social shows. Now Caesar was made praetor for 62 B.C.
and he was given a command in Spain—the chance he needed to
make his name as a soldier.

62 B.C. Pompey Returns from the East.

Not long after all this, Pompey returned to Italy. He
could have had anything he wanted at this point, including
the dictatorship, but he chose instead to break up his army.
All he asked for was land for his veterans and approval of
what he had done in the East. Cicero, appreciating what
Pompey might have done, urged the Senate to give the general
what little he asked. The Senate, listening instead to Cato,
refused. Stupidly and meanly, the Optimates in the Senate
defied Pompey. In doing so, they killed the Republic.

The Senate's foolishness extended even beyond this. Within a short time, it also angered both Crassus and Caesar:
—The tax-farmers responsible for the taxes of the province of
Asia had made a bad deal with the state; having bid too high
for the right to collect, they were now trying to get a rebate
from the state. Crassus, their good friend, supported them.
In refusing the request, the Senate took a step it could not
afford, whatever the merits of its attitude otherwise. Crassus,
embarrassed by the Catiline affair and now openly humiliated,
was ready to make a move.
—Caesar returned from a successful period in Spain in 60 B.C.
He wanted to be a consul for 59 B.C. The Senate, associating
him with the Populares, refused Caesar a triumph for his
Spanish victories. More importantly, the Senate had the job
of deciding ahead of time what military commands would be
given to those who should be elected consuls for the next year
(59 B.C.). Knowing that Caesar was sure to be a candidate,
the Senate decided to keep the two consuls for 59 B.C. in
Italy rather than to give them foreign campaigns. Caesar was
very angry. Having discovered in Spain that he had a great
military talent, he was anxious to get the chance to build up
his military reputation—the sure passport to bigger things.

Pompey and Crassus united once more, as they had in 71 B.C., to dominate the Republic. This time, though, they accepted the increasingly important Caesar as a third party to their arrangements. This combination of the three men in 60 B.C. is called the IST TRIUMVIRATE (system of three men). Cicero refused to support the Triumvirate, but such a combination could not be stopped. From now on, the Republic was lost. For if Pompey and Crassus did not look to the dictatorship, Caesar did.

THE GENERAL WHO WOULD: CAESAR AND THE TRIUMVIRATES, 60-49 B.C.

Pompey, Crassus, and Caesar, the Triumvirs (the members
of the Triumvirate) had agreed upon a number of specific objectives:
--Pompey was to get what the Senate had refused him--land for
his veterans and approval for what he had done in the East;
--Crassus was to get the rebate on the tax deal for the
province of Asia, along with a general restoration of his position at Rome;
--Caesar was to become a consul for 59 B.C. and to get a big
military command.

In 60 B.C., against the opposition of the Senate, Caesar
was elected one of the consuls for 59 B.C. The other consulship, though, went to a friend of the Senate, Bibulus. In
59 B.C., the year of his consulship, Caesar gave his daughter
Julia in marriage to Pompey.

To carry the program the Triumvirs had agreed on, Caesar
as consul had to be willing to act illegally and to use violence. All this he did, showing that he was a very different
man from Pompey and Crassus. Frustrated in the Senate by
Cato and others, Caesar often took business to the Assembly
instead. He had the proceedings of both the Senate and the
Assembly published, so that there could be no more secret
meetings. The Senate used its influence over the priests to
try to hold up Caesar by interpreting the signs (auspices)
unfavorably; bad signs meant that no public business could be
transacted. Caesar, illegally, merely ignored the signs.
There was considerable fighting in the streets. Caesar had
his gangs beat up Bibulus, the other consul. This was to
discourage Bibulus and others from using their veto powers.
From this time until the end of the Republic there was constant disorder in the streets. The Senate had lost all ability to control the city.

The Triumvirs won their way. The entire program was
passed. For himself, Caesar took at first a five-year command
in Cisalpine Gaul and Illyria, ignoring the Senate's duty to
make these appointments. He intended to look for glory toward
the Danube in the northeast. Then the governor of Narbonese
Gaul (southern France) died. Taking the better opportunity,
Caesar had that area added to his command. He now looked to

win fame by conquering the rest of Gaul (France) to the
Rhine river.

58-50 B.C. Caesar in Gaul.

In the most splendid series of campaigns in the history
of the Republic, Caesar conquered the area north of Narbonese
Gaul between the Atlantic Ocean and the Rhine river. These
campaigns are known to us in detail from Caesar's own description of them in The Gallic Wars. Written in a deliberately
simple style, these accounts were rushed off to Rome to
serve their propaganda purpose. They show Caesar as a super-
man, but in any case he had little need to exaggerate his
achievements. For what he did in Gaul, Romans recognized
Caesar as the greatest military talent they had produced. We
can compare Caesar's rapid conquest of Gaul with the terrible
and drawn-out problems the Romans had met with in conquering
Spain, an area of similar size and much of it inhabited by
the same Celts/Gauls.

The Celts of Gaul had at this time the most advanced
society which had yet developed north of the Alps. Yet they
were still generally primitive, not yet settled in towns, and
they had no literacy beyond a Greek-based alphabet which was
used for limited official purposes. Politically, they were
split up into many tribes. These tribes spent a great deal
of time fighting one another, something which was of much
advantage to the Romans. Most of the tribes were ruled by
warrior aristocracies, the earlier kings generally having
lost their power. The area inhabited by the Gauls was very
fertile, with a temperate climate. and it had good communi-
cations, with many usable rivers and few mountains. To the
east, toward the Rhine, the Celts gave way to the more backward German peoples. It was these Germans who gave Caesar
the excuse to move north from Narbonese Gaul.

58 B.C.: A Celtic tribe from Switzerland, the Helvetii, was
being pressured by Germans from the north. The Helvetii
tried to move west away from this threat. This brought them
into Narbonese Gaul. Caesar refused to let the Helvetii
move through the province. He almost exterminated the
Helvetii and drove the rest back into Switzerland (which is
still called the Helvetic Confederation.)
58 B.C.: Then Caesar answered appeals from tribes of Gauls
in central France which felt threatened by another German
people, the Suevi, and their leader Ariovistus. The Suevi
had been asked into Gaul in 61 B.C. to help out one of the

Celtic tribes in a local war. Rome had not then objected;
in fact, for Rome, Caesar as a consul in 59 B.C. had accepted the Suevi as allies. Now Caesar's aims had changed.
Caesar defeated the Suevi and occupied central France.
57 B.C.: Caesar took northern France, defeating the Belgae,
a mixed German-Celt people who dominated the northeast. Over
the next two years, Caesar occupied the rest of Gaul.
55 B.C.: Caesar went to Britain, a land also inhabited by
Celts, including many of the same Belgae. The British tribes
were much more primitive; most were still ruled by kings.
Caesar's descriptions of the island are our first good look
at what it was like. Caesar's motives probably were curi-
osity and continuing ambition, although the British tribes
had been giving some aid to those in France. Caesar stayed
only 18 days.
54 B.C.: Caesar returned to Britain with 5 legions (30,000
men). He conquered southeast England, and captured
Wheathampstead, which was the capital of the major British
Celtic king, Cassivelaunus of the Catuvellauni tribe.
Caesar stayed three months this time; long enough, it seems,
for him to decide that the thing was not worth the bother.
He did not return.
52 B.C.: A great revolt broke out among the Gauls of central
France. The leader was Vercingetorix of the Arverni tribe.
Caesar put down this revolt in heavy fighting.

This revolt is misleading. The remarkable thing is how
secure Roman control was in Gaul by the time Caesar had finished. Some part of this may have resulted from the great brutality with which Caesar worked in Gaul at first. Anxious
to win quickly, he terrorized the Celts; whole peoples were
all but exterminated, or relocated around Gaul. Caesar took
little bother to hide this kind of behavior in his writings,
for it was not something to bother Romans. At the same time,
by virtue of his extraordinary personality, Caesar was able
despite all this violence to promote himself as a friend to
the Gauls. The area accepted him, and he found many fine
troops there to serve him alongside his legions.

58-56 B.C. The 1st Triumvirate.
Caesar's wonderful successes in Gaul tilted things his
way, to the disadvantage of Pompey and Crassus. Caesar's
style early had raised the possibility that he might be willing to overthrow the state, and now his army gave him the

means to do it. The booty Caesar picked up in Gaul also
allowed him to finance an organization of his own in Rome
and so to cut himself loose to some extent from the other
Triumvirs.

Caesar's chief aide in Rome from 58 B.C. was P. Clodius
Pulcher, a wild young man who turned the trade of street
gangs and political terror into a fine art. As a tribune
of 58 B.C. (the patrician Clodius made himself eligible for
the position by getting himself adopted into a plebeian
family--his adopted father being younger than himself),
Clodius:
--exiled Cicero for his part in the Catilinarian Conspiracy.
This was partly a warning to the Senate, partly personal ill-
feeling. Cicero had earlier prosecuted Clodius unsuccessfully in a sex/religious scandal. Clodius had dressed as a
woman to attend the Good Goddess festival, an event closed
to men. What he had done there was also in some dispute,
but Clodius' reputation made any immorality seem reasonable.
Caesar's wife had been involved, and Caesar had taken the
opportunity to divorce her: "Caesar's wife must be above
suspicion." Caesar did not think that Clodius needed to be
above suspicion. Nor, for that matter, did Caesar himself:
he chased women eagerly and changed wives for political purposes quite regularly. Clodius had been acquitted of the
charges against him, presumably as a result of bribery.
--outlawed the use of bad signs to prevent government business.
--turned the corn law into a great give-away program. By
46 B.C., 320,000 citizens were receiving free grain.
--grabbed Cyprus from its king and used the king's treasury
to enrich himself and his gangs and to pay for the corn program. Clodius sent Cato, the Senate champion, to Cyprus,
hoping to get Cato to dirty his hands there, but Cato could
not be tempted.
Crassus seems to have gone along with Caesar, and probably was helping to bankroll Clodius. Pompey however, as the
greatest name in the Republic and a man who disliked meddling
in politics, had more to lose. Jealous of Caesar's military
successes, he was also upset by the street violence, and he
worked up some gangs of his own to match Clodius.

Some elements in the Senate began to look to Pompey for
a possible agreement. They knew they could rely on Pompey
not to overthrow the government: they were not nearly so sure

about Caesar. Cicero encouraged the moves toward Pompey.
He had always had a genuine admiration for Pompey, and he
knew that only a military man could save the Republic against
a military man. Pompey paid some attention. He helped secure
the recall of Cicero from exile. He obtained for himself a
five-year command (without an army) to organize the corn
program—an obvious move to compete with Clodius in the give-
away business.

It seemed that the Triumvirate might fall apart, but in
56 B.C., calculating their interests, all three members decided that it suited them to stay together. The 2nd
Triumvirate was established. The three men made their deal
at Lucca, in Cisalpine Gaul in Caesar's command. Under
Sulla's law, Caesar could not leave his provinces without the
permission of the Senate.

56-52 B.C. The 2nd Triumvirate.
The new arrangement was:
--Caesar was to have his command extended for five years,
although the date when it was to end is not known and in
fact none may have been named;
--Pompey and Crassus were to be the consuls of 55 B.C.;
--Pompey was to have the command of the two Spanish provinces
for five years. This would give him a little army. He did
not, though have to go to Spain; he could remain in Italy:
--Crassus was to get a five year command in Syria-Mesopotamia,
to fight the Parthians who controlled Iran and Mesopotamia.

Things had obviously shifted in Caesar's favor. Both
Pompey and Crassus wanted armies to match Caesar's. The
Triumvirate once again got its way. Since the arrangements
were made after the candidates for the consulships of 55 B.C.
had been nominated, and the commands they were to receive
settled, it took some rearranging to get Pompey and Crassus
what they wanted.

Caesar went off to greater glories in France and Britain.
Crassus, however, proved himself no Caesar. He was killed in
53 B.C. at the battle of CARRHAE, a great defeat at Mesopotamia.
The story is that, facing defeat, he was tempted into a con-
ference with the Parthian king and murdered. Pompey and
Caesar were left to face one another.

Pompey and Caesar were not able to work together for long in Rome. This was apparent long before Crassus got himself killed. The death in 54 B.C. of Pompey's wife Julia, the daughter of Caesar, came at a time when the two men were already near a break. Violence between their rival gangs became very serious. No consuls could be elected for 54 B.C. or for the first half of 53 B.C. In riots in 52 B.C. in which the Senate House and many other public buildings were destroyed Clodius was murdered. The Senate, looking again to Pompey, declared a state of emergency. Pompey was made sole consul, which was illegal, and was given soldiers to restore order in the city. His command in Spain, from which he was drawing his funds, was extended for five more years.

It is not surprising that Pompey, who was on the scene, could outmatch Caesar, who was not. Caesar was in the position Sulla had been in 30 years before during his campaign in the East. From now on, Caesar and Pompey were on a collision course, although Pompey, in his typically hesitant way, was not eager for trouble, and Caesar was willing to wait his time. Pompey found himself moving closer to the Senate, to some degree in spite of himself. The Senate had little choice but to deal with Pompey, who dominated the city. In 52 B.C. Pompey turned down Caesar's offer of a new marriage alliance. Instead, he married into the Optimates, taking a woman descended from the Metelli and the Scipiones.

The Crisis of 50 B.C.

The year 50 B.C. was dominated by the problem of what to do when Caesar's command in Gaul should end. While we do not know precisely when he was due to leave Gaul, it is clear enough what was at stake. Caesar wanted to be elected a consul for 49 B.C. This would allow him to move from his existing command directly into office as consul at Rome, with no period between when he would be out of office. As long as he held office, he was safe from prosecution; he believed that his enemies were waiting to charge him with his many illegal actions as consul in 59 B.C. if they could get him out of office. Unfortunately, he had to be present in Rome to stand for election as consul. He could not leave his provinces and go to Rome to do this without the consent of the Senate, which he could not get, or without giving up his command, which he would not risk.

Caesar wanted the Seante to let him run for consul while he remained in Gaul. Some senators were on Caesar's side; most senators, aware of the risks involved, were willing to try to work out a deal. The diehards, though, led by Cato, would not yield. And the diehards won the support of Pompey for their cause, although Pompey probably never was sure what he wanted to do. Caesar, for his part, had no intention of backing down. Like Sulla, he understood that the alternative to protecting himself was death; unlike Sulla, he had no objection to replacing the Republic permanently with a dictatorship.

546

THE DICTATORSHIP OF CAESAR, 49-44 B.C.

The crisis came in the winter of 50-49 B.C.:
December, 50 B.C.: Pompey accepted the Senate's call to protect the Republic and took command of all the soldiers in Italy.
January 1, 49 B.C.: The Senate voted to order Caesar to surrender his provinces. Tribunes friendly to Caesar, including MARK ANTONY, vetoed this.
January 10, 49 B.C.: Caesar brought his army across the Rubicon, moving from his province in Cisalpine Gaul into Italy proper. This was treason, being against Sulla's law. "The die is cast" is the phrase credited to Caesar at this moment (from Suetonius). "Crossing the Rubicon" to us means going beyond the point of no return, going for broke.

Caesar knew what he was doing. In contrast, neither Pompey nor many of the senators supporting him had much faith in their own chances. Pompey withdrew east to Greece at once, lacking the means to fight the great army of veterans Caesar was bringing out of Gaul. L. Domitius Ahenobarbus, of the family of the later dictator Nero, fought Caesar unsuccessfully in Italy. Caesar let him and his soldiers off lightly, being anxious to show that he did not intend to wipe out the Optimates. He did not want to repeat the massacres of Marius and Sulla. Unpredictable charity was Caesar's style; he had used it already in Gaul.

48 B.C.: Securing Italy, Caesar went next to Spain, Pompey's province, and defeated the opposition there.
48 B.C.: Caesar then went after Pompey himself in Greece. Pompey was defeated at the battle of Pharsalus. Pompey fled to Egypt, but the Egyptians assassinated him, not wishing to offend Caesar. When Caesar arrived in Egypt in pursuit of Pompey he found time instead to love CLEOPATRA. The 21 years old princess, who wanted Caesar's support in her struggle for power with her 13 years old half-brother and husband, needed no pursuing.
48-47 B.C.: An infatuated Caesar spent the winter with Cleopatra holed up in the palace at Alexandria, where they were besieged by supporters of Cleopatra's brother.
47 B.C.: This strange spectacle ended in the spring of 47 B.C. when more Roman and allied troops reached Alexandria. Cleopatra was given Egypt, her half-brother was killed (she

had to marry a still younger half-brother, however).
47 B.C.: Caesar then campaigned briefly in Asia Minor, including a five-day campaign against a rebellion in Pontus
which gave rise to the most famous phrase associated with
him, "I came, I saw, I conquered" (Veni, vidi, vici), reported in Suetonius and Plutarch.
47 B.C.: Caesar finally returned to Italy.
47-46 B.C.: The following winter Caesar campaigned in the
province of Africa, the one remaining stronghold of the
opposition. Cato committed suicide there, and became the
great martyr of the Republican cause.
45 B.C.: After another period in Rome, Caesar campaigned
in Spain again against Pompey's sons. One was killed, one
escaped. There was now order in the state.

Caesar was the authority across the empire. The Republic was as good as dead--killed, as any Roman could have
predicted, by an ambitious patrician reformer. At first,
Caesar held power simply as a great rebel. Then he held
brief dictatorships and the sole consulship. In 47 or 46 B.C.
he became dictator for 10 years. In February, 44 B.C. he
became dictator for life. He then issued coins with the
word Perpetuus--for ever. Lacking a son, Caesar adopted as
his son his closest male relative, his young great nephew
Octavius, who had been born in 63 B.C. It was Caesar's
intention to take for his family permanent control of the
state. He toyed with the idea of becoming king,but this was
a very un-Roman idea. In January, 44 B.C. a crowd saluted
him as king, and in February at the Lupercalia his closest
associate Mark Antony offered him a crown which he refused.
This kind of thing may have been staged to test public reaction.

Caesar's intentions are not known. He was no Sulla,
looking for an easy retirement after a brief dictatorship.
Caesar said that Sulla had been a fool not to keep power,
and he certainly intended to stay on top. Probably, he
was playing things by ear, while all the time showing his
power more and more openly. There was in Caesar, another
Epicurean, a strain of rash showmanship. His flamboyant
charity toward his enemies was one expression of this.

Caesar used all of the great titles of later dictators:

548

imperator, greatest general (from which we get emperor);
princeps, first or chief citizen; father of the country.
As father of the country, senators swore an oath of allegiance
to Caesar personally, as though they were his clients or children. A little while before his death he put his own head
on coins, the first time a living human had appeared on
Roman coins. There was also a good business in busts of
Caesar, which were distributed widely in Italy and the East
to be placed in public buildings and temples.

   Caesar did a great deal in the days of his power. Beyond his wish to promote stability and order, the impression
his actions give is that Caesar wanted to emphasize his
generosity and his reputation as a reformer:
--the Senate's membership was increased from 600 to 900, so
that his friends were in the majority. Some of the new
members were from Gaul, as Caesar kept up his line of being
a friend to the provinces.
--he secured land for his veterans, the great obligation of
the general. Many new colonies were founded in Italy, and
at least 40 elsewhere, including Spain, Corinth, and Carthage.
The last was a nod to the memory of Caius Gracchus. More
than 3/4ths of the colonies were in the West. Ordinary citizens were allowed in the colonies as well as vererans.
Caesar was anxious to find some way of moving some of the
large numbers of poor citizens out of the swelling city of
Rome. Some 80,000 of these poor were given land.
--partly as a result of the land program, the number receiving the corn hand-out was reduced from 320,000 to 150,000.
--great public works were begun, including a new Forum at
Rome. Caesar planned to construct a canal across the
isthmus at Corinth. Such activity showed the dictator in
good light--it also provided opportunities for both the poor
and the equites.
--steps were taken to settle the debt problem which had mush-
roomed in the civil war. Caesar favored debtors against
creditors, a traditional reformer position. At first, he
forced lenders to accept any property in repayment and to
take such property at its prewar assessment. While he was
in Egypt, proposals that all debts simply be cancelled produced riots in Rome. On his return, Caesar cancelled all
interest payments due since the start of the civil war. Any
interest paid in that period could be applied to what was
due in the future.

--he dropped the class immediately below the equites in wealth from the privilege of <u>jury service</u> which it had enjoyed since 70 B.C.

--<u>citizenship</u> was extended to Italy north of the Po river.

--with the help of a scientist brought in from <u>Alexandria</u>, Caesar introduced our <u>solar calendar</u>. One month, July, was named in his honor.

The open scorn of Caesar for the Republic, even while he treated his opponents generously, was too much for some, including a number who had been on his side in the struggle. Angered by Caesar's acceptance of the permanent dictatorship in February, 44 B.C. and by the talk of his becoming king, they plotted to kill Caesar before he left for the East on March 18. He intended to make a great campaign out there, including a defeat of the <u>Parthians</u> to avenge the defeat of <u>Crassus</u> at <u>Carrhae</u>. About 60 senators were in the plot. They were led by two brothers-in-law, CASSIUS and BRUTUS. <u>Cassius</u> was from a great old family. <u>Brutus</u> was a son-in-law of the "martyred" <u>Cato</u> and claimed descent from the <u>Brutus</u> who had overthrown the last Etruscan king of Rome, <u>Tarquin the Proud</u>. His wife was the widow of <u>Bibulus</u>, Caesar's unfortunate partner as consul in 59 B.C. She had also been one of the many mistresses of Caesar. Both men had been strong <u>Pompey</u> supporters in the civil war; many in the plot, though, had earlier supported Caesar. Dictatorship was still widely disliked.

Caesar was murdered in the Senate House on March 15, 44 B.C. (<u>the Ides of March</u>). There is no good basis for the remark, "You too, Brutus?" (Et tu, Brute?), credited to him by <u>Shakespeare</u> in the play <u>Julius Caesar</u>.

OCTAVIAN AND MARK ANTONY, 44-31 B.C.

The friends of the Republic gained little from the death of Caesar. No reasonable alternative to dictatorship could be found. It soon became clear that the real question was who would succeed Caesar in power.

One serious candidate was available immediately in Mark Antony, one of the consuls of 44 B.C. From an old and famous family, Mark Antony was a close associate of Caesar and a good soldier, although he had a reputation as something of a playboy. At first he tried to work with the Senate, offering amnesty to the assassins. This was a strange course, one likely to upset Caesar's veterans. Caesar's other chief lieutenant, Marcus Lepidus, the son of the ambitious consul of 78 B.C., moved to use violence against the Senate. Mark Antony restrained him.

Another possibility was Octavius, the adopted son of Caesar, aged 18 at this time. He is known to us as OCTAVIAN, or Octavianus, meaning the adopted Octavius. Few took the young and inexperienced Octavian seriously at first. Rome had no tradition of such young men playing big roles. Octavian stood for an eastern-style "Hereditary" idea, an un-Roman thing. Mark Antony patronized him. The Senate played up to him in order to weaken Mark Antony, the biggest name in the field. As Cicero said, "the young man is to be praised, honored, and set aside." With his series of speeches against Mark Antony, the Philippics (shades of Demosthenes and Philip of Macedon), Cicero played a big part in bringing on a break between Mark Antony and the Senate, pushing the latter toward an arrangement with Octavian. Once again, the Senate was wasting its time.

Early in 43 B.C. the forces of Octavian and the Senate defeated Mark Antony at Mutina in north Italy. Mark Antony withdrew into Gaul, where he was joined by Lepidus. Octavian then found that the Senate no longer wanted him. In anger he reversed directions. Octavian seized Rome and offered a deal to Mark Antony and Lepidus. This led to a Triumvirate in late 43 B.C. Lepidus was a good deal less important than the other two parties to the deal.

The three men had themselves voted control of the state for <u>five years</u>. Caesar was recognized as a <u>god</u> and there was a purge, the biggest so far, of those the <u>Triumvirs</u> did not like. Some 300 senators died. Among them, at Mark Antony's insistence, was <u>Cicero</u>. His head and hands were cut off and displayed at Rome.

The next task was to defeat the friends of the Senate who were concentrating their forces in the East, just as Pompey had done in 49 B.C. This proved to be no difficult task. Mark Antony and Octavian went east in 42 B.C. and defeated <u>Brutus</u> and <u>Cassius</u> and the Senate army in two battles at <u>Philippi</u>. Both Brutus and Cassius committed suicide. Most of the credit for these victories went to Mark Antony, much the most prominent military figure among the Triumvirs.

Mark Antony and Octavian next conspired to drop Lepidus from their arrangements. They planned a division of Rome's possessions which gave Mark Antony the East and Gaul; Octavian most of the rest of the West; and Lepidus only the province of Africa. Mark Antony, appropriately, had the lion's share. Octavian married Mark Antony's step-daughter. For so young a man he had done remarkably well since 44 B.C.

It was not long before Octavian and Mark Antony were again at odds. A brother of Mark Antony challenged Octavian in the West. This was not of Mark Antony's doing, and he did not give help to the challenge, but Octavian was greatly angered. In 40 B.C. he divorced his wife, a rejection of his connection with Mark Antony. The two men were on the edge of civil war, and there actually was some minor fighting. Then both thought better of it. The Triumvirate was renewed. Octavian now received the entire West, save for Lepidus' province of Africa; Mark Antony held the East. Mark Antony married <u>Octavia</u>, Octavian's sister.

The new arrangement survived for <u>eight</u> years, although the two chief parties were soon ill-disposed to one another. It was an odd situation, with the state practically divided into two.

In the West, Octavian had to fight major campaigns against remaining Republican forces, the most important of which were led by Pompey's surviving son, <u>Sextus</u>, who was based in <u>Sicily</u>. Victory in this struggle came in 36 B.C.

as the result of the work of AGRIPPA, Octavian's leading
soldier. Lepidus then revolted, but was defeated without any
great problem. He lost Africa, but was left as Chief Priest,
a position in which he had succeeded Caesar in 44 B.C.
Octavian also campaigned in Illyria. He was not much of a
soldier, but he recognized that it was very important for him
to build up a personal relationship with the legions.

In the East, Mark Antony led a very strange existence.
His great aim was to lead a big force against the Parthians,
the task to which Caesar had been looking at the time of his
assassination. Infatuation with Cleopatra, Caesar's old
flame, distracted him. Cleopatra, who had a son she claimed
was Caesar's, had murdered her last brother-husband and was
running Egypt herself. By 38 B.C. Mark Antony was very much
in love with Cleopatra, an affection she returned with a
great deal more calculation than existed on his part. In
37 B.C. Mark Antony sent his wife Octavia back to the West
and actually married Cleopatra, an act of bigamy that was
not recognized in Roman law. Over the next several years,
Mark Antony and Cleopatra had three children. None of this
looked any good at Rome. It could be made to look as if a
foolish Mark Antony, tucked away in the East, was forgetting
all about the state while proposing to set up himself and
his whore as eastern-style rulers of one half of what Rome
possessed.

When he did get around to it, Mark Antony's campaign
of 36-33 B.C. against the Parthians was no great success.
It was easy to say that this too came from his not having
all his mind on the job. The final touch came in 32 B.C.
when Mark Antony formally divorced Octavia, whom he had not
seen for years. Octavian, with the West solidly under his
control and Mark Antony badly discredited, was ready to move.

31 B.C.: The civil war which followed did not amount
to much. At the battle of ACTIUM in Greece Mark Antony and
Cleopatra were defeated. The circumstances of the battle
are difficult to follow; Cleopatra apparently ran off with
her Egyptian fleet in fear, and Mark Antony seems to have
been barely interested. The outcome, however, was very clear.
Mark Antony and Cleopatra went back to Egypt, and there they
both committed suicide. Octavian, at 32, was now the master
of the Roman state and the Mediterranean world. Dictatorship was alive and well.

THE ESTABLISHMENT OF THE PERMANENT DICTATORSHIP
(THE 'ROMAN EMPIRE'): AUGUSTUS, 31 B.C.-14 A.D.

The dictatorship of Octavian marks the beginning of
the period we call the Roman Empire, a period which covers
several centuries until the "fall of Rome." Empire really
indicates the area under Rome's control--the area over
which Rome had imperium. So we can talk about the Empire
of the Roman Republic, before Octavian, or about the
American "Empire," without indicating that any emperor,
any particular type of government, is involved. Beginning with Octavian, though, we also call the individuals
who ran Rome emperors, indicating a type of one-man rule.
Our word emperor comes from imperator, by which the Romans
meant great general. It was used by men like Caesar and
Octavian, but it meant little special beyond a big military name. The Romans, in fact, had no particular name
for these men who controlled them, or for the system
itself. There is no problem in using the words emperor
and empire if this is understood. Often the first 200
years after Octavian won power are called by historians
the PRINCIPATE. This comes from Princeps (first or chief,
as in our use of words like principal), which was one of
the titles by which the men who ran Rome were known (first
citizen). Its usefulness was and is that it is a lot more
low-key than the words emperor or dictator, and for a long
time the style of Octavian and the men who succeeded him
was surprisingly low-key. This was why the term was
popular with the Romans, and the dictators, themselves.
Dictatorship/tyranny still seemed un-Roman. The Romans
tended to avoid the word, except in criticism, and we do
the same: we call Sulla and Caesar dictators; we call
Octavian the first of the emperors.

Octavian intended to establish a permanent and
hereditary system of one-man rule. There is no question
about that. It was a principle he himself embodied, since
he had succeeded, after many ups and downs, his own adopted father, Caesar. In this aim he was successful. In the
course of his own long life he was able to make his system
reasonably attractive to almost everyone, so that few
could deny that it was superior in its stability and its
efficiency to the old Republican system. His achievement

indicates both his own great talents and the awful weaknesses of the old Republic which had brought Rome to such disorders. It was important that Octavian enjoyed such a long life. At his death in 14 A.D., when he was nearly 80, there were few alive who could remember any other form of government than the one he offered. Republicanism by then had become an ancient memory, and it seemed natural to go on with the dictatorship which had served so well under Octavian. The system which Octavian established lasted for over 200 years. It not only lasted: from the beginning it flourished, and Rome and the provinces flourished with it. These 200 years are the greatest success story, in administration and economics, in the history of our civilization before recent times. Truly, Octavian did great things.

The "Restoration of the Republic"

Many in the traditional governing and intellectual classes disliked dictatorship: Caesar had annoyed many of his own supporters by his high-flying style and had ended a victim of murder. Octavian wished to avoid this end, and these problems, by encouraging the old ruling class, including the Republican sympathizers who were at their strongest in the Senate, to cooperate with him. To achieve this, he took pains to avoid the outright appearance of dictatorship--including avoiding the very word.

This line of Octavian's was called, misleadingly but significantly, the Restoration of the Republic. It worked well. Octavian was skillful at this kind of thing, lacking the dramatic streak which had characterized Caesar; it was less of an effort for Octavian to avoid flaunting his powers. He also had the advantage that by the time of Actium, 31 B.C., there was a great longing for peace after all the troubles since 49 B.C. It was much easier for Octavian than it had been for Caesar to convince the Republicans that what he offered them was the best they could get.

So it was that Octavian lived in a modest house on the Palatine hill. Close by was the ancient round hut of sticks and reeds, the so-called Cottage of Romulus, where Virgil has Aeneas in the Aeneid (see below) spend his first

555

night in Rome; close by, too, was the Lupercal, where the wolf was supposed to have suckled the twins Romulus and Remus. Octavian beautified Rome, but he did not live splendidly himself, not wishing to appear too prominent. We can see the same deliberate low profile in the procession scene on the Altar of Peace, which provides us with some of the best-known surviving Roman sculpture; Octavian is just one in the crowd.

We should not make too much of this—it is a pretty obvious tactic. The same can be said of Octavian's refusal to consider himself a god. Such a thing, of course, was against all Roman tradition. In the East, where kings were commonly seen as gods, people quite naturally built shrines to Octavian. He did not approve or encourage this, but he did not prevent it. Even in the West, at Lyons in France for example, a number of such altars were set up. On the other hand, Octavian did secure the recognition of the dead Caesar as a god, so that he could appear as the son of a god. Toward the end of his life, Octavian's "divine power" (numen) was worshipped at Rome. Similarly, his spirit or genius was on guard in little shrines maintained at public expense all over Rome. There were also clear religious implications to the title AUGUSTUS which was given to him in 27 B.C. The word Angustus suggests growth, good fortune, as well as power and majesty. Octavian took this title as his preferred name. As a result, for example, the month named in his honor was called August. It is the name by which he will be called here from this point. The word was also used as a title by the later rulers.

Augustus also tried to give the appearance of respecting the old Republican traditions in his morality laws. He introduced:
—restrictions on flashy dress and habits (sumptuary laws)
—severe punishment for adultery
—penalties for remaining unmarried (celibacy) and for deliberately childless marriages
—privileges for the parents of three or more children.
Conservatives and traditionalists at Rome saw the decline of the family, of marality, and of simplicity, as all springing from the same corrupting eastern influence that broght in dictatorship. For them, wealth and eastern

(Greek) influence combined to undermine the qualities which had made Rome great. The traditionalists objected to a group of things which are coinciding in our own time also: growing sexual permissiveness (men and women getting together too much--adultery--or not enough--homosexuality) and a declining birth rate. Childlessness, it was assumed, indicated indifference to one's public responsibilities.

To pass morality laws was to honor the Republic and the old ways of the Senate. The old ways, though, could not be brought back by laws, any more than the dictatorship could be made to go away. In 9 A.D. a law gave preference in the government service to fathers--both of the consuls of that year who brought forward the bill were unmarried. Augustus himself took women in adultery often enough, although he was strongly attached to his wife Livia. In 2 B.C. his daughter Julia was sent into exile for immorality (the man she was sinning with was also believed to be intriguing against Augustus and his system). Later, Julia's own daughter, another Julia of course, suffered the same punishment. Neither one was called back.

Apart from these social and moral tactics, Augustus took a lot of care to leave the old political system largely intact, at least on the surface. His willingness to do this was first made very clear in 27 B.C.

Augustus did not return to Rome from the East until 29 B.C. In the East, he had restored order, generally changing little; he did, however, grab Egypt, and with it Cleopatra's treasury, which he kept for himself so that for a while he was wealthier than was the Roman government. He came back to Rome to a great triumph, and to a private reading of Virgil's Georgics, then unpublished, in which the coming golden age was welcomed. He then broke up most of his army. Many of his veterans were settled in a large number of colonies (he liked to boast that he had paid a fair price to obtain the land for these colonies). Most were in the West, including a number of what later were famous cities: Saragossa (Caesaraugusta) in Spain, Nimes and Avignon in France. By 27 B.C. he was ready to attempt a political settlement.

;

Augustus then announced "the transfer of the state
to the free disposal of the Senate and people." This was
the so-called Restoration of the Republic. It was for
this act that he was given the title Augustus. His
willingness to take Augustus as his preferred name itself
indicates his desire to show his pride in "restoring" the
Republic.

Augustus had been reelected consul each year (in his
absence, Augustus taking as a matter of course what
Caesar had been unable to obtain in 50 B.C.). He continued
to be reelected annually to that position. In addition,
the Senate, supported by the Assembly, gave Augustus
proconsular powers (the powers of a consul) and the command
of the provinces of Egypt, Gaul, Spain, and Syria. Since
nearly all the legions were stationed in those areas, he
had the bulk of the army directly under his orders. He
was also given control of the new areas in the north which
were being conquered (see below). Augustus governed
these provinces through governors who were his subordinates. These governors were always senators, save
in the case of Egypt, which was governed by a man of the
equites class. Augustus was very jealous of Egypt, which
was a source of great wealth to him and his family.
Senators were not allowed into Egypt at all without
permission from Augustus. All financial matters in the
various provinces of Augustus were kept separate and were
placed in the hands of the equites. This class Augustus
clearly considered to be more reliable and more efficient
than the senators. Drawn from all over Italy, the equites
were now finally coming into their own as servants of the
state.

The other provinces, those at peace and long settled
(and with few troops), were left under the control of the
Senate, which picked the governors for them. At first,
the Senate controlled only the provinces of Africa, Cyrene,
Sicily, Macedonia, Asia, and Bithynia and Pontus.
Augustus later handed some other pacified provinces,
Narbonese Gaul (southern France), Baetica (southern Spain),
and Cyprus, to the Senate.

A number of areas remained as client kingdoms under
their own rulers. These were Mauretania (ruled by the old

558

royal family of Numidia, although Numidia itself had been
added to the province of Africa); Thrace; Cappadocia, and
Armenia. Galatia and Judaea, however, lost their
independence and were added to the provinces of Augustus.

In 23 B.C. there was a major revision of the arrangements which had been made in 27 B.C. This followed a
serious illness of Augustus, when it had been thought that
he was dying. He seems to have decided that the man in
charge of the system (himself and his successors) needed
more power. He gave up the consulship, which he had held
every year since 31 B.C. In exchange, he took several new
powers. He assumed the imperium maius (the greatest
authority). This ranked him above all other officials,
consuls, governors, etc. While it was not used much,
this power, renewed at intervals, gave Augustus the right
to interfere anywhere, to issue orders to anyone. He
also took the right to make war and peace on his own, without asking the Senate or the Assembly, and the right to
speak first in the Senate (a big aid to the senators in
knowing what line they had to fall in with). At the same
time, Augustus took permanently the powers of a tribune.
This allowed him to deal directly with the people and to
exercise the tribune's traditional right of veto. In
practice, though, its importance was restricted mostly
the psychological benefit which from appearing as the
champion of the people.

Together, the arrangements of 27 B.C. and 23 B.C.
were the basis of Augustus' system. They gave him control
of the army, the frontiers, most of the Empire's lands,
and the right to order any other official. With these
powers he was content. In 22 B.C. he refused the office
of dictator; in 19 B.C. he refused general censorship
powers. Later changes were mostly cosmetic. In 12 B.C.,
on the death of Lepidus, the old triumvir, Augustus
became Chief Priest, an appointment for life (which
explains why Lepidus had held it since 44 B.C. through all
his troubles). In 2 B.C. Augustus became father of the
country. With this title, copied from Caesar, he took the
whole population of the Empire as his clients. Augustus
had done this kind of thing much earlier in the West, in
the late 30's B.C. before going east to fight Mark Antony,

when he had asked the population to take an oath to support him.

Within this system, we have to think of Augustus attending the Senate, keeping up the niceties with its members, spending a good portion of his time trying to give the impression that he was not a dictator. It was mostly sham, of course. Augustus could use a harsh touch when he needed. He purged the Senate of his opponents (by killing) when he wanted, and he reduced the Senate in overall size from around 1,000 to 600, getting rid of many members he did not like. Nonetheless, he helped to keep the Senate alive, and the Senate remained the center of such opposition as there was to the system, even long after Republicanism—and the old Republican ruling class—had disappeared.

From the Senate's point of view, it must have been apparent that, while things could not have been much better, they could have been a great deal worse. Pressure from below, from the equites, the Assemblies, the plebeians generally, aimed persistently at giving Augustus more, rather than less, power. This pressure produced occasional disorders in the city, particularly in the early period when Augustus was often abroad. On its own, the Senate could hardly have stood at all. Augustus protected it, patronized it, and discouraged the traditional rivals of the Senate, the "reformers."

Reformers found that they had no future at all. The same was true of the Assemblies. Augustus allowed the Assemblies to go on meeting, often permitting even a certain degree of free elections. They were so irrelevant to the new situation, though, that they withered away over a few generations. By the end of the 1st century A.D. we hear no more of the Assemblies at all. They had met their deaths. The same could have happened to the Senate, and the Senate surely knew it. Instead, the senators, splendid in their togas with the tell-tale broad purple stripe, pampered in their privileges and their apparent powers, were allowed to associate themselves with the glory of the state. To the dictator's advantage, between the declining birth rate, the effects of inbreeding, and the ravages of the civil wars, many of the patrician families were self-

destructing. It was not long before a large majority in
the Senate were the dictator's own men.

The Assemblies were sacrificed to Augustus' desire
for order. He did want, though, to show that he stood
with Caesar in the tradition of the Populares; after all,
he had taken power as the enemy of the Seante. Therefore:
--the corn law was kept. The number receiving corn was
fixed at 200,000 in a total population of perhaps more than
1,000,000. Fuel and drink were also distributed.
--many entertainments were provided--wild beast fights,
gladiators, a great mock sea battle with 30 big ships and
3,000 men. The bathing facilities Augustus built had the
same purpose. In undertaking to amuse the masses in the
city, Augustus showed that in a way they were his clients,
These amusements went on growing under the later rulers
and they spread to cities all across the Empire.
--a great number of public works were undertaken at Rome,
Rome for the first time became a city worthy of its
Empire, so that Suetonius said Rome "was dressed as the
glory of the Empire demanded." It was said that Augustus
had found a Rome of brick and left it a city of marble:
  -the marble Temple of Apollo on the Palatine hill.
  Apollo was given custody here of the old Sibylline Books.
  -the Forum (or square) of Augustus, with a temple of
  Mars the Avenger (in memory of avenging Caesar). The
  Forum included also a Hall of Fame of Rome's great
  names. There the Senate discussed war and the granting
  of triumphs; from there commanders made their official
  departures for the front,
  -Temple of the God Caesar, built soon after Actium.
  -Theater of Marcellus, named for the nephew of Augustus,
  This is our first surviving standing stone theater--
  one, that is, not built into a hillside.
  -the Baths of Agrippa, Rome's first public baths,
  -the Altar of Peace, 13-9 B.C. with its famous sculptures,
  -a great mausoleum (burial house) for the family of
  Augustus.

The generosity of Augustus toward the plebeians
extended to the freedmen (ex-slaves), who must have made
up a substantial portion of the poor. It was an age in
which, for reasons we do not know, slavery was becoming
less profitable in Italy and so less common. Slaves were

being allowed to buy their freedom more often, owners were granting freedom in their wills. The slave proportion of the population certainly was declining; correspondingly, freedmen were on the increase. Freedmen were still not allowed to vote, although their sons were. In any case, voting was a less and less interesting exercise. Freedmen and their children were allowed to marry ordinary citizens. In addition, Augustus made some use of freedmen in his bureaucracy, for example in the imperial religious practices (such as the worship of his genius). Later emperors used freedmen even more, so that the next generations became a sort of golden age for freedmen. Some became very wealthy, as we see in the Satyricon of Petronius.

Freedmen were accepted; but emancipation, the sign of the declining slave system, which produced the freedmen, was to be discouraged. Slaves still made up perhaps 40% of Italy's total population (4 out of 9 or 10 millions). Elsewhere in the Empire they were much less numerous. Augustus believed that freeing slaves increased the chance of disorder and made more mouths for the government to feed. So.
—2 B.C.: The number of slaves a man can free in his will is limited.
—5 A.D.: An owner's right to free his slaves during his own lifetime is severely limited.
The movement away from slavery could not be halted—it was indeed one of the great achievements of the Empire that it produced prosperity in a largely free population.

All these activities produced a Rome in which there was employment, security, and entertainment for the people, and good contracts for the equites. In case this would not do, Augustus introduced the city's first regular police force. He also formed a special guard, the PRAETOR- IAN GUARD, soldiers highly paid and drawn from the cream of the legions, whose job it was to stay in Italy to keep order. Augustus did not wish the city, his own residence and the showpiece of the Empire, to be too disorderly; nor did he want to rely on the old private client armies to keep order.

The building program, of course, also provided the right, kind of splendid image for the new system. It

served as a visible sign of success, just as the same kind
of activity had been exploited by men as diverse as
Caesar, Sulla, Pericles, and Peisistratus. The desire
to work up the image of success also lay behind the support Augustus gave to Latin literature (see below).
Success in that area made him look successful. At the
same time, given the attitudes prevalent in Rome, Augustus
had to be careful in such an area. Intellect was suspect
in itself as something Greek rather than Roman, and
writers were identified with the moral decay which conservatives associated with Greeks. Praising Rome's past
(Virgil, Livy) or the natural splendor and wealth of Italy
(Virgil) was alright, but Augustus was troubled by the
scandals into which writers (Ovid) could get themselves.
Still, he succeeded in his essential aim. The same desire
motivated the ambitious and aggressive foreign policy that
Augustus followed (see below). For all of his low-key
approach, Augustus was convinced of the importance of
looking as well as being great.

The Family of Augustus.
        The existence of the dictatorship, and the determina-
tion to make the system hereditary, put the family of
Augustus at the center of attention. Augustus had little
luck with his family. He had no son. He did have one
daughter, JULIA, by his second wife (this wife, the one
he took after divorcing Mark Anthony's step-daughter, was
actually connected to Pompey's family). Like many in the
old aristocracy, the family of Augustus, inbred over
generations, had trouble producing offspring--which was
how Augustus, a great-nephew, had come to be Caesar's
closest male relative. The family was troubled also by
epilepsy, a typical product of in-breeding. It was common
to take epilepsy as a sign of good birth and great genius
(as in Caesar's case).

        Augustus' closest male relative was Marcellus, the
only sone of his only sister Octavia (but born of a marriage
before that to Mark Antony). Marcellus was married to his
cousin Julia, the daughter of Augustus. Marcellus died as
a youth, however, in 23 B.C., before there were any children to the marriage. The widowed Julia, then aged 16,
was married next to a very different type--the middle-
aged Agrippa, a noted soldier, Augustus' right-hand man,

563

and a <u>new</u> <u>man</u>. This marriage produced three sons and two
daughters. The succession seemed assured.

The two older grandsons, <u>Gaius</u> and <u>Lucius</u>, were taken
up by Augustus as his own sons and were raised to succeed
him. Both, however, died early deaths, Lucius in 2 A.D. of
illness at the age of 19, <u>Gaius</u> in 4 A.D. of wounds at
24. Neither left children. The third son of Julia's
marriage, <u>Agrippa</u> <u>Postumus</u> (posthumous), called so because
his mother Julia was pregnant with him at the time of the
father Agrippa's death in 12 B.C., was never considered.
He seems to have been a fool, a physical misfit, and a
moral degenerate. He was kept from the public eye, was
sent into exile, and eventually was murdered in 14 A.D.
at the time of Augustus' death, on the orders of either
the dying Augustus or his successor <u>Tiberius</u>. Since
Augustus could not wait for great-grandchildren from
Julia's daughters, he had to look elsewhere.

He had in fact already done this as a matter of
insurance. Following Agrippa's death in 12 B.C., Augustus
pushed Julia into another marriage. Her new husband was
TIBERIUS, the older <u>stepson</u> of Augustus by his third and
last wife LIVIA. <u>Livia</u>, a great beauty, had left her
husband, by whom she was pregnant at the time, for Augustus
when the young leader had become infatuated with her in
the 30's B.C. She had no children by Augustus, but there
was already <u>Tiberius</u> and his younger brother <u>Nero</u> <u>Drusus</u>.
These two men served Augustus as his major generals while
his grandsons <u>Gaius</u> and <u>Lucius</u> were growing up, especially
after the death of the dependable Agrippa. Nero Drusus,
however, died in 9 B.C. Tiberius' marriage to Julia was
a precaution taken in case something happened to Gaius
and Lucius. The marriage did not suit Tiberius. He was
forced to give up a wife he loved for Julia, a woman of
loose morals for whom he never cared. There were no
children from their marriage. The experience added to
the nastiness and pessimism of Tiberius' nature; he had
very great abilities, but he looked to the dark side of
things. With Gaius and Lucius coming of age, Tiberius
could see the pointlessness of his position. In 6 B.C. he
retired to the island of <u>Rhodes</u>, believing that his time
had gone.

When Lucius and Gaius died, Augustus turned to
Tiberius. He adopted Tiberius as his son. Augustus
probably took this step because of his respect for
Tiberius' mother, Livia, for whom he had great admiration.
While at the time Augustus had no great-grandchildren to
consider, there was one possibility. This was GERMANICUS.
Germanicus was the son of Tiberius' younger brother, the
dead Nero Drusus, and of Antonia, daughter of Octavia and
Mark Antony and so a step-sister to Marcellus, the first
husband of Julia. As Augustus' great-nephew, Germanicus
was the oldest male remaining in the family. In addition,
he was married to AGRIPPINA, daughter of Julia and Agrippa
(so her name) and thus grand-daughter of Augustus himself.
Their children, when they were born, would be the only
flesh of Augustus in the third generation. The first son
of this marriage, Nero, was born in 6 A.D., two years
after Gaius died.

Germanicus was 19 in 4 A.D. when Gaius died.
Augustus passed him over, but kept his eye on him. The
ruler forced Tiberius, who had a son of his own, to adopt
Germanicus as his son. Clearly, Germanicus was intended
by Augustus to succeed Tiberius. As time passed, with
Augustus surviving 10 more years (4-14 A.D.), the situation grew more strained. Germanicus grew into a young man,
a very talented one; Tiberius came to look more expendable.
Many preferred Germanicus to the aging and unsociable
Tiberius. But Augustus made no change. He stuck with
Tiberius, leaving Germanicus to take his lumps, ignoring
the call of blood. Thus power passed to Tiberius on the
death of Augustus in 14 A.D., in circumstances which make
it easy to understand why he was a bitter man.

The Army.
For all of the talk about restoring the Republic, the
basis of the power of Augustus was the army. The experience of the late Republic indicated the need to keep the
army and its generals reasonably happy. Augustus was
remarkably successful in doing this, producing a situation
in which, while he could rely confidently upon the army,
the army was effectively taken out of politics, allowing
him to run things as he pleased within reason.

The era of civil wars ended very abruptly after the
victory over Mark Antony at Actium in 31 B.C. Roman
soldiers did not again fight one another for 100 years.
Some part of this can be credited to the careful policy
of Augustus, but the sharpness of the change shows up the
oddity of the situation in the late Republic when the
state had effectively become headless. Soldiers had not
lost the habit of doing what they were told; they had
simply obeyed their generals rather than the Senate--not
an unreasonable step in the circumstances. Now, since in
fact the army had in a sense won, with the state in the
hands of the army's choice, the army obeyed the state in
obeying its general, the imperator.

In 31 B.C. after Actium, Rome's army was Augustus'
army. It was to remain thus. It was to Augustus that
the soldiers swore their allegiance; it was his image
which they carried in the legions, even though the standards proclaimed SPQR (Senatus Populusque Romanus)--the
Roman Senate and People. There is no doubt that, in
a basic way, the soldiers served the Emperor rather than
the state. Potentially this was very dangerous, but for
a long time it made little difference--beyond, that is,
the very great difference that normally the Emperor had
a near-monopoly on military power in the state.

Augustus reduced the size of the army, some 60 legions
after Actium, to 28 legions. The army did not grow much
beyond this figure for a very long time. This meant an
army of about 280,000 men. For so big an area (some
2,000,000 square miles, not much smaller than the continental U.S.A.), the number was not great, although it was
larger than the armies of the Republic had been before
the recent civil wars. It was a permanent army, which did
not fluctuate in size with need. Augustus preferred a
relatively small army, as being less expensive and less
troublesome. At the same time, he wanted an army large
enough to keep order, protect the frontiers, and add
further territories when such were desired.

Most of the legions were stationed on the frontiers.
We have (from Tacitus) the legion postings for the year
23 A.D. under the next ruler, Tiberius. There were then
25 legions rather than the 28 of Augustus' day. Of the

566

25, 8 were on the Rhine and 6 in the Danube area, giving
14 altogether on the northern borders. There were 4 in
Syria on the eastern border with the Parthians. Of the
rest, 3 were in Spain, 2 in Africa, and 2 in Egypt. Only
2 of the 25 (those in Africa) were under the supervision
of the Senate. The troops in Spain were the only ones
clearly on garrison duty, away from any frontier; Spain
was still a very troublesome place. Augustus had kept 5
legions there for a long while. After another generation
of peace and prosperity, however, 2 of the 3 legions
stationed in Spain in 23 A.D. were removed. Rome was at
peace in 23 A.D., but at any time, aside from some shifting between frontiers, the arrangement was much the same.
There were not enough legions to do anything else. There
was too little manpower to have a large central army in
reserve to use at discretion, and serious trouble in more
than one place at a time caused major problems. Augustus
and his successors had no interest in bankrupting the
state through a swollen military.

The army was a professional volunteer force.
Augustus did not want to annoy people with a draft.
This completed the trend we associate in its early stages
with Marius. A man in the army of Augustus who didn't
like things had only himself to blame.

The legionary soldiers made up about half the army's
manpower. A legion usually contained about 5,000 men.
A soldier in the legions had to be a citizen. Citizens
numbered about 5,000,000 (males and females of all ages)
at the beginning under Augustus; over 6,000,000 when he
died in 14 A.D.—censuses were taken of the citizens.
Perhaps some 4,000,000 of these citizens, the large
majority certainly, were in Italy; many of the others, too,
were Italians who had moved to the provinces. This was
out of a total population of perhaps 75,000,000, although
the overall figure is just an estimate—the general
censuses were only of citizens. In the East there were
very few citizens. Italians still provided under Augustus
a very large majority of the legionaries, overall perhaps
80%, but more and more, over the next generations, and
particularly in the East, men were simply given citizenship if they enlisted. This made it easier to obtain men
locally for the legions, since they were stationed out of

Italy; it also grew naturally out of the fact that it was the poorer and more backward peoples who tended to volunteer rather than the Italians. Within a couple of generations, half the legionaries were non-Italians; by the 100's A.D. this was true of a large majority of them.

The legions, infantry armed in the old Roman fashion, made up the heart of the army. Associated with them was a similar number of auxiliaries, non-citizen volunteers from the rougher sections of the Empire who were equipped and trained in ways they found more to their liking--archers, cavalrymen, spearmen, light infantry. The northern border areas and places like Spain produced many auxiliaries (and, of course, non-citizen volunteers for the legions too). The auxiliaries were usually given citizenship when they left the service.

As a result of this system, the army was much more diverse in its make-up than any of the Empire's political institutions--or the old Italian Republican ruling class. It was in this way more representative of the people who made up the Empire--a condition which made it easier to justify the military basis of the system, since the army in a sense represented the people against the old state. The army command was dominated by the Italian ruling class, however. The commander of a legion was always a senator. Some auxiliary forces, though, were put into the hands of their own leaders, tribal chiefs, etc.--of course, these men were made citizens.

The period of was long, 16 or 20 or 25 years depending on the needs and the law of the moment, but the terms were reasonably attractive. Pay was good, booty often available, and benefits after retirement were wonderful, with large bonuses and land grants. In theory, legionaries could not marry--the better to keep them willing to die--but the state turned a blind eye to all kinds of things in this direction. A legion camp was generally surrounded by the homes of the women attached to the soldiers, and the state legitimized these unions and their offspring after the soldier involved retired or was killed on service. In any case, it was still an age when homosexuality was widely accepted and could have overtones of masculinity. Many of the emperors were homosexuals--few of them were effeminate.

568

This made it easier to put up with the military life.
The centurions, 60 of them to each legion, made the army
tick. Professional master-sergeants, who knew their men
well and had shown great individual ability and courage
in combat, they were treated well enough that a centurion who survived his service could expect to be rich
(in the class of equites). This was for the right type
a wonderful chance to move up the ladder socially--
in fact, the centurion rank was attractive enough to
bring in actual volunteers from the equites.

Wars and Expansion.
        Augustus wanted to keep this army busy and successful.
Success in war would strengthen his name within the army
and his hold upon the state as a whole. He was anxious
to be a worthy successor of Caesar. Augustus personally
was an unmilitary figure, small of frame and often ill,
and he did not care much for campaigning. He had forced
himself to it in the 30's B.C., and he continued to do
so for a while in the 20's B.C. More and more, though,
he relied on subordinates to command in campaigns he
planned. This increased the chance that generals who
won wars in his absence might begin to fancy themselves
as his rivals for power--always a possibility in successful
wars. Augustus tried to avoid this danger by giving high
command to his close relatives and associates, the men he
thought he could trust best. That Augustus could get away
with this is a sign of the security of his position--the
army did see itself as his, to hand around within his
family as he wished.

        Augustus organized a series of wars which ranked him
with the great conquerors of Rome's past. Because of the
limited size of the army, however, he had to pick his way
with care. In addition, by the nature of his position, the
one thing he could not afford, at least early on, was a
substantial defeat. In many ways, what he did consituted
the first organized and thought-out foreign policy Rome
had had.

        Basically, his plan was to concentrate on expanding
the frontiers to the north. This meant ignoring the other
major possible threat, the Parthians to the East. In 20
B.C. Augustus reached an agreement with the Parthians.

They gave him the prisoners and the banners taken at Carrhae in 53 B.C. and recognized Armenia as a Roman protected client. For the Parthians, this was a reasonable enough way of getting Rome to leave them alone. Augustus made great propaganda use of this deal, trying to make it look like a victory. In truth, it was only a way of freeing himself to turn to the Rhine-Danube area.

Between 27 and 19 B.C. there was heavy fighting in Spain as Augustus took the northwest, completing the conquest of the peninsula. Augustus supervised some of the Spanish campaign personally, his last appearance in the field.

Then he began a great move forward to the north:
16-15 B.C.: Tiberius and Nero Drusus, his two stepsons, conquered the area of the Alps up to the Danube river.
12-9 B.C.: Tiberius conquered the great angle of the Danube river (present-day Hungary). Nero Drusus moved east across the Rhine into Germany.
It is likely that the objective was to move to the Elbe river, and to link the head of the Elbe with the Danube. In 9 B.C. Nero Drusus died an accidental death. Tiberius was transferred to Germany but did little more than send a series of raids forward to the Elbe.
6-9 A.D.: The conquest of Germany was taken up again in 6 A.D. Tiberius, now marked as the next ruler, took 12 legions into Bohemia. Then came news of a big rebellion by the tribes in Illyria and Pannonia. Tiberius had to spend the three years crushing the rebellion. This left the forces in Germany weak.
9 A.D.: A force of three legions (30,000 men) under Quinctilius Varus was wiped out in north-central Germany in the battle of the Teutoburger Forest by the German chief Arminius (from whose name we have the name Herman). Tiberius was sent into Germany to restore order, but the defeat convinced Augustus to give up Germany and Bohemia. The setback may have unnerved Augustus, who was now over 70. There is a story of him wandering the palace in the middle of the night crying "Quinctilius Varus, give me back the legions." The three legions were not replaced, the total number being reduced from 28 to 25. Augustus gave up expansion, taking the Rhine-Danube line as the frontier. His final advice to drop expansion became a

gospel with his successors, leading to a great oddity—
that the arrival of military rule coincided with the end
of expansion. The system was by this time too well-
entrenched and respected to be shaken by such a loss, but
the defeat did point out the fact that the army was too
small to allow much in the way of wars of conquest.

The Provinces.

Beyond Rome and the army, it took little more than
what came most easily to an efficient one-man system to
guarantee the acceptance of the hereditary dictatorship.
In restoring order and bringing the armies under control,
Augustus freed the provinces from the ravages of the late
Republic. The orderly and fair administration which
followed was a great improvement over the notorious
sloppiness, inconsistencies, amateurishness, and corruption of Republican administration, which had never done
much for the provinces except exploit them. Even critics
of the dictators, such as the historian Tacitus, admitted
that the provinces were generally handled well.

There is no doubt that from the beginning the new
system was popular across the Empire. Stable and predictable, strong enough to fight off any enemies outside its
borders and to put down any trouble within its borders,
the system produced the 200-year PAX ROMANA, the Roman
Peace, allowing a great era of prosperity and order. This
is what Pliny the Elder called "The immense majesty
of the Roman peace." In light of the tremendous variety
of peoples under Roman control, so diverse in language,
customs, religions, and levels of development, so large
in numbers, over so large an area, this may be the greatest
political achievement of our civilization.

So obvious to the provinces were the advantages of
the new system compared to the old that force was hardly
needed. It is misleading to think of the Empire as a
military state. The army was small and in most provinces
there were no soldiers at all. Extensive self-government
was allowed to continue, along with the diverse legal,
social, and religious customs, under the supervision of
the governors sent out from Rome. Most of those
governors now were chosen by Augustus; and he had the
power to check the others. The impact of the state often

did not go much beyond providing order. In many ways, then, the Empire was hardly a country at all in the modern sense, but rather a haphazard collection of peoples supervised by a common authority. Some specific steps were taken by the government, however, to improve things in the provinces: all direct taxes, for example, were taken out of the hands of the tax-farmers, and virtually all taxes were collected by the state itself by the 100's, and a strong currency was established which flourished for several generations. Caesar himself, in his propaganda in Gaul and in admitting men from Gaul into the Senate in the 40's B.C., had set the pattern which Augustus now followed of being the friend of the provinces. Citizenship was extended slowly as a sign of favor, until it became common; eventually, in 212 A.D., almost the entire free population of the Empire was given citizenship. Power was extended too, as non-Italians came into the Senate, the army, and the administartion. Italians long were much the biggest group at the top, but by the 100's they no longer were a majority. Eventually, the rulers themselves were not Italians. The new system always showed itself to be more flexible and responsive toward the desires of the provinces than the old Republic had been, and vastly more efficient and fair in its handling of them.

ART IN THE AGE OF AUGUSTUS, 31 B.C.-14 A.D.

We have more of the art and architecture of the Age of
Augustus than of any earlier period in Rome's history.
Augustus encouraged and patronized these arts, as he did
literature, in order to provide himself and his new system
with a splendid image. He undertook a big program in Rome
itself and a substantial number of major projects in the
provinces; with this example, other towns followed suit.
A lot of the work was not distinguishable from the mixed
Italian-Hellenistic styles the Romans had worked up in the
late Republic. Augustus did, though, have a preferred style,
which showed through particularly clearly in sculpture--it
was a revival of the calm, cool, detached style of the Greek
Classical period. To him, very clearly, this style was the
most efficient way of dramatizing the glory of the state and
the dignity of the First Citizen.

Several great aqueducts constructed (with concrete now)
in the Age of Augustus survive. The most famous is the one
at Nimes in southern France (Gallia Narbonensis), which
manages to be graceful as well as imposing in its great size.
The lower arches supported a bridge which is still in use.
Nimes seems to have been the busiest provincial center of
the period in terms of building. There also we find the
Square House, which is the most complete temple building of
the age. It is in Corinthian style, with the usual Italian
high podium and large vestibule. We also have at Nimes an
amphitheater, a sports stadium, from this period.

We have a number of other temples from elsewhere in the
western provinces, including one at Pola in modern Yugoslavia.
This, too, was in mixed Corinthian and Italian style; the
Corinthian columns in this case, though, were unfluted in
the early Italian fashion. The temple to Mercury (the Roman
Hermes) at Baiae is our earliest surviving domed building.
There was an opening at the top of the dome and four large
rectangular windows to give light. Domes had a great future
before them at Rome, as the ability to construct barrel vaults
allowed the Romans to add more and more interior space.

Other pieces from the provinces worth noting, as interesting or as pointers for the future, are the monument (badly

573

preserved) at La Turbie in France, which is a cylindrical
structure built on a great square podium, some 100' high in
all; the Palatine Gate at Augustus' colony of Turin in north
Italy, which with its enormous 16-sided brick towers looks
like something from a grim castle of the Middle Ages; and
the Sergian Arch at Pola, an early (and private) example of
the free-standing Arch built in honor of famous men. This
kind of arch, too, had a great future ahead of it.

In Rome itself, where the work done must surely have
been catered carefully to Augustus' desires, the two best-
known surviving architectural works are (1) the Temple of
Mars the Avenger, of marble in the Corinthian style, which
was built directly into the wall of the Forum or city-center
which Augustus planned, and (2) the Altar of Peace, a small
building intended to express the services of the dictatorship
in restoring order. The altar inside rested on a podium
reached by the usual frontal steps. The whole was surrounded
by a wall around which ran a frieze. The frieze showed a
procession, of religious officials, Augustus and his family
and friends, and the great men of Rome, moving around the
building toward the entrance (which reminds us in its subject
of the Parthenon and in its location of the Temple of Zeus).

This frieze, less than 2' high, is characteristic of the
sculpture of the day. The frieze is uneven in quality, but
some of the work is of high technical quality. There is some
use of perspective, but the Romans had only a limited command
of that technique--at best, they knew no more about it than
had the Classical Greeks. Partly to substitute for perspective, partly because it was a traditional Italian style,
figures in the background were brought forward by making them
larger than those to the front. This was a way of asserting
frontality, as in their temples--the figures came right out
at you. The same value was indicated in the Roman habit of
placing their statues in niches in their buildings, with
their backs to the wall and the backs often only roughly
done. The figures were not to be seen in the round. We
can see the same idea in the Vicomagistri frieze of about
20 A.D., which also shows a procession.

The frieze on the Altar of Peace has some elements of
Classical restraint: the figures do not leap out in the
style of the Temple of Zeus, and the layout is orderly and

574

matter-of-fact. At the same time, the frieze is overloaded with figures in a Hellenistic manner, and there are odd little bits of individualizing and sentiment: children stand aimlessly about, a woman (Augustus' sister?) hushes one with a finger to her mouth. In more general terms, the whole scene was about real people--a very clear departure from the Parthenon procession. The Romans seem to have been far too Romantic ever to do much of a job of recreating the spirit of the Greece of the 400's B.C. This is seen even more clearly in the various statues of Augustus which we have from the period. The intent of these statues is always clear, but they generally manage to seem a little ridiculous.

The best-known of the protraits of Augustus is the Porta Prima Statue with Augustus as the great conqueror and leader. His feet are bare, which is probably a sign that he was dead, but the work seems to be a variation of a type produced in Augustus' life. He is in flashy uniform, in a pose clearly copied from Greek art of the 400's B.C. and with a face intended to look very imposing and Classical. Mostly, he looks silly--and very self-conscious. The cupid on a dolphin by his right leg is an unbearable Hellenistic/ Romantic touch; it was intended to indicate his descent from Aeneas, founder of Rome, who was a son of Venus. There are many traces of color remaining about the statue. Usually the Romans painted their statues gaudily (most often with red and gold). This can hardly have helped the statue to look cool. The great man in this kind of pose was to remain a favorite style. We have one from Pompeii at this time of a locally important man, and one of Tiberius, the next emperor, done while Augustus was still alive. They all look like Greek youths. We also have Augustus as chief priest (a role in which he looks quite lost and a work which is of very poor quality), and Augustus as naked god-like figure. The Romans were definitely more at home running up massive and useful public buildings.

575

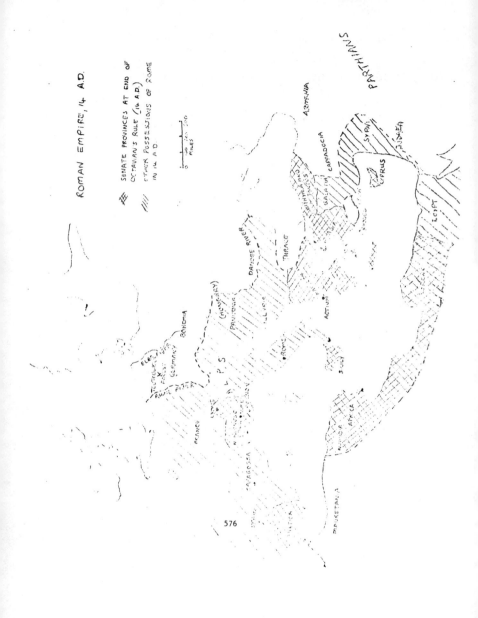

ROMAN EMPIRE, 14 A.D.

SENATE PROVINCES AT END OF OCTAVIAN'S RULE (14 A.D.)

OTHER POSSESSIONS OF ROME IN 14 A.D.

0 100 200 300
MILES

PARTHIANS

ARMENIA

BITHYNIA

GALATIA   CAPPADOCIA

SYRIA

CYPRUS

JUDAEA

EGYPT

THRACE

DANUBE RIVER

PANNONIA (HUNGARY)

ILLYRIA

ACTIUM

ROME

SICILY

A L P S

BOHEMIA

ELBE

GERMANY

RHINE RIVER

LYONS

GARANCE

SARAGOSSA

AFRICA

NUMIDIA

MAURETANIA

BAETICA

THE JULIO-CLAUDIAN DYNASTY, FROM THE DEATH OF AUGUSTUS TO 68 A.D.

Augustus was recognized as a god within hours of his death in 14 A.D. A senator was found to swear that he had seen Augustus' soul going up into the heavens. Augustus was succeeded by <u>Tiberius</u>. Since Tiberius was descended on his father's side from the great clan of the <u>Claudii</u>, the line of rulers from Augustus through <u>Nero</u> are known as the <u>Julio-Claudians</u>, men of the clans of <u>Julius</u> and <u>Claudius</u>. These rulers are well known to us through the writings of <u>Tacitus</u> and <u>Suetonius</u> particularly. They were:

Augustus	31 B.C.	- 14 A.D.
Tiberius	14 A.D.	- 37 A.D.
Caligula	37 A.D.	- 41 A.D.
Claudius	41 A.D.	- 54 A.D.
Nero	54 A.D.	- 68 A.D.

<u>Tiberius, 14-37.</u>

Tiberius was in his mid-fifties when he became emperor, a man of great talents and solid reputation. He was accepted in Rome without problem, although in line with his sour nature he played out a game of reluctance, having the Senate plead with him to take the position. On the frontiers, though, it seems to have been a different story. There were mutinies in both of the major legion concentrations, on the <u>Rhine</u> and on the <u>Danube</u>. We do not know the details, and there may not have been much more involved than a wish to make it clear to Tiberius that the legions wanted to be active, having been held back since the defeat at the <u>Teutoburger Forest</u> in 9. It is hard to believe that anything serious was involved.

The trouble was settled by the two chief generals, Drusus, the son of Tiberius, in <u>Pannonia</u>, and <u>Germanicus</u>, his adopted son, in <u>Germany</u>. Then Germanicus, perhaps as a way of pleasing the soldiers, fought three big campaigns in Germany (14-16). He may have begun these campaigns without permission from Tiberius. In 15, Germanicus reached the Teutoburger Forest and buried the dead. The <u>Elbe</u> river was reached again, but Tiberius was unwilling to get involved in a great expansion of territory. With honor satisfied, and the legions happy, Tiberius withdrew the army to the Rhine.

577

He would allow no further big campaigns anywhere.

Germanicus was then sent East. Cappadocia, a client-kingdom, was annexed as a province. An incident arose when Germanicus visited Egypt without permission, something which was illegal for a senator. This encouraged the talk that Germanicus, by virtue of his blood claim and his popularity with the soldiers, was a possible replacement for Tiberius. Germanicus died in the East in 19. His death seems to have been natural, but there were suggestions that Tiberius had arranged an event which was so welcome to him. Agrippina, the aggressive widow of Germanicus and the ranking living offspring of Augustus' own flesh, made free with the charge that Tiberius had been involved. Perhaps to head off the talk, the governor of Syria, who had had an argument with Germanicus, was called back to Rome to stand trial for murdering Germanicus. The governor was acquitted, but he committed suicide anyway, knowing that he was expected to do so.

Over the next decade, Tiberius showed that he did not know how to get along with either the Senate or his own family. Moody, nasty, and suspicious, he was jealous of his privileges and very insecure. He fell under the influence of SEJANUS, a new man and the commander (prefect) of the Praetorian Guard. The Guard was now gathered at Rome instead of being stationed around Italy. Fear dominated the city. Conspiracies, real and invented, were everywhere, and savage laws were introduced to control them.

23: Tiberius' only son Drusus died. Tiberius does not seem to have liked Drusus, and he had made more use of Germanicus earlier. The ruler was suspected of murdering his son to remove a possible rival. There seems to be no truth to this, but there is a likelihood that Drusus was murdered by Sejanus, the Praetorian Prefect, who had taken the wife of Drusus as his mistress. Drusus left a son, but Tiberius seems to have felt no great interest in the boy.
26: Tiberius retired to Capri. He never again visited Rome--a remarkable state of affairs. Sejanus became virtually his only link with the government.
29-30: Agrippina, the widow of Germanicus and a woman much hated by Tiberius, was arrested along with her two older sons, Nero and Drusus. All three were killed or forced into suicide in the next few years. To take this step, Tiberius

waited until after the death of his mother <u>Livia</u>, the widow
of Augustus, who remained until her death in 29, when she
was almost 90, a powerful figure. These killings, and
Tiberius' strange willingness to ignore his own grandson
by Drusus, pointed to CALIGULA, the remaining son of
Agrippina and Germanicus, as the intended successor. Otherwise, why was Caligula left alive?
31: <u>Sejanus</u> became consul, even though he was not eligible
under the law, being only an equites and not a senator. He
was promised Tiberius' granddaughter in marriage. But then
Sejanus fell suddenly from power. Tiberius from Capri
appointed a new Praetorian Prefect, <u>Macro</u>, and ordered him
to murder Sejanus and his friends. This was done, in very
bloody fashion, as the guard proved to be loyal to the ruler
rather than to its old commander. Sejanus may have been
suspected of plotting against <u>Caligula</u>, the intended
successor--perhaps aiming at taking over himself.

The last years of Tiberius were gloomy and fear-filled.
Later, they became the source of scandalous stories involving
Tiberius' relationship with Caligula, a most famous pervert.
Tiberius died at Capri in 37, aged almost 80, and he was
succeeded by Caligula as planned. His faults are known to
us in exaggerated detail from the writings of <u>Tacitus</u> and
<u>Suetonius.</u> The tone is set by Tacitus, the most brilliant
of all Roman historians, who lived at the end of the 1st
century and who was a strong supporter of the Senate tradition. Tiberius was drawn as a tyrant, mean and unfair
and murderous, who terrorized the Senate and his own
relatives. For such reasons, the Senate failed to declare
him a god after his death. Tiberius' failings sprang
probably from personal weaknesses rather than from incompetence or miscalculation. He seems to have tried to work
with the Senate at first, for example. He gave it the power
to elect the chief officials--a sure sign, incidentally, of
the decline of the Assemblies. But Tiberius found that he
could not get along. Things like the retirement to Capri
are difficult to understand in any other light. The
<u>Claudians</u> were famous for being excitable, strange, even
crazy; this may have had something to do with the problem.
Certainly there was, as we shall see, plenty of sheer lunacy
around among Tiberius' relatives.

There is no way to deny the efficiency of Tiberius's government, however, or the practicality and economy of his quiet foreign policy. Economy, though, could be carried too far. Tiberius was accused of being cheap, particularly in that, unlike Augustus, he did not go in for a great wave of public construction. Yet he did begin to build the first great palace for the rulers--of course, such a step did not sit well with Republican sympathizers. All in all, it was a great tribute to the strength of the new system that it could work so well in such circumstances and not be seriously challenged.

(Gaius) Caligula, 37-41.

Caligula is a nickname, meaning "little boots," which the new ruler had picked up as a child in the legion camps in Germany where his father Germanicus had been stationed. His name was Gaius. Caligula, a great-grandson of Augustus, succeeded Tiberius without problem, but he was in a very different position from either of the two rulers before him. Only 25 years old, he lacked all qualifications other than birth, being known only for his fantastic sexual preferences and his general instability. Here is the first of the mad emperors. The best that can be said of Caligula is that he may have grown crazy only in stages.

Tiberius had injected into the ruling family the poison of murder and intrigue. Such habits came easily to Caligula. He soon murdered the grandson of Tiberius, who appeared to be the only possible replacement for himself. He also murdered Macro, who had served Tiberius so well in 31. Caligula liked to have sex with his sisters, one of whom figured among his four wives (in succession, not as a harem). He was convinced that he was a god, a claim flatly contrary to Roman tradition. He even ordered his own statue put up in the Temple at Jerusalem, although the officials there had the good sense not to do it. The Senate and the old Republican traditions generally he treated with contempt, giving rise to the story that he enrolled one of his horses in the Senate. After he discovered a genuine plot in the Senate and the German legions in 39, he killed very widely. A lazy playboy, Caligula depended on ex-slaves, usually Greeks or Hellenized Easterners, to run the administration. He was also a coward. He backed out of planned expeditions into Germany and Britain, partly from fear, partly because he disliked the hardships of campaigning. This was very

unwise on his part. Since he lacked a military reputation
and was known as a playboy, a victory or two would have
helped him a great deal. As it was, the popularity he
enjoyed at first in the legions as the son of Germanicus
was soon squandered. The legions were ashamed of him.

Caligula was murdered in his palace in 41 by the
Praetorian Guards. It was the most efficient way to get
rid of such a ruler. It is at least comforting to think
that the impact of Caligula on most parts of the Empire
was probably close to nil--the system could run itself by
this time.

Claudius, 41-54.
The Guard recognized CLAUDIUS as the new emperor,
by one account finding him hiding in the palace afraid for
his life. Aged 51, Claudius was Caligula's uncle, being
a younger brother of Germanicus and thus a nephew of
Tiberius. He was the only grown male surviving in the
family. What needs explaining is why Claudius was passed
over in so many killings over so many years to reach this
status. The reason was simple--he had not been thought
worth killing. As Suetonius said, Caligula had left him
alone "only because he was a laughing-stock." Claudius
had serious physical defects. He would stutter and spit
when he spoke; when he walked he dragged his leg; his head
shook, his face twitched. Here was the price of inbreeding.
Claudius may have been spastic--in truth there is no telling
what was wrong with him. A harmless, if embarrassing,
oddity, Claudius had survived because he had not been
considered eligible to rule. He had been little used in
the public service, although he had been a consul of 37.
Instead, he had made for himself a reputation as a historian
of Rome's past. He was intelligent--the whole family was
remarkable for this quality.

The Senate made some objections to accepting Claudius.
There were objections to the way he had been chosen by the
Guard: there was, of course, no set method for selecting
a new ruler, but the Senate thought that under the circumstances of 41 it was entitled to an important, perhaps the
chief, part. In addition, many of the senators perhaps had
given Claudius reason to dislike them over so many years of
ridicule. Claudius was very sensitive about his condition;
as ruler, that could be dangerous. The Senate actually

discussed restoring the old Republican system—the only
episode of its kind, it seems, through the whole period.
Senators soon found, though, that this kind of talk was
totally unrealistic. They had no choice but to accept
Claudius and keep the hereditary dictatorship. The armies
in the provinces accepted him also.

The Senate was right to worry about Claudius. He disliked the Senate a great deal. In 42, some senators got
involved in a half-hearted rebellion by the governor of
Illyria. Claudius, who had been careful toward the Senate
at first, used the opportunity to kill many senators—and
then he went on doing so. He worked through secret trials—
or no trials at all. Using the powers of a censor in 47 he
threw out many senators. It was a more dangerous climate
in fact than that under Tiberius. As part of the same
process, Claudius relied heavily for advice on equites and,
more notably, on freedmen. With such freedmen, who owed
everything to him, he felt much more secure and at ease.
The most famous of the freedmen were Narcissus and Pallas.
These, like most of their kind, were from the Hellenized
East. Such use of freedmen was a great insult to the Senate.

The fear which dominated Rome again had little effect
elsewhere. Claudius won a reputation as an efficient
administrator and a sensible ruler. He pleased the provinces
by giving more promotions to provincials, especially Gauls.
This included putting them into the Senate—which for
Claudius also pleasantly annoyed the senators. Citizenship,
always an attractive prize, was extended into the provinces
more willingly than under the earlier rulers.

Claudius moved quickly to obtain for himself a military
reputation. In showing himself in good light to the soldiers, he could expect to benefit from the contrast with
Caligula. He selected Britain to conquer, a task Caligula
had shunned as well as one which recalled the exploits of
Caesar. In 43 southern England was conquered easily.
Claudius trailed in after the troops, getting credit for the
victory, being charitably excused from the rigors of actual
campaigning. Claudius also annexed the client-kingdoms of
Mauretania, Thrace, and Lycia. At first he gave Judaea to
his friend, Herod Agrippa, but when that man died in 44 the
area was reannexed.

Claudius had many wives. For obvious reasons, he had problems with them. At the time he became emperor, in 41, he was married to Messalina. By her he had a daughter, Octavia, and a son, the latter born in 41 and known to us by the nickname Britannicus in honor of the conquest of Britain. Messalina had many lovers. In 48 she foolishly allowed a lover to talk her into some kind of plot against Claudius—perhaps to replace him with the child Britannicus. The freedman Narcissus took the biggest role in stopping the trouble; the plotters were killed. Narcissus had a replacement for Messalina lined up, a girl who would do his bidding, but Claudius instead married in 49 AGRIPPINA, the surviving daughter of Germanicus and Agrippina the Elder. His new wife was a great-granddaughter of Augustus. As a sister of Caligula, Agrippina had suffered her share of abuse, and she had been in exile at the time of Caligula's assassination in 41. Agrippina was all calculation, a hard-headed woman in the fashion of her mother. By a previous marriage to a Domitius Ahenobarbus, member of one of the great old families of the Republic, Agrippina had a son, born in 37. This was NERO. Nero was the great-great-grand-son of Augustus—the last remnant of his blood.

Agrippina, in league with the freedman Pallas and the Praetorian Prefect Burrus, dominated Claudius to her own purposes. In 50, the year after the marriage, the 13 years old Nero was adopted by Claudius and given preference over his own son Britannicus, who was then aged 9. This remark-able step went beyond even Tiberius' neglect of his own offspring. Nero was married to Claudius' daughter (and his own aunt) Octavia.

Nero, 54-68.
Claudius died in 54. It is highly likely that he was assassinated by his wife Agrippina to clear the way for Nero, then 16. The story is that she fed Claudius poisoned mushrooms. Now Rome had a boy emperor. Still, the Senate and the army accepted the change without problem.

Nero, very intelligent and, it seems, pleasant enough at first, had learned in a very hard school. It was not long before he made it clear to his mother that he would run things himself. In 55 Nero had Britannicus killed. In 59 Agrippina herself was killed. Then Nero divorced, and later killed, Octavia. He married Poppaea, a great beauty

583

who had been the wife of his good friend <u>Otho</u>. Poppaea gave
Nero a daughter in 63. The child died in 65—the family of
Augustus was at an end.

Nero also threw off the influence of his early advisors,
who had been picked for him by Agrippina. Chief among these
were the Prefect Burrus and Nero's tutor SENECA, the most
famous Stoic philosopher Rome produced. The idea of the
Stoic, emphasizing duty and dignity and brotherhood, bringing up Nero has been a source of wonder ever since, and a
source of concern to those who admire Seneca. Burrus died
in 62 and was replaced by the nasty Tigellinus, who became
Nero's chief advisor. Seneca retired.

Perhaps under the influence of Burrus and Seneca, Nero
was a serious and efficient ruler in his first years. In
foreign policy, though, he was very cautious. There was
trouble in the East with the Parthians, the first of any
seriousness in 100 years. It grew out of a quarrel over
Rome's client kingdom of Armenia. A successful war was
fought out there (58-60) by Domitius Corbulo. Nero was
not interested in campaigning himself and he settled with
the Parthians without pressing them too hard. A Parthian
appointee was accepted as king of Armenia after he agreed
to be a Roman client. More aggression was shown in the
less important area of Britain. Wales was occupied; it had
been providing refuge for the British Celt leader Caratacus,
the son of the last king of the Catuvellauni, the great
tribe in southern England. Northern England was occupied
also, after a series of revolts in the south, the most
famous of them led by the Queen Boudicca of the Iceni (60),
had been encouraged from the north by Queen Cartimandua of
the Brigantes, the big northern tribe. These fighting
women are striking and unusual figures in the Roman story.
Boudicca particularly has become a great figure in British
legend.

It seems a good deal clearer in Nero's case than in
Caligula's that he became crazy by degrees. Toward the end
there was rapid worsening. He became a mad sensualist like
Caligula, but he found quite new ways to show himself up:
64: Fire destroyed most of Rome. The dwelling units were
mostly wooden tenements several storeys high, packed tightly
together in the low-lying areas. Suspicion centered on Nero,
who was not above a good caper and who had been planning an

enormous new palace complex (his Golden Palace). Could he have jumped the gun on clearing the site for the project? Nero tried to turn aside the talk with his customary imagination. He accused the Christians, of whom there were already some in Rome, of doing the dirty deed. He killed the Christians in various ways for the amusement of the masses. One of the variations was to use them to light the stadium at night to allow evening chariot races. Tied to poles around the track, the Christians were covered in tar and set on fire. Tradition says that Peter--and perhaps Paul--were killed at this time.

65: Nero gave his first public performance on stage, shocking "respectable" opinion. He was very proud of his high-pitched voice, but few others seem to have shared his opinion. He was also a fat, ugly man.

66: Nero made an artistic tour of Greece, appearing in all kinds of contests there, including the Olympic Games. He won all the first prizes--among them many for competitions he did not even enter. The Greeks were being careful. In return, Nero "freed" Greece--that is, he exempted it from Roman taxes. (It is only fair to say that Nero did enter many chariot races, another of his passions and a dangerous one. Those, too, he always won; in fact, one of the races had to be stopped when he fell off his chariot so that he could get aboard and win.) It takes little imagination to understand what the army, Senate, and Guard thought of all this kind of thing.

Nero took to killing senators in good numbers in these years. Plots were discovered everywhere--some at least were real. Seneca was killed, the general Corbulo was forced to commit suicide. Finally in 68 everyone deserted Nero at the same time. It may have taken so long to reach this moment because there was no other male in the family to turn to. Vindex, governor of Central Gaul, revolted against Nero but was killed when the Rhine army was brought in. As the descendent of Celtic chiefs, Vindex was not the man to make such a move. He did manage to talk a very different type into the field, though, before he was put down. This was GALBA, governor of Nearer Spain, aged 71 and from a great family. Galba, encouraged by the discovery that Nero had ordered him killed, announced his rebellion. The Senate recognized Galba as ruler and sentenced Nero to death. It was safe for the Senate to do this, since the Guard approved. When the Guard went to kill Nero in his palace, the ruler killed himself, although he had to get someone to help him. One version of his last words is, "What an artist dies when I perish." It deserves to be true.

THE YEAR OF THE FOUR EMPERORS, 68-69: GALBA, VITELLIUS, OTHO, VESPASIAN

Galba reached Rome on October 28, 68. Once there, he soon lost the popularity he had had at a distance. The collapse of his position is difficult to understand; the story that his cruelty and stinginess annoyed the Romans does not explain much. It was important that Galba had not been the choice of the legions, for in this kind of situation that was where the final power lay.
January 2, 69: VITELLIUS, governor of Lower Germany, was hailed as ruler by his legions. Here was the first move by the great army groups on the frontiers.
To improve his position, Galba now adopted a son, having none of his own. He took a young man of high aristocratic background. This enraged OTHO. The Etruscan Otho, aged 37, had been married to Poppaea, Nero's second wife. As governor of Lusitania, Otho had supported Galba strongly, hoping in return to get adopted into the succession.
January 15, 69: Otho murdered Galba, his newly adopted son, and his associates, and had himself declared emperor in Rome.
The army groups on the Danube and in the East accepted Otho, leaving only the third big army group, that on the Rhine, supporting Vitellius. Vitellius' men, however, struck first.
April 16, 69: Vitellius defeated Otho at the first battle of Bedriacum in north Italy. This was the return of civil war after 100 years. Otho committed suicide. He should have waited for the friendly legions from the Danube to come up in his support before risking battle.
The Senate accepted Vitellius as emperor, and he occupied Rome. The legions in the East, though, now took their own commander, VESPASIAN, as emperor. The Danube legions also accepted Vespasian.
October 69: Vitellius was beaten at the second battle of Bedriacum by Danube legions supporting Vespasian. Rome was taken and Vitellius killed. Vespasian himself stayed in the East, waiting to see if his forces would win. He did not reach Rome until the summer of 70.

The disorder had not been great. The Senate had been irrelevant; the Guard equally so. The legions decided the matter, their first serious meddling in politics in 100 years. Tacitus, who gives us our detailed knowledge of these events, said that what happened taught everyone that an emperor could be made outside Rome. It can only have reminded them of this--the army had been at all times the final source of power, Having been forced to intervene, the army would now support the hereditary principle in the new ruling family.

THE FLAVIAN DYNASTY, 69-96

Flavian is the name of the new dynasty, the founder's name being T. Flavius Vespasianus. The Flavian rulers were:

Vespasian	69-79	and his two sons;
Titus	79-81	
Domitian	81-96	

Vespasian, 69-79.

Vespasian, aged 60 when he became emperor, was a veteran soldier. He had commanded a legion in the invasion of Britain in 43. Most recently, he had been sent to the East to put down the Jewish rebellion which broke out in 67. This rebellion is known to us through the writings of Josephus, a Jewish general who went over to the Roman side. Vespasian was steady but not brilliant. Nero may have given him the command in the east because he seemed unlikely to get ambitious for himself (Nero had recently done away with the general Corbulo, a far more talented man). Vespasian was said to have annoyed Nero once by falling asleep during one of the madman's musical performances.

Vespasian was from the equites. His father had been a Sabine tax-collector. He was a very different type from the patrician Julio-Claudians, who had been products of the city of Rome, flashy, cynical, amoral, unstable. Vespasian's busts show him as a hard, mean, very determined, and very ordinary man (although the Flavian women are shown as elegant and ornate). Vespasian's victory showed that the circle of power was broadening, in a way that would have been much more difficult under the old Republic. The next 100 years would produce a much more serious and sober line of emperors, of upper middle class background, drawn from the small towns of Italy and the provinces.

587

Vespasian has a good reputation as emperor. He put the
finances of the empire back into order (which took some
doing after Nero), and he was carefully aggressive in foreign
policy. He had to put down a revolt on the Rhine among the
legions which had lost the civil war. The four legions
involved were put out of the service and replaced by new
ones. Vespasian proceeded to annex the angle between the
Rhine and Danube in order to shorten the defensive line.
He also continued a forward movement to the north in Britain.
Elsewhere, his son TITUS stormed Jerusalem and crushed the
Jewish rebellion. The Jews, however, were allowed to keep
their privileges (which included exemption from military
service and from the official Roman religious practices),
but they now paid a tax for those privileges. This war left
one of the great archaeological remains of the period in
the ruins of the Jewish rock fortress at Masada.

It was difficult for Vespasian, given his background,
to get along with the Senate, many of whose members were
his social superiors. He was keen to discover plots among
the senators. As censor of 73-74, with Titus, he threw out
many members. New senators were added from all over Italy,
with many from the provinces also, as Vespasian and his sons
speeded up the process of admitting the provinces to power.
In 90 there was the first known eastern consul; in 94 both
consuls were provincials. Often, the new senators came from
the same kind of background in the equites as Vespasian
himself. It was the equites he relied on most heavily for
his associates. This also meant that the role of freedmen
was much reduced. Such types did not appeal to the rough
and ready Vespasian.

Vespasian began the construction of the famous
COLOSSEUM, which seated about 50,000. Titus, his son, was
to finish it. The name Colosseum is a nickname picked up
from the colossal statue of Nero which had stood nearby.
Vespasian rebuilt the Capitoline Temple, which had been
burnt in 69. This new one, though, was itself destroyed
by fire in 80, and was then rebuilt on a bigger scale by
Domitian. Vespasian also put up a Temple of Peace in the
Forum. He introduced a further refinement of concerned
emperors—public toilets. Street urinals in France today
are still called "vespasiennes."

Vespasian died a peaceful death in 79, the first dictator to manage that feat since Tiberius. His deathbed phrases, "A Roman emperor should die on his feet," "Oh dear, I think I'm becoming a god," reveal the man.

Titus, 79-81

Vespasian was followed as emperor by his older son Titus, aged 40. Titus had shared much of the work of Vespasian over the previous 10 years. Popular, able, Titus had all the marks of a great emperor, but he died after a couple of years. He is best known to us for
--His love affair with the Jewish princess Berenice, who had lived with him in Rome for several years. Titus sent her away when he became emperor, being anxious to avoid comparisons with Mark Antony and that great schemer and queen from the East, Cleopatra.
--The eruption of the volcano VESUVIUS in 79, which buried POMPEII and other towns. This catastrophe preserved our best evidence of Roman town and domestic life in the period.

Domitian, 81-96.

Titus had no son. He was succeeded as emperor by his younger brother DOMITIAN. Since Domitian wound up as one of the "bad" emperors, there were stories that he had poisoned Titus. There is no evidence to such effect. Domitian built the great Arch of Titus in Rome to show that he wanted people to remember his brother's victories over the Jews.

Domitian was in many ways an efficient and hard-working emperor. Lacking the prestige of his father and brother, he wanted to make a military name for himself. To that end, he called off the movement northward which had been going on in Britain since late in Vespasian's rule. Under the command of Agricola, Roman armies had moved into northern Scotland. They now consolidated their hold up to southern Scotland only. This decision was one of the things which made the historian Tacitus dislike Domitian. Tacitus was Agricola's son-in-law. Tacitus' biography of Agricola is a great source of information about Britain at this time. Domitian's aim was to concentrate his forces elsewhere to bigger purposes. Between 83 and 89 Domitian campaigned in southern Germany, extending the frontier a little, and in

589

Dacia, where the king Decebalus was building himself up. Decebalus agreed to become a Roman client; he kept his territories and received grants of money from Domitian.

Any serious military efforts were called off after 89, when the commander of Upper Germany rebelled. From that point on, Domitian got very bloody, although this was a style he had liked from the start. He was not crazy, in the way of Caligula and Nero, but he created the same atmosphere of terror in Rome. He took the title of "perpetual censor" so that he could throw men out of the Senate at will.

Domitian was also not able to resist letting his position go to his head in ways that were still thought of as un-Roman. He seems to have had his officials call him "Lord and God," although he did not use the style himself, and the oath upon his genius or guiding spirit seems to have been compulsory in some matters. It is not surprising that the Senate hated him, but it is important to note that Domitian was not in the position of Caligula and Nero. To the end, he was efficient, and he was popular with the army.

One odd aspect of Domitian's rule is his old-fashioned "morality" legislation. He passed laws against plays and against the freeing of slaves. He revived the death penalty for Vestal Virgins caught in adultery—and even buried one alive in the ancient fashion. From a man who liked his fun— and one of his mistresses was his niece—this did not look very good.

Domitian was assassinated in September 96. At the center of the plot was his wife, a daughter of the general Corbulo from Nero's days. She was afraid that Domitian was going to kill her. Others in on the thing were some officers of the guard and, most probably, some senators. Domitian had no son; the only males in his family were young children of a cousin. The line of Vespasian could not be maintained. Noone would make a child emperor.

"THE FIVE GOOD EMPERORS": THE ADOPTIVE EMPERORS, 96-180

Nerva, 96-98.
     The Senate quickly produced a candidate to take Domitian's place. This was NERVA, aged 66, of an old but

not very distinguished family, a man of great experience who had survived in politics since Nero's days. It is likely that Nerva and those who brought him forward had been in on the plot to kill Domitian. This was a high point of achievement for the Senate, although there can have been little hope for any substantial change in the system.

Neither the Guard as a whole, nor the legions, had been involved in the overthrow of Domitian. The soldiers had liked the dead emperor and were not happy with what had been done. Nerva found that he could not ignore this feeling in the army. To satisfy the Guards, he allowed the "plotters" to be killed. To satisfy the legions, and avoid a repeat of 68-69, he adopted as his son and intended successor a leading general of the day. This was TRAJAN, who was commander of the army on the upper Rhine river—the army closest to Rome. It was Nerva's good fortune that he did not have a son of his own to keep him from this course (although Galba in 68 had squandered a similar opportunity). With Nerva old and in poor health, the armies proved willing to wait things out. Nerva died in January 98, after only 16 months in office. Trajan then became the emperor.

Nerva is the first of those rulers known as the "Five Good Emperors." These were:

Nerva	96-98
Trajan	98-117
Hadrian	117-138
Antoninus Pius	138-161
Marcus Aurelius	161-180

They are also known as the adoptive emperors. Each one, beginning with Nerva, lacked a son and so was able to choose his successor. Adoption ended when Marcus Aurelius had a son. The adoptive period was one of successful and very efficient government. These decades are usually seen as the high point of the Roman Empire, its golden age. 200 years ago Edward Gibbon, in writing the most famous history of Rome that we have, The Decline and Fall of the Roman Empire, identified the 100's as "the period in the history of the world during which the condition of the human race was most happy and prosperous."

While the general outline of the period is known to us, much is missing. We do not have the detailed knowledge that exists for much of the 1st century A.D.

Trajan, 98-117.

    Nerva hardly belongs on the list of "Good Emperors,"
other than to credit him with beginning adoption, an act
which was born only of need. With TRAJAN, however, we meet
one of the greatest of the emperors--the one with perhaps
the biggest reputation of all after Augustus. The Senate
voted him Best First Citizen (Optimus Princeps), a wonderful
acknowledgement of his reputation, particularly considering
the source. Best was a term reserved usually for Jupiter,
mightiest of the gods.

    Trajan was 44 in 98. He was descended from Romans who
had settled in Spain; his mother was a Spaniard. His father
had been consul under Vespasian in the 70's. Here was
further evidence of the broadening of power--the first
emperor from outside Italy, and one with some non-Italian
blood.

    Trajan was not willing to give more power to the
Senate, but he did swear, as had Nerva, not to kill any
senators. He kept his word. This, along with some tact,
allowed him to be as popular with the Senate as was possible
for a dictator. By this time, non-Italians (mostly from the
West) made up about 40% of the Senate, although the Italians
did not actually lose their majority until 200. Trajan
and his successors, like the Flavians, preferred to rely
on provincials of the equites class, rather than senators--
or freedmen. One of his generals, for example, was a Moor
from North Africa.

    He constructed great public works, including an
enormous Forum of Trajan which was virtually a new city
center. We still have the famous Column of Trajan, which
commemorated his victories in Dacia (see below). Trajan
was lavish with games and entertainments, which occurred
more and more frequently. His games of 107, also intended
to commemorate the conquest of Dacia, lasted 126 days.
Trajan was generous with handouts to the poor, which had
grown to include wine and oil and even cash, in addition to
corn. The city of Rome was now at the peak of its growth,
with perhaps well over 1,000,000 population.

    A different kind of expression of the dictator's
concern for the poor was the alimenta, a program to provide

maintenance allowances for poor children across Italy.
Begun probably by Trajan (though perhaps by Nerva), this
program grew steadily in the 100's. The dictators were
very proud of it.

Despite his expenditures on such things and on his
wars, Trajan was able to reduce taxes in the provinces.
This reflected the great underlying economic strength of
the Empire--and the fact that Trajan's wars were successful.

The most remarkable thing about Trajan, the one which
set him apart from other emperors, was that for the first
time since Augustus a full century before Rome undertook
deliberate major expansion. The reason was probably as
simple as could be--as a professional soldier in the prime
of his life, Trajan wanted to campaign.

Trajan increased the army to 30 legions (Augustus
had finished with 25). The legions were now bigger, too.
The regular legions and the auxiliaries were supported by
numeri, native troops from tribal units often lying beyond
the frontiers. The numeri contracted with the Romans, fighting in their own fashion and under their own commanders.
101-106: Trajan conquered DACIA, which is modern Romania.
He took 13 legions with him. The fighting was very heavy.
In the end, the Dacian king, the same Decebalus of Domitian's
day, committed suicide. Dacia was annexed as a province.
It contained large gold and silver deposits and became for
a while a wonderful source of profit for the Romans. Only
Caesar's conquest of Gaul ranks with what Trajan did in
Dacia.
113-116: Trajan annexed Armenia, closing out the existence
of the troublesome client state. This step led to war with
the Parthians. Trajan conquered Mesopotamia from them,
including their summer capital at Ctesiphon. He went as
far as the Persian Gulf. A client kingdom was set up in
Mesopotamia, although the situation there was far from
settled. This brought the Empire to its greatest territorial
extent.
115: Rebellion broke out among Jews across the East,
upsetting Trajan's plan to concentrate against the Parthians.

Trajan turned home in 116. He perhaps had already
suffered a stroke, and may have wanted to get back to Rome
to make sure that things were in order at the end. He died

in Asia Minor in 117 on the way home.

It will not have seemed odd to Romans that this most military of their emperors was a homosexual. We get a glimpse of Trajan in his correspondence with Pliny the Younger when the latter was governor of Bithynia in Asia Minor. His attitudes seem reasonable, his approach calm and, in a distant and cool way, concerned. The knowledge of his power is overwhelmingly present, but Trajan was at pains to keep a low-profile. With Pliny, who was very anxious to please, this took some doing. Pliny usually addressed Trajan as "Lord" (dominus); sometimes he was more flowery, with Best Imperator and even Most Virtuous (Sanctissimus) Imperator. Trajan talked in turn about "our republic" and "our times." At one point Trajan said flatly, "It is not my plan by fear and terror and by making up charges of treason to make men hold my name in awe." He liked to refer frequently to "my fellow-soldiers," an indication of companionship with the soldiers that earlier emperors would have avoided. He referred to "the justice of our times," expressing his concern for the people. However, Trajan kept a careful eye on what counted. After a big fire at Nicomedia, Pliny asked if he should allow the city to set up a guild of firemen. The answer was no: "Whatever name or cause we give them, before long those who act together will turn themselves into a political club." When two runaway slaves were discovered among the recruits for the legions, Trajan's response was--kill them. The correspondence is a good insight into the nature of the system at this time--and the pressure upon Trajan to become more like a dictator. In this connection, it was the dictators themselves who were dragging their feet. We also see the conventional Roman attitude toward the Greeks. Pliny wrote that Nicaea wanted to build a big new gymnasium. Trajan noted that "The little Greeks like their Gymnasiums." He had no architect available to do the job in Rome--Pliny should look around where he was: "usually it's from Greece that they come here."

Hadrian, 117-138.
        Trajan had no children. The new emperor, HADRIAN, was Trajan's closest male relative (although the relationship was a distant one, Hadrian being the grandson of Trajan's aunt). Hadrian claimed that Trajan on his deathbed

adopted him as a son. While this may be invention, it is
all but certain that Trajan intended Hadrian to succeed
him--it was the closest Trajan could come to the hereditary
principle. Hadrian had been closely associated with Trajan
over the previous 20 years. He had been left behind in
charge of the legions in the East in 117 when Trajan set
out for Rome--a dangerous thing for Trajan to do if he
intended to pick someone else to succeed him.

The second emperor from Spain was aged 41 in 117. He
has a great name, primarily as an efficient administrator
and as a highly cultivated patron of the arts. Our impression is that Hadrian came closest among the emperors to
being an intellectual. He was a famous homosexual, in an
age when that took some doing. This taste is often associated with his preference for the arts, although the very
different Trajan had the same tastes. The busts of Hadrian
show a cute, effeminate type, while those of Trajan reveal
a hard and businesslike man.

Hadrian definitely abandoned military expansion.
Perhaps he thought that what he had seen Trajan do in the
East was not worth the bother. He gave up Mesopotamia and
let it go back into Parthian hands. He kept Armenia, however. He is said to have wanted to give up Dacia also, but
he did not do so.

Hadrian's defensive attitude is expressed in the lines
of defense he encouraged around the frontiers of the Empire.
The most famous of these is HADRIAN'S WALL across the north
of Britain. This stone wall was 73 miles long. Hadrian
planned its construction himself when he visited Britain in
the 120's following local revolts. He was the first emperor
to go there since Claudius at the time of the conquest in the
40's. He build a wooden line across the angle between the
Rhine and the Danube in Germany, a stone wall in Numidia
against desert tribesmen, etc.

He seems to have disliked Jews more actively than most
emperors, perhaps because he was such a friend of Hellenistic
learning (or perhaps because of the way the Jews had embarrassed Trajan). He put down the Jewish rebellion which was
still going on when he became emperor. Later, in 132-135,
there was a great Jewish revolt in Palestine. After

595

capturing Jerusalem, Hadrian renamed the city Aelia
Capitolina (after his family name, Aelius), built a
Roman temple and a Roman colony there, and banned
circumcision. This was the end of the great Jewish
problem in their homeland.

Hadrian's attitude, and the weakness of Rome's
enemies, meant that there was relatively little fighting.
Hadrian, however, became famous for tightening up the
training of the legions. Some of this he supervised himself on his many travels around the Empire. Less than half
his time as emperor was spent in Rome. One of his motives
in this travel was simple curiosity--he was a great tourist.
His travels also emphasized the point that more and more
the Empire was a commonwealth, not just a great piece of
real estate owned by Italy. On one of these trips, to
Egypt in 130, Hadrian's most famous lover, the young man
Antinous, drowned in the Nile Delta.

Hadrian, like Trajan, was a great builder. We can
note:
--the Temple of Venus and Rome (Venus was the "mother" of
Aeneas).
--the enormous Tomb of Hadrian, which is now the Castle
Sant'Angelo.
--the rebuilt Pantheon, a great wonder of ancient architecture, with the first great dome the world had seen.
--his country estate at Tivoli near Rome, where he spent
most of the last few years of his life. This was a series
of buildings spread out over a mile of ground.

Hadrian's relations with the Senate were not very good.
Like Trajan, he took the oath not to kill senators, but he
broke the promise. In 118, while Hadrian was in the Danube
river area, his associates at Rome killed four leading
senators, all of them ex-consuls. The plot involved may
have been imaginary, with the intention being to scare
opposition to Hadrian into silence. The emperor may not
even have known of the killings ahead of time; they may
have been the work of his too eager friends. Hadrian,
hindered by this poor beginning, never became popular with
the Senate--an odd thing in light of the efficiency and
good government he offered.

Relations with the Senate at the end were very bad.
Hadrian, like Trajan, had no children. His nearest male
connection was his brother-in-law, Servianus. While this
man was over 80, he did have a grandson who seemed the most
likely choice for the succession. Hadrian, though, had no
such intention. In fact, in 136, both Servianus and his
grandson, with others, were killed as Hadrian broke up an
apparently genuine plot to replace him. In preference to
his own relatives, Hadrian in the same year (136) adopted
as his son and intended successor a senator of good family
but of no special distinction. This man took the name
Aelius Caesar, Aelius being Hadrian's family name. The
Senate did not approve; we do not know why. It was suggested that Aelius Caesar was Hadrian's own illegitimate
son. The adopted Aelius died in January 138, 6 months
before Hadrian. Passing over Aelius' son, who at the age
of 8 was too young to be considered, Hadrian next adopted
ANTONINUS PIUS, who at age 51 was only 10 years younger
than himself. The new "son" of Hadrian was the most distinguished senator of his day, a man of much experience,
although he had little of a military name. This adoption
pleased the Senate and was satisfactory to everyone else.
Hadrian required Antoninus Pius, who had no son of his own,
to adopt as his sons
--Lucius Verus, the young son of Aelius Caesar;
--Marcus Aurelius, who was a nephew of Antoninus Pius' wife
and the next emperor's closest male connection. Marcus
Aurelius was already the fiancé of Lucius Verus' sister.
Aged 16 at this time, Marcus Aurelius already showed outstanding promise. His own father had recently died.

The adoption of Marcus Aurelius was a step Antoninus
Pius probably would have taken anyway, since it coincided
with the hereditary principle. The adoption of Lucius
Verus was to Hadrian a vindication of his earlier selection
of the boy's father, Aelius Caesar, as his successor.
Hadrian was providing ahead for two generations here,
but in a way likely to cause only confusion.

Antoninus Pius, 138-161.
The family of Antoninus Pius were Italians from the
old colony of Nîmes in southern France. His father had been
a consul. Like Trajan and Hadrian, therefore, the new
emperor evidenced the widening circle of power. They all

came from the successful provincial families which had been
encouraged and brought forward by Vespasian, the first
ruler from outside the old aristocracy.

Antoninus Pius has a very solid reputation, although
we know little about him. He was very friendly to the
Senate, where he had many old associates, and he had the kind
of quiet dignity and old-fashioned virtues that the Senate
liked. These qualities won him the title Pius from the
Senate, a word meaning true to one's duty (to the gods and
the state). One example of this quality, in this case
involving duty as an (adopted) son, was his insistence
that the Senate recognize the dead Hadrian as a god. The
Senate agreed, after resisting, and later the incident was
used to show that Antoninus Pius was a man to do what was
"right" for him in his situation. Coming right after
Hadrian's death, it also, of course, helped to show the
Senate who was in charge.

Antoninus Pius was lucky. The times were quiet and
prosperous. He had no wish to change them. In contrast
to Hadrian, Antoninus Pius stayed in and around Rome.
There was little fighting, though he did advance the Roman
line in Britain a little to a new wall, the Antonine Wall
(only 37 miles long). He did not visit Britain himself.
In many ways, this was the best of the good times, with the
Empire thriving, well-governed, and apparently secure
beyond challenge. On the last day of his life, Antoninus
Pius selected as the password for the Guards "peace of mind."

Marcus Aurelius, 161-180.
When Antoninus Pius died, Marcus Aurelius, his closest
male connection and his adopted son, was 40. Marcus
Aurelius, like Trajan and Hadrian, was from an Italian
family which had long before moved to Spain. Since his
adoption, Marcus Aurelius had been raised to become emperor.
He had married Antoninus Pius' daughter, his earlier
engagement to the sister of Lucius Verus being called off.
Since 147 he had been co-emperor, in the way of Titus with
Vespasian.

The second adopted son of Antoninus Pius, Lucius Verus,
had been more or less ignored, that adoption being a
concession to Hadrian rather than a voluntary act. In 161,
however, Marcus Aurelius voluntarily made Lucius Verus

598

co-emperor, producing a new kind of situation in the state. This may have been an expression of "piety" in doing his duty to his brother by adoption. It seems that Marcus Aurelius liked Lucius Verus. We do not know how the two men divided up their duties. Lucius Verus is often seen as something of a lightweight, much the less important of the two. This may be hindsight. In 163–166 he commanded a large and successful campaign in the East—no easy or unimportant job. He died in 169, though, leaving Marcus Aurelius on his own.

Marcus Aurelius has a wonderful reputation, built in part on his exploits and in part on his surviving writings, the MEDITATIONS. These Meditations, ideas or impressions written down at the end of his busy days, give us our best glimpse of the personality of a Roman emperor. We do not know if they were meant to be totally private—they soon became very famous. The impression they give is a strange one. On the one hand, they establish Marcus Aurelius as an outstanding Roman Stoic, revealing both the hard sense of duty of the type and the more attractive belief in human brotherhood. At the same time, the emperor appears terribly pessimistic, flatly contemptuous of human nature, very proud of his own qualities. Among the people he did not like were the Christians—he made this point in the Meditations (see below). He wrote in Greek, a sign of the bilingualism (use of two languages, here Latin and Greek) of the people running the empire.

Marcus Aurelius' luck was bad. Oddly, this suited his sour personality and prompted the general tone of his writings—the man of virtue struggling against great odds. This ill-luck was responsible for the heroic quality of his reign. Because of what they knew of his character and talents, and because they sympathized with his bad luck, something they understood well, later Romans made a great favorite of Marcus Aurelius, admiring him above all others. To us, his rule is something of a turning point—the end of the great age of the Empire after 200 years, the beginning of harder times.

There is no question that Marcus Aurelius wished to make a great reputation as emperor. He meant to do this by fighting, intending to make the first major additions of territory to the Empire since <u>Trajan</u>. Fighting was not something he was much interested in by nature. It suited him to force himself to it, just as he had worked hard at improving his own weak and sickly body.

163-166: A great campaign in the East against the <u>Parthians</u> was commanded by <u>Lucius Verus</u>, the co-emperor. The real force on the Roman side, though, was the general <u>Avidius Cassius</u>, a <u>Syrian</u> (again, the expanding circle of power). <u>Mesopotamia</u> was reconquered with no great problem. In 166 a mission was sent on to <u>China</u>, looking for markets in the other great empire of the world.

167: Unfortunately, in <u>Mesopotamia</u> the legions picked up a <u>disease</u> which over the next years swept through the Empire, reducing the population considerably and dealing the administration and the economy blows from which they never fully recovered. Rome never was the same again. This disease is usually called the <u>plague</u>, but we do not know what it was. <u>Smallpox</u> and <u>typhus</u> are possibilities.

The effect on the <u>army</u> was probably substantial, with men huddled tightly together, often in unsanitary conditions, not able to escape contact with one another. The military weakness which resulted, the shortage of both soldiers and officers, made it difficult for a while to hold the frontiers to the <u>north</u>. The plague struck at a time when the <u>Danube</u> area was already giving more trouble than at any time since <u>Trajan</u>.

Marcus Aurelius had probably intended originally to move north of the Danube in a new expansion of territory, one to match the gains in the East:

166: German tribes slipped past Marcus Aurelius on the Danube and reached across the <u>Alps</u> into Italy itself, reaching <u>Aquileia</u>. Rome had not seen this kind of thing since the days of <u>Marius</u> almost 300 years before. Soon, with the scourge of the plague in his legions, Marcus Aurelius was forced flatly on to the defensive. Most of <u>Dacia</u> was lost and the tribes raided widely through the <u>Balkans</u>, even reaching ancient <u>Eleusis</u>, very close to <u>Athens</u>.

By great efforts, Marcus Aurelius, and Lucius Verus until his death in 169, restored the northern frontier over the next several years. This was a tribute both to their

efficiency and to the enormous remaining strength of Rome--
although it was fortunate that the Parthians, perhaps as
badly off as the Romans, were quiet at this time. The
fighting was commemorated on the Column of Marcus Aurelius
at Rome. The scenes on this column are much more bloody
and nasty and grim than those on the earlier Column of
Trajan.

Marcus Aurelius had to <u>draft</u> soldiers when he needed
them, including slaves and gladiators, and he hired many
German tribesmen to fight against their own kind, offering
good lands which were now vacant because of the reduced
population. Hiring foreign tribesmen was not a new thing,
but probably it had not been done before on such a scale.
These circumstances added to Marcus Aurelius's dislike of
Christians, as he found that they resisted the draft. With
the times not normal, he could not afford the normal easy-
going attitude toward the Christians.

By 175, the <u>Danube</u> border was restored. Marcus Aurelius
intended to push on north into <u>Bohemia</u> and the <u>Carpathians</u>,
returning to his first plan of expansion. Prospects looked
bright, but then:
175: The general <u>Avidius Cassius</u>, who was in charge of all
Roman forces in the East, declared himself emperor. This
was a very new kind of thing; in fact, there had been little
trouble of any kind since the incident under Hadrian in 118.
It seems that Avidius Cassius had heard that Marcus Aurelius
had died and was simply making a bid to replace him. Marcus
Aurelius made terms with the Germans and gathered his Danube
armies for a move to the East. Civil war was avoided when
Avidius Cassius' men murdered him. Their hearts were not in
it when they found that the emperor was alive; neither,
probably, was that of Avidius Cassius himself. Marcus
Aurelius decided in any case to make a tour of the East.
Among other things, like <u>Hadrian</u>, he was initiated into the
<u>Mysteries of Eleusis</u> in Greece. His wife died in the East.
178-180: Marcus Aurelius returned to war against the German
tribes along the <u>Danube</u>. They had caused some trouble during
his absence. He restored the river line again and was moving
north beyond the Danube when he died in camp at <u>Vienna</u> in 180.

THE END OF ADOPTION: COMMODUS, THE NO-GOOD EMPEROR,
180-192

Marcus Aurelius left the Empire to his son COMMODUS.

Aged only 18, Commodus was the first emperor who had been born to the job, and only the second (after Titus) to succeed his father as emperor. Marcus Aurelius thus ended the period of "adoptive" emperors by returning to the hereditary principle (actually, of course, only Hadrian had ignored his own relatives in adopting--both Trajan and Antoninus Pius had adopted their closest male connection).

In leaving Commodus to follow him, Marcus Aurelius put an end also to the era of "good" emperors. In doing this, Marcus Aurelius did a great and knowing disservice to Rome, for his son had already shown himself the lazy, crazy playboy type--the first of that kind since Nero more than 100 years earlier. So abrupt was the change from the father to the son that Dio Cassius, a contemporary, in writing of the transitions said "our story now declines from a kingdom of gold to one of iron and rust, as things did for the Romans in that day." It seems that Marcus Aurelius' idea of duty did not extend to passing over his own son in the interests of the state (he would have had to kill Commodus, of course). Many poorer men had ignored their own offspring in the previous 200 years.

Wishing to spend his time in Rome, Commodus abandoned the idea of expansion to the north, settling for the old line of the Danube river. The German tribes, though, had been mauled badly enough by Marcus Aurelius that they were reasonably quiet for 50 years to come.

Things at Rome went downhill rapidly, although as usual the impact on the provinces was minimal. Plots against Commodus began almost at once; he killed his sister for such plotting in 182. He also killed his wife. Commodus treated the Senate very harshly, killing widely. In his laziness, he allowed his Praetorian Prefects to run things, something not seen since Nero's day.

Commodus' craziness was expressed in the usual ways. Like Caligula, he claimed to be a god, specifically a reincarnation of Hercules, the strong man. He had his name changed to Hercules. There was also the standard quota of sex-scandals. The most interesting is that one of his mistresses, Marcia, in Dio Cassius's words, "greatly favored the Christians and did them many kindnesses, so far as she could have any influence over Commodus." A wonderful new element was Commodus' insistence that he was a great fighter (which explains his belief that he was Hercules). He performed in public many times, providing the people with

A real breakthrough in entertainment--the chance to watch the god-emperor in the arena. He always won. The animals he fought (sometimes with a club, in the manner of Hercules) were drugged. He engaged in play-fighting with the gladiators, but did not risk himself too much in that direction.

On December 31, 192 Commodus met his inevitable end. The latest Praetorian Prefect, Laetus--who seems to have been the first North African to hold the position--hired a professional athlete to murder Commodus while he was taking a bath. Marcia seems to have been in on the plot. Commodus had no son, and none seems to have been interested in trying to keep the job of ruler within his family.

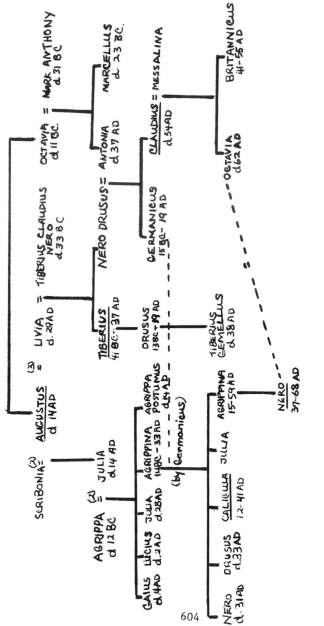

The Family of Augustus
(The Julio-Claudian Dynasty)

ROMAN LITERATURE

Roman literature begins with borrowings from the Greek literary traditions. The earliest known attempts at literature in Latin are by a Greek slave, Livius Andronicus (taken prisoner in 272 B. C.) who wrote a Latin translation of some of Homer, and introduced the Greek dramatic tradition to Romans. He was soon followed by a native Roman, Naevius (born 280? B. C.) who, like Andronicus, imitated the Greek New Comedy tradition of Menander instead of the Old Comedy of Aristophanes. New Comedy emphasizes general satire of human errors such as greed, lust, cowardice and so forth rather than satire of specific public figures. Even so, Naevius seems to have gotten into trouble with a powerful family because of his plays. Ennius (born 239 ? B. C.) wrote Latin imitations of Aeschylus and Euripides. Nothing has survived of the work of any of these writers.

The first Roman literary figure whose work has come down to us is Plautus (born 240? B. C.) who cintinued the Roman imitation of Menender in his best play The Captives. Next came Terence (born 190 ? B. C.) who was probably brought to Rome from North Africa as a slave. Terence added some interesting devices (prologues, asides, narrators, etc.) to Plautus, but still the satire and humor concerned broad topics like old bragging soldiers, smart-aleck servants, cases of mistaken identity between twins, mothers-in-law and so forth. There is no criticism of Roman customs or of Roman leaders.

Catullus (84-54 B. C.) made a truly original and truly Roman contribution to the literary history of the Western world. He is the Hank Williams of the ancient world. The Greeks have no poet of love who pictures himself as a slave to an unworth woman who treats him with contempt. In his poems Catullus pictures himself in love with "Lesbia," who seems really to have been Clodia, the wife of a powerful Roman politician. Lesbia, like Clodia, seems to have been given to all manner of depravity and abandon, but not very interested in Catullus. For this poet, love seems to have been like slavery, being in chains, being tortured, or being sick. He is constantly saying, "I can't help it if I'm still in love with you." The most typical poems is "Odi

et Amo," meaning "I Love You and I hate You." In another, "Catullus Struggles to be Free," the poet concludes that he really loves his chains. Here we recognize,
in full bloom, the tradition of which almost all modern love
songs are a part, the lover in love with an unworthy partner.
As in Catullus, almost all country songs are about lovers who
are married to the wrong partner.

Propertius (born 54? B. C.) brought originality to his
imitations of Hellenistic pastorals and love poems. He is
witty and often obscure, but very talented. Since he was not
a member of the Augustan "in-group" of his time, he does not
survive as well as we would like.

Augustus continued a Roman tradition of being nice to
literary figures and intellectuals, but, being more aware
of the political value of such patronage, he exploited the
relationship more carefully, and supported literary people
more royally. Augustus had an un-official minister of culture
(or minister of propagand, as you choose) named Maecenas. It
was Maecenas' job to find and enlist the support of the finest
writing talent. He was very successful.

Three poets, Virgil (70-19 B. C.), Horace (65-8 B. C.),
and Tibullus (55-19 B. C.), were all sons of families which
had supported the wrong side in the conflicts between Caesar
and his enemies, and as a result they found their land confiscated. Tibullus took his business to Messalla, thus making
a second mistake in two generations, and he is therefore less
well remembered than the other two. Horace and Virgil wrote
their way into financial security and into western history.

Horace wrote love poems, poems about literature, poems
about parties and drink, and poems flattering Maecenas and
Augustus. Even with the flattery, his poems are always cute,
original and interesting. He seems to hade led a contented
life and wound up with a nice pension.

O Virgil we shall have more to say later. Another poet,
Ovid (43 B. C,-17 A. D.) should have been more careful. He
specialized in Roman re-tellings of Greek mythological stories,
was exiled for offending someone in his writings. It has been
suggested that his sex manual, the _Art of Love_, brought his
into disgrace, but that seems unlikely, given the general depravity of Rome at that time. His _Metamorphoses_, on the ᕪ

606

great changes that occur because of love, gives us the first version of "Romeo and Juliet."

Seneca (1-65), and adviser to Nero, added to ghe tragic drama the elements we missed in the Greek version. In all his tragdies, seneca includes mad people who torture and kill, all on stage, and he includes stage blood and props to aid the violence. He wrote of Heracles when he was insane (Hercules Furens) and a play Thyestes, about the man who ate the flesh of his own children. His dramas would make wonderful horror movies today.

After Augustus poets had a more difficult time. Martial (40-104) flattered Domitian with as much gusto as Horace had lavished on Augustus, but with less success. He had no shame, no morals, and no self-respect, and his satires are filthy even by modern standards. Juvenal (60-127) was a bitter man made more bitter by the decadent age he lived in. He seems to have hated women, and he gives us an insight into the wide range of sexual perversion known to the Romans.

As we have noted, Virgil, like Horace, found his family's land confiscated. At first, he tried to repair his fortunes by practicing law, but he failed at it. He tried literature, writing in the Hellenistic tradition about the glories of the countryside, nature and the shepherd's life. These Poemsare the Eclogues and Bucolics. He then wrote a book on farming, the Georgics, which showed him a master of Latin verse. By this time he had become a member of Maecenas' group of poets, and was therefore known to Augustus.

Augustus suggested (strongly) that Virgil write a long epic poem which would be for the Romans what the Iliad and the Odyssey had been for the Greeks. Such a book would be a source of good Latin language and grammar, and would provide patterns of good Roman behavior for children to follow. The hero of the poem would embody what the Romans thought of as the manly virtues.

Furthermore, such a book could give the Romans some "class," some culture. It could show how the Romans were intended to be the rulers of the world. It could, in short, "Romanti-cize" their history.

The word "romantic" is troublesome to define, but it really means only "Roman-like." It means that the thing

607

described was meant to evoke strong emotions and will be sentimental. The dominant emotion will be "love," according to the Roman definition. The Aeneid is a highly Romantic document. It contains a one-sided love affair which is followed by the suicide of the rejected lover. Like all romantic stories, it ends with a marriage. It makes the difficulties between Carthage and Rome a matter of "love," not an economic and military rivalry.

In writing the poem Virgil faced at least four serious problems. In the first place, he was not interested in military things, in soldiers and campaigns, and he knew little about them. Thus, he tends to compare soldiers to ants and bees, not horses as Homer did. Secondly, Virgil was an effeminate kind of sexual pervert, very shy and retiring, and had difficulty "relating to" combat and bloodletting. Thirdly, the Iliad and the Odyssey are very different in structure, and he had to take elements from both.

But most important was his difficulty with the Roman conception of things. The romans were at one time sentimental and cruel, law-abiding and ungoverned, strictly disciplined and orgiastically abandoned. The character of Aeneas, the super-Roman, reflects these contradictions. He is frequently called "pious," meaning very conscious of his duty. Readers for centuries, however, have found him a little too good, and suspected that he used the concept of duty to justify doing whatever he wanted to do.

But in spite of these difficulties, Virgil did a spectacular job. He was still polishing the verse when he died, and he wanted it destroyed. Augustus prevailed, and the Aeneidbecame one of the most important documents in western literature. From 19 B. C. until 1930 or so, going to high school meant studying Virgil. Instead of taking the SAT examinations, students who applied to college were given a passage from Virgil to read at sight. This method made a great deal of sense, because all college-trained professionals in all countries, lawyers, doctors, preachers and scholars, read and wrote in Latin. When the modern world gave up Latin, it lost a great deal.

The Aeneid tells of the advantures of Aeneas, Trojan and the son of Venus and a mortal, Anchises, who leaves Troy after its fall to establish a new home for the Trojan gods and the Trojan way of life. By Creusa, his wife (who dies), he has a son, Ascanius (sometimes called Iulus). Aeneas then finds himself in North Africa (Libya), in Carthage. Carthage was a colony of the city of Tyre in Phoenicea. There he meets Dido, widow of Sychaeus, and sister of Anna. After that, he fights the native Latins and their hero Turnus for the right to establish Rome.

If aeneas is too moral, the hero of Petronius' Satyricon certainly does not have that problem. Our second reading illustrates the opposite pole of Roman literature, the degenerate side. Petronius was an arbiter (umpire) of good behavior under Nero, when good taste meant good taste in depravity. His novel satirizes the romances of his day, for instead of the virtuous man and maid, it feature the depraved homosexual and his lover, Encolpius and Giton. In the first of four episodes, they impersonate the statues used in fertility rites. The second, in our test, involves a gross dinner given by a crude ex-slave of no taste. In the third, Encolpius becomes impotent after over-indulgence, and seeks various remedies for his condition(he explains that he is a "bankrupt in the market of love" and a "soldier without a weapon"). In the fourth episode, he pretends to be an old rich man who is looking for someone to leave his money to, and thereby gets a great deal of attention from everyone. When an episode from the Satyrican appeared in Playboy as a "Ribald Classic," io was cleaned up--the original was much too raunchy. Petronius was eventually forced by Nero to commit suicide, which he did in his typical elegant fashion by bleeding himself to death.

THE AENEID

BOOK ONE

   Arms and the man I sing, who at the first from Troy's
shores as an exile of Fate won his way to Italy and her
Latian coast--a man much knocked about on land and on the
deep sea by violence from gods, to satisfy the unforgetting anger of Juno the cruel--much hurt too in was, as
he struggled to build him a city, and find his gods a home
in Latium--himself the father of the Latian people, and
of the chiefs of Alba's houses, and of the walls of high
towering Rome.
   Bring to my mind, O Muse, the causes--for what treason
against her godhead, or what pain received, the queen of
heaven drove a man of piety so true to turn the wheel of
so many difficulties to bear the brunt of so many hardships! Can heavenly natures hate so fiercely and so long?
   Of old there was a city, its people emigrants from
Tyre, Carthage, over against Italy and Tiber's mouth, yet
far removed--rich and mighty, and formed to all roughnes
by war's iron trade--a spot where Juno, it was said, loved
to dwell more than in all the world beside, Samos
holding but the second place. Here was her armor, here
her chariot--her to fix by her royal act the empire of the
nations, could Fate be brought to agree, was even then
her aim, her cherished scheme. But she had heard that
the blook of Troy was sowing the seed of a race to over-
turn one day those Tyrian towers--from that see a nation,
monarch of broad realms and glorious in war, was to bring
ruin on Libya--such the turning of Fate's wheel. With
that old war wihch at first she had waged at Troy for her
loved Argos' sake--nor indeed had the causes of that feud
and the bitter pangs they roused yet vanished from her
mind--no, stored up in her soul's depths remains the
judgment of Paris, and the wrong done to their slighted
beauty, andthe race hated from the womb, and the state
enjoyed by the raped Ganymede. With this fuel added to
the fire, the Trojans, poor remnants of Danaan havoc and
Achilles' ruthless spear, she was tossing from sea to sea,

and keeping far away from Latium; and for many long years they, the Trojans, were wandering, with destiny still driving them, the whole ocean round. So vast the effort it cost to build up the Roman nation!

Scarce out of sight of the land of Sicily were they spreading their sails merrily to the sea, and scattering their brazen prows the briny spray, when Juno, the everlasting wound still rankling in her heart's core, thus communed with herself;"And am I to give up what I have taken in hand, frustrated, nor have power to prevent the king of the Teucrians from reaching Italy--because, forsooth, the Fates forbid me? What! was Pallas Athena strong enough to burn up utterly the Grecian fleet, and whelm the crews in the sea, for the offense of a single man, the frenzy of Ajax, Oileus' son? Yes, she with her own hand launched fro the clouds Jove's winged fire, dashed the ships apart, and turned up the sea-floor with the wind--him, gasping out the flame which pierced his bosom, she caught in the blast, and impaled on a rock's point--while I, who walk the sky as its queen, Jove's sister and wife, both, am battling with a single nation these many years. And will there be any found to pray to Juno's deity after this, or lay on her altar a suppliant gift?

With such thoughts swooping through the solitude of her firely breast, the goddess comes to the storm-cloud's birthplace, the teeming womb of fierce southern blasts, Aeolia. Here, in a vast cavern, King Aeolus of the winds bowing to his sway struggling winds and howling tempests, and bridling them with bond and prison. They, in their passion, are raving at the closed doors, while the huge rock roars responsive; Aeolus is sitting aloft in his fortress, his sceptre in his hand, soothing their moods and allaying their rage; were he to fail in this, then sea and land, and the deep of heaven, would all be forced along by their blast, and swept through the air. But the almighty father has buried them in caverns dark and deep, with this fear before his eyes, and placed over them giant bulk of his compact, should know how to tighten or slacken the reins at his patron's will. To him it was that Juno then, in these words, made her humble request:

"Aeolus--for it is to thee that the father of gods and king of men has given it with the winds now to calm, now to rouse the billows--there is a race which I hate now sailing the Tyrrhene sea, carrying Ilion into Italy and Ilion's vanquished gods; do thou lash the winds to fury, sink and whelm their ships, or scatter them apart, and strew the ocean with their corpses. Twice seven nymphs are of my train, all of surpassing beauty; of these her whose form is fairest, Deiopea, I will unite to thee in lasting wedlock, and consecrate her thy own, that all her days, for a service so great, she may pass with thee, and make thee father of many children."

Aeolus returns:"Thine, great Queen, is the task to search out what thou mayest fix the hear; for me to do thy bidding is but right. Thou makest this poor realm mine, mine the sceptre and Jove's smile; thou givest me a couch at the banquets of the gods, and makest me lord of the stor-cloud and the tempest."

So soon as this was said, he turned his spear, and pushed the hollow mountain on its side; and the winds, as though in column fourmed, rush forth where they see an outlet, and sweep over the earth in hurricane. Heavily they fall on the sea, and from its very bottom crash down the whole expanse--one and all east and south, and sout-west, with his storms thronging at his back, roll huge billows shore-ward. Hark to the shrieks of the crew, and the creaking of the cables! In an instant, the clouds snatch sky and day-light from the Teucrians' eyes--night lies on the deep, black and heavy--pole thunders pole; heaven flashes thick with fires, and all nature brandishes instand death in the seaman's face. At once Aeneas' limbs are unstrung and chilled--he groans aloud, and, stretching his clasped hands to the stars, fetches from his breast words like these: "O happy, thrice and again, whose lot it was, in their fathers' sight, under Troy's high walls to meet death! O thou, the bravest of the Danaan race, Tydeus' son, why was it not mine to lay me low on Ilion's plains, and yield this fated life to thy right hand? Yes, there it is that

Simois seizes and sweeps down her channel those many shields and helmets, and bodies of the brave!"

Such words as he flung wildly forth, a blast roaring from the north strikes his sail full in front and lifts the billows to the stars. Shattered are the oars; then the prow turns and presents the ship's side to the waves; down crashes in a heap a craggy mountain of water. Look! these are hanging on the surge's crest--to those the yawning deep is giving a glimpse of land down among the billows; surf and sand are raving together. Three ships the south catches, and flings upon hidden rocks--rocks which, as they stand with the waves all about them, the Italians call Altars, an enormous ridge rising above the sea. Three the east drives from the main on to the shallows and Syrtes, a piteous sight, and dashes them on shoals, and embarks them in mounds of sand. On in which the Lycians were sailing, and true Orontes, a mighty sea strikes from high on the stem before Aeneas' very eyes; and down goes the helmsman, washed from his post, and topples on his head, while the ship is turned round by the billow in the spot where she lay, and swallowed at once by the greedy gulf. You might see them here and there swimming in that vast abyss--heroes' arms, and planks and Troy's treasures glimmering through the water. Already Ilioneus' stout ship, already brave Achates', and that in which Abas sailed, and that which carrid old Aletes, are worsted by the storm; their sid-jointings loosened, one and all give entrance to the wattery foe, and part failingly asunder.

Meanwhile, the roaring riot of the ocean and the storm let loose reached the sense of Neptune, and the still disgorged from their deep beds, troubling him grievously; and casting a broad glance over the main he raised at once his tranquil brow from the water's surface. There he sees Aeneas' fleet tossed hither and thither over the whole expanse--the Trojans tossed by the waves, and the crashing ruin of the sky --nor failed the brother to read Juno's craft and hatred there. East and West he calls before him, and Neptune speaks to them thus:

"Are you then so wholly overmasterd by the pride of your birth? Have you come to this, you Winds, that, without sanc-

tion from me, you dare to confound sea and land, and up-
heave these mighty mountains? You! Whom I--but it were
best to calm the billows you have troubled. Henceforth, you
shall pay me for your crimes in different coin. Get out
quick, and give your king Aeolus this massage. Not to him
did I the lot assign to decide the time and place of storms,
but to me. His sway is over those enormous rocks, where you
Eurus, dwell, and such as you; in that court let Aeolus lord
it, and rule in the prison house of the winds when its doors
are barred."

Neptune speaks and ere his words are done soothes the
swelling waters, and rounts the mustered clouds, and brings
back the sun in triumph. Cymothee and Triton combine their
efforts to push off the vessels from the sharp-pointed rock.
The god himself upheaves them with his own trident, and
levels the great quicksands, and allsys the sea, and on
chariot wheels of lightest motion glides along the water's
top. Even as when in a great crowd tumult is oft stirred
up, and the base herd becomes wild and frantic, and brands
and stones are flying already, rage suiting the weapon to
the hand--at that moment, should their eyes fall on some man
of weight, for duty done and public worth, tongues are
hushed and ears fixed in attention, while his words sway
the spirit and soothe the breast--so fell all the thunders
of the oceaan, so soon as the great father, with the waves
before him in prospect, and the clear sky all about him,
buides his steeds at will, and as he flies flings out the
reins freely to his obedient car.

Spent with toil, the family of Aeneas labor to gain the
shore that may be nearest, and are carried to the coasts
of Libya. There is a spot retiring deep into the land,
where an island forms a harbor by the barrier of its sides,
which break every billow from the main and send it shattered
into the deep indented hollows. On either side of the bay
are huge rocks, and two great crags rising in menace to the
sky; under their summits far and wide the water is hushed in
shelter, while a theatric backgroudn of waving woods, a black
forest of stiffening shade, overhangs it from the height
Under the brow that fronts the deep is a cave with hanging
crags; within there are fresh springs and seats in the living
rock--the home of the nymphs; no need of cable here to con-

fine the weary ship or anchor's crooked tooth to grapple
her to shore. Here with seven ships mustered from his
whole fleetAeneas enters; and with intense yearning for dry
land the Trojans disembark and take possession of the wished-
for shore, and lay their sea-soaked limbs umpon the beach.
And first Achates from a flint struck out a spark, and
received the fire as it dropped in a cradle of leaves, and
placed dry food all about it, and spread the strong blaze
among the tinder. Then their corn, soaked and spoiled as
it was, and the corn-goddess; armory they bring out, sick of
fortune; and make ready tp parch the rescued grain at the fire
and crush it with the millstone.

Aeneas meanwhile took his bow and arrows and clambered
up the rocky hillside to look for game. He did not return
until he and his party had seven huge deer. Next he divides
the little wine they rescued from the wreck at sea, and as
his comrades drink, Aeneas addresses them thus:

Comrades! for comrades we are, no strangers to hardships
already; hearts that have felt deeper wounds! for these too
heaven will find a balm. Why, men, you have even looke on
Scylla in her madness, and heard those yells that thrill
the rocks; You have even made trial of the crags of the
Cyclops. Come, call your spirits back, and banish these
doleful fears--who knows but someday this too will be remembered with pleasure? Boar up, and reserve yourselves for
better days."

Such were the words his tongue uttered; heart-sick with
overwholming care, he wears the semblance of hope in his
face, but has grief deep buried in his heart. Tho men cook
the deer meat and with the food they recall their strength.
But Aeneas' sorrow exceeds the rest, and he thinks of his
lost companions--Orontes the bold, Amycus, Lycus, gallant
Gyas and Cloanthus.

And now at last their mourning had an end, when
Jupiter from the height of ether, looking down on the sea
with its fluttering sails, on the flat surface of earth,
the shores, and the broad tribes of men, paused thus upon
heaven's summit, and fixed his downward gaze on Libya's
realms. To him, revolving in his breast such thoughts as
these, sad beyond her usual habit, and with tears on her face,

Venus, mother of Aeneas, speaks to mighty Jupiter:

"O, Jupiter, who by thy everlasting laws swayest the two commonwealths of men and gods, and awest them by thy lightning! What can my poor Aeneas have done to merit thy anger? What can the Trojans have done? and yet they, after the many deaths they have suffered already, still find the whole world barred against them for Italy's sake. From them assuredly it was that the Romans, as years rolled on, from them were to spring those warrior chiefs, yes, from Teucer's blood revived, who should rule sea and land with absolute sway--such was thy promise; how has thy purpose, o my father, made a change in thee? This, I know, was my constant solace when Troy's star set in grievous ruin, as I sat balancing destiny agaist destiny. And now here is the same Fortune, pursuing the brave men she has so oft ruined already. Mighty king, what end of suffering have you to give them? The Trojan ships and men are divided and scattered. Is This the reward of piety? Is this to restore a king to his throne?"

Smiling on her, Jupiter with that face which calms the fitful moods of the sky, touched with a kiss his daughter's lips, then said thus to her: "Give thy fears a rest, Lady of Cythera; thy people's destiny abides still unchanged for thee; thine eyes shall see the city of thy heart, the promised walls of Lavinium; thine arms shall bear aloft to the stars of heaven thy hero Aeneas; nor has my purpose changed in me. Thy hero shall wage a mighty war in Italy, crush its haughty races and tribes, and set up for his warriors a polity and a city, till the third summer shall have seen him king of Latium, the three winters in camp shall have passed. And the boy Ascanius, Aeneas son, shall let thirty years of the sun's great courses fulfil their monthly rounds while he is sovereign, the transfer the empire from Lavinium's seat, and build Alba the long, with power and might. After a while there shall be one, proud to wear the tawny hide of the wolf that nursed him, Romulus, who will take up the sceptre, and build a new city, the city of mars, and give the people his own name of Roman. To them I assign no limit, no date of empire; my grant to them is dominion without end. No, Juno, your savage foe, who now, in her blind terror, lets neither sea, land, nor heaven rest, shall amend her thoughts, and work with me in watching over the Romans, lords of earth, the great nation. So it is willed. The time shall come, as Rome's years roll on, when the house of Assaracus shall bend to its yoke Phthia and renowned Mycenae, and be king over vanquished Argos. Then shall be born the child of an illustrious line, one of thine own Trojans, Caesar, born to extend his empire to the ocean, his glory to the stars,--Julius, in name as in blood the heir of great Iulus, as Ascanius was once known. Him shall you one day welcome in safety to the sky, a warrior laden with Eastern spoils; to him, as to Aeneas, men shall pray and make their vows. In his days war shall cease, and savage times grow mild. Faith with her hoary head, and Vesta, Quirinus, and Remus his brother shall give law to the world; grim, iron bound, closel welded, the gates of war shall be closed; the fiend of Discord prisoner within, seated on a pile of arms deadly as himself, his hands bound behind his back with a hundred brazen chains, shall roar ghastly from his throat of blood.'

So saying Jupiter sends down from on hin Mercury, that Carthage the new may open her lands, her towers and her people to Aeneas and his men, and welcome the Teucrians, lest Dido, in her ignorance of Fate, should drive them from her borders. Mercury flies down to accomplish his purpose, and quickly does.

But Aeneas the good, revolving many things the whole night through, soon as he sees the gracious dawn, resolves to go out and explore this new region; to inquire what shores be these on which the wind has driven him. His ships he hides in a wooded cove, and moves with Achates, his single companion, to wxplore the region. He soon meets with his mother Venus, who appears to him in the disguise of a Carthegenian maiden out hunting in the woods. Aeneas, struck by her beauty, asks if she is some goddess, perhaps Phoebus sister. To him Venus in disguise thus replied:

"No, I can make no claim to such high honors. I am a simple Tyrian maiden, lost from her sisters in the course of the hunt."

Aeneas then to her replied, "Utter strangers are we to this place, driven here by the fury of the storm. Can you tell us where we are, the country and its rulers?"

Said Venus: "This that you now see is the Punic realm, the nation tyrian and the town of Agener; but on the frontiers are the Libyans, a race ill to handle in war. The queen is Dido, who left her home in Tyre to escape from her brother Pygmalion. Lengthy is her tale of wrong, but I will pass rapidly from point to point. Her husband was Sychaeus, wealthiest of Phoenician landowners, and loved by his poor wife with great passion; on him her father had given her in maiden bloom, linking them together by the omens of a first bridal. But the crown of Tyre was on the head of her brother Pygmalion, in crime monstrous beyond the rest of men. They were at odds, and fury came between them. Impious that he was, at the very altar of the palace, the love of gold blinding his eyes, he surprises Sychaeus with his stealthy knife, and lays him low, without a thought for his sister's passion. He kept the deed long hidden and with many a base coinage sustained the mockery of false hope in her pining love-lorn heart. But lo! in her sleep there came to her the dream-form of Sychaeus; he showed her his breast gored with the steel, and unveiled the dark domestic crime. Then he urged her to escape, and revealed a hoard of treasure long hid in the earth, a mass of silver and gold which none knew but she. Dido's soul was stirred; she began to make ready her flight, and friends to share it. There they meet, all whose hate of the tyrant was great or whose fear was bitter; ships that chanced to lie ready in the harbor they seize, and freight with godl. Away it floats over the deep sea, the greedy Pygmalion's wealth; and who heads the enterprise? a woman! So they came to the spot where you now see yonder those lofty walls, and rising citadel of Carthage the new. there they bought ground which got from the transaction the name of Byrse, for they bought as much ground as they could compass round with a string made from the hide of a single bull. But now tell me, who are you, after all? What coast are you come from, or whither are you holding on your journey?

Aeneas then told her his long story of suffering, and the goddess drank in and loved his telling of it, and when he had finished, Venus in disguise said to her son, " Go now, and make your way to the queen's palace, for I give you news that your comrades are there, wafted into shelter by the shifting gales."

Thus she said, and as she turned away, flashed on their
sight her neck's lovely pink color, her ambrosial locks,
and breathed from her bosom a heavenly fragrance; her robe
streamed down to her very feet; and in her walk was revealed
the true goddess. Soon as he knew his mother, he pursued
her flying steps with words like these; "Why will you be
cruel like the rest, mocking your son these many times with
disguises? Why is it not mine to grasp your hand in mine,
and hear and return the true language of the heart?" Such
are his words, while he het bends his way to the town. But
Venus fenced them round with a dim cloud as they moved, and
wrapped them as a goddess only can in a spreading mantle of
fog, that none might be able to see them, none to touch
them, or put hindrances in their path, or ask the reason
of their coming. Venus then took her way to Paphos, glad
again to visit the realm she loved.

Meanwhile Aeneas and Achates have made their way to the
city of Carthage. Aeneas marvels at the mass of building,
once a mere village of huts; marvels at the gates, and
the civic din, and the paved ways. The Tyrians are alive
and on fire--intent, som on carrying the walls aloft and
up heaving the citadeal, and rolling stones from underneath by force of hand; some on making choice of a site
for a house and enclosing it with a trench. They are
ordaining the law and its guardians, and the senate's
sacred majesty. Here are some diggine out havens; there
are others laying deep the foundations of a theatre, and
making from the rocks enormous columns, the lofty ornaments of a stage that is to be. Such are the toils that
keep the commonwealth of bees at work in the sun among
the flowery fields when summer is new, what time the bees
lead out the nations's hope, the young now grown, or mass
together honey, clear and flowing, and strain the cells
to bursting with its nectarous sweets, or relieve those
coming in of their burdens, or collect a troop and expel
from their stalls the drones, that lazy, thriftless herd.
The work is all afire, and a scent of thyme breathes from
the gragrant honey. Aeneas cries, "O happy they, whose
city is rising already," and in he goes, protected by the
mist, miraculously unperceived of all.

619

On the way to the palace, Aeneas sees a sight which stabs
his heart. In a shadey Grove, Dido is having built a lovely
temple for Juno, and now the workmen devote their skills to
putting into marble the sotry of the Trojan war, for the
tory of that war is already widespread. Aeneas examines
each scene in tears and then moves on to the palace.
Hefinds Dido seated on her throne, giving laws and judgments to her citizens, and equalising the burden of their
tasks by fair partition. Suddenly Aeneas sees coming among
the great crowd Antheus and Sergestus, and brave Cloanthus,
and other of his friends, whom the black storm had scattered
over the deep, and carried far away to toehr coasts.
Astounded was he, overwhelmed, too was Achates, all for joy
and fear; eagerly were they burning to join hands with
theirs, but the unexplained mystery confounds their minds.
They carry on the concealment and look out from the hollow
fog that wraps them, to learn what fortune their friends
have had, on what shore they are leaving their fleet, and
what errand they are on here. Aeneas listens as Ilioneus
begs from the Queen the right to repair their ships with
wood from the Carthegenian forests, that they might set to
sea again. Ilioneus asks only the right to have the chance
to die at sea.

Then briefly Dido, with downcast look, makes reply:
"Teucrians! unberden your hearts of fear, lay your anxieties aside. It is the stress of danger and the infancy
of my kingdom that make me put this policy in motion and
protect my frontiers with a guard all about. The men of
Aeneas and the city of Troy--who can be ignorant of them?--
the deeds and the doers, and all the blaze of that mighty
war? Not so blunt are the wits   we Punic folk carry
with us, not so wholly does the sun turn his back on our
Tyrian town when he harnesses his horses. Whether you make
your choice of Hesperia the great, and the old realm of
Saturn, or of the borders of Eryx and their king Acestes,
I will send you on your way with an escort to protect you,
and will supply you with stores. Or would you like to
settle along with me in my kingdom here? Look at the city
I am building, it is yours, lay up your ships, Trojan and
Tyrian shall be dealt with by me as if your had always lived
here. Would to heaven your king were here too, driven by

the gale that drove you hither--Aeneas himself! For myself,
I will send trusty messengers along the coast, with orders
to go over the furtherest part of Libya, in case he should
be shipwrecked and wandering anywhere in forest or town."

Excited by her words, brave Achates and Aeneas too,
were burning long ere this to break out of their cloud.
Achates first says to Aeneas:"Goddess-born, what purpose now
is foremost in your mind? All you see is safe, our fleetand
our friends are restored to us. One is missing, whom our
own eyes saw in the midst of the sea swallowed up, all the
rest is even as your mother told us."

Scarce had he spoken when the cloud that enveloped them
suddenly parts and lcears into the open sky. Out stood
Aeneas, and shone again in the bright sunshine, his face
and his body the image of a god, for his great mother had
shed graceful tresses over her son's brow, and the glowing
flush of youth, and had breathed the breath of beauty and
gladness into his eyes, loveliness such as the artist's
touch imparts to ivory. Then he addresses the queen, and
speaks suddenly to the astonishment of all;"Here am I whom
you aro seeking, here before you,--Aeneas, the Trojan,
snatched from the jaws of the Libyan wave. O heart that
alone of all has found pity for Troy's cruel agonies--
that makes us, poor remnants of Danaan fury, utterly spent
by all the chances of land and sea, destitue of all,
partners of its city, of its very palace! To repay such
a debt of gratitude, Dido, is more than we can do. May
the gods--if there are powers that regard the pious, if
justice and conscious rectitude count for anything on earth--
may you receive from those gods the reward you deserve,
what age had the happiness to bring you forth? What godlike parents gave such nobleness to the world? While the
rivers run into the sea, while the shadows sweep along the
mountain-sides, while the stars draw life from the sky,
your glory and your name and your praise shall still
endure, whatever the land whose call I must obey." So
saying, he stretches out his right hand to his friend
Ilioneus, his left to Serestus, and so on to others, gallant
Gyas and gallant Cloanthus.

Astounded was Dido, Sidon's daughter, first at the hero's

presence, then at his enormous sufferings, and she bespoke
him thus: "What chance is it, goddess-born, that is hunting
you through such a wilderness of perils? What violence
throws you on our savage coast? I, too, have had a fortune
like yours, which, after the buffeting of countless
sufferings, has been pleased that I should find rest in
this land at last. Myself no stranger to sorrow, I am
learning to help the unhappy." With these words, at the
same moment she ushers Aeneas into her queenly palace, and
orders a solemn sacrifice at the temples of the gods.
Meanwhile, as if this were nothing, she sends to his comrades at the shore twenty bulls , a hundred huge swine, a
hundred fat lambs with their mothers, and much wine.

But the palace within is laid out with all the splendour
of regal luxury, and in the center of the mansion they are
making ready for the banquet.

Aeneas, because his fatherly love would not leave his
heart at rest, sends on Achates with speed to the ships to
tell his son Ascanius the news and to contuct him to the
city. On Ascanius all a fond parent's anxieties are
centered. Presents, morevoer, rescued from the ruins of
Troy, he bids Achates bring--a pall stiff with figures of
gold, and a veil with a border of yellow acanthus, adrnments
of Argive Helen, which she carried away from Mycenae, when
she went to Troy and to her unblessed bridal, her mother
Leda'a marvelous gift; the sceptre too, which Ilione had
once borne, the eldest of Prima's daughters, and the string
of pearls for the neck, and the double coronal of jewels
and gold. With this to do, Achates was bending his way to
the ships.

t the lady Venus is casting new schemes. She decides
that Cupid should be made into an exact copy of Ascanius,
who could, as Cupid, by the presents he brings, influence
the queen to madness, and turn the very marrow of her bones
to fire. Venus fears the two-faced generation, the double
tongued sons of Tyre; Juno's hatred scorches her like a
flame, and as night draws on the care comes back to her. So
then with these words she addresses Cupid: "My son, who art
alone my strength and my mighty power, my son who laughest
to scorn our great father's Typhoesn thunderbolts, to thee

622

I fly for aid, and make supplient prayer to they majesty.
How thy brother Aeneas is tossed on the ocean the whole
world over by Juno"s anger I need not tell thee--no, thou
hast often mingled thy grief with mine. He is not the guest
of Dido, and the spell of a courteous tongue is laid on him,
and I fear what may be the end of taking shelter under Juno's
wing; she will never be idle at a time on which so much
hangs. Thus then I am planning to be first in the field,
surprising the queen by trick, and encompassing her with
love's fire, that no power may be able to work a change in
her, but that a mighty passion for Aeneas may keep her on
my side. For the way in which thou mayest bring this about,
listen to what I have been thinking. The young Ascanius, at
his loved father's summons, is making ready to go to Carthage, the bearer of presents that have survived the sea
and the flames of Troy. Him will lull in deep sleep and
hide him. Do thou then for a single night, no more ,
put on the boy's usual look, thyself a boy, that when Dido,
at the height of her joy, shall take thee into her lap
while the princely board is laden and the vine-god's
liquor flowing, when she shall be caressing thee and
printing her fondest kisses on they cheek, thou mayest
breathe concealed into her veins, and steal upon her with
love's firey passion.

At once Cupid obeyed his mother's words, puts off his
wings, and walks rejoicing in the gait of Ascanius. As for
Ascanius, Venus sprinkles his form all over with the dew
of slumber, and carries him , as a goddess may, lapped in
her bosom, into Idalia's lofty groves, where a soft couch
enfolds him with its flowers, and the fragrant breath of
its sweet shade.

All the guests marvel at the gifts of Aeneas to Dido.
But chiefly Dido cannot satisfy herself with gazing, and
kindles as she looks, charmed with the boy and the presents alike. After he has long hung in his father's arms,
Capid as Ascanius finds his way to the queen. She is
riveted by him--riveted, eye and heart, and ever and anon
fondles him in her lap--poor Dido, unconscious how great a
god is sitting heavy on her bosom. But Cupid is beginning
to erase the name of Sychaeus letter by letter, and en-
deavoring to surprize by a living passion affections long

623

asleep, and a heart long unused to love.

When the banquet's first lull was come, and the board removed, then they set up the huge bowls and wresthe the wine. The the queen called for a cup, heavy with jewels and gold, and filled it with unmixed wine and said, "Jupiter, for thou hast the name of lawgiver for guest and host, grant that this day may be happy alike for the Tyrians and the voyagers from Troy, and that its memory may long live among our children. Be with us, Bacchus, the giver of jollity, and Juno, the queen of our blessings; and you, the lords of Tyre, may your goodwill grace this meeting." She said thus, and poured on the table an offering of the wine, and, the libation made, touched the cup first with her lips, then handed it to Bitias, rallying his slowness. Then the other lords drank in order. With varied talk, Dido kept lengthening out the night, unhappy Dido, drinking deep of love long and deep, as she asked about Priam, about Hector, and the events at Troy. Finally, she said, "Tell us, gentle guest, the story from the very first--all about the stratagems of the Danaans, and the sad fate of your country, and your own wanderings--for this is now the seventh summer that is wafting you a wanderer still over every land and wave."

BOOK II

Every tongue was hushed, and every eye fixed intently when from his high couch Aeneas began thus:

"Too cruel to be told, great queen, is the sorrow you bid me tell about--how the ;ower of Troy and its empire met with horrid overthrow from the Danaans--the heartrending sights which my own eyes saw, and the scenes where I had a large part to play. Who, in such telling would refrain from tears? But I will try to tell the story.

Broken by war and foiled by destiny, the chiefs of the Danaans, now that the flying years were numbering many, Build a horse of mountain size, by the inspiration of Minerva's skill, and interlace its ribs with planks of fir. A vow for their safe journey home is the pretest; such the fame the spreads. In this they secretly enclose chosen men sinew, picked out by lot, in the depth of its sides, and fill every conrner of those mighty caverns, the belly of the

the monster, with armed warriors.

"In sight of Troy lies Tenedos, and island powerful and rich while Priam's empire was prospering but which was now a mere bay, a treacherous harbor for ships. Thus far the Greeks sail out, and hide themselves on the forsaken coast. We thought them gone off with a fair wind for Mycenae. And so all Trojan land shakes off the agony of years/ Open fly the gates; what pleasure to go and see the Dorian camp, and the places deserted and the shore forsaken. Yes here were the troops of the Dolopes, and here the tent of that savage Achilles. Some of us are standing gazing at the fatal offering to the virgin goddess, and wondering at the hugeness of the wooden horse; and Thumoetes takes the lead, urging to havo it dragged within the walls, and lodged in the citadel, either with treasonable intent, or that the fate of Troy had begun to set that way. But Capys, and the men of saner judgment, suggts that se send this gift of the Greeks headlong into the sea, or light a fire under it and burn it; or if not that, to pierce and probe that hollow womb that might hide so much. The populace, unstable as over, cannot decide.

"Throwing himself before all, with a great crowd at his back, Laocoon, all on fire, comes running down the steep of the citadel, crying in the distance, "What strange madness is this, my unhappy countrymen? Think you that the enemy has sailed oof, or that a Greek could ever make a presont that had no treachery in it? Is this your knowledge of Ulysses? Either the Achaeans are shut up and hiding in this piece of wood, or it is an engine fromed against our walls to command the houses and come down on the city from above, or there is some other secret trick. Men of Troy, put no faith in the horse. Whatever it be, I fear a Greek, especially with a gift in his hand." With these words he hurled a mighty spear with all his force against the beast's side, the jointed arch of its belly. It lodged, and stood quivering; the womb shook again, and an echo and a groan rang hollow from its caverns; and then, had but heaven's destiny and man's judgment been warped, he had led us to carry sword and havoc into the Greek lurking-place within the horse; then Troy would still be standing, and Priam's tall towers still in being.

"But there were two reasons why we did not do the pru-

625

dent thing. First, some shepherds are draggin with loud
shouts a young man before the king. This young man was
said to have tried to betray us by sneakily letting the
Greeks into Troy. We questioned the traitor, and he told
us his story (or at least what he said was his story).
He told us that his father had been forced to send him as a
soldier to the wars at a young age. He told us of falling
out with Ulysses, and of having been marked as a sacrifice
for the gods, and of escaping on the day when he was to be
sacrificed. and of living since then in the Trojan hills.
He appealed to us for mercy, and asked to become a citizen
of our city. Priam took pity on the young man, and then
questioned him about the meaning of the mountainous horse.
The young man replied with infinite guile the young
traitor, whose name was Sinon, thus replied to Priam

"'Calchas told the Greeks that unless they returned to
Mycenae for fresh omens, they would never conquer Troy.
Therefore they have returned to Argos for new supplies and
new consultation with the omens. As for this Image, he
warned them to set it up in exchange for the Palladium,
the shrine which Ulysses so horribly desecrated. In ex-
piation of injured deity, to atone for the fatal crime,
Calchas told them to raise it to the vast height you see,
knitting plank to plank, till it was brought near to
heaven, that it might not be admitted at the gates or
dragged within the walls, and thus restore to the people
the bulwark of thier old worship. For if your hand should
profane Minerva"s offering, then Calchas told them, a
mighty destruction would come to the empire of Priam and
the Phrygian nation. But if these hands of yours should
help it to scale your city's height, Asia would roll the
mighty tide of invasion on the walls of Pelops, and the
Greeks would see no more of prosperity.'
    "Thus lied the deceitful Sinon; and while we pondered his
words, the second horrible and misleading event took place.
Laocoon, drawn by lot as Neptune's priest, was sacrificing
a mighty bull at the usual altar--when behold from Tenedos,
over the still deep--I shudder as I recount the tale--two
serpents coiled in vast circles are seen breasting the sea,
and moving side by side towards the shore. Their breasts
rise erect among the waves; their manes, of bloo-red color,
tower over the water, the rest of them floats behind on the

626

sea, trailing a huge curling length; the sea boams and
dashes about them; they are already on shore, in the plain,
with their glowing eyes blooshot and fiery, and their forked
tongues playing in their hissing mouths. We fly all ways in
pale terror; they, in an answering line, make for Laocoon,
and first each serpent folds round one of his two sons,
clasping the youthful body, and greedily devouring the poor
limbs. Afterwards, as the father comes to the rescue,
weapon in hand, they fasten on him and lash their enormous
bodies tight round him--and now twice folded round
his middle, twide embracing his neck and his body. He is
straining with agonizing clutch to pull the knots asunder,
his priestly hair wet with gore and black poison, and all
the while crying dreadfully to heaven. Then the two serpents
glide to the temple top, making for the height where
Tritonia Neptune is enthroned, and there shelter themselves
under the feet of the idol. Then every breast among the
Trojans is cowed and thrilled through by a new terror--
every voice cries that Laocoon has been duly punished for
his crime, profaning the sacred horse with his weapon's
point and hurling his guilty lance against the back of the
horse. Everyone cries, "Let the image be drawn to her
temple, and let prayer be made to the goddess"--we break
through the walls and open the town within. All of us
work, putting wheels to run easily under its feet, and
throwing lengths of rope round its neck. It scales the walls,
that fateful engine, with its armed brood. Oh my country!
O Troy, how sad! Four times on the gateway's very thre-
hold it stopped, and four times the arms rattled in its
womb. On, however, we press, unheeding in the blindness
of our frenzy, and lodge the ill-starred portent in our
hallowed city. Even then Cassandra unseals to speak of
future fate those lips which by the god's command no Trojan
ever believed--while we, alas! we spend the day that was to
be our last in crowning the temples of the gods with festal
leaves the whole city through.

"When night comes on, all the Trojans repose their joy-
filled limbs in peaceful repose. The sneaky Greeks sail
back toward Troy, and Ulysses and his men slither down a
rope from the belly of the horse and open the gates to their
companions. The Greeks rush on the town as it lies drowned
in sleep and revelry. The watchers are put to the sword,

and a general carnage follows.

"Lo! as I slept, before my eyes, I see the ghost of Hector, in deepest sorrow, and he seemed to be standing by me, shedding rivers of tears--mangled from dragging at the car, as I remember him of old, and black with bloody dust, and with swollen feet gashed by the thong. Ay me! The ghost cries, 'Fly, goddess-born! and escape these flames--the walls are in the enemy's jamd--Troy is tumbling from the summit--the claims of country and king upon you are now satisfied--if Troy could be defended by force of hand,it would have been defended by mine. Your country's worship and her gods are what whe gives to you now--take them to share your destiny--seek for them a mighty city, which you shall one day build when you have wandered the ocean over.' With these words he brings to my mind a picture of the sacred altar.

But then I hear the sounds of shouting and the braying of trumpets. To arms I rush, ignoring the words of the ghost of Hector, and think only to muster a troop for fight, and I run to the citadel with my comrades , burning with madness and rage, and I think how glorious it is to die with arms in my hand!

"In the streets I am joined by many valiant companions, and we fight the Greeks with all our might. Our fighting takes us even to Priam's palace, where, helpless against the overwhelming numbers of the Greeks, I am powerless to prevent the murder of Priam by Pyrrhus. The old man winessed the death of the last of his sons,Polites, and then ho put on his sword like a young warrior and forces Pyrrhus to kill him. Hecuba is in a sea of the blood of her son and husband.

"Now, for the first time grim horror prisoned me round-- I was insane--there rose up the image of my dear father, as I saw the death of the aged king and his ghastly wounds. I saw my wife Creusa, unprotected, guarding my little son.

"But before I could leave, I saw the guilty Hele, the source of all our woes. The thought of her returning to lead a long and happy life in Argos drove me insane. I said to myself, 'Although there are no proud memories to be won by vengeance on a woman, no laurels to be reaped from a conquest like this, yet the extinction of so base a life and the exaction of vengeance so needed will count as a praise,

and it will be a joy to have glutted my spirit with the
flame of revenge and watered the thirsty ashes of those I
love." Such were the wild thought I was thinking , when
suddenly there appeared to me, brighter than I have ever
seen her before, and shone forth in clear radiance through
the night, my gracious mother, all her deity confessed, with
the same beauty and stature by which she is known to the
dwellers in heaven. My mother said to me, 'My son, what
mighty agony is it that stirs up this untamed passion? What
means your frenzy? or whither has fled your care of me?
Will you not first see where you have left your father
Anchises, spent with age as he is? Whether your wife Creusa
be yet alive? and your child Ascanius? All about them the
Greek army is raging to and fro, and were not my care exerted to rescue them, ere this they had been snatched by the
flame, devoured by the foeman's sword. It is not the hated
beauty of Helen, and not the Hated Paris which has brought
this about. No it is heaven, unpitying heaven that is over-
turning this great empire of Troy. Come, my son, escape
while you can, and bring the struggle to an end. I will not
leave you, till I have set you in safety at your father's
door.' She ceased, and veiled herself at once in night's
shadows.

"Then, indeed, I beheld all Troy sinking into flame, and
Neptune's city overthrown totally. I come down , and,
following my heavenly guide, thread my way through flames
and foemen, while weapons glance aside and flames retire.

"Now when at last I had reached the door of my father's
house, that old house I knew so well, my father, whom it was
my first resolve to carry away high up to the hills--
who was the first object I sought--refuses to survive the
burning of Troy and submit to banishment. Anchises says,
'You, whose young blood is untinted, whose strength is
firmly based, it is for you to think of flight. For me,
had the gods in heaven wanted me to prolong my life, they
would have preserved for me a home. It is enough and more
than enough to have witnessed one home destroyed. Here, O
here as I lie, bid farewell to my corpse and begone. I
will find me a warrior's death. Long, long have I been a
clog on time, hated of heaven and useless to earth, and I

am ready for my death.'

"such words Anchises kept repeating and continued un-
shaken, while we were shedding our hearts in tears--
Creusa, my wife, and Ascanius and my whole house, imploring
my father not to be bent on draggin all with him to ruin.
I think to return to the battle and find for myself an
early grave, but Creusa sees my thoughts, and says, 'If
it is to death you are going, then carry us with you to
death; to whom, do you think, you are leaving your little
son--your father and me, who was once called your wife.'

My father then raised his eyes to heaven, and said,
'Almighty Jove! if any prayer can cnage thy will, look down
on us and send us an omen to guide us.' No sooner had he
spoken when there came a sudden peal of thunder on the left,
and a star fell from heaven and swept through the gloom
with a torchlike train and blaze of light. Then my father
said, 'Yours is this sign--Yes, my son, I give way, and
shrink not from your flight.'

"Instantly I take my father upon my back and my son by
the hand and we set out, my wife comes on behind. On we
go, keeping in the shade--and I, who for a moment never
worried about spears and arrows that rained upon me or at
the masses of Greeks that barred my path, am now scared by
every breath of air, startled by every sound, upset as I
am, and fearing alike for him who holds my and and him I
carry. And now I am nearing the gates, and the whole
journey seems accomplished, when suddenly the noise of
heavy feet came to my ear, and my father looks onward
through the darkness. He cries, 'Son, Son, fly; they are
upon us. I distinguish the flashing of their shields
and the gleam of their steel.' in this alarm some un-
friendly power perplexed me and took away my judgment.
For, while I was tracking places where no track was, and
swerving from the line of road, woe is me! destiny tore
from me my wife Creusa. Whether she stopped, or strayed
from the road, or sat down tired, I never knew--nor was she
ever restored to my eyes in life. When I discovered my
loss, I take my father and son to a place of safety, and
turning them over to my comrades, I go again to the city .
My mind is to retrace my steps and to rescue my wife. I

filled the streets with shouts, and in my agony called again and again on my Dreusa. As I was thus making my search and raving, the ghost, the spectre of my own Creusa appeared in my presence--a likeness larger than life. I was aghast, my hair stood erect, my tongue stuck to my mouth, while she began thus to address me:'Why this strange pleasure in indulging frantic grief, my darling husband? It is not without heaven's will that these things are ha;pening; that you should carry your Creusa with you on your journey is forbidden by fate, borbidden by the mighty ruler of heaven above. You have long years of exile, a vast expanse of ocean to go over--and then you will arrive at the land of Hesperia, where Tiber, Lyda's river, rolls his gentle waters through rich and cultured plains. There you have a smiling future, a kingdom and a royal bride waiting your coming. Dry your tears for me, your heart's choice though I am. I am not to see the face of the victorious Greeks, I am not to be a servant in their haughty homes, and am not to be in the service of some Greek matron--in that I am lucky. No, I am kept in this country by heaven's mighty mother. And now farewell, and continue to love your son and mine.' Thus having spoken, in spite of my tears, in spite of the thousand things I longed to say, she left me and vanished into the air. Three times, as I stood, I tried to fling my arms around her neck. Three times the phantom escaped the hands that caught at it in vain.

"So passed the night, and such was my return to my comrades. Arrived there, I find with wonder their band swelled by a vast multitude of new companions, matrons and warriors both, an army mustered for exile, a crowd of the defeated. From every side they were met, prepared in heart as in fortune to follow me over the sea to any land where I might take them to settle. And now the morning star was rosong pver Ida's loftiest ridge with the day in its train. Greek sentinels were blocking up the entry of the gates, and no hope of help appeared. I retired at last, took up my father and made for the mountains.

BOOK THREE

BOOK THREE

(Vergildevotes all of Book Three to Aeneas' re-telling of
his advaentures after leaving Troy. these advantures are
rather fantastic in nature, and sound very much like the adventures of Odysseus in Homer's Odyssey. At the end of Book
Three, Aeneas loses his father Anchises to death. Soon after
he meets the storm which brought him to Carthage.)

Book Four

Aeneas ended his story. But the queen,pierced long since
by love's cruel shaft, is feeding the wound with her life-
blood, and wasting under a hidden fire. Many times the
hero's own worth comes back to her mind, many times the glory
of his race; his every look remains imprinted on her breast,
and his every word, nor will trouble let soothing sleep rest
her mind.

At dawn Dido seeks out her sister Anna, and says to her,
"Who is this guest that has entered out door! What a face
and carriage! Had I not sworn after the death of Sychaes
never to consent to join myself with any in wedlock's bands,
I might have stooped to this one reproach. Anna, since the
death of my husband, Aeneas and he alone has touched my heart
and shaken my sesolution. I recognise the traces of the old
flame. But first I would pray that earth may yawn for me
from her foundations before I violate my woman's honor, or
unknit the bonds I have tied. He who first wedded me has
carried off my heart--let him keep it all his own, and keep
it in his grave."

Anna replies: "Sweet love, dearer than the light to your
sister's eye, are you to pine and grieve in loneliness
through life's long spring, nor know anything of a mother's
joy in her children, nor the prizes Venus gives? Think you
of that before you swear. Do you think that dead ashes and
ghosts low in the grave take this to heart? No husband has
here touched your heart, and you have rejected Iarbas and
the other chieftains of Afric Remember, you are threatened
by many dangers, on all sides by jealous Numidians, to say
nothing of the threats from Tyre and Pygmalion. It is under
he blessings of Juno that the vessels of Troy have made this
voyage hither. What a city, my sister, will ours become
before your eyes! What an empire will grow out of a

marriage like this! With the arms of the Trojans at its back, to what a height will the glory of Carthage soar!"

By these words Anna added fresh fuel to the fire of love, gave confidence to the wavering mind, and loosed the ties of woman's honor. Dido struggled fiercely against her desire, but alas! what can vows, what can temples do for the madness of love? All the while a flame is preying on the very marrow of her bones, and deep in her breast a wound keeps noiselessly alive. She is on fire, the ill-fated Dido, and in her madness, she ranges the whole city through, like a doe from an arrow-shot whom, unguarded in the thick of the Dretan woods, a shepherd, chasing her with his darts, has pierced from a distance, and left the flying steel in the wound, unknowing his prize; she at full speed runs through the forest, the deadly reed still stuck in her side. So was Dido. Now she leads Aeneas with her through the heart of the town, and displays the wealth of her city. She begins to speak, and stops midway in the utterance. Now, as the day fades, she seeks again the banquet of yestercay, and once more in frenzy asks to hear of the agonies of Troy, and hangs once more on the lips of the teller of the tale. Afterwards, when the guests are gone, and the dim moon in turn is hiding her light, and the setting stars invite to slumber, alone she mourns in the empty hall, and presses the couch he has just left; him far away she sees and hears, herself far away; or in memory she holds Ascanius in her lap, spellbound by his father's image.

When the goddesses Venus and Juno see the results of their scheme, they are very pleased. To Venus Juno says: "Dido is ablaze with love, and the madness of love is coursing through her frame. Jointly let us then rule this nation, each with full sovereignty. Let her stoop to be the slave of a Trojan husband, and make over her Tyrians in place of dowry to your control."

To Juno Venus thus replied:"Who would be so mad as to spurn offers like these, and prefer your hatred to your friendship, were it but certain that the issue that you name would bring good fortune in its train? The only question is this: can we persuade Jupiter, your husband, to allow this change in destiny. You are his wife--it is your place to approach him about this arrangement."

Said imperial Juno:"That task shall rest with me. Now here is what I propose at present. Tomorrow Dido, Aeneas and the nobility of the Trojans and the Carthegenians will go hunting. I will arrange that a black storm will force Dido and Aeneas into the same cave for shelter. I leave it to you to be sure that they are united in lasting wedlock. Do you agree to this plan?"

Venus makes no objection, but nods assent.

The next day, after Aurora has risen and left the ocean, the Trojans and the Tyrians join to hunt, each in his finest array, and on beauteous horses. The queen is conspicuous in purple and gold. Young Ascanius is filled with joy over his powerful horse. They take to the fields.

Lightnings blaze, and heaven flashes in sympathy with the thunder. That day was the birthday of death, the birthday of woe. From that time on, Dido has no thought for the common eye or the common tongue; it is not a stolen passion that Dido now in her mind--no, she call it marriage; that name is the screen of her sins.

Instantly Fame takes her journey through Libya's great cities,--Fame, a monster surpassed in speed by none; Fame's speed gains strength as she goes.

As the news of Dido and Aeneas spreads, many of the chief of Africa, whom Dido has rejected as suitors, are offended, most especially Iarbas. Iarbas prayed thus: "Jove, the Almighty, to wom during my kingship the Moorish race has given many sacrifices, do you see this? This woman, to whom we made over a strip of land for tillage, she has re jected an alliance with us, and received Aeneas into her kingdom, to be its lor and hers. Now he is enjoying his prize, while we who make offerings to you suffer."

Thus he prayed, and Jupiter heard him. Jupiter calls his messenger Mercury to him and says to him: "Go, haste, summon the Zephyrs, and float on your wings; tell Aeneas, who is now dallying in Tyrian Carthage, and giving no thought to the city which Destiny makes his own. Carry him my commands through the flying air. Tell him he is to govern Italy, with its brood of unborn empires, and the line of his blood

shall force the whole world to bow to the laws he makes. If
he is fird by no spark of ambition for greatness like this,
and will not rear a monument to his own praise, tell him he
should do it for the sake of Ascanius. Tell him to get to
the sea. This is our sentence; be the proper messenger of it."

Thus spoke Jupiter, and Mercury was off to deliver the
message. Soon his winged feet alight among the huts of
Carthage, and he sees Aeneas founding towers anf making
houses new. A sword was at his side, starred with yellow
jespers, and a mantle drooped from his shoulders, ablaze
with Tyrian purple--a costly gift which Dido made, varying
the web with threads of gold. Instantly Mercury assails
him--"And are you at a time like this laying the foundations
of stately Carthage, and building, like a fond husband, your
wife's goodly city, forgotting your own kingdom and the cares
that should be yours? It is no less than the ruler of the
gods who sends me down to you from bright Olympus--he whose
nod sways through the are. What are you building? Why are
you squandering your leisure here in Libyan land?"

The sight left Aeneas dumb and aghast indeed; his hair
stood shudderingly erect. He instantly burns to take flight
and leave the land of pleasure, as his ears righ with the
thunder of heaven's stern warning. What to do? How can he
speak to the impassioned queen? As he thinks, he sends
Sergestus and many others to prepare his ships for leaving,
and to quietly muster the crews on the shores, hiding the
reason for so sudden a change. Meantime, he, while Dido,
kindest of friends, is in ignorance, deeming love's chain too
strong to be snapped, goes about her business in bliss.

But the queen, scented the plot (who can cheat a lover's
senses?), and caught the first sound of the coming stir,
alive to fear in the midst of safety. Fame, as before, the
same hideous fiend, whispered in her angry ear that the
fleet was being equipped and the voyage got ready. She storms
in impotence of sould, and all on fire, goes raving through
the city. At last finding Aeneas she spoke to him before he
had a chance to speak to her: "To hide, yes, hide your enormous crimes, lying scoundrel, did you holpe that might be
done? To steal away in silence from my realm was your sneaky
plan. Has our love no power to keep you? has our wedding

vow no meaning for you? No, you are fitting out your fleet
with winter's sky overhead, and hastening to cross the ocean
in the dead of winter. Flying from me! By the tears I shed
and by your plighted hand, since my own act, alas! has
left me nothing else to beg--by our union--by the nuptial
rites thus performed--if I have ever deserved well of you, or
anything of mine ever gave you pleasure--have pity on a
falling house, and strip off, I beg you, if prayer be not
too late, the mind that clothes you. It is owing to you that
the Libyan tribes and the Nomad chiefs hate me, that my
own Tyrians are strangers to me; owing to you, yes, you,
that my woman's honor has been put out, and that which was
my one passport to immortality, my former reputation, is
lost. To whom are you abandoning a dying woman, my guest?
I call you 'guest' because the name of husband has dwindled
to that. Why do I live any longer?--since now my brother
Pygmalion will now batter down my walls, or Iarbas the Moor
carry me away a captive? Had I but given birth to any
offspring of you before your flight, were there some tiny
Aeneas to play in my hall, and remind me of you, though but
in looks, I should not feel utterly forlorn."

   She finally ceased. He all the while, at Jove's command,
was keeping his eyes unmoved, and shutting up in his heart
his great love. At length he answers thus--"Fair queen,
name all the claims to gratitude you can. I shall never
say you are not entitled to them all, nor will I ever regret any of my memories of Carthage while the flame of life
burns within me. A few words I will say, as the case ad-
mits. I never counted--do not dream it--on stealthily concealing my flight. I never came to you with a bridegroom's
torch in my hand, nor did I ever agree to any for of
marriage. For me, were the Fates to allow me to live anywhere I would like, I would have continued to live at Troy.
But now to Italy I am ordered by Apollo. There is my heart,
my fatherland. If your are riveted here by the sight of
your stately Carthage, a daughter of Phoenicia by a Libyan
town, why I would ask, should jealousy forbid the Trojans to
settle in Italy? We, like you, have the right of looking
for a foreign realm. I do my son Ascanius an injustice
every day that I do not secure for him his kingdom in Italy.
Now, this very day, the messenger of the gods, sent down
from Jupiter himself (I swear by both our lives) has brought

---

me orders through the air. With my own eyes I saw the god
Mercury in broad daylight, and I took in his words with the
ears that hear you now. STop then these reproaches, for
they only make us both feel worse. It is god's will, not
my own, that forces me to go to Italy."

Long ere he had done this speech she was glaring at him,
rolling her eyes this way and that, and scanning the whole
man with her silent glances, and thus she burts forth, all
ablaze--"Go goddess was your mother, lying scoundrel--no,
your parent was was the Caucasus mountains, rugged and
craggy, and a Hyrcanian tigress put her breast to your lips.
A shipwrecked beggar, I welcomed you, and insanely gave
him a share of my realm; Now you say a god forces you to go
away. How mad I have been to trust you. I will not hold
you by force nor bother to argue with your reasons. Go,
chase to Italy with the winds at your back; look for realms
with the whole sea between you and me. I hope you will
wreck on the rocks between here and there, and get what you
deserve for your behavior. I will follow you as a ghost
and haunt you, and when you suffer as you shall, I will hear
the story down among the dead."

She ceased, and her maidens support her, and carry her
sinking frame into the marble chamber, and lay her on her
bed.

But pious Aeneas, though yearning to solace and soothe
her suffering spirit, and by his words to check the onset
of sorrow, with many a groan, his whole soul overturned by
the force of love, goes nevertheless about the commands of
heaven, and repairs to his fleet. The Trojans increase their
efforts, and along the shore crag their tall ships to the
sea. You may see them all in motion, streaming from every
part of the city. Even as aunts when they are sacking a
huge heap of wheat, provident of winter days, and laying up
the stores; a black column is seen moving through the plain.
They convey their loot along the grass in a narrow path; some
are putting their shoulders to the big grains, and pushing
them along; others are rallying the force and punishing the
stragglers; the whole track is in a glow of work. What were
your feelings, Dodo, at the sight of the Trojans working like
ants to launch their ships? Tyrant love! What force does
love impose on human hearts! She goes back and forth between

637

weeping and begging. First Dido asks Anna her sister to
go to Aeneas and beg him to come back for just a little
while. But Aeneas is firm in his resolve, and sets sail.
When she realizes that Aeneas is finally and truly gone,
Dido makes a pyre of the garments worn by Aeneas, and picks
up the sword made a gift. Then, after looking at the
Trojan garments and the bed, too well known, and pausing
awhile to weep and think, she pressed her bosom to the bed
and uttered her last words_"Relics, once carlings of mine,
while Fate and heaven gave leave, receive thismy soul, and
release me from these my sorrows. I have lived my life--the
course assigned me by fortuen is run, and now the stately
phatom of Dido shall pass underground. I have built a
lovely city. I have seen my walls completed. In vengeance
for a husband, I have punished a brother that hated me--
blessed, ah, blessed beyond human bliss, if only Trojan ship
had never touched coast of ours!" She spoke--and kissing
the bed--"this, this is the road by which I love to pass
to the shades. Is it to be death without revenge? Oh, let
the heartless Trojan suffer for the wrongs he has done me."

She spoke, and even while she was yet speaking, her
attendants see her fallen on the sword, the blade spouting
blook, and her hands dabbled in it. The shrieks of the
attendants rise to the lofty roof. Fame runs wild through
the convulsed city. With wailing and groaning, and screams
ow women the palace rings; the sky resounds with mighty
cries and beating of breasts.

Her sister heard it. Breathless and frantic, with wild
speed disfiguring her cheeks with her nails, her bosom with
her fists, she bursts through the attendants, and calls by
name on the dying queen. Anna says, "Did you not want your
sister's company in death? You should have called me to
share your fate. The same keen sword pain, and the same
hour, should have been the end of both. Yes, sister, you
have destroyed yourself and me, the people and the elders
of Carthage and your own fair city. Let in the water to
the wounds. Let me cleanse them, and if any remains of
breath be still flickering, catch them in my mouth."

As she spoke, she was at the top of the lofty steps, and
was embracing and fondling in her bosom her dying sister,

ᴸ

and staunching with her robe the black streams of blood,
Dido strives to raise her heavy eyes, and sinks down again,
the deep stab gurgles in her breast. Three times, with an
effort, she lifted and reared herself up on her elbow.
Three times she fell back on the couch, and with helpless
wandering eyes aloft in the sky, sought for the light and
groaned when she found it.

Then Juno almighty, in compassion for her lengthened
agony and her trouble in dying, sent down Iris from Olympus
to part the struggling soul and its prison of flesh. For,
as she was dying, not in the course of fate, nor for any
crime of hers, but in mere misery, before her time, the
victim of sudden frenzy and madness, no yet had Proserpine
carried off a lock of her yellow hair, and thus doomed her
head to Styx and the place of death. So then Iris glides
down the sky with saffron wings , trailing a thousand
various colors of her rainbow, and alights above her head.
"This I am ordered to bear away as an offering to Pluto,
and hereby set you free from the body." So saying, she
stretches her hand and cuts the lock of hair. At once all
heat parts from the frame, and the life passes into the
air.

BOOK FIVE

(In Book Five through Book Twelve, Virgil follows
Aeneas through many adventures. With the help of the Sibyl
at Cumae and armed with a magical Golden Bough reserved for
great heroes, Aeneas visits the realm of the dead (this is
clearly an imitation of Homer and the Odyssey). In the
place of the dead, Aeneas talks to his father and gets a
detailed picture of the future of the empire Aeneas is to
found in Rome. He speaks to Dido's ghost, but she scorns
him. When he arrives in Italy, he becomes engaged to the
daughter of the local resident kind, Latinus, a girl named
Lavinia. But Lavinia had previously been engaged to a local
leader, Turnus. The gods give many signs that Lavinia
should not marry Turnus, but he persists in causing trouble,
and a long war breaks out between the resident population
of Italy and the allies of the Trojans. Among these allies
is Evander and his son Pallas. Pallas becomes a very close
friend to Aeneas, but is killed by Turnus on his first day
in battle. Turnus is aided by his sister, a nymph named
Juturna, and Aeneas is aided by his mother Venus. After

many, many complications, Turnus and Aeneas meet in single combat, a fight that recalls the single combats between Paris and Menelaus and between Achilles and Hector. Turnus shows himself to be a very brave warrior. Virgil closes the poem with this scene.)

Aeneas presses on, front to front, shaking his massy, tree-like spear, and thus speaks in the fierceness of his spirit: "What is to be the next delay? Why does Turnus still hand back? Ours is not contest of speed, but of stern soldiership, hand to hand. Take all disguises you can: muster all your powers of courage or of skill; mount on wing, if you want to, or to the stars above, or hide in the cavernous depth of earth."

Shaking his head, Turnus replies:"I am not afraid of your fiery words, insulting enemy. It is heaven that makes me afraid, and Jove is my enemy." No more he spoke, but sweeping his eyes round, espies a huge stone, a stone ancient and huge, which chanced to be lying on the plain, set as some field's boundary, to settle disputes of ownership. Scarce could twelve picked me lift it on their shoulders, such puny frames as earth now produces in these times we now live in. Turnus caught it up with hurried grasp and flung it at this foe, rising as he threw, and running rapidly, as a hero might. And yet all the while he knows not that he is running or moving, lifting up or stirring the enormous stone; his knees totter under him, and his blood chills and freezes; and so the mass from the warrior's hand, whirled throu the empty void, passed not through through all the space between the two fighters, nor carried home the blow. Even as in dreams, at night, when slumber has weighed down the eyes, we seem vainly wishing to make eager progress forward and midway in the effort fail helplessly; our tongue has no power, our usual strength stands not our frames in use, nor do words or utterances come to our call; so it is with Turnus;whatever means his valor tries, the fiend of tiredness makes him unable to do what he wants. And now confused images whirl through his brain; he looks to his friends and to his city, and falters with dread, and shrinks before the threatening spear; how to escape he knows not, nor how to

640

confront his enemy, nor see he anywhere his car or the sister who drives it.

Full in that shrinking face Aeneas shakes his fatal weapon, taking aim with his eye, and with an effort of his whole frame hurls it forth. Never stone flung from engine of siege roars so loud, never peal so rending follows the thunderbolt. On flies the spear like dark whirlwind with horrid destruction on its wing, pierces the edge of the corselet, and the outermost circle of the seven fold shield, and with a rush cuts through to the thigh. Down with he knee doubled under him comes Turnus to earth, all his length prostrated by the blow. Up jump Rutulian friends of Turnus, groaning as one man; the whole mountain around resounds, and the depths of the forest send back the sound far and wide. He in lowly supplicance lifts up eye and entreating hand: "it is my due," he says, "And I ask not to be spared it; take what fortune gives you. Yet, if you can feel for a parent's misery--your father, Anchises, was once in like situation--have mercy on my father's white hair, and let me, or if you choose my breathless body, be restored to my kin. You are conqueror; My Friends have seen my conquered hands outstretched; the royal bride is yours, the fair Lavinia. Let hatred by pressed no further."

Aeneas stood still, a fiery warrior, his eyes rolling, and checked his hand; and those prayerful words were working more and more on his faltering purpose, when-- alas! the ill-starred belt that was seen high on the shoulder, and light flashed from the well-known studs-- it was the belt of young Pallas, whom Turnus conquered and struck down to earth, and bore on his breast the badge of triumphant enmity. Soon as his eyes caught the spoil and drank in the recollection of that cruel grief, kindled into madness and terrible in anger: "What, with my friend's trophies upon you, you would escape my hand? It is Pallas, Pallas, who with this blow makes you his victim." With these words, Aeneas plunged the steel into the breast before him, and Turnus' soul flies groaningly to the shades.

THE END

The third day had now arrived, the date appointed
for the free banquet at Trimalchio's; but with so many
wounds as we had, we deemed it better policy to fly
than to remain where we were. So we made the best
of our way to our inn, and our hurts being only skin-
deep after all, we lay in bed and dressed them with
wine and oil.

Still one of the rascals was lying on the ground
disabled, and we were afraid we might yet be discovered.
Whilst we were still debating sadly with ourselves how
we might best escape the storm, a slave of Agamemnon's
broke into our trembling conclave, crying, "What! don't
you recollect whose entertainment it is this day?—
Trimalchio's, a most elegant personage; he has a time-
piece in his dining-room and a trumpeter specially
provided for the purpose keeps him constantly informed
how much of his lifetime is gone." So, forgetting all
our troubles, we proceed to make a careful toilette,
and bid Giton, who had always hitherto been very ready
to act as servant, to attend us at the bath.

Meantime in our gala dresses, we began to stroll
about, or rather to amuse ourselves by approaching
the different groups of ballplayers. Amongst these
we all of a sudden catch sight of a baldheaded old
man in a russet tunic, playing ball amid a troupe of
long-haired boys. It was not however so much the
boys, though these were well worth looking at, that
drew us to the spot, as the master himself, who wore
sandals and was playing with green balls. He never
stooped for a ball that had once touched ground, but
an attendant stood by with a sackful, and supplied
the players as they required them. We noticed other
novelties too. For two eunuchs were stationed at
opposite points of the circle, one holding a silver
chamber-pot, while the other counted the balls,—
not those that were in play and flying from hand to
hand, but such as fell on the floor.

We were still admiring these refinements of elegance when Menelaus runs up, saying, "See! that's the gentleman you are to dine with; why! this is really nothing else than a prelude to the entertainment." He had not finished speaking when Trimalchio snapped his fingers, and at the signal the eunuch held out the chamber-pot for him, without his ever stopping play. After easing his bladder, he called for water, and having dipped his hands momentarily in the bowl, dried them on one of the lads' hair.

There was no time to notice every detail; so we entered the bath, and after stewing in the sweating-room, passed instantly into the cold chamber. Trimalchio, after being drenched with unguent, was being rubbed down, not however with ordinary towels but with pieces of blanketing of the softest and finest wool. Meanwhile three bagnio doctors were swilling Falernian under his eyes; and seeing how the fellows were brawling over their liquor and spilling most of it, Trimalchio declared it was a libation they were making in his particular honour.

Presently muffled in a wraprascal of scarlet frieze, he was placed in a litter, preceded by four running-footmen in tinselled liveries, and a wheeled chair, in which his favourite rode, a little old young man, sore-eyed and uglier even than his master. As the latter was borne along, a musician took up his place at his head with a pair of miniature flutes, and played softly to him, as if he were whispering secrets in his ear. Full of wonder we follow the procession and arrive at the same moment as Agamemnon at the outer door, on one of the pillars of which was suspended a tablet bearing the words:

ANY SLAVE
GOING ABROAD WITHOUT THE MASTER'S
PERMISSION
SHALL RECEIVE ONE HUNDRED LASHES

Just within the vestibule stood the doorkeeper, dressed in green with a cherry-coloured sash, busy picking pease in a silver dish. Over the threshold

643

hung a gold cage with a black and white magpie in it,
which greeted visitors on their entrance.

But as I was staring open-eyed at all these fine
sights, I came near tumbling backwards and breaking
my legs. For to the left hand as you entered, and not
far from the porter's lodge, a huge chained dog was
depicted on the wall, and written above in capital
letters: 'WARE DOG! 'WARE DOG! My companions made
merry at my expense; but soon regaining confidence,
I fell to examining the other paintings on the walls.
One of these represented a slave-market, the men
standing up with labels round their necks, while in
another Trimalchio himself, wearing long hair, holding
a caduceus in his hand and led by Minerva, was entering Rome. Further on, the ingenious painter had shown
him learning accounts, and presently made steward of
the estate, each incident being made clear by explana-
tory inscriptions. Lastly at the extreme end of the
portico, Mercury was lifting the hero by the chin and
placing him on the highest seat of a tribunal. Fortune
stood by with her cornucopia, and the three Fates,
spinning his destiny with a golden thread.

I noticed likewise in the portico a gang of running-
footmen exercising under a trainer. Moreover I saw
in a corner shrine inside were ranged a marble statue
of Venus, and a golden casket of ample dimensions, in
which they said the great man's first beard was preserved. I now asked the hall-keeper what were the
subjects of the frescoes in the atrium itself. "The
Iliad and Odyssey," he replied, "and on your left the
combat of gladiators given under Laenas."

We had no opportunity of examining the numerous
paintings more minutely, having by this time reached
the banquet-hall, at the outer door of which the house-
steward sat receiving accounts. But the thing that
surprised me most was to notice on the doorposts of
the apartment fasces and axes fixed up, the lower part
terminating in an ornament resembling the bronze beak
of a ship, on which was inscribed:

644

```
                TO GAIUS POMPEIUS TRIMALCHIO,
                     AUGUSTAL SEVIR
                 CINNAMUS HIS TREASURER.
```

Underneath this inscription hung a lamp with two
lights, depending from the vaulting. Two other tablets were attached to the doorposts. One, if my memory serves me, bore the following inscription:

```
             ON DECEMBER THIRTIETH AND
                    THIRTY-FIRST
             OUR MASTER GAIUS DINES ABROAD.
```

The other showed the phases of the moon and the
seven planets, while lucky and unlucky days were
marked by distinctive studs.

When, sated with all these fine sights, we were just
making for the entrance of the banquet-hall, one of
the slaves, stationed there for the purpose, called out,
"Right foot first!" Not unnaturally there was a moment's
hesitation, for fear one of us should break the rule.
But this was not all; for just as we stepped out in line
right leg foremost, another slave, stripped of his
outer garments, threw himself before our feet, beseech-
ing us to save him from punishment. Not indeed that
his fault was a very serious one; in point of fact the
Intendant's clothes had been stolen when in his charge
at the bath,—a matter of ten sesterces or so at the
outside. So facing about, still right foot in front,
we approached the Intendant, who was counting gold in
the hall, and asked him to forgive the poor man. He
looked up haughtily and said, "It's not so much the
loss that annoys me as the rascal's carelessness. He
has lost my dinner robes, which a client gave me
on my birthday,—genuine Tyrian purple, I assure you,
though only once dipped. But there! I will pardon the
delinquent at your request."

Deeply grateful for so signal a favour, we now
returned to the banquet-hall, where we were met by
the same slave for whom we had interceded, who to our

                         645

astonishment overwhelmed us with a perfect storm of
kisses, thanking us again and again for our humanity.
"Indeed," he cried, "you shall presently know who it
is you have obliged; the master's wine is the cup-
bearer's thank-offering."

Well! at last we take our places, Alexandrian slave-
boys pouring snow water over our hands, and others
succeeding them to wash our feet and cleanse our toe
nails with extreme dexterity. Not even while engaged
in this unpleasant office were they silent, but sang
away over their work. I had a mind to try whether
all the house servants were singers, and accordingly
asked for a drink of wine. Instantly an attendant
was at my side, pouring out the liquor to the accom-
paniment of the same sort of shrill recitative. Demand
what you would, it was the same; you might have
supposed yourself among a troupe of pantomime actors
rather than at a respectable citizen's table.

Then the preliminary course was served in very elegant style. For all were now at table except Trimalchio,
for whom the first place was reserved,—by a reversal
of ordinary usage. Among the other hors d'oeuvres
stood a little ass of Corinthian bronze with a pack-
saddle holding olives, white olives on one side, black
on the other. The animal was flanked right and left
by silver dishes, on the rim of which Trimalchio's
name was engraved and the weight. On arches built up
in the form of miniature bridges were dormice seasoned
with honey and poppy-seed. There were sausages too
smoking hot on a silver grill, and underneath (to
imitate coals) Syrian plums and pomegranate seeds.

We were in the middle of these elegant trifles when
Trimalchio himself was carried in to the sound of
music, and was bolstered up among a host of tiny
cushions,—a sight that set one or two indiscreet guests
laughing. And no wonder; his bald head poked up out
of a scarlet mantle, his neck was closely muffled,
and over all was laid a napkin with a broad purple
stripe of laticlave, and long fringes hanging down
either side. Moreover he wore on the little finger

of his left hand a massive ring of silver gilt, and on
the last joint of the next finger a smaller ring, apparently of solid gold, but starred superficially with
little ornaments of steel. Nay! to show this was not
the whole of his magnificence, his left arm was bare,
and displayed a gold bracelet and an ivory circlet
with a sparkling clasp to put it on.

After picking his teeth with a silver toothpick, "My
friends," he began, "I was far from desirous of coming
to table just yet, but that I might not keep you waiting
by my absence, I have sadly interfered with my own
amusement. But will you permit me to finish my game?"
A slave followed him in, carrying a draught-board of
terebinth wood and crystal dice. One special bit of
refinement I noticed; instead of the ordinary black
and white men he had medals of gold and silver res-
pectively.

Meantime, whilst he is exhausting the vocabulary
of a tinker over the game, and we are still at the
hors d'oeuvres, a dish was brought in with a basket on
it, in which lay a wooden hen, her wings outspread
round her as if she were sitting. Instantly a couple
of slaves came up, and to the sound of lively music
began to search the straw, and pulling out a lot of peafowl's eggs one after the other, handed them round to
the company. Trimalchio turns his head at this, saying,
"My friends, it was by my orders the hen was set on the
peafowl's eggs yonder; but by God! I am very much
afraid they are half-hatched. Still we can but try
whether they are still eatable." For our part, we
take our spoons, which weighed at least half a pound
each, and break the eggs, which were made of paste.
I was on the point of throwing mine away, for I thought
I discerned a chick inside. But when I overheard a
veteran guest saying, "There should be something good
here!" I further investigated the shell, and found
a very fine fat baccafico swimming in yolk of egg
flavoured with pepper.

Our applause was interrupted by the second course,
which did not by any means come up to our expectations.

Still the oddity of the thing drew the eyes of all.
An immense circular tray bore the twelve signs of the
zodiac displayed round the circumference, on each of
which the Manoiple or Arranger had placed a dish of
suitable and appropriate viands: on the Ram ram's-
head pease, on the Bull a piece of beef, on the Twins
fried testicles and kidneys, on the Crab simply a
Crown, on the Lion African figs, an a Virgin a sow's
haslet, (on Libra a balance with a tart in one scale
and a cheese-cake in the other, on Scorpio a small
sea-fish, on Sagitarius an eye-seeker, on Capricornus
a lobster, on Aquarius a wild goose, on Pisces two
mullets. In the middle was a sod of green turf) cut
to shape and supporting a honeycomb. Meanwhile an
Eqyptian slave was carrying bread round in a miniature oven of silver, crooning to himself in a horrible
voice a song in praise of wine and laserpitium.

Seeing us look rather blank at the idea of attacking
such common fare, Trimalchio cried, "I pray you
gentlemen, begin; the best of your dinner is before
you." No sooner had he spoken than four fellows ran
prancing in, keeping time to the music, and whipped
off the top part of the tray. This done, we beheld
underneath, on a second tray in fact, stuffed capons,
a sow's paps, and as a centrepiece a hare fitted with
wings to represent Pegasus. We noticed besides four
figures of Marsyas, one at each corner of the tray,
carrying little wine-skins which spouted out peppered
fish-sauce over the fishes swimming in the Channel of
the dish.

We all join in the applause started by the domestics
and laughingly fall to on the choice viands. Trimalchio, as pleased as anybody with a device of the sort,
now called out, "Cut!" Instantly the Carver advanced,
and posturing in time to the music, sliced up the
joint with such antics you might have thought him a
jockey struggling to pull off a chariot-race to the
thunder of the organ. Yet all the while Trimalchio
kept repeating in a wheedling voice, "Cut! Cut!"
For my part, suspecting there was some pretty jest
connected with this everlasting reiteration of the word,

I made no bones about asking the question of the guest
who sat immediately above me. He had often witnessed
similar scenes and told me at once, "You see the man
who is carving; well; his name is Cut. The master is
calling and commanding him at one and the same time."

Unable to eat any more, I now turned towards my
neighbour in order to glean what information I could,
and after indulging in a string of general remarks,
presently asked him, "Who is that lady bustling up and
down the room yonder?" "Trimalchio's lady," he replied;
"her name is Fortunata, and she counts her coin by
the bushelful! Before? what was she before? Why! my
dear Sir! saving your respect, you would have been
mighty sorry to take bread from her hand. Now, by hook
or by crook, she's got to heaven, and is Trimalchio's
factotum. In fact if she told him it was dark night
at high noon, he'd believe her. The man's rolling
in riches, and really can't tell what he had and what
he hasn't got; still his good lady looks keenly after
everything, and is on the spot where you least expect
to see her. She's temperate, sober and well advised,
but she has a sharp tongue of her own and chatters
like a magpie between the bed-curtains. When she
likes a man, she likes him; and when she doesn't,
well! she doesn't.

"As for Trimalchio, his lands reach as far as the
kites fly, and his money breeds money. I tell you, he
has more coin lying idle in his porter's lodge than
would make another man's whole fortune. Slaves! why,
heaven and earth! I don't believe one in ten knows
his own master by sight. For all that, there's never
a one of the fine fellows a word of his wouldn't
send scutting into the nearest rat-hole. And don't you
imagine he ever buys anything; every mortal thing is
home grown,—wool, rosin, pepper; call for hen's milk
and he'd supply you! As a matter of fact his wool was
not first rate originally; but he purchased rams at
Tarentum and so improved the breed. To get homemade
Attic honey he had bees imported direct from Athens,
hoping at the same time to benefit the native insects
a bit by a cross with the Greek fellows. Why! only

the other day he wrote to India for mushroom spawn. He
has not a single mule but was got by a wild ass. You
will see all these mattresses; never a one that is not
stuffed with the finest wool, purple or scarlet as the
case maybe. Lucky, lucky dog!

"And look you, don't you turn up your nose at the
other freedmen, his fellows. They're very warm men.
You see the one lying last on the last couch yonder?
He's worth his eight hundred thousand any of these
days. A self-made man; once upon a time he carried
wood on his own two shoulders. They do say,—I don't
know how true it may be, but I've been told so,—he
snatched an Incubo's hat, and so discovered a treasure.
I grudge no man's good fortune, whatever God has seen
good to give him. He'll still take a box o' the ear
for all that, and keeps a keen eye on the main chance.
Only the other day he placarded his house with this
bill:

C. POMPEIUS DIOGENES
IS PREPARED TO LET HIS GARRET
FROM JULY FIRST,
HAVING BOUGHT THE HOUSE HIMSELF.

This agreeable gossip was here interrupted by Trimalchio; for the second course had now been removed,
and the company being merry with wine began to engage
in general conversation. Our host then, lying back
on his elbow and addressing the company, said, "I
hope you will all do justice to this wine; you must
make the fish swim again. Come, come, do you suppose
I was going to rest content with the dinner you saw
boxed up under the cover of the tray just now? 'Is
Ulysses no better known?' Well, well! even at table
we mustn't forget our scholarship. Peace to my worthy
patron's bones, who was pleased to make me a man amongst
men. For truly there is nothing can be set before
me that will nonplus me by its novelty. For instance
the meaning of that tray just now can be easily enough
explained. This heaven in which dwell the twelve
gods resolves itself into twelve different configur-
ations, and presently becomes the Ram. So whosoever

is born under this sign has many flocks and herds and
much wool, a hard head into the bargain, a shameless
brow and a sharp horn. Most of your schoolmen and
pettifoggers are born under this sign."

We recommended and learned expounder's graceful
erudition, and he went on to add: "Next the whole
sky becomes Bull; then are born obstinate fellows and
neatherds and such as think of nothing but filling their
own bellies. Under the Twins are born horses in a pair,
oxen in a yoke, men blessed with a sturdy brace of
testicles, all who manage to keep in with both sides.
I was born under the Crab myself. Wherefore I stand
on many feet, and have many possessions both by sea
and land; for the Crab is equally adapted to either
element. And this is why I never put anything on that
sign, so as not to eclipse my horoscope. Under the
Lion are born great eaters and wasters, and all who
love to domineer; under the Virgin, women and run-
aways and jailbirds; under the Scales, butchers and
perfumers and all retail traders; under the Scorpion,
poisoners and cut-throats; under the Archer, squint-
eyed folks, who look at the greens and whip off with
the bacon; under Capricorn, the 'horny-handed sons of
toil'; under Aquarius or the Waterman, innkeepers and
pumpkin-heads; under Pisces, or the Fishes, fine cooks
and fine talkers. Thus the world goes round like a
mill, and is for ever at some mischief, whether making
men or marring them. But about the sod of turf you
see in the middle, and the honeycomb atop of it, I
have a good reason to show too. Our mother Earth is
in the middle, round-about like an egg, and has all
good things in her inside, like a honeycomb!"

"Clever! clever!" we cry in chorus, and with hands
uplifted to the ceiling, swear Hipparchus and Aratus
were not to be named in the same breath with him. This
lasted till fresh servants entered and spread carpets
before the couches, embroidered with pictures of fowling
nets, prickers with their hunting spears, and sporting
gear of all kinds. We were still at a loss what to
expect when a tremendous shout was raised outside the
doors, and lo! and behold, a pack of Laconian dogs

came careering round and round the very table. These
were succeeded by another huge tray, on which lay a
wild boar of the largest size, with a cap on its head,
while from the tushes hung two little baskets of woven
palm leaves, one full of Syrian dates, the other of
Theban. Round it were little piglets of baked sweet-
meats, as if at suck, to show it was a sow we had
before us; and these were gifts to be taken home with
them by the guests.

To carve the dish however, it was not this time our
friend Cut who appeared, the same who had dismembered
the capons, but a great bearded fellow, wearing leggings
and a shaggy jerkin. Drawing his hunting knife, he
made a furious lunge and gashed open the boar's flank,
from which there flew out a number of field-fares.
Fowlers stood ready with their rods and immediately
caught the birds as they fluttered about the table.
Then Trimalchio directed each guest to be given his
bird, and this done, added "Look what elegant acorns
this wild-wood pig fed on." Instantly slaves ran to
the baskets that were suspended from the animal's
tushes and divided the two kind of dates in equal
proportions among the diners.

Meantime, sitting as I did a little apart, I was
led into a thousand conjectures to account for the
boar's being brought in with a cap on. So after
exhausting all sorts of absurd guesses, I resolved to
ask my former "philosopher and friend" to explain the
difficulty that tormented me so. "Why! said he, "your
own servant could tell you that much. Riddle? it's as
plain as daylight. The boar was presented with his
freedom at yesterday's dinner; he appeared at the
end of the meal and the company gave him his conge.
Therefore today he comes back to table as a freedman."
I cursed my own stupidity, and asked no more questions,
for fear of their thinking I had never dined with good
company before.

We were still conversing, when a pretty boy entered,
his head wreathed with vine-leaves and ivy, announcing
himself now as Bromius, anon as Lyaeus and Evous. He

proceeded to hand round grapes in a small basket,
and recited in the shrillest of voices some verses of
his master's composition. Trimalchio turned round at
the sound, and, "Dionysus," said he, "be free (Liber)!"
The lad snatched the cap from the boar's head and stuck
it on his own. Then Trimalchio went on again, "Well!
you'll not deny," he cried, "I have a Father Liber (a
freeborn father) of my own." We praised Trimalchio's
joke, and heartily kissed the fortunate lad, as he went
round the company to receive our congratulations.

At the end of this course Trimalchio left the table
to relieve himself, and so finding ourselves free from
the constraint of his overbearing presence, we began
to indulge in a little friendly conversation. Accordingly Dama began first, after calling for a cup of wine.
"A day! what is a day?" he exclaimed, "before you can
turn round, it's night again! So really you can't
do better than go straight from bed to board. Fine
cold weather we've been having; why! even my bath
has hardly warmed me. But truly hot liquor is a good
clothier. I've been drinking bumpers, and I'm down-
right fuddled. The wine has got into my head."

Seleucus then struck into the talk: "I don't bathe
every day," he said; "your systematic bather's a mere
fuller. Water's got teeth, and melts the heart away,
a little every day; but there! when I've fortified my
belly with a cup of mulled wine, I say 'Go hang!' to
the cold. Indeed I couldn't bathe to-day, for I've been
to a funeral. A fine fellow he was too, good old
Chrysanthus, but he's given up the ghost now. He was
calling me just this moment, only just this moment;
I could fancy myself talking to him now. Alas! alas!
what are we but blown bladders on two legs? We're
not worth as much as flies! they are some use, but
we're no better than bubbles." "He wasn't careful
enough in his diet?" "I tell you, for five whole days
not one drop of water, or one crumb of bread, passed
his lips. Nevertheless he has joined the majority.
The doctors killed him,—or rather his day was come;
the very best of doctors is only a satisfaction to the
mind. Anyhow he was handsomely buried, on his own

653

best bed, with good blankets. The wailing was first class,—he did a trifle of manumission before he died; though no doubt his wife's tears were a bit forced. A pity he always treated her so well. But woman! woman's of the kite kind. No man ought ever to do 'em a good turn; just as well pitch it in the well at once. Old love's an eating sore!"

Whilst we were still acclaiming these and similar remarks, Trimalchio returned, and instantly started talking again, "Pray my dearest Agamemnon, do you recollect by any chance the twelve labours of Hercules, or the story of Ulysses, how the Cyclops twisted his thumb out of joint, after he was turned into a pig. I used to read these tales in Homer when I was a lad. Then the Sibyl! I saw her at Cumae with my own eyes hanging in a jar; and when the boys cried to her, 'Sibyl, what would you?' she would answer, 'I would die,'—both of 'em speaking Greek."

He was still in the middle of this nonsense when a tray supporting an enormous hog was set on the table. One and all we expressed our admiration at the expedition shown, and swore a mere ordinary fowl could not have been cooked in the time,—the more so as the hog appeared to be a much larger animal than the wild boar just before. Presently Trimalchio, staring harder and harder, exclaimed, "What! what! isn't he gutted? No! by heaven! he's not. Call the cook in!"

The cook came and stood by the table, looking sadly crestfallen and saying he had clean forgotten. "What! forgotten!" cried Trimalchio; "to hear him, you would suppose he'd just omitted a pinch of pepper or a bit of cummin. Strip him!"

Instantly the cook was stripped, and standing between two tormentors, the picture of misery. But we all began to intercede for him, saying, "Accidents will happen; do forgive him this once. If ever he does it again, not one of us will say a word in his favour." For my own part I felt mercilessly indignant, and could not hold myself, but bending over to Agamemnon's ear, I whispered, "Evidently he must be a villainous bad servant. To think of anybody forgetting to bowel a hog, by Gad! I would not let the fellow off, if he'd shown such carelessness about a fish."

Not so Trimalchio, for with a smile breaking over his face, "Well! well!" said he, "as you have such a bad memory, bowel him now, where we can all see."

Thereupon the cook resumed his tunic, seized his knife and with a trembling hand slashed open the animal's belly. In a moment, the apertures widening under the weight behind, out tumbled a lot of sausages and black-puddings.

At this all the servants applauded like one man, and chorussed, "Gaius for ever!" Moreover the cook was gratified with a goblet of wine and a silver wreath, and received a drinking cup on a salver of Corinthian metal. This Agamemnon scanned with some attention, and Trimalchio observed, "I am the only man possessing the genuine Corinthian plate."

The thing was getting positively sickening, when Trimalchio, now in a state of disgusting intoxication, commanded a new diversion, a company of horn-blowers, to be introduced; and then stretching himself out along the edge of a couch on a pile of pillows, "Make believe I am dead," he ordered. "Play something fine." Then the horn-blowers struck up a loud funeral dirge. In particular one of these undertaker's men, the most conscientious of the lot, blew so tremendous a fanfare he roused the whole neighbourhood. Hereupon the watchmen in charge of the surrounding district, thinking Trimalchio's house was on fire, suddenly burst open the door, and rushing in with water and axes, started the much admired confusion usual under such circumstances. For our part, we seized the excellent opportunity thus offered, snapped our fingers in Agamemnon's face, and away helter-skelter just as if we were escaping from a real conflagration.

655

Having turned Stoicism, the preferred style of thought,
into little more than a dignified-sounding but generally
irrelevant way of life, the Roman state had little further
interest in philosophy other than to make sure that it did
not get out of line. Dictators often liked to give the
impression that they were progressive, in step with what
Trajan called "the justice of our times," but there was
little more involved than ritual recitings of the brotherhood angle of Stoicism—none of it seems to have had much
to do with anything. Seneca, for example, advisor to Nero
(50's-60's) and our chief source for Stoic thought through
the first 200 years after Christ, is both superficial and
confusing. Looking at his work in literature—at the
unchained Romantic style of his drama about Hercules,
for example—it is difficult to believe that the Stoic
line was not being worked up mostly because it was generally reasonably acceptable to the system. Seneca has the
usual bits about brotherhood and sympathy for others,
including the standard criticism of the evils possible in
slavery—everyone knew by this time that it was all nice
and safe. When the Greek freedman Epictetus in the next
generation tried to breathe a little life into Stoicism,
mixing the usual line about accepting fate with an emotional concern with the benevolent, warm-hearted God which
ran things (something which didn't belong in Stoicism anyway), Domitian threw him, and other philosophers, out of
Rome. Epictetus had to go back to Asia Minor (90). This
was one of the elements in Domitian's "conservative"
program—an old-fashioned cleansing out of philosophers.

With philosophy unattractive, Roman intellectual
talent still tended to go into law. The 100's were a
golden age of Roman law. The major names are:
Salvius Julianus d. 169
Gaius - late 100's
Scaevola - advisor to Marcus Aurelius and Septimius Severus
Papitian - executed by Caracalla in 212
Ulpian - killed by practorians in 220's
Paulus - early 200's. Few of the leading figures were
Westeners, although we do not know where all of them were
from. The most famous, Papirian was from North Africa or

Syria. In line with Stoic brotherhood and the desire to look progressive, the law became more humane—particularly where the rights of women and slaves were concerned. Ulpian, for example, stated that all human beings were born free, so slavery was "unnatural." The lawyers liked to talk, in Stoic fashion, about a natural law, a set of principles valid everywhere and for everyone—for the total brotherhood of man. This can look good. At the same time, though, citizens (almost all free men from 212) were being divided more and more clearly into two groups, with very different legal rights. The upper group, the honestiores (wealthy, officials, soldiers) were much more secure than the humiliores, who actually suffered many punishments that only non-citizens had suffered before (flogging, torture, execution without appeal). Little of this shows up in the works of the lawyer-intellectuals.

The most interesting Stoic figure of the era is the dictator Marcus Aurelius (161-180) in his Meditations—interesting as a study in psychology and as an indication of what had happened to Stoicism. Marcus Aurelius is not a philosopher at all. He uses stock Stoic phrases to defend a hard, self-punishing lifestyle with which he feels at home and about which he likes to complain. The tone varies amazingly from grim reality to an annoying whine, with plenty of reason for worry about Marcus Aurelius' state of mind (the daily drugs prescribed by Galen cannot have helped). It is other-worldly (in the fashion of Epictetus, Marcus Aurelius agrees that there is a guiding intelligence —a God, to which our soul is related), but he insists that there is no life after death. Sometimes he can look very sympathetic—in an aimless way. This Stoic philosopher stuck Rome with his crazy son Commodus and provided 135 days of free public shows a year in the city. This is the equivalent of what we saw in the late Greek period—the widening of concern to all as the dictatorship takes freedom away from all. The following pieces will indicate the tone and some of the ideas:

Let everything you do and say and think be as if you were to leave the world this moment. But going away from here is no terrible thing, if there are Gods; for they are above evil. If there are no Gods, or if they don't care about men, then what is the point of living in a Universe without Gods or Providence? But there are Gods, and they do care about people.

A man's true work is to show goodwill to others, to be above his senses, to be suspicious of them, to keep in mind the entire nature of the Universe and all that she makes happen.

Death reduced to the same condition Alexander of Macedon and the man who took care of his mules. They were taken back into the same Reason of the Universe or they were scattered into atoms.

I seek the truth, which never hurts man. But he hurts himself who remains ignorant and self-deceived.

Be as a great rock, on which the waves break endlessly; but it stands fast and all around it the troubled waters sink to rest.

Always remember that the Universe is one living Being, a single substance and a single soul.

Get rid of opinion and you are safe. And who is there to keep you from getting rid of it.

Be your own master.

How strong is the brotherhood between a man and all men.

We can see that Marcus Aurelius uses a strong mystic ("religious") tone, after the manner of Epictetus. It seems to have few consequences for him, and he uses words like Reason, Universe, Nature, God, Gods, interchangeably in a haphazard fashion, so that it is impossible to tell what the nature of significance of these elements were. There is no way for large numbers of people to obtain much emotional satisfaction from Marcus Aurelius' way of looking at things. His work shows, though, that even in Stoicism emotional needs did make themselves felt. In philosophy, one way of handling this problem was to give more attention to the mystic elements of the Pythagorean and Platonic styles—a typical piece of looking back, but to a quite specific source. It was easier for men in the Roman period to do this because, as in their art, the general attitude was electric--a willingness to take ideas or styles from a wide variety of sources (eclecticism). Seneca did this, as did Epictetus. Marcus Aurelius will throw in ideas or slogans from all sorts of sources (Heraclitus, Parmenides, etc.), in a way that suggests that it is all much the same to him. In particular, this allowed Stoicism to pick mystical-magical elements (we saw this already in the late Republic) and to borrow from the otherworldliness, the nonmaterialism, of Pythagoreans and Platonists. The result was more Romantic and could offer more emotional satisfaction--to educated types, at least.

The result was that through the first two centuries and more after Christ Stoicism not only took on more and more mystery-religious elements from Platonism but actually gave ground to a resurgent Neo-Platonism (neo meaning new). Platonism had had a hard time of it in the Hellenistic centuries, tending to wander off in a variety of directions, such as astrology/magic and word-mongering (skepticism, which is doubting everything and taking pride in cleverness). At times, it is almost lost from sight. By the 100's A.D. it was reviving, although by that time, while calling itself Neo-Platonism, it had taken on bits and pieces from many sources, in the typical Roman eclectic fashion. Neo-Platonism, more than anything else, was at this time a theology (a system of religion). It could be intensely devotional and pious, as with the Greek biographer Plutarch in the late 1st century; it could be more or less casual, as with the satirical writer Apuleius of the 2nd century. In any event, it was, in a way that no Greek system of thought had been since at least Pythagoras, religious. Its revival indicated the dissatisfaction of many educated people of the 100's (Marcus Aurelius, say) with the matter-of-factness of Stoicism.

Neo-Platonism reached its climax in the 200's, during the anarchy, when it perhaps looked like a way of escaping from the horrors of the real world. It then produced PLOTINUS, who has the greatest reputation of any philosopher of the Roman Empire (in fact the only great reputation among philosophers of that period). Plotinus,

205-270, was an Egyptian--we would expect him to be from
the East. After studying at the great center of Alexandria,
he settled in Rome. He was befriended by Gallienus and
was a very influential figure at the center of power in
the 250's and 260's. His discussions with his students
were published, in Greek, by one of them, Porphyry of
Tyre, about 300. Much of Plotinus' system is vague,
some of it contradictory, but the general outline is
clear. There is a First Principle, the One or the Good
or the Father (he rarely calls it God, but his student
Porphyry uses that word for it all the time. This One
is beyond all thought, all definition; we cannot say what
it is or "describe" it. It has always been; it always
will be: it is "all will and loves Itself and creates
Itself." It is all reality and goodness; it never changes.
It is entirely outside the world, and it does not
interfere in what goes on in the world. It is a thing so
removed from us that it can be reached only through
intermediaries which are its creations. It is the source
of the infinitely powerful Divine Mind and of the World of
Forms (from Plato, the essences of the things we see).
The One also creates the material universe, which also
is eternal and unchanging; an idea from Aristotle, and
perhaps Plato too. The universe is linked to the Forms,
and so to the One, by Soul. All of these things, Divine
Mind, Forms, Soul, the universe, are created spontaneously
(from the beginning--and there is no beginning), inevitably, unplanned, and without the One changing. Why?
Because what is perfect is productive--a most peculiar and
unsatisfying answer to explain why things are as they are.

The basic suppositions in this system are generally
Pythagorean/Platonic. There is the insistence on order,
everything being from the One; the belief that things
proceed teleologically (toward an end), there being always
an impulse toward the One. It is not certain whether
Plotinus believed in the old style that matter is actually
evil, that it is the product of a separate inferior or
evil Soul. Many people think so, and such a belief was
common among his followers. In any case, the theory
includes clearly a heavy dose of the old anti-matter
attitudes. A person should direct his efforts toward
uniting with the One. This could be done by contemplation,
by turning inward upon oneself--and by such practices as

vegetarianism. Plotinus, the quiet mystic with the strange habits, reminds us unmistakeably of Pythagoras stretching across the centuries. If you try hard and go about it right, you may catch flashes of the One, achieving even a moment of union with it; Plotinus thought that he had achieved this mystic union more than once. The mystic element in Plotinus is very powerful and insistent; it is indeed the whole purpose of the thing. This note was relatively new—Neo-Platonism of the 100's had not used it so eagerly.

Plotinus' view of the One had enormous impact on the Christians' way of looking at their God. Neo-Platonism is in fact the single greatest intellectual influence on the Christian church of the late Roman Empire. Where Plotinus, or any philosopher, could not match Christianity was in the emotional satisfaction of a personal Savior, who intervened actively in the world and who operated a system of rewards and punishments. What Plotinus offered, in contrast, had all the limitations of its type: high-toned, unexciting, and irresponsible from the Christian viewpoint. In the Plotinus system, the Christian will look generally in vain for "goodness." Contemplation, not doing good, was the thing, although Plotinus talks sometimes about right actions. Personally, if the impression of the writings is anything to go by, he seems to have been arrogant and superior as well as weird. He does seem to have won a large circle of admiring friends, though, and he bore with great bravery the horrible sufferings of a drawn-out death, perhaps from leprosy.

For us, the most important thing to realize is that with Plotinus philosophy had turned into theology, a journey back to its old home. The intellectual world was a long way toward the habits of mind which made Christianity possible. Plotinus does not offer a great intellectual framework to understand the universe; he offers a way of communing with the divine. This is the Christian way. The existence of this kind of Neo-Platonism in the 200's, its appeal to the educated of the day (and even to the dictator Gallienus), is a sign that there was tremendous interest in the spiritual. This interest dated from long before the anarchy of the 200's, although the bad times then may well have encouraged the drift.

660

It is related to the movement in art toward the new abstracted style aimed at expressing, releasing the "inner" man.

Many who felt this kind of need could find little comfort in the complicated and highly personal explanations of Plotinus and the Neo-Platonists. At a more emotional and popular level the same purpose was provided for in the mystery religions which thrived in the age of the Roman Empire. These existed independently of the state religion, which centered on the Greek-Roman combined gods like Zeus/Jupiter and the worship of dead emperors and of the genius of the living emperor. There was no emotional satisfaction to be found in what the state offered. For centuries, Romans had been looking for more rewarding religious forms, always under the careful eye of the state. In the 100's and 200's this movement reached great proportions across the Empire, producing a number of major emotional religious forms.

There was a very extensive degree of religious freedom in the Empire. The state, which had always watched the religions of Rome itself very carefully, had found that in general there was little enough social and political content to most of the religions across the area of the Empire that an easy-going attitude could be afforded. Those religions were local and not exclusive; that is, their followers were polytheists, aware that their preferred god or goddess was only one among many and willing to tolerate (and to participate in) other religions. The social elite of the Empire did not for the most part share in these religions, finding them ridiculous. For the earlier rulers, as had been the case with the elite since at least the late Greek Classical period, religion was a matter of considering the Divine, or the Good, or Nature, or the One, etc. There is, for example, plenty of superstition in Marcus Aurelius, but he is contemptuous of the many gods of the masses. The state used the officially supported gods like Jupiter and the cult of the emperors to promote unity, loyalty, and obedience-- religion was hardly involved at all. The popular religions were watched, but interference came only when the state found a particular item of devotion too objectionable. The Druids, for example, a body of Celtic priests in Gaul

661

and Britain, were banned from offering human sacrifices to their gods. Many purely local gods were merged with the gods of Roman/Greek myth. The Celtic water-god Nemausus became Apollo at Nimes in southern France (the Roman name for the town, Nemausus, was that of the god). A special case was the Jews, since they had only the one God and could neither tolerate other faiths nor share in the official religions of the empire, including the emperor-cult. The Jews were also a nation, with a sense of oneness and separateness which made them unique in the Roman world. A large majority of Jews, though, even at the time of Christ, lived outside Israel, generally in the Hellenized cities of the eastern Mediterranean—particularly Alexandria. The Roman state was, from its own point of view, generous toward the Jews, exempting them from the official religions and from military service. Jews were also allowed to administer themselves in Israel; they could not take the many oaths which were required in the course of the normal administrative and judicial operations of the state. Eventually, though, in the 100's, the Romans cracked down sharply on the Jews, after many serious Jewish revolts. The Jewish privileges were generally withdrawn and their home in Israel was broken up. The Romans would have argued that this reflected simply Jewish unreasonableness.

Some of the religions were more appealing and had wider followings than the others. By the 200's, a number had become very widespread, across virtually the entire Empire, although we cannot even guess at the numbers who supported them. The greatest of these was the cult of Isis, an Egyptian goddess originally. The worship of Isis was described by Apuleius in The Golden Ass, where it is presented as the dominant religion of the day (100's). With no barriers of wealth or sex or race, Isis was attractive to women, freedmen, and slaves. Isis had a brother and husband, Osiris, god of the underworld, who died each year and was revived and who offered salvation (immortality) to the faithful. A temple to Isis was built at Rome in 42 B.C. by the Triumvirs (Mark Antony, Octavian, and Lepidus) who succeeded Caesar. Augustus later put Isis out of the city, but she was readmitted by Caligula. There was also the worship of the Great Mother, Cybele, from Asia Minor, a religious form which, as we saw, came

662

to Rome as early as the 2nd Punic War (218-201 B.C.).
Claudius (41-54) restored the temple of Cybele at Rome
and opened her priesthood to Roman citizens. Cybele crops
up frequently in the Roman cities of the West. She too,
like Isis, began as a fertility figure; she too had her
associate who died and offered salvation to the followers.
The third of the most successful pagan cults was different.
This was Mithraism, the worship of Mithras. Mithras was
of Persian origin; for Persians he was an assistant to the
chief god and provided salvation to the human race. For
Romans, Mithras was related to the sun and to astrology.
Mithraism was popular in the legions. He was a super-
hero, hard, bold, and brave, simple in tastes, honest,
and highly moral. It offered a series of physical tests
to initiates, enduring heat, cold, etc., as a way of
moving closer to salvation. There was a baptism ceremony,
communal meals, strict rules against immorality. Women
were not admitted to membership in the faith. There
seems to have been no professional priesthood in the
religion, little extensive organization, and it was not
supported by the state (Mithras does not appear on coins,
for example).

While we know very little about these religions (the
victory of Christianity made sure of that), certain
features are evident, particularly the hope of immortality,
the use of a savior as an associate of the chief figure in
the religion, and the idea of "members" of the faith
worshipping the same god at temples or churches over an
extended area. You can recognize these things as items
shared by the Christians. In a different category was
the old Greek worship of Dionysius, which continued to
flourish widely, especially in the West. Dionysius, with
time, had become a good-time god--parties here and parties
for evermore in the afterlife. This had its attractions,
but it was not nearly serious or mysterious enough for
the times. It is very notable that none of the three
great pagan cults were Greek in origin--they appealed to
the masses and often existed below the officially supported
Hellenized leading layer of society.

The Roman state never showed much interest in any of
these major pagan religions: Mithraism it ignored, the
others it supported only weakly. The state was interested,

663

though, in promoting answers to the religious needs of the 100's and 200's. This attitude was in line with Rome's traditional adaptability to new religions as need arose (as in the 2nd Punic War). The favorite answer of the state in the 200's was the worship of the SUN. This had an ancient heritage and had long been found in one variation or another over a very wide area. Often it verged on the magical, in relationship to astrology. The Sun also had the virtue of long association with the Good, the Divine in Greek/Hellenistic philosophy. It had long occupied a place in Roman religious life, although we can say very little about it. People wonder, for example, about the implications of Hadrian's Pantheon, with its great opening to the sky--was it related to sun worship or astrology. Worship of the Sun began to flourish with the Severi. Both Septimius Severus and his wife Julian Domna, a noted religious enthusiast, were devoted to the Sun; it occurs frequently on their coins. The Sun continued to appeal to the primitive soldier-emperors of the anarchy (235-284). In that period it became virtually a state-preferred religion. Aurelian (270-275) was especially devoted to the Sun, and built a great temple of the Sun (the Unconquerable Sun, as it was called) at Rome. In the late 200's, unquestionably, reverence for the Sun was very widespread. The dictator Constantine was a follower of the Sun before he became a Christian, and sun worship was probably the most common religious form among the men and the soldiers who ran the Empire by 300. It is difficult to say more than this. The virtue of the sun worship was that it could be associated with many other types of faith--a lot of things could be given an association with the sun, the life-providing force, without much difficulty. This happened to Mithras, another favorite of the soldiers. The same thing happened after 300 with Christianity. Constantine seems to have decided that the Son and the Christian God were the same thing--in other words, he had been right all along. To the state, it was an obvious, if crude, symbol of power, and so it served in a way that Mithras, Cybele, and Isis could not (the last two even being women--hardly the appropriate symbols for a military dictatorship). The success of sun worship, by any standard, is an appalling example of the primitivism of the men who were running the Roman state by 300. What would have been the attitude of Augustus or Marcus

Aurelius to this kind of thing?

The great difficulty with the Sun was that, while
it could create awe and fear and respect, it was short of
human interest. It is hard to "relate" to the Sun. The
Sun was given a birthday (December 25, signifying the
"return" of the Sun as the days again began to grow longer);
Mithras was picked up to put a little life in Sun worship.
This would hardly do. The religion could not generate
enough emotional and spiritual satisfaction to command
the willing and committed support of large numbers of
ordinary people.

All of these forms, Neo-Platonism, the mystery-
religions of Isis, Cybele, Mithras, the worship of the
Sun, had something to offer. It was the triumph of
Christianity that it combined the attractions of all
three, along with much more, in a religion which had no
counterpart in the Roman world: In this sense, Christianity deserved to succeed; it was the most efficient
example of religious syncretism (merging of different
religious ideas and habits) in its era. It combined
emotional and intellectual appeal, and offered in addition
a heavy emphasis on organization and a willingness to
accept the direction of the state. Soon after 300, finding
that the Sun did not serve, the Roman state, in the person
of the dictator Constantine, decided to give Christianity
a try.

665

ART AND ARCHITECTURE IN THE ROMAN EMPIRE, 14-300

The conquests of Alexander the Great in the 300's B.C.,
and the survival of the Macedonian successor states, had
produced a common Hellenistic cultural style around the
eastern Mediterranean--so that Alexandria, in Egypt, was
perhaps the most important single center of that·Greek/
Hellenistic style. The cultural effect of the Roman Empire
was to spread that style to the western Mediterranean, with
appropriate adjustments made to the Romans' satisfaction.
It is easy to say this, but if you think of the great
variety of peoples who lived in the Empire it is easy to
realize that this was a very considerable achievement, that
it was an influential (which is not to say important) way of
promoting a sense of oneness. From Britain to Egypt a common
cultural framework existed (with local variations). **This did
not come only from the spread of Greek artists and** workmen
across the area--most of the work in Italy and the West was
done by non-Greeks. It was an "official" Roman style,
sponsored and encouraged, and often paid for, by the state
(central and local). Often the quality of work was high,
but there is always the feeling that it is a copied style,
lacking originality, creativity; much of it, of course, was
in fact outright copy, of statue formats and architectural
forms. Often, it looks silly, even mindless. It arose not
from any desire of artists for self-expression but from the
desire of the state to "have" a culture. Compared to the
Greeks, as one result, we know the names of hardly any
artists from this long period--it seems likely that from the
state's own point of view men who merely turned out a potted
Hellenistic style were hacks who did not deserve recognition.
Another result was that we find the most surprising mixing-
up of Hellenistic elements in the same period. Some rulers
preferred certain elements, others had different preferences--
but across the Empire at any one time it is difficult to say
which elements were dominant. This is one of the clearest
signs that noone--neither those doing the work nor those
paying for it--cared a great deal about what was done. Nobody
much looked for coherence or unity of expression in art. The
Hellenistic style in its entirety, after all, was only being
copied because it was already there. We have the impression
with the Romans that they would just as well have copied a
Japanese style. The only reasonably secure comment we can

make about change over time through these generations is
that there was a movement toward the more flamboyant and
emotional Hellenistic elements--toward a greater Romanticism.
Roman art tended over time to "lose its cool"--although it
never had had much of that quality. Then, in the 200's,
for the first time, there emerged, hesitantly and inconsist-
ently at first, but with great and gathering impact, a new
style, abstracted and deliberately "primitive" looking. By
300, we have works which for the first time do not seem to
belong in the Greek/Hellenistic framework.

Architecture.

    Architecture was where Romans continued to be at their
best. It appealed to their sense of the useful and let them
express their taste for big things. With the arch and vault
they could do wonderful things, achieving enormous size in
their buildings, and in particular being able to build up
to great heights--to achieve very impressive interiors. It
is hard not to see in the Roman love of bigness an expression
of the power of the state and its people. In the same
direction, we notice that the Romans built to last--to last,
in fact, far longer than was necessary. Apart from a pride
in the work, this looks like another assertion of the state's
image of itself--the Empire was to be eternal. This is why
we have so very much more Roman architecture than we do
Greek. Roads, aqueducts, theaters, temples, exist in numbers.
Some of the most impressive remains are those of cities
abandoned since the Romans--particularly places on the fringes
of the desert in North Africa and the Near East such as
Timgad and Palmyra--and also the Lepcis Magna of Septimius
Severus.

    There was plenty of temple construction, but such build-
ings were no longer the overwhelming focus of art work which
they had been in the Classical Greek period. The Romans
perhaps were more at home with the "useful"--although the
gods, of course, were useful to the Romans, under controlled
circumstances. Temple work remained heavily Greek in form,
with a typical willingness to go on mixing up the traditional
Doric, Ionic, and Corinthian orders. The Romans developed,
by the late 1st century A.D., a Composite Order for columns,
which mixed the Ionic and Corinthian together. This was
hardly an achievement--more an indication that they didn't
care. The temples, even in the East, usually had the Italian

667

high podium and large vestibule, and unfluted columns were
common. There was a tendency toward big, high temples in a
nod to the Roman liking for size. The best example is the
temple to Bacchus (the Greek Dionysius) at Baalbek in Lebanon
of about 150, with columns 52' high. There was also a very
large temple complex to Jupiter of the Capitoline, chief
among the Roman gods, at Baalbek--the date of its construction
is not known. By the 100's temple decoration, particularly
of interiors, had become very busy, in a crowded, excessive
Hellenistic way.

Temples generally continued to rely heavily on the
Greek post-and-lintel style--they were the most old-fashioned,
the most traditional of Roman architectural styles. Arches
were used to some degree, though, and there continued to be
some variety of appearance (round temples, etc.). The only
temple of the period which ranks among the great wonders of
Roman construction--and it occupies a very prominent place--
is the PANTHEON of Hadrian at Rome from the 130's. This is
in fact the best preserved of all Roman buildings. It was
a temple to all the gods (presumably holding a great collection of statues), replacing an earlier pantheon built by
Agrippa under Augustus. It is a very large round structure
topped by a gigantic dome--a wonderful example of the Romans'
ability to use the arch and vault to provide great amounts
of free interior space. Both the interior diameter and the
height of the dome measure some 140'. The use of concrete
arches allowed the walls to be thin enough to put substantial
niches into them where the statues of the gods could be
located. The sole source of light is the single 29' opening
in the middle of the dome. The ceiling was faced with gilded
sheet bronze, which stars painted upon the panels, for strange
lighting effects. The original exterior was also done in
gilded bronze tiles. People wonder about the religious significance of the building--whether it was connected to a
worship of the sun and stars. This is probably not necessary.
The Senate met in the Pantheon--an activity which, even if
not useful, was not religious. The Pantheon was raised up
and approached by steps, with a frontal aspect even to this
round building, in the traditional Roman fashion. Later,
before 200, a very big vestibule was added. This altered
totally the appearance of the building and is a fine example
of the Roman hodge-podge approach and their indifference to
aesthetic concerns. So is the fact that the Pantheon was

built right out of surrounding walls (in the fashion of Augustus' temple of Mars the Avenger); it did not stand on its own to be admired.

More effort went into the construction of large works for the direct and practical use of the public--a sign that the state was splendid and that it cared. Aqueducts and roads ran all over; the dictator Trajan for example (98-117) constructed a new aqueduct at Rome and built a road across the mountains (200 miles) from Rome to Brindisium, to replace the old, roundabout Via Appia. Many sizeable towns had a theater for drama shows, some of them free-standing (not built into hillsides). The orchestra area for the chorus became a semi-circle standing in front of a high and heavily decorated backdrop wall which connected with the semi-circle of seats, providing an enclosed structure. The biggest towns in the West (the East does not seem to have taken to this part of Roman life) had stadiums for the fight shows (animals and man). The most famous is the Colosseum at Rome, which is the work of Vespasian and Titus (69-81). This could seat about 45,000. It is 157' high with 4 stories (the 4th added later by Domitian (81-96). It was built of concerete with a marble face. The 80 archways show a wide variety of column types. It was a sensible filling: the entrance and seating arrangements were planned so that the building could be emptied in minutes. Like many stadiums, and theaters, it had a canvas awning which could be drawn across the top for protection against the sun. This open style, of course, only worked where people could rely on sunny and dry weather--a Mediterranean climate. We do not find theaters or stadiums in northern Gaul or Britain. We have a fine stadium at Nimes in southern France which seated about 25,000; it had only two stories. The biggest form of stadium was the circus, which was used for chariot races, the biggest sport of the period. A circus featured two long, straight sides linked by two narrow and tight turns, making for a sport that was dangerous as well as exciting. The Circus Maximus (the Chief Circus) was able to seat perhaps 200,000 people. Only the biggest towns had this kind of thing. City authorities also provided bathing facilities for citizens. This was a Greek idea, but it was done in the larger Roman towns on a scale that was very characteristic of the Empire. The most famous baths are those built at Rome. Those of Trajan (98-117) reveal in the main hall the earliest surviving use of concrete cross-vaulting. More famous, being larger and better preserved, are the Baths of Caracalla from a century later (211-217). The entire building complex measures 1050' by 1080' and the main building 720' by 370'. This was another of the mighty Roman interiors--the central hall was 183' long, with an open space between the walls of 79'. The Baths were very gaudily and heavily decorated inside, with statues and paintings and mosaics. Another century later, the Baths of Diocletian (284-305) at Rome were larger still--the commitment to size was increasing. These baths provided many kinds of facilities, including swimming pools, hot baths, gymnasiums, etc. Romans seem to have bathed regularly--the last people to do so for a very long time. The centre of activities in towns was the Forum or city-center/market-place. Rome had a whole series of these, as emperors competed with one another is redesigning large parts of the downtown areas. The most famous is Trajan's Forum, covering some 25 acres. Like most such centers, this one included a large open square and a basilica or public office building. These basilicas were usually elongated rectangular structures--this plan was adopted later for Christian churches. Our chief surviving basilica is that of Maxentius in Rome (completed by Constantine) from right at the end of the period, around 300. It has a raised central hall, 150' high, springing from buttresses supported by spurs. The Corinthian columns of the interior are only for show; they are not needed for support. The material was the usual concrete faced with brick.

Other well-known architectural relics from the Rome of this period that we can mention are (1) Hadrian's Tomb (130's), which lay across the river from downtown at the end of the new Bridge of Aelius (Hadrian's family name); (2) Hadrian's Villa at Tivoli outside the city, a rambling collection of buildings covering a tremendous area and containing a wide variety of styles copied from Greece (such as the maidens from the Erechtheum); (3) the Wall of Aurelian, from the 270's, 55' high and extending over almost 10 miles. We have little architectural evidence of the private residences of the dictators. The early relatively simple living style of Augustus gave way fairly soon to enormous and flashy palaces, built in a predictable variety of shapes. Examples are Nero's planned Golden Palace (60's) and the heavily ornamented palace of Domitian (80's). Even the rural "retreat" of Hadrian, the Villa at Tivoli, which has survived, is built to great excess. From the very end of the period we have the fortified palace complex that Diocletian built for his retirement at Split on the coast of his native Illyria. It is very large (some 700' x 600') but it is built on the rectangular lines of a legion base, and it has very much the look of a fortress. The contrast between this construction, so clearly showing the insecurity of the age, and the rambling ease of Hadrian's country place could not be more obvious. Split complex, though, seem to have been relatively squat. Very different is the great palace which Constantine built at about the same time at Trier near the German border. It was 220' long and 106' high, heated with the hypocaust system (for this is a long way from the Mediterranean). This blocky, elongated style grew out of the customary style for the basilicas or public buildings.

The tendency to build up, to exploit the arch and concrete, was seen also in private structures. Some of the best-preserved private architecture comes from the Roman port of Ostia. Many people there lived in high-rise apartment houses, with little balconies, in a style that would not be out of place now. The Forum which Trajan built at Rome was also surrounded by high-rise stores. For such buildings concrete with a bricked surface was a favorite material, the bricks being colored bright red or yellow. Poorer structures, though, still were often made out of wood, and fires were common. Normally, there were no private water supplies; water was supplied publicly to many points around the towns. The wealthy lived in villas substantial individual houses. Large numbers of these have survived in some shape. The chief source is the group of towns, the most important among them Pompeii, destroyed by the eruption of Vesuvius in 79. The villas had broken away from the old atrium style into a variety of ground plans. They still contained extensive painting, by the 1st century A.D. often rich figure drawings. At no point can we say much at all about Roman painting, through, for so little of it survives. The most famous house painting is of a nature scene from the country house of Livia, wife of Augustus. We should remember that the public buildings we talk about would be lavishly painted--it was part of Hellenistic/Romantic excess. Mosaics were becoming more popular, sometimes on walls as well as floors, and contained figures as well as the older vivid patterns.

One popular form of public architecture which merged with sculpture was the Arch, put up to commemorate achievements of the emperors. These arches were free-standing and served no purpose at all beyond propaganda. We have a small one at Orange in southern France from the 20's (under Tiberius). It has three gateways and is a little more than 60' high. The first of the great arches (with a single gateway) is that of Titus, built by his brother Domitian in the 80's. This has attached Composite statues, the first in the new mixed Ionic-Corinthian style. We have an Arch of Trajan from Benevento, boasting of his road across south Italy. The Composite columns on this work are nearly 50' high. There is an Arch of Septimius Severus from a century later (about 200), commemorating his victories against the Parthians and others. It has three arches and is 65' high. We also have an Arch of Galerius from Thessalonica around 300; it has three arches but is much smaller than the others. For the great Arch of Constantine (early 300's), older pieces of sculpture were taken from many earlier pieces, a strange process of cannibalism which produced an absurd effect on the new arch. A closely related architectural style is the Column, simply an alternative way of offering imperial propaganda. We have two famous Columns at Rome. One is Trajan's, built in honor of his conquest of Dacia, which was placed in his Forum. It is in white marble, 128' high (18' base, 97' shaft, with a 13' statue of Trajan on top—the last lost and replaced now by St. Peter). The diameter shaft diminishes from a 12' diameter at the base to 10' at the top, to give the correct visual impression. According to tradition, Trajan's ashes were buried in the base of the column. There is also the Column of Marcus Aurelius, in honor of his wars against the Germans (170's).

Sculpture.
The Arch and the Column were also major works of Roman sculpture, deliberate expressions of how the system wished to present itself. The arches are stuffed with sculpture, the columns feature sculptural spirals running all the way up the shafts. All concentrate on action scenes, presenting the emperor doing a variety of worthwhile things. Usually this means war—the exception is the Arch of Trajan at

672

Benevento. The columns can do this by telling a story, in a sequence of single shots or episodes, much as a cartoon does for us.

Among the Arches, that of Titus has the highest reputation for quality of work. It is carved in deep relief, with good use of perspective (a complex thing which the Romans had great difficulty mastering). It follows the processional style of Augustus' Altar of Peace. The sculpture is likely to look "busy" or over-loaded to us, in a way that is characteristically Hellenistic/Romantic. The same is true of the Domitian frieze of the 80's, which is generally restrained in the Classic manner but which is far "busier" than the scenes on the Altar of Peace of Augustus. In the Arch of Septimius Severus, excess explodes all over the place—the figures are all but swamped by decoration and ornament. It has the look about it of the worst elements of the Hellenistic style; and it is not very well done either. The Column of Trajan has a low-relief spiral band which is 50" high and 660' long, the subject is Trajan's conquest of Dacia. In all, some 2,500 figures are shown. A quick calculation will show you that the work is very crowded. To us, it looks like a jungle of figures. Perspective often is simply ignored, and in many ways the work appears ridiculous to us. The Column of Marcus Aurelius of half-a-century later (170's), with a similar spiral telling how the dictator gave the barbarian Germans what they deserved, is much weaker in technical efficiency; many sections are plain badly done. It creates the same feeling of suffocating business, however. The difference in the attitude toward war which is expressed in these two columns, for Trajan's gives a gung-ho impression, while the other has something of a war-is-hell attitude. This may reflect the attitudes of the two rulers—Trajan the eager conqueror, Marcus Aurelius the Stoic suffering his way through life. There is a chance that residents of Rome paid more or less no attention to the sculptures—little can be seen from the ground level. Perhaps only the scale, the bigness, counted.

Roman statues of the centuries of the dictatorship reflect the wide variety of the Hellenistic style, coupled with the Roman tradition of more or less realistic personal, individual portraits. There was a substantial market in statues of the emperors and members of the ruling families.

673

Sometimes we have the impression that emperors wished to create a particular image of themselves; at other times we seem to be looking at just "stuff," created because figures of the emperor were needed. Often, the statues are only roughed in at the back, because they were intended to stand in niches rather than out in the open.

The line of naked male statues continued, often using poses copied from the Greeks. Emperors could be represented naked, as we saw with Augustus. At times, this style had laughable results, as in the statue of Claudius, in which the very plain and middle-aged head of that worthy is stuck on top of a cute young body. This tradition lasted well into the 200's; we have one of Alexander Severus as naked Greek athlete. The most striking of all the naked male figures is that of Antinous, lover of Hadrian (117-138). Females were generally clothed--the Romans were not nearly as easy-going in this direction as the Hellenistic Greeks. Goddesses, however, could be naked, and it seems to have been acceptable to give to naked goddesses the heads of empresses. We have a statue of Sabina (wife of Hadrian) in a very strange-looking see-through outfit, and one of Faustina, wife of Marcus Aurelius and a famous beauty, as naked Aphrodite in the manner of Praxiteles of the 300's B.C. Faustina, though, has a cloth in front of herself. Neither work is done very skillfully; both look ridiculous. Christianity, of course, was going to kill the representation of the naked body.

The most impressive element about the formal, clothed statues or busts of the emperors is the note of individualism, of realism. We see Nero as the soft playboy; Vespasian as the hard-headed non-aristocratic, tough and mean; Titus his son as a softer version of the same; Trajan, with upper body naked, as the great statesman, hard but concerned; Hadrian as the weak dandy in flashy armor and very fancy headgear; Marcus Aurelius, on horseback, as the concerned Stoic leader. Perhaps the most impressive piece of all in this line is the head of Caracalla (211-217), brutal, mean-looking, heavily wrinkling. This was possibly patterned after a style set by Lysippus in the 300's B.C. Caracalla seems to have liked the piece--it was distributed widely. There is a fine bust of Elagabalus, strangest of the strange, showing him very clearly as a chinless, characterless sensualist. The most

674

ridiculous piece is the head of <u>Commodus</u> as Hercules. Commodus, with a flashy hair-style painted in gold, is soft and weak; the paws of the animal skin he is wearing on his head reach perversely down to scratch at his nipples. Female figures are generally much less expressive, and are much more idealized. Flavian women, for example, are shown as very different from the down-to-earth Flavian men (Vespasian and Titus). The wife of Marcus Aurelius (the Faustina of the Aphrodite statue) is not used to indicate an association with her husband's style. Julia Domna, wife of Septimius Severus and mother of Caracalla, is shown composed and good-looking in a very abstracted way, quite unlike the Caracalla work. It is impossible to calculate what this tells us about the propaganda system at work--the extensive realism in showing dictators, the restraints in the female representations.

The figures tell us something about the changes in style. Beards came in with <u>Hadrian</u>; he is said to have grown one because he had scars on his face. Rich beards remained popular for nearly a century. At much the same time, men's hair-styles became much more ornate and full; this had happened earlier with women. By Marcus Aurelius' time (161-180) hair styles for both sexes were very dandified-- a great change from the days of Augustus. It is harder to use the sculptural work to "interpret" the rulers or the age. Hadrian, for example, is associated with a revival of the cool Classical style (117-138). His villa at Tivoli is used as evidence, along with a series of sculptural pieces which from this period which were later stuck on to the Arch of Constantine (early 300's). Where does this leave the beard, the wilder hairstyles, the representation of Hadrian himself as the dandy-soldier? The same mixed-up effects mark the period of Marcus Aurelius, which is sometimes associated with the early stages of the movement away from Hellenistic realism toward a new abstract style. The significance of any of this as political propaganda, let alone as art, is beyond us.

In very general terms, over the first two centuries after Christ there was a movement toward greater flashiness, ornamentation, business--toward the richer, more Romantic elements of the Hellenized style. By 200, in general, style had moved a long way from the attempted detachment of the

period of Augustus. Compare the Caracalla bust to those of
Augustus. This movement had its counterpart in architecture,
in the steady trend toward more and more bigness. All these
varieties, though, were just variations of the Hellenistic
style. At the same time, there were signs toward the end of
the 100's of a new style, more abstract, more impressionistic--
a style that tried to get at the inner man in some other way
than the brutal realism of the head of Caracalla. The statue
of Marcus Aurelius on horseback is an early example of this.
Another is provided by the figures from an Arch of Septimius
Severus from his home town of Lepcis Magna in north-central
Africa. These figures are done bluntly frontally, all on
one level, with a lack of interest in detail. The deliberate
crudeness of technique was an attempt to indicate character
and meaning, to get away from the centuries-old traditions
of technical proficiency and "realism."

This newer style emerged over several generations,
through the 200's, for a long time coexisting with the
traditional Hellenistic style in a confusing way. By the
mid-200's, though, it had pushed a new element of simplicity
into statues that were obviously meant to be traditionally
Hellenistic. From the mid-200's we have new-style heads of
Philip the Arab (244-249) and Decius (249-251), the second
particularly being a very clear example of the deliberate
crudity of technique which was associated with the new
style. Decius is very worried, very uncertain--the ruler in
the Anarchy. Gallus is shown on another piece with his
forehead horribly furrowed. A Gallienus bust of a few years
later is deliberately traditional in intent and provides a
sharp contrast to the earlier works; even it, though, is
hard and rough in the new style. We have the emperor
Hostilianus in a relief sculpture of the same period which
is very traditional in the crowded and overdone way that had
been common in the 100's.

As late as the 280's we have a bust of the emperor Carus
which looks very traditional--it would have looked much out
of place 200 years before. By this time, though, the new
style was widespread. Figure carvings on what may be the
tomb of Carus' son Carinus are very abstracted, with the deep
drilling into the surface of the head which was becoming
common. The Eros and Psyche among Cupids from another tomb
of about the same period (late 200's) is very strange looking,

676

being tremendously abstracted and impressionistic.

Over the next generation, the new style won out. Famous examples of the abstract style are the groups of the Tetrachs (Diocletian and those he picked to rule with him) and the amazing colossal head of Constantine (early 300's), 9' high and weighing 9 tons. To see the difference, the figure of Victory from the Column of Trajan (98-117), a purely traditional work in a more-or-less busy Hellenistic manner, can be compared with the representations of Victory on the Arch of Galerius, on the Arch of Constantine, and on the Decennial Base at Rome (a work of 305 marking the 10th anniversary of the selection of Galerius and Constantius Chlorus as Caesars). The plundering of older works to provide sculptures for the Arch of Constantine is an indication of how much the old style had declined by this time.

Here a Roman style emerged, at last, as the Empire fell on hard times. What happened is clear--detail and technique were given up for impression and "inner" meaning. How the change was related to what was happening in the Empire in the horrible 200's we can only guess at? Did it spring naturally from an unhappiness with the old forms which had prevailed for so long? Did it spring from a decline in ability, with a wish to make a virtue of necessity by favoring abstraction over realism? Abstraction may not spring from a lack of technical ability; but it makes it easier to put up with that lack, and over time it will cripple that ability. How any of what happened was related to spiritual or political trends in the 200's we also cannot say. Escapism was common, as we see in the philosophy and religion of the day; there was plenty to escape from. Certainly, Christianity in the 300's, when it had been adopted by the Roman state, found the new style suited to its purpose--the abstraction, the search for the "inner" man, could be easily turned into a spiritual search or wondering in statues. Immense eyes, looking up, for example, became a token of devotion in 300's sculpture. Did the new style begin as a means of spiritual expression, and as a protest against the spiritual poverty of the old? And where were the dictators in all this, poor, uneducated soldiers that most of them were? Did the change come because they saw themselves differently?

677

THE SEVERI DYNASTY, 193-235

The most important source for this period is the work of Dio Cassius, who witnessed many of the events himself. A member of the Senate class, the son of a governor, himself a consul, Dio Cassius has little good to say about the period. He wrote in Greek. His writings indicate a surprising superstition and lack of sophistication. His work is very romantic, often entertaining, but not impressive in any other way. It is a great pity that we do not know more about the Severi (plural of Severus) period, since in many ways it was very important and revealing.

Septimius Severus, 193-211.

193: Those who killed Commodus had their replacement ready. This was Pertinax, a great name from the days of Marcus Aurelius. The Senate approved happily. After three months, however, Pertinax was murdered by the Guards. Laetus, who had gotten rid of Commodus, may have been responsible. The explanation given is the same one used to explain the death of Galba in 69: the emperor annoyed his soldiers by his stinginess and discipline.

193: The Guard now held a sort of auction in their camp, offering the position of emperor at bid. The winner was Didius Julianus, who then sensibly killed the Prefect Laetus. These sorry episodes at least show how weak the Senate was by this time; the circumstances were very different from those after the murder of Domitian in 96. Once again, though, as in 69 and 97, the legions beyond Italy were not willing to accept the choices made in Rome—and again the final power rested with them. Generals in the provinces now declared themselves, finding it much easier to oppose Didius Julianus than Pertinax. This led to the first civil war since 68-69.

193: The two chief hopefuls outside Italy were Pescennius Niger in Syria and SEPTIMIUS SEVERUS on the Danube front. Severus had the double advantage of being closer to Rome and having more legions. With Severus marching on Rome, the Senate decided to obey his order to kill poor Didius Julianus, who had been "ruler" (of very little) for 9 weeks. Occupying Rome, Severus carefully settled for the time being with a minor hopeful in the West. This was Albinus, governor of Britain. Severus adopted Albinus as his heir, even though he had two sons of his own.

678

194: Severus then went East and defeated <u>Pescennius</u> <u>Niger</u>,
his major rival. He stayed a while to settle the East.
197: Dropping <u>Albinus</u>, Severus took his own children as his
heirs. He then defeated and killed Albinus at the battle of
<u>Lyons</u>. Lyons, the biggest town in Gaul, was looted and
destroyed, and never was the same again.

     This gave Severus control of the Empire. The episode
had been the longest and worst outbreak of disorder since
the wars of the 30's B.C. The victory of Severus was the
first political victory for the <u>Danube</u> armies and indicated
the increased importance of that front which dated from
<u>Marcus</u> <u>Aurelius</u>.

     Severus, aged 48 in 193, was from <u>Lepcis</u> <u>Magna</u> in <u>North</u>
<u>Africa</u>. While he was descended on his father's side from
Italian settlers, he probably had <u>Carthaginian</u> (<u>Punic</u>) blood.
He spoke Latin with a definite accent. Severus had been
born into the class of <u>equites</u>; his family was even more
obscure than that of <u>Vespasian</u>, the only comparable case.
Severus certainly was the most <u>untraditional</u> emperor to this
point, particularly since his wife was a <u>Syrian</u> woman (JULIA
DOMNA).

     Severus' background explains certain developments of
his rule:
--He was very suspicious of the Senate and the old ruling
class (themselves actually mostly new families since
<u>Vespasian</u>'s day). The old Republican traditions perhaps
meant less to Severus than to earlier emperors. Many senators were killed (29, for example, for being friendly to
<u>Albinus</u>). Severus preferred to depend on the equites, the
group with which he identified best. They, rather than
senators, provided his administrators; they commanded the
extra legions he raised. In the same way, he took away most
of the duties of the permanent courts, which were dominated
by men of the senatorial class, and gave them to his own
officials, who were usually equites. This was a return to
the highly personal control of justice by officials which
had been the style of the early Republic.
--As an expression of this hostility to the Senate, and at
the same time a sensible extension of the old process of
broadening the circle of power, Severus speeded up the
<u>provincialization</u> of the Empire. For example, he increased

the number of non-Italians in the Senate, giving them a
majority for the first time. Africans and Easterners were
especially favored--about 1/6th of the senators now were
Africans.
--Above all, Severus militarized the Empire much more bluntly and clearly than had been done before.
   1. He replaced the highly-political Praetorian Guard at
Rome with a force of his own troops from the Danube--and
in the process doubled the numbers involved to about
15,000. He also stationed one legion in Italy, close to
the capital--a very revealing break with tradition.
   2. He increased the size of the army from 30 to 33 legions
and hired more auxiliaries and, especially, tribal soldiers
from outside the Empire. The total now under arms was
about 400,000 in an Empire smaller in population since the
plague and weaker in its economic structure.
   3. He was "nice" to the soldiers in many ways. Their pay
was increased greatly; they were allowed to marry. The
nonlegionary troops were given land around their camps in
the border areas and so were turned into a frontier militia.
This was not the best thing for efficiency, but it suited
the troops well. Since Severus disliked the old ruling
groups, there were many opportunities in his armies for
men of talent from humble backgrounds.

   All of this was summed up in his supposed dying advice
to his sons: "Be generous to the soldiers and don't bother
about anything else!" More clearly than ever before, the
political power of the army was recognized. In view of what
happened later, it is easy to criticize Severus in this
connection; the immediate impact, however, was to produce
under his strong leadership a large and very efficient army,
well capable of coping with any problem. At no other point,
perhaps, was Rome stronger militarily in relation to surrounding peoples.

   Severus liked to fight and wanted a military reputation.
He had served on the Danube with Marcus Aurelius, a man he
admired greatly--although the desire for glory must have been
one of the very few things the two men had in common:
197-199: Following the defeat of Albinus in the West (197),
Severus campaigned in the East against the Parthians. He
overran Mesopotamia and annexed the northern part of it. So
heavy were his blows that the Parthian Empire fell apart. At

the time this looked like a wonderful service to the state—the destruction of an enemy who had troubled Rome for 300 years. He rewarded himself with a great victory <u>Arch</u> <u>of</u> <u>Severus</u> at Rome.

Back in Rome, Severus was not so comfortable. The details of administration seem to have bored him. He depended heavily on the commanders of his new Guard (who were still called Praetorian Prefects). The most prominent of these was <u>Plautanias</u>, another product of the town of <u>Lepcis</u> <u>Magna</u>. Plautanias enjoyed 10 years of power, even managing to get his daughter married to CARACALLA, the older son of Severus, before he died violently in 208 (<u>Caracalla</u>, it seems, was jealous of his father-in-law). Severus' wife, <u>Julia</u> <u>Domna</u>, was also an important figure—a rare thing for an emperor's wife. We have to go back to <u>Agrippina</u> in <u>Nero</u>'s day for a previous example of such a woman. Julia Domna was a patron of learning and had a great interest in all varieties of religion.
208-211: Severus, with his wife and two sons, campaigned in <u>Britain</u>, restoring the northern border and the line of <u>Hadrian's</u> <u>Wall</u>. The <u>Wall</u> <u>of</u> <u>Antoninus</u> further north was abandoned. Severus was the first emperor since <u>Hadrian</u> to put himself to the trouble of going to Britain. He died in Britain, at <u>York</u>, in 211, aged 66. The body was taken back to Rome for burial.

<u>Caracalla, 211-217.</u>
<u>Caracalla</u>, the older son of Severus, was 23 when his father died; his brother <u>Geta</u> was a year younger. Severus intended them to share the Empire, in the way of <u>Marcus</u> <u>Aurelius</u> and <u>Lucius</u> <u>Verus</u> in the 160's. Instead, Caracalla murdered his brother almost as soon as they were back in Rome. Caracalla is a nickname meaning a long cloak of the Celtic fashion—it was a style of dress he liked.

Caracalla has a bad name with us, perhaps unreasonably. He was active and ambitious; he seems to have been popular with the legions and successful militarily:
—He issued the EDICT OF CARACALLA, the most famous law of the Empire. It gave <u>citizenship</u> to <u>all</u> <u>free</u> <u>men</u> in the Empire except one group. This group (the <u>dediticii</u>) were perhaps native peoples who had been allowed only recently into the Empire—we do not know for sure. This step brought

681

to its logical conclusion the steady expansion of citizenship which had been going on for centuries. We do not know
how far citizenship had spread before the Edict. The Empire
was now one universal society.
--He completed the great public baths which his father had
begun. These BATHS OF CARACALLA are among the greatest
relics of Rome.
--To raise money for his campaigns and for the larger army,
Caracalla introduced a new income tax. He also began the
serious weakening of the currency, reducing the vital metal
content. With time, this kind of thing would get out of
hand and help to produce tremendous inflation. One purpose
of the extension of citizenship, in fact, may have been to
manufacture more people to pay the income tax, since only
citizens were liable. Here were the unavoidable consequences of having a large and well-treated army.

     Caracalla, like his father, wanted a great military
reputation. He campaigned with some success on the German
border and then went East. Despite some setbacks he fought
through Mesopotamia and on into Persia. Then:
217: Caracalla was assassinated near Carrhae (site of the
battle of 55 B.C.). The culprit was his Praetorian Prefect,
MACRINUS, a Mauretanian (a new Guard, an old story).
Macrinus apparently thought that Caracalla was about to have
him killed. When Macrinus the Prefect proceeded to set himself up as emperor, though, he did break new ground. The
legions in the East approved; the Senate at Rome rubber-
stamped the change. Macrinus had risen from the ranks and
was still only in the equites class--so that he was the first
person not of Senate rank to become emperor. Here was a
further broadening of the circle of power.

Elagabalus, 218-222.
     Macrinus soon lost his hold on the legions. Further
fighting went badly and he settled for unfavorable terms
with the Parthians, allowing Armenia to remain in the hands
of a Parthian prince as a Roman client (just as Nero had done
in the 60's). In 218 the legions in the East transferred
their support to Caracalla's closest male relative--his
nephew ELAGABALUS, aged 14. Elagabalus was the grandson of
Julia Maesa, sister to Julia Domna (now dead). Once again,
female influence was very important, Julia Maesa being the
moving force behind Elagabalus. To make the young man more

acceptable, he was presented as the bastard son of Caracalla.
The hereditary principle won out; Macrinus was defeated and
killed. After a settlement was made in the East, Elagabalus
came, or was brought, to Rome.

For all the wrong reasons, Elagabalus is among the most
remarkable of the emperors. He was the youngest to reach
that positon, taking the record from Nero, who had been 16.
Since both his father and his mother were Syrians, he was
the first non-Italian emperor. In addition, he proved to be
the craziest of the crazy emperors. In loving detail, Dio
Cassius describes Elegabalus' sexual oddities: his wild
homosexuality (he "married" a male lover), his mad trans-
vestism, his obsession with being a whore, his sado-masochism.
Along with all this, he took the time to marry a large number
of women, and he had one shocking affair with a Vestal Virgin
(theoretically impossible). Here is a sample from Dio
Cassius:

> He would go to the bars at night, wearing a wig, to hustle
> as a woman. He hung around the worst brothels, throwing
> out the whores in order to take their place himself. He
> also had a room in the palace set apart for his filth. He
> always stood nude by the door of the room, as a whore does,
> shaking the curtain and its golden rings, softly solicit-
> ing those who passed by.
> He wanted to be known for committing adultery, so that he
> could be like the filthiest women in this way too. He
> often let himself be caught having sex, so that his
> "husband" would scold him and beat him up, leaving him
> with black eyes.

Elagabalus' religion was a further weakness. At home at
Emesa in Syria he had been a priest in a local religion
devoted to the god Elagabalus (hence the emperor's nickname,
by which we know him). This god was a black stone, probably
a meteorite--very much a thing of the East. Elagabalus
brought his god with him in great splendor to Rome. The god
had many strange sexual tastes (obviously), although it seems
that Elagabalus resisted the god's order to do away with his
sexual organs.

His mother and her lover were the chief influences over
Elagabalus; they do not seem to have been much better than
he was. In 222 his grandmother Julia Maesa and her second

daughter Julia Mamaea had Elagabalus and his mother killed.
They had a replacement at hand in Julia Mamaea's son
ALEXANDER, cousin to Elagabalus. Alexander was offered as
another of Caracalla's bastards.

Alexander Severus, 222-235.

Julia Maesa, the grandmother, died in 226. Her death
left Julia Mamaea as the chief influence, as the unusual
female prominence continued. Alexander, also only 14 when
he became emperor, never asserted himself, becoming one of
the rare do-nothing emperors. He seems to have been weak,
but not depraved. He had some of his family's philosophical
and religious interests, and it is said that among the
figures he admired and prayed to and whose statues he kept
in his prayer room was Christ (along with Socrates). The
story of the revival of Senate influence under Alexander
probably has little to it. The Senate had become almost
irrelevant, and it was only natural that the body should
become more visible in a period of peace under so weak an
emperor.

What would be the attitude of the soldiers toward such
an un-military person? Under the Severi, this was a more
critical question than it had been earlier. In 228 the
Praetorian Guards murdered their Prefect Ulpian, an important
figure in Roman law (see below), inside the palace and were
not punished.

Alexander's mother, Julia Mamaea, tried. She surely was
aware of the importance of the military to the Severi:
231-232: Alexander and his mother campaigned in the East
against the new kingdom of PERSIA which had arisen on the
ruins of the Parthians. The last Parthian ruler was overthrown in the 220's by Artaxerxes, the founder of the new
Persian Empire. The Persians ruled from the Parthian city
of Ctesiphon in Mesopotamia, but their "religious" capital
was near Persepolis, the ancient capital of the Achaemenid
kings of Persia who had threatened Classical Greece 700 years
earlier. The Persians were to be much more troublesome to
the Romans than the Parthians had been.
The intention if the Roman campaign was a grand one--the outright invasion of Persia. It did not work out well. Still,
the Persians were pushed out of Mesopotamia.
234-235: Alexander and his mother went to the Rhine border

in Germany to fight the tribes. They found the soldiers
very unsettled. When Alexander tried to settle with the
Germans in order to avoid fighting, the legions, angered at
such an insult from the weakling, killed him and his mother.
The story is that they were cornered in the legion latrines
and killed and left there. That was the end of the Severi.

- \.

What followed the murder of <u>Alexander</u> <u>Severus</u> was horrible beyond description. For the next half-century, it was
as if the Romans had lost all their talents for government
and good sense. At times it seemed even as if the Empire
would not survive. It did survive, but what came out of the
chaos and weakness of the period was an Empire much changed
and much reduced. The cost of the recovery was enormous;
the extent of the recovery was very limited. The old Rome
could not be brought back. It is unfortunate that we have
no major historical source at all for this period. Much of
it is very little known to us.

Two specific elements in the difficulties were:
--There was a sudden failure to provide reasonably for the
<u>succession</u> to the position of emperor. Under a system of
one-man rule, the succession obviously is the most important
of all political questions. There had been difficulties
earlier (in 68-69, 96, 192-197, 217-218), but what happened
after 235 was new. In the period 235-284, there were 21
"regular" emperors. Of these, only one escaped a violent
death. Most were killed by their own supporters. There
were in addition large numbers of other claimants, pretend-
ers, setting themselves up all over the Empire. One emperor
alone, <u>Gallienus</u> (260-268), had to overcome, or ignore, 18
rivals. The biggest source of this trouble was the loss of
self-control by the armies, which now interfered in politics
much more openly and much more frequently than ever before.
The armies now exercised as a matter of habit that power
which had always potentially been theirs. The military
changes made by <u>Septimius</u> <u>Severus</u> may have played a big role
in this although he may only have been doing what was
becoming inevitable. The armies were bigger, more pampered,
more political, more independent of control by the traditional Senate ruling class. Already, since the death of
Septimius Severus in 211, instability and murder had been on
the increase. The murder of Alexander Severus in 235 was
totally without precedent. Things did not collapse because
of the end of the <u>Severi</u> dynasty; the changes that were
taking place overwhelmed the Severi as their first victims.
The Severi had responded to and encouraged those changes;
they had not invented them. Out of all this came great civil
wars which devastated much of the Empire, and instability and

inefficiency at the top since the emperors were removed so
frequently. In addition, many of the emperors were new
types--soldier-emperors, often from primitive backgrounds,
whose success resulted from the armies' asserting themselves.
Some of these emperors were men of enormous talent and honest
effort with a great love of Rome, but they all had very
different values and attitudes from the men of the old ruling
class.
--Feeding on the weaknesses caused by the civil wars and the
chaos at the top of the Roman system, and also adding greatly to it, were the foreign enemies to the north and in the
East: the German tribes beyond the Rhine and Danube rivers
and the new Persian Empire. The balance of power tilted
very heavily against the Romans in this period, the Empire
for the first time finding itself very clearly weaker than
these enemies. Parts of the East were ravaged repeatedly by
the Persians and the Rhine-Danube frontier became irrelevant
for a while, with the Germans raiding deep into the Empire
almost at will. There is no question about the enormous
damage suffered in the provinces--the Empire's economy was
never the same again (although of course the civil wars
played their parts in this too). There is a great deal of
question about whether and to what extent these difficulties
could have been avoided by reasonably strong emperors and the
disciplined, orderly armies of old. It is hard to say much
in this connection about the German tribes, because we know
so little about the circumstances which affected them. A
new German people, the GOTHS, appeared in the Danube area
soon after 200, giving trouble for the first time under
Caracalla. There was more trouble from the Goths in the
230's, but nothing serious. The big problems here did not
arise until the late 240's, when Rome was already self-
destructing. In the case of the Persians, the suspicion is
stronger that they were reacting to the problems the Romans
were creating for themselves. In the East, also, the problems did not become serious until the 240's. The Empire
under the Severi, it seems, had been as secure as ever. It
was much stronger than the Persians and there had been no
serious difficulties with the Germans since the days of Marcus
Aurelius in the 170's. Even in the anarchy, the Germans and
the Persians do not seem to have been strong enough to do
anything more than raid and pillage. When the Empire began
to get itself back into orfer in the 270's, it was again
apparent that Rome still had the strength to assert itself

against both the Persians and the Germans. By the 280's
the foreign situation had been brought under control, and
for another 100 years Roman military strength was superior
to that of its enemies, singly or in combination.

Maximin, 235-238.

MAXIMIN was chosen in 235 by the legions on the Rhine
to replace the murdered Alexander Severus as emperor. The
choice indicates a lot about what was happening. Maximin
was from a peasant background from the primitive Balkans,
the great breeding ground of volunteers for the army and the
most important of the border areas. He may not even have
been a Roman citizen by birth (the Edict of Caracalla,
giving citizenship to nearly everyone, dated only from 212).
Maximin was a giant of a man, with tremendous physical
strength. He is said to have been taken into the army by
Septimius Severus, who saw him in a wrestling match while
passing through the Balkans. His ability in battle and his
good relations with the soldiers, who were mostly from his
kind of background, had brought him to the rank of general
and equestrian status. There is no earlier emperor at all
to compare to Maximin--Macrinus, who had assassinated
Caracalla in 217, comes closest.

After some hesitation, the legions along the Rhine and
Danube accepted Maximin. He campaigned successfully in both
areas against the German tribes. He seems to have had no
desire at all to visit Rome, a place which must have seemed
very alien to such a man. This was an early sign that the
city of Rome would suffer greatly in importance from the
change in the kind of men who ran the state.

238: Revolt broke out in the Senate province of Africa. The
governor, aged 80, and his son declared as co-emperors
(GORDIAN I and II). The purpose of this arrangement was to
prevent objections to the age of the father. The Gordians
claimed to be descended from the Gracchi brothers and from
Trajan. This had the look of a protest by the old ruling
class, and by the older and wealthier parts of the Empire,
against the primitive Maximin. The Senate at Rome declared
for Gordian I and II, but the two were both killed in battle
against the governor of Numidia who was loyal to Maximin.
The Senate then picked two replacements for the Gordians,
elderly senators named BALBINUS and PUPIENUS. In selecting

688

two men, like the two consuls of old, the Senate indicated a desire to end one-man rule.

Maximin brought his army into Italy from the north, entering it almost as a foreign country. Before he could do anything, though, his soldiers murdered him. This is hard to explain. He had promised to double the pay of his soldiers--a tactic of the Severi and one which, repeated often enough, would have sad economic consequences--and he may not have been able to deliver on his promise. For the legions simply to kill an emperor for no special political purpose--not even to select his successor--was a totally new thing. It did prevent, though, a big civil war.

Balbinus and Pupienus did not benefit much from Maximin's death. Soon the Praetorian Guard, which had played little part so far, killed them both, again it seems for no special reason. The Guard picked GORDIAN III, 13 years old son of the dead Gordian II, as a replacement. The Guard Prefect, Timesitheus, figured to be the dominant influence over the boy (the youngest ruler so far). The Senate went along. More surprisingly, so did the armies. It had been a very strange year.

Gordian III, 238-244.
Timesitheus did become the power behind the boy-emperor. He took Gordian III East in 242-243. There they successfully dealt with the first troubles from the Persians, who had moved close to Antioch, the third city of the Empire after Rome and Alexandria. Then, in 243, Timesitheus died. The new Prefect was PHILIP the ARAB, the son of an Arab chief. In 244, the Guard murdered Gordian III, almost certainly at the bidding of Philip, who was recognized as the new emperor.

Philip the Arab, 244-249.
However odd he seemed as a Roman emperor, this Arab was efficient. He settled things with the Persians, campaigned on the Danube (246-247), and returned to Rome to celebrate in magnificent style the 1000th birthday of Rome (248). Things looked promising, particularly since Philip had a son to succeed him. Then in 249 the Danube armies recognized one of their commanders, DECIUS, as emperor. We do not know why. Decius took the job and marched his army into Italy. In the brief war, both Philip and his son were killed.

Decius, 249-251.

Decius was from the Balkans, but he seems to have been born there of a prosperous Italian family. Under Decius came the first serious results of the disorder. With the Danube army gone off to the war in Italy, the Goths were able to raid widely across the Balkans. They destroyed Philippopolis, a long way south of the border. At the same time, perhaps, the Persians began to cause trouble again, although our chronology is not certain on this point. Decius campaigned hard in the Balkans, largely clearing the area, but in 251 he was killed in battle against the Goths in the marshes of the Dobrudja at Abrittus. His son died with him. To be killed in battle against foreign enemies was a novelty for an emperor. It is likely that Decius risked himself foolishly when he was weak in numbers. GALLUS, governor of Moesia, was deliberately refusing to help him. Gallus was then recognized as emperor by the soldiers.

One very important thing is associated with Decius--the first substantial persecution of the Christians. This we will look at below.

Gallus, 251-253, and Aemilianus, 253.

Gallus was a soldier-emperor from the Balkans of the Maximin type. He made peace with the Goths. It may have been at this time that the plague (or whatever it was) struck the Empire again. The impact was as great as during the outbreak of the 160's, and the epidemic lasted until about 270.

In 253, AEMILIANUS, who had succeeded Gallus as governor of Moesia, came out as emperor. He had won popularity with his legions by some victories against the Goths. Off to Italy he went with his troops, in the manner of Decius in 249. Gallus and his son were killed in the civil war. Then, three months later, while he was still in Italy, Aemilianus was murdered by his own soldiers. We do not know what lay behind this. The soldiers replaced him with VALERIAN. Like the Gordians, Valerian came from one of the old noble families of the Republic. He was to be the last of his kind. What steps he took to help himself to his new position (he was in Germany at the time) we cannot say.

690

<u>Valerian, 253-260, and Gallienus, 253-268.</u>
     Valerian took his son GALLIENUS as co-emperor. He
intended to make a lot of use of <u>Gallienus</u>. Both men had
ability and dedication, but their luck was bad. This period
marks both the low point and in some ways the beginning of
recovery.

     The plague continued all through these years, with far-
reaching effect. On the frontiers, both to the north and the
East, there was greater weakness than ever. The <u>Goths</u> overran the <u>Balkans</u> repeatedly, raiding even into <u>Asia</u> <u>Minor</u>.
For a decade and a half they had the better of things here.
Their last big success was in 268, when, arriving by sea,
they ravaged <u>Asia</u> <u>Minor</u> and <u>Greece</u> (including <u>Athens</u>), and
then returned to the <u>Danube</u> area by land. The year 253, when
Valerian came to power, also saw the <u>Rhine</u> frontier seriously
broken for the first time. The <u>Franks</u> (which means "free
men," indicating a grouping of German tribes) could hardly
be stopped after that. They raided all the way through <u>Gaul</u>
and <u>Spain</u> and even into <u>North</u> <u>Africa</u>. Other Germans, the
<u>Saxons</u>, moving by water, attacked <u>northern</u> <u>Gaul</u> and <u>Britain</u>.
More Germans got into Italy (attacking <u>Ravenna</u> in 254, for
example). In the East, the Persian king <u>Shapur</u> <u>I</u> made yearly
expeditions deep into Roman lands. Shapur had had to wait
his moment for up to 20 years, but after 250, with Rome's
attention centered almost entirely on the Balkans and civil
war, there was little to stop him. He took <u>Antioch</u> at least
twice. The greatest Persian attacks came between 250 and
256, and then again in 259-260.

     It may have been beyond the Empire's ability for a while
to handle all these problems, particularly with the plague
running its course. One response, one with great potential
for evil, was for local army commanders to go their own way
and declare themselves emperors in charge of a certain area,
ignoring or defying the central government. This kind of
thing was commonest on the <u>Rhine</u> border and in the <u>East</u>;
there was a feeling that the <u>Danube</u> armies had been getting
too much attention and had been playing too big a part in
picking emperors since 249. The most important examples are:
--<u>Postumus</u>, 259-268. <u>Postumus</u> set up his capital at <u>Trier</u> on
the <u>Rhine</u> frontier. He and his successors held <u>Gaul</u>, <u>Britain</u>,
and <u>Spain</u> for 14 years.
--<u>Odenathus</u> <u>of</u> <u>Palmyra</u>. <u>Palmyra</u> was an oasis city on the

Syrian border which had grown rich servicing the desert trade
routes. It had been annexed by Rome in the 1st century A.D.,
but it was still administered by its own chiefs. Odenathus
was such a chief. A man of great ability, he had an important place in the Roman military system in the East in the
250's. He defeated Shapur of Persia in the big war of
259-260--a great service to Rome. In the 260's Gallienus
gave him virtual control of all the Roman possessions in the
East. Odenathus played with the idea of deserting Rome and
grabbing much of the East for himself, but he decided against
it. After he was assassinated (267), though, his widow
ZENOBIA did declare herself independent of Rome. In behalf
of her young son, she grabbed Egypt, Syria, and most of Asia
Minor. Here was another of the remarkable women from the
East after the manner of the Severi.

Men like Postumus and Odenathus performed real services,
but they threatened the unity of the state. Over the long
run, they could not be allowed to survive. Even in the short
run, their defensive efforts against foreign enemies left
the central government without the means to do the same thing
(as they saw it, of course, they existed only because of the
collapse of the central government and were doing things
which otherwise would not be done at all). There is by every
account less to be said for the large number of lesser names
who set themselves up as the emperors of various pieces of
the Roman Empire in these years. Their existence reflected
simply the breakdown of discipline; most of them were too
weak to do much beyond fight one another and pillage.
Against Rome's enemies they were useless.

In the 250's, Valerian and Gallienus had a very hard
time of it. Gallienus took the West, including both the
Rhine and Danube borders. He controlled little of the area
outside Italy, and may have had little choice but to try to
ride things out. He campaigned energetically, but to little
effect that we can see. His father Valerian took an army to
the East, certainly by 256. He was able to push the Persians
back and restore order. Valerian remained in the East. In
the next heavy fighting against the Persians, in 259-260,
Valerian was captured (260). Perhaps he was tricked into
negotiating and seized. The Persians carried Valerian off
into slavery, a condition in which he lived out the rest of
his life. A giant Persian rock sculpture shows Valerian

kneeling at the feet of king <u>Shapur</u>. It is easy to imagine
how stunning this event must have seemed to Romans, even
though they did again manage, under the leadership of
Odenathus, to drive off the Persians.

Valerian is also associated with the <u>second</u> <u>major</u> <u>perse-</u>
<u>cution</u> <u>of</u> <u>Christians</u>; the first having been under <u>Decius</u>.
<u>Gallienus</u> halted the persecution after the capture of his
father.

Gallienus was now sole emperor--but he was not in control of much. This moment, 260, was the bottom of the pit.
Gallienus made no attempt to rescue his father; his only way
of restoring order in the East was to give the area into the
care of Odenathus. Postumus in the West he generally avoided.
Instead, he concentrated on the <u>Danube</u> frontier, fighting the
Goths and a whole line of rivals.

In these efforts, Gallienus did well by Rome. Trying
to improve the military situation, he took two important
steps:
--He extended the separation of the senators from the army,
refusing to allow them a military career. This strengthened
professionalism in the army but separated it further from
the old ruling class; it also encouraged the concentration of
political power in the army. For a man of Gallienus's background, it was a strange step to take.
--He set up a new mobile central army reserve, located at
<u>Milan</u> in northern Italy. This army contained a very large
cavalry force. Such a reserve was something the Empire had
always lacked. Its development now indicated the difficulty
of holding the actual frontier lines. The heavy use of
cavalry indicated the need to cover great distances and the
shift away from the old Roman dependence on legionary infantry. It was hardly the old army in any sense. This new
force, being directly under the emperor's control, was a way
of getting round the fact that he did not control many of
the troops on the frontiers.

The new central army played a big part in the improvement
in the situation in the <u>Balkans</u> which can be seen in the late
260's. At that point, it can be said, things began to turn
at last in Rome's favor. In 268, the Romans defeated the
Goths, who were on their way back from the great raid in Asia

Minor and Greece, at the battle of Nis, probably the biggest
battle of the century. Gallienus may still have been emperor
at that time. If so, he was murdered soon afterwards. The
new army, being so close to the ruler, offered obvious opportunities to ambitious men. Its first commander had already
tried to make himself emperor. In 268 Gallienus was removed
in a plot led by the central army's second commander,
AURELIAN, and the general CLAUDIUS, who became the new
emperor.

Claudius II Gothicus, 268-270, and Quintillus, 270.

Claudius was another of the primitive soldier-emperors
from the Balkans. He defeated German tribes as they raided
into north Italy and then savaged the Goths in a number of
battles in the Balkans (including perhaps Nis)--so his nickname Gothicus. This ended the worst of the troubles with the
Goths. The Danube frontier was restored and made secure for
the next 100 years. Elsewhere, though, things were still in
bad shape. Zenobia was becoming dominant in the East and
after Postumus's death in 268 a variety of rebels held most
of the West.

Claudius died of the plague in 270, which made a change,
if hardly an attractive one, from the violent deaths which
had become so common. He was the first emperor to die a
non-violent death since Septimius Severus in 211. An army in
Italy recognized Claudius' brother QUINTILLUS as emperor.
The central army, though, chose the late emperor's right-hand
man, the man who had helped him get rid of Gallienus--
Aurelian. Quintillus was murdered.

Aurelian, 270-275.

Aurelian, another of the Balkan peasant soldier-emperors,
has a great reputation as a hard man of action, the ablest of
his kind. "Hand-on-Sword" was his nickname. While he did
great things, we should remember that the recovery had already
begun; the Danube front had just about been stabilized.
--He completed the restoration of the Danube border, fighting
off more German raids into north Italy and continuing to
batter the Goths.
--At the same time (270-271) he gave up Dacia, which had been
Roman for 160 years, since the conquest by Trajan. Aurelian
decided that the area was not worth the bother it took to
defend it. The Danube river line was easier to defend. The

mines of Dacia were played out, but the area had developed
under Roman control and a large farming population had to
be brought out with the legions, to be resettled south of
the river. In some ways, obviously, this is a very clear
sign of Rome's decline, even if it was done voluntarily.
--He constructed a great wall (the Wall of Aurelian) around
Rome, the first such wall in 600 years. Built of concrete
and faced with brick, the wall was 12 miles long and 20 feet
high, with 381 towers. It enclosed an area smaller than the
Rome of 100 years earlier, a sign that Rome, like the rest
of the Empire, had suffered heavily from the economic hardships and the plague. The Wall, like giving up Dacia, was
a sign of the times-the German tribes had raided into Italy
a number of times. The sense of security of the old days,
of the Pax Romana (Roman Peace), was gone.
--271-273: Aurelian restored authority in the East.
Palmyra was defeated (and savagely destroyed when it rebelled
again a short time later). Zenobia was brought to Rome to
walk in golden chains in Aurelian's grand triumph of 274.
These victories indicated the strength that Rome still had
when guided by an efficient hand. Aurelian did not, though,
do anything about the Persians except scare them off. They
knew that their time had passed; the borders in the East were
now secure too.
--273-274: Aurelian restored authority in the West, crushing
those who still supported the successors of Postumus.

    With some justification, even if the situation was still
unsettled, this remarkable man now took the title "RESTORER
OF THE WORLD." He had restored the unity of the Empire. He
made a beginning also on restoring the economy, trying to
reestablish a strong coinage to build up confidence and
reduce inflation (which had reached 1000% since 258).
Aurelian also promoted heavily, perhaps as a way of encouraging unity, the worship of the SUN (Sol Invictus, The
Unconquerable Sun), and surrounded himself with a great deal
of deliberate splendor. We will look at these things below.

    In 275 Aurelian, finding the fate of many another, was
murdered by his soldiers. We do not know the circumstances.

Tacitus, 275-276, and Florianus, 276.
    The elderly TACITUS was chosen to replace Aurelian. A
story says that the soldiers, disgusted with themselves for

having killed Aurelian, asked the Senate to name a successor
--with the 70 years old Tacitus as the surprised, and unwilling, result. Tacitus may have been another Danube general.
He died the next year in Asia Minor campaigning against some
raiding Goths. The soldiers probably murdered him; he may
have died a natural death. His half-brother, FLORIANUS, was
brought forward in Italy and was accepted in the West. The
Danube and eastern armies, though, recognized the leading
general PROBUS, who had been an associate of Aurelian.
Florianus was murdered by his own troops, who did not wish
to face the armies from the East. Whatever part the Senate
had played since 275, it now fell back into irrelevance.

Probus, 276-282.
Probus was another soldier-emperor from the Balkans.
He fought off a big German attack on Gaul, but not before it
had done much damage to most of the province. He also stopped
further raids on the Balkans. Rival emperors continued to
crop up here and there. The experience of Probus shows that
Aurelian's work was far from completed; but Probus certainly
did his share to continue the good work.

Carus, 282-283.
CARUS probably came from the same Danube background,
although there is a chance that he was from Narbonese Gaul.
He was the Praetorian Prefect to Probus. Some of the legions
declared for Carus in 282. This led the legions in Pannonia
to murder Probus, allegedly for working them too hard on land
reclamation. Carus became the first emperor not even to
bother to ask the Senate for its approval of his position.

Carus campaigned against the Germans. He then left one
of his sons, CARINUS, to look after the West while he went
East with his other son, NUMERIAN. He campaigned against the
Persians, even occupying the capital at Ctesiphon. This
marked another very clear step in the restoration of Rome's
power and self-respect. At this point, the story has it,
Carus was struck dead by lightning. Almost surely he was
murdered by his soldiers.

Numerian, 283-284, and Carinus, 283-285.
Carus had meant to have himself succeeded by his sons,
Carinus in the West and Numerian in the East. Numerian ended
the Persian war and turned for Rome. On the way, in 284, he

was murdered by his father-in-law, his Praetorian Prefect, Aper. If Aper had ambitions for himself, they came to nothing. The army took as emperor the general DIOCLETIAN. Diocletian moved into the West and defeated and killed Carinus the following year. Diocletian followed Carus in not asking for Senate approval.

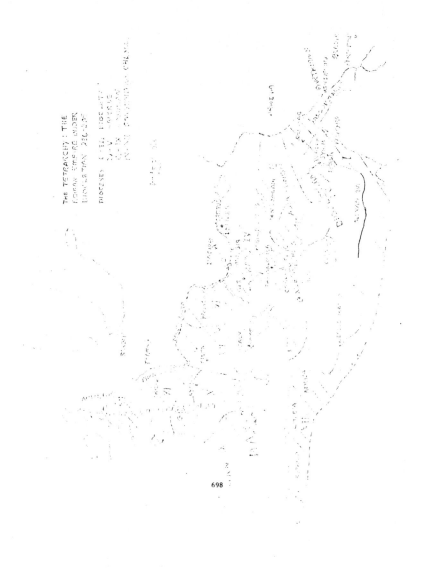

THE TETRARCHY : THE
ROMAN EMPIRE UNDER
DIOCLETIAN 284-305

THE DOMINATE: DIOCLETIAN, 284-305, AND
MAXIMIAM, 285-305

The new emperor, <u>Diocletian</u>, was another of the soldiers from simple peasant background in the <u>Balkans</u>. With
Diocletian, order finally was restored in the Empire and
the frontiers were made secure. With better cause than
<u>Aurelian</u>, he could call himself the "Restorer of the World."
Diocletian also carried out the greatest reorganization of
the state since <u>Augustus</u>, a reorganization which was made
permanent by his successor CONSTANTINE and which established
the character of the late Empire.

It is not difficult to understand how the security
against outside threats came about. It had been returning
since the late 260's; the Empire clearly was still immensely
strong compared to its enemies. It is much more difficult
to understand how the chain of murders at the top, resulting
from the indiscipline of the legions and the ambitions of
generals, was broken so abruptly, allowing stability to
return. All concerned may have been tired, even ashamed, of
the mess, but this does not explain why the change should
have taken hold, and so abruptly, at this point rather than
another. The personal impact of Diocletian, unmistakably a
very great figure, must have had its effect, but this we can
only guess at. Some specific steps were taken to encourage
stability and discipline and efficiency:

1. Diocletian deliberately chose from the beginning to
<u>share</u> power. He did this in two stages:
286: He made another Balkan general, MAXIMIAN, co-Emperor
(or <u>Augustus</u>, as it was called). Diocletian took the East,
<u>Maximian</u> the West. The Empire was still one, but despite
the prestige of Diocletian, who was very much the dominant
figure, there must have been a lot of independent activity
by the two men. There had been such divisions earlier, as
far back as <u>Marcus Aurelius</u> and <u>Lucius Verus</u> in the 160's.
They had become more common during the anarchy (<u>Valerian</u>
and <u>Gallienus</u>; <u>Carinus</u> and <u>Numerian</u>). But there had been
nothing as formal as the present arrangement. One purpose
may have been to discourage assassinations by buying over a
potential rival. In so far as the purpose was to increase
efficiency, the division was a comment on how things had

declined--why were two necessary? The division worked well under Diocletian, but it set a pattern for the future which in many ways had more bad effects than good. As a result of the prestige of Diocletian, this kind of division, usually between East and West, became common in the late Empire. Unfortunately, rivalry between emperors often outran cooperation; in any case, the weakening of the system of one-man control tended to hurt the spirit of unity in the Empire, and particularly to push apart the two great sections, the Latin West and the Hellenized East.

The arrangement of 286 points to some other developments which had taken place:
--Diocletian took the East, the wealthier and more populated, as well as the more highly cultured, part of the Empire. The anarchy since 235 may have tilted the Empire more to the East. The Empire was to take on more and more of a Hellenized Eastern appearance--Christianity was to be one example of this.
--The city of Rome lost much of its importance. Diocletian, the chief force in the Empire, was far away; in fact, he only visited Rome once in the 20 years of his power. Even Maximian had his capital at <u>Milan</u> in north Italy, a city which had grown in importance during the anarchy as a forward base for the soldier-emperors and the base for the central reserve army. All this reflected the shift to the East, as well as the lack of interest of these Balkan emperors in the old city and its traditions. It also reflected the personal wishes of Diocletian. Emperors of the anarchy generally had gone on using Rome as their capital-- what Diocletian did now was (as was his sharing power with Maximian) abrupt and new.

293: After 286, there were some years of busy fighting on all the frontiers and a number of rebellions (particularly that of the general <u>Carausius</u>, who between 287 and 293 carved out for himself an area in <u>Britain</u> and <u>northern Gaul</u> in the old style of the anarchy, only to be murdered and replaced, also in the old style, by an associate, who fell in his turn to the regular emperors). In 293, Diocletian decided to increase the number of rulers to four, by bringing in two more Balkan generals. He shared the East with GALERIUS: Maximian shared the West with CONSTANTIUS CHLORUS. This might make it easier to cope with the various troubles.

At the same time, Diocletian hoped to secure the succession and so avoid trouble. The two new men were called Caesar rather than Augustus. In theory, each one was the subordinate of the Augustus of his region. In each half of the Empire, the Caesar would eventually succeed the Augustus as emperor. In effect, what resulted was a four-way territorial split, with the two subordinates having a great deal of independence. This was a very strange system. It held together well under Diocletian but it collapsed almost as soon as he was out of the way. This system of four men is known as the TETRARCHY.

The Tetrarchy foundered on the good old hereditary principle. Diocletian had no son; he married his daughter to Galerius, with whom he shared power in the East, so that in the fashion of the "adoptive emperors" of the 100's he was trying to preserve the hereditary idea, which had survived the anarchy. Maximian, in the West, married his step-daughter to his Caesar, Constantius Chlorus. Maximian, however, had a son—he was being asked to make a sacrifice of his flesh, as Diocletian was not. Others, too, had sons, including Constantius Chlorus. Diocletian could claim that the idea was to pick the best men—those with sons neither agreed with him nor approved of the principle of preferring merit to blood. As soon as Diocletian was out of the way (305), the blood principle led to civil war. From the wars came CONSTANTINE, son of Constantius Chlorus, as the sole ruler. He divided the Empire after his death (337), keeping Diocletian's idea there, but he divided it only among his sons.

Yet the Tetrarchy did work well as long as Diocletian was around. In the East, Diocletian took Asia Minor, the Near East, and Egypt, living at Nicomedia. Galerius, from Thessalonica, had charge of the Balkan front; being trusted by Diocletian, who regarded him as his heir, Galerius was also allowed to operate widely across the East. He campaigned north of the Danube against the Germans and led a successful war against the Persians in 296. In the West, there was naturally less trust between the two men in power. Maximian stayed at Milan. Constantius Chlorus, based at Trier, looked after the Rhine frontier, where he campaigned successfully, and Gaul and Britain, where in 296 he crushed the break-away state which had been founded by Carausius.

2. A number of changes were introduced in administration:
--The number of provinces was raised from around 50 to
about 100. One purpose was to make their governors too
weak to rebel.
--The provinces were grouped into a dozen larger units
called dioceses, controlled by governors-general. These
were now the critical figures.
--The governors-general depended on the four Praetorian
Prefects, one attached to each ruler.
--All of these officials, up to the Praetorian Prefects,
supervised only civilian matters. The army was kept
separate under the direct control of the rulers, in a clear
separation of civil and military powers. The aim was to
make it harder for the officials to rebel, since they did
not have armies. This transferred the problem into the
army, which was carefully controlled--the generals lacked
the financial resources and the territorial bases which
they would have had as governors.
--The army was overhauled, in the direction taken during
the anarchy. We do not know how much of this was done by
Diocletian and how much by Constantine, who won the civil
war, after the retirement of Diocletian. A large mobile
field army, perhaps 200,000 strong, was built up, with a
portion of it attached to each ruler. This force depended
heavily on cavalry, much of it drawn from German tribes
brought in to fight for pay. By Constantine's day, there
were many German generals. All this put the four rulers,
rather than the commanders on the frontier, directly in
control of the backbone of the army, and so served a clear
political purpose as well as a sensible military one. A
central army made the Praetorian Guard unnecessary--
Constantine did away with it. Now the dictator always had
troops within reach. The rest of the army, perhaps 300,000
men, was an inferior frontier force, stationed at permanent
posts along the now heavily fortified borders. The frontier
troops were obtained partly by drafting citizens, usually
with fixed quotas for an area and with terrible penalties
attached for failure to meet a quota. There were also many
barbarian volunteers in these frontier armies.

3. The rulers became more splendid and remote than before.
This, too, had been seen during the anarchy--indeed in many
ways it was only the result of the drift away from the simple
Republican style which had been going on ever since the time

of Augustus 300 years before. Aurelian in the 270's had
worn a crown (diadem) and had put the slogan "born Lord and
God" on his coins. His encouragement of the worship of the
Sun (he constructed a great Temple of the Sun at Rome) was
intended to benefit himself by association with that god,
although he had not claimed that he should be identified
with the Sun. Under Diocletian and Maximian it was common
to refer to matters concerning the rulers as "sacred" and
"divine." They claimed a special relationship with gods,
Diocletian with Jupiter (the greatest of the old gods),
Maximian with Hercules. Constantine later made precisely
the same kind of claim about himself and the Christian God.
Their advisors stood in their presence; lesser people knelt
down before them; they seldom appeared in public. With
their jewels and their crowns and their haloes (to indicate
mightiness and closeness to the gods), they looked a good
deal closer to the kings of the East than to old Rome--
another example of the growing influence of the East. The
new style may have been intended to discourage assassination
and rebellion by making the emperor more than a man. It
probably appealed to the simple-mindedness of the Balkan
soldier-emperors, who were much less sophisticated and clear-
headed than the old Roman emperors. Augustus would have
wept to see what was going on.

The new style surrounding the rulers was part of a
deliberate response to the enormous problems of restoring
order and stability and prosperity in the Empire after all
the trouble of the anarchy. Diocletian's method was to
impose a savage totalitarian terror state on the Empire,
using force and fear to work his way. In so doing, he
speeded up the movement away from the old Roman state
toward the kind of thing we mean by dictatorship. From this
point, the Empire's system is often called the DOMINATE,
from the word dominus, meaning lord or master (the same
word was used for the Christian god), in contrast to the
Principate, the more low-key system of first citizen. The
Dominate was the work of both Diocletian and Constantine.
In describing its elements, we often do not know which
emperor to associate with particular points.

This approach may have seemed the obvious way to go to
the soldier-emperors--to replace the old complex relationships with a more outright military dictatorship. At very

best, though, it did little more than paper over the cracks. The deeper problems simply were ignored. These emperors seem to have known that they could only hope that such problems would go away.

We have seen an example of the new system in the military. The army was bigger than ever (500,000) among a much reduced population and a battered economy. Soldiers, like all servants of the state, had to be treated well, in order to emphasize their dignity (and in the case of the army head off rebellion). They were well paid and, like all civil servants, were made exempt from the ordinary courts. To make sure that they got enough, in a period of inflation and hardship, the state paid the soldiers in kind (in goods, not money), particularly food, gathered from the areas in which they served. Still, there were not enough volunteers, so that troops had to be obtained by draft of citizens and by hiring barbarians.

The problems with the army were typical. A swollen state was existing off a much reduced economic foundation, defending itself by force and fear. Lacking the sophistication and perhaps the desire to do anything else, the state tried to solve all problems by more force, thereby adding to its own size and expense and to the degradation of the people:
—Diocletian (294) tried to restore a stable coinage as a way of fighting inflation. He failed, but Constantine later had more success in this area, so that the restoration of the currency is one of the few success stories of the era.
—Diocletian (301) introduced a system of maximum wages and prices as another weapon against inflation. This step, the most famous economic law of the ancient world, was a failure. The threats of mutilation and terror were not nearly as effective in this larger area as they were eventually in controlling tampering with the coinage. The effort was given up later, probably by Constantine. A substitute policy was for the government to become more reliant on payments in kind rather than in money.
—Diocletian and Constantine (especially the latter) froze the population into hereditary place and status. People could not change their line of work without permission; many could not move. This included those in the army (providing

704

an hereditary class of soldiers), the civil service, local government, as well as groups such as peasants, blacksmiths, etc. Steps toward this kind of thing had already been taken in the anarchy. One purpose was to guarantee that each district would be able to go on supplying its quotas of manpower and taxes and goods to the state. In terms of the economic situation which existed after the anarchy and the plague, it was a confession that the state intended to protect itself by the simple exercise of trying to keep things from getting worse. This program is the clearest evidence of the changed nature of the state, indicating an attitude close to contempt toward the pppulation. We can look at a couple of examples:

1. In much of the countryside peasants had been driven off their lands by civil war, enemy raids, inflation, the plague, etc. They often took refuge on the great estates of the rich landowners, which became fortified and self-sufficient. The landless peasants found themselves clamped hereditarily into their new and very undesirable situation. To get out, they had to escape and remain unfound for 30 years (women only for 20). We are looking at the beginning of the SERF system of the Middle Ages, when the mass of the population was tied to a particular piece of land, unfree to move, controlled by whoever held that land. This freezing of the peasant population was probably the work of Diocletian rather than Constantine. In devastated frontier areas, many Germans were brought in and turned into such unfree peasants. The large areas of abandoned land, from which the population had fled, passed into the hands of the state and then into the hands of the friends of the state, producing a movement toward the concentration of landed wealth.

2. Local government service became hereditary and compulsory. Many towns had been hurt badly by the anarchy and the plague. The soldier-emperors served themselves by forcing the wealthier groups (normally Roman local government units were outright plutocracies) to continue to serve in local administration. This bankrupted many, since the wealthy had always been expected, in the Greek fashion, to make large contributions out of their own pockets as a substitute for taxation. Local governments were also required to make up out of their own pockets any shortages in the annual

705

quotas of money and kind required by the state; the private property of the local government officials could be confiscated for failure or inability to do this. As a result, it became one of the chief purposes of the wealthy to win exemption, by purchase or whatever, from the burdens of local government. The rich diversity of Roman local government, the old pride in local achievement and independence, collapsed and was replaced by fear and uniformity and the heavy hand of the state.

One of the clearest losers from the new kind of state was the old senatorial class. The soldier-emperors were not the men to bother much about pretending to share power. The Senate lost most of its remaining scraps of influence. Gallienus had refused to allow senators a military career; now under Diocletian the Senate lost its influence over provincial and local government, as all governors were appointed by the rulers. Finally, Constantine ended even the existence of the senatorial class, merging it with the equites. Privilege was now something granted only by the ruler.

The system of the Dominate worked reasonably well under Diocletian, at least in comparison to the sufferings of the anarchy. In the longer run, the system may have played a part in preserving the strength of the Empire for a century until the collapse began in the late 300's. There is little else to be said for it, though--it could provide no way of building the Empire back up, so that everything save the swollen size of the government remained on a scale much reduced from the great days of the Principate. And there is no doubt that the cost of the Dominate in the simplest human terms was enormous and terrible. A more or less primitive military dictatorship controlled an unfree population, offering no hope beyond the promise of security. We can suppose that this promise was seen as no very great deal by the mass of the population. Beginning in the late 300's, even the promise of security could not be kept. Between that point and the late 400's there took place what we often call the Fall of the Roman Empire--specifically the loss of the western portions of the Empire to collections of tribes from beyond the northern borders. Along the way, Rome itself was captured and pillaged twice, in 410 and 455. The Roman Empire survived, but by 500 it was reduced to the old, Hellenized East and it lacked the city of Rome—an amazing spectacle, the ultimate victory of the East. It is difficult to understand how this could have happened, since we know that the successful barbarian tribes of the 400's were not very numerous. They may well have been less of a menace in themselves than the tribes which had been contained in the 200's. We need to remember that by the 400's the Roman population had been battered by a century of dictatorship into the hopelessness of the unfree. The will to resist must have been weak. Quite reasonably, that Roman population could decide that it gained too little from the Empire to put out much of an effort at resistance. In addition, the failure of the 400's indicated that the soldier-emperors had had no solutions. They had only held things together for a while. With a great deal lying beyond their abilities, and a great deal more perhaps beyond their comprehension, they had "restored the World" only in a very limited way, so that the Empire remained very much weaker in 400 than it had been in 200. It is difficult to believe that the soldier-emperors had done the best job possible under the circumstances, specializing in the military techniques of terror and force which they knew allowed them to turn away from the great problems of the Empire.

ROMAN EMPIRE
OF 500

☰ ROMAN EMPIRE

0 100 200 300
MILES

CONSTANTINOPLE

ROME

708